Entrepreneurship and Economic Growth

Edited by

Martin Carree

Professor of Industrial Organisation
University of Maastricht, The Netherlands

and

A. Roy Thurik

Professor of Economics and Entrepreneurship
Erasmus University Rotterdam, The Netherlands

THE INTERNATIONAL LIBRARY OF ENTREPRENEURSHIP

An Elgar Reference Collection
Cheltenham, UK • Northampton, MA, USA

Published by
Edward Elgar Publishing Limited
Glensanda House
Montpellier Parade
Cheltenham
Glos GL50 1UA
UK

Edward Elgar Publishing, Inc.
136 West Street
Suite 202
Northampton
Massachusetts 01060
USA

A catalogue record for this book is available from the British Library.

Library of Congress Cataloging-in-Publication Data

Entrepreneurship and economic growth / edited by Martin Carree and A. Roy Thurik.
    p. cm. — (International library of entrepreneurship ; 6.)
   Includes bibliographical references and index.
   1. Entrepreneurship. 2. Economic development.   I. Carree, Martin Anthony.
II. Thurik, A. R. (A. Roy). III. Series.

  HB615.E64242   2006
  338'.04—dc22   2006040649

ISBN-10: 1 84542 134 5
ISBN-13: 978 1 84542 134 2

Printed and bound in Great Britain by MPG Books Ltd, Bodmin, Cornwall.

Contents

Acknowledgements

The editors and publishers wish to thank the authors and the following publishers who have kindly given permission for the use of copyright material.

American Economic Association for article: John McMillan and Christopher Woodruff (2002), 'The Central Role of Entrepreneurs in Transition Economies', *Journal of Economic Perspectives*, **16** (3), Summer, 153–70.

Blackwell Publishing Ltd for article: Claudio Michelacci (2003), 'Low Returns in R&D Due to the Lack of Entrepreneurial Skills', *Economic Journal*, **113** (484), January, 207–25.

Elsevier for articles: Kathleen M. Eisenhardt and Naushad Forbes (1984), 'Technical Entrepreneurship: An International Perspective', *Columbia Journal of World Business*, **XIX** (4), Winter, 31–8; Thomas J. Prusa and James A. Schmitz, Jr. (1991), 'Are New Firms an Important Source of Innovation? Evidence from the PC Software Industry', *Economics Letters*, **35**, 339–42; Tony Fu-Lai Yu (1998), 'Adaptive Entrepreneurship and the Economic Development of Hong Kong', *World Development*, **26** (5), May, 897–911.

Harvard University Press and the President and Fellows of Harvard College for excerpt: Joseph A. Schumpeter ([1934] 1961), 'The Fundamental Phenomenon of Economic Development', in *The Theory of Economic Development: An Inquiry into Profits, Capital, Credit, Interest, and the Business Cycle*, Translated by Redvers Opie, Chapter II, 57–94.

Oxford University Press for article: Michael Gort and Nakil Sung (1999), 'Competition and Productivity Growth: The Case of the U.S. Telephone Industry', *Economic Inquiry*, **37** (4), October, 678–91.

Review of Economic Studies Ltd for article: Huw Lloyd-Ellis and Dan Bernhardt (2000), 'Enterprise, Inequality and Economic Development', *Review of Economic Studies*, **67** (1), January, 147–68.

Senate Hall Academic Publishing for article: David Audretsch and Roy Thurik (2004), 'A Model of the Entrepreneurial Economy', *International Journal of Entrepreneurship Education*, **2** (2), 143–66.

Springer Science and Business Media for articles: Wesley M. Cohen and Steven Klepper (1992), 'The Tradeoff Between Firm Size and Diversity in the Pursuit of Technological Progress', *Small Business Economics*, **4** (1), March, 1–14; Sharon Gifford (1998), 'Limited Entrepreneurial Attention and Economic Development', *Small Business Economics*, **10** (1),

February, 17–30; Pietro F. Peretto (1998), 'Technological Change, Market Rivalry, and the Evolution of the Capitalist Engine of Growth', *Journal of Economic Growth*, **3** (1), March, 53–80; Peter Howitt and Philippe Aghion (1998), 'Capital Accumulation and Innovation as Complementary Factors in Long-Run Growth', *Journal of Economic Growth*, **3** (2), June, 111–30; Murat F. Iyigun and Ann L. Owen (1999), 'Entrepreneurs, Professionals, and Growth', *Journal of Economic Growth*, **4** (2), June, 213–32; Sander Wennekers and Roy Thurik (1999), 'Linking Entrepreneurship and Economic Growth', *Small Business Economics*, **13** (1), August, 27–55; Stefan Fölster (2000), 'Do Entrepreneurs Create Jobs?', *Small Business Economics*, **14** (2), March, 137–48; Martin Carree, André van Stel, Roy Thurik and Sander Wennekers (2002), 'Economic Development and Business Ownership: An Analysis Using Data of 23 OECD Countries in the Period 1976–1996', *Small Business Economics*, **19** (3), November, 271–90.

Taylor and Francis Ltd (http://www.tandf.co.uk/journals) for articles: Zoltan J. Acs and Catherine Armington (2004), 'Employment Growth and Entrepreneurial Activity in Cities', *Regional Studies*, **38** (8), November, 911–27; David B. Audretsch and Max Keilbach (2004), 'Entrepreneurship Capital and Economic Performance', *Regional Studies*, **38** (8), November, 949–59.

University of Chicago Press for articles: James A. Schmitz, Jr. (1989), 'Imitation, Entrepreneurship, and Long-Run Growth', *Journal of Political Economy*, **97** (3), June, 721–39; William J. Baumol (1990), 'Entrepreneurship: Productive, Unproductive, and Destructive', *Journal of Political Economy*, **98** (5, Part 1), October, 893–921; Stephen J. Nickell (1996), 'Competition and Corporate Performance', *Journal of Political Economy*, **104** (4), August, 724–46.

Every effort has been made to trace all the copyright holders but if any have been inadvertently overlooked the publishers will be pleased to make the necessary arrangement at the first opportunity.

In addition the publishers wish to thank the Library of Indiana University at Bloomington, USA, for their assistance in obtaining these articles.

Understanding the Role of Entrepreneurship for Economic Growth

Martin Carree[a] and A. Roy Thurik[b]

Introduction

Throughout the first three-quarters of the last century, the economies of scale and scope present in production, distribution, management and R&D dictated increasing firm size (Chandler, 1990). Moreover, the growing but relatively low level of economic development went together with high price elasticities stimulating price competition that again favoured large-scale production. Statistical evidence points towards an increasing presence and role of large enterprises in the economy during this period (Caves, 1982; Teece, 1993; Brock and Evans, 1989). This development towards large-scale activity was visible in most of the OECD countries (Audretsch, Thurik, Verheul and Wennekers, 2002). The importance of entrepreneurship and small business seemed to be fading. At the same time, it was recognized that the small business sector was in need of protection for both social and political reasons, but not on the grounds of economic efficiency (Audretsch and Thurik, 2000).

Entrepreneurship and small business are related but far from synonymous concepts. On the one hand, entrepreneurial activity (defined, for instance, as behaviour concentrating on opportunities) may occur in both small and large businesses but also outside the business world (Stevenson and Gumpert, 1991; Low, 2001; Davidsson, 2004). On the other hand, small businesses can be a vehicle for both Schumpeterian entrepreneurs introducing new products and processes that change industry, as well as for people who simply run and own a business for a living (Wennekers and Thurik, 1999; Chapter 1, this volume). The latter group includes many franchisees, shopkeepers and people in professional occupations. The prominent example of entrepreneurship and small business overlapping is in the area of new, small and often fast-growing businesses. During the first decades of the last century, small businesses were both a vehicle for entrepreneurship and a source of employment and income. This is the era in which Schumpeter (1934) wrote *The Theory of Economic Development*, emphasizing the role of the entrepreneur as prime cause of economic development. He describes how the innovating entrepreneur challenges incumbent firms by introducing new inventions that make current technologies and products obsolete. This process of creative destruction is the main characteristic of what has been called the Schumpeter Mark I regime.

[a] Faculty of Economics and Business Administration, University of Maastricht.
[b] Centre for Advanced Small Business Economics (CASBEC) at Erasmus University Rotterdam, EIM Business and Policy Research, Zoetermeer and Max Planck Institute of Economics, Jena.

During the post-war years, small business still mattered. It was obvious that this was less on the grounds of economic efficiency but more for social and political purposes. In a time when large firms had not yet gained the powerful position of the 1960s and 1970s, small businesses were the main supplier of employment and hence of social and political stability (Thurik and Wennekers, 2004). Scholars, such as Chandler (1977, 1990), Galbraith (1956) and Schumpeter (1942), were convinced that the future was in the hands of large corporations and that small business would fade away as the victim of its own inefficiencies. Policy in the United States was divided between allowing for the demise of small business on economic grounds, on the one hand, and preserving at least some semblance of a small business sector for social and political reasons, on the other hand. It was argued that small business was essential to maintaining American democracy in the Jeffersonian tradition. The passage of the Robinson-Patman Act (providing some measure of protection to small independent retailers and their independent suppliers from possibly unfair competition from vertically integrated, multi-location chain stores) and the creation of the United States Small Business Administration were policy responses to protect less-efficient small businesses and maintain their viability. These policy responses are typical for a Schumpeter Mark II regime. In *Capitalism, Socialism and Democracy*, Schumpeter (1942) focuses on innovative activities by large and established firms. He describes how large firms outperform their smaller counterparts in the innovation and appropriation process through a strong positive feedback loop from innovation to increased R&D activities. This process of creative accumulation is the main characteristic of the Schumpeter Mark II regime.

In Audretsch and Thurik (2004; Chapter 2, this volume) the two Schumpeterian regimes are used in the framework of two broader concepts of economic organization: the *managed* and the *entrepreneurial economies*. They introduce the concept of the managed economy that flourished for most of the last century. It was based on relative certainty in outputs, which consisted mainly of manufactured products, and in the traditional inputs of labour, capital and land. The joint effect of globalization and the ICT revolutions have drastically reduced the cost of shifting not just capital but also information out of the high-cost locations of Europe and into lower-cost locations around the globe. This means that economic activity in a high-cost location is no longer compatible with routinized tasks. Rather, globalization has shifted the comparative advantage of high-cost locations to knowledge-based activities, which cannot be transferred without cost around the globe. Knowledge as an input into economic activity is inherently different from land, capital and labour. It is characterized by high uncertainty, high asymmetries across people and is costly to transact. The response to a trend establishing knowledge as the main source of comparative advantage is the entrepreneurial economy. Audretsch and Thurik identify 15 characteristics that differ between the entrepreneurial and managed economies and provide a framework for understanding how the entrepreneurial economy fundamentally differs from the managed economy.

Entrepreneurship is an ill-defined, multidimensional concept (Wennekers and Thurik, 1999, table 4; Chapter 1, this volume). This complicates the measurement of the extent of entrepreneurial activities and hence that of their impact on economic performance. Understanding their role in the process of growth requires a framework because there are various intermediate variables or linkages to explain how entrepreneurship influences economic growth (Carree and Thurik, 2003; Karlsson, Friis and Paulsson, 2005). The collection of articles in the present volume gives an image of the domain of the study of the consequences of entrepreneurship for economic growth. We present this collection below, but, first, we discuss the changes in the economy leading to the entrepreneurial economy. We also distinguish between two frameworks of the impacts of entrepreneurial capital: one based upon Carree and Thurik (2003) distinguishes between three entrepreneurial roles, and one following Audretsch and Thurik (2004; Chapter 2, this volume) distinguishes between three impacts of entrepreneurial capital.

In creating this collection of articles we sought originality and spread rather than tradition and reputation. This strategy allowed us to go beyond the traditional 'A' journals and to give ample attention to recent material. The collection contains a selection of both theoretical contributions, mainly in the field of endogenous growth theory, and of empirical contributions. The collection also pays separate attention to two key intermediate variables, namely innovation and competition. The present collection complements that of Acs (1996), where a small business perspective rather than an entrepreneurship view is taken.

The Re-emergence of Entrepreneurship

In view of the general belief that large-scale production was driving out small firms, it seemed paradoxical when scholars first began to document that the inevitable demise of small business had not only stopped, but even reversed. Following the work of Blau (1987); both Loveman and Sengenberger (1991) and Acs and Audretsch (1993) carried out international analyses of the re-emergence of small business and entrepreneurship in North America and Europe. Two major findings emerged from these studies. First, the relative importance of small business varies strongly across countries, and secondly, in many European countries and North America the prevalence of small business increased in the past several decades.

The reversal of the trend away from large enterprises towards the re-emergence of small business started in North America in the late 1970s but was not limited to that part of the world. It was also seen in parts of Europe. A study by EIM (2002) documents show how the relative importance of small firms in Europe (19 countries), measured in terms of employment shares, had continued to increase between 1988 and 2001. In a study by Van Stel (2003) the development of the self-employment rates (defined in terms of business ownership rates) for 23 OECD countries is reported. See Figure 1 for the development of this rate in a selection of countries. A distinct U-shape can be observed for these countries. This may be interpreted as a manifestation of the change from the managed to the entrepreneurial economy. In the first years of the twenty-first century, the upward trend started levelling off in such countries as the UK and the USA. See Van Stel (2003) or Audretsch, Thurik, Verheul and Wennekers (2002) for precise data and figures of the US development. In the UK this levelling off may be due to policy measures favouring incumbent growth businesses rather than start-ups (Thurik, 2003). In the USA this may be due to the shake-out in industries that are in a more advanced stage than elsewhere in the area of modern OECD countries.

As the empirical evidence documenting the re-emergence of entrepreneurship increased, scholars began to look for explanations and to develop a theoretical basis. Carlsson (1989, 1992) advances two explanations for the shift toward smallness in manufacturing industries. The first deals with fundamental changes in the world economy from the 1970s onwards. These changes relate to intensifying global competition, the increasing degree of uncertainty and market fragmentation. The second explanation deals with changes in the character of

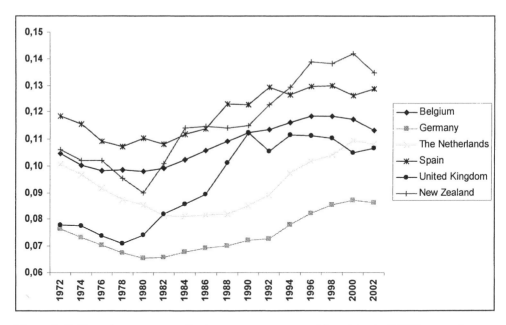

Figure 1: Self-employment rates (business owners per workforce) in six OECD countries

technological progress. Piore and Sabel (1984) argue that the market instability of the 1970s resulted in the demise of mass production and promoted flexible specialization. This fundamental change in the path of technological development generated important diseconomies of scale. The shift away from large firms was not just confined to manufacturing industries. Brock and Evans (1989) show that this trend has occurred in more sectors of the economy in the United States. They provide four more reasons why this shift has occurred: the increase of labour supply leading to lower real wages and coinciding with an increasing level of education; changes in consumer tastes; relaxation of (entry) regulations; and the current period of creative destruction ('Third Industrial Revolution').

Loveman and Sengenberger (1991) stress the influence of two industrial restructuring trends: that of decentralization and vertical disintegration (the breaking up of large plants and businesses), and the formation of new business communities. These intermediate forms of market coordination flourish owing to declining costs of transaction. They also emphasize the role of public and private policies promoting the small business sector. Audretsch and Thurik (2000, 2001) explain the re-emergence of entrepreneurship in Europe and North America on the basis of increased globalization, which has shifted the comparative advantage of economically advanced countries towards knowledge-based economic activity.

Consequences of Entrepreneurship

The causes of the shift are one domain. Its consequences also cover a broad area of research. For example, Acs (1992) distinguishes four consequences of the increased importance of small firms: a vehicle for entrepreneurship, routes of innovation, industry dynamics and job generation. Baumol (1993) deals with the role of entrepreneurial activities and the different effects it may have. The role of smallness in the process of innovative activities is investigated extensively by Acs and Audretsch (1990) and Audretsch (1995). A discussion of the relation between the role of small firms and industry dynamics can be found in Audretsch (1995). Acs and Armington (2004; Chapter 20, this volume) and Fölster (2000; Chapter 21, this volume) are examples of studies of job generation. The Global Entrepreneurship Monitor (GEM) project has recently made internationally comparable data on entrepreneurial activity available for research. In Reynolds *et al.* (2000, 2001, 2002) growth and entrepreneurial activity are found to have a strong positive correlation. Using GEM data in the context of a model controlling for several alternative drivers of growth, van Stel, Carree and Thurik (2005) find that entrepreneurial activity affects economic growth, but that this effect depends upon the level of per capita income, in that entrepreneurship has a negative impact on GDP growth for developing countries and a positive one for developed countries.

Audretsch and Keilbach (2004; Chapter 22, this volume) emphasize that entrepreneurship capital may be a missing link in explaining variations in economic performance. An alternative and wider view of this missing link may be that it is the institutional fabric that makes the difference between high and low performance. For example, Saxenian (1990, 1994) attributes the superior performance of Silicon Valley to a high capacity for promoting entrepreneurship. While entrepreneurs undertake a definitive action – i.e. they start a new business or introduce a new product – this action cannot be viewed in a vacuum devoid of context. Rather, as Audretsch, Thurik, Verheul and Wennekers (2002) show, entrepreneurship is shaped by a number of forces and factors, including legal and institutional as well as cultural and social factors. The study of social capital and its impact on economic decision-making and behaviour dates back to the classic economics and sociology literature where it is argued that social and relational structures influence market processes (Granovetter, 1985). Thorton and Flynne (2003) and Saxenian (1994) argue that entrepreneurial environments are characterized by thriving supportive networks that provide the institutional fabric linking individual entrepreneurs to organized sources of learning and resources.

Carree and Thurik (2003) focus on three entrepreneurial roles, emphasized by Schumpeter, Kirzner and Knight respectively. The first is the role of innovator. Schumpeter was the economist who has most prominently drawn attention to the 'innovating entrepreneur'. He or she carries out 'new combinations we call enterprise; the individuals whose function it is to carry them out we call entrepreneurs' (Schumpeter, 1934, p. 74). The second is the role of perceiving profit opportunities. We label this role as Kirznerian (or neo-Austrian) entrepreneurship (see e.g. Kirzner, 1997). The third role is that of assuming the risk associated with uncertainty. This role can be called Knightian entrepreneurship. The Knightian entrepreneur has also been interpreted as the 'neo-classical entrepreneur' (Shane, 2000). In the neo-classical (equilibrium) framework, entrepreneurship is explained by fundamental attributes of people (like 'taste' for uncertainty). When an individual introduces a new product or starts a new firm, this can be interpreted as an entrepreneurial act in terms of each of the three types of entrepreneurship. The individual is an innovator, has perceived a hitherto unnoticed profit opportunity and takes the risk that the product or venture may turn out to be a failure. A lack of entrepreneurial activity or alertness is therefore directly connected to low rates of innovation, to unused profit opportunities and to risk-averse attitudes. These are important barriers for a healthy economic development.

Audretsch and Thurik (2004; Chapter 2, this volume) distinguish three ways in which entrepreneurial capital affects growth. The first way is by creating knowledge spillovers. Romer (1986), Lucas (1988, 1993) and Grossman and Helpman (1991) established that knowledge spillovers are an important mechanism driving growth. Insight into the process of knowledge diffusion is important, especially since a policy implication commonly drawn from new economic growth theory is that, due to the increasing role of knowledge and the resulting increasing returns, knowledge factors, such as R&D, should be publicly supported. However, they shed little light on the actual mechanisms by which knowledge is transmitted across firms and individuals.

The literature identifying the creation of knowledge spillover mechanisms is underdeveloped. However, entrepreneurship is an important area where some of the transmission mechanisms have been identified. Cohen and Levinthal (1989) suggest that firms develop the capacity to adapt new technology and ideas developed in other firms and are therefore able to appropriate some of the returns accruing to investments in new knowledge made externally – i.e. outside their own organization. Audretsch (1995) proposes a shift in the unit of observation away from exogenously assumed firms towards individuals, such as scientists, engineers or other knowledge workers – i.e. agents with endowments of new economic knowledge. When the focus is shifted from the firm to the individual as the relevant unit of observation, the appropriability issue remains, but the question becomes: how can economic agents with a given endowment of new knowledge best appropriate the returns from that knowledge? In this spillover process, where a knowledge worker may exit the firm or university in order to create a new company, the knowledge production function is reversed. Knowledge is exogenous and embodied in a worker and the firm is created endogenously through the worker's effort to appropriate the value of his knowledge by way of innovative activity. Hence, entrepreneurship serves as a mechanism by which knowledge spills over to a new firm in which it is commercialized.

The second way in which entrepreneurship capital generates economic growth is through augmenting the number of enterprises and increasing competition. Jacobs (1969) and Porter (1990) argue that competition is more conducive to knowledge externalities than local monopolies. With local competition, Jacobs (1969) is not referring to competition within product markets as traditionally envisioned by the industrial organization literature, but rather to the competition for new ideas embodied in economic agents. Not only does an increase in the number of firms enhance the competition for new ideas, but greater competition across firms also facilitates the entry of new firms specializing in a particular new product niche. This is because the necessary complementary inputs are more likely available from small specialist niche firms than from large, vertically integrated producers. Glaeser, Kallal, Scheinkman and Shleifer (1992) and Feldman and Audretsch (1999) found empirical evidence supporting the hypothesis that an increase in competition within a city, as measured by the number of enterprises, is accompanied by higher growth performance of that city. Van Stel and Nieuwenhuijsen (2004) found that this competition effect may prevail, in particular, for manufacturing industries.

A third way in which entrepreneurship capital generates economic output is by providing diversity among firms (Cohen and Klepper, 1992; Chapter 8, this volume). Not only does entrepreneurship capital generate a greater number of enterprises, it also increases the variety of enterprises in a certain location. There has been a series of theoretical arguments suggesting that the degree of diversity, as opposed to homogeneity, will influence the growth potential of a location.

The basis for linking diversity to economic performance is provided by Jacobs (1969), who argues that the most important sources of knowledge spillovers are external to the industry in which the firm operates and that cities are a source of considerable innovation because there the diversity of knowledge sources is greatest (Jaffe, Trajtenberg and Henderson, 1993; Audretsch and Feldman, 1996). According to Jacobs, it is the exchange of complementary knowledge across diverse firms and economic agents that yields an important return on new economic knowledge. She develops a theory emphasizing the role of the geographic environment in promoting knowledge externalities which lead to innovative activity and economic growth. In this environment entrepreneurship capital can contribute to growth by injecting diversity and serving as a conduit for knowledge spillovers, leading to increased competition. The entrepreneurial economy is characterized by a high reliance on this third role of entrepreneurship capital.

The Collection

The collection of 22 articles in this volume can be divided into six broad categories of subjects. The first group of articles can be described as providing a general introduction to the effect of entrepreneurial activity on economic growth and development. There are three papers in Part I by Wennekers and Thurik (1999; Chapter 1), Audretsch and Thurik (2004; Chapter 2) and Schumpeter ([1934] 1961; Chapter 3). The paper by Wennekers and Thurik gives an overview of how different kinds of entrepreneurship may influence economic progress, and sketches a causal scheme relating several entrepreneurial aspects to macro-economic performance. Audretsch and Thurik concentrate on the entrepreneurial economy, building on their earlier work (Audretsch and Thurik, 2000). They show that this economy differs from the previous economy where progress was based upon economies of scale and scope (Chandler, 1990). It goes without saying that Joseph Schumpeter has been highly influential in our understanding of the role of entrepreneurs in technological and economic progress. We have incorporated the second chapter of *The Theory of Economic Development* in which the prominent role of entrepreneurial activity is explained. Holcombe (1998) provides a good overview of the role of the entrepreneur in economic development from an (neo)-Austrian viewpoint, combining insights from Kirzner and Schumpeter.

The articles in Part II also deal with the general issue of the effect of entrepreneurial activity, and focus on historical and country-specific contexts. The four papers included are by Baumol (1990; Chapter 4), Eisenhardt and Forbes (1984; Chapter 5), McMillan and Woodruff (2002; Chapter 6) and Yu (1998; Chapter 7). Baumol stresses the historical context and shows that entrepreneurial activity has not always had a productive contribution to economic welfare, and has on many occasions been unproductive or destructive. He shows how the institutional framework is crucial to have entrepreneurship positively impacting economic progress. Eisenhardt and Forbes provide an early contribution on the oft-cited Silicon Valley cluster of high-tech firms. They provide an international comparison of 'technical' entrepreneurship. McMillan and Woodruff deal with the importance of entrepreneurship in the transition economies. These formerly centrally planned economies have had little or no experience with entrepreneurial ventures, making the transition towards a capitalist economy more challenging. Yu studies entrepreneurial activity in Hong Kong, and especially deals with adaptive (Kirznerian) entrepreneurship (partly) explaining how the Hong Kong economy progresses over time.

The papers in Part III deal with the issue of innovation. While Acs and Audrestch (1990) already provided ample evidence of small firms being an important source of innovative activity, we introduce three additional viewpoints: those of Cohen and Klepper (1992; Chapter 8), Gifford (1998; Chapter 9) and Prusa and Schmitz (1991; Chapter 10). Cohen and Klepper discuss the trade-off for technological progress between an industry having many small firms or having a few large firms. On the one hand, the presence of many small firms guarantees variety of innovative approaches. On the other hand, large firms have the capacity to invest and make use of economies of scale in R&D (e.g. Klepper, 1996). Gifford investigates the issue of the allocation of entrepreneurial attention to different kinds of activity, including innovation. The extent to which entrepreneurs have the ability and attention for innovative activities will be highly influential for future economic development. Prusa and Schmitz provide a short, empirical example of small and new firms in the PC software industry being more likely than their larger and older counterparts to introduce radical innovation. It is in line with the ideas of 'dynamic complementarity', as introduced by Rothwell (1983, 1984), suggesting different roles for small and large firm in the innovation process.

Consequences for growth is the common denominator of the fourth group of articles. The study of economic growth and development has radically altered since the introduction of endogenous growth models in the late 1980s (Romer, 1986; Lucas, 1988). Elements of entrepreneurship and firm size distribution have been introduced into these growth models. Although mathematical tractability limits the way in which entrepreneurial activity can be incorporated, there have been some important contributions in this area. In Part IV we include six articles by Schmitz (1989; Chapter 11), Howitt and Aghion (1998; Chapter 12), Michelacci (2003; Chapter 13), Iyigun and Owen (1999; Chapter 14), Lloyd-Ellis and Bernhardt (2000; Chapter 15) and Peretto (1998; Chapter 16). Schmitz made an early contribution introducing one aspect of entrepreneurial activity (imitation) into an endogenous growth model. An interesting outcome is that the socially optimal rate of entrepreneurship is higher than the market equilibrium rate providing a rationale for policies promoting entrepreneurial activity. Howitt and Aghion extend upon their famous article of 1992 introducing a (mathematical) form of creative destruction into an endogenous growth framework. They add capital accumulation complementing the innovative element in achieving progress. Michelacci makes a case for entrepreneurship by investigating circumstances in which innovation should be promoted by encouraging entrepreneurship rather than research. His model shows that the growth process may stagnate because of the lack of entrepreneurial skills. The three papers by Iyigun and Owen, Lloyd-Ellis and Bernhardt and by Peretto all consider the changing role of small versus large firms over the stages of economic development. Iyigun and Owen show that countries that initially have too little of either entrepreneurial or professional human capital may end up in a development trap. Lloyd-Ellis and Bernhardt as well as Peretto take more aspects of economic development into consideration. The former show that the average firm size tends to increase through the first stages of development but then tends to decrease during the later stages. Peretto shows that there is an optimum (in terms of promoting progress) in the size distribution of firms, in line with Cohen and Klepper's (1992) paper.

It has been argued that the presence of new and small firms promotes competition which is often seen as stimulating economic growth. Competition is the central element in the fifth group of articles. Kirzner already argued that entrepreneurship and competition may be considered identical notions (see for a summary of these thoughts Kirzner, 1997). In Part V we include two contributions illustrating the role of competitive pressure on productivity growth by Nickell (1996; Chapter 27) and Gort and Sung (1999; Chapter 18). Nickell finds that competition measured by either number of competitors or by lower level of rent has a positive effect on productivity growth. Gort and Sung consider a special case, namely the US telephone industry, and also find confirmation for competition to boost productivity.

In the final group of articles in Part VI we present four empirical contributions directly measuring the impact of entrepreneurial activity on economic performance: Carree, van Stel, Thurik and Wennekers (2002; Chapter 19), Acs and Armington (2004; Chapter 20), Fölster (2000; Chapter 21) and Audretsch and Keilbach (2004; Chapter 22). Carree *et al.* investigate whether countries that have a self-employment rate deviating from a 'natural' rate given the level of economic development suffer in terms of economic performance. They find confirmation of a growth penalty to exist for these countries. Countries may have too high self-employment rates (e.g. Italy) or too low self-employment rates (e.g. Scandinavian countries). Audretsch *et al.* (2002) show that deviating from an 'optimal' economy-wide small firm presence may negatively influence subsequent economic growth. Acs and Armington find evidence for US Local Market Area data that the level of entrepreneurial activity has a positive effect on the employment growth rate. Fölster uses Swedish data for the 1976–95 period and finds that self-employment has a positive effect on total employment. Lastly, Audretsch and Keilbach introduce the factor of entrepreneurship capital and find evidence for German regions that this positively influences productivity.

References

Acs, Z.J. (1992), 'Small Business Economics: A Global Perspective', *Challenge*, **35**, 38–44.
Acs, Z.J. (1996), *Small Firms and Economic Growth*, The International Library of Critical Writings in Economics 61. Cheltenham, UK, and Brookfield, MA: Edward Elgar.
Acs, Z.J. and D.B. Audretsch (1990), *Innovation and Small Firms*. Cambridge, MA: MIT Press.
Acs, Z.J. and D.B. Audretsch (1993), 'Conclusion', in Z.J. Acs and D.B. Audretsch (eds), *Small Firms and Entrepreneurship: an East–West Perspective*. Cambridge: Cambridge University Press.
Aghion, P. and P. Howitt (1992), 'A Model of Growth through Creative Destruction', *Econometrica*, **60**, 323–51.
Audretsch, D.B. (1995), *Innovation and Industry Evolution*. Cambridge, MA: MIT Press.
Audretsch, D.B., M.A. Carree, A.J. van Stel, and A.R. Thurik (2002), 'Impeded Industrial Restructuring: the Growth Penalty', *Kyklos*, **55**(1), 81–97.
Audretsch, D.B., M.A. Carree, and A.R. Thurik (2001), *Does Entrepreneurship Reduce Unemployment?* Tinbergen Institute Discussion Paper TI 2001-074/3. Rotterdam: Tinbergen Institute.
Audretsch, D.B. and M.P. Feldman (1996), 'R&D Spillovers and the Geography of Innovation and Production', *American Economic Review*, **86**(3), 630–40.
Audretsch, D.B. and A.R. Thurik (2000), 'Capitalism and Democracy in the 21st Century: From the Managed to the Entrepreneurial Economy', *Journal of Evolutionary Economics*, **10**, 17–34.
Audretsch, D.B. and A.R. Thurik (2001), 'What Is New about the New Economy: Sources of Growth in the Managed and Entrepreneurial Economies', *Industrial and Corporate Change*, **19**, 795–821.
Audretsch, D.B., A.R. Thurik, I. Verheul, and A.R.M. Wennekers (eds) (2002), *Entrepreneurship:*

Determinants and Policy in a European–US Comparison. Boston, MA, and Dordrecht: Kluwer Academic Publishers.

Baumol, W.J. (1993), *Entrepreneurship, Management and the Structure of Payoffs*. Cambridge, MA: MIT Press.

Blanchflower, D.G. (2000), 'Self-employment in OECD Countries', *Labor Economics*, **7**, 471–505.

Blau, D. (1987), 'A Time Series Analysis of Self-employment', *Journal of Political Economy*, **95**, 445–67.

Brock, W.A. and D.S. Evans (1989), 'Small Business Economics', *Small Business Economics*, **1**(1), 7–20.

Carlsson, B. (1989), 'The Evolution of Manufacturing Technology and its Impact on Industrial Structure: an International Study', *Small Business Economics*, **1**(1), 21–38.

Carlsson, B. (1992), 'The Rise of Small Business: Causes and Consequences', in W.J. Adams (ed.), *Singular Europe, Economy and Policy of the European Community after 1992*. Ann Arbor, MI: University of Michigan Press, 145–69.

Carree, M.A. and A.R. Thurik (2003), 'The Impact of Entrepreneurship on Economic Growth', in D.B. Audretsch and Z.J. Acs (eds), *Handbook of Entrepreneurship Research*. Boston, MA, and Dordrecht: Kluwer Academic Publishers, 437–71.

Caves, R. (1982), *Multinational Enterprise and Economic Analysis*. Cambridge: Cambridge University Press.

Chandler, A.D. (1977), *The Visible Hand: The Managerial Revolution in American Business*. Cambridge, MA: Harvard University Press.

Chandler, A.D. Jr. (1990), *Scale and Scope: the Dynamics of Industrial Capitalism*. Cambridge, MA: Harvard University Press.

Cohen, W. and D. Levinthal (1989), 'Innovation and Learning: the Two Faces of R&D', *Economic Journal*, **99**(3), 569–96.

Davidsson, P. (2004), *Researching Entrepreneurship: International Studies in Entrepreneurship*. New York and Heidelberg: Springer.

EIM (2002), *SMEs in Europe. Report Submitted to the Enterprise Directorate-General of the EC by KPMG Special Services*. Zoetermeer: EIM Business and Policy Research.

Feldman, M.P. and D.B. Audretsch (1999), 'Innovation in Cities: Science-based Diversity, Specialization and Localized Monopoly', *European Economic Review*, **43**, 409–29.

Galbraith, J.K. (1956), *American Capitalism: the Concept of Countervailing Power*. Boston, MA: Houghton Mifflin.

Glaeser, E., H. Kallal, J. Scheinkman, and A. Shleifer (1992), 'Growth in Cities', *Journal of Political Economy*, **100**, 1126–52.

Granovetter, M.S. (1985), 'Economic Action and Social Structure: the Problem of Embeddedness', *American Journal of Sociology*, **91**(3), 481–510.

Grossman, G.M. and Helpman, E. (1991), *Innovation and Growth in the Global Economy*. Cambridge, MA: MIT Press.

Holcombe, R.G. (1998), 'Entrepreneurship and Economic Growth', *Quarterly Journal of Austrian Economics*, Summer, **1**(2), 45–62.

Jacobs, J. (1969), *The Economy of Cities*. New York: Vintage Books.

Jaffe, A., M. Trajtenberg, and R. Henderson (1993), 'Geographic Localization of Knowledge Spillovers as Evidenced by Patent Citations', *Quarterly Journal of Economics*, **63**, 577–98.

Karlsson, C., C. Friis, and T. Paulsson (2005), 'Relating Entrepreneurship to Economic Growth', in B. Johansson, C. Karlsson, and R.R. Stough (eds), *The Emerging Digital Economy: Entrepreneurship, Clusters and Policy*, Berlin: Springer-Verlag.

Kirzner, I.M. (1997), 'Entrepreneurial Discovery and the Competitive Market Process: an Austrian Approach', *Journal of Economic Literature*, **35**, 60–85.

Klepper, S. (1996), 'Entry, Exit, Growth, and Innovation Over the Product Life Cycle', *American Economic Review*, **86**, 562–83.

Loveman, G. and W. Sengenberger (1991), 'The Re-emergence of Small-scale Production: an International Comparison', *Small Business Economics*, **3**(1), 1–37.

Low, M.B. (2001), 'The Adolescence of Entrepreneurship Research: Specification of Purpose', *Entrepreneurship: Theory and Practise*, June, 17–25.

Lucas, R.E. (1988), 'On the Mechanics of Economic Development', *Journal of Monetary Economics*, **22**, 3–39.

Lucas, R.E. (1993), 'Making a Miracle', *Econometrica*, **61**(2), 251–72.

Piore, M.J. and C.F. Sabel (1984), *The Second Industrial Divide: Possibilities for Prosperity*. New York: Basic Books.

Porter, M. (1990), *The Comparative Advantage of Nations*. New York: Free Press.

Reynolds, P.D., W.D. Bygrave, E. Autio, L.W. Cox, and M. Hay (2002), *Global Entrepreneurship Monitor: 2002 Executive Report*, Ewing Marion Kauffman Foundation.

Reynolds, P.D., S.M. Camp, W.D. Bygrave, E. Autio, and M. Hay (2001), *Global Entrepreneurship Monitor: 2001 Executive Report*, Kauffman Centre for Entrepreneurial Leadership at the Ewing Marion Kauffman Foundation.

Reynolds, P.D., M. Hay, W.D. Bygrave, S.M. Camp, and E. Autio (2000), *Global Entrepreneurship Monitor: 2000 Executive Report*, Kauffman Centre for Entrepreneurial Leadership at the Ewing Marion Kauffman Foundation.

Romer, P.M. (1986), 'Increasing Returns and Long-run Growth', *Journal of Political Economy*, **94**(5), 1002–37.

Rothwell, R. (1983), 'Innovation and Firm Size: a Case of Dynamic Complementarity; or, Is Small Really So Beautiful?' *Journal of General Management*, **8**, 5–25.

Rothwell, R. (1984), 'The Role of Small Firms in the Emergence of New Technologies', *OMEGA*, **12**, 19–29.

Saxenian, A. (1990), 'Regional Networks and the Resurgence of Silicon Valley', *California Management Review*, **33**, 89–111.

Saxenian, A. (1994), *Regional Advantage*. Cambridge, MA: Harvard University Press.

Schumpeter, J.A. (1934), *The Theory of Economic Development*. Cambridge, MA: Harvard University Press; originally published, 1912.

Schumpeter, J.A. (1942), *Capitalism, Socialism and Democracy*. New York: Harper and Row.

Shane, S. (2000), 'Prior Knowledge and the Discovery of Entrepreneurial Opportunities', *Organization Science*, **11**, 448–69.

Stel, A.J. van (2003), *Compendia 2000.2: a Harmonized Data Set of Business Ownership Rates in 23 OECD Countries*. EIM Research Report H200302. Zoetermeer: EIM Business and Policy Research.

Stel, A.J. van, M.A. Carree, and A.R. Thurik (2005), 'The Effect of Entrepreneurial Activity on National Economic Growth', *Small Business Economics*, **24**, 311–21.

Stel, A.J. van and H.R. Nieuwenhuijsen (2004), 'Knowledge Spillovers and Economic Growth: an Analysis Using Data of Dutch Regions in the Period 1987–1995, *Regional Studies*, **38**, 393–407.

Stevenson, H.H. and D.E. Gumpert (1991), 'The Heart of Entrepreneurship', in W.A. Sahlman and H.H. Stevenson (eds), *The Entrepreneurial Venture*. Boston, MA: McGraw-Hill.

Teece, D.J. (1993), 'The Dynamics of Industrial Capitalism: Perspectives on Alfred Chandler's "Scale and Scope"', *Journal of Economic Literature*, **31**, 199–225.

Thorton, P.H. and K.H. Flynne (2003), 'Entrepreneurship, Networks and Geographies', in Z.J. Acs and D.B. Audretsch (eds), *Handbook of Entrepreneurship Research*. Boston, MA, and Dordrecht: Kluwer Academic Publishers, 401–33.

Thurik, A.R. (2003), 'Entrepreneurship and Unemployment in the UK', *Scottish Journal of Political Economy*, **50**(3), 264–90.

Thurik, A.R. and S. Wennekers (2004), 'Entrepreneurship, Small Business and Economic Growth', *Journal of Small Business and Enterprise Development*, **11**(1), 140–49.

Part I
General Overview

[1]

Linking Entrepreneurship and Economic Growth

Sander Wennekers
Roy Thurik

ABSTRACT. In the 1980s stagflation and high unemployment caused a renewed interest in supply side economics and in factors determining economic growth. Simultaneously, the 1980s and 1990s have seen a reevaluation of the role of small firms and a renewed attention for entrepreneurship. The goal of this survey is to synthesize disparate strands of literature to link entrepreneurship to economic growth. This will be done by investigating the relationship between entrepreneurship and economic growth using elements of various fields: historical views on entrepreneurship, macro-economic growth theory, industrial economics (Porter's competitive advantage of nations), evolutionary economics, history of economic growth (rise and fall of nations) and the management literature on large corporate organizations. Understanding the role of entrepreneurship in the process of economic growth requires the decomposition of the concept of entrepreneurship. A first part of our synthesis is to contribute to the understanding of the dimensions involved, while paying attention to the level of analysis (individual, firm and aggregate level). A second part is to gain insight in the causal links between these entrepreneurial dimensions and economic growth. A third part is to make suggestions for future empirical research into the relationship between (dimensions of) entrepreneurship and economic growth.

1. Introduction

Economic growth is a key issue both in economic policy making and in economic research. In Europe in particular, the interest in economic growth is growing fast in view of the persistently high rates of unemployment. In most OECD countries the first decades after World War II showed historically high rates of economic growth. Following the first oil crisis in 1973 a period of

Final version accepted on February 22, 1999

EIM Small Business Research and Consultancy,
The Netherlands and Centre for
Advanced Small Business Economics (CASBEC),
Erasmus University Rotterdam,
The Netherlands
E-mail: awe@eim.nl

stagflation set in, characterized by a combination of inflation and slow growth. Since the mid-1980s economic growth in some countries – such as the Netherlands – has picked up again.

In the 1960s and 1970s academic and political interest in many Western countries gradually turned to matters of demand management and income equality, whereas the interest in the causes of economic growth waned. Neo-classical theory explained economic growth by accumulation of production factors and by exogenous technological change. Mainstream economics however did not show any substantial interest in the ultimate causes underlying long-term factor accumulation and technological development.

In the 1980s stagflation and high unemployment caused a renewed interest in supply side economics and its underlying factors. As clearly exposed by North and Thomas (1973), Olson (1982) and more recently by Van de Klundert (1997) the institutional foundations of an economy are among the most prominent of these factors. These authors focus attention on factors such as incentives, regulation of markets and social rigidities. Somewhat understated in their analysis is the primal role of the economic agents who link the institutions at the micro level to the economic outcome at the macro level. It remains veiled how exactly institutions and cultural factors frame the decisions of the millions of entrepreneurs in small firms and of entrepreneurial managers working within large companies. And little is known about how these individuals materialize their decisions into the kind of actions that aggregate into economic growth. This directs our attention to two related phenomena of the 1980s and 1990s: the resurgence of small business and the revival of entrepreneurship.

There is ample evidence that economic activity moved away from large firms to small firms in the

1970s and 1980s. The most impressive and also the most cited is the share of the 500 largest American firms, the so-called Fortune 500. Their employment share dropped from 20 per cent in 1970 to 8.5 per cent in 1996 (Carlsson, 1992 and 1999). European data dealing with the size distribution of firms were not available in a systematic manner until recently. However, Eurostat has begun publishing yearly summaries of the firm size distribution of (potential) EU-members at the two-digit level for the entire business sector. See Eurostat (1994), for instance. The efforts of Eurostat are supplemented by the European Network for SME Research (ENSR), a cooperation of 19 European institutes. This organization publishes a yearly report on the structure and the developments of the small business sectors in the countries of the EU including Iceland, Norway, Liechtenstein and Switzerland. See EIM (1993/4/5/6/7). In its 1997 issue (EIM, 1997, p. 15) it is shown that small business employment growth in Europe is in excess of that of their large counterparts in the period 1988–1998.

Acs and Audretsch (1993) and Carlsson (1992) provide evidence concerning manufacturing industries in countries in varying stages of economic development. Carlsson advances two explanations for the shift toward smallness. The first deals with fundamental changes in the world economy from the 1970s onwards. These changes relate to the intensification of global competition, the increase in the degree of uncertainty and the growth in market fragmentation. The second deals with changes in the character of technological progress. He shows that flexible automation has various effects resulting in a shift from large to smaller firms. The pervasiveness of changes in the world economy, and in the direction of technological progress result in a structural shift affecting the economies of all industrialized countries. Also Piore and Sable (1984) argue that the instability of markets in the 1970s resulted in the demise of mass production and promoted flexible specialization. This fundamental change in the path of technological development led to the occurrence of vast diseconomies of scale.

This shift away from large firms is not confined to manufacturing industries. Brock and Evans (1989) show that this trend has been economy-wide at least for the United States. They provide

four more reasons why this shift has occurred: the increase of labor supply leading to lower real wages and coinciding with an increasing level of education; changes in consumer tastes; relaxation of (entry) regulations and the fact that we are in a period of creative destruction. Loveman and Sengenberger (1991) stress the influence of two trends of industrial restructuring: that of decentralization and vertical disintegration and that of the formation of new business communities. These intermediate forms of market coordination flourish owing to declining costs of transaction. Furthermore, they emphasize the role of public and private policies promoting the small business sector.[1] Audretsch and Thurik (1998) point at the necessary shift towards the knowledge based economy being the driving force behind the move from large to smaller businesses. In their view globalization and technological advancements are the major determinants of this challenge of the Western countries. See Loveman and Sengenberger (1991), Acs et al. (1999) and Carree et al. (1999) for a further documentation of industrial changes and their causes.

The causes of this shift are one thing. Its consequences cover a different area of research. Acs (1992) has discussed them. He distinguishes four consequences of the increased importance of small firms: entrepreneurship, routes of innovation, industry dynamics and job generation. His claims are that small firms play an important role in the economy serving as agents of change by their entrepreneurial activity, being the source of considerable innovative activity, stimulating industry evolution and creating an important share of the newly generated jobs. Baumol (1993a) amply deals with the role of entrepreneurial activities and the different effects it may have. The role of smallness in the process of innovative activities is investigated extensively in Acs and Audretsch (1990) and Audretsch (1995). The discussion of the relation between the role of small firms and industry dynamics is spread out: examples can be found in Audretsch (1993, 1995). Cohen and Klepper (1992) zoom in on the role of number of firms and diversity for obtaining progress. The role of small firms in the job creation process is controversial.[2]

Clearly, there are many more consequences of the increased share of small firms than the four mentioned by Acs (1992). For instance, an increase in the share of small firms may lead, ceteris paribus, to a lower orientation towards exports, a lower propensity to export employment, a qualitative change in the demand for capital and consultancy inputs, more variety in the supply of products and services or in the manner and aims of conducting research and development. The literature of the consequences of smallness is complemented by some empirical exercises by Thurik (1996) and Carree and Thurik (1998 and 1999) for some European countries. They show that a rise in the share of smallness in a certain economy, respectively a high share of smallness in a certain industry generates additional output in the entire economy, respectively industry. Schmitz (1989) provides a theoretical model with a similar result. Audretsch and Thurik (1999) show that an increase of the rate of entrepreneurship (number of business owners per labor force) leads to lower levels of unemployment in 23 OECD countries in the period 1984 through 1994.

The reevaluation of the role of small firms is related to a renewed attention to the role of entrepreneurship. If the size class distribution has an influence on growth, it must be differences in organization that matter. The major difference between the organization of a large firm and a small one is the role of ownership and management. In a small firm usually there is one person or a very small group of persons which is in control and which shapes the firm and its future. The role of such a person is often described with the term "entrepreneurship".

In recent years renewed attention has been given to the role of entrepreneurship in economic development. This is related to the aforementioned shift to supply side economics. Many economists and politicians now have an intuition that there is a positive impact of entrepreneurship on the growth of GDP and employment. Furthermore, many stress the role of the entrepreneur in implementing innovations. This renewed interest of politicians and professional economists coincides with a revival of entrepreneurship rates in most, though not in all, Western economies.[3]

A related question is whether small firms and entrepreneurship are synonymous. We will argue that this is not the case.[4] Small firms certainly are a vehicle in which entrepreneurship thrives. There

are more such vehicles, for instance business units within large companies. Clearly, this broader interpretation of entrepreneurship implies measurement difficulties.

"Small business has to save us" is a slogan often heard from European politicians and representatives of social and institutional groups. They fear for a further rise of the already unacceptably high level of unemployment caused by the sheer endless series of efficiency and cost-cutting operations of the public and large business sectors. They seek salvation with the residual sector, being the small business sector. They hope that stimulating smallness can fight unemployment. There is probably some truth in their hopes and slogans. The literature cited above points decisively it this direction. However, there are more ways for entrepreneurship to contribute to growth than through small firms. Recent studies on the role of competition (Nickell, 1996), of deregulation (Koedijk and Kremers, 1996) and of the nature of innovation (Cohen and Klepper, 1996) support this view.

The objective of this article is to synthesize disparate strands of literature in order to link entrepreneurship to economic growth. This will be done by investigating the relationship between entrepreneurship and economic growth in the following fields: historical views on entrepreneurship, macro-economic growth theory, industrial economics (Porter's competitive advantage of nations), evolutionary economics, history of economic growth (rise and fall of nations) and the management literature on large organizations. This last body of literature is taken into account because management techniques within large organizations have tried to learn from their smaller counterparts. This led to a wave of downsizing, the creation of business units, forms of intrapreneurship, etc. Furthermore, as we have argued above, our approach to entrepreneurship will not be confined to its role in the arena of small firms.

Entrepreneurship is an ill-defined, at best multidimensional, concept. Understanding its role in the process of growth requires the decomposition of the concept of entrepreneurship. A *first* goal of this paper is to contribute to the understanding of the dimensions involved, while paying attention to the level of analysis (individual, firm and aggregate level). A *second* goal is to provide insight in the causal links between these entrepreneurial dimensions and economic growth. These insights, however valuable, are not a goal in itself but should be viewed in a broader framework. Empirical research of the role of entrepreneurship as a driving force of economic development still is not well developed. Therefore, a *third* goal of our paper is to suggest ways in which to measure entrepreneurship and to suggest ways in which the relationship between dimensions of entrepreneurship and growth might be empirically investigated. This might shed light on the way the capitalist market engine works.

The preliminary framework of this article is given in Figure 1. This framework is adopted because there is not usually a direct link between entrepreneurship and economic growth. And secondly, entrepreneurship is an ill-defined concept. That is why we need *intermediate variables* or *linkages* to explain how entrepreneurship influences economic growth. Examples of these intermediate variables are innovation, and entry and exit of firms (competition). We will also attempt to provide some *conditions* for entrepreneurship. This is done for several reasons. First personal traits lie at the origin of entrepreneurship. Furthermore, both entrepreneurship and the intermediate linkages may depend upon underlying cultural and institutional conditions. The relevance of these conditions will be looked into in some detail. Finally, the possibility of feedbacks will be considered.

Conditions

(personal, cultural, institutional)

Entrepreneurship

(multidimensional; different levels of analysis)

Intermediate linkages

(innovation, competition)

Economic growth

Figure 1. Preliminary framework.

This article is structured as follows. In section 2 introductory remarks will be made on current and historical views on entrepreneurship. This section also contains a part on the explanation of the disappearance of entrepreneurship from economic theory during the post war period, and closes with the explanation of the revival of interest in entrepreneurship since the 1980s. Section 3 is concerned with understanding economic growth. First, the significance of the rejuvenation of macro-economic growth theory for entrepreneurship research will be examined. This theory focuses on the importance of (human) capital formation and innovation. Next, some seminal literature in the field of economic history, in particular concerning the rise and decline of nations, is discussed in order to search for the underlying causes of economic growth such as the cultural setting, legal framework and entrepreneurial activity. In a final section some modern views regarding economic growth, as formulated in industrial economics and in evolutionary economics are considered. Section 4 focuses on the role of entrepreneurship, downsizing and intrapreneurship within large organizations. Section 5 attempts to bring it all together. Some conclusions will be drawn from the literature research reported in sections 2 through 4, viewed through the framework as it has developed in the course of our investigations. This section also presents proposals for further research.

2. Economic literature on entrepreneurship

In section 2.1 we will give an introduction to the historical views of economists on entrepreneurship, particularly by summarizing Hébert and Link (1989) which again is a summary of Hébert and Link (1982). In section 2.2 we will describe the disappearance and the revival of the interest in entrepreneurship. In section 2.3 we will expand on two main aspects of entrepreneurship: start-ups and innovation.

2.1. *Historical views on entrepreneurship*

Throughout intellectual history, the entrepreneur has worn many faces and fulfilled many roles. At least thirteen distinct roles for the entrepreneur can be identified in the economic literature (Hébert and Link, 1989, but also Van Dijk and Thurik, 1995 and Van Praag, 1996):

1. The person who assumes the risk associated with uncertainty.
2. The supplier of financial capital.
3. An innovator.
4. A decision-maker.
5. An industrial leader.
6. A manager or a superintendent.
7. An organizer and coordinator of economic resources.
8. The owner of an enterprise.
9. An employer of factors of production.
10. A contractor.
11. An arbitrageur.
12. An allocator of resources among alternative uses.
13. The person who realizes a start-up of a new business.

Once we focus on the dynamic role of the entrepreneur – a role most directly linked with change and growth, implied in statements 1, 3, 4, 5, 7, 10, 11, 12, and 13 – the taxonomy of entrepreneurial theories can be condensed into three major intellectual traditions, each tracing its origin to Richard Cantillon (Hébert and Link, 1989). The first is the German tradition of von Thünen, Schumpeter and Baumol, the second the (neo-)classical tradition of Marshall, Knight and Schultz and the third the Austrian tradition of Menger, von Mises, and Kirzner. These traditions share a heritage and common language but they point at different aspects of the function of the entrepreneur. Representing differences in style and emphasis, they can be summarized as follows. The (neo-)classicals stress the role of the entrepreneur in leading markets to equilibrium through their entrepreneurial activities. The Austrians concentrate on the abilities of the entrepreneur to perceive profit opportunities, usually after some exogenous shock. The "Austrian" entrepreneur combines resources to fulfill currently unsatisfied needs or to improve market inefficiencies or deficiencies. In the German or Schumpeterian tradition economists concentrate on the entrepreneur as a creator of instability and creative destruction. The difference between the German (Schumpeterian) and Austrian tradition can be summarized as follows: "The creation of potential may be seen as Schumpeterian and its realization as Austrian" (Nooteboom 1993, p. 1).

The entrepreneur first appeared in the writings of Cantillon (1680–1734). Cantillon recognized three classes of economic agents: landowners, entrepreneurs and employees. Cantillon's entrepreneur is someone who exercises business engagements in the face of uncertainty. He argued that the origin of entrepreneurship lies in the lack of perfect foresight. Von Thünen also sharply discriminates between the entrepreneur and the supplier of financial capital, who is similar to Cantillon's landowner. Menger, being one of the founders of the Austrian school, also makes this distinction. See Hébert and Link (1989). He saw the entrepreneur primarily as a person combining production factors. This draws attention to the personality of the entrepreneur. See also Lumpkin and Dess (1996).

Marshall describes the function of "superintendence". This superintendent organizes the production in a firm. Marshall attached a more important role to entrepreneurs, "the pioneers of new paths" (Marshall, 1961), than any other neoclassical theorist. The mainstream modern neoclassical economists apparently have not cared to include the entrepreneur in their formalized model. Knight and Schumpeter distinguished this managerial or superintendent role from the role of the "entrepreneur". Since the writings of Knight, it is customary to distinguish between risk and uncertainty. The latter is unique and uninsurable. We will discuss the disappearance of the entrepreneur from economic theory in section 2.2. We will also see that Knight's distinction between risk and uncertainty parallels information problems within firms, increasing the need for entrepreneurial coordination.

Based on their study of the history of economic thought about entrepreneurship, Hébert and Link (1989, p. 47) propose the following "synthetic" definition of who an entrepreneur is and what he does: *"the entrepreneur is someone who specializes in taking responsibility for and making judgmental decisions that affect the location, form, and the use of goods, resources, or institutions"*. When searching for links between entrepreneurship and growth, this definition does not fully suffice. The dynamics of perceiving and creating new economic opportunities and the competitive dimensions of entrepreneurship need more attention. We will return to the definition of entrepreneurship in section 5.

2.2. *Disappearance and revival*

In the traditional interpretation of the neo-classical model, all individual agents have perfect information. Their economic objectives are clearly and rationally stated. In equilibrium, consumers and producers reach one set of prices at which demand for each good equals its supply. All markets that are implicitly assumed to exist and to work perfectly well are cleared at this set of equilibrium prices. Given this definition of a firm's task, there is no need for innovative alertness and risk bearing initiative.

The neo-classical model, with its production function, the internal logic of rational choice and perfect information, leaves no room for an active entrepreneur.[5] As neo-classical economics became more formalized and as the mathematics of equilibrium theory became more important, references to the entrepreneur receded from the micro textbooks. The model left no room for aspects like initiative, charisma, stubbornness and the struggle with new ideas and uncertainty. "The model is essentially an instrument of optimality analysis of well defined problems which need no entrepreneur for their solution" (Van Praag, 1996, p. 17, referring to Baumol, 1968 and 1993a). Also see Barreto, 1989 and Kirchhoff (1984, p. 30).

Reality, however, does not consist of well-defined problems alone. The neo-classical model constrained the decision making of the entrepreneur, in terms of product quality and price, technology, within limits wholly alien to the context in which real world entrepreneurs characteristically operate (Kirzner, 1985). It is now some twenty years since economic theorists have come to feel uncomfortable about the absence of entrepreneurship from their models. A number of circumstances have contributed to this discomfort.

Firstly, the importance of the entrepreneur in the real world became more and more difficult to ignore. Some economists had predicted that large firms would prevail in economic life, due to their higher efficiency and superior technology (Galbraith, 1967). In the 1980s it became clear that firms of different size continued to coexist in each industry. The importance of mass-producing,

"Fordist" firms declined (Piore and Sabel, 1984). Flexibility of (groups of) small firms was shown to result in competitive advantages. In some circumstances, like in a very turbulent environment, small firms can act more resolutely. Also, large firms have created more room for entrepreneurial employees to act within the firm. We will expand on this "corporate entrepreneurship" in section 4.

The share of small firms expanded in the 1980s in many industries in many industrialized countries. This generated an increased interest in the concept of entrepreneurship. Another reason why the interest in entrepreneurship has grown, is the employment problem in Western Europe. Many politicians and economists have the intuition that new possibilities for growth, innovation and creating jobs will come from small and new firms.

Two theoretical developments outside the realm of established neo-classical theory brought entrepreneurship within the focus of attention (Casson, 1991). Leibenstein in formulating his X-efficiency theory distinguished himself from the neo-classicals. Basically, X-efficiency is the degree of inefficiency in the use of resources within the firm: it measures the extent to which the firm fails to realize its productive potential. Four differences can be identified between the X-efficiency theory and neo-classical theory. One is that contracts are incomplete. This leads to the second main difference, which can be compared to the principal-agent problem. According to Leibenstein, there is a tension between the employee and the employer over how hard the former should work. Thirdly, effort and alertness are required to change old routines and production techniques. Finally, Leibenstein differs from neo-classical theory in regarding the firm as an organization of different individuals that have no consensus on their objectives. Leibenstein sees entrepreneurship as a creative response to X-efficiency (Leibenstein, 1968 and 1979).

A second addition to neo-classical theory was offered by institutionalism. Coase (1937) saw the entrepreneur as a coordinator of production within the firm. This coordination is needed because the price mechanism is mostly not used to allocate resources within the firm itself. Outside the firm, price movements direct production. Williamson (1975) elaborated on this approach with his thesis that firms concentrate on economizing on transaction costs. Institutionalism also focused attention on information problems and hierarchical tensions within an organization. An important question is how entrepreneurial individuals can "appropriate" the gains of their specific abilities. Is it within a firm as an "intrapreneur" or by starting a new firm as an entrepreneur? We will expand on this in the section on corporate entrepreneurship.

In sum, we see that the importance of entrepreneurship increased by developments in the economic process itself and was recognized by theories serving as a supplement or an alternative to the established neo-classical paradigm.

2.3. *Entrepreneurship: new entry and newness*

Hébert and Link (1989) show that many different roles[6] of the entrepreneur can be distinguished. However, from a viewpoint of linking entrepreneurship to economic growth, two major roles of entrepreneurship can be singled out. The first has to do with "new entry" and the second with "newness" in general. First, the entrepreneur as the founder of a new business: ". . . someone who creates and then, perhaps, organizes and operates a new business firm, whether or not there is anything innovative in those acts". Secondly, entrepreneurship plays a more general innovative role in economic life: ". . . the entrepreneur as the innovator – as the one who transforms inventions and ideas into economically viable entities, whether or not, in the course of doing so they create or operate a firm" (Baumol, 1993b, p. 198). The latter approach can be embodied in the former, i.e. an innovation implemented by a firm start-up (see Kirchhoff, 1994 p. 37, who regards entrepreneurship as "innovation by newly formed independent firms").

The management literature has a broader view upon entry. In surveying this literature, Lumpkin and Dess (1996) integrate the renewing aspects of entrepreneurship. "New entry can be accomplished by entering new or established markets with new or existing goods or services. New entry is the act of launching a new venture, either by a start-up firm, through an existing firm or via internal corporate venturing" (Lumpkin and Dess, 1996, p. 136). In their view, the essential act of entrepreneurship is more than new entry as we see

it. In section 4 we will see that entrepreneurial activities in existing, large firms often take place by mimicking smallness. Usually, new-firm start-ups and innovative entrepreneurship are treated separately. In the next two sections we will pay attention to both appearances of entrepreneurship.

2.3.1. *New entry: start-ups*

To some the creation of new organizations is what entrepreneurship is all about. This view is clearly expressed by Gartner (1989, p. 62). A firm start-up is a major form of (new) entry into an industry. Both macro and micro-economic factors influence start-ups. Since measuring the number of new-firm start-ups has not been done systematically at the industry level, but mostly at the macro-level (Audretsch, 1995, p. 56), separating macro-economic influences from microeconomic causes of new-firm start-ups is difficult. Three major points can be emphasized (Audretsch, 1995). Firstly, the number of new-firm start-ups and its importance relative to the total number of firms differs considerably across industries. Secondly, the number of start-ups differs significantly from year to year. Thirdly, the impact of macro-economic developments varies from industry to industry.

The traditional view on why firms enter says that firms are attracted by excess profitability in an industry because of lack of competitors. Start-ups play a more important role than reestablishing market equilibrium. Antitrust regulation determines the legal structure for the role entrepreneurship can play in stimulating competitiveness. We will return to this in section 3. New-firm start-ups do not take place at the same rate in every industry. Audretsch (1995, p. 63) finds that, due to differences in the underlying knowledge structure, new-firm start-ups tend to be more important in industries that can be characterized as having an entrepreneurial technological regime. New firms tend to be less important in industries with a routinized technological regime. This difference is caused by higher expected profits when starting up in an industry with an entrepreneurial technological regime.

To start as an entrepreneur both "willingness" and "opportunity" are essential (Van Praag, 1996, p. 39). She defines opportunity as "the possibility to become an entrepreneur if one wants to".

Sander Wennekers and Roy Thurik

n starting capital, entrepre-
(economic) environment.
illingness to start as an
ndent on both individual
ecial features of entrepre-
i the alternative available
options and their perceived attractiveness".

Although reliable data are scant, there are indi-
cations that since the mid-1980s start-ups have
increased in several Western countries. This rise
was particularly strong in The Netherlands.[7]

2.3.2. *Newness: innovating entrepreneurship*

Schumpeter[8] was the economist who has most
prominently drawn attention to the "innovating
entrepreneur". He or she carries out "new combinations we call enterprise; the individuals whose
function it is to carry them out we call entrepreneurs" (Schumpeter, 1934, p. 74). Dess and
Lumpkin write that: "Innovativeness reflects a
firm's tendency to engage in and support new
ideas, novelty, experimentation, and creative
processes that may result in new products,
services, or technological processes. Although
innovations can vary in their degree of radicalness,
innovativeness represents a basic willingness to
depart from existing technologies or practices and
venture beyond the current state of the art"
(Lumpkin and Dess, 1996, p. 142). Innovativeness
can be distinguished between product-market
innovation and technological innovation. The
latter which until recently enjoyed the main focus
of research into this field, "consists primarily of
product and process development, engineering,
research, and an emphasis on technical expertise
and industry knowledge. Product-market innovativeness suggests an emphasis on product design,
market research and advertising and promotion"
(Lumpkin and Dess, 1996, p. 143). Using a broad
definition of new entry, Dess and Lumpkin point
out that entrepreneurship can be innovative
without new products or production processes
being introduced.

Enlarging the amount of innovative entrepreneurship has long been the aim of government
policy. Schumpeter does not formulate any
concepts for the role of government in stimulating
"innovative entrepreneurship". Baumol states that
this is the main shortcoming of Schumpeter's
theory: ". . . the paucity of insights on policy that

emerge from it". Baumol finds that institutional
arrangements or other social phenomena affect the
quantity of entrepreneurial effort. These structural
and cultural factors can also determine the allocation of entrepreneurship. Essential for economic
development is ". . . that the exercise of entrepreneurship can sometimes be unproductive or
even destructive, and that whether it takes one of
these directions or one that is more benign
depends heavily on the structure of payoffs in the
economy – the rules of the game" (Baumol, 1990,
p. 899). Some examples can clarify this: Baumol
describes various types of rent seeking, like the
wars in the early Middle Ages in Western Europe
over land and castles. "Such violent economic
activity inspired frequent and profound innovation
. . . its net effect may be a . . . net reduction in
social income and wealth" (Baumol, 1990, p. 904).
A more recent example is that in Japan, when
compared to the United States, ". . . the rules of
the game have been designed to discourage the
allocation of entrepreneurial talent into rent-
seeking litigation" (Baumol, 1993a, p. 240). In
section 3 we will return to the role of entrepreneurship in the economic history of various
countries.

2.4. *Conclusions from the literature on entrepreneurship*

The different historical views of economists offer
a broad perspective on the concept of entrepreneurship as well as on the intermediate variables
that form the connection between entrepreneurship
and economic growth. The neo-classicals stress
the role of the entrepreneur in leading markets to
equilibrium. In the Austrian tradition, the alertness
for profit opportunities and the importance of
competition are emphasized. Schumpeter sees the
entrepreneur as the innovator in economic life.
Table I provides our conclusions in terms of the
preliminary framework proposed in section 1.

Entrepreneurship has to do with individuals,
both with their traits and their actions (roles).
Newness through start-ups and innovations as well
as competition are the most relevant factors
linking entrepreneurship to economic growth.

Many questions remain, like what is the
influence of basic conditions on entrepreneurship
and on the intermediate linkages? Which is the

TABLE I
Conclusions based upon the historical views of economists

Items from the framework	Relevant variables found in the literature	Relevant disciplines	Focal unit of observation
Conditions	– (only indirect links were found in the literature; to be discussed in section 3)		
Entrepreneurship	– traits (alertness, perception) – roles of the entrepreneur	– psychology – economics	– individuals – individuals
Intermediate linkages	– newness through start-ups and innovation – markets and competition – equilibrium versus disequilibrium	– industrial economics – industrial economics – economics	– firms – firms and industries – aggregate levels
Economic growth	– (only indirect links were found in the literature; to be discussed in section 3)		

role of smallness and what are the opportunities for entrepreneurship within large organizations? Which intermediate linkages are still missing from the analysis? These questions will be touched upon in the following sections.

3. Economic growth and entrepreneurship

Where entrepreneurship was the focus in the preceding section, we will now focus upon economic growth. In section 3.1 we briefly deal with growth theories. Some aspects of the history of economic growth are surveyed in section 3.2. Finally, in section 3.3, some modern views as formulated in industrial economics and in evolutionary economics are discussed.

3.1. *Growth theory*

In this section, the distinction will be made between the "old" neo-classical growth theory and the "new", endogenous growth theory. For a long period neo-classical growth theory concentrated solely on the contribution of labor and capital to the process of economic expansion. In its different forms, either as growth accounting (Denison, 1985) or as a theory of long-run tendencies (Solow, 1970), there remained much to explain. Both forms generate a substantial residual, which was ascribed to the effects of technological change. This change is unaccounted for and is viewed as exogenous "manna from heaven" (Van de Klundert and Smulders, 1992, p. 177).

The basic idea of the new growth theory is to endogenize the long-run rate of economic expansion. Baumol (1993a, pp. 259–260) suggests ". . . that so far as capital investment, education, and the like are concerned, one can best proceed by treating them as *endogenous* variables in a sequential process – in other words, these variables affect productivity growth, but productivity growth, in turn, itself influences the value of these variables, after some lag. These endogenous influences are, then, critical components of a feedback process". Baumol (p. 260) continues: "To some degree, the same story can be told about the exercise of entrepreneurship, investment in innovation, and the magnitude of activity directed to the transfer of technology. These too, clearly, are influenced by past productivity growth achievements and they also, in their turn, influence future growth. Yet it would seem plausible that there is a strong streak of exogeneity in these variables, which can help to account for the outbreak and spread of industrial revolutions and for the relative decline and even for the collapse of economies that formerly were models of success". These statements describe both the contribution of endogenous growth theory and the dilemma this theory is confronted with.

Few attempts have been made to incorporate entrepreneurship in growth models. Entrepreneurship did not fit in the traditional, theoretical neo-classical models for two reasons. Firstly, the neo-classical axiom of perfect competition implies that there are no profit opportunities for entrepreneurs left. Secondly, models of general equilibrium do not take into account the dynamics of

Sander Wennekers and Roy Thurik

ating entrepreneurship", as described in 1 2. The axioms of the endogenous growth theory have created new possibilities for fitting entrepreneurship and/or innovation into growth models. A first example is Romer's version (1990) in which the engine of growth is the research sector which produces blueprints for new varieties of capital goods that are in turn produced and used in the goods-producing sector. The model assumes increasing returns to scale. By assuming monopolistic competition (Chamberlin, 1933), rents can be assigned to the research activities that generate knowledge. Secondly, the model pertains to some features of Schumpeter's later work:[9] growth is driven by monopoly rents obtained by the introduction of new products, economic change is the result of purposeful activities of profit-seeking entrepreneurs.

Van de Klundert and Smulders (1992, p. 191) state that Schumpeter's "creative destruction" gives a much richer description of entrepreneurship and economic dynamics. A recent attempt to capture "creative destruction" in a formal model can be found in Aghion and Howitt (1992). The R&D sector invents new production techniques making existing techniques obsolete. Producers shift to this new technique and the innovator is rewarded until a new technique is found which replaces his invention. The intermediate variable of innovativeness, enlarging the long-term growth, can be seen as valuable in the endogenous growth theory.

A connection between historical views on entrepreneurship (Schultz, 1980) and the endogenous growth theory (Lucas, 1988) can be made using the concept of "enlarging entrepreneurial ability", as a form of human capital. Schultz stated that the quantity and quality of entrepreneurial efforts can be enhanced by investment in entrepreneurial ability: ". . . the abilities of entrepreneurs to deal with the disequilibria that are pervasive in a dynamic economy are a part of the stock of human capital. . . . Many of the disequilibria that are associated with economic growth are endogenous. An innovation by a business enterprise (Schumpeter's innovator) is an endogenous event" (Schultz, 1980, p. 437 and p. 444). Schultz is a scholar of the Anglo-American tradition, since he concentrates on the abilities of entrepreneurship to restore equilibrium. Eliasson (1995)

contests this view. He stresses the importance of entry and exit and selection mechanisms. Lucas (1988) concludes from his models that structurally divergent rates of growth can occur, due to the external effects of human capital (spillovers). In our view the external effects of entrepreneurship, a special form of human capital, can be seen as an additional intermediate variable derived from the "new" growth theory.

The new growth theory puts emphasis on the endogenous role of innovation and human capital formation in explaining economic growth. On the other hand, in spite of the strong technological dynamism of today it is well to remember that in world history technological creativity has been an exception rather than a rule (Mokyr, 1990). Underlying political, social and economic conditions have time and again been seen to play a vital role.

Summing up, the endogenous growth theory focuses explicit attention on the intermediate variables (human) capital formation and innovation. However, entrepreneurship remains largely implicit and this theory does not shed light on the underlying conditions of the entrepreneurial activity needed for (human) capital formation and innovation. This will be the subject of the next section.

3.2. *Economic history and the causes of long term growth*

Growth accounting in a neo-classical framework can disentangle economic growth into contributing factors such as labor inputs (correcting for hours of work and education), capital formation, economies of scale and advances in the state of knowledge. But it leaves a residual, and more importantly it misses the fundamental causes governing capital formation and innovation. Lewis (1955) already distinguishes between the proximate causes of economic growth (the effort to economize, increase of knowledge and increase of the amount of capital per head) and the underlying "causes of these causes", which are to be found in beliefs and institutions. North and Thomas (1973) put it even more bluntly: "The factors we have listed (innovation, economies of scale, education, capital accumulation, etc.) are not causes of growth; they *are* growth". According to them the causes of economic growth are to be found in the factors which determine the efficiency of the economic organization: incentives, property rights etc.

An interesting approach focusing on these factors is chosen by economists studying historical processes of economic growth. An introduction to this approach which aims at ". . . comprehending the economy as a dynamic, historical process' is provided by Lazonick (1991, pp. 115–117 and pp. 303–321). The time span covered in these historical investigations is usually quite long (a century or more). This time span encompasses large differences in average growth rates between periods (usually referred to in terms of the "rise and decline of nations"). It keeps track of slowly changing factors in the culture, the legal framework and the external organization of markets, and it covers the full length of time it may take for new technologies to disseminate through the economic system.

Paraphrasing Cipolla (1981) who regards growth accounting as highly artificial, because in reality "everything flows together" can summarize their approach. Referring to Schumpeter he states that economic growth cannot be understood without taking the role of entrepreneurship into account. Cipolla (p. 120) however continues: "Entrepreneurial activity is a necessary ingredient, but not a sufficient one. It is the human vitality of a whole society which, given the opportunity, comes into play and sets loose the 'creative responses of history'".

This field of "the rise and fall of nations" is extremely wide and diverse.[10] Below we will certainly do no full justice to the analysis of each of the authors whom we cite. However, all is well if we will have succeeded in painting a picture of the role of entrepreneurship in the historical analysis of economic growth. We follow two approaches: historical case studies and generalizations (Lewis, 1955). First some major periods in European history will be summarized one by one, while another short case study will discuss the so-called East Asian miracle. Secondly, some general views on the role of culture and institutions will be discussed and the main findings will be integrated in our final framework.

3.2.1. *Role of entrepreneurship in European history*

Between 1000 and 1500 the European economy seemed locked in the feudal system. Property rights were not secure, the rendering of many services in the so-called manorial system (Cipolla, 1981, p. 114) was not monetarized, local tolls hindered a free flow of goods. These conditions improved slowly. Gradually, a system evolved in which entrepreneurship was primarily embodied by a class of merchants advancing raw materials to the craftsmen and marketing the finished goods. Also, the rise of the cities created a frontier for experimentation and innovation.[11]

The Italian city states took the lead in this development, and their commercial success went hand in hand with a Renaissance of arts and sciences. Gradually the center of gravity moved to the Low Countries. In the seventeenth century conditions in the Northern Netherlands were highly conducive for an upsurge of entrepreneurship. The legal framework was advanced, property rights were secure and the economy had been monetarized to a great extent. Markets for final goods and production factors were reasonably accessible. Social mobility was relatively high. The rate of urbanization was far ahead of the rest of Europe, and in these cities demand conditions were favorable for economic expansion. According to De Vries and Van der Woude (1985) the resulting Golden Age can be regarded as the first round of modern economic growth.

As is well known, in this period also the arts and sciences bloomed. Again we quote Cipolla (1981, p. 120): "In the seventeenth century, when the Low Countries became the prime movers in international trade while producing great entrepreneurs such as De Geer or the Tripps, they also produced jurists like Grotius, experimentalists such as Huyghens and Leeuwenhoek, and painters such as Rembrandt." Regarding periods of economic rise in general he continues: "In order to understand what happened in certain societies, it is necessary to understand an atmosphere of collective enthusiasm, of exaltation and of cooperation".

Jane Jacobs (1984) has a great deal to offer when dealing with entrepreneurship. While it is fair to say that "cities" and not "entrepreneurship" form the central theme of her writing, it is clear from her analysis that the all-important growth of import-replacing cities must be viewed as a highly entrepreneurial process. Historically, she finds two major patterns or motifs: reliance of backward cities upon one another and economic improvisation. Her views on the rise of Venice and subsequently many other hitherto backward European cities may serve to bear this out. Essentially the Veneti used their initial trade with the rich city of Constantinople as a springboard to start re-exporting and selling their imitations to other backward cities in Europe. They were able to replace more imports by home production and to shift to more sophisticated imports as their wealth increased. Meanwhile, other cities used Venice as a springboard. Finally, a volatile network of inter-city trade developed, constantly changing in content and stimulating new markets for city-made innovations. According to Jacobs there were no "ready-made schemes of producing predetermined choices of products" underlying these developments. On the contrary, the entrepreneurs in the backward cities of Europe had to experiment and to improvise in order to develop and sell cheaper substitutes for more sophisticated import-goods.

According to Cipolla (1981, p. 276), at the end of the fifteenth century England was still an "underdeveloped country" in comparison to countries such as Italy, the Low Countries, France and Southern Germany. Between 1500 and 1700 considerable changes occurred. At first British exports were dominated by wool and woolen cloth only. After 1550, gradually the many immigrants from France and the southern Low Countries brought many other "industrious manufactures" with them. English society at the time showed a striking cultural receptiveness and open-mindedness for new ideas and techniques. Increasingly young men were sent abroad to study at foreign universities. English society showed an ability to give positive and innovative responses to challenges and difficulties such as increasing competition and scarcity of raw materials. Entrepreneurs adopted other methods of production, diversified into other manufactures and penetrated new markets. Gradually the English developed a worldwide commercial network. The notable development of international trade, according to Cipolla (p. 295) "proved to be a great school of entrepreneurship".

By 1700 the legal and institutional conditions had also considerably changed and were favorable for factor mobility and innovation in economic activity (North and Thomas, 1973). The elimination of feudalism, the declining power of the guilds, the burgeoning of the joint stock company and the development of a banking system are some important examples they cite. North and Thomas (p. 156) conclude: "England . . . had developed an efficient set of property rights embedded in common law . . . and had begun to protect private property in knowledge with its patent law. The stage was now set for the industrial revolution". The Industrial Revolution was both a revolution in production techniques (mechanization) and in organization (the factory system). A great variety of innovations, mutually reinforcing each other, yielded an unprecedented increase in productivity (Landes, 1969, p. 41). There is apparently no full consensus why this revolution came about first in Britain, but some factors seem beyond doubt. Among these is the technological leadership (Mokyr, 1990, p. 239) which Britain showed between 1750 and 1850.

In explaining this leadership British superiority in implementation (innovation) was more decisive than their strength in inventions. It was not based on scientific leadership although British inventors and manufacturers were in constant contact with scientists. Another factor was its endowment of technically skilled labor, which had more to do with on-the-job training than with schooling. Mokyr (p. 254) sums it all up in one sentence: "It is arguable that though Britain may have had an absolute advantage in both inventors and entrepreneurs, it had a comparative advantage in entrepreneurs and skilled workers, and thus imported inventions and inventors and exported entrepreneurs and technicians to the industrializing enclaves of the Continent".

In Britain a free flow of entrepreneurship between lines of business was also manifest, and the allocation of resources was more responsive to new opportunities than in Continental economies which were characterized by occupational exclusiveness (Landes, 1969, p. 71). Also in these countries social and psychological attitudes, viewing the family business as a way of life and not as a means to an end, were unfavorable to effective entrepreneurship and competition

(Landes, pp. 131–132). The inevitable conclusion is that during the Industrial Revolution Britain excelled in entrepreneurship.

During the 19th century decline set in. Some figures from Maddison (1995, pp. 23–24) may serve to illustrate this. During the period 1870 through 1973 real growth of GDP per capita in Britain was only 1.3% annually and lagged behind that in the U.S.A. (1.9%) and Germany (1.9%), and certainly behind that in Japan (2.7%). Consequently, in 1973 per capita income in Britain, once the richest nation in the world, had fallen substantially behind that in countries such as Switzerland, Denmark, Germany and the U.S.A.

It is beyond the scope of this paper to consider all the possible causes of this decline. We will only view this retardation through the perspective of entrepreneurship and some underlying factors. Wiener (1981) paints a vivid picture of how the Industrial Revolution seems to have caused a strong cultural reorientation. Part of this was a romantic reaction to industrial society ("our England is a garden"). Another part has to do with what Wiener calls "the gentrification of the entrepreneurial class", in which values such as zeal for work, invention and money making gave way to a preference for comfort, enjoyment and public service. This was reinforced by the school system which, modeling itself on the public schools, separated the middle class from technology and business. Quite contrary to the U.S.A. where Henry Ford was a folk hero, in Britain a successful entrepreneur like William Morris "has received largely uninformed and unenthusiastic acceptance" (Wiener, 1981, p. 131). Wiener also gives two examples illustrating how this cultural reorientation permeated deeply into the 1960s and the 1970s. First, several surveys among students and graduates then showed a "combination of ignorance and distaste" towards industry. Secondly, a poll revealed that a large majority of directors of leading British companies felt that television and universities were "biased against business and private enterprise". At the same time the legal and institutional framework – with high marginal tax rates, public monopolies, shop stewards, and collusive tendering among its prominent features – had become less conducive to entrepreneurship and competition.

Another authoritative source in this area is

Landes who also argues that the major reasons why Britain declined when compared to Germany were ". . . not material, but rather social and institutional" (Landes, 1969, p. 334). As examples he mentions the control of well-organized craft workers and the limited organizational capabilities of the entrepreneurs as major obstacles to innovation.

Porter (1990, p. 502) sums it all up for the postwar period: "British firms have, too often, a management culture that works against innovation and change . . . Combined with such managerial attitudes has been a debilitating relationship between labor and management. . . . Unions have had great power to negotiate restrictive practices, which have inhibited innovation and retarded productivity." According to Porter also the motivation of managers and workers to work hard and to earn a great deal of money was traditionally low in Britain, and absenteeism into the early 1980s was high. High personal tax rates contributed to dulled incentives. Finally domestic rivalry according to Porter has long been lacking. Instead of competing fiercely British firms would rather attempt to protect a monopoly or to merge with another firm. Up to the early 1980s rivalry was also limited by a slow rate of new business formation.

Summarizing one can say that entrepreneurship has played a vital role both in the take off stages of the European economy and during the Industrial Revolution. Moreover, it is likely that economic decline, such as experienced in late 19th and most of 20th century Britain, was aggravated by the cultural and institutional framework becoming less conducive to entrepreneurship.[12]

3.2.2. *The East Asian miracle*[13]

One of the most interesting recent growth experiences is the superior achievement of the East Asian economies in the last decades. In a World Bank policy research report, titled "The East Asian Miracle; economic growth and public policy", the rapid and sustained growth of the Republic of Korea, Taiwan, Singapore, Hong Kong, Japan, Indonesia, Malaysia and Thailand in the period 1965–1990 is analyzed. See World Bank (1993). These eight so-called High-performing Asian economies (HPAEs) experienced an average annual growth rate of real GNP per capita of 5.5%, more than twice that of the OECD countries. At the same time the HPAEs diminished the inequality of their income distributions.

In fact, the analysis of the World Bank fits well into our framework. The remarkable growth achievements manifest themselves in both exports and domestic demand, and can directly be linked to superior accumulation of physical and human capital, allocation of resources to productive investment, and the acquisition and mastering of technology. These investment activities were supported by public policies promoting macro-economic stability, diminishing inequality and universal primary and secondary education, as well as by a reliable legal framework conducive to competition and international trade. In spite of this attention for fundamentals it is fair to say that the analysis is primarily macroeconomic and somehow does not convey that innovation, private investment and marketing all are manifestations of entrepreneurial activity. Apart from a factual section on the profusion of small and medium-size enterprises there is no analysis of the rise of entre-preneurship. Nor is there an extensive analysis of the role of cultural factors such as attitudes towards risk and uncertainty, and openness to foreign technology.

Support for an alternative view on the East Asian miracle can be found with Phelps in his comments on a paper by Mankiw (1995, pp. 312–313) concerning "The Growth of Nations". We quote Phelps: "The alternative view also has implications for the demand for human capital. Why is it that several countries have, in only a few short decades, experienced a rapid accumulation of human capital – the Asian miracle economies – while other countries at about the same place in the poverty ranking have not? Surely the answer is the emergence of entrepreneurship, encouraged and sanctioned by the government". Porter (1990) endorses this alternative view in his section on Emerging Korea. Two of the key factors he mentions are the willingness to take risk and the intensity of competition. Primary focus of the central government has been to promote interna-tional competitiveness. Finally, Hofstede (1995, pp. 208–209) points at the comparatively strong long-term orientation prevalent in these countries, which may have determined their remarkable growth performance.

3.2.3. *Culture and the legal framework*

Values are often seen as the hard core of a culture. The outer layers of a culture are then made up by rituals, heroes and symbols. See Hofstede[14] (1995, pp. 18–20). Other authors, such as Lynn (1991), speak of attitudes rather than of values. The atti-tudes and values toward work, production, wealth and saving, toward new information, invention and strangers, and finally toward risk and failure seem particularly relevant for economic growth. Probably, these values are active through all players be they consumers, workers, business men or government officials. As we have seen from the historical case studies, they may also influence growth through the degree and quality of entre-preneurship in a society.

Jane Jacobs has made some additional obser-vations about culture and economic growth. In her view: "In its very nature, successful economic development has to be open-ended rather than goal-oriented, and has to make itself up expedi-ently and empirically as it goes along" (Jacobs, 1984, p. 221). Entrepreneurs have to find impro-vised solutions for unforeseeable problems. And this has little to do with "long-range planning" and meeting "targets". Jacobs also cites Cyril Stanley Smith from MIT, who points out that the roots of invention are to be found in curiosity, and espe-cially "esthetic curiosity". Smith also gives examples how many industrial products and tech-nologies first started out with frivolities and luxuries.

A classic study of the relationship between culture and economic development is Max Weber's famous essay (1958)[15] on "The Protestant ethic and the spirit of capitalism". Weber studies how psychological conditions may have facilitated the development of capitalism. In his view the ascetic Calvinist ethic with its emphasis on piety, industry and zeal, was greatly conducive to the spirit of modern capitalism that emphasizes rationality and discipline. Already contemporary authors (Sir William Petty as quoted by Weber, p. 179) attributed the economic success of seven-teenth century Holland to that the numerous protestants in that country "are for the most part thinking, sober men, and such as believe that Labour and Industry is their duty towards God". In retrospect however, De Vries and Van der Woude (1995, pp. 198–213) contend that much of the capitalist spirit was already present in (late) medieval Holland and was mainly reinforced by Calvinism.

Several authors have also considered the relationship between culture and economic growth during the 20th century. Hofstede (1995, pp. 208–217) points out that a long term orientation as expressed by thrift, investment and perseverance may be particularly conducive to economic growth. Some support for this hypothesis was found in a sample of 23 countries for the years 1965–1987. Hofstede (1995, p. 211) also regards this long-term orientation as conducive to entrepreneurship. Lynn (1991) has conducted an empirical study linking economic growth to several work attitudes in 41 nations. Lynn reports a significant positive correlation between "competitiveness" in each country (measured as a positive attitude towards competition) and the growth performance of these countries over the years 1970 through 1985.

Recently, however, Wildeman et al. (1998) reported that relationships could also be counterintuitive, where they found a positive relationship between uncertainty avoidance (at the national level) in 23 developed countries and the rate of self-employment in these countries. They explain this result as further proof that dissatisfaction may be a source of entrepreneurship.

In summarizing the literature we conclude that the impact of cultural dimensions on entrepreneurship and economic growth, while probably significant, is not straightforward. The role of the following traits deserves further investigation while distinguishing between the individual level, the firm level and the country level:

- open-mindedness towards other cultures;
- curiosity, creativity and experimentation;
- perseverance;
- valuation of wealth and savings;
- acceptance of risk and failure;
- competitiveness.

From the historical case studies we have already seen the relevance of the legal framework and economic institutions for economic growth. Lewis (1955) offers a general framework to study the role of institutions. He distinguishes:

- the right to reward; this has to do with property rights and the structure of incentives;

- possibilities for trade and specialization; in history as well as today the extent of the market is determined by the presence or absence of prohibitions such as tolls, guilds, tariffs, quota and other barriers to the mobility of goods and productive factors;
- economic freedom, i.e. the freedom a society permits for seeking out and seizing economic opportunities; first of all this has to do with the possibilities to make a profit and to go bankrupt; also relevant is the legal framework determining the access to resources through the functioning of the labor market and the capital market; finally economic freedom has to do with the possibilities (both legal and cultural) for vertical mobility.

The seminal contribution by Olson (1982) adds a vital element to this perspective. His central thesis is that special interest groups slow down a society's capacity to adopt new technologies and to reallocate resources in response to changing conditions, and thereby reduce the rate of economic growth. Further evidence is found in Mokyr (1990). Some major examples of these coalitions are labor unions blocking labor saving innovations, professional groups regulating entry to their profession and price cartels. Olson contends that the harm for society is often much greater than is the gain for the interest group. As he demonstrates through an extensive historical tour d'horizon, stable societies accumulate more collusion over time, and see their growth rates falter. Whereas societies in which these narrow interest groups have been destroyed (by war or revolution) enjoy a period of great gains in economic growth. Far from advocating "war and revolution", Olson does recommend to repeal special interest legislation and regulation, and to apply anti-trust law to cartels and forms of collusion that fix wages or prices above competitive levels.

We conclude that the legal and institutional framework is another vital factor hidden behind entrepreneurship and indispensable for a good understanding of economic growth. Viewed from the angle of entrepreneurship and economic growth the most vital concepts seem to be the incentives and the competition rules. Legal incentives for entrepreneurship are mainly rooted in the fiscal regime (replacement ratio, flat or steep tax rates) and in the laws concerning bankruptcies. Competition rules have to do with entry (de)regulation, anti-trust policy, removal of trade barriers and market intransparancies, and finally with union power in the labor market.

3.2.4. *Conclusions from economic history*
Economic history offers many insights with which to fill in and expand the framework as proposed in section 1. Our conclusions are summarized in Table II. A major addition to our conclusions in section 2.4 has to do with cultural and institutional conditions stimulating entrepreneurial traits and behavior within a population, as well as influencing the intermediate linkages (such as interaction between invention and innovation). A second addition is the evidence that, far from denying the vital role of capital formation and technological change for economic growth, for a real understanding of long-term growth it is necessary to explicitly take into account the role of entrepreneurial activity underlying these intermediary processes.

Remaining questions have to do with the role of smallness and selection and the possibilities for entrepreneurship within large organizations. They will be dealt with below. First we discuss the relevance of the historical view for modern economies.

3.3. *Relevance of historical views at the threshold of the new millennium*

Why are the historical views on the role of culture, the legal framework and entrepreneurial activity still relevant for understanding economic growth at the threshold of the new millennium? In this section we will first consider some views on economic growth as formulated in Porter's "The competitive advantage of nations" (1990). Next, we will discuss the views on economic growth as developed by evolutionary economics.

3.3.1. *Entrepreneurship and the competitive advantage of nations*
The conclusions from economic history, as exposed in Table II, can be related to the more recent analysis of Porter (1990). In his analysis four interrelated sets of factors or conditions determine the competitive strength of nations and thereby the possibilities for sustained productivity growth. These four sets of factors make up the so-called national "diamond". The four determinants are

- factor conditions. Porter distinguishes basic factors (e.g. natural resources and cheap, unskilled labor) from advanced factors (highly skilled personnel, modern networks infrastructure);
- demand conditions. These have three main elements: the nature of buyer needs (e.g. sophisticated instead of basic), the size and the pattern of growth and the existence of mecha-

TABLE II
Conclusions from economic history

Framework	Variables	Relevant disciplines	Focal unit of observation
Conditions	– culture (open-mindedness, acceptance of risk, long term orientation etc.)	– social psychology, anthropology and sociology	– groups and societies
	– institutions (incentives, competition rules)	– law and economics	– macro framework influencing micro behavior
Entrepreneurship	– traits and behavior	– psychology and managerial economics	– individual persons
Intermediate linkages	– conquest of new markets – invention and innovation – new business formation – competition	– industrial economics	– firms and industries
Economic growth	– rise and decline of nations	– economics	– national economies

nisms by which a nation's domestic preferences are transmitted to foreign markets;

- related and supporting industries. The presence of internationally competitive supplier and related industries stimulates rivalry and partial cooperation;
- the structure and culture of domestic rivalry. This encompasses a wide scope such as opportunities provided to possible new entrants, the nature of competition between incumbent firms, dominant business strategies and management practices.

The relevance of Porter's diamond for our analysis can be summed up in one sentence: "Invention and entrepreneurship are at the heart of national advantage" (Porter, 1990, p. 125). More specifically, Porter's "diamond" can help investigating the interface between entrepreneurship and economic growth. Demand conditions signal needs better in some nations than in others. National factor creation mechanisms affect the pool of knowledge and talent. Supplier industries provide crucial help or are the source of new entrants. Domestic rivalry creates a good "incubation environment" for entrepreneurs, but it can also be a mechanism by which entrepreneurship contributes to growth. Finally, feedback mechanisms are relevant because entrepreneurship can enhance the quality of the factor conditions through the learning process which starting a business provides.

In terms of our framework Porter's diamond offers several extensions. First, invention or rather innovation is best viewed as a direct manifestation of entrepreneurship, more than an intermediate process linking entrepreneurship to growth. Secondly, international competitiveness is a crucial intermediate linkage between entrepreneurship (innovation) and economic growth; however domestic rivalry is an essential precondition for international competitiveness; so competition comes in as an intermediate linkage at two levels. Thirdly, whereas in the short run there is a straight direct line of causation as in our preliminary framework in section 1, in the long run feedbacks are active. Finally, it is also clear from his analysis that entrepreneurship is not restricted to small firms.

3.3.2. *Evolutionary economics*

The economy is entering a world governed by a new technological paradigm. Like the steam machine during the first Industrial Revolution, Information and Communication Technology is a pervasive new technology (or in terms of Mokyr: a macro-invention) which will radically alter the economy. A wave of micro-inventions and innovations based on ICT is gaining momentum and will sweep the world in the decades to come. The implications of this radical transition for the growth of nations will not only depend on macro-economic conditions, but primarily on cultural and organizational factors and on the adaptability of institutions and the legal framework. An analysis of the diffusion of the many applications of this new technology will also have to include micro-economic processes of new start-ups and of entry by firms from outside the industry.

This ICT revolution makes it increasingly necessary to distinguish between information and knowledge. On the one hand information will become more cheaply and readily available. In some cases this will weaken existing entrepreneurial edges. On the other hand information has to be selected, upgraded and combined with other information in order to become useful for economic application. Only then may it be called "knowledge". Whereas the raw material information will become abundant, knowledge will remain scarce. Undoubtedly, new entrepreneurial edges will be based on knowledge. In this way an economy may develop which is driven by ideas and in which entrepreneurship equates to competition between ideas.

A framework helpful when analyzing this transition at the level of sectors of industry is evolutionary economics[16] as developed by Nelson and Winter (1982), and the related theory of the experimentally organized economy developed by Eliasson (1995). These lines of thinking will be briefly discussed in the following section.[17] The seminal book by Nelson and Winter (1982), bearing the title of this section, argues that in order to understand how technical change functions as the key driving force of long-run economic development, it is necessary to incorporate the realities of firm decision making as well as the dynamics of the competitive process. In developing their theory they acknowledge their intellectual debts with Schumpeter (economic development) and Simon (human and organizational behavior).

Nelson and Winter contend that the concepts of optimization and equilibrium which are the core of orthodox theory are unfruitful abstractions and simplifications from reality. Instead of maximizing behavior of firms they use the concept of decision rules, and instead of equilibrium they see tendencies. Next, in their evolutionary theory, they borrow some major ideas from biology such as from Darwin and Lamarck. Individual firms have a kind of genetic endowment in terms of technical routines, procedures etc. These routines usually can evolve only gradually. However searching for new routines (innovation) is itself also a routine. Besides, exogenous shocks can press incumbent firms or outsiders to search for new organizational and technical routines. In the end the competitive process at the sector level selects the most successful routines and weeds out the routines which are no longer suitable. So innovation ("mutations") and selection are the catchwords in this approach.

Although the approach chosen by Nelson and Winter is strongly based on the premise of variety of behavior and performance of individual firms, there is not much explicit attention for the role of the entrepreneur. More explicit scope for the entrepreneur is to be found in the work of Eliasson. He argues that market competition and economic growth cannot be understood without recourse to non-linear selection mechanisms and the discontinuities of technical change (Eliasson, 1995). In his view the major production factor is competence capital embodied in people. This capital accumulates through education and learning on the job. It is allocated and reallocated through the labor market and the market for mergers and acquisitions, through entry of new enterprises – often by entrepreneurial people leaving large firms – and through the exit of failing enterprises. These processes make up the mechanism of "competitive selection among business experiments". Eliasson has incorporated these ideas into his micro-to-macro model of the Swedish economy called MOSES. In his model the long-term growth rate is determined by the institutions regulating the mechanisms of selection and the allocation of competence. Eliasson also argues that 30 years of post war mistreatment of the market mechanism

show up in a decline of the percentage share of new firms and are responsible for the slow growth of the Swedish economy since the 1970s.

Viewed from the perspective of "linking entrepreneurship and growth" we may now distinguish between two lines of thinking. The first is the neo-classical paradigm. The second we will call the entrepreneurial paradigm. See Figure 2.

The neo-classical paradigm seems most applicable in the more mature sectors of the economy, the entrepreneurial paradigm seems most relevant for understanding the rise of new, technology-driven industries. Audretsch and Thurik (1997) would call these sectors the "managed" and the "entrepreneurial" sectors, respectively. Our expanded framework as developed in Table II remains valid. An essential addition is the crucial role of diversity (variety) and of selection as an intermediate linkage between entrepreneurship and economic growth.

4. Entrepreneurship in large firms

Entrepreneurial activity not only takes place in small firms. It also happens in large organizations.[18] Entrepreneurship not only occurs in the form of new small firms but also in the form of corporate entrepreneurship, new ideas and responsibilities implemented in existing large organizations. According to Drucker (1985, p. 144) today's large businesses will not even survive "unless they acquire entrepreneurial competence".

Stopford and Baden-Fuller (1994, p. 521) sum-

Neo-classical paradigm	*Entrepreneurial paradigm*
• homo economicus	• homo ludens
• technocratic	• (esthetic) curiosity
• rational	• creativity
• goal-oriented	• open-minded
• perfect information	• improvising
• equilibrium	• uncertainty
• optimization	• diversity
• price-competition	• selection
	• competition of ideas

Figure 2. Two paradigms.

marize how the strategy literature identifies three types of corporate entrepreneurship. The first type is the creation of new businesses or business units within an existing organization – corporate venturing or intrapreneurship as it is sometimes called. Another is the more pervasive activity associated with the transformation or strategic renewal of existing organizations. The third type is where the enterprise changes the "rules of competition" for its industry, for example by carrying out an innovation that fundamentally alters the industry. Stopford and Baden-Fuller (1994, p. 523) distinguish five attributes that are common to all types of (corporate) entrepreneurship: proactiveness, aspirations beyond current ability, team-orientation, capability to resolve dilemmas and learning capacity. Despite the classification of Stopford and Baden-Fuller we will use the terms corporate entrepreneurship and intrapreneurship interchangeably.

Stevenson and Jarillo (1990, pp. 23–25) also regard corporate entrepreneurship as wider than corporate venturing and include the "ability of corporations to act entrepreneurially". In their view ". . . pursuing opportunity, whether through specific company structures or not, constitutes the core of entrepreneurship, both individual and corporate". In order to create corporate entrepreneurship top management is heavily dependent on other individuals within the firm. As relevant elements promoting corporate entrepreneurship Stevenson and Jarillo mention "a conscious effort to lessen negative consequences of failure when opportunity is pursued" and facilitating "the emergence of informal internal and external networks". This points again to the importance of (business) culture. Furthermore they state "The crux of corporate entrepreneurship is, then, that opportunity for the firm has to be pursued by individuals within it, who may have perceptions of personal opportunity more or less at variance with opportunity for the firm."

Bridge et al. (1998, p. 190) also point out that "Inventors are usually individuals, but intrapreneurship is frequently carried out by groups or teams". This underlines the need of what we have called a vehicle for entrepreneurship. Regarding the fostering of innovation they do not only mention the toleration of failure but add the reward of success. More generally speaking we

would consider both business culture and incentives as potentially stimulating factors.

Of course there are also dilemmas in corporate entrepreneurship in so far that there may be an intrinsic tension between hierarchies and entrepreneurial behavior. Also there is the appropriability dilemma of individuals that possess "new knowledge". The question may be put forward whether entrepreneurial employees who can realize their ideas within the firm may be less likely to create a spin off or start working for another existing firm. On the other hand a firm may have to explicitly offer the option of spinning off when it wants to keep and attract entrepreneurial employees.

Regarding the possible effects of corporate entrepreneurship we conclude that it plays an essential role in the process of strategic renewal of large and incumbent firms. It can be associated with the typical growth enhancing features of entrepreneurial behavior: alertness, finding new product-market combinations and innovation. In the short run corporate entrepreneurship can occur simultaneously with corporate downsizing, which is associated with the process of job destruction. In the long run though, it is expected to stimulate competitiveness and sales growth of the firm. Furthermore, viewed in a macro-economic perspective downsizing creates opportunities for growth by enhancing the creation of new ventures. Wherever entrepreneurial employees reap the benefits of their abilities, within the firm or in a spin-off, their activities are likely to enhance growth at the macro-level.

There seems to be a strong case to hypothesize a positive impact of corporate entrepreneurship on economic growth. On the other hand corporate entrepreneurship remains an elusive concept. Innovative empirical research will therefore be needed to investigate this hypothesis. In that respect it will be necessary to develop a scale for measuring corporate entrepreneurship.

Conclusion

In this section we assert that entrepreneurship occurs irrespective of the size of organizations.[19] A crucial element in organizing corporate entrepreneurship is the necessity of an organizational "vehicle" such as teams, business units or other

TABLE III
Conclusions regarding individual and corporate entrepreneurship

Framework	Individual entrepreneurship	Corporate entrepreneurship
Conditions	– national culture: open-mindedness, acceptance of risk, etc. – institutions: property rights, incentives, competition rules, entry barriers	– business culture: open-mindedness, proactiveness, trust in employees etc. – internal rules and procedures, incentives
Entrepreneurship	– personal traits: alertness, creativity, ambition, perseverance – vehicle: smallness (autonomous role of owners of small firms) – manifestations or behavior: newness through innovation, entry of new markets, start-ups	– idem – vehicle: mimicking smallness (autonomous role of entrepreneurial individuals through teams and business units) – manifestation or behavior: newness through innovation, entry of new markets, spin-offs, joint ventures
Intermediate linkages between entrepreneurial actions and performance	– domestic and international competition – variety and selection of viable ideas and replacement of obsolete enterprises	– idem – variety and selection of viable ideas and re-engineering of corporations
Economic growth	– higher productivity; new niches and industries – international competitiveness	– higher productivity; improving best practice; new industries – idem

ways of decentralization. This is sometimes called "mimicking smallness". Corporate entrepreneurship may also stimulate spin-offs. Our conclusions are summarized in Table III.

5. Synthesis

We have investigated the relationship between entrepreneurship and economic growth from various perspectives: historical views on entrepreneurship, macro-economic growth theory, industrial economics (in particular, Porter's competitive advantage of nations), evolutionary economics, history of economic growth (in particular, rise and fall of nations) and the management literature on large corporate organizations. The challenge is to synthesize these insights to provide a broad picture of how economic growth is linked to entrepreneurship. We will do so defining entrepreneurship and considering its inherent heterogeneity. We will present a framework for linking economic growth to entrepreneurship while including conditions for entrepreneurship. This framework is meant to help setting an agenda for further research.

5.1. *Definition of entrepreneurship*

At least three levels of analysis can be distinguished when discussing the relationship between entrepreneurship and economic growth: the level of the individual entrepreneurs operating on their own or in teams and partnerships, the firm level and the aggregate levels of industries, regions and national economies. Basically, entrepreneurship has to do with activities of individual persons. The concept of economic growth is relevant at levels of firms, industries and nations. Linking entrepreneurship to economic growth means linking the individual level to the aggregate levels.

First we will define entrepreneurship. Inspired by Hébert and Link (1989), Bull and Willard (1993) and Lumpkin and Dess (1996), we propose the following definition of entrepreneurship:

Entrepreneurship is the manifest ability and willingness of individuals, on their own, in teams, within and outside existing organizations, to:
- *perceive and create new economic opportunities (new products, new production methods, new organizational schemes and new product-market combinations) and to*
- *introduce their ideas in the market, in the face of uncertainty and other obstacles, by making*

decisions on location, form and the use of resources and institutions.

Essentially, entrepreneurship is a behavioral characteristic of persons. This behavior has an input and an output side: where on the one hand entrepreneurial behavior requires entrepreneurial skills and qualities, it also implies the participation in the competitive process on the other.

It should be noted that entrepreneurship is not an occupation and that entrepreneurs are not a well-defined occupational class of persons. Even obvious entrepreneurs may exhibit their entrepreneurship only during a certain phase of their career and/or concerning a certain part of their activities. In this respect we agree with Gartner (1988, p. 64) who asserts that "The entrepreneur is not a fixed state of existence, rather entrepreneurship is a role that individuals undertake to create organizations". See also Schumpeter (1934, p. 78) who states "Because being an entrepreneur is not a profession and as a rule not a lasting condition, entrepreneurs do not form a social class in the technical sense as, for example, landowners or capitalists or workmen do".

Entrepreneurship is not synonymous with small business. Certainly, small firms are an outstanding vehicle by which individuals can channel their entrepreneurial ambitions. The small firm is an extension of the individual who is in charge (Lumpkin and Dess, 1996, p. 138). However, as we have seen, entrepreneurship is not restricted to persons starting or operating an (innovative) small firm. Enterprising individuals in large firms, the so-called "intrapreneurs" or "corporate entrepreneurs", undertake entrepreneurial actions as well. In these environments there is a tendency of "mimicking smallness", for instance using business units, subsidiaries or joint ventures.

Strictly speaking, entrepreneurship is a behavioral characteristic of persons. By creating opportunities for entrepreneurial behavior of their employees, organizations can also become entrepreneurial. In the popular press Europe's current economic problems are often attributed to a lack of entrepreneurial firms. This term is sometimes used also in the academic literature. See Audretsch (1995), Audretsch and Thurik (1997 and 1998) and Carree et al. (1999).

Our survey suggests that entities at the macro level such as industries, cities, regions and nations can be entrepreneurial to a certain extent. Therefore, we need to define and operationalize concepts of entrepreneurship at the aggregate levels of firms, industries and nations. These concepts are usually intuitive and need further developing. Probably, entrepreneurship at these levels of analysis is a multidimensional concept. Where entrepreneurs tend to reside at the tails of the distribution of the dimensions of personal characteristics, entrepreneurship is an inherent complex phenomenon to capture. The development of these concepts should be the subject of future, probably multidisciplinary, research.

5.2. *Measuring entrepreneurship*

Clearly, it is difficult to measure entrepreneurship, both at the individual level and at the aggregate level. The concepts involved have to be operationalized. Meanwhile proxies are needed to help researchers and policy makers to take their bearings. At the aggregate level it seems pragmatic to count numbers. However, because in colloquial speech many terms like entrepreneurs, self-employed and businessmen are used indiscriminately, it is not immediately clear which numbers to count.

However, we can make some pragmatic distinctions. First, we distinguish between the concepts *entrepreneurial*, as defined in section 5.1, and *managerial* in the sense of organizing and coordinating. Secondly, we make a distinction between business-owners or *self-employed* (including owner-managers of incorporated firms)[20] and *employees*. Based on this double dichotomy of self-employed versus employee and entrepreneurial versus managerial, three types of entrepreneurs may be distinguished. These three types are the Schumpeterian entrepreneurs, the

TABLE IV
Three types of entrepreneurs

	Self-employed	Employee
Entrepreneurial	**Schumpeterian entrepreneurs**	**Intrapreneurs**
Managerial	**Managerial business owners**	Executive managers

intrapreneurs and the managerial business owners who are entrepreneurs in a formal sense only. This is illustrated in Table IV.

Schumpeterian entrepreneurs are to be found mostly in small firms. They own and direct independent firms that are innovative and creatively destroy[21] existing market structures. After realizing their goals Schumpeterians often develop into managerial business owners, but some may again start new ventures or new firms. *Intrapreneurs or entrepreneurial managers* also belong to the core of real entrepreneurship. By taking commercial initiatives on behalf of their employer, and by risking their time, reputation and sometimes their job in doing so, they are the embodiment of leadership resulting in entrepreneurial ventures in larger firms. Sometimes these entrepreneurial employees, either in teams or on their own, spin off, start new enterprises and become Schumpeterian entrepreneurs. *Managerial business owners (entrepreneurs in a formal sense)* are to be found in the large majority of small firms. They include many franchisees, shopkeepers and people in professional occupations. They belong to what Kirchhoff (1994) calls "the economic core" and sometimes entrepreneurial ventures grow out of them.

While the managerial business owners fulfill many useful functions in the economy such as the organization and coordination of production and distribution, they cannot be viewed as the engine

of innovation and creative destruction. This is the major function of Schumpeterian entrepreneurs and intrapreneurs. How all three groups can make a contribution to economic growth, we will briefly touch upon in section 5.3.

First however we want to consider the feedbacks from economic development to both the total number of self-employed and the number of real entrepreneurs (the sum of Schumpeterians and intrapreneurs). Figure 3 illustrates in a tentative way how these numbers may depend on the stage of economic development.

Figure 3 is based upon the assumption that the number of self-employed includes an unknown but probably relatively modest share of Schumpeterian entrepreneurs. Clearly, this share depends on various historical, institutional and structural factors. Up to the late 1970s, most industrialized economies experienced a long period of secular decline in the number of self-employed per population. Since the late 1970s the number of self-employed in several of these countries is increasing again (Wildeman et al., 1998). This mirrors both a resurgence of entrepreneurship in the intrinsic sense (Schumpeterian entrepreneurship) as well as an increase of franchisees and marginal start-ups.

Further evidence of this U-shaped trend of self-employment rates over time (1965–1990) is presented in Acs, Audretsch and Evans (1994).[22] In their analysis a U-shaped trend is a net effect of

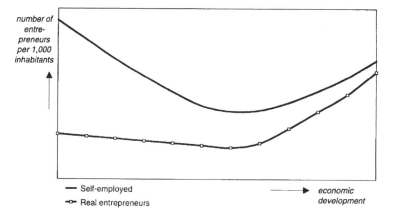

number of entre-preneurs per 1,000 inhabitants

— Self-employed
-o- Real entrepreneurs

economic development

Figure 3. The hypothesized number of self-employed and of real entrepreneurs.

(among others) the negative influence of rising per capita income and a positive one of the rising share of the service sector. Further research should dig more deeply into this relationship between economic development and this U-shaped trend (Carree et al., 1999). To what extent do stages of economic development matter? And to what extent is economic development over specific time intervals[23] involved?

In Figure 3 it is hypothesized that the number of real entrepreneurs will increase even more steeply. It is hypothesized that the revival of Schumpeterian start-ups the Western world is now experiencing is matched or even surpassed by an upsurge of intrapreneurship in its many forms.

The number of self-employed is the only yardstick of entrepreneurship because statistical information is available only along the ownership dimension. This can be misleading. For instance, it is unknown whether the relatively high number of self-employed in Italy as compared to the Netherlands expresses a high level of Schumpeterian entrepreneurship or merely a time-lag in economic development influencing the number of marginal establishments. In recent empirical studies other approximations are brought forward. Audretsch (1995) uses the employment share of surviving young firms as a proxy for entrepreneurial activity in manufacturing industries. This variable may well express the comparative entrepreneurial positions of these industries. Outside the manufacturing sector this variable may be biased due to the occurrence of franchising firms and marginal or part-time start-ups. Audretsch and Thurik (1997) and Carree and Thurik (1998) use the share of small firms as proxies. Also these proxies have obvious shortcomings. Moreover, the rate of intrapreneurship, both in new and incumbent firms, is still lacking in these approaches.

The number of real entrepreneurs would approach the level of entrepreneurial activity more closely. Measuring their number will necessitate further conceptual development taking into account personal capabilities and a wide array of behavioral aspects. This implies a need to define typologies of entrepreneurs, for instance based on entrepreneurial dimensions (Lumpkin and Dess, 1996) and on the vehicle they use for materializing their goals.

Of course counting numbers, in however sophisticated a manner, will always remain an approximation of the rate of entrepreneurship. Hopefully other ways can be found to measure the intensity of entrepreneurial activity.

5.3. *Linking entrepreneurship to economic growth*

5.3.1. *Views in the economic literature*
Entrepreneurship is "at the heart of national advantage" (Porter, 1990, p. 125). It is of eminent importance for carrying out innovations. Concerning the role of entrepreneurship in stimulating economic growth, many links have been discussed. Both the role of the entrepreneur in carrying out innovations and in enhancing rivalry are important for economic growth. Our assessment of the role of entrepreneurship as expressed in several fields of research which we have drawn from (such as historical views; management literature; growth theory; evolutionary economics), is shown in Table V. Competition is interpreted in the broad sense: contestability of markets, domestic rivalry and international competition.

In the historical views of the Schumpeterians and the Austrians entrepreneurship is explicitly relevant for explaining economic growth. On the other hand, the neo-classicals have no explicit room for the role of an active entrepreneur. The endogenous growth theory may offer new theoretical perspectives for entrepreneurship. As yet it does not offer many concrete starting-points. Economic history is the foremost field in which entrepreneurship is considered crucial for the economic growth of nations. On the microeconomic level the management literature of large organizations devotes explicit attention to the importance of entrepreneurship for performance. Porter's work offers distinctive starting points for the role of entrepreneurship in explaining economic development and growth of nations. Entrepreneurship can be attached to the determinants of his "diamond". In the work of Eliasson entrepreneurship is also considered crucial for economic growth.

5.3.2. *Final framework*
Figure 4 presents our final framework inspired by the many insights reaped from the fields of literature. In discussing this framework we concentrate

TABLE V
Assessment of the role of entrepreneurship, drawn from several fields of research

Field of literature	Specific domain	Competition	Innovation	Firm start-ups	Importance of entrepreneurship for economic growth
Historical views	Schumpeter/Baumol	++	+++	+	++
	Neo-classicals	++	+	0	+
	Austrians	++	+	0	++
Endogenous growth theory		+	+++	0	+
Economic history		++	+++	+	+++
Management literature		+	+++	++	++
Industrial economics	Porter	+++	+++	++	+++
Evolutionary economics	Eliasson	+++	+++	+++	+++

0   Not present in the writings.
+   Implicitly present in the writings.
++   Explicitly present in the writings.
+++ Pivotal element in the writings.

on entrepreneurship, economic growth and what links them together. We also take into account some wider ranging relationships. As we have seen in section 5.1, it is crucial that three levels of analysis be distinguished. More precisely, *linking entrepreneurship to economic growth also means linking the individual level to the firm and the macro level.*

Strictly speaking, entrepreneurship as defined in section 5.1, is a concept operational at the individual level. While requiring skills and other qualities, essentially entrepreneurship has to with behavior.

Entrepreneurial action takes us to the firm level. Entrepreneurs need a vehicle transforming their personal qualities and ambitions into actions. Small firms where the entrepreneur has a controlling stake provide such a vehicle. Larger firms often mimic smallness (using organizational forms like business units, subsidiaries and joint ventures) to introduce corporate entrepreneurship. The outcome of these entrepreneurial manifestations at the firm level generally has to do with newness. This can be newness through product, process and organizational innovation, entry of new markets and innovative business start-ups.

At the aggregate level of industries, regions and national economies the many individual entrepreneurial actions compose a mosaic of new experiments. In evolutionary terms this can be called variety. A process of competition between these various new ideas and initiatives takes place continuously, leading to the selection of the most viable firms and industries. Variety, competition, selection and also imitation (for the latter see Baumol, 1993a, p. 260) expand and transform the productive potential of a regional or national economy (by replacement or displacement of obsolete firms, by higher productivity and by expansion of new niches and industries). They enhance its international competitiveness and thereby its market share. Viewed from within a closed economy or the world economy as a whole, one could say that the additional productive potential in a competitive environment would create its own demand.[24] We assume that the outcome of this chain of variables linking the individual level to the macro level, will be economic growth.[25]

In this process Schumpeterian entrepreneurs, intrapreneurs and managerial business owners all play their part. Assuming that the secular trends in Figure 3 may be regarded as equilibrium rates, this implies "optimal" proportions for both real entrepreneurs and self-employed.[26] Deviations from these rates can be expected to frustrate the growth rate of an economy. A shortage of real entrepreneurs will hamper innovation, whereas a glut of self-employed may result in an average scale of business below optimum levels. Besides both the number of real entrepreneurs and that of self-employed may influence the intensity of competition.

Next to the linkages from the individual level to the aggregate level, it is likely that there are important feedback mechanisms. Competition and selection amidst variety undoubtedly enable individuals (and firms) to learn from both their own and other's successes and failures.[27] These learning processes enable individuals to increase their skills and adapt their attitudes. The outcome of these so-called spillovers will be new entrepreneurial actions, creating a recurrent chain of linkages.

Clearly, the outcome of these dynamic processes depends on a set of conditions referred to in Figure 4. Given the psychological endowments of the population, conditions refer to the environment in which an individual carries out his or her entrepreneurial activities. First, this refers to the national (or regional) cultural environment, and to the internal culture of corporations. The linkages between culture and entrepreneurship are by no means simple and straightforward, and much is still unknown about these processes. As we have seen in section 3, the history of the rise and fall of nations has shown that cultural vitality, thriving sciences and high tide in entrepreneurship often coincide. Second, the institutional frame-

work, both on the national level and within firms, defines the incentives for individuals to turn their ambitions into actions, and determines to what extent unnecessary barriers will hamper them. The importance of institutions for the development of entrepreneurship is paramount and deserves further study.

5.4. *Research conclusions*

Entrepreneurship matters. In modern open economies it is more important for economic growth than it has ever been. The reason is that globalization and the ICT-revolution imply a need for structural change, requiring a substantial real-location of resources. This induces an intense demand for entrepreneurship (Audretsch and Thurik, 1998 and Casson, 1995, p. 94). When it comes to how the mechanisms operate, little is known, either on how entrepreneurship can best be promoted or on how entrepreneurship influences economic performance. Our paper has to be viewed in exactly this broader framework of unanswered questions. It attempts to be a starting point for an agenda of research into the field of entrepreneurship and economic development. In formulating such an agenda, we propose to distinguish three main fields of research.

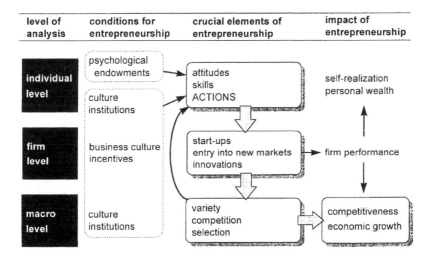

Figure 4. Final framework: linking entrepreneurship to economic growth.

The *first* field is that of measuring entrepreneurship. Much work has yet to be done in two directions. First, that of the development of typologies of entrepreneurship at the micro level. Second, that of operationalization of a multidimensional concept of entrepreneurship at higher levels of aggregation such as industries and national economies; possibly a scale can be devised tracking the amount of entrepreneurship over time or comparing it between national economies.

The *second* field is that of the determinants of entrepreneurship. Both culture and the institutional framework are important conditions codetermining the amount of entrepreneurship in an economy and the way in which entrepreneurs operate in practice. But also technological, demographic and economic forces are at play.[28] Several questions remain, such as

- how do cultural variables influence the decisions of individuals to start a business, and how do cultural variables interact with economic and technological developments or with policies designed to promote entrepreneurship; what is the role of the educational system in this respect?
- how do differences in incentive structures contribute to the explanation of differences in entrepreneurship?
- which role is played by business dynamics (entry and exit) originating from deviations between the actual and an equilibrium rate of self-employment (entrepreneurship)?

Future research should attempt to explain the statistical number of the self-employed, but will also have to deal with explaining more qualitative aspects such as the rise of Schumpeterian entrepreneurship and that of intrapreneurship.

The *third* field is that of the impact of entrepreneurship on economic development. This major field opens up many highly relevant questions for research, both at the level of firm performance and that of the development of industries and national economies:

- knowing that many new start-ups fail and that only few develop into gazelles, which then are the major determinants of failure, of mere survival and of real success?
- which specific contributions to the post war

performance of national economies were made by Schumpeterian entrepreneurship, intrapreneurship and self-employment, respectively; which role have institutions and policies played?
- how can the results of these studies be incorporated in the econometric models[29] which are now being used in policy analysis?

Acknowledgements

The authors would like to thank Folkert Buis for his contributions, in particular to the references system and to sections two and four. They are also grateful to David Audretsch for his comments and encouragement while visiting EIM in 1996 and 1997 and to three anonymous referees.

Notes

[1] De Koning en Snijders (1992) provide an overview of the various public policies in countries of the European Union which have been introduced during the 1980s. You (1995) attempts to use various lines of economic theory in explaining the shift. Finally, Carree (1997) brings it all together in his extensive survey of the determinants of the shift building upon the literature on the determinants of firm size and firm-size distribution and complemented with empirical material.

[2] See Davis, Haltiwanger and Schuh (1996), Carree and Klomp (1996) and Kleijweg and Nieuwenhuijsen (1996) for a recent discussion.

[3] Equating the growth of entrepreneurship by the number of new firm start-ups and taking the Netherlands, for which we have reliable figures, as an illustration, we observe that the number of new start-ups in the Netherlands almost doubled between 1986 and 1994. See Wennekers (1997).

[4] Here we differ from Kirchhoff (1994, p. 37 and p. 62).

[5] As Lazonick (1991, p. 309) points out, the neo-classicals in fact use the terms "entrepreneur" and "manager" interchangeably.

[6] These roles are also corroborated by colloquial speech in Germanic languages such as Dutch and German. The first meaning of the Dutch word "ondernemen" is "to undertake" but it also means "to dare", "to attempt" and "to start".

[7] See Wennekers (1997) for more information about this revival.

[8] Schumpeter's "Theory of Economic Development" was published in German in 1911, and in English in 1934.

[9] See Schumpeter (1996), which was first published in 1943.

[10] Important publications concerning "the rise and fall of nations" include Cipolla (1981), Jacobs (1984), Landes (1969), Lewis (1955), Mokyr (1990), North and Thomas (1973), Olson (1982) and Wiener (1981). A useful survey is presented in De Jong and Van Paridon (1989).

[11] "Stadtluft machts frei" (Cipolla. p. 146).

[12] For a partly conflicting view on the quality of British entrepreneurship in the period 1870-1914, see Pollard who argues: "In short, some failures there undoubtedly were, but they were surely not characteristic of the period as a whole. The entrepreneurs who had got to the top in late Victorian and Edwardian Britain could hold their own with the very best abroad" (Pollard, 1994, p. 89).

[13] The economic problems that many countries in East Asia are presently facing do not nullify their remarkable growth performance in the past decades. It is yet too early to decide whether the present setback is temporary or is another example of "rise and fall".

[14] This publication builds upon Hofstede (1980) but also includes new material.

[15] Weber's essay was first published in German in 1904–1905.

[16] Also see Witt (1993).

[17] Also see Magnusson (1994).

[18] We will focus our discussion on entrepreneurship in large firms, but note that there is also a literature on "entrepreneurial government" (see Osborne and Gaebler, 1992).

[19] See also Stevenson and Gumpert (1991).

[20] We will use the terms self-employed and business owners interchangeably. For definitions see SBA, The state of small business: a report of the president 1986, Washington: U.S. Government Printing Office, chapter 4.

[21] The concept of creative destruction was introduced by Schumpeter (1996) which was first published in 1943.

[22] See also Acs et al. (1999).

[23] For instance, when Greece will have reached the 1990 per capita income of the U.S.A., its number of self-employed will also have been influenced by global technological and cultural trends. Besides, country-specific demographic, social and institutional conditions will be relevant for its number of self-employed.

[24] Cf. Say's law.

[25] As the figure indicates there will also be an outcome at the individual level (self-realization and personal wealth) and at the firm level (performance).

[26] There is an analogy with the work of Allen (1988, p. 116) who asserts that the success of the overall system is determined by the balanced existence between "stochasts" (representing the adaptive capacity) and "cartesians" (representing efficient performance).

[27] Also see Dosi (1988, p. 235).

[28] For an overview of possible determinants of the level of entrepreneurship, see Wennekers (1997).

[29] These models will have to incorporate the two-way relationship between entrepreneurship and economic development. See Carree et al. (1999).

References

Acs, Z. J., 1992, 'Small Business Economics: A Global Perspective', *Challenge* 35 (November/December), 38–44.

Acs, Z. J. and D. B. Audretsch, 1990, *Innovation and Small Firms*, Cambridge, MA: MIT Press.

Acs, Z. J. and D. B. Audretsch, 1993, 'Conclusion', in Z. J. Acs and D. B. Audretsch (eds.), *Small Firms and Entrepreneurship: An East-West Perspective*, Cambridge, U.K.: Cambridge University Press.

Acs, Z. J., D. B. Audretsch and D. S. Evans, 1994, *The Determinants of Variations in the Self-Employment Rates Across Countries and Over Time*, mimeo (fourth draft).

Acs, Z. J., B. Carlsson and Ch. Karlsson, 1999, 'The Linkages Among Entrepreneurship, SMEs and the Macroeconomy', in Z. J. Acs, B. Carlsson and Ch. Karlsson (eds.), *Entrepreneurship, Small and Medium-Sized Enterprises and the Macroeconomy*, Cambridge, U.K.: Cambridge University Press.

Aghion, P. and P. Howitt, 1992, 'A Model of Growth Through Creative Destruction', *Econometrica* 60, 323–351.

Allen, P. M., 1988, 'Evolution, Innovation and Economics', in G. Dosi, C. Freeman, R. Nelson, G. Silverberg and L. Soete (eds.), *Technical Change and Economic Theory*, London and New York: Pinter Publishers, pp. 95–115

Audretsch, D. B., 1993, *Kleinunternehmen in der Industrieökonomiek; ein neuer Ansatz*, Discussion paper FS IV 93-26, Berlin: Wissenschaftszentrum.

Audretsch, D. B., 1995, *Innovation and Industry Evolution*, Cambridge, MA: MIT Press.

Audretsch, D. B. and A. R. Thurik, 1997, *Sources of Growth: the Entrepreneurial versus the Managed Economy*, Discussion paper TI97-109/3, Tinbergen Institute, Erasmus University Rotterdam.

Audretsch, D. B. and A. R. Thurik, 1998, *The Knowledge Society, Entrepreneurship and Unemployment*, Research Report 9801/E, Zoetermeer: EIM.

Audretsch, D. B. and A. R. Thurik, 1999, 'Capitalism and Democracy in the 21st Century: From the Managed to the Entrepreneurial Economy', *Journal of Evolutionary Economics*, forthcoming.

Barreto, H., 1989, *The Entrepreneur in Economic theory: Disappearance and Explanation*, London: Routledge.

Baumol, W. J., 1968, 'Entrepreneurship and Economic Theory', *American Economic Review* 58, 64–71.

Baumol, W. J., 1990, 'Entrepreneurship: Productive, Unproductive, and Destructive', *Journal of Political Economy* 98, 893–921.

Baumol, W. J., 1993a, *Entrepreneurship, Management and the Structure of Payoffs*, Cambridge, MA: MIT-Press.

Baumol, W. J., 1993b, 'Formal Entrepreneurship Theory in Economics: Existence and Bounds', *Journal of Business Venturing* 8, 197–210.

Bridge, S., K. O'Neill and S. Cronie, 1998, *Understanding Enterprise, Entrepreneurship and Small Business*, Houndmills: MacMillan Press.

Brock, W. A. and D. S. Evans, 1989, 'Small Business Economics', *Small Business Economics* 1, 7–20.

Bull, I. and G. E Willard, 1993, 'Towards a Theory of Entrepreneurship', *Journal of Business Venturing* 8, 183–195.

Carlsson, B., 1992, 'The Rise of Small Business: Causes and Consequences', in W. J. Adams (ed.), *Singular Europe, Economy and Policy of the European Community after 1992*, Ann Arbor, MI: University of Michigan Press, pp. 145–169.

Carlsson, B., 1999, 'Small Business, Entrepreneurship, and Industrial Dynamics', in Z. Acs (ed.), *Are Small Firms*

Important?, Dordrecht: Kluwer Academic Publishers, forthcoming.

Carree, M. A., 1997, *Market Dynamics, Evolution and Smallness*, Amsterdam: Thesis Publishers and Tinbergen Institute.

Carree, M. A. and L. Klomp, 1996, 'Small Business and Job Creation: A Comment', *Small Business Economics* **8**, 317–322.

Carree, M. A. and A. R. Thurik, 1998, 'Small Firms and Economic Growth in Europe', *Atlantic Economic Journal* **26**(2), 137–146.

Carree, M. A. and A. R. Thurik, 1999, 'Industrial Structure and Economic Growth', in D. B. Audretsch and A. R. Thurik (eds.), *Innovation, Industry Evolution and Employment*, Cambridge, U.K.: Cambridge University Press, forthcoming.

Carree, M. A., A. van Stel, A. R. Thurik and A. R. M. Wennekers, 1999, *Business Ownership and Economic Growth: An Empirical Research*, Research Report 9809/E, Zoetermeer: EIM.

Casson, M., 1991, The *Entrepreneur: An Economic Theory*, Aldershot, England: Gower House.

Casson, M., 1995, *Entrepreneurship and Business Culture: Studies in the Economics of Trust*; Vol. 1, Edward Elgar.

Chamberlin, E., 1933, *The Theory of Monopolistic Competition*, Cambridge, MA: MIT Press.

Cipolla, C. M., 1981, *Before the Industrial Revolution: European Society and Economy, 1000–1700*, 2nd edition, Cambridge, U.K.: Cambridge University Press.

Coase, R. H., 1937, 'The Nature of the Firm', *Economica* **4**, 386–405.

Cohen, W. M. and S. Klepper, 1992, 'The Trade-Off Between Firm Size and Diversity in the Pursuit of Technological Progress', *Small Business Economics* **4**, 1–14.

Cohen, W. M. and S. Klepper, 1996, 'A Reprise of Size and R&D', *Economic Journal* **106**, 925–951.

Davis, S. J., J. Haltiwanger and S. Schuh, 1996, 'Small Business and Job Creation: Dissecting the Myth and Reassessing the Facts', *Small Business Economics* **8**, 297–315.

Denison, E. F., 1985, *Trends in American Economic Growth 1929–1982*, Washington, DC: Brookings Institution.

Dosi, G., 1988, 'The Nature of the Innovative Process', in G. Dosi, C. Freeman, R. Nelson, G. Silverberg and L. Soete (eds.), *Technical Change and Economic Theory*, London and New York: Pinter Publishers, pp. 221–238.

Drucker, P. F., 1985, *Innovation and Entrepreneurship; Practice and Principles*, New York: Harper and Row.

Dijk, B. van and A. R. Thurik, 1995, *Entrepreneurship: visies en benaderingen*, Research Report 9510/N, Zoetermeer: EIM.

EIM, 1993, *The European Observatory for SMEs*; first annual report, Zoetermeer.

EIM, 1994, *The European Observatory for SMEs*; second annual report, Zoetermeer.

EIM, 1995, *The European Observatory for SMEs*; third annual report, Zoetermeer.

EIM (1996), *The European Observatory for SMEs*; fourth annual report, Zoetermeer.

EIM (1997), *The European Observatory for SMEs*; fifth annual report, Zoetermeer.

Eliasson, G. E., 1995, *Economic Growth Through Competitive Selection*, paper presented at 22nd Annual E.A.R.I.E. Conference 3–6 September 1995, mimeo.

Eurostat, 1994, *Enterprises in Europe*, 3rd edition, Luxembourg.

Floud, R. and D. McCloskey (eds.), 1994, *The Economic History of Britain Since 1700*; Vol. 2: 1860–1939, Cambridge, U.K.: Cambridge University Press.

Galbraith, J. K., 1967, *The New Industrial State*, London: Routledge.

Gartner, W. B., 1989, '"Who is an Entrepreneur?" is the Wrong Question', *Entrepreneurship Theory and Practice* **13**, 47–68.

Hébert, R. F. and A. N. Link, 1982, *The Entrepreneur*, New York: Praeger.

Hébert, R. F. and A. N. Link, 1989, 'In Search of the Meaning of Entrepreneurship', *Small Business Economics* **1**, 39–49.

Hofstede, G., 1980, *Culture's Consequences; International Differences in Work-Related Values*, Beverley Hills: Sage.

Hofstede, G., 1995, *Allemaal andersdenkenden; omgaan met cultuurverschillen*, Amsterdam: Contact.

Jacobs, J., 1984, *Cities and the Wealth of Nations: Principles of Economic Life*, New York: Random House.

Jong, A. H. M. de and C. W. A. M. van Paridon, 1989, *De economische geschiedenis van West-Europa in vogelvlucht; een speurtocht naar groeibepalende factoren*, Onderzoeks-memorandum no 55, Den Haag: Centraal Planbureau.

Kirchhoff, B. A., 1994, *Entrepreneurship and Dynamic Capitalism*, Westport CT: Praeger.

Kirzner, I. M., 1985, 'The Entrepreneur in Economic Theory', in E. Dahmén, L. Hannah and I. M. Kirzner (eds.) (1994), *The Dynamics of Entrepreneurship*, Lund: Lund University Press.

Kleijweg, Aad and Henry Nieuwenhuijsen, 1996, *Job Creation by Size-Class: Measurement and Empirical Investigation*, Research Report 9604/E, Zoetermeer: EIM

Klundert, Th. van de and S. Smulders (1992), 'Reconstructing Growth Theory: A Survey', *De Economist* **140**, 177–203.

Klundert, Th. van de, 1997, *Groei en institutes: over de oorzaken van economische ontwikkeling*, Tilburg University Press

Koedijk, K. and J. J. M. Kremers, 1996, *Market Opening, Regulation and Growth in Europe*, Research memorandum 9607, Research Centre for Economic Policy, Rotterdam: Erasmus University Rotterdam.

Koning, A. de and J. Snijders, 1992, Policy on Small and Medium-Sized Enterprises in Countries of the European Community', *International Small Business Journal* **10**, 25–39.

Landes, D. S., 1969, *The Unbound Prometheus: Technological Change and Industrial Development in Western Europe from 1750 to the Present*, Cambridge, U.K.: Cambridge University Press.

Lazonick, W., 1991, *Business Organization and the Myth of the Market Economy*, Cambridge, U.K.: Cambridge University Press.

Leibenstein, H., 1968, 'Entrepreneurship and Development', *American Economic Review* **58**, 72–83.

Leibenstein, H., 1979, 'The General X-Efficiency Paradigm and the Role of the Entrepreneur', in Mario Rizzio (ed.), *Time, Uncertainty and Disequilibrium*, Lexington: Heath, 127–139.

Lewis, W. A., 1955, *The Theory of Economic Growth*, London: George Allen & Unwin.

Loveman, G. and W. Sengenberger, 1991, 'The Re-Emergence of Small-Scale Production: An International Comparison', *Small Business Economics* **3**, 1–37.

Lucas, R. E., 1988, 'On the Mechanics of Economic Development', *Journal of Monetary Economics* **22**, 3–42.

Lumpkin, G. T. and G. G. Dess, 1996, Clarifying the Entrepreneurial Orientation Construct and Linking It to Performance', *Academy of Management Review* **21**, 135–172.

Lynn, Richard, 1991, *The Secret of the Miracle Economy: Different National Attitudes to Competitiveness and Money*, London: Crowley Esmonde Ltd.

Maddison, Angus, 1995, *Monitoring the World Economy 1820–1992*, Development Center Studies, Paris: OECD.

Magnusson, L. (ed.), 1994, *Evolutionary and Neo-Schumpeterian Approaches to Economics*, Dordrecht: Kluwer Academic Publishers.

Mankiw, N. G., (1995), 'The Growth of Nations', *Brookings Papers on Economic Activity* **1**, 275–326.

Marshall, A., 1961, *Principles of Economics*, 9th edition, London: Macmillan.

Mokyr, Joel, 1990, *The Lever of Riches: Technological Creativity and Economic Progress*, Oxford, U.K.: Oxford University Press.

Nelson, R. R. and S. Winter, 1982, *An Evolutionary Theory of Economic Change*, Cambridge, MA: Harvard University Press.

Nickell, S. J., 1996, 'Competition and Corporate Performance', *Journal of Political Economy* **104**, 724–746.

Nooteboom, B., 1993, *Schumpeterian and Austrian Entrepreneurship: A Unified Process of Innovation and Diffusion*, Research report nr. 1993-01, Groningen: Groningen University.

North, D. C. and R. P. Thomas, 1973, *The Rise of the Western World: A New Economic History*, Cambridge, U.K.: University Press.

Olson, M., 1982, *The Rise and Decline of Nations: Economic Growth, Stagflation and Social Rigidities*, New Haven/London: Yale University Press.

Osborne, D. and T. Gaebler, 1992, *Reinventing Government: How the Entrepreneurial Spirit is Transforming the Public Sector*, Reading, MA: Addison-Wesley.

Piore, M. and C. Sable, 1984, *The Second Industrial Divide: Possibilities for Prosperity*, New York: Basic Books.

Pollard, S., 1994, 'Entrepreneurship 1870–1914', in Floud, Roderick and Donald McCloskey (eds.) (1994), *The Economic History of Britain since 1700; Volume 2: 1860–1939*, Cambridge, U.K.: Cambridge University Press.

Porter, M. E., 1990, *The Competitive Advantage of Nations*, New York: Free Press.

Praag, C. M., 1996, *Determinants of Successful Entrepreneurship*, Amsterdam: Thesis Publishers.

Romer, P. M., 1990, 'Endogenous Technical Change', *Journal of Political Economy* **98**, 71–102.

Rostow, W. W., 1960, *The Stages of Economic Growth: A Non-Communist Manifesto*, Cambridge, U.K.: Cambridge University Press.

SBA, 1986, *The State of Small Business*, Washington DC.

Schmitz, Jr., J. A., 1989, 'Imitation, Entrepreneurship, and Long-Run Growth', *Journal of Political Economy* **97**, 721–739.

Schultz, T. W., 1980, 'Investment in Entrepreneurial Ability', *Scandinavian Journal of Economics* **82**, 437–448.

Schumpeter, J. A., 1934, *The Theory of Economic Development*, Cambridge, MA: Harvard University.

Schumpeter, J. A., 1996, *Capitalism, Socialism and Democracy*, London: Routledge.

Solow, R. M., 1970, *Growth Theory: An Exposition*, Oxford, U.K.: Oxford University Press.

Stevenson, H. H. and D. E. Gumpert, 1991, 'The Heart of Entrepreneurship', in W. A. Sahlmann and H. H. Stevenson (eds.), *The Entrepreneurial Venture*, Boston, MA: Harvard Business School Publications, pp. 9–25.

Stevenson, H. H. and J. C. Jarillo, 1990, A Paradigm of Entrepreneurship: Entrepreneurial Management', *Strategic Management Journal* **11**, 17–27.

Stopford, J. M. and C. W. F. Baden-Fuller, 1994, 'Creating Corporate Entrepreneurship', *Strategic Management Journal* **15**, 521–536.

Thurik, A. R., 1996, 'Small Firms, Entrepreneurship and Economic Growth', in P. H. Admiraal (ed.), *Small Business in the Modern Economy*, Oxford, U.K.: Basil Blackwell Publishers.

Vries, J. de and A. van der Woude, 1995, *Nederland 1500-1815; de eerste ronde van moderne economische groei*, Amsterdam: Uitgeverij Balans.

Weber, M., 1958, *The Protestant Ethic and the Spirit of Capitalism*, New York: Charles Scribner's Sons.

Wennekers, A. R. M., 1997, *The Revival of Entrepreneurship in the Netherlands*, Updated version of a paper presented at the EIIW Conference on business start-ups and SME-policy in Europe, Potsdam 13–14 March 1997, mimeo.

Wiener, M. J., 1981, *English Culture and the Decline of the Industrial Spirit, 1850–1980*, Cambridge, U.K.: Cambridge University Press.

Wildeman, R. E., G. Hofstede, N. G. Noorderhaven, A. R. Thurik, W. H. J. Verhoeven and A. R. M. Wennekers, 1998, *Culture's Role in Entrepreneurship: Self-Employment out of Dissatisfaction*, RIBES paper 9815, Erasmus Universiteit Rotterdam.

Williamson, O. E., 1975, *Markets and Hierarchies: Analysis and Antitrust Implications*, New York: the Free Press.

Witt, U. (ed.), 1993, *Evolutionary Economics*, Aldershot: Edward Elgar Publishing.

World Bank, 1993, *The East Asian Miracle: Economic Growth and Public Policy*, World Bank Policy Report, Oxford University Press.

You, J. I., 1995, 'Small Firms in Economic Theory', *Cambridge Journal of Economics* **19**, 441–462.

[2]

International Journal of Entrepreneurship Education 2(2): 143-166.
© 2004, Senate Hall Academic Publishing.

A Model of the Entrepreneurial Economy

David Audretsch[1]

Indiana University and Max Planck Institute for Research into Economic Systems (Entrepreneurship, Growth and Public Policy Group)

Roy Thurik

Erasmus University and Max Planck Institute for Research into Economic Systems (Entrepreneurship, Growth and Public Policy Group)

Abstract: The present paper deals with the distinction between the models of the managed and entrepreneurial economies. It explains why the model of the entrepreneurial economy may be a better frame of reference than the model of the managed economy in the contemporary, developed economies. This is done by contrasting the most fundamental elements of the managed economy model with those of the entrepreneurial economy model. Building upon Audretsch and Thurik (2000 and 2001), Audretsch, Thurik, Verheul and Wennekers (2002) and Thurik and Verheul (2003), fourteen dimensions are identified as the basis for comparing models of the entrepreneurial and the managed economy.

Keywords: entrepreneurship, innovation, knowledge economy and globalization.

1. Introduction

Robert Solow (1956) was awarded a Nobel Prize for identifying the sources of growth – the factors of capital and labor. These were factors best utilized in large scale production. Throughout the first three-quarters of the last century, the increasing level of transaction costs (Coase, 1937) incurred in large-scale production dictated increasing firm size over time. Certainly, statistical evidence points towards an increasing presence and role of large enterprises in the economy in this period (Caves, 1982; Teece, 1993; Brock and Evans, 1989). This development towards large-scale activity was visible, not just in one country, but in most of the OECD countries. In this same period, the importance of entrepreneurship and small business seemed to be fading. Although it was recognized that the small business sector was in need of

---

1.   The present paper benefited from a visit by Roy Thurik to Bloomington in the framework of the BRIDGE (Bloomington Rotterdam International Doctoral and Graduate) program in April 2003. Comments by Andrew Burke, Ingrid Verheul and two anonymous referees are gratefully acknowledged.

protection for both social and political reasons, there were few that made this case on the grounds of economic efficiency.

Romer (1986), Lucas (1988 and 1993) and Krugman (1991) discovered that the traditional production factors of labor and capital are not sufficient in explaining growth and that knowledge instead has become the vital factor in endogenous growth models. Knowledge has typically been measured in terms of R&D, human capital and patented inventions (Audretsch and Thurik, 2000 and 2001). Many scholars have predicted that the emergence of knowledge as an important determinant of growth and competitiveness in global markets would render new and small firms even more futile. Conventional wisdom would have predicted increased globalization to present an even more hostile environment to small business (Vernon, 1970). Caves argued that the additional costs of knowledge activity that would be incurred by small businesses in a global economy *"constitute an important reason for expecting that foreign investment will be mainly an activity of large firms"* (Caves, 1982, p. 53). As Chandler (1990, p. 78) concluded: *"to compete globally you have to be big"*. Furthermore, Gomes-Casseres (1997, p. 33) observed that *"students of international business have traditionally believed that success in foreign markets required large size"*. In a world that became dominated by exporting giant firms, global markets, global products, global players became the focus of interest. Small firms were thought to be at a disadvantage vis-à-vis larger firms because of the fixed costs of learning about foreign environments, communicating at long distances, and negotiating with national governments.

Despite these counteracting forces, entrepreneurship has emerged as the engine of economic and social development throughout the world.[2] The role of entrepreneurship has changed dramatically, fundamentally shifting between what Audretsch and Thurik (2001) introduced as the model of the managed economy and that of the entrepreneurial economy. In particular, Audretsch and Thurik (2001) argue that the model of the managed economy is the political, social and economic response to an economy dictated by the forces of large-scale production, reflecting the predominance of the production factors of capital and (unskilled) labor as the sources of competitive advantage. By contrast, the model of the entrepreneurial economy is the political, social and economic response to an economy dictated not just by the dominance of the production factor of knowledge – which Romer (1990, 1994) and Lucas (1988) identified as replacing the more traditional factors as the source of competitive advantage – but also by a very different, but complementary, factor they had overlooked: entrepreneurship capital, or the capacity to engage in and generate entrepreneurial activity. It is not straightforward that knowledge or R&D always spills over due to its mere existence (Audretsch and Keilbach, 2003).

---

2. See Carree and Thurik (2003) for a literature survey spanning different strands.

The purpose of this paper is to discuss the distinction between the models of the managed and entrepreneurial economies and to explain why the model of the entrepreneurial economy may be a better frame of reference than the model of the managed economy when explaining the role of entrepreneurship in the contemporary, developed economies. This is done by contrasting the most fundamental elements of the managed economy model with those of the entrepreneurial economy model. Building upon Audretsch and Thurik (2000 and 2001), Audretsch, Thurik, Verheul and Wennekers (2002) and Thurik and Verheul (2003), fourteen dimensions are identified as the basis for comparing models of the entrepreneurial and the managed economy. The common thread throughout these dimensions is the more important role of new and small enterprises in the entrepreneurial economy model (as compared to that of the managed economy). Understanding the distinction between the models of the entrepreneurial and managed economies is vital for entrepreneurship education explaining why the causes and consequences of entrepreneurship differ in the managed and the entrepreneurial economies (Wennekers, Uhlaner and Thurik, 2002; Thurik, Wennekers and Uhlaner, 2002). This suggests that the conditions for, and aspects of, teaching entrepreneurship under the model of the entrepreneurial economy may not be the same as under the managed economy model. While the paradigm prevalent across the management curricula was a response to managing production in the managed economy model, the model of the entrepreneurial economy dictates new approaches.

2. The Era of the Managed Economy

Throughout the first three-quarters of the last century large enterprise was clearly the dominant form of business organization (Schumpeter, 1934). The systematic empirical evidence, gathered from both Europe and North America, documented a sharp decreased in the role of small business in the post-war period. This was the era of mass production when economies of scale seemed to be the decisive factor in dictating efficiency. This was the world described by John Kenneth Galbraith (1956) in his theory of countervailing power, where the power of 'big business' was balanced by that of 'big labor' and 'big government'. This was the era of the man in the gray flannel suit and the organization man, when virtually every major social and economic institution acted to reinforce the stability and predictability needed for mass production (Piore and Sabel, 1984; Chandler, 1977).[3] Stability, continuity and homogeneity were the cornerstones of the managed economy (Audretsch and Thurik, 2001). Large firms dominated this economy. Large corporations in the

---

3.   See Whyte (1960) and Riesman (1950) for a description of the gray flannel suit and the
     organization man.

managed economy are described in *The Economist* (December 22nd, 2001, p. 76): *"They were hierarchical and bureaucratic organizations that where in the business of making long runs of standardized products. They introduced new and improved varieties with predictable regularity; they provided workers with life-time employment; and enjoyed fairly good relations with the giant trade unions"*. In organization studies this modernism is referred to as Fordism.[4]

Small firms and entrepreneurship were viewed as a luxury, as something Western countries needed to ensure a decentralization of decision making, obtained only at the cost of efficiency. A generation of scholars, spanning a broad spectrum of academic fields and disciplines, has sought to create insight into the issues surrounding this perceived trade-off between economic efficiency on the one hand and political and economic decentralization on the other (Williamson, 1968). These scholars have produced a large number of studies focusing mainly on three questions: (i) What are the gains to size and large-scale production?, (ii) What are the economic and welfare implications of an oligopolistic market structure, i.e., is economic performance promoted or reduced in an industry with just a handful of large-scale firms?, and (iii) Given the overwhelming evidence that large-scale production and economic concentration is associated with increased efficiency, what are the public policy implications?

This literature has produced a series of stylized facts about the role of small business in the post-war economies of North America and Western Europe:

- *Small businesses were generally less efficient than their larger counterparts.* Studies from the United States in the 1960s and 1970s revealed that small businesses produced at lower levels of efficiency than larger firms (Weiss, 1966, 1964 and Pratten, 1971).

- *Small businesses were characterized by lower levels of employee compensation.* Empirical evidence from both North America and Europe found a systematic and positive relationship between employee compensation and firm size (Brown, Hamilton and Medoff, 1990; Brown and Medoff, 1989).

- *Small businesses were only marginally involved in innovative activity.* Based on R&D measures, small businesses accounted for

---

4. Early contributions of organization studies have shown that changes in the external organization affect the type of organization that is successful. For instance, Lawrence and Lorsch (1967) show that the more homogeneous and stable the environment, the more formalized and hierarchical the organization.

only a small amount of innovative activity (Chandler, 1990; Scherer, 1991; Acs and Audretsch, 1990; Audretsch, 1995).

- *The relative importance of small businesses was declining over time in both North America and Europe* (Scherer, 1991).

3. The Emergence of the Entrepreneurial Economy

Given the painstaking and careful documentation that large-scale production was driving out entrepreneurship, it was particularly startling and seemingly paradoxical when scholars first began to document that – what had seemed like – the inevitable demise of small business, began to reverse itself from the 1970s onwards. Loveman and Sengenberger (1991) and Acs and Audretsch (1993) carried out systematic international analyses examining the re-emergence of small business and entrepreneurship in North America and Europe. Two major findings emerged from these studies. First, the relative importance of small business varies largely across countries, and, secondly, in most European countries and North America the importance of small business increased since the mid-1970s. In the United States the average real GDP per firm increased by nearly two-thirds between 1947 and 1989 – from $150,000 to $245,000 – reflecting a trend towards larger enterprises and a decreasing importance of small firms. However, within the subsequent seven years it had fallen by about 14 percent to $210,000, reflecting a sharp reversal of this trend and the re-emergence of small business (Brock and Evans, 1989). Similarly, small firms accounted for one-fifth of manufacturing sales in the United States in 1976, but by 1986 the sales share of small firms had risen to over one-quarter (Acs and Audretsch, 1993).

The reversal of the trend away from large enterprises towards the re-emergence of small business was not limited to North America. It was also seen in Europe. For example, in the Netherlands the business ownership rate (business owners per workforce) fell during the post-war period, until it reached the lowest point at 8.1 percent in 1984 (Verheul et al., 2002). The downward trend was subsequently reversed, and a business ownership rate of 10.4 percent was reached by 1998 (Verheul et al., 2002). Similarly, the employment share in manufacturing of small firms in the Netherlands increased from 68.3 percent in 1978 to 71.8 percent in 1986. In the United Kingdom this share increased from 30.1 percent in 1979 to 39.9 percent in 1986; in (Western) Germany from 54.8 percent in 1970 to 57.9 percent by 1987; in Portugal from 68.3 percent in 1982 to 71.8 percent in 1986; in the North of Italy from 44.3 percent in 1981 to 55.2 percent in 1987, and in the South of Italy from 61.4 percent in 1981 to 68.4 percent in 1987 (Acs and Audretsch, 1993). A study of EIM (2002) documents how the relative importance of small firms in Europe (19 countries), measured in terms of employment shares, has continued to increase between 1988 and 2001. See Figure 1 for the development of the entrepreneurship rates (business ownership rates) in a selection of countries taken from van Stel (2003). A distinct U-shape can be observed for these countries. The upward trend of the entrepreneurship rate is leveling off in such countries as the UK and the US.[5] In the UK this may be due to policy measures favoring incumbent growth businesses rather than startups (Thurik, 2003). In the US this may be due to the high level of economic development and to shake out of industries that are in a more advanced stage than elsewhere in the area of modern OECD countries.[6]

Figure 1: Entrepreneurship rates (business owners per workforce) in six OECD countries

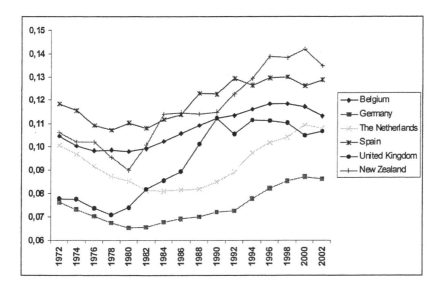

As the empirical evidence documenting the re-emergence of entrepreneurship increased, scholars began to look for explanations and to develop a theoretical basis. Early explanations (Brock and Evans, 1989) revolved around six hypotheses regarding the increased role of small firms:

5.   See van Stel (2003) or Verheul et al. (2002) for precise data and figures of the US development.
6.   See also Kwoka and White (2001) who observe that despite its importance in absolute and relative terms the small business sector accounts for a diminishing share of US private sector activity. In van Stel (2003) it can be observed that the entrepreneurship rate in countries like Japan and France has dropped over a long period including the 1990s.

- Technological change reduces the importance of scale economies in manufacturing.[7]

- Increased globalization and the accompanying competition from a greater number of foreign rivals render markets more volatile.

- The changing composition of the labor force, towards a greater participation of women, immigrants, young and old workers, is more conducive to smaller than larger enterprises, due to the greater premium placed on work flexibility.

- A proliferation of consumer demand away from standardized and mass-produced goods towards tailor-made and personalized products facilitates small producers serving niche markets.

- Deregulation and privatization facilitate the entry of new and small firms into markets previously protected and inaccessible.

- The increased importance of innovation in high-wage countries reduces the relative importance of large-scale production, fostering entrepreneurial activity instead.

Audretsch and Thurik (2001) explain the re-emergence of entrepreneurship in Europe and North America on the basis of increased globalization, which has shifted the comparative advantage towards knowledge-based economic activity. They discuss the consequences for economic performance: entrepreneurship capital may be a missing link in explaining variations in economic performance (Audretsch and Keilbach, 2003). An alternative and wider view of this missing link may be that it is the institutional fabric that makes the difference between high and low performance. For example, Saxenian (1994) attributes the superior performance of Silicon Valley to a high capacity for promoting entrepreneurship. While the traditional production factors of labor and capital, as well as knowledge capital, are important in shaping output, the capacity to harness new ideas by creating new enterprises is also essential to economic output.

While entrepreneurs undertake a definitive action, i.e., they start a new business, this action can not be viewed in a vacuum devoid of context. Rather, as Audretsch et al. (2002) show, entrepreneurship is shaped by a number of

---

7.   The influence of technological change on the shaping of business conditions has been widely discussed elsewhere in the late 1980s. See Piori and Sable (1984) and Tushman and Anderson (1986).

forces and factors, including legal and institutional as well as social factors. The study of social capital and its impact on economic decision making and behavior dates back to classic economics and sociology literature where it is argued that social and relational structures influence market processes (Granovetter, 1985). Thorton and Flynne (2003) and Saxenian (1994) argue that entrepreneurial environments are characterized by thriving supportive networks that provide the institutional fabric linking individual entrepreneurs to organized sources of learning and resources. Studying networks located in California's Silicon Valley, Saxenian (1990, p. 96/7) emphasizes that it is the communication between individuals that facilitates the transmission of knowledge across agents, firms, and industries, and not just a high endowment of human capital and knowledge in the region: "*It is not simply the concentration of skilled labor, suppliers and information that distinguish the region. A variety of regional institutions – including Stanford University, several trade associations and local business organizations, and a myriad of specialized consulting, market research, public relations and venture capital firms – provide technical, financial, and networking services which the region's enterprises often cannot afford individually. These networks defy sectoral barriers: individuals move easily from semiconductor to disk drive firms or from computer to network makers. They move from established firms to startups (or vice versa) and even to market research or consulting firms, and from consulting firms back into startups. And they continue to meet at trade shows, industry conferences, and the scores of seminars, talks, and social activities organized by local business organizations and trade associations. In these forums, relationships are easily formed and maintained, technical and market information is exchanged, business contacts are established, and new enterprises are conceived...This decentralized and fluid environment also promotes the diffusion of intangible technological capabilities and understandings.*"

Such contexts generating a high propensity for economic agents to start new firms can be characterized as being rich in entrepreneurship capital. Other contexts, where the startup of new firms is inhibited, can be characterized as being weak in entrepreneurship capital.[8]

Entrepreneurship capital exerts a positive impact on competitiveness and growth in a number of ways. The *first* way is by creating knowledge spillovers. Romer (1986), Lucas (1988 and 1993) and Grossman and Helpman (1991) established that knowledge spillovers are an important mechanism underlying endogenous growth. However, they shed little light on the actual mechanisms by which knowledge is transmitted across firms and individuals. Insight into the process of knowledge diffusion is important, especially since a policy

---

8.   While this may seem like a tautology, we are using the concept of entrepreneurial capital to characterize locations exhibiting a high degree of entrepreneurial capital.

implication commonly drawn from new economic growth theory is that, due to the increasing role of knowledge and the resulting increasing returns, knowledge factors (e.g., R&D) should be publicly supported. It is important to recognize that also the mechanisms for spillovers may play a key role and, accordingly, should serve as a focus for public policy enhancing economic growth and development.[9]

The literature identifying mechanisms creating knowledge spillovers is sparse and remains underdeveloped. However, entrepreneurship is an important area where transmission mechanisms have been identified. This will be explained below.

Cohen and Levinthal (1989) suggest that firms develop the capacity to adapt new technology and ideas developed in other firms and are therefore able to appropriate some of the returns accruing to investments[10] in new knowledge made externally (i.e., outside the own organization). This view of spillovers is consistent with the traditional knowledge production function, where firms exist exogenously, and then make (knowledge) investments to generate innovative output. Audretsch (1995) proposes a shift in the unit of observation away from exogenously assumed firms towards individuals, such as scientists, engineers or other knowledge workers, i.e., agents with endowments of new economic knowledge. When the focus is shifted from the firm to the individual as the relevant unit of observation, the appropriability issue remains, but the question becomes: How can economic agents with a given endowment of new knowledge best appropriate the returns from that knowledge? Albert O. Hirschman (1970) argues that if voice proves to be ineffective within incumbent organizations, and loyalty is sufficiently weak, a knowledge worker may exit the firm or university where the knowledge is created in order to create a new company. In this spillover process the knowledge production function is reversed. Knowledge is exogenous and embodied in a worker and the firm is created endogenously through the worker's effort to appropriate the value of his knowledge by way of innovative activity. Hence, entrepreneurship serves as a mechanism by which knowledge spills over from the source to a new firm in which it is commercialized. There is a large history of people who only started their firms after large firms were disinterested in the innovation. This applies particularly to competence-destroying industries. Chester Carlsson started Xerox after his proposal to produce a new copy machine was rejected by Kodak. Steven Jobs started Apple Computer after his proposal to produce a new personal computer was turned down by Xerox.

---

9. For instance, see Scarpetta et al. (2002) where a firm-level database for ten OECD countries is used to present empirical evidence on the role that policy measures and institutions in product and labor markets play for firm dynamics and productivity. Moreover, different features of entrant and exiting firms across countries are observed.

10. As Audretsch and Feldman (1996) point out knowledge spillovers occur in the context of networks and clusters.

A *second* way in which entrepreneurship capital generates economic growth is through augmenting the number of enterprises and increasing competition. Jacobs (1969) and Porter (1990) argue that competition is more conducive to knowledge externalities than is local monopoly.[11] With local competition Jacobs (1969) is not referring to competition within product markets as has traditionally been envisioned within the industrial organization literature, but rather to the competition for new ideas embodied in economic agents. Not only does an increase in the number of firms enhance the competition for new ideas, but greater competition across firms also facilitates the entry of new firms specializing in a particular new product niche. This is because the necessary complementary inputs are more likely to be available from small specialist niche firms than from large, vertically integrated producers. Feldman and Audretsch (1999) as well as Glaeser et al. (1992) found empirical evidence supporting the hypothesis that an increase in competition in a city, as measured by the number of enterprises, is accompanied by higher growth performance of that city.[12]

A *third* way in which entrepreneurship capital generates economic output is by providing diversity among firms (Cohen and Klepper, 1992). Not only does entrepreneurship capital generate a greater number of enterprises, it also increases the variety of enterprises in a certain location. A key assumption of Hannan and Freeman (1989) in the population ecology literature is that each new organization represents a unique formula.[13] There has been a series of theoretical arguments suggesting that the degree of diversity, as opposed to homogeneity, will influence the growth potential of a location.

The theoretical basis for linking diversity to economic performance is provided by Jacobs (1969), who argues that the most important sources of knowledge spillovers are external to the industry in which the firm operates and that cities are a source of considerable innovation because here the diversity of knowledge sources is greatest (Audretsch and Feldman, 1996; Jaffe et al., 1993). According to Jacobs (1969) it is the exchange of complementary knowledge across diverse firms and economic agents that yields an important return on new economic knowledge. Jacobs (1969) develops a theory emphasizing the argument that the variety of industries within a geographic environment promotes knowledge externalities and, ultimately, innovative activity and economic growth. In this environment

11. An anonymous referee pointed out that saying that competition is more conducive to knowledge externalities than a local monopoly is not the same as that new firms create more knowledge externalities.
12. See also Acs (2002) who hints at the dual causality between the growth of cities and that of the number of firms.
13. As opposed to the organizational ecology approach of Hannan and Freeman institutional theorists in organization studies also point to strong pressures on new firms to conform (Dimaggio and Powell, 1983).

International Journal of Entrepreneurship Education 2(2)   153

entrepreneurship capital can contribute to growth and development by injecting diversity and serving as a conduit for knowledge spillovers, leading to increased competition. The entrepreneurial economy is characterized by a high reliance on this third role of entrepreneurship capital.[14]

4. Contrasting the Entrepreneurial and Managed Economy Models

The era of the managed economy is being supplanted by the emergence of the entrepreneurial economy. This suggests two contrasting models with differing roles of entrepreneurship. The model of the managed economy revolves around the links between stability, specialization, homogeneity, scale, certainty and predictability on the one hand and economic growth on the other. By contrast, the model of the entrepreneurial economy focuses on the links between flexibility, turbulence, diversity, novelty, innovation, linkages and clustering on the one hand and economic growth on the other. The models of the managed and the entrepreneurial economy can be compared distinguishing between different groups of characteristics, including underlying forces, external environment characteristics, internal or firm characteristics and policy characteristics. See Table 1 at the end of the present article.

4.1. Underlying Forces

The first group of characteristics contrasts the forces underlying the models of the entrepreneurial and managed economy: localization *versus* globalization; change *versus* continuity; and jobs and high wages *versus* jobs or high wages.

In the model of the managed economy production results from the inputs of labor and capital (Solow, 1956). Geography provides a platform to combine (mobile) capital with (immobile) lower-cost labor (Kindleberger and Audretsch, 1983). In the model of the entrepreneurial economy knowledge is the dominant factor of production. The comparative advantage in the knowledge economy is dependent on innovative activity. Knowledge spillovers are an important source of this innovative activity. Hence, in the model of the entrepreneurial economy local proximity is important, with the region being the most important locus of economic activity, as knowledge tends to be developed in the context of localized production networks embedded in innovative clusters.

While the model of the managed economy focuses more on *continuity* (Chandler, 1977), the model of the entrepreneurial economy provokes and

---

14. A different view on the role of knowledge and its spillovers is offered in the "systems of innovations" approach (Nelson, 1993).

thrives on *change*. Although innovation is present under the conditions of both change and continuity, the locus of innovative activity differs. A distinction can be made between incremental and radical innovations. Innovations are considered incremental when they are compatible with the core competence and technological trajectory of the firm (Teece, Rumult, Dosi and Winter, 1994). By contrast, a radical innovation can be defined as extending beyond the boundaries of the core competence and technological trajectory of the firm. In the model of the managed economy change is absorbed within a given technological paradigm: the average firm excels at incremental innovation. By contrast, in the model of the entrepreneurial economy, the capacity to break out of the technological lock-in imposed by existing paradigms is enhanced by the ability of economic agents to start new firms. Thus, incremental innovative activity along with diffusion plays a more important role in the model of the managed economy. While often requiring large investments in R&D, this type of innovative activity generates incremental changes in products along the existing technological trajectories. In the entrepreneurial economy model, the comparative advantage of the high-cost location demands innovative activity earlier in the product life cycle and which is of a more radical nature.

One of the most striking policy dilemmas in the model of the managed economy is that unemployment can be reduced only at the cost of lower wages. In the model of the entrepreneurial economy high employment can be combined with high wages and a low wage level does not imply high employment.[15] An indication of the absence of a trade-off between high wages and employment is the fact that although corporate downsizing has been rampant throughout the OECD countries, there is a large variance in unemployment rates. Audretsch et al. (2002) show that economies of OECD countries exhibiting characteristics in conformity with the entrepreneurial economy model have been more successful at creating new jobs to compensate for jobs lost in the process of corporate downsizing. Small firms in general, and new ventures in particular, are the engine of employment creation.[16] Under the model of the managed economy the job creation by small firms is associated with lower wages. However, the growth of new firms may not only generate greater employment, but also higher wages. New firm growth ensures that higher employment does not come at a cost of lower wages, but rather the opposite – higher wages. Hence, while small firms generate employment at a cost of lower wages in the model of the managed economy, in the entrepreneurial economy model small firms may create both more jobs and higher wages.[17]

---

15. An anonymous referee pointed out that, clearly, the trade-off between involuntary unemployment and wages requires a ceteris paribus condition: if the productivity of workers increases than both employment and wages can increase.
16. Carree and Thurik (1999) show that a higher share of small business in European manufacturing industries leads to higher growth of value added in the subsequent years.

International Journal of Entrepreneurship Education 2(2)   155

4.2. External Environment

The second group of characteristics contrasts the external environment characteristics of the models of the managed and the entrepreneurial economies. Turbulence, diversity and heterogeneity are central to the model of the entrepreneurial economy. By contrast, stability, specialization and homogeneity are the cornerstones in the model of the managed economy.

Stability in the model of the managed economy results from a homogeneous product demand, resulting in a low turnover rate of jobs, workers and firms. The model of the entrepreneurial economy is characterized by a high degree of *turbulence*. Each year many new firms are started and only a subset of these firms survives. Nelson and Winter (1982) argue that the role of diversity and selection is at the heart of generating change. This holds for both the managed and the entrepreneurial economy model. However, what differs in these models is the management and organization of the process by which diversity is created as well as the selection mechanism. In the model of the managed economy research activities are organized and scheduled in departments devoted to developing novel products and services. The management of change fits into what Nelson and Winter (1982) refer to as the firm's routines. The ability of existing businesses to manage the process of change pre-empted most opportunities for entrepreneurs to start new firms, resulting in a low startup rate and a stable industrial structure. In the model of the entrepreneurial economy the process of generating new ideas, both within and outside of R&D laboratories, creates a turbulent environment with many opportunities for entrepreneurs to start new firms based upon different and changing opinions about different and changing ideas.

A series of theoretical arguments has suggested that the degree of *diversity* versus *specialization* may account for differences in rates of growth and technological development. While *specialization* of industry activities is associated with lower transaction costs and, therefore, greater (static) efficiency, *diversity* of activities is said to facilitate the exchange of new ideas and, therefore, greater innovative activity and (dynamic) efficiency. Because knowledge spillovers are an important source of innovative activity, diversity is a prerequisite in the model of the entrepreneurial economy where lower transaction costs are preferably sacrificed for greater opportunities for knowledge spillover. In the model of the managed economy, there are less gains from knowledge spillovers. The higher transaction costs associated with diversity yield little room for opportunities in terms of increased innovative activity, making specialization preferable in the model of the managed economy.

---

17. See Acs, Fitzroy and Smith (2002) and Scarpetta, Hemmings, Tressel and Woo (2002) for illustrating data material.

Whereas the trade-off between diversity and specialization focuses on firms, that between *homogeneity* and *heterogeneity* focuses on individuals. There are two dimensions shaping the degree of homogeneity versus heterogeneity. The first dimension refers to the genetic make-up of individuals and their personal experiences (Nooteboom, 1994) and the second dimension refers to the information set to which individuals are exposed. The model of the managed economy is based on homogeneity, that of the entrepreneurial economy on heterogeneity. In a heterogeneous population communication across individuals tends to be more difficult and costly than in a homogenous population: transaction costs are higher and efficiency is lower. At the same time, new ideas are more likely to emerge from communication in a heterogeneous than in a homogeneous world. Although the likelihood of communication is lower in a heterogeneous population, communication is this environment is more prone to produce novelty and innovation. The lower transaction costs resulting from a homogeneous population in the model of the managed economy are not associated with high opportunity costs because knowledge spillovers are relatively unimportant in generating innovative activity. However, knowledge spillovers are a driving force in the model of the entrepreneurial economy, offsetting the higher transaction costs associated with a heterogeneous population.

4.3. Firm Behavior

The third group of characteristics contrasts firm behavior of the models of the managed and the entrepreneurial economy: control *versus* motivation; firm transaction *versus* market exchange; competition and cooperation as substitutes *versus* complements; and scale *versus* flexibility.

Under the model of the managed economy labor is considered as indistinguishable from the other input factors, as long as management is able to extract a full day's worth of energy for a full day's pay (Wheelwright, 1985). It is considered homogeneous and easily replaceable. In the managed economy model firms organize their labor according to the principles of *command and control*. Management styles emphasize the maintenance of tasks through direct forms of employee control. Under the model of the entrepreneurial economy, the command and control approach to labor is less effective as the comparative advantage of the advanced industrialized countries tends to be based on new knowledge. *Motivating* workers to facilitate the discovery process and implementation of new ideas is more important than requiring an established set of activities from knowledge workers. Management styles emphasize the nurturing of interpersonal relationships facilitating rather than supervising employees. In the entrepreneurial economy model the focus of activities is on exploring new abilities, rather than exploiting existing ones. Hence, under the

International Journal of Entrepreneurship Education 2(2)   157

model of the entrepreneurial economy motivating employees to participate in the creation and commercialization of new ideas is more important than simply controlling and regulating their behavior. The distinction between controlling and motivating employees can be traced back to, and corresponds with, McGregor's (1960) Theory X and Y, autocratic versus democratic decision-making (Lewin and Lippitt, 1938), task-oriented versus interpersonal-oriented styles (Blake and Mouton, 1964), and transactional versus transformational leadership (Bass et al., 1996).[18] It has also been suggested that controlling versus motivating employees can be viewed as more masculine versus more feminine management styles (Van Engen, 2001), although a recent study by Verheul (2003) suggests that women are more control-oriented than men when managing employees.

Dating back to Coase (1937), and more recently to Williamson (1975), an analytical distinction can be made between *exchange via the market* and *intra-firm transactions*. Both Coase and Williamson emphasize that uncertainty and imperfect information increase the cost of intra-firm transactions. As Knight (1921) argued, low uncertainty combined with transparency and predictability of information, make intra-firm transactions efficient relative to market exchange. In the managed economy model, where there is a high degree of certainty and predictability of information, transactions within firms tend to be more efficient than market exchange. By contrast, in the entrepreneurial economy model market transactions are more efficient because of the high uncertainty. Since the mid-1970s the economic arena has become increasingly uncertain and unpredictable (Carlsson, 1989; Carlsson and Taymaz, 1994), witnessed by a decrease in both mean firm size and the extent of vertical integration and conglomeration.

While models of *competition* generally assume that firms behave autonomously, models of *cooperation* assume linkages among firms. These linkages take various forms, including joint ventures, strategic alliances, and (in)formal networks (Gomes-Casseres, 1996 and 1997; Nooteboom, 1999). In the model of the managed economy competition and cooperation are viewed as being substitutes. Firms are vertically integrated and primarily compete in product markets. Cooperation between firms in the product market reduces the number of competitors and reduces the degree of competition. In the model of the entrepreneurial economy firms are vertically independent and specialized in the product market. The higher degree of vertical disintegration under the model of the entrepreneurial economy implies a replacement of internal transactions within a large vertically integrated corporation with cooperation among independent firms. At the same time, there are more firms, resulting in an increase in both the competitive and cooperative interface. The likelihood

---

18. An anonymous referee refers to Ackroyd and Thomson (1999) for some entertaining examples on the subject within UK firms.

of a firm competing or cooperating with other firms is higher in the entrepreneurial economy model.

Under the model of the managed economy costs-per-unit are reduced through expanding the scale of output, or through exploiting economies of *scale*. In product lines and industries where a large scale of production translates into a substantial reduction in average costs, large firms will have an economic advantage, leading to a concentrated industrial structure. The importance of scale economies has certainly contributed to the emergence and dominance of large corporations in heavy manufacturing industries, such as steel, automobiles, and aluminum (Chandler, 1977). The alternative source of reduced average costs is *flexibility* (Teece, 1993), characterizing the entrepreneurial economy model. Industries where demand for particular products is shifting constantly, require a flexible system of production that can meet such a whimsical demand.

4.4. Government Policy

The final group of contrasting dimensions of the models of the entrepreneurial economy and the managed economy refers to government policy, including the goals of policy (enabling *versus* constraining), the target of policy (inputs *versus* outputs), the locus of policy (local *versus* national) and financing policy (entrepreneurial *versus* incumbent).

Under the model of the managed economy public policy towards the firm is essentially *constraining* in nature. There are three[19] general types of public policy towards business: antitrust policy (competition policy), regulation, and public ownership. All three of these policy approaches restrict the firm's freedom to contract. Under the model of the managed economy the relevant policy question is: *How can the government withhold firms from abusing their market power?* The entrepreneurial economy model is characterized by a different policy question: *How can governments create an environment fostering the success and viability of firms?* Whereas the major issues in the model of the managed economy are concerns about excess profits and abuses of market dominance, in the model of the entrepreneurial economy the issues of international competitiveness, growth and employment are important. In the managed economy model the emphasis is *constraining* market power through regulation, whereas the focus in the entrepreneurial economy model is on stimulating firm development and performance through *enabling* policies.

---

19. As an anonymous referee pointed out: enabling one section in society may entail constraining other sections. For instance, a major policy issue for small businesses in the UK is how government can withhold banks from abusing power in the market from small business banking, thereby fostering an environment in which small businesses can succeed.

Another governmental policy dimension involves targeting selected *outputs* in the production process versus targeting selected *inputs*. Because of the relative certainty regarding markets and products in the model of the managed economy, the appropriate policy response is to target outcomes and outputs. Specific industries and firms can be promoted through government programs. Whereas in the model of the managed economy production is based on the traditional inputs of land, labor and capital, in the entrepreneurial economy model it is mainly based on knowledge input. There is uncertainty about what products should be produced, how and by whom. This high degree of uncertainty makes it difficult to select appropriate outcomes and increases the likelihood of targeting the wrong firms and industries. Hence, the appropriate policy in the model of the entrepreneurial economy is to target inputs, and in particular those inputs related to the creation and commercialization of knowledge.

The *locus* of policy is a third dimension on which the models of the managed and entrepreneurial economy can be compared. Under the model of the managed economy the appropriate locus of policy making is the *national or federal* level. While the targeted recipients of policy may be localized in one or a few regions, the most important policy making institutions tend to be located at the national level. By contrast, under the model of the entrepreneurial economy, government policy towards business tends to be decentralized and *regional or local* in nature. This distinction in the locus of policy results from two factors. *First*, because the competitive source of economic activity in the model of the entrepreneurial economy is knowledge, which tends to be localized in regional clusters, public policy requires an understanding of regional-specific characteristics and idiosyncrasies. *Secondly*, the motivation underlying government policy in the entrepreneurial economy is growth and the creation of jobs (with high pay), to be achieved mainly through new venture creation. New firms are usually small and pose no oligopolistic threat in national or international markets. In the model of the entrepreneurial economy no external costs – in the form of higher prices – are imposed on consumers in the national economy as is the case in the model of the managed economy. The promotion of local economies imposes no cost on consumers in the national economy. Hence, local intervention is justified and does not result in any particular loss incurred by agents outside of the region.

Finally, financing policies vary between the two models. Under the model of the managed economy, the systems of finance provide the existing companies with just liquidity for investment.[20] Liquidity is seen as a homogeneous input factor. The model of the entrepreneurial economy requires a system of finance that is different from that in the model of the managed

---

20. See Hughes and Storey (1994), Storey (1994), Reid (1996) and the special issue of Small Business Economics devoted to European SME Financing (Cressy and Olofsson, 1997).

economy. In the model of the managed economy there is certainty in outputs as well as inputs. There is a strong connection between banks and firms, fostering growth. In the entrepreneurial economy model certainty has given way to uncertainty requiring different (or differently structured) financial institutions. In particular the venture and informal capital markets, providing finance for high-risk and innovative new firms (Gaston, 1989; Gompers, 1999), play an important role in the model of the entrepreneurial economy. In this model liquidity looses its homogeneous image and is often coupled with forms of advice, knowledge and changing levels of involvement.

Storey (2003) has painstakingly documented examples of policies predicted by the entrepreneurial model like access to loan finance and equity capital, access to markets, administrative burdens, managed workspace, university spin-offs, science parks, stimulating innovation and R&D and training in small firms. See Storey (2003, table 3).

5. Discussion

The model of the managed economy seems to characterize most economies throughout the first three-quarters of the previous century. It is based on relative certainty in outputs (mainly manufactured products) and inputs (mainly land, labor and capital). The twin forces of globalization have reduced the ability of the managed economies of Western Europe and North America to grow and create jobs. On the one hand there is the advent of new competition from low-cost, but highly educated and skill-intensive, countries in Central and Eastern Europe as well as Asia. On the other hand, the telecommunications and computer revolutions have drastically reduced the cost of shifting not just capital but also information out of the high-cost locations of Europe and into lower-cost locations around the globe. Taken together, these twin forces of globalization imply that economic activity in high-cost locations is no longer compatible with routinized tasks. Rather, globalization has shifted the comparative advantage of high-cost locations to knowledge-based activities, and in particular intellectual search activities. These activities cannot be costlessly transferred around the globe. Knowledge as an input into economic activity is inherently different from land, labor and capital. It is characterized by high uncertainty, high asymmetries across people and high transaction costs. An economy where knowledge is the main source of comparative advantage is more consistent with the model of the entrepreneurial economy.

This paper has identified fourteen dimensions that span the difference between the models of the entrepreneurial and managed economies and provides a framework for understanding how the entrepreneurial economy fundamentally differs from the managed economy. See Table 1 for a overview. Building upon Audretsch and Thurik (2001) these contrasting models provide a lens through which economic events can be interpreted and policy formulated. Using the wrong lens leads to the wrong policy choice. For example, under the model of the managed economy firm failure is viewed negatively, representing a drain on society's resources. In the model of the managed economy resources are not invested in high-risk ventures. In the model of the entrepreneurial economy firm failure is viewed differently, i.e., as an experiment, an attempt to go in a new direction in an inherently risky environment (Wennekers and Thurik, 1999). An externality of failure is learning. In the model of the entrepreneurial economy the process of searching for new ideas is accompanied by failure. Similarly, the virtues of long-term relationships, stability and continuity under the model of the managed economy give way to flexibility, change, and turbulence in the model of the entrepreneurial economy. What is a liability in the model of the managed economy is, in some cases, a virtue in the model of the entrepreneurial economy.

Table 1: Fourteen dimensions of the difference between the model of the entrepreneurial and the managed economy

Category	Entrepreneurial economy	Managed economy
Underlying forces		
	Localization	Globalization
	Change	Continuity
	Jobs and high wages	Jobs or high wages
External environment		
	Turbulence	Stability
	Diversity	Specialization
	Heterogeneity	Homogeneity
How firms function		
	Motivation	Control
	Market exchange	Firm transaction
	Competition and cooperation	Competition or cooperation
	Flexibility	Scale
Government policy		
	Enabling	Constraining
	Input targeting	Output targeting
	Local locus	National locus
	Entrepreneurial	Incumbent

The implication for teaching entrepreneurship is that the role of and context for new and small firms is strikingly different in the entrepreneurial economy than in the managed economy. While small business was a follower in the managed economy, it has emerged as the engine of growth in the entrepreneurial economy. Also, ever more teaching efforts have the small-scaled environment as case example regardless of whether the education aims at training people for small or large firms.

References:

Ackroyd, S. and P. Thomson, 1999, *Organizational Misbehaviour*, London: Sage Publications.

Acs, Z.J., 2002, *Innovation and the Growth of Cities*, Cheltenham, UK: Edward Elgar.

Acs, Z.J. and D.B. Audretsch, 1990, *Innovation and Small Firms*, Cambridge, MA: MIT Press.

Acs, Z.J. and D.B. Audretsch, 1993, Conclusion, in: Z.J. Acs and D.B. Audretsch (eds.), *Small Firms and Entrepreneurship; an East-West Perspective*, Cambridge, UK: Cambridge University Press.

Acs, Z.J., F.R. Fitzroy and I. Smith, 2002, "High-technology employment and R&D in cities: heterogeneity vs specialization", *Annals of Regional Science* 36 (3), 373-386.

Aldrich, H.E. and M. Martinez, 2003, "Entrepreneurship as social construction", in: Z.J. Acs and D.B. Audretsch (eds.), *The International Handbook of Entrepreneurship*, Boston/ Dordrecht: Kluwer Academic Publishers.

Audretsch, D,B., 1995, *Innovation and Industry Evolution*, Cambridge, MA: MIT Press

Audretsch, D.B. and M.P. Feldman, 1996, "R&D spillovers and the geography of innovation and production", *American Economic Review* 86 (3), 630-640.

Audretsch, D.B. and M. Keilbach, 2003, "Entrepreneurship capital and economic performance", Centre for Economic Policy Research Discussion Paper DP3678, London: CEPR.

Audretsch, D.B. and A. R. Thurik, 1999, *Innovation, Industry Evolution and Employment*, Cambridge: Cambridge University Press.

Audretsch, D.B. and A. R. Thurik, 2000, "Capitalism and democracy in the 21st century: from the managed to the entrepreneurial economy", *Journal of Evolutionary Economics* 10, 17-34.

Audretsch, D.B. and A.R. Thurik, 2001, "What is new about the new economy: sources of growth in the managed and entrepreneurial economies", *Industrial and Corporate Change* 19, 795-821.

Audretsch, D.B., M.A. Carree and A.R. Thurik, 2001, "Does entrepreneurship reduce unemployment?" Tinbergen Institute Discussion Paper TI 2001-074/3, Rotterdam: Tinbergen Institute.

Audretsch, D.B., M.A. Carree, A.J. van Stel and A.R. Thurik, 2002, "Impeded industrial restructuring: the growth penalty", *Kyklos* 55 (1), 81-97.

Audretsch, D.B., A.R. Thurik, I. Verheul and A.R.M. Wennekers (eds.), 2002, *Entrepreneurship: Determinants and Policy in a European - US Comparison*, Boston/ Dordrecht: Kluwer Academic Publishers, 2002.

Bass, B.M., Avolio, B.J. and L.E. Atwater, 1996, "The transformational and transactional leadership style of men and women", *Applied Psychology* 45, 5-34.

Blake, R.R. and J.S. Mouton, 1964, *The Managerial Grid*, Houston: Gulf Publishing Company.

Brock, W.A. and D.S. Evans, 1989, "Small business economics", *Small Business Economics* 1 (1), 7-20.

Brown, C. and J. Medoff, 1989, "The employer size-wage effect", *Journal of Political Economy* 97 (5), 1027-1059.

Brown, C., Hamilton, J. and J. Medoff, 1990, *Employers Large and Small*, Cambridge, MA: Harvard University Press.

Carlsson, B., 1989, "The evolution of manufacturing technology and its impact on industrial structure: an international study", *Small Business Economics* 1 (1), 21-38.

Carlsson, B. and E. Taymaz, 1994, "Flexible technology and industrial structure in the U.S.", *Small Business Economics* 6 (3), 193-209.

Carree, M.A. and A.R. Thurik, 1999, "Industrial structure and economic growth, in: D.B. Audretsch and A. R. Thurik (eds.)", *Innovation, Industry Evolution and Employment*, Cambridge, UK: Cambridge University Press, 86-110.

Carree, M.A. and A.R. Thurik, 2003, "The impact of entrepreneurship on economic growth", in: Z.J. Acs and D.B. Audretsch (eds.), *Handbook of Entrepreneurship Research*, Boston/ Dordrecht: Kluwer Academic Publishers.

Caves, R., 1982, *Multinational Enterprise and Economic Analysis*, Cambridge: Cambridge University Press.

Chandler, A.D., 1977, *The Visible Hand: The Managerial Revolution in American Business*, Cambridge, MA: Harvard University Press.

Chandler, A.D. Jr., 1990, *Scale and Scope: The Dynamics of Industrial Capitalism*, Cambridge, MA: Harvard University Press.

Coase, R.H., 1937, "The nature of the firm", *Economica* 4 (4), 386-405.

Cohen, W.M. and S. Klepper, 1992, "The trade-off between firm size and diversity in the pursuit of technological progress", *Small Business Economics* 4 (1), 1-14.

Cohen, W. and D. Levinthal, 1989, "Innovation and learning: the two faces of R&D", *Economic Journal* 99 (3), 569-596.

Cressy, R.C. and C. Olofsson, 1997, "European SME financing: an overview", *Small Business Economics* 9 (2), 87-96.

Dimaggio, P.J. and W. Powell, 1983, "The iron cage revisited: institutional isomorphism and collective rationality in organizational fields", *American Sociological Review* 48, 147-160.

Dosi, G., 1988, "Sources, procedures and microeconomic effects of innovations", *Journal of Economic Literature* 26, 1120-1171.

EIM, 2002, *SMEs in Europe*, Report submitted to the Enterprise Directorate General by KPMG Special Services, Zoetermeer: EIM Business & Policy Research.

Feldman, M.P. and D.B. Audretsch, 1999, "Innovation in cities: science-based diversity, specialization and localized monopoly", *European Economic Review* 43, 409-429.

Galbraith, J.K., 1956, "American Capitalism: The Concept of Countervailing Power", Boston: Houghton Mifflin Co.

Gaston, R.J., 1989, "The scale of informal capital markets", *Small Business Economics* 1 (3), 223-230.

Glaeser, E., Kallal, H., Sheinkman, J. and A. Schleifer, 1992, "Growth in cities", *Journal of Political Economy* 100, 1126-1152.

Gomes-Casseres, B., 1997, "Alliance strategies of small firms", *Small Business Economics* 9 (1), 33-44.

Gomes-Casseres, B., 1996, *The Alliance Revolution: The New Shape of Business Rivalry*, Cambridge, MA: Harvard University Press.

Gompers, P., 1999, *The Venture Capital Cycle*, Cambridge, MA: MIT Press.

Granovetter, M.S., 1985, "Economic action and social structure: the problem of embeddedness", *American Journal of Sociology* 91 (3), 481-510.

Grossman, G.M. and Helpman, E., 1991, *Innovation and Growth in the Global Economy*, Cambridge, MA: MIT Press.

Hannan, M.T. and J. Freeman, 1989, *Organizational Ecology*, Cambridge, MA: Harvard University Press.

Hirschman, A.O., 1970, *Exit, Voice, and Loyalty*, Cambridge, MA: Harvard University Press.

Hughes, A. and D.J. Storey, 1994, *Finance and the Small Firm*, London: Routledge.

Jacobs, J., 1969, *The Economy of Cities*, New York: Vintage Books.

Jaffe, A., Trajtenberg, M. and R. Henderson, 1993, "Geographic localization of knowledge spillovers as evidenced by patent citations", *Quarterly Journal of Economics* 63, 577-598.

Kindleberger, C.P. and D.B. Audretsch (eds.), 1983, *The Multinational Corporation*, Cambridge, MA: MIT Press.

Knight, F.H., 1921, *Risk, Uncertainty and Profit*, New York: Houghton Mifflin.

Krugman, P., 1991, *Geography and Trade*, Cambridge, MA: MIT Press.

Kwoka, J.E. and L.J. White, 2001, "The new industrial organization and small business", *Small Business Economics* 16 (1): 21-30.

Lawrence, P. and J. Lorsch, 1967, *Organization and Environment*, Cambridge, MA: Harvard Universty Press.

Lewin, A. and R. Lippitt, 1938, "An expirimental approach to the study of autocracy and democracy: a preliminary note", *Sociometry* 1, 292-300.

Loveman, G. and W. Sengenberger, 1991, The re-emergence of small-scale production; an international comparison, *Small Business Economics* 3 (1), 1-37.

Lucas, R.E. Jr., 1993, "Making a miracle", *Econometrica* 61 (2), 251-272.

Lucas, R.E., 1988, "On the mechanics of economic development", *Journal of Monetary Economics* 22, 3-39.

McGregor, D., 1960, *The Human Side of Enterprise*, New York: McGraw-Hill.

Nelson, R.R., (ed.), 1993, *National Innovation Systems: A Comparative Analysis,* Oxford, UK: Oxford University Press.

Nelson, R.R. and S.G. Winter, 1982, *An Evolutionary Theory of Economic Change*, Cambridge, MA: Harvard University Press.

Nooteboom, B., 1994, "Innovation and diffusion in small firms", *Small Business Economics* 6, 327-347.

Nooteboom, B., 1999, *Inter-Firm Alliances; Analysis and Design*, London: Routledge.

Piore, M.J. and C.F. Sabel, 1984, *The Second Industrial Divide: Possibilities for Prosperity*, New York: Basic Books.

Porter, M., 1990, *The Comparative Advantage of Nations*, New York: Free Press.

Pratten, C.F., 1971, *Economies of Scale in Manufacturing Industry*, Cambridge: Cambridge University Press.

Reid, G.C., 1996, "Financial structure and the growing small firm: theoretical underpinning and current evidence", *Small Business Economics* 8 (1), 1-7.

Riesman, D., 1950, "The Lonely Crowd: A Study of the Changing American Character", New Haven: Yale University Press.

Romer, P.M., 1986, "Increasing returns and long-run growth", *Journal of Political Economy* 94 (5), 1002-1037.

Romer, P.M., 1990, "Endogenous technological change", *Journal of Political Economy* 98, 71-101.

Romer, P.M., 1994, "The origins of endogenous growth", *Journal of Economic Perspectives* 8 (1), 3-22.

Saxenian, A., 1994, *Regional Advantage*, Cambridge, MA: Harvard University Press.

Saxenian, A., 1990, "Regional networks and the resurgence of Silicon Valley", *California Management Review* 33, 89-111.

Scherer, F.M., 1991, "Changing perspectives on the firm size problem", in Z.J. Acs and D. B. Audretsch, (eds.), *Innovation and Technological Change: An International Comparison*, Ann Arbor: University of Michigan Press, 24-38.

Schumpeter, J.A., 1934, *The Theory of Economic Development*, Cambridge, MA: Harvard University Press.

Solow, R., 1956, "A contribution to the theory of economic growth", *Quarterly Journal of Economics* 70, 65-94.

Van Stel, A.J., 2003, "COMPENDIA 2000.2: a harmonized data set of business ownership rates in 23 OECD countries", EIM Research Report H200302, Zoetermeer: EIM Business and Policy Research.

Scarpetta, S., Ph. Hemmings, T. Tressel and J. Woo, 2002, "The role of policy and institutions for productivity and firm dynamics: evidence from micro and industry data", OECD Economics Department Working Paper 329, Paris: OECD.

Storey, D.J., 1994, *Understanding the Small Business Sector*, London: Routledge.

Storey, D.J., 2003, "Entrepreneurship, small and medium sized enterprise and public policies", in: Z.J. Acs and D.B. Audretsch (eds.), *Handbook of Entrepreneurship Research*, Boston/ Dordrecht: Kluwer Academic Publishers.

Teece, D.J., 1993, "The dynamics of industrial capitalism: perspectives on Alfred Chandler's "Scale and Scope"", *Journal of Economic Literature* 31, 199-225.

Teece, D.J., R. Rumult, G. Dosi and S. Winter, 1994, "Understanding corporate coherence: theory and evidence", *Journal of Economic Behavior and Organization* 23 (1), 1-30.

Thorton, P.H. and K.H. Flynne, 2003, "Entrepreneurship, networks and geographies", in: Z.J. Acs and D.B. Audretsch (eds.), *Handbook of Entrepreneurship Research*, Boston/ Dordrecht: Kluwer Academic Publishers.

Thurik, A.R., 2003, "Entrepreneurship and unemployment in the UK", *Scottish Journal of Political Economy*, 50 (3), 264-290.

Thurik, A.R. and I. Verheul, 2003, "The relationship between entrepreneurship and unemployment: the case of Spain", in: E. Genesca, D. Urbano, J.L. Capelleras, C. Guallarte, J. Verges (eds.), *Creacion de Empresas. Entrepreneurship*, Barcelona, Spain: Servei de Publicacions de la UAB.

Thurik, A.R., Wennekers, A.R.M. and L.M. Uhlaner, 2002, "Entrepreneurship and economic growth: a macro perspective", *International Journal of Entrepreneurship Education* 1 (2), 157-179.

Tushman, M.L. and Ph. Anderson, 1986, "Technological discontinuities and organizational environments", *Administrative Science Quarterly* 31 (3), 439-465.

Van Engen, 2001, *Gender and Leadership: a Contextual Perspective*, Tilburg University: Dissertation Social and Behavioral Sciences.

Verheul, I., 2003, "Commitment or control? Human resource management in female- and male-led businesses", Strategic Study B200206, Zoetermeer: EIM Business and Policy Research.

Verheul, I., Wennekers, A.R.M., Audretsch, D.B. and A.R. Thurik, 2002, "An eclectic theory of entrepreneurship: policies, institutions and culture", in: Audretsch, D.B., Thurik, A.R., Verheul, I. and A.R.M. Wennekers (eds.), *Entrepreneurship: Determinants and Policy in a European-US Comparison*, Boston/Dordrecht: Kluwer Academic Publishers, 11-82..

Vernon, R., 1970, "Organization as a scale factor in the growth of firms", in: J. W. Markham and G. F. Papanek (eds.), Industrial Organization and Economic Development, Boston: Houghton Mifflin, 47-66.

Weiss, Leonard W., 1976, "Optimal plant scale and the extent of suboptimal capacity", in R.T. Masson and P.D. Qualls, (eds.), *Essays on Industrial Organization in Honor of Joe S. Bain*, Cambridge, Mass.: Ballinger.

Wennekers, A.R.M. and A.R. Thurik, 1999, "Linking entrepreneurship and economic growth", *Small Business Economics* 13 (1), 27-55.Weiss, Leonard W., 1964, "The survival technique and the extent of sub-optimal capacity", *Journal of Political Economy*, 72(3), 246-261.

Wennekers, A.R.M., Uhlaner, L.M. and A.R. Thurik, 2002, "Entrepreneurship and its conditions: a macro perspective", *International Journal of Entrepreneurship Education* 1 (1), 25-64.

Wheelwright, S.C., 1985, "Restoring competitiveness in U.S. manufacturing", *California Management Review* 27, 113-121.

Whyte, W.H., 1960, *The Organization Man*, Hammondsworth, Middlesex: Penguin.

Williamson, O.E., 1968, "Economies as an antitrust defense: the welfare trade-offs", *American Economic Review* 58 (1), 18-36.

Williamson, O.E., 1975, *Markets and Hierarchies: Analysis and Antitrust Implications*, New York: The Free Press.

[3]

THE FUNDAMENTAL PHENOMENON OF
ECONOMIC DEVELOPMENT

I

THE social process, which rationalises [1] our life and thought, has
led us away from the metaphysical treatment of social development and taught us to see the possibility of an empirical treatment; but it has done its work so imperfectly that we must be
careful in dealing with the phenomenon itself, still more with the
concept in which we comprehend it, and most of all with the word
by which we designate the concept and whose associations might
lead us astray in all manner of undesirable directions. Closely
connected with the metaphysical preconception — more precisely
with the ideas which grow out of metaphysical roots and become
preconceptions if, neglecting unbridgeable gulfs, we make them
do the work of empirical science — even if not itself such a metaphysical preconception, is every search for a "meaning" of
history. The same is true of the postulate that a nation, a civilisation, or even the whole of mankind, must show some kind of uniform unilinear development, as even such a matter-of-fact mind
as Roscher assumed and as the innumerable philosophers and
theorists of history in the long brilliant line from Vico to Lam-
precht took and still take for granted. Here, too, belong all kinds
of evolutionary thought that centre in Darwin — at least if this
means no more than reasoning by analogy — and also the psychological prejudice which consists in seeing more in motives and
acts of volition than a reflex of the social process. But the evolutionary idea is now discredited in our field, especially with his-

---

[1] This is used here in Max Weber's sense. As the reader will see, "rational" and
"empirical" here mean, if not identical, yet cognate, things. They are equally different from, and opposed to, "metaphysical," which implies going beyond the reach
of both "reason" and "facts," beyond the realm, that is, of science. With some it
has become a habit to use the word "rational" in much the same sense as we do
"metaphysical." Hence some warning against misunderstanding may not be out of
place.

58   *THE THEORY OF ECONOMIC DEVELOPMENT*

torians and ethnologists, for still another reason. To the reproach of unscientific and extra-scientific mysticism that now surrounds the "evolutionary" ideas, is added that of dilettantism. With all the hasty generalisations in which the word "evolution" plays a part, many of us have lost patience.

We must get away from such things. Then two facts still remain: first the fact of historical change, whereby social conditions become historical "individuals" in historical time. These changes constitute neither a circular process nor pendulum movements about a centre. The concept of social development is defined by these two circumstances, together with the other fact: that whenever we do not succeed in adequately explaining a given historical state of things from the preceding one, we do indeed recognise the existence of an unsolved but not insoluble problem. This holds good first of all for the individual case. For example, we understand Germany's internal political history in 1919 as one of the effects of the preceding war. It also holds good, however, for more general problems.

Economic development is so far simply the object of economic history, which in turn is merely a part of universal history, only separated from the rest for purposes of exposition. Because of this fundamental dependence of the economic aspect of things on everything else, it is not possible to explain *economic* change by previous *economic* conditions alone. For the economic state of a people does not emerge simply from the preceding economic conditions, but only from the preceding total situation. The expository and analytical difficulties which arise from this are very much diminished, practically if not in principle, by the facts which form the basis of economic interpretation of history; without being compelled to take a stand for or against this view, we can state that the economic world is relatively autonomous because it takes up such a great part of a nation's life, and forms or conditions a great part of the remainder; wherefore writing economic history by itself is obviously a different thing from writing, say, military history. To this must be added still another fact which facilitates the separate description of any of the divisions of the social process. Every sector of social life is, as it were, inhabited by a distinct set of people. The heteronomous elements generally do not affect the social process in any such sector directly as the bursting of a bomb "affects" all things which happen to be in the room in which it explodes, but only through its data and the conduct of its inhabitants; and even if an event occurs like the one suggested by our metaphor of a bursting bomb, the effects only occur in the particular garb with which those primarily concerned dress them. Therefore, just as describing the effects of the Counter Reformation upon Italian and Spanish painting always remains history of art, so describing the economic process remains economic history even where the true causation is largely non-economic.

The economic sector, again, is open to an endless variety of points of view and treatments, which one can array, for example, according to the breadth of their scope — or we might just as well say according to the degree of generalisation which they imply. From an exposition of the nature of the economic life of the Niederaltaich monastery in the thirteenth century to Sombart's exposition of the development of economic life in western Europe, there runs a continuous, logically uniform thread. Such an exposition as Sombart's is theory, and indeed theory of economic development in the sense in which we intend it for the moment. But it is not economic theory in the sense in which the contents of the first chapter of this book are economic theory, which is what has been understood by "economic theory" since Ricardo's day. Economic theory in the latter sense, it is true, plays a part in a theory like Sombart's, but a wholly subordinate one: namely, where the connection of historical facts is complicated enough to necessitate methods of interpretation which go beyond the analytic powers of the man in the street, the line of thought takes the form offered by that analytical apparatus. However, where it is simply a question of making development or the historical outcome of it intelligible, of working out the elements which characterise a situation or determine an issue, economic theory in the traditional sense contributes next to nothing.[1]

[1] If economists, nevertheless, have always had something to say on this theme, this is only because they did not restrict themselves to economic theory, but — and

60   THE THEORY OF ECONOMIC DEVELOPMENT

We are not concerned here with a theory of development in this sense. No historical evolutionary factors will be indicated — whether individual events like the appearance of American gold

indeed quite superficially as a rule — studied historical sociology or made assumptions about the economic future. Division of labor, the origin of private property in land, increasing control over nature, economic freedom, and legal security — these are the most important elements constituting the "economic sociology" of Adam Smith. They clearly relate to the social framework of the economic course of events, not to any immanent spontaneity of the latter. One can also consider this as Ricardo's theory of development (say in Bücher's sense), which, moreover, exhibits the line of thought which earned the characterisation of "pessimist" for him: namely the "hypothetical prognosis" that in consequence of the progressive increase of population together with the progressive exhaustion of the powers of the soil (which can according to him only temporarily be interrupted by improvements in production) a position of rest would eventually appear — to be distinguished *toto coelo* from the ideal momentary position of rest of the equilibrium of modern theory — in which the economic situation would be characterised by an hypertrophy of rent, which is something totally different from what is understood above by a theory of development, and still more different from what we shall understand by it in this book. Mill worked out the same line of thought more carefully, and also distributed color and tone differently. In essence, however, his Book IV, "Influence of the Progress of Society on Production and Distribution," is just the same thing. Even this title expresses how much "progress" is considered as something non-economic, as something rooted in the data that only "exercises an influence" upon production and distribution. In particular his treatment of improvements in the "arts of production" is strictly "static." Improvement, according to this traditional view, is something which just happens and the effects of which we have to investigate, while we have nothing to say about its occurrence *per se*. What is thereby passed over is the subject matter of this book, or rather the foundation stone of its construction. J. B. Clark (Essentials of Economic Theory), whose merit is in having consciously separated "statics" and "dynamics," saw in the dynamic elements a disturbance of the static equilibrium. This is likewise our view, and also from our standpoint an essential task is to investigate the effect of this disturbance and the new equilibrium which then emerges. But while he confines himself to this and just like Mill sees therein the meaning of dynamics, we shall first of all give a theory of these causes of disturbances in so far as they are more than mere disturbances for us and in so far as it seems to us that essential economic phenomena depend upon their appearance. In particular: two of the causes of disturbance enumerated by him (increase of capital and population) are for us, as for him, merely causes of disturbance, however important as "factors of change" they may be for another kind of problem just indicated in the text. The same is true of a third (changes in the direction of consumers' tastes) which will later be substantiated in the text. But the other two (changes in technique and in productive organisation) require special analysis and evoke something different again from disturbances in the theoretical sense. The non-recognition of this is the most important single reason for what appears unsatisfactory to us in economic theory. From this insignificant-looking source flows, as we shall see, a new conception of the economic process, which overcomes a series of fundamental difficulties and thus justifies the new statement of the problem in the text. This statement of the problem is more nearly parallel to that of Marx. For according to him there is an *internal* economic development and no mere adaptation of economic life to changing data. But my structure covers only a small part of his ground.

production in Europe in the sixteenth century, or "more general" circumstances like changes in the mentality of economic men, in the area of the civilised world, in social organisation, in political constellations, in productive technique, and so forth — nor will their effects be described for individual cases or for groups of cases.[1] On the contrary, the economic theory the nature of which was sufficiently expounded to the reader in the first chapter will simply be improved for its own purposes, by building onto it. If this were also to enable this theory to perform better than hitherto its service to the other kind of theory of development, the fact would still remain that the two methods lie in different planes.

Our problem is as follows. The theory of the first chapter describes economic life from the standpoint of a "circular flow," running on in channels essentially the same year after year — similar to the circulation of the blood in an animal organism. Now this circular flow and its channels do alter in time, and here we abandon the analogy with the circulation of the blood. For although the latter also changes in the course of the growth and decline of the organism, yet it only does so continuously, that is by steps which one can choose smaller than any assignable quantity, however small, and always within the same framework. Economic life experiences such changes too, but it also experiences others which do not appear continuously and which change the framework, the traditional course itself. They cannot be understood by means of any analysis of the circular flow, although they are purely economic and although their explanation is obviously among the tasks of pure theory. Now such changes

---

[1] Therefore one of the most annoying misunderstandings that arose out of the first edition of this book was that this theory of development neglects all historical factors of change except one, namely the individuality of entrepreneurs. If my representation were intended to be as this objection assumes, it would obviously be nonsense. But it is not at all concerned with the concrete factors of change, but with the method by which these work, with the *mechanism of change.* The "entrepreneur" is merely the bearer of the mechanism of change. And I have taken account not of one factor of historical change, but of none. We have still less to do here with the factors which in particular explain the changes in the economic organisation, economic custom, and so on. This is still another problem, and although there are points at which all these methods of treatment collide, it means spoiling the fruit of all if they are not kept apart and if each is not allowed the right to grow by itself.

and the phenomena which appear in their train are the object of our investigation. But we do not ask: what changes of this sort have actually made the modern economic system what it is? nor: what are the conditions of such changes? We only ask, and indeed in the same sense as theory always asks: how do such changes take place, and to what economic phenomena do they give rise?

The same thing may be put somewhat differently. The theory of the first chapter describes economic life from the standpoint of the economic system's tendency towards an equilibrium position, which tendency gives us the means of determining prices and quantities of goods, and may be described as an adaptation to data existing at any time. In contrast to the conditions of the circular flow this does not mean in itself that year after year "the same" things happen; for it only means that we conceive the several processes in the economic system as partial phenomena of the tendency towards an equilibrium position, but not necessarily towards the same one. The position of the ideal state of equilibrium in the economic system, never attained, continually "striven after" (of course not consciously), changes, because the data change. And theory is not weaponless in the face of these changes in data. It is constructed so as to be able to deal with the consequences of such changes; it has special instruments for the purpose (for example the instrument called quasi-rent). If the change occurs in the non-social data (natural conditions) or in non-economic social data (here belong the effects of war, changes in commercial, social, or economic policy), or in consumers' tastes, then to this extent no fundamental overhaul of the theoretical tools seems to be required. These tools only fail — and here this argument joins the preceding — where economic life itself changes its own data by fits and starts. The building of a railway may serve as an example. Continuous changes, which may in time, by continual adaptation through innumerable small steps, make a great department store out of a small retail business, come under the "static" analysis. But "static" analysis is not only unable to predict the consequences of discontinuous changes in the traditional way of doing things; it can neither explain the occurrence of such productive revolutions nor the phenomena which accompany them. It can only investigate the new equilibrium position after the changes have occurred. It is just this occurrence of the "revolutionary" change that is our problem, the problem of economic development in a very narrow and formal sense. The reason why we so state the problem and turn aside from traditional theory lies not so much in the fact that economic changes, especially, if not solely, in the capitalist epoch, have actually occurred thus and not by continuous adaptation, but more in their fruitfulness.[1]

By "development," therefore, we shall understand only such changes in economic life as are not forced upon it from without but arise by its own initiative, from within. Should it turn out that there are no such changes arising in the economic sphere itself, and that the phenomenon that we call economic development is in practice simply founded upon the fact that the data change and that the economy continuously adapts itself to them, then we should say that there is *no* economic development. By this we should mean that economic development is not a phenomenon to be explained economically, but that the economy, in itself without development, is dragged along by the changes in the surrounding world, that the causes and hence the explanation of the development must be sought outside the group of facts which are described by economic theory.

Nor will the mere growth of the economy, as shown by the growth of population and wealth, be designated here as a process of development. For it calls forth no qualitatively new phenomena, but only processes of adaptation of the same kind as the changes in the natural data. Since we wish to direct our attention to other phenomena, we shall regard such increases as changes in data.[2]

---

[1] The problems of capital, credit, entrepreneurial profit, interest on capital, and crises (or business cycles) are the ones in which this fruitfulness will be demonstrated here. Yet it is not thereby exhausted. For the expert theorist I point, for example, to the difficulties which surround the problem of increasing return, the question of multiple points of intersection between supply and demand curves, and the element of time, which even Marshall's analysis has not overcome.

[2] We do this because these changes are small per annum and therefore do not stand in the way of the applicability of the "static" method. Nevertheless, their appearance is frequently a condition of development in our sense. But even though they often make the latter possible, yet they do not create it out of themselves.

64   *THE THEORY OF ECONOMIC DEVELOPMENT*

Every concrete process of development finally rests upon preceding development. But in order to see the essence of the thing clearly, we shall abstract from this and allow the development to arise out of a position without development. Every process of development creates the prerequisites for the following. Thereby the form of the latter is altered, and things will turn out differently from what they would have been if every concrete phase of development had been compelled first to create its own conditions. However, if we wish to get at the root of the matter, we may not include in the data of our explanation elements of what is to be explained. But if we do not do this, we shall create an apparent discrepancy between fact and theory, which may constitute an important difficulty for the reader.

If I have been more successful than in the first edition in concentrating the exposition upon essentials and in guarding against misunderstandings, then further special explanations of the words "static" and "dynamic," with their innumerable meanings, are not necessary. Development in our sense is a distinct phenomenon, entirely foreign to what may be observed in the circular flow or in the tendency towards equilibrium. It is spontaneous and discontinuous change in the channels of the flow, disturbance of equilibrium, which forever alters and displaces the equilibrium state previously existing. Our theory of development is nothing but a treatment of this phenomenon and the processes incident to it.[1]

---

[1] In the first edition of this book, I called it "dynamics." But it is preferable to avoid this expression here, since it so easily leads us astray because of the associations which attach themselves to its various meanings. Better, then, to say simply what we mean: economic life changes; it changes partly because of changes in the data, to which it tends to adapt itself. But this is not the only kind of economic change; there is another which is not accounted for by influence on the data from without, but which arises from within the system, and this kind of change is the cause of so many important economic phenomena that it seems worth while to build a theory for it, and, in order to do so, to isolate it from all the other factors of change. The author begs to add another more exact definition, which he is in the habit of using: what we are about to consider is that kind of change arising from within the system *which so displaces its equilibrium point that the new one cannot be reached from the old one by infinitesimal steps*. Add successively as many mail coaches as you please, you will never get a railway thereby.

II

These spontaneous and discontinuous changes in the channel of the circular flow and these disturbances of the centre of equilibrium appear in the sphere of industrial and commercial life, not in the sphere of the wants of the consumers of final products. Where spontaneous and discontinuous changes in consumers' tastes appear, it is a question of a sudden change in data with which the businessman must cope, hence possibly a question of a *motive* or an opportunity for other than gradual adaptations of his conduct, but not of such other conduct itself. Therefore this case does not offer any other problems than a change in natural data or require any new method of treatment; wherefore we shall neglect any spontaneity of consumers' needs that may actually exist, and assume tastes as "given." This is made easy for us by the fact that the spontaneity of wants is in general small. To be sure, we must always start from the satisfaction of wants, since they are the end of all production, and the given economic situation at any time must be understood from this aspect. Yet innovations in the economic system do not as a rule take place in such a way that first new wants arise spontaneously in consumers and then the productive apparatus swings round through their pressure. We do not deny the presence of this nexus. It is, however, the producer who as a rule initiates economic change, and consumers are educated by him if necessary; they are, as it were, taught to want new things, or things which differ in some respect or other from those which they have been in the habit of using. Therefore, while it is permissible and even necessary to consider consumers' wants as an independent and indeed the fundamental force in a theory of the circular flow, we must take a different attitude as soon as we analyse *change*.

To produce means to combine materials and forces within our reach (cf. *supra*, Chapter I). To produce other things, or the same things by a different method, means to combine these materials and forces differently. In so far as the "new combination" may in time grow out of the old by continuous adjustment in small steps, there is certainly change, possibly growth, but neither a

66   *THE THEORY OF ECONOMIC DEVELOPMENT*

new phenomenon nor development in our sense. In so far as this is not the case, and the new combinations appear discontinuously, then the phenomenon characterising development emerges. For reasons of expository convenience, henceforth, we shall only mean the latter case when we speak of new combinations of productive means. Development in our sense is then defined by the carrying out of new combinations.

This concept covers the following five cases: (1) The introduction of a new good — that is one with which consumers are not yet familiar — or of a new quality of a good. (2) The introduction of a new method of production, that is one not yet tested by experience in the branch of manufacture concerned, which need by no means be founded upon a discovery scientifically new, and can also exist in a new way of handling a commodity commercially. (3) The opening of a new market, that is a market into which the particular branch of manufacture of the country in question has not previously entered, whether or not this market has existed before. (4) The conquest of a new source of supply of raw materials or half-manufactured goods, again irrespective of whether this source already exists or whether it has first to be created. (5) The carrying out of the new organisation of any industry, like the creation of a monopoly position (for example through trustification) or the breaking up of a monopoly position.

Now two things are essential for the phenomena incident to the carrying out of such new combinations, and for the understanding of the problems involved. In the first place it is not essential to the matter — though it may happen — that the new combinations should be carried out by the same people who control the productive or commercial process which is to be displaced by the new. On the contrary, new combinations are, as a rule, embodied, as it were, in new firms which generally do not arise out of the old ones but start producing beside them; to keep to the example already chosen, in general it is not the owner of stage-coaches who builds railways. This fact not only puts the discontinuity which characterises the process we want to describe in a special light, and creates so to speak still another kind of discontinuity in addition to the one mentioned above, but it also explains important features of the course of events. Especially in a competitive economy, in which new combinations mean the competitive elimination of the old, it explains on the one hand the process by which individuals and families rise and fall economically and socially and which is peculiar to this form of organisation, as well as a whole series of other phenomena of the business cycle, of the mechanism of the formation of private fortunes, and so on. In a non-exchange economy, for example a socialist one, the new combinations would also frequently appear side by side with the old. But the economic consequences of this fact would be absent to some extent, and the social consequences would be wholly absent. And if the competitive economy is broken up by the growth of great combines, as is increasingly the case to-day in all countries, then this must become more and more true of real life, and the carrying out of new combinations must become in ever greater measure the internal concern of one and the same economic body. The difference so made is great enough to serve as the water-shed between two epochs in the social history of capitalism.

We must notice secondly, only partly in connection with this element, that whenever we are concerned with fundamental principles, we must never assume that the carrying out of new combinations takes place by employing means of production which happen to be unused. In practical life, this is very often the case. There are always unemployed workmen, unsold raw materials, unused productive capacity, and so forth. This certainly is a contributory circumstance, a favorable condition and even an incentive to the emergence of new combinations; but great unemployment is only the consequence of non-economic events — as for example the World War — or precisely of the development which we are investigating. In neither of the two cases can its existence play a fundamental rôle in the explanation, and it cannot occur in a well balanced circular flow from which we start. Nor would the normal yearly increment meet the case, as it would be small in the first place, and also because it would normally be absorbed by a corresponding expansion of production within the circular flow, which, if we admit such increments, we must think of as adjusted

68   *THE THEORY OF ECONOMIC DEVELOPMENT*

to this rate of growth.[1] As a rule the new combinations must draw the necessary means of production from some old combinations — and for reasons already mentioned we shall assume that they *always* do so, in order to put in bold relief what we hold to be the essential contour line. The carrying out of new combinations means, therefore, simply the different employment of the economic system's existing supplies of productive means —which might provide a second definition of development in our sense. That rudiment of a pure economic theory of development which is implied in the traditional doctrine of the formation of capital always refers merely to saving and to the investment of the small yearly increase attributable to it. In this it asserts nothing false, but it entirely overlooks much more essential things. The slow and continuous increase in time of the national supply of productive means and of savings is obviously an important factor in explaining the course of economic history through the centuries, but it is completely overshadowed by the fact that development consists primarily in employing existing resources in a different way, in doing new things with them, irrespective of whether those resources increase or not. In the treatment of shorter epochs, moreover, this is even true in a more tangible sense. Different methods of employment, and not saving and increases in the available quantity of labor, have changed the face of the economic world in the last fifty years. The increase of population especially, but also of the sources from which savings can be made, was first made possible in large measure through the different employment of the then existing means.

The next step in our argument is also self-evident: command over means of production is necessary to the carrying out of new combinations. Procuring the means of production is one distinct problem for the established firms which work within the circular flow. For they *have* them already procured or else can procure them currently with the proceeds of previous production as was explained in the first chapter. There is no fundamental gap here

[1] On the whole it is much more correct to say that population grows slowly up to the possibilities of any economic environment than that it has any tendency to outgrow it and to become thereby an independent cause of change.

between receipts and disbursements, which, on the contrary, necessarily correspond to one another just as both correspond to the means of production offered and to the products demanded. Once set in motion, this mechanism works automatically. Furthermore, the problem does not exist in a non-exchange economy even if new combinations are carried out in it; for the directing organ, for example a socialist economic ministry, is in a position to direct the productive resources of the society to new uses exactly as it can direct them to their previous employments. The new employment may, under certain circumstances, impose temporary sacrifices, privations, or increased efforts upon the members of the community; it may presuppose the solution of difficult problems, for example the question from which of the old combinations the necessary productive means should be withdrawn; but there is no question of procuring means of production not already at the disposal of the economic ministry. Finally, the problem also does not exist in a competitive economy in the case of the carrying out of new combinations, if those who carry them out have the necessary productive means or can get them in exchange for others which they have or for any other property which they may possess. This is not the privilege of the possession of property *per se*, but only the privilege of the possession of disposable property, that is such as is employable either immediately for carrying out the new combination or in exchange for the necessary goods and services.[1] In the contrary case — and this is the rule as it is the fundamentally interesting case — the possessor of wealth, even if it is the greatest combine, must resort to credit if he wishes to carry out a new combination, which cannot like an established business be financed by returns from previous production. To provide this credit is clearly the function of that category of individuals which we call "capitalists." It is obvious that this is the characteristic method of the capitalist type of society — and important enough to serve as its *differentia specifica* — for forcing the economic system into new channels, for putting its means at

---

[1] A privilege which the individual can also achieve through saving. In an economy of the handicraft type this element would have to be emphasised more. Manufacturers' "reserve funds" assume an existing development.

the service of new ends, in contrast to the method of a non-exchange economy of the kind which simply consists in exercising the directing organ's power to command.

It does not appear to me possible to dispute in any way the foregoing statement. Emphasis upon the significance of credit is to be found in every textbook. That the structure of modern industry could not have been erected without it, that it makes the individual to a certain extent independent of inherited possessions, that talent in economic life "rides to success on its debts," even the most conservative orthodoxy of the theorists cannot well deny. Nor is the connection established here between credit and the carrying out of innovations, a connection which will be worked out later, anything to take offence at. For it is as clear *a priori* as it is established historically that credit is primarily necessary to new combinations and that it is from these that it forces its way into the circular flow, on the one hand because it was originally necessary to the founding of what are now the old firms, on the other hand because its mechanism, once in existence, also seizes old combinations for obvious reasons.[1] First, *a priori*: we saw in the first chapter that borrowing is not a necessary element of production in the normal circular flow within accustomed channels, is not an element without which we could not understand the essential phenomena of the latter. On the other hand, in carrying out new combinations, "financing" as a special act is fundamentally necessary, in practice as in theory. Second, historically: those who lend and borrow for industrial purposes do not appear early in history. The pre-capitalistic lender provided money for other than business purposes. And we all remember the type of industrialist who felt he was losing caste by borrowing and who therefore shunned banks and bills of exchange. The capitalistic credit system has grown out of and thrived on the financing of new combinations in all countries, even though in a different way in each (the origin of German joint stock banking is especially characteristic). Finally there can be no stumblingblock in our speak-

---

[1] The most important of which is the appearance of productive interest, as we shall see in Chapter V. As soon as interest emerges somewhere in the system, it expands over the whole of it.

ing of receiving credit in "money or money substitutes." We certainly do not assert that one can produce with coins, notes, or
bank balances, and do not deny that services of labor, raw materials, and tools are the things wanted. We are only speaking of
a method of procuring them.

Nevertheless there is a point here in which, as has already been
hinted, our theory diverges from the traditional view. The accepted theory sees a problem in the existence of the productive
means, which are needed for new, or indeed any, productive processes, and this accumulation therefore becomes a distinct function or service. We do not recognise this problem at all; it appears
to us to be created by faulty analysis. It does not exist in the circular flow, because the running of the latter presupposes given
quantities of means of production. But neither does it exist for
the carrying out of new combinations,[1] because the productive
means required in the latter are drawn from the circular flow
whether they already exist there in the shape wanted or have first
to be produced by other means of production existing there. Instead of this problem another exists for us: the problem of detach-
ing productive means (already employed somewhere) from the
circular flow and allotting them to new combinations. This is
done by credit, by means of which one who wishes to carry out
new combinations outbids the producers in the circular flow in the
market for the required means of production. And although the
meaning and object of this process lies in a movement of goods
from their old towards new employments, it cannot be described
entirely in terms of goods without overlooking something essential, which happens in the sphere of money and credit and upon
which depends the explanation of important phenomena in the
capitalist form of economic organisation, in contrast to other
types.

Finally one more step in this direction: whence come the sums

---

[1] Of course the productive means do not fall from heaven. In so far as they are
not given by nature or non-economically, they were and are created at some time by
the individual waves of development in our sense, and henceforth incorporated in
the circular flow. But every individual wave of development and every individual
new combination itself proceeds again from the supply of productive means of the
existing circular flow — a case of the hen and the egg.

needed to purchase the means of production necessary for the new combinations if the individual concerned does not happen to have them? The conventional answer is simple: out of the annual growth of social savings plus that part of resources which may annually become free. Now the first quantity was indeed important enough before the war — it may perhaps be estimated as one-fifth of total private incomes in Europe and North America — so that together with the latter sum, which it is difficult to obtain statistically, it does not immediately give the lie quantatively to this answer. At the same time a figure representing the range of all the business operations involved in carrying out new combinations is also not available at present. But we may not even start from total "savings." For its magnitude is explicable only by the results of previous development. By far the greater part of it does not come from thrift in the strict sense, that is from abstaining from the consumption of part of one's regular income, but it consists of funds which are themselves the result of successful innovation and in which we shall later recognise entrepreneurial profit. In the circular flow there would be on the one hand no such rich source, out of which to save, and on the other hand essentially less incentive to save. The only big incomes known to it would be monopoly revenues and the rents of large landowners; while provision for misfortunes and old age, perhaps also irrational motives, would be the only incentives. The most important incentive, the chance of participating in the gains of development, would be absent. Hence, in such an economic system there could be no great reservoirs of free purchasing power, to which one who wished to form new combinations could turn — and his own savings would only suffice in exceptional cases. All money would circulate, would be fixed in definite established channels.

Even though the conventional answer to our question is not obviously absurd, yet there is another method of obtaining money for this purpose, which claims our attention, because it, unlike the one referred to, does not presuppose the existence of accumulated results of previous development, and hence may be considered as the only one which is available in strict logic. This method of obtaining money is the creation of purchasing power by banks. The form it takes is immaterial. The issue of bank-notes not fully covered by specie withdrawn from circulation is an obvious instance, but methods of deposit banking render the same service, where they increase the sum total of possible expenditure. Or we may think of bank acceptances in so far as they serve as money to make payments in wholesale trade. It is always a question, not of transforming purchasing power which already exists in someone's possession, but of the creation of new purchasing power out of nothing — out of nothing even if the credit contract by which the new purchasing power is created is supported by securities which are not themselves circulating media — which is added to the existing circulation. And this is the source from which new combinations *are* often financed, and from which they would have to be financed *always*, if results of previous development did not actually exist at any moment.

These credit means of payment, that is means of payment which are created for the purpose and by the act of giving credit, serve just as ready money in trade, partly directly, partly because they can be converted immediately into ready money for small payments or payments to the non-banking classes — in particular to wage-earners. With their help, those who carry out new combinations can gain access to the existing stocks of productive means, or, as the case may be, enable those from whom they buy productive services to gain immediate access to the market for consumption goods. There is never, in this nexus, granting of credit in the sense that someone must wait for the equivalent of his service in goods, and content himself with a claim, thereby fulfilling a special function; not even in the sense that someone has to accumulate means of maintenance for laborers or land-owners, or produced means of production, all of which would only be paid for out of the final results of production. Economically, it is true, there is an essential difference between these means of payment, if they are created for new ends, and money or other means of payment of the circular flow. The latter may be conceived on the one hand as a kind of certificate for completed production and the increase in the social product effected through it, and on the other hand as a kind of order upon, or claim to, part of this social product. The former have not the first of these two characteristics. They too are orders, for which one can immediately procure consumption goods, but not certificates for previous production. Access to the national dividend is usually to be had only on condition of some productive service previously rendered or of some product previously sold. This condition is, in this case, not yet fulfilled. It will be fulfilled only after the successful completion of the new combinations. Hence this credit will in the meantime affect the price level.

The banker, therefore, is not so much primarily a middleman in the commodity "purchasing power" as a *producer* of this commodity. However, since all reserve funds and savings to-day usually flow to him, and the total demand for free purchasing power, whether existing or to be created, concentrates on him, he has either replaced private capitalists or become their agent; he has himself become the capitalist par excellence. He stands between those who wish to form new combinations and the possessors of productive means. He is essentially a phenomenon of development, though only when no central authority directs the social process. He makes possible the carrying out of new combinations, authorises people, in the name of society as it were, to form them. He is the ephor of the exchange economy.

III

We now come to the third of the elements with which our analysis works, namely the "new combination of means of production," and credit. Although all three elements form a whole, the third may be described as the fundamental phenomenon of economic development. The carrying out of new combinations we call "enterprise"; the individuals whose function it is to carry them out we call "entrepreneurs." These concepts are at once broader and narrower than the usual. Broader, because in the first place we call entrepreneurs not only those "independent" businessmen in an exchange economy who are usually so designated, but all who actually fulfil the function by which we define the concept, even if they are, as is becoming the rule, "dependent" employees of a company, like managers, members of boards of directors, and so forth, or even if their actual power to perform the entrepreneurial function has any other foundations, such as the control of a majority of shares. As it is the carrying out of new combinations that constitutes the entrepreneur, it is not necessary that he should be permanently connected with an individual firm; many "financiers," "promotors," and so forth are not, and still they may be entrepreneurs in our sense. On the other hand, our concept is narrower than the traditional one in that it does not include all heads of firms or managers or industrialists who merely may operate an established business, but only those who actually perform that function. Nevertheless I maintain that the above definition does no more than formulate with greater precision what the traditional doctrine really means to convey. In the first place our definition agrees with the usual one on the fundamental point of distinguishing between "entrepreneurs" and "capitalists" — irrespective of whether the latter are regarded as owners of money, claims to money, or material goods. This distinction is common property to-day and has been so for a considerable time. It also settles the question whether the ordinary shareholder as such is an entrepreneur, and disposes of the conception of the entrepreneur as risk bearer.[1] Furthermore, the ordinary characterisation of the entrepreneur type by such expressions as "initiative," "authority," or "foresight" points entirely in our direction. For there is little scope for such qualities within the routine of the circular flow, and if this had been sharply separated

---

[1] Risk obviously always falls on the owner of the means of production or of the money-capital which was paid for them, hence never on the entrepreneur *as such* (see Chapter IV). A shareholder *may* be an entrepreneur. He may even owe to his holding a controlling interest the power to act as an entrepreneur. Shareholders *per se*, however, are never entrepreneurs, but merely capitalists, who in consideration of their submitting to certain risks participate in profits. That this is no reason to look upon them as anything but capitalists is shown by the facts, first, that the average shareholder has normally no power to influence the management of his company, and secondly, that participation in profits is frequent in cases in which everyone recognises the presence of a loan contract. Compare, for example, the Graeco-Roman *foenus nauticum*. Surely this interpretation is more true to life than the other one, which, following the lead of a faulty legal construction — which can only be explained historically — attributes functions to the average shareholder which he hardly ever thinks of discharging.

76   THE THEORY OF ECONOMIC DEVELOPMENT

from the occurrence of changes in this routine itself, the emphasis in the definition of the function of entrepreneurs would have been shifted automatically to the latter. Finally there are definitions which we could simply accept. There is in particular the well known one that goes back to J. B. Say: the entrepreneur's function is to combine the productive factors, to bring them together. Since this is a performance of a special kind only when the factors are combined for the first time — while it is merely routine work if done in the course of running a business — this definition coincides with ours. When Mataja (in Unternehmergewinn) defines the entrepreneur as one who receives profit, we have only to add the conclusion of the first chapter, that there is no profit in the circular flow, in order to trace this formulation too back to ours.[1] And this view is not foreign to traditional theory, as is shown by the construction of the *entrepreneur faisant ni bénéfice ni perte*, which has been worked out rigorously by Walras, but is the property of many other authors. The tendency is for the entrepreneur to make neither profit nor loss in the circular flow — that is he has no function of a special kind there, he simply does not exist; but in his stead, there are heads of firms or business managers of a different type which we had better not designate by the same term.

It is a prejudice to believe that the knowledge of the historical origin of an institution or of a type immediately shows us its sociological or economic nature. Such knowledge often leads us to understand it, but it does not directly yield a theory of it. Still more false is the belief that "primitive" forms of a type are also *ipso facto* the "simpler" or the "more original" in the sense that they show their nature more purely and with fewer complications than later ones. Very frequently the opposite is the case, amongst other reasons because increasing specialisation may allow functions and qualities to stand out sharply, which are more difficult to recognise in more primitive conditions when mixed with others.

---

[1] The definition of the entrepreneur in terms of entrepreneurial profit instead of in terms of the function the performance of which creates the entrepreneurial profit is obviously not brilliant. But we have still another objection to it: we shall see that entrepreneurial profit does not fall to the entrepreneur by "necessity" in the same sense as the marginal product of labor does to the worker.

So it is in our case. In the general position of the chief of a primitive horde it is difficult to separate the entrepreneurial element from the others. For the same reason most economists up to the time of the younger Mill failed to keep capitalist and entrepreneur distinct because the manufacturer of a hundred years ago was both; and certainly the course of events since then has facilitated the making of this distinction, as the system of land tenure in England has facilitated the distinction between farmer and landowner, while on the Continent this distinction is still occasionally neglected, especially in the case of the peasant who tills his own soil.[1] But in our case there are still more of such difficulties. The entrepreneur of earlier times was not only as a rule the capitalist too, he was also often — as he still is to-day in the case of small concerns — his own technical expert, in so far as a professional specialist was not called in for special cases. Likewise he was (and is) often his own buying and selling agent, the head of his office, his own personnel manager, and sometimes, even though as a rule he of course employed solicitors, his own legal adviser in current affairs. And it was performing some or all of these functions that regularly filled his days. The carrying out of new combinations can no more be a *vocation* than the making and execution of strategical decisions, although it is this function and not his routine work that characterises the military leader. Therefore the entrepreneur's essential function must always appear mixed up with other kinds of activity, which as a rule must be much more conspicuous than the essential one. Hence the Marshallian definition of the enterpreneur, which simply treats the entrepreneurial function as "management" in the widest meaning, will naturally appeal to most of us. We do not accept it, simply because it does not bring out what we consider to be the salient point and the only one which specifically distinguishes entrepreneurial from other activities.

---

[1] Only this neglect explains the attitude of many socialistic theorists towards peasant property. For smallness of the individual possession makes a difference only for the petit-bourgeois, not for the socialist. The criterion of the employment of labor other than that of the owner and his family is economically relevant only from the standpoint of a kind of exploitation theory which is hardly tenable any longer.

Nevertheless there are types — the course of events has evolved them by degrees — which exhibit the entrepreneurial function with particular purity. The "promoter," to be sure, belongs to them only with qualifications. For, neglecting the associations relative to social and moral status which are attached to this type, the promoter is frequently only an agent intervening on commission, who does the work of financial technique in floating the new enterprise. In this case he is not its creator nor the driving power in the process. However, he *may* be the latter also, and then he is something like an "entrepreneur by profession." But the modern type of "captain of industry" [1] corresponds more closely to what is meant here, especially if one recognises his identity on the one hand with, say, the commercial entrepreneur of twelfth-century Venice — or, among later types, with John Law — and on the other hand with the village potentate who combines with his agriculture and his cattle trade, say, a rural brewery, an hotel, and a store. But whatever the type, everyone is an entrepreneur only when he actually "carries out new combinations," and loses that character as soon as he has built up his business, when he settles down to running it as other people run their businesses. This is the rule, of course, and hence it is just as rare for anyone always to remain an entrepreneur throughout the decades of his active life as it is for a businessman never to have a moment in which he is an entrepreneur, to however modest a degree.

Because being an entrepreneur is not a profession and as a rule not a lasting condition, entrepreneurs do not form a social class in the technical sense, as, for example, landowners or capitalists or workmen do. Of course the entrepreneurial function will *lead* to certain class positions for the successful entrepreneur and his family. It can also put its stamp on an epoch of social history, can form a style of life, or systems of moral and aesthetic values; but in itself it signifies a class position no more than it presupposes one. And the class position which may be attained is not as such an entrepreneurial position, but is characterised as landowning or

---

[1] Cf. for example the good description in Wiedenfeld, Das Persönliche im modernen Unternehmertum. Although it appeared in Schmoller's Jahrbuch in 1910 this work was not known to me when the first edition of this book was published.

capitalist, according to how the proceeds of the enterprise are used. Inheritance of the pecuniary result and of personal qualities may then both keep up this position for more than one generation and make further enterprise easier for descendants, but the function of the entrepreneur itself cannot be inherited, as is shown well enough by the history of manufacturing families.[1]

But now the decisive question arises: why then is the carrying out of new combinations a special process and the object of a special kind of "function"? Every individual carries on his economic affairs as well as he can. To be sure, his own intentions are never realised with ideal perfection, but ultimately his behavior is moulded by the influence on him of the results of his conduct, so as to fit circumstances which do not as a rule change suddenly. If a business can never be absolutely perfect in any sense, yet it in time approaches a relative perfection having regard to the surrounding world, the social conditions, the knowledge of the time, and the horizon of each individual or each group. New possibilities are continuously being offered by the surrounding world, in particular new discoveries are continuously being added to the existing store of knowledge. Why should not the individual make just as much use of the new possibilities as of the old, and, according to the market position as he understands it, keep pigs instead of cows, or even choose a new crop rotation, if this can be seen to be more advantageous? And what kind of special new phenomena or problems, not to be found in the established circular flow, can arise there?

While in the accustomed circular flow every individual can act promptly and rationally because he is sure of his ground and is supported by the conduct, as adjusted to this circular flow, of all other individuals, who in turn expect the accustomed activity from him, he cannot simply do this when he is confronted by a new task. While in the accustomed channels his own ability and experience suffice for the normal individual, when confronted with innovations he needs guidance. While he swims with the stream in the circular flow which is familiar to him, he swims against the

---

[1] On the nature of the entrepreneurial function also compare my statement in the article "Unternehmer" in the Handwörterbuch der Staatswissenschaften.

80   THE THEORY OF ECONOMIC DEVELOPMENT

stream if he wishes to change its channel. What was formerly a help becomes a hindrance. What was a familiar datum becomes an unknown. Where the boundaries of routine stop, many people can go no further, and the rest can only do so in a highly variable manner. The assumption that conduct is prompt and rational is in all cases a fiction. But it proves to be sufficiently near to reality, if things have time to hammer logic into men. Where this has happened, and within the limits in which it has happened, one may rest content with this fiction and build theories upon it. It is then not true that habit or custom or non-economic ways of thinking cause a hopeless difference between the individuals of different classes, times, or cultures, and that, for example, the "economics of the stock exchange" would be inapplicable say to the peasants of to-day or to the craftsmen of the Middle Ages. On the contrary the same theoretical picture [1] in its broadest contour lines fits the individuals of quite different cultures, whatever their degree of intelligence and of economic rationality, and we can depend upon it that the peasant sells his calf just as cunningly and egotistically as the stock exchange member his portfolio of shares. But this holds good only where precedents without number have formed conduct through decades and, in fundamentals, through hundreds and thousands of years, and have eliminated unadapted behavior. Outside of these limits our fiction loses its closeness to reality.[2] To cling to it there also, as the traditional theory does, is to hide an essential thing and to ignore a fact which, in contrast with other deviations of our assumptions from reality, is theoretically important and the source of the explanation of phenomena which would not exist without it.

[1] The same *theoretical* picture, obviously not the same sociological, cultural, and so forth.

[2] How much this is the case is best seen to-day in the economic life of those nations, and within our civilisation in the economics of those individuals, whom the development of the last century has not yet completely drawn into its stream, for example, in the economy of the Central European peasant. This peasant "calculates"; there is no deficiency of the "economic way of thinking" (Wirtschaftsgesinnung) in him. Yet he cannot take a step out of the beaten path; his economy has not changed at all for centuries, except perhaps through the exercise of external force and influence. Why? Because the choice of new methods is not simply an element in the concept of rational economic action, nor a matter of course, but a distinct process which stands in need of special explanation.

Therefore, in describing the circular flow one must treat combinations of means of production (the production-functions) as data, like natural possibilities, and admit only small [1] variations at the margins, such as every individual can accomplish by adapting himself to changes in his economic environment, without materially deviating from familiar lines. Therefore, too, the carrying out of new combinations is a special function, and the privilege of a type of people who are much less numerous than all those who have the "objective" possibility of doing it. Therefore, finally, entrepreneurs are a special type,[2] and their behavior a special

[1] Small disturbances which may indeed, as mentioned earlier, in time add up to great amounts. The decisive point is that the businessman, if he makes them, never alters his routine. The usual case is one of small, the exception one of great (*uno actu* great), disturbances. Only in this sense is emphasis put upon "smallness" here. The objection that there can be no difference in principle between small and large disturbances is not effective. For it is false in itself, in so far as it is based upon the disregard of the principle of the infinitesimal method, the essence of which lies in the fact that one can assert of "small quantities" under certain circumstances what one cannot assert of "large quantities." But the reader who takes umbrage at the large-small contrast may, if he wishes, substitute for it the contrast adapting-spontaneous. Personally I am not willing to do this because the latter method of expression is much easier to misunderstand than the former and really would demand still longer explanations.

[2] In the first place it is a question of a type of *conduct* and of a type of *person* in so far as this conduct is accessible in very unequal measure and to relatively few people, so that it constitutes their outstanding characteristic. Because the exposition of the first edition was reproached with exaggerating and mistaking the peculiarity of this conduct, and with overlooking the fact that it is more or less open to every businessman, and because the exposition in a later paper ("Wellenbewegung des Wirtschaftslebens," Archiv für Sozialwissenschaft) was charged with introducing an intermediate type ("half-static" businessmen), the following may be submitted. The conduct in question is peculiar in two ways. First, because it is directed towards something different and signifies doing something different from other conduct. One may indeed in this connection include it with the latter in a higher unity, but this does not alter the fact that a theoretically relevant difference exists between the two, and that only one of them is adequately described by traditional theory. Secondly, the type of conduct in question not only differs from the other in its object, "innovation" being peculiar to it, but also in that it presupposes aptitudes differing *in kind* and not only in degree from those of mere rational economic behavior.

Now these aptitudes are presumably distributed in an ethically homogeneous population just like others, that is the curve of their distribution has a maximum ordinate, deviations on either side of which become rarer the greater they are. Similarly we can assume that every healthy man can sing if he will. Perhaps half the individuals in an ethically homogeneous group have the capacity for it to an average degree, a quarter in progressively diminishing measure, and, let us say, a quarter in a measure above the average; and within this quarter, through a series of continually increasing singing ability and continually diminishing number of people

82   *THE THEORY OF ECONOMIC DEVELOPMENT*

problem, the motive power of a great number of significant phenomena. Hence, our position may be characterised by three corresponding pairs of opposites. First, by the opposition of two real processes: the circular flow or the tendency towards equilibrium on the one hand, a change in the channels of economic routine or a spontaneous change in the economic data arising from within the system on the other. Secondly, by the opposition of two theoretical *apparatuses*: statics and dynamics.[1] Thirdly, by the opposi-

who possess it, we come finally to the Carusos. Only in this quarter are we struck in general by the singing ability, and only in the supreme instances can it become the characterising mark of the person. Although practically all men can sing, singing ability does not cease to be a distinguishable characteristic and attribute of a minority, indeed not exactly of a type, because this characteristic — unlike ours — affects the total personality relatively little.

Let us apply this: Again, a quarter of the population may be so poor in those qualities, let us say here provisionally, of economic initiative that the deficiency makes itself felt by poverty of their moral personality, and they play a wretched part in the smallest affairs of private and professional life in which this element is called for. We recognise this type and know that many of the best clerks, distinguished by devotion to duty, expert knowledge, and exactitude, belong to it. Then comes the "half," the "normal." These prove themselves to be better in the things which even within the established channels cannot simply be "dispatched" (erledigen) but must also be "decided" (entscheiden) and "carried out" (durchsetzen). Practically all business people belong here, otherwise they would never have attained their positions; most represent a selection — individually or hereditarily tested. A textile manufacturer travels no "new" road when he goes to a wool auction. But the situations there are never the same, and the success of the business depends so much upon skill and initiative in buying wool that the fact that the textile industry has so far exhibited no trustification comparable with that in heavy manufacturing is undoubtedly partly explicable by the reluctance of the cleverer manufacturers to renounce the advantage of their own skill in buying wool. From there, rising in the scale we come finally into the highest quarter, to people who are a type characterised by super-normal qualities of intellect and will. Within this type there are not only many varieties (merchants, manufacturers, financiers, etc.) but also a continuous variety of degrees of intensity in "initiative." In our argument types of every intensity occur. Many a one can steer a safe course, where no one has yet been; others follow where first another went before; still others only in the crowd, but in this among the first. So also the great political leader of every kind and time is a type, yet not a thing unique, but only the apex of a pyramid from which there is a continuous variation down to the average and from it to the sub-normal values. And yet not only is "leading" a special function, but the leader also something special, distinguishable — wherefore there is no sense in our case in asking: "Where does that type begin then?" and then to exclaim: "This is no type at all!"

[1] It has been objected against the first edition that it sometimes defines "statics" as a theoretical construction, sometimes as the picture of an actual state of economic life. I believe that the present exposition gives no ground for this opinion. "Static" theory does not assume a stationary economy; it also treats of the effects of changes in data. In itself, therefore, there is no necessary connection between static theory and stationary reality. Only in so far as one can exhibit the fundamental form of the

tion of two types of conduct, which, following reality, we can picture as two types of individuals: mere managers and entrepreneurs. And therefore the "best method" of producing in the theoretical sense is to be conceived as "the most advantageous among the methods which have been empirically tested and become familiar." But it is not the "best" of the methods "possible" at the time. If one does not make this distinction, the concept becomes meaningless and precisely those problems remain unsolved which our interpretation is meant to provide for.

Let us now formulate precisely the characteristic feature of the conduct and type under discussion. The smallest daily action embodies a huge mental effort. Every schoolboy would have to be a mental giant, if he himself had to create all he knows and uses by his own individual activity. And every man would have to be a giant of wisdom and will, if he had in every case to create anew all the rules by which he guides his everyday conduct. This is true not only of those decisions and actions of individual and social life the principles of which are the product of tens of thou-

economic course of events with the maximum simplicity in an unchanging economy does this assumption recommend itself to theory. The stationary economy is for uncounted thousands of years, and also in historical times in many places for centuries, an incontrovertible fact, apart from the fact, moreover, which Sombart emphasised, that there is a tendency towards a stationary state in every period of depression. Hence it is readily understood how this historical fact and that theoretical construction have allied themselves in a way which led to some confusion. The words "statics" and "dynamics" the author would not now use in the meaning they carry above, where they are simply short expressions for "theory of the circular flow" and "theory of development." One more thing: theory employs two methods of interpretation, which may perhaps make difficulties. If it is to be shown how all the elements of the economic system are determined in equilibrium by one another, this equilibrium system is considered as not yet existing and is built up before our eyes *ab ovo*. This does not mean that its coming into being is genetically explained thereby. Only its existence and functioning are made logically clear by mental dissection. And the experiences and habits of individuals are assumed as existing. How just these productive combinations have come about is not thereby explained. Further, if two contiguous equilibrium positions are to be investigated, then sometimes (not always), as in Pigou's Economics of Welfare, the "best" productive combination in the first is compared with the "best" in the second. And this again need not, but may, mean that the two combinations in the sense meant here differ not only by small variations in quantity but in their whole technical and commercial structure. Here too the coming into being of the second combination and the problems connected with it are not investigated, but only the functioning and the outcome of the already existing combination. Even though justified as far as it goes, this method of treatment passes over our problem. If the assertion were implied that this is also settled by it, it would be false.

84   *THE THEORY OF ECONOMIC DEVELOPMENT*

sands of years, but also of those products of shorter periods and of a more special nature which constitute the particular instrument for performing vocational tasks. But precisely the things the performance of which according to this should involve a supreme effort, in general demand no special individual effort at all; those which should be especially difficult are in reality especially easy; what should demand superhuman capacity is accessible to the least gifted, given mental health. In particular within the ordinary routine there is no need for leadership. Of course it is still necessary to set people their tasks, to keep up discipline, and so forth; but this is easy and a function any normal person can learn to fulfil. Within the lines familiar to all, even the function of directing other people, though still necessary, is mere "work" like any other, comparable to the service of tending a machine. All people get to know, and are able to do, their daily tasks in the customary way and ordinarily perform them by themselves; the "director" has his routine as they have theirs; and his directive function serves merely to correct individual aberrations.

This is so because all knowledge and habit once acquired becomes as firmly rooted in ourselves as a railway embankment in the earth. It does not require to be continually renewed and consciously reproduced, but sinks into the strata of subconsciousness. It is normally transmitted almost without friction by inheritance, teaching, upbringing, pressure of environment. Everything we think, feel, or do often enough becomes automatic and our conscious life is unburdened of it. The enormous economy of force, in the race and the individual, here involved is not great enough, however, to make daily life a light burden and to prevent its demands from exhausting the average energy all the same. But it is great enough to make it possible to meet the ordinary claims. This holds good likewise for economic daily life. And from this it follows also for economic life that every step outside the boundary of routine has difficulties and involves a new element. It is this element that constitutes the phenomenon of leadership.

The nature of these difficulties may be focussed in the following three points. First, outside these accustomed channels the individual is without those data for his decisions and those rules of conduct which are usually very accurately known to him within them. Of course he must still foresee and estimate on the basis of his experience. But many things must remain uncertain, still others are only ascertainable within wide limits, some can perhaps only be "guessed." In particular this is true of those data which the individual strives to alter and of those which he wants to create. Now he must really to some extent do what tradition does for him in everyday life, viz. consciously plan his conduct in every particular. There will be much more conscious rationality in this than in customary action, which as such does not need to be reflected upon at all; but this plan must necessarily be open not only to errors greater in degree, but also to other kinds of errors than those occurring in customary action. What has been done already has the sharp-edged reality of all the things which we have seen and experienced; the new is only the figment of our imagination. Carrying out a new plan and acting according to a customary one are things as different as making a road and walking along it.

How different a thing this is becomes clearer if one bears in mind the impossibility of surveying exhaustively all the effects and counter-effects of the projected enterprise. Even as many of them as could in theory be ascertained if one had unlimited time and means must practically remain in the dark. As military action must be taken in a given strategic position even if all the data potentially procurable are not available, so also in economic life action must be taken without working out all the details of what is to be done. Here the success of everything depends upon intuition, the capacity of seeing things in a way which afterwards proves to be true, even though it cannot be established at the moment, and of grasping the essential fact, discarding the unessential, even though one can give no account of the principles by which this is done. Thorough preparatory work, and special knowledge, breadth of intellectual understanding, talent for logical analysis, may under certain circumstances be sources of failure. The more accurately, however, we learn to know the natural and social world, the more perfect our control of facts becomes; and the greater the extent, with time and progressive

86   *THE THEORY OF ECONOMIC DEVELOPMENT*

rationalisation, within which things can be simply calculated, and indeed quickly and reliably calculated, the more the significance of this function decreases. Therefore the importance of the entrepreneur type must diminish just as the importance of the military commander has already diminished. Nevertheless a part of the very essence of each type is bound up with this function.

As this first point lies in the task, so the second lies in the psyche of the businessman himself. It is not only objectively more difficult to do something new than what is familiar and tested by experience, but the individual feels reluctance to it and would do so even if the objective difficulties did not exist. This is so in all fields. The history of science is one great confirmation of the fact that we find it exceedingly difficult to adopt a new scientific point of view or method. Thought turns again and again into the accustomed track even if it has become unsuitable and the more suitable innovation in itself presents no particular difficulties. The very nature of fixed habits of thinking, their energy-saving function, is founded upon the fact that they have become subconscious, that they yield their results automatically and are proof against criticism and even against contradiction by individual facts. But precisely because of this they become drag-chains when they have outlived their usefulness. So it is also in the economic world. In the breast of one who wishes to do something new, the forces of habit rise up and bear witness against the embryonic project. A new and another kind of effort of will is therefore necessary in order to wrest, amidst the work and care of the daily round, scope and time for conceiving and working out the new combination and to bring oneself to look upon it as a real possibility and not merely as a day-dream. This mental freedom presupposes a great surplus force over the everyday demand and is something peculiar and by nature rare.

The third point consists in the reaction of the social environment against one who wishes to do something new. This reaction may manifest itself first of all in the existence of legal or political impediments. But neglecting this, any deviating conduct by a member of a social group is condemned, though in greatly varying degrees according as the social group is used to such conduct or not. Even a deviation from social custom in such things as dress or manners arouses opposition, and of course all the more so in the graver cases. This opposition is stronger in primitive stages of culture than in others, but it is never absent. Even mere astonishment at the deviation, even merely noticing it, exercises a pressure on the individual. The manifestation of condemnation may at once bring noticeable consequences in its train. It may even come to social ostracism and finally to physical prevention or to direct attack. Neither the fact that progressive differentiation weakens this opposition — especially as the most important cause of the weakening is the very development which we wish to explain — nor the further fact that the social opposition operates under certain circumstances and upon many individuals as a stimulus, changes anything in principle in the significance of it. Surmounting this opposition is always a special kind of task which does not exist in the customary course of life, a task which also requires a special kind of conduct. In matters economic this resistance manifests itself first of all in the groups threatened by the innovation, then in the difficulty in finding the necessary cooperation, finally in the difficulty in winning over consumers. Even though these elements are still effective to-day, despite the fact that a period of turbulent development has accustomed us to the appearance and the carrying out of innovations, they can be best studied in the beginnings of capitalism. But they are so obvious there that it would be time lost for our purposes to dwell upon them.

There is leadership *only* for these reasons — leadership, that is, as a special kind of function and in contrast to a mere difference in rank, which would exist in every social body, in the smallest as in the largest, and in combination with which it generally appears. The facts alluded to create a boundary beyond which the majority of people do not function promptly by themselves and require help from a minority. If social life had in all respects the relative immutability of, for example, the astronomical world, or if mutable this mutability were yet incapable of being influenced by human action, or finally if capable of being so influenced this type of action were yet equally open to everyone, then there would be

88   *THE THEORY OF ECONOMIC DEVELOPMENT*

no special function of leadership as distinguished from routine work.

The specific problem of leadership arises and the leader type appears only where new possibilities present themselves. That is why it is so strongly marked among the Normans at the time of their conquests and so feebly among the Slavs in the centuries of their unchanging and relatively protected life in the marshes of the Pripet. Our three points characterise the nature of the *function* as well as the *conduct* or behavior which constitutes the leader type. It is no part of his function to "find" or to "create" new possibilities. They are always present, abundantly accumulated by all sorts of people. Often they are also generally known and being discussed by scientific or literary writers. In other cases, there is nothing to discover about them, because they are quite obvious. To take an example from political life, it was not at all difficult to see how the social and political conditions of France at the time of Louis XVI could have been improved so as to avoid a breakdown of the *ancien régime*. Plenty of people as a matter of fact did see it. But nobody was in a position to *do* it. Now, it is this "doing the thing," without which possibilities are dead, of which the leader's function consists. This holds good of all kinds of leadership, ephemeral as well as more enduring ones. The former may serve as an instance. What is to be done in a casual emergency is as a rule quite simple. Most or all people may see it, yet they want someone to speak out, to lead, and to organise. Even leadership which influences merely by example, as artistic or scientific leadership, does not consist simply in finding or creating the new thing but in so impressing the social group with it as to draw it on in its wake. It is, therefore, more by will than by intellect that the leaders fulfil their function, more by "authority," "personal weight," and so forth than by original ideas.

Economic leadership in particular must hence be distinguished from "invention." As long as they are not carried into practice, inventions are economically irrelevant. And to carry any improvement into effect is a task entirely different from the inventing of it, and a task, moreover, requiring entirely different kinds of aptitudes. Although entrepreneurs of course *may* be inventors just as they may be capitalists, they are inventors not by nature of their function but by coincidence and vice versa. Besides, the innovations which it is the function of entrepreneurs to carry out need not necessarily be any inventions at all. It is, therefore, not advisable, and it may be downright misleading, to stress the element of invention as much as many writers do.

The entrepreneurial kind of leadership, as distinguished from other kinds of economic leadership such as we should expect to find in a primitive tribe or a communist society, is of course colored by the conditions peculiar to it. It has none of that glamour which characterises other kinds of leadership. It consists in fulfilling a very special task which only in rare cases appeals to the imagination of the public. For its success, keenness and vigor are not more essential than a certain narrowness which seizes the immediate chance and *nothing else*. "Personal weight" is, to be sure, not without importance. Yet the personality of the capitalistic entrepreneur need not, and generally does not, answer to the idea most of us have of what a "leader" looks like, so much so that there is some difficulty in realizing that he comes within the sociological category of leader at all. He "leads" the means of production into new channels. But this he does, not by convincing people of the desirability of carrying out his plan or by creating confidence in his leading in the manner of a political leader — the only man he has to convince or to impress is the banker who is to finance him — but by buying them or their services, and then using them as he sees fit. He also leads in the sense that he draws other producers in his branch after him. But as they are his competitors, who first reduce and then annihilate his profit, this is, as it were, leadership against one's own will. Finally, he renders a service, the full appreciation of which takes a specialist's knowledge of the case. It is not so easily understood by the public at large as a politician's successful speech or a general's victory in the field, not to insist on the fact that he seems to act — and often harshly — in his individual interest alone. We shall understand, therefore, that we do not observe, in this case, the emergence of all those affective values which are the glory of all other kinds of social leadership. Add to this the precariousness of the economic position both of the individual entrepreneur and of entrepreneurs as a group, and the fact that when his economic success raises him socially he has no cultural tradition or attitude to fall back upon, but moves about in society as an upstart, whose ways are readily laughed at, and we shall understand why this type has never been popular, and why even scientific critique often makes short work of it.[1]

We shall finally try to round off our picture of the entrepreneur in the same manner in which we always, in science as well as in practical life, try to understand human behavior, viz. by analysing the characteristic motives of his conduct. Any attempt to do this must of course meet with all those objections against the economist's intrusion into "psychology" which have been made familiar by a long series of writers. We cannot here enter into the fundamental question of the relation between psychology and economics. It is enough to state that those who on principle object to *any* psychological considerations in an economic argument may leave out what we are about to say without thereby losing contact with the argument of the following chapters. For none of the results to which our analysis is intended to lead stands or falls with our "psychology of the entrepreneur," or could be vitiated by any errors in it. Nowhere is there, as the reader will easily satisfy himself, any necessity for us to overstep the frontiers of observable behavior. Those who do not object to *all* psychology but only to the *kind* of psychology which we know from the traditional textbook, will see that we do not adopt any part of the time-honored picture of the motivation of the "economic man."

In the theory of the circular flow, the importance of examining motives is very much reduced by the fact that the equations of the system of equilibrium may be so interpreted as not to imply any psychic magnitudes at all, as shown by the analysis of Pareto

---

[1] It may, therefore, not be superfluous to point out that our analysis of the rôle of the entrepreneur does not involve any "glorification" of the type, as some readers of the first edition of this book seemed to think. We do hold that entrepreneurs *have* an economic function as distinguished from, say, robbers. But we neither style every entrepreneur a genius or a benefactor to humanity, nor do we wish to express any opinion about the comparative merits of the social organisation in which he plays his rôle, or about the question whether what he does could not be effected more cheaply or efficiently in other ways.

and of Barone. This is the reason why even very defective psychology interferes much less with results than one would expect. There may be rational *conduct* even in the absence of rational *motive*. But as soon as we really wish to penetrate into motivation, the problem proves by no means simple. Within given social circumstances and habits, most of what people do every day will appear to them primarily from the point of view of duty carrying a social or a superhuman sanction. There is very little of conscious rationality, still less of hedonism and of *individual* egoism about it, and so much of it as may safely be said to exist is of comparatively recent growth. Nevertheless, as long as we confine ourselves to the great outlines of constantly repeated economic action, we may link it up with wants and the desire to satisfy them, on condition that we are careful to recognise that economic motive so defined varies in intensity very much in time; that it is society that shapes the particular desires we observe; that wants must be taken with reference to the group which the individual thinks of when deciding his course of action — the family or any other group, smaller or larger than the family; that action does not promptly follow upon desire but only more or less imperfectly corresponds to it; that the field of individual choice is always, though in very different ways and to very different degrees, fenced in by social habits or conventions and the like: it still remains broadly true that, within the circular flow, everyone adapts himself to his environment so as to satisfy certain *given* wants — of himself or others — as best he can. In *all* cases, the *meaning* of economic action is the satisfaction of wants in the sense that there would be no economic action if there were no wants. In the case of the circular flow, we may also think of satisfaction of wants as the normal *motive*.

The latter is not true for our type. In one sense, he may indeed be called the most rational and the most egotistical of all. For, as we have seen, conscious rationality enters much more into the carrying out of new plans, which themselves have to be worked out before they can be acted upon, than into the mere running of an established business, which is largely a matter of routine. And the typical entrepreneur is more self-centred than other types, because he relies less than they do on tradition and connection and because his characteristic task — theoretically as well as historically — consists precisely in breaking up old, and creating new, tradition. Although this applies primarily to his economic action, it also extends to the moral, cultural, and social consequences of it. It is, of course, no mere coincidence that the period of the rise of the entrepreneur type also gave birth to Utilitarianism.

But his conduct and his motive are "rational" in no other sense. And in *no* sense is his characteristic motivation of the hedonist kind. If we define hedonist motive of action as the wish to satisfy one's wants, we may indeed make "wants" include any impulse whatsoever, just as we may define egoism so as to include all altruistic values too, on the strength of the fact that they also mean something in the way of self-gratification. But this would reduce our definition to tautology. If we wish to give it meaning, we must restrict it to such wants as are capable of being satisfied by the consumption of goods, and to that kind of satisfaction which is expected from it. Then it is no longer true that our type is acting on a wish to satisfy his wants.

For unless we assume that individuals of our type are driven along by an insatiable craving for hedonist satisfaction, the operations of Gossen's law would in the case of business leaders soon put a stop to further effort. Experience teaches, however, that typical entrepreneurs retire from the arena only when and because their strength is spent and they feel no longer equal to their task. This does not seem to verify the picture of the economic man, balancing probable results against disutility of effort and reaching in due course a point of equilibrium beyond which he is not willing to go. Effort, in our case, does not seem to weigh at all in the sense of being felt as a reason to stop. And activity of the entrepreneurial type is obviously an obstacle to hedonist enjoyment of those kinds of commodity which are usually acquired by incomes beyond a certain size, because their "consumption" presupposes leisure. Hedonistically, therefore, the conduct which we usually observe in individuals of our type would be irrational.

This would not, of course, prove the absence of hedonistic motive. Yet it points to another psychology of non-hedonist character, especially if we take into account the indifference to hedonist enjoyment which is often conspicuous in outstanding specimens of the type and which is not difficult to understand.

First of all, there is the dream and the will to found a private kingdom, usually, though not necessarily, also a dynasty. The modern world really does not know any such positions, but what may be attained by industrial or commercial success is still the nearest approach to medieval lordship possible to modern man. Its fascination is specially strong for people who have no other chance of achieving social distinction. The sensation of power and independence loses nothing by the fact that both are largely illusions. Closer analysis would lead to discovering an endless variety within this group of motives, from spiritual ambition down to mere snobbery. But this need not detain us. Let it suffice to point out that motives of this kind, although they stand nearest to consumers' satisfaction, do not coincide with it.

Then there is the will to conquer: the impulse to fight, to prove oneself superior to others, to succeed for the sake, not of the fruits of success, but of success itself. From this aspect, economic action becomes akin to sport — there are financial races, or rather boxing-matches. The financial result is a secondary consideration, or, at all events, mainly valued as an index of success and as a symptom of victory, the displaying of which very often is more important as a motive of large expenditure than the wish for the consumers' goods themselves. Again we should find countless nuances, some of which, like social ambition, shade into the first group of motives. And again we are faced with a motivation characteristically different from that of "satisfaction of wants" in the sense defined above, or from, to put the same thing into other words, "hedonistic adaptation."

Finally, there is the joy of creating, of getting things done, or simply of exercising one's energy and ingenuity. This is akin to a ubiquitous motive, but nowhere else does it stand out as an independent factor of behavior with anything like the clearness with which it obtrudes itself in our case. Our type seeks out difficulties, changes in order to change, delights in ventures. This group of motives is the most distinctly anti-hedonist of the three.

Only with the first groups of motives is private property as the result of entrepreneurial activity an essential factor in making it operative. With the other two it is not. Pecuniary gain is indeed a very accurate expression of success, especially of *relative* success, and from the standpoint of the man who strives for it, it has the additional advantage of being an objective fact and largely independent of the opinion of others. These and other peculiarities incident to the mechanism of "acquisitive" society make it very difficult to replace it as a motor of industrial development, even if we would discard the importance it has for creating a fund ready for investment. Nevertheless it is true that the second and third groups of entrepreneurial motives may in principle be taken care of by other social arrangements not involving private gain from economic innovation. What other stimuli could be provided, and how they could be made to work as well as the "capitalistic" ones do, are questions which are beyond our theme. They are taken too lightly by social reformers, and are altogether ignored by fiscal radicalism. But they are not insoluble, and may be answered by detailed observation of the psychology of entrepreneurial activity, at least for given times and places.

Part II
History and Countries

[4]

Entrepreneurship: Productive, Unproductive, and Destructive

William J. Baumol

New York University and Princeton University

The basic hypothesis is that, while the total supply of entrepreneurs varies among societies, the productive contribution of the society's entrepreneurial activities varies much more because of their allocation between productive activities such as innovation and largely unproductive activities such as rent seeking or organized crime. This allocation is heavily influenced by the relative payoffs society offers to such activities. This implies that policy can influence the allocation of entrepreneurship more effectively than it can influence its supply. Historical evidence from ancient Rome, early China, and the Middle Ages and Renaissance in Europe is used to investigate the hypotheses.

> It is often assumed that an economy of private enterprise has an automatic bias towards innovation, but this is not so. It has a bias only towards profit. [HOBSBAWM 1969, p. 40]

When conjectures are offered to explain historic slowdowns or great leaps in economic growth, there is the group of usual suspects that is

I am very grateful for the generous support of the research underlying this paper from the Division of Information Science and Technology of the National Science Foundation, the Price Institute for Entrepreneurial Studies, the Center for Entrepreneurial Studies of the Graduate School of Business Administration, New York University, and the C. V. Starr Center for Applied Economics. I am also very much indebted to Vacharee Devakula for her assistance in the research. I owe much to Joel Mokyr, Stefano Fenoaltea, Lawrence Stone, Constance Berman, and Claudia Goldin for help with the substance of the paper and to William Jordan and Theodore Rabb for guidance on references.

[*Journal of Political Economy*, 1990, vol. 98, no. 5, pt. 1]

regularly rounded up—prominent among them, the entrepreneur. Where growth has slowed, it is implied that a decline in entrepreneurship was partly to blame (perhaps because the culture's "need for achievement" has atrophied). At another time and place, it is said, the flowering of entrepreneurship accounts for unprecedented expansion.

This paper proposes a rather different set of hypotheses, holding that entrepreneurs are always with us and always play *some* substantial role. But there are a variety of roles among which the entrepreneur's efforts can be reallocated, and some of those roles do not follow the constructive and innovative script that is conventionally attributed to that person. Indeed, at times the entrepreneur may even lead a parasitical existence that is actually damaging to the economy. How the entrepreneur acts at a given time and place depends heavily on the rules of the game—the reward structure in the economy—that happen to prevail. Thus the central hypothesis here is that it is the set of rules and not the supply of entrepreneurs *or the nature of their objectives* that undergoes significant changes from one period to another and helps to dictate the ultimate effect on the economy via the *allocation* of entrepreneurial resources. Changes in the rules and other attendant circumstances can, of course, modify the composition of the class of entrepreneurs and can also alter its size. Without denying this or claiming that it has no significance, in this paper I shall seek to focus attention on the allocation of the changing class of entrepreneurs rather than its magnitude and makeup. (For an excellent analysis of the basic hypothesis, independently derived, see Murphy, Shleifer, and Vishny [1990].)

The basic proposition, if sustained by the evidence, has an important implication for growth policy. The notion that our productivity problems reside in "the spirit of entrepreneurship" that waxes and wanes for unexplained reasons is a counsel of despair, for it gives no guidance on how to reawaken that spirit once it has lagged. If that is the task assigned to policymakers, they are destitute: they have no means of knowing how to carry it out. But if what is required is the adjustment of rules of the game to induce a more felicitous allocation of entrepreneurial resources, then the policymaker's task is less formidable, and it is certainly not hopeless. The prevailing rules that affect the allocation of entrepreneurial activity can be observed, described, and, with luck, modified and improved, as will be illustrated here.

Here, extensive historical illustrations will be cited to impart plausibility to the contentions that have just been described. Then a short discussion of some current issues involving the allocation of entrepreneurship between productive and unproductive activities will be offered. Finally, I shall consider very briefly the means that can be used to change the rules of the game, and to do so in a manner that stimulates the productive contribution of the entrepreneur.

I. On the Historical Character of the Evidence

Given the inescapable problems for empirical as well as theoretical study of entrepreneurship, what sort of evidence can one hope to provide? Since the rules of the game usually change very slowly, a case study approach to investigation of my hypotheses drives me unavoidably to examples spanning considerable periods of history and encompassing widely different cultures and geographic locations. Here I shall proceed on the basis of historical illustrations encompassing all the main economic periods and places (ancient Rome, medieval China, Dark Age Europe, the Later Middle Ages, etc.) that the economic historians almost universally single out for the light they shed on the process of innovation and its diffusion. These will be used to show that the relative rewards to different types of entrepreneurial activity have in fact varied dramatically from one time and place to another and that this seems to have had profound effects on patterns of entrepreneurial behavior. Finally, evidence will be offered *suggesting* that such reallocations can have a considerable influence on the prosperity and growth of an economy, though other variables undoubtedly also play substantial roles.

None of this can, of course, be considered conclusive. Yet, it is surely a standard tenet of scientific method that tentative confirmation of a hypothesis is provided by observation of phenomena that the hypothesis helps to explain and that could not easily be accounted for if that hypothesis were invalid. It is on this sort of reasoning that I hope to rest my case. Historians have long been puzzled, for example, by the failure of the society of ancient Rome to disseminate and put into widespread practical use some of the sophisticated technological developments that we know to have been in its possession, while in the "High Middle Ages," a period in which progress and change were hardly popular notions, inventions that languished in Rome seem to have spread like wildfire. It will be argued that the hypothesis about the allocability of entrepreneurial effort between productive and unproductive activity helps considerably to account for this phenomenon, though it certainly will *not* be claimed that this is all there was to the matter.

Before I get to the substance of the discussion, it is important to emphasize that nothing that follows in this article makes any pretense of constituting a contribution to economic history. Certainly it is not intended here to try to explain any particular historical event. Moreover, the analysis relies entirely on secondary sources, and all the historical developments described are well known to historians, as the citations will indicate. Whatever the contribution that may be offered by the following pages, then, it is confined to enhanced understanding and extension of the (nonmathematical) theory of entrepreneurship in general, and not to an improved analysis of the historical events that are cited.

II. The Schumpeterian Model Extended: Allocation of Entrepreneurship

The analysis of this paper rests on what seems to be the one theoretical model that effectively encompasses the role of the entrepreneur and that really "works," in the sense that it constitutes the basis for a number of substantive inferences.[1] This is, of course, the well-known Schumpeterian analysis, whose main shortcoming, for our purposes, is the paucity of insights on policy that emerge from it. It will be suggested here that only a minor extension of that model to encompass the *allocation* of entrepreneurship is required to enhance its power substantially in this direction.

Schumpeter tells us that innovations (he calls them "the carrying out of new combinations") take various forms besides mere improvements in technology:

> This concept covers the following five cases: (1) the introduction of a new good—that is one with which consumers are not yet familiar—or of a new quality of a good. (2) The introduction of a new method of production, that is one not yet tested by experience in the branch of manufacture concerned, which need by no means be founded upon a discovery scientifically new, and can also exist in a new way of handling a commodity commercially. (3) The opening of a new market, that is a market into which the particular branch of manufacture of the country in question has not previously entered, whether or not this market has existed before. (4) The conquest of a new source of supply of raw materials or half-manufactured goods, again irrespective of whether this source already exists or whether it has first to be

[1] There has, however, recently been an outburst of illuminating writings on the theory of the innovation process, analyzing it in such terms as *races* for patents in which the winner takes everything, with no consolation prize for a close second, or treating the process, alternatively, as a "waiting game," in which the patient second entrant may outperform and even survive the first one in the innovative arena, who incurs the bulk of the risk. For an overview of these discussions as well as some substantial added insights, see Dasgupta (1988).

created. (5) The carrying out of the new organization of any industry, like the creation of a monopoly position (for example through trustification) or the breaking up of a monopoly position. [(1912) 1934, p. 66]

The obvious fact that entrepreneurs undertake such a variety of tasks all at once suggests that theory can usefully undertake to consider what determines the *allocation* of entrepreneurial inputs among those tasks. Just as the literature traditionally studies the allocation of other inputs, for example, capital resources, among the various industries that compete for them, it seems natural to ask what influences the flow of entrepreneurial talent among the various activities in Schumpeter's list.

Presumably the reason no such line of inquiry was pursued by Schumpeter or his successors is that any analysis of the allocation of entrepreneurial resources among the five items in the preceding list (with the exception of the last—the creation or destruction of a monopoly) does not promise to yield any profound conclusions. There is no obvious reason to make much of a shift of entrepreneurial activity away from, say, improvement in the production process and toward the introduction of new products. The general implications, if any, for the public welfare, for productivity growth, and for other related matters are hardly obvious.

To derive more substantive results from an analysis of the allocation of entrepreneurial resources, it is necessary to expand Schumpeter's list, whose main deficiency seems to be that it does not go far enough. For example, it does not explicitly encompass innovative acts of technology transfer that take advantage of opportunities to introduce already-available technology (usually with some modification to adapt it to local conditions) to geographic locales whose suitability for the purpose had previously gone unrecognized or at least unused.

Most important for the discussion here, Schumpeter's list of entrepreneurial activities can usefully be expanded to include such items as innovations in rent-seeking procedures, for example, discovery of a previously unused legal gambit that is effective in diverting rents to those who are first in exploiting it. It may seem strange at first blush to propose inclusion of activities of such questionable value to society (I shall call them acts of "unproductive entrepreneurship") in the list of Schumpeterian innovations (though the creation of a monopoly, which Schumpeter does include as an innovation, is surely as questionable), but, as will soon be seen, this is a crucial step for the analysis that follows. If entrepreneurs are defined, simply, to be persons who are ingenious and creative in finding ways that add to their own wealth, power, and prestige, then it is to be expected that not all of them will be overly concerned with whether an activity that achieves these goals adds much or little to the social product or, for that matter, even whether it is an actual impediment to production (this notion goes back, at least, to Veblen [1904]). Suppose that it turns out, in addition, that at any time and place the magnitude of the benefit the economy derives from its entrepreneurial talents depends *substantially,* among other variables, on the allocation of this resource between productive and unproductive entrepreneurial activities of the sorts just described. Then the reasons for including acts of the latter type in the list of entrepreneurial activities become clear.

Here no exhaustive analysis of the process of allocation of entrepreneurial activity among the set of available options will be attempted. Rather, it will be argued only that at least *one* of the prime determinants of entrepreneurial behavior at any particular time and place is the prevailing rules of the game that govern the payoff of one entrepreneurial activity relative to another. If the rules are such as to impede the earning of much wealth via activity A, or are such as to impose social disgrace on those who engage in it, then, other things being equal, entrepreneurs' efforts will tend to be channeled to other activities, call them B. But if B contributes less to production or welfare than A, the consequences for society may be considerable.[2]

As a last preliminary note, it should be emphasized that the set of active entrepreneurs may be subject to change. Thus if the rules of the game begin to favor B over A, it may not be just the same individuals who switch their activities from entrepreneurship of type A to that of type B. Rather, some persons with talents suited for A may simply drop out of the picture, and individuals with abilities adapted to B may for the first time become.entrepreneurs. Thus the allocation of entrepreneurs among activities is perhaps best described in the way Joan Robinson (following Shove's suggestion) analyzed the allocation of heterogeneous land resources (1933, chap. 8): as the solution of a jigsaw puzzle in which the pieces are each fitted into the places selected for them by the concatenation of pertinent circumstances.

III. Entrepreneurship, Productive and Unproductive: The Rules Do Change

Let us now turn to the central hypothesis of this paper: that the exercise of entrepreneurship can sometimes be unproductive or even

---

[2] There is a substantial literature, following the work of Jacob Schmookler, providing strong empirical evidence for the proposition that even the allocation of inventive effort, i.e., the directions pursued by inventive activities, is itself heavily influenced by relative payoff prospects. However, it is now agreed that some of these authors go too far when they appear to imply that almost nothing but the demand for the product of invention influences to any great extent which inventions will occur. For a good summary and references, see Abramovitz (1989, p. 33).

destructive, and that whether it takes one of these directions or one that is more benign depends heavily on the structure of payoffs in the economy—the rules of the game. The rather dramatic illustrations provided by world history seem to confirm quite emphatically the following proposition.

PROPOSITION 1. The rules of the game that determine the relative payoffs to different entrepreneurial activities *do* change dramatically from one time and place to another.

These examples also suggest strongly (but hardly "prove") the following proposition.

PROPOSITION 2. Entrepreneurial behavior changes direction from one economy to another in a manner that corresponds to the variations in the rules of the game.

A. Ancient Rome

The avenues open to those Romans who sought power, prestige, and wealth are instructive. First, it may be noted that they had no reservations about the desirability of wealth or about its pursuit (e.g., Finley 1985, pp. 53–57). *As long as it did not involve participation in industry or commerce,* there was nothing degrading about the wealth acquisition process. Persons of honorable status had three primary and acceptable sources of income: landholding (not infrequently as absentee landlords), "usury," and what may be described as "political payments":

> The opportunity for "political moneymaking" can hardly be over-estimated. Money poured in from booty, indemnities, provincial taxes, loans and miscellaneous extractions in quantities without precedent in Graeco-Roman history, and at an accelerating rate. The public treasury benefited, but probably more remained in private hands, among the nobles in the first instance; then, in appropriately decreasing proportions, among the *equites,* the soldiers and even the plebs of the city of Rome. . . . Nevertheless, the whole phenomenon is misunderstood when it is classified under the headings of "corruption" and "malpractice", as historians still persist in doing. Cicero was an honest governor of Cilicia in 51 and 50 B.C., so that at the end of his term he had earned only the legitimate profits of office. They amounted to 2,200,000 sesterces, more than treble the figure of 600,000 he himself once mentioned (*Stoic Paradoxes* 49) to illustrate an annual income that could permit a life of luxury. We are faced with something structural in the society. [Finley 1985, p. 55]

Who, then, operated commerce and industry? According to Veyne (1961), it was an occupation heavily undertaken by freedmen— former slaves who, incidentally, bore a social stigma for life. Indeed, according to this writer, slavery may have represented the one avenue for advancement for someone from the lower classes. A clever (and handsome) member of the lower orders might deliberately arrange to be sold into slavery to a wealthy and powerful master.[3] Then, with luck, skill, and drive, he would grow close to his owner, perhaps managing his financial affairs (and sometimes engaging in some homosexual activity with him). The master then gained cachet, after a suitable period, by granting freedom to the slave, setting him up with a fortune of his own. The freedmen, apparently not atypically, invested their financial stakes in commerce, hoping to multiply them sufficiently to enable them to retire in style to the countryside, thereafter investing primarily in land and loans in imitation of the upper classes.

Finally, regarding the Romans' attitude to the promotion of technology and productivity, Finley makes much of the "clear, almost total, divorce between science and practice" (1965, p. 32). He goes on to cite Vitruvius's monumental work on architecture and technology, in whose 10 books he finds only a single and trivial reference to means of saving effort and increasing productivity. Finley then reports the following story:

> There is a story, repeated by a number of Roman writers, that a man—characteristically unnamed—invented unbreakable glass and demonstrated it to Tiberius in anticipation of a great reward. The emperor asked the inventor whether anyone shared his secret and was assured that there was no one else; whereupon his head was promptly removed, lest, said Tiberius, gold be reduced to the value of mud. I have no opinion about the truth of this story, and it is only a story. But is it not interesting that neither the elder Pliny nor Petronius nor the historian Dio Cassius was troubled by the point that the inventor turned to the emperor for a reward, instead of turning to an investor for capital with which to put his invention into production?[4] . . . We must

---

[3] Stefano Fenoaltea comments that he knows no documented cases in which this occurred and that it was undoubtedly more common to seek advancement through adoption into an upper-class family.

[4] To be fair to Finley, note that he concludes that it is *not* really interesting. North and Thomas (1973, p. 3) make a similar point about Harrison's invention of the ship's chronometer in the eighteenth century (as an instrument indispensable for the determination of longitude). They point out that the incentive for this invention was a large governmental prize rather than the prospect of commercial profit, presumably because of the absence of effective patent protection.

> remind ourselves time and again that the European experi-
> ence since the late Middle Ages in technology, in the econ-
> omy, and in the value systems that accompanied them, was
> unique in human history until the recent export trend com-
> menced. Technical progress, economic growth, productivity,
> even efficiency have not been significant goals since the be-
> ginning of time. So long as an acceptable life-style could be
> maintained, however that was defined, other values held the
> stage. [1985, p. 147]

The bottom line, for our purposes, is that the Roman reward system, although it offered wealth to those who engaged in commerce
and industry, offset this gain through the attendant loss in prestige.
Economic effort "was neither the way to wealth nor its purpose. Cato's
gods showed him a number of ways to get more; but they were all
political and parasitical, the ways of conquest and booty and usury;
labour was not one of them, not even the labour of the entrepreneur"
(Finley 1965, p. 39).

B. Medieval China

In China, as in many kingdoms of Europe before the guarantees of
the Magna Carta and the revival of towns and their acquisition of
privileges, the monarch commonly claimed possession of all property
in his territories. As a result, particularly in China, when the sover-
eign was in financial straits, confiscation of the property of wealthy
subjects was entirely in order. It has been claimed that this led those
who had resources to avoid investing them in any sort of visible capital
stocks, and that this, in turn, was a substantial impediment to economic expansion (see Balazs 1964, p. 53; Landes 1969, pp. 46–47;
Rosenberg and Birdzell 1986, pp. 119–20; Jones 1987, chap. 5).

In addition, imperial China reserved its most substantial rewards in
wealth and prestige for those who climbed the ladder of imperial
examinations, which were heavily devoted to subjects such as Confu-
cian philosophy and calligraphy. Successful candidates were often
awarded high rank in the bureaucracy, high social standing denied to
anyone engaged in commerce or industry, even to those who gained
great wealth in the process (and who often used their resources to
prepare their descendants to contend via the examinations for a position in the scholar bureaucracy). In other words, the rules of the game
seem to have been heavily biased against the acquisition of wealth *and
position* through Schumpeterian behavior. The avenue to success lay
elsewhere.

Because of the difficulty of the examinations, the mandarins
(scholar-officials) rarely succeeded in keeping such positions in their

own families for more than two or three generations (see Marsh 1961, p. 159; Ho 1962, chap. 4 and appendix). The scholar families devoted enormous effort and considerable resources to preparing their children through years of laborious study for the imperial examinations, which, during the Sung dynasty, were held every 3 years, and only several hundred persons in all of China succeeded in passing them each time (E. A. Kracke, Jr. in Liu and Golas [1969, p. 14]). Yet, regularly, some persons not from mandarin families also attained success through this avenue (see, e.g., Marsh [1961] and Ho [1962] for evidence on social mobility in imperial China).

Wealth was in prospect for those who passed the examination and who were subsequently appointed to government positions. But the sources of their earnings had something in common with those of the Romans:

> Corruption, which is widespread in all impoverished and backward countries (or, more exactly, throughout the pre-industrial world), was endemic in a country where the servants of the state often had nothing to live on but their very meager salaries. The required attitude of obedience to superiors made it impossible for officials to demand higher salaries, and in the absence of any control over their activities from below it was inevitable that they should purloin from society what the state failed to provide. According to the usual pattern, a Chinese official entered upon his duties only after spending long years in study and passing many examinations; he then established relations with protectors, incurred debts to get himself appointed, and then proceeded to extract the amount he had spent on preparing himself for his career from the people he administered—and extracted both principal and interest. The degree of his rapacity would be dictated not only by the length of time he had had to wait for his appointment and the number of relations he had to support and of kin to satisfy or repay, but also by the precariousness of his position. [Balazs 1964, p. 10]

Enterprise, on the other hand, was not only frowned on, but may have been subjected to impediments deliberately imposed by the officials, at least after the fourteenth century A.D.; and some historians claim that it was true much earlier. Balazs tells us of

> the state's tendency to clamp down immediately on any form of private enterprise (and this in the long run kills not only initiative but even the slightest attempts at innovation), or, if it did not succeed in putting a stop to it in time, to take over

and nationalize it. Did it not frequently happen during the course of Chinese history that the scholar-officials, although hostile to all inventions, nevertheless gathered in the fruits of other people's ingenuity? I need mention only three examples of inventions that met this fate: paper, invented by a eunuch; printing, used by the Buddhists as a medium for religious propaganda; and the bill of exchange, an expedient of private businessmen. [P. 18]

As a result of recurrent intervention by the state to curtail the liberty and take over any accumulated advantages the merchant class had managed to gain for itself, "the merchant's ambition turned to becoming a scholar-official and investing his profits in land" (p. 32).

C. The Earlier Middle Ages

Before the rise of the cities and before monarchs were able to subdue the bellicose activities of the nobility, wealth and power were pursued primarily through military activity. Since land and castles were the medieval forms of wealth most highly valued and most avidly sought after, it seems reasonable to interpret the warring of the barons in good part as the pursuit of an economic objective. For example, during the reign of William the Conqueror (see, e.g., Douglas 1964), there were frequent attempts by the barons in Normandy and neighboring portions of France to take over each other's lands and castles. A prime incentive for William's supporters in his conquest of England was their obvious aspiration for lands.[5] More than that, violent means also served to provide more liquid forms of income (captured treasure), which the nobility used to support both private consumption and investment in military plant and equipment, where such items could not easily be produced on their own lands and therefore had to be purchased from others. In England, with its institution of primogeniture (the exclusive right of the eldest son to inherit his father's estate), younger sons who chose not to enter the clergy often had no socially acceptable choice other than warfare as a means to make their fortunes, and in some cases they succeeded spectacularly. Thus note the case of William Marshal, fourth son of a minor noble, who rose

---

[5] The conquest has at least two noteworthy entrepreneurial sides. First, it involved an innovation, the use of the stirrup by the Normans at Hastings that enabled William's warriors to use the same spear to impale a series of victims with the force of the horse's charge, rather than just tossing the spear at the enemy, much as an infantryman could. Second, the invasion was an impressive act of organization, with William having to convince his untrustworthy allies that they had more to gain by joining him in England than by staying behind to profit from his absence by trying to grab away his lands as they had tried to do many times before.

through his military accomplishments to be one of the most powerful and trusted officials under Henry II and Richard I, and became one of the wealthiest men in England (see Painter 1933).

Of course, the medieval nobles were not purely economic men. Many of the turbulent barons undoubtedly enjoyed fighting for its own sake, and success in combat was an important avenue to prestige in their society. But no modern capitalist is a purely economic man either. What I am saying here is that warfare, which was of course pursued for a variety of reasons, was *also* undertaken as a primary source of economic gain. This is clearly all the more true of the mercenary armies that were the scourge of fourteenth-century France and Italy.

Such violent economic activity, moreover, inspired frequent and profound innovation. The introduction of the stirrup was a requisite for effective cavalry tactics. Castle building evolved from wooden to stone structures and from rectangular to round towers (which could not be made to collapse by undermining their corners). Armor and weaponry became much more sophisticated with the introduction of the crossbow, the longbow, and, ultimately, artillery based on gunpowder. Military tactics and strategy also grew in sophistication. These innovations can be interpreted as contributions of military entrepreneurs undertaken at least partly in pursuit of private economic gains.

This type of entrepreneurial undertaking obviously differs vastly from the introduction of a cost-saving industrial process or a valuable new consumer product. An individual who pursues wealth through the forcible appropriation of the possessions of others surely does not add to the national product. Its net effect may be not merely a transfer but a net reduction in social income and wealth.[6]

---

[6] In saying all this, I must not be interpreted as taking the conventional view that warfare is an unmitigated source of impoverishment of any economy that unquestionably never contributes to its prosperity. Careful recent studies have indicated that matters are more complicated (see, e.g., Milward 1970; Olson 1982). Certainly the unprecedented prosperity enjoyed afterward by the countries on the losing side of the Second World War suggests that warfare need not always preclude economic expansion, and it is easy to provide earlier examples. The three great economic leaders of the Western world preceding the United States—Italy in the thirteenth–sixteenth centuries, the Dutch Republic in the seventeenth and eighteenth, and Great Britain in the eighteenth and nineteenth—each attained the height of their prosperity after periods of enormously costly and sometimes destructive warfare. Nevertheless, the wealth gained by a medieval baron from the adoption of a novel bellicose technique can hardly have contributed to economic growth in the way that resulted from adoption of a new steelmaking process in the nineteenth century or the introduction of a product such as the motor vehicle in the twentieth.

D. The Later Middle Ages

By the end of the eleventh century the rules of the game had changed from those of the Dark Ages. The revival of the towns was well under way. They had acquired a number of privileges, among them protection from arbitrary taxation and confiscation and the creation of a labor force by granting freedom to runaway serfs after a relatively brief residence (a year and a day) in the towns. The free-enterprise turbulence of the barons had at least been impeded by the church's pacification efforts: the peace and the (later) truce of God in France, Spain, and elsewhere; similar changes were taking place in England (see, e.g., Cowdrey [1970]; but Jones [1987, p. 94] suggests that some free-enterprise military activity by the barons continued in England through the reigns of the earlier Tudors in the sixteenth century). All this subsequently "gave way to more developed efforts to enforce peace by the more organized governments of the twelfth century" (Brooke 1964, p. 350; also p. 127). A number of activities that were neither agricultural nor military began to yield handsome returns. For example, the small group of architect-engineers who were in charge of the building of cathedrals, palaces, bridges, and fortresses could live in great luxury in the service of their kings.

But, apparently, a far more common source of earnings was the water-driven mills that were strikingly common in France and southern England by the eleventh century, a technological innovation about which more will be said presently. An incentive for such technical advances may have been the monopoly they conferred on their owners rather than any resulting improvement in efficiency. Such monopoly rights were alike sought and enforced by private parties (Bloch 1935, pp. 554–57; Brooke 1964, p. 84) and by religious organizations (see below).

The economic role of the monks in this is somewhat puzzling—the least clear-cut part of our story.[7] The Cistercian abbeys are generally assigned a critical role in the promotion of such technological advances. In some cases they simply took over mills that had been constructed by others (Berman 1986, p. 89). But the Cistercians improved them, built many others, and vastly expanded their use; at

---

[7] Bloch (1935) notes that the monasteries had both the capital and the large number of consumers of flour necessary to make the mills profitable. In addition, they were less likely than lay communities to undergo military siege, which, Bloch notes, was (besides drought and freezing of the waterways) one of the main impediments to adoption of the water mill, since blocking of the waterway that drove the mill could threaten the besieged population with starvation (pp. 550–53).

least some writers (e.g., Gimpel 1976, pp. 3–6) seem to suggest that the Cistercians were the spearhead of technological advance.

Historians tell us that they have no ready explanation for the entrepreneurial propensities of this monastic order. (See, e.g., Brooke [1964, p. 69] and also a personal communication to me from Constance Berman. Ovitt [1987, esp. pp. 142–47] suggests that this may all have been part of the twelfth-century monastic drive to reduce or eliminate manual labor in order to maximize the time available for the less onerous religious labors—a conclusion with which Bloch [1935, p. 553] concurs.) But the evidence suggests strongly that avid entrepreneurs they were. They accumulated vast tracts of land; the sizes of their domesticated animal flocks were enormous by the standards of the time; their investment rates were remarkable; they sought to exercise monopoly power, being known, after the erection of a water mill, to seek legal intervention to prevent nearby residents from continuing to use their animal-powered facilities (Gimpel 1976, pp. 15–16); they were fierce in their rivalrous behavior and drive for expansion, in the process not sparing other religious bodies—not even other Cistercian houses. There is a "record of pastoral expansionism and monopolies over access established by the wealthiest Cistercian houses . . . at the expense of smaller abbeys and convents . . . effectively pushing out all other religious houses as competitors" (Berman 1986, p. 112).

As with early capitalists, the asceticism of the monks, by keeping down the proportion of the monastery's output that was consumed, helped to provide the resources for levels of investment extraordinary for the period (pp. 40, 83). The rules of the game appear to have offered substantial economic rewards to exercise of Cistercian entrepreneurship. The order obtained relatively few large gifts, but instead frequently received support from the laity and from the church establishment in the form of exemptions from road and river tolls and from payment of the tithe. This obviously increased the *marginal* yield of investment, innovation, and expenditure of effort, and the evidence suggests the diligence of the order in pursuing the resulting opportunities. Their mills, their extensive lands, and their large flocks are reported to have brought scale economies and extraordinary financial returns (chap. 4). Puritanical, at least in earlier years, in their self-proclaimed adherence to simplicity in personal lifestyle while engaged in dedicated pursuit of wealth, they may perhaps represent an early manifestation of elements of "the Protestant ethic." But whatever their motive, the reported Cistercian record of promotion of technological progress is in diametric contrast to that of the Roman empire.

E. Fourteenth Century

The fourteenth century brought with it a considerable increase in military activity, notably the Hundred Years' War between France and England. Payoffs, surely, must have tilted to favor more than before inventions designed for military purposes. Cannons appeared as siege devices and armor was made heavier. More imaginative war devices were proposed: a windmill-propelled war wagon, a multibarreled machine gun, and a diving suit to permit underwater attacks on ships. A pervasive business enterprise of this unhappy century of war was the company of mercenary troops—the *condottiere*—who roamed Europe, supported the side that could offer the most attractive terms, and in lulls between fighting, when unemployment threatened, wandered about thinking up military enterprises of their own, at the expense of the general public (Gimpel 1976, chap. 9; see also McNeill 1969, pp. 33–39). Clearly, the rules of the game—the system of entrepreneurial rewards—had changed, to the disadvantage of productive entrepreneurship.

F. Early Rent Seeking

Unproductive entrepreneurship can also take less violent forms, usually involving various types of rent seeking, the type of (possibly) unproductive entrepreneurship that seems most relevant today. Enterprising use of the legal system for rent-seeking purposes has a long history. There are, for example, records of the use of litigation in the twelfth century in which the proprietor of a water-driven mill sought and won a prohibition of use in the vicinity of mills driven by animal or human power (Gimpel 1976, pp. 25–26). In another case, the operators of two dams, one upstream of the other, sued one another repeatedly at least from the second half of the thirteenth century until the beginning of the fifteenth, when the downstream dam finally succeeded in driving the other out of business as the latter ran out of money to pay the court fees (pp. 17–20).

In the upper strata of society, rent seeking also gradually replaced military activity as a prime source of wealth and power. This transition can perhaps be ascribed to the triumph of the monarchies and the consequent imposition of law and order. Rent-seeking entrepreneurship then took a variety of forms, notably the quest for grants of land and patents of monopoly from the monarch. Such activities can, of course, sometimes prove to contribute to production, as when the recipient of land given by the monarch uses it more efficiently than the previous owner did. But there seems to have been nothing in the structure of the land-granting process that ensured even a tendency toward transfer to more productive proprietors, nor was the individual who sought such grants likely to use as an argument in favor of his suit the claim that he was likely to be the more productive user (in terms of, say, the expected net value of its agricultural output).

Military forms of entrepreneurship may have experienced a renaissance in England in the seventeenth century with the revolt against Charles I. How that may have changed the structure of rewards to entrepreneurial activity is suggested by Hobsbawm (1969), who claims that at the end of the seventeenth century the most affluent merchants earned perhaps three times as much as the richest "master manufacturers."[8] But, he reports, the wealthiest noble families probably had incomes more than 10 times as large as those of the rich merchants. The point in this is that those noble families, according to Hobsbawm, were no holdovers from an ancient feudal aristocracy; they were, rather, the heirs of the Roundheads (the supporters of the parliamentary, or puritan, party) in the then-recent Civil War (pp. 30–32). On this view, once again, military activity would seem to have become the entrepreneur's most promising recourse.

But other historians take a rather different view of the matter. Studies reported in Thirsk (1954) indicate that ultimately there was little redistribution of property as the result of the Civil War and the restoration. Rather it is noted that in this period the "patrician élites depended for their political power and economic prosperity on royal charters and monopolies rather than on talent and entrepreneurial initiative" (Stone 1985, p. 45). In this interpretation of the matter, it was rent seeking, not military activity, that remained the prime source of wealth under the restoration.

By the time the eighteenth-century industrial revolution ("the" industrial revolution) arrived, matters had changed once again. According to Ashton (1948, pp. 9–10), grants of monopoly were in good part "swept away" by the Monopolies Act of 1624, and, we are told by Adam Smith (1776), by the end of the eighteenth century they were rarer in England than in any other country. Though industrial activity continued to be considered somewhat degrading in places in which industry flourished, notably in England during the industrial revolution there was probably a difference in degree. Thus Lefebvre (1947, p. 14) reports that "at its upper level the [French] nobility . . . were envious of the English lords who enriched themselves in bourgeois

---

[8] The evidence indicates that the wealth of affluent families in Great Britain continues to be derived preponderantly from commerce rather than from industry. This contrasts with the record for the United States, where the reverse appears to be true (see Rubinstein 1980, pp. 22–23, 59–60).

ways," while in France "the noble 'derogated' or fell into the common mass if [like Mirabeau] he followed a business or profession" (p. 11). (See, however, Schama [1989], who tells us that "even a cursory examination of the eighteenth-century French economy . . . reveals the nobility deeply involved in finance, business and industry—certainly as much as their British counterparts. . . . In 1765 a royal edict officially removed the last formal obstacles to their participation in trade and industry" [p. 118].) In England, primogeniture, by forcing younger sons of noble families to resort to commerce and industry, apparently was imparting respectability to these activities to a degree that, while rather limited, may have rarely been paralleled before.

The central point of all the preceding discussion seems clear— perhaps, in retrospect, self-evident. If entrepreneurship is the imaginative pursuit of position, with limited concern about the means used to achieve the purpose, then we can expect changes in the structure of rewards to modify the nature of the entrepreneur's activities, sometimes drastically. The rules of the game can then be a critical influence helping to determine whether entrepreneurship will be allocated predominantly to activities that are productive or unproductive and even destructive.

IV. Does the Allocation between Productive and Unproductive Entrepreneurship Matter Much?

We come now to the third proposition of this article.

PROPOSITION 3. The allocation of entrepreneurship between productive and unproductive activities, though by no means the only pertinent influence, can have a profound effect on the innovativeness of the economy and the degree of dissemination of its technological discoveries.

It is hard to believe that a system of payoffs that moves entrepreneurship in unproductive directions is not a substantial impediment to industrial innovation and growth in productivity. Still, history permits no test of this proposition through a set of anything resembling controlled experiments, since other influences *did*, undoubtedly, also play important roles, as the proposition recognizes. One can only note what appears to be a remarkable correlation between the degree to which an economy rewarded productive entrepreneurship and the vigor shown in that economy's innovation record.

Historians tell us of several industrial "near revolutions" that occurred before *the* industrial revolution of the eighteenth century that are highly suggestive for our purposes (Braudel [1986, 3:542–56]; for a more skeptical view, see Coleman [1956]). We are told that two of the incipient revolutions never went anywhere, while two of them were rather successful in their fashion. I shall report conclusions of some leading historians on these episodes, but it should be recognized by the reader that many of the views summarized here have been disputed in the historical literature, at least to some degree.

A. Rome and Hellenistic Egypt

My earlier discussion cited ancient Rome and its empire as a case in which the rules did not favor productive entrepreneurship. Let us compare this with the evidence on the vigor of innovative activity in that society. The museum at Alexandria was the center of technological innovation in the Roman empire. By the first century B.C., that city knew of virtually every form of machine gearing that is used today, including a working steam engine. But these seem to have been used only to make what amounted to elaborate toys. The steam engine was used only to open and close the doors of a temple.

The Romans also had the water mill. This may well have been the most critical pre-eighteenth-century industrial invention because (outside the use of sails in transportation by water) it provided the first significant source of power other than human and animal labor: "it was able to produce an amount of concentrated energy beyond any other resource of antiquity" (Forbes 1955, 2:90). As steam did in more recent centuries, it offered the prospect of providing the basis for a leap in productivity in the Roman economy, as apparently it actually did during the eleventh, twelfth, and thirteenth centuries in Europe. Yet Finley (1965, pp. 35–36), citing White (1962), reports that "though it was invented in the first century B.C., is was not until the third century A.D. that we find evidence of much use, and not until the fifth and sixth of general use. It is also a fact that we have no evidence at all of its application to other industries [i.e., other than grinding of grain] until the very end of the fourth century, and then no more than one solitary and possibly suspect reference . . . to a marble-slicing machine near Trier."

Unfortunately, evidence of Roman technical stagnation is only spotty, and, further, some historians suggest that the historical reports give inadequate weight to the Roman preoccupation with agricultural improvement relative to improvement in commerce or manufacture. Still, the following quotation seems to summarize the weight of opinion: "Historians have long been puzzled as to why the landlords of the Middle Ages proved so much more enterprising than the landlords of the Roman Empire, although the latter, by and large, were much better educated, had much better opportunities for making technical and scientific discoveries if they had wished to do so"

(Brooke 1964, p. 88). It seems at least plausible that some part of the explanation is to be found in the ancient world's rules of the game, which encouraged the pursuit of wealth but severely discouraged its pursuit through the exercise of productive entrepreneurship.[9]

B. Medieval China

The spate of inventions that occurred in ancient China (before it was conquered by the barbarian Yuan dynasty in 1280) constituted one of the earliest potential revolutions in industry. Among the many Chinese technological contributions, one can list paper, (perhaps) the compass, waterwheels, sophisticated water clocks, and, of course, gunpowder. Yet despite the apparent prosperity of the Sung period (960–1270) (see, e.g., Liu and Golas 1969), at least some historians suggest that none of this spate of inventions led to a flowering of *industry*[10] as distinguished from commerce and some degree of general prosperity. And in China too, as we have seen, the rules did not favor productive entrepreneurship. Balazs (1964, p. 53) concludes that

> what was chiefly lacking in China for the further development of capitalism was not mechanical skill or scientific aptitude, nor a sufficient accumulation of wealth, but scope for individual enterprise. There was no individual freedom and no security for private enterprise, no legal foundation for rights other than those of the state, no alternative investment other than landed property, no guarantee against being penalized by arbitrary exactions from officials or against intervention by the state. But perhaps the supreme inhibiting

[9] It has been suggested by historians (see, e.g., Bloch 1935, p. 547) that an abundance of slaves played a key role in Roman failure to use the water mill widely. However, this must imply that the Romans were not efficient wealth seekers. As the cliometric literature has made clear, the cost of maintaining a slave is not low and certainly is not zero, and slaves are apt not to be efficient and dedicated workers. Thus if it had been efficient to replace human or animal power by the inanimate power of the waterways, failure to do so would have cut into the wealth of the slaveholder, in effect saddling him with the feeding of unproductive persons or keeping the slaves who turned the mills from other, more lucrative, occupations. Perhaps Roman landowners *were* fairly unsophisticated in the management of their estates, as Finley (1985, pp. 108–16) suggests, and, if so, there may be some substance to the hypothesis that slavery goes far to account for the failure of water mills to spread in the Roman economy.

[10] Also, as in Rome, none of this was associated with the emergence of a systematic body of science involving coherent theoretical structure and the systematic testing of hypotheses on the basis of experiment or empirical observation. Here, too, the thirteenth-century work of Bishop Grosseteste, William of Henley, and Roger Bacon was an early step toward that unique historical phenomenon—the emergence of a systematic body of science in the West in, say, the sixteenth century (see Needham 1956).

factor was the overwhelming prestige of the state bureaucracy, which maimed from the start any attempt of the
bourgeoisie to be different, to become aware of themselves
as a class and fight for an autonomous position in society.
Free enterprise, ready and proud to take risks, is therefore
quite exceptional and abnormal in Chinese economic history.

C. Slow Growth in the "Dark Ages"

An era noted for its slow growth occurred between the death of
Charlemagne (814) and the end of the tenth century. Even this period
was not without its economic advances, which developed slowly, including the beginnings of the agricultural improvements that attended the introduction of the horseshoe, harness, and stirrup, the
heavy plow, and the substitution of horsepower for oxen, which may
have played a role in enabling peasants to move to more populous
villages further from their fields (see White 1962, p. 39 ff.). But, still,
it was probably a period of significantly slower growth than the industrial revolution of the eleventh–thirteenth centuries (Gimpel 1976),
about which more will be said presently. We have already seen that
this was a period in which military violence was a prime outlet for
entrepreneurial activity. While this can hardly pretend to be *the* explanation of the relative stagnation of the era, it is hard to believe that it
was totally unimportant.

D. The "High Middle Ages"

A good deal has already been said about the successful industrial
revolution (and the accompanying commercial revolution sparked by
inventions such as double-entry bookkeeping and bills of exchange
[de Roover 1953]) of the late Middle Ages, whose two-century duration makes it as long-lived as our own (see Carus-Wilson 1941; White
1962; Gimpel 1976).

Perhaps the hallmark of this industrial revolution was that remarkable source of productive power, the water mills, that covered the
countryside in the south of England and crowded the banks of the
Seine in Paris (see, e.g., Gimpel 1976, pp. 3–6; Berman 1986, pp. 81–
89). The mills were not only simple grain-grinding devices but accomplished an astonishing variety of tasks and involved an impressive
variety of mechanical devices and sophisticated gear arrangements.
They crushed olives, ground mash for beer production, crushed cloth
for papermaking, sawed lumber, hammered metal and woolens (as
part of the "fulling" process—the cleansing, scouring, and pressing of

woven woolen goods to make them stronger and to bring the threads closer together), milled coins, polished armor, and operated the bellows of blast furnaces. Their mechanisms entailed many forms of ingenuity. Gears were used to translate the vertical circular motion of the efficient form of the waterwheel into the horizontal circular motion of the millstone. The cam (a piece attached, say, to the axle of the waterwheel, protruding from the axle at right angles to its axis of rotation) served to lift a hammer and to drop it repeatedly and automatically (it was apparently known in antiquity, but may not have been used with waterwheels). A crank handle extending from the end of the axle transformed the circular motion of the wheel into the back and forth (reciprocating) motion required for sawing or the operation of bellows. The most sophisticated product of all this mechanical skill and knowledge was the mechanical clock, which appeared toward the end of the thirteenth century. As White (1962, p. 129) sums up the matter, "the four centuries following Leonardo, that is, until electrical energy demanded a supplementary set of devices, were less technologically engaged in discovering basic principles than in elaborating and refining those established during the four centuries before Leonardo."[11]

In a period in which agriculture probably occupied some 90 percent of the population, the expansion of industry in the twelfth and thirteenth centuries could not by itself have created a major upheaval in living standards.[12] Moreover, it has been deduced from what little we know of European gross domestic product per capita at the beginning of the eighteenth century that its average growth in the preceding six or seven centuries must have been very modest, since if the poverty of that later time had represented substantial growth from

[11] As was already noted, science and scientific method also began to make an appearance with contributions such as those of Bishop Grosseteste and Roger Bacon. Walter of Henley championed controlled experiments and observation over recourse to the opinions of ancient authorities and made a clear distinction between economic and engineering efficiency in discussing the advisability of substituting horses for oxen. Bacon displayed remarkable foresight when he wrote, circa 1260, that "machines may be made by which the largest ships, with only one man steering them, will be moved faster than if they were filled with rowers; wagons may be built which will move with incredible speed and without the aid of beasts; flying machines can be constructed in which a man . . . may beat the air with wings like a bird . . . machines will make it possible to go to the bottom of seas and rivers" (as quoted in White [1962, p. 134]).

[12] But then, much the same was true of the first half century of "our" industrial revolution, which, until the coming of the railways, was centered on the production of cotton that perhaps constituted only some 7–8 percent of national output (Hobsbawm 1969, p. 68). Initially, the eighteenth-century industrial revolution was a very minor affair, at least in terms of investment levels and contributions to output and to growth in productivity (perhaps 0.3 percent per year) (see Landes 1969, pp. 64–65; Feinstein 1978, pp. 40–41; Williamson 1984).

eleventh-century living standards, much of the earlier population would surely have been condemned to starvation.

Still, the industrial activity of the twelfth and thirteenth centuries was very substantial. By the beginning of the fourteenth century, according to Gimpel (1976), 68 mills were in operation on less than one mile of the banks of the Seine in Paris, and these were supplemented by floating mills anchored to the Grand Pont. The activity in metallurgy was also considerable—sufficient to denude much of Europe of its forests and to produce a rise in the price of wood that forced recourse to coal (Nef [1934]; other historians assert that this did not occur to any substantial degree until the fifteenth or sixteenth century, with some question even about those dates; see, e.g., Coleman [1975, pp. 42–43]). In sum, the industrial revolution of the twelfth and thirteenth centuries was a surprisingly robust affair, and it is surely plausible that improved rewards to industrial activity had something to do with its vigor.

E. The Fourteenth-Century Retreat

The end of all this period of buoyant activity in the fourteenth century (see the classic revisionist piece by Lopez [1969] as well as Gimpel [1976, chap. 9]) has a variety of explanations, many of them having no connection with entrepreneurship. For one thing, it has been deduced by study of the glaciers that average temperatures dropped, possibly reducing the yield of crops (though recent studies indicate that the historical relation between climatic changes and crop yields is at best ambiguous) and creating other hardships. The plague returned and decimated much of the population. In addition to these disasters of nature, there were at least two pertinent developments of human origin. First, the church clamped down on new ideas and other manifestations of freedom. Roger Bacon himself was put under constraint.[13] The period during which new ways of thinking brought rewards and status was apparently ended. Second, the fourteenth century included the first half of the devastating Hundred Years' War. It is implausible that the associated renewal of rewards to military enterprise played no part in the economic slowdown.

F. Remark on "Our" Industrial Revolution

It need hardly be added, in conclusion, that *the* industrial revolution that began in the eighteenth century and continues today has brought

---

[13] The restraints imposed by the church had another curious effect: they apparently made bathing unfashionable for centuries. Before then, bathhouses had been popular as centers for social and, perhaps, sexual activity; but by requiring separation of the sexes and otherwise limiting the pleasures of cleanliness, the church undermined the inducements for such sanitary activities (see Gimpel 1976, pp. 87–92).

to the industrialist and the businessperson generally a degree of wealth and a respect probably unprecedented in human history. The fact that this period yielded an explosion of output at least equally unprecedented is undoubtedly attributable to a myriad of causes that can probably never be discovered fully and whose roles can never be disentangled. Yet the continued association of output growth with high financial and respectability rewards to productive entrepreneurship is surely suggestive, even if it can hardly be taken to be conclusive evidence for proposition 3, which asserts that the allocation of entrepreneurship *does* really matter for the vigor and innovativeness of an economy.

V. On Unproductive Avenues for Today's Entrepreneur: A Delicate Balance

Today, unproductive entrepreneurship takes many forms. Rent seeking, often via activities such as litigation and takeovers, and tax evasion and avoidance efforts seem now to constitute the prime threat to productive entrepreneurship. The spectacular fortunes amassed by the "arbitrageurs" revealed by the scandals of the mid-1980s were *sometimes,* surely, the reward of unproductive, occasionally illegal but entrepreneurial acts. Corporate executives devote much of their time and energy to legal suit and countersuit, and litigation is used to blunt or prevent excessive vigor in competition by rivals. Huge awards by the courts, sometimes amounting to billions of dollars, can bring prosperity to the victor and threaten the loser with insolvency. When this happens, it must become tempting for the entrepreneur to select his closest advisers from the lawyers rather than the engineers. It induces the entrepreneur to spend literally hundreds of millions of dollars for a single legal battle. It tempts that entrepreneur to be the first to sue others before those others can sue him. (For an illuminating quantification of some of the social costs of one widely publicized legal battle between two firms, see Summers and Cutler [1988].)

Similarly, taxes can serve to redirect entrepreneurial effort. As Lindbeck (1987, p. 15) has observed, "the problem with high-tax societies is not that it is impossible to become rich there, but that it is difficult to do so by way of productive effort in the ordinary production system." He cites as examples of the resulting reallocation of entrepreneurship " 'smart' speculative financial transactions without much (if any) contribution to the productive capacity of the economy" (p. 15) as well as "illegal 'business areas' such as drug dealing" (p. 25).

In citing such activities, I do not mean to imply either that rent-seeking activity has been expanding in recent decades or that takeover bids or private antitrust suits are always or even preponderantly unproductive. Rather, I am only suggesting where current rent-seeking activities are likely to be found, that is, where policy designers should look if they intend to divert entrepreneurial talents into more productive channels.

The main point here is to note that threats of takeovers are sometimes used as a means to extract "greenmail" and that recourse to the courts as a means to seek to preserve rents through legally imposed impediments to competition does indeed occur, and to suggest that it is no rare phenomenon. This does, then, become an attraction for entrepreneurial talent whose efforts are thereby channeled into unproductive directions. Yet, to the extent that takeovers discipline inefficient managements and that antitrust intervention sometimes is legitimate and sometimes contributes to productivity, it would seem that it will not be easy to change the rules in a way that discourages allocation of entrepreneurial effort into such activities, without at the same time undermining the legitimate role of these institutions. Some promising proposals have been offered, but this is not a suitable place for their systematic examination. However, a few examples will be reported in the following section.

VI.   Changes in the Rules and Changes in Entrepreneurial Goals

A central point in this discussion is the contention that if reallocation of entrepreneurial effort is adopted as an objective of society, it is far more easily achieved through changes in the rules that determine relative rewards than via modification of the goals of the entrepreneurs and prospective entrepreneurs themselves. I have even gone so far as to use the same terms to characterize those goals in the very different eras and cultures referred to in the discussion. But it would be ridiculous to imply that the attitudes of a wealth-seeking senator in Rome, a Sung dynasty mandarin, and an American industrialist of the late nineteenth century were all virtually identical. Still, the evidence suggests that they had more in common than might have been expected by the casual observer. However, even if it were to transpire that they really diverged very substantially, that would be of little use to the designer of policy who does not have centuries at his or her disposal and who is notoriously ineffective in engendering profound changes in cultural influences or in the structure of preferences. It is for this reason that I have chosen to take entrepreneurial goals as given and to emphasize modification in the structure of the rewards to different activities as the more promising line of investigation.

This suggests that it is necessary to consider the process by which those rules are modified in practice, but I believe that answers to even this more restricted question are largely beyond the powers of the historians, the sociologists, and the anthropologists into whose domains it falls. One need only review the disputatious literature on the influences that led to the revival of trade toward the end of the early Middle Ages to see how far we still are from anything resembling firm answers. Exogenous influences such as foreign invasions or unexpected climatic changes can clearly play a part, as can developments within the economy. But the more interesting observation for our purposes is the fact that it is easy to think of measures that *can* change these rules quickly and profoundly.[14]

For example, the restrictions on royal grants of monopolies imposed by Parliament in the Statute of Monopolies are said to have reduced substantially the opportunities for rent seeking in seventeenth- and eighteenth-century England and may have moved reluctant entrepreneurs to redirect their efforts toward agricultural improvement and industry. Even if it did not succeed to any substantial extent in reallocation of the efforts of an unchanged body of entrepreneurs from one of those types of activity to the other, if it increased failure rates among the rent seekers while not impeding others who happened to prefer productive pursuits, the result might have been the same. Similarly, tax rules can be used to rechannel entrepreneurial effort. It has, for instance, been proposed that takeover activity would be reoriented substantially in directions that contribute to productivity rather than impeding it by a "revenue-neutral" modification in capital gains taxes that increases rates sharply on assets held for short periods and decreases them considerably for assets held, say, for 2 years or more. A change in the rules that requires a plaintiff firm in a private antitrust suit to bear both parties' legal costs if the defendants are found not to be guilty (as is done in other countries) promises to reduce the frequency with which such lawsuits are used in an attempt to hamper effective competition.

As has already been said, this is hardly the place for an extensive discussion of the design of rational policy in the arena under consideration. The objective of the preceding brief discussion, rather, has been to suggest that there are identifiable means by which the rules of the game can be changed effectively and to illustrate these means concretely, though hardly attempting to offer any generalizations about their character. Certainly, the few illustrations that have just been offered should serve to confirm that there exist (in principle)

---

[14] Of course, that still leaves open the critical metaquestion, How does one go about changing the society's value system so that it will *want* to change the rules? But that is not the issue with which I am grappling here, since I see no basis on which the economist can argue that society *ought* to change its values. Rather, I am positing a society whose values lead it to favor productivity growth and am examining which instruments promise to be most effective in helping it to pursue this goal.

testable means that promise to induce entrepreneurs to shift their attentions in productive directions, *without any major change in their ultimate goals.* The testability of such hypotheses indicates that the discussion is no tissue of tautologies, and the absence of references to the allocability of entrepreneurship turned up in extensive search of the literature on the entrepreneur suggests that it was not entirely self-evident.

VII. Concluding Comment

There is obviously a good deal more to be said about the subject; however, enough material has been presented to indicate that a minor expansion of Schumpeter's theoretical model to encompass the determinants of the *allocation* of entrepreneurship among its competing uses can enrich the model considerably and that the hypotheses that have been associated with the model's extension here are not without substance, even if none of the material approaches anything that constitutes a formal test of a hypothesis, much less a rigorous "proof." It is also easy to confirm that each of the hypotheses that have been discussed clearly yields some policy implications.

Thus clear guidance for policy is provided by the main hypothesis (propositions 1–3) that the rules of the game that specify the relative payoffs to different entrepreneurial activities play a key role in determining whether entrepreneurship will be allocated in productive or unproductive directions and that this can significantly affect the vigor of the economy's productivity growth. After all, the prevailing laws and legal procedures of an economy are prime determinants of the profitability of activities such as rent seeking via the litigative process. Steps such as deregulation of the airlines or more rational antitrust rules can do a good deal here.

A last example can, perhaps, nail down the point. The fact that Japan has far fewer lawyers relative to population and far fewer lawsuits on economic issues is often cited as a distinct advantage to the Japanese economy, since it reduces at least in part the quantity of resources devoted to rent seeking. The difference is often ascribed to national character that is said to have a cultural aversion to litigiousness. This may all be very true. But closer inspection reveals that there are also other influences. While in the United States legal institutions such as trebled damages provide a rich incentive for one firm to sue another on the claim that the latter violated the antitrust laws, in Japan the arrangements are very different. In that country any firm undertaking to sue another on antitrust grounds must first apply for permission from the Japan Fair Trade Commission. But such permission is rarely given, and, once denied, there is no legal avenue for appeal.

The overall moral, then, is that we do not have to wait patiently for slow cultural change in order to find measures to redirect the flow of entrepreneurial activity toward more productive goals. As in the illustration of the Japanese just cited, it may be possible to change the rules in ways that help to offset undesired institutional influences or that supplement other influences that are taken to work in beneficial directions.

References

Abramovitz, Moses. *Thinking about Growth, and Other Essays of Economic Growth and Welfare.* New York: Cambridge Univ. Press, 1989.
Ashton, Thomas S. *The Industrial Revolution, 1760–1830.* London: Oxford Univ. Press, 1948.
Balazs, Etienne. *Chinese Civilization and Bureaucracy: Variations on a Theme.* New Haven, Conn.: Yale Univ. Press, 1964.
Berman, Constance H. "Medieval Agriculture, the Southern French Countryside, and the Early Cistercians: A Study of Forty-three Monasteries." *Trans. American Philosophical Soc.* 76, pt. 5 (1986).
Bloch, Marc. "Avènement et conquêtes du moulin a eau." *Annales d'Histoire Économique et Sociale* 7 (November 1935): 538–63.
Braudel, Fernand. *Civilization and Capitalism, 15th–18th Century.* Vols. 2, 3. New York: Harper and Row, 1986.
Brooke, Christopher N. L. *Europe in the Central Middle Ages, 962–1154.* London: Longman, 1964.
Carus-Wilson, Eleanora M. "An Industrial Revolution of the Thirteenth Century." *Econ. Hist. Rev.* 11, no. 1 (1941): 39–60.
Coleman, Donald C. "Industrial Growth and Industrial Revolutions." *Economica* 23 (February 1956): 1–22.
———. *Industry in Tudor and Stuart England.* London: Macmillan (for Econ. Hist. Soc.), 1975.
Cowdrey, H. E. J. "The Peace and the Truce of God in the Eleventh Century." *Past and Present,* no. 46 (February 1970), pp. 42–67.
Dasgupta, Partha. "Patents, Priority and Imitation or, the Economics of Races and Waiting Games." *Econ. J.* 98 (March 1988): 66–80.
de Roover, Raymond. "The Commercial Revolution of the 13th Century." In *Enterprise and Secular Change: Readings in Economic History,* edited by Frederic C. Lane and Jelle C. Riemersma. London: Allen and Unwin, 1953.
Douglas, David C. *William the Conqueror: The Norman Impact upon England.* Berkeley: Univ. California Press, 1964.
Feinstein, C. H. "Capital Formation in Great Britain." In *The Cambridge Economic History of Europe,* vol. 8, pt. 1, edited by Peter Mathias and M. M. Postan. Cambridge: Cambridge Univ. Press, 1978.
Finley, Moses I. "Technical Innovation and Economic Progress in the Ancient World." *Econ. Hist. Rev.* 18 (August 1965): 29–45.
———. *The Ancient Economy.* 2d ed. London: Hogarth, 1985.
Forbes, Robert J. *Studies in Ancient Technology.* Leiden: Brill, 1955.

Gimpel, Jean. *The Medieval Machine: The Industrial Revolution of the Middle Ages.* New York: Holt, Reinhart and Winston, 1976.

Ho, Ping-Ti. *The Ladder of Success in Imperial China, 1368–1911.* New York: Columbia Univ. Press, 1962.

Hobsbawm, Eric J. *Industry and Empire from 1750 to the Present Day.* Harmondsworth: Penguin, 1969.

Jones, Eric L. *The European Miracle: Environments, Economies, and Geopolitics in the History of Europe and Asia.* Cambridge: Cambridge Univ. Press, 1987.

Landes, David S. *The Unbound Prometheus: Technological Change and Industrial Development in Western Europe from 1750 to the Present.* New York: Cambridge Univ. Press, 1969.

Lefebvre, Georges. *The Coming of the French Revolution, 1789.* Princeton, N.J.: Princeton Univ. Press, 1947.

Lindbeck, Assar. "The Advanced Welfare State." Manuscript. Stockholm: Univ. Stockholm, 1987.

Liu, James T. C., and Golas, Peter J., eds. *Change in Sung China: Innovation or Renovation?* Lexington, Mass.: Heath, 1969.

Lopez, Robert S. "Hard Times and Investment in Culture." In *The Renaissance: A Symposium.* New York: Oxford Univ. Press (for Metropolitan Museum of Art), 1969.

McNeill, William H. *History of Western Civilization.* Rev. ed. Chicago: Univ. Chicago Press, 1969.

Marsh, Robert M. *The Mandarins: The Circulation of Elites in China, 1600–1900.* Glencoe, Ill.: Free Press, 1961.

Milward, Alan S. *The Economic Effects of the Two World Wars on Britain.* London: Macmillan (for Econ. Hist. Soc.), 1970.

Murphy, Kevin M.; Shleifer, Andrei; and Vishny, Robert. "The Allocation of Talent: Implications for Growth." Manuscript. Chicago: Univ. Chicago, 1990.

Needham, Joseph. "Mathematics and Science in China and the West." *Science and Society* 20 (Fall 1956): 320–43.

Nef, John U. "The Progress of Technology and the Growth of Large-Scale Industry in Great Britain, 1540–1640." *Econ. Hist. Rev.* 5 (October 1934): 3–24.

North, Douglass C., and Thomas, Robert Paul. *The Rise of the Western World: A New Economic History.* Cambridge: Cambridge Univ. Press, 1973.

Olson, Mancur. *The Rise and Decline of Nations: Economic Growth, Stagflation, and Social Rigidities.* New Haven, Conn.: Yale Univ. Press, 1982.

Ovitt, George, Jr. *The Restoration of Perfection: Labor and Technology in Medieval Culture.* New Brunswick, N.J.: Rutgers Univ. Press, 1987.

Painter, Sidney. *William Marshal: Knight-Errant, Baron, and Regent of England.* Baltimore: Johns Hopkins Press, 1933.

Robinson, Joan. *The Economics of Imperfect Competition.* London: Macmillan, 1933.

Rosenberg, Nathan, and Birdzell, L. E., Jr. *How the West Grew Rich: The Economic Transformation of the Industrial World.* New York: Basic Books, 1986.

Rubinstein, W. D., ed. *Wealth and the Wealthy in the Modern World.* London: Croom Helm, 1980.

Schama, Simon. *Citizens: A Chronicle of the French Revolution.* New York: Knopf, 1989.

Schumpeter, Joseph A. *The Theory of Economic Development.* Leipzig: Duncker and Humblot, 1912. English ed. Cambridge, Mass.: Harvard Univ. Press, 1934.

ENTREPRENEURSHIP 921

Smith, Adam. *An Inquiry into the Nature and Causes of the Wealth of Nations.* 1776. Reprint. New York: Random House (Modern Library), 1937.
Stone, Lawrence. "The Bourgeois Revolution of Seventeenth-Century England Revisited." *Past and Present,* no. 109 (November 1985), pp. 44–54.
Summers, Lawrence, and Cutler, David. "Texaco and Pennzoil Both Lost Big." *New York Times* (February 14, 1988).
Thirsk, Joan. "The Restoration Land Settlement." *J. Modern Hist.* 26 (December 1954): 315–28.
Veblen, Thorstein. *The Theory of Business Enterprise.* New York: Scribner, 1904.
Veyne, Paul. "Vie de trimalcion." *Annales: Économies, Societés, Civilisations* 16 (March/April 1961): 213–47.
White, Lynn T., Jr. *Medieval Technology and Social Change.* Oxford: Clarendon, 1962.
Williamson, Jeffrey G. "Why Was British Growth So Slow during the Industrial Revolution?" *J. Econ. Hist.* 44 (September 1984): 687–712.

[5]

Technical Entrepreneurship: An International Perspective

Kathleen M. Eisenhardt
Naushad Forbes

An analysis of technical entrepreneurship in the United States, Great Britain, Japan and India makes clear—a regenerative capital cycle, incubator companies, social and technical volatility and a supportive culture are the common denominators of high rates of technical entrepreneurship throughout the world.

TECHNICAL ENTREPRENEUR-SHIP is an increasingly popular topic in many parts of the world. Following the dramatic success of such ventures in the US, governments such as those of Ireland, Sweden, Taiwan, and Korea are attempting to foster technical entrepreneurs through myriad ideas such as industrial centers, tax incentives, government loan programs, and expanded stock market opportunities. For many regions and countries, the start-up of technically innovative companies is seen as a source of continuing technical and economic vitality, and possibly even the source of a technical renaissance. All start-ups create jobs and, in the long term, technical firms seem to perform particularly well in this regard. Technical start-ups also play an important role

Ms. Eisenhardt is an assistant professor in the Department of Industrial Engineering and Engineering Management at Stanford University. Her research interests are design, decision-making and performance, especially in high-technology firms.

Mr. Forbes is a Ph.D. candidate of the Department of Engineering and Engineering Management at Stanford. His research interest is technical entrepreneurship.

in innovation and have generated a disproportionate share of the commercial innovations in industries such as electronics and biotechnology. Although the size of their importance to innovation is debated, start-ups appear to have several advantages. They are better able to exploit new market niches which may initially be too small for larger, more established firms. They often have fewer commitments to the status quo and their tenuous economic position keeps them very close to the actual needs of the marketplace. One has only to think of the government's inability to pick "technology winners" in the UK to see the merits of the start-up company approach to innovation. Add these considerations to those of the importance of a native-owned industrial base and a slowdown of the "brain drain" in many countries, then it is not surprising to see world-wide interest in technical entrepreneurship.

Despite widespread interest in technical start-ups, the question of how to encourage their formation remains an elusive problem. Are financial resources such as venture capital, the

existence of an over-the-counter market, or a wealthy elite the key? Or are other resources, such as universities, a scientifically trained labor pool, or incubator companies, more important? What role does government play? Does culture really constitute a barrier and if so does entrepreneurship require economic, technological, or social instability to get people to move in new ways?

This paper begins to grapple with these questions. Our approach is to review some of the experience with technical entrepreneurship in four countries: the United States, United Kingdom, Japan, and India. We focus on the US because it is the world leader in technical entrepreneurship. We focus on the UK because it is the "birthplace" of technical entrepreneurship, and it has a moderate but increasing rate of technical entrepreneurship. Our third case, Japan, is clearly a successful industrial power, but has a low rate of technical entrepreneurship. Japan has a large number of small companies but few that grow beyond the subcontractor stage and generate much in the way of technical innovation. Finally, India represents the special problems of technical entrepreneurship in the post-colonial environment and the Third World. India has a significant industrial base and a large, technically trained workforce, but as yet, few new high growth and high technology firms.

For each country, we examine the major factors which influence the rate of technical entrepreneurship. These are:

- financial factors such as availability of venture capital, the savings rate, existence of a wealthy elite, and access to a stock market;

- government factors such as tax incentives, loan programs, and procurement policies;

- infrastructure factors such as major universities, scientific labor pool, and incubator companies;

- factors which contribute to volatility such as immigration, industrial diversity, and technological change;

- cultural factors such as attitudes towards risk and status, and entrepreneurial role models.

For each country, we highlight what has spurred technical entrepreneurship, what has retarded it, and what has had little effect.

The major points of our analysis are summarized in Table 1. A regenerative venture capital cycle stimulated by a favorable tax structure and an active OTC market, appropriate incubator companies, technical and social volatility, and entrepreneurial role models all promote high rates of technical entrepreneurship. Other factors such as major universities, scientific labor pool, wealthy elite, and government loan programs explain few differences in rates of technical entrepreneurship across regions and countries.

TABLE 1

Major Factors Related to Rates of Technical Entrepreneurship

	United States	United Kingdom	Japan	India
Rate of Technical Entrepreneurship	High	Moderate	Low	Low
Tax Structure	Favorable	Recently changed to be more favorable	Mixed	Not Favorable
Venture Capital Pool	Large	Small, growing	Small	Small
Activity of OTC Market	High	Moderate, Increasing	Low	Low
Number of Appropriate Incubators	High	Moderate to Low	Low	Unknown, probably Low
Social Volatility (e.g. immigration, migration, class mobility, diversity)	High	Moderate to Low	Low	Unknown
Entrepreneurial Culture	Yes	Yes/No, Changing	No	No

UNITED STATES

In the past twenty years, the United States has generated the largest number of technically based start-ups in the world—more than every other country combined. While several thousand technical start-ups have occurred in the US in the last two decades, Silicon Valley (Santa Clara Valley) in California and the Route 128 complex near Boston are the leading regions. However, technical entrepreneurship activity is increasing in Florida, Texas, the Research Triangle in North Carolina, and other locations.

The Role of Venture Capital

Many observers credit the wealth of venture capital in the US, and in the Silicon Valley/Route 128 regions in particular, with having an important influence on the rate of technical entrepreneurship. A recent review by Bruno and Tyebjee (1980) states that venture capital is the single most often cited reason for high entrepreneurial activity. While initial start-up capital is usually provided personally by the entrepreneur, substantial inputs of venture capital have become the norm for the "high fliers" among start-ups. Since the quadrupling of venture capital availability after the 1979 reduction in the capital gains tax, sums well in excess of $1 billion per year have been made available by some 600 venture capital firms. After studying the 51 almost active venture capitalists, Timmons (1983) estimates that 30-35% of this venture capital is invested in start-ups, with some firms specializing in start-up funding. Moreover, much of US venture capital is provided by successful technical entrepreneurs who "follow-through" on their investments by taking an active part in managing.

Another important aspect of providing capital for young companies is easy access to an active market in unlisted securities. The over-the-counter (OTC) market, or Nasdaq, is by far the most active unlisted securities market in the world. 3,700 stocks were traded on the OTC market in 1983, and the annual turnover doubled that in 1982. The trading volume of 3.7 billion shares was approximately two-thirds that of the NYSE. Aside from providing young companies with additional capital, the OTC also enables stockholders in unlisted companies to capitalize on their investments. This not only provides a powerful incentive to other would-be entrepreneurs and venture capitalists, but also frees up capital for reinvestment in other ventures. Indeed, an important source of capital in the US is the successful technical entre-

32

preneur who thinks that he or she can pick the next "winners" (Cooper 1970). As such, venture capital in the US increasingly constitutes a regenerative cycle in which successful ventures generate the financial and human capital to seed new ventures.

A good example of this cycle is Apple Computer. A major source of early funding and management for Apple was A.C. Markkula. Markkula "retired" from Intel as a millionaire in his thirties. Steve Jobs, co-founder of Apple, has continued the cycle by investing in a Small Space satellite company.

The Role of Government

Some observers (e.g., Vesper and Albaum 1979) argue that the government is an important source of financial resources for young companies as well. However, only 3% of funded government R&D goes to small business, and government loan programs are targeted to small (not necessarily new) firms. The government's prime role in fostering technical entrepreneurship has been through procurement and tax policy. For example, government procurement played an important role in the success of Route 128. As Roberts and Wainer (1968) note, a substantial number of the companies in their sample began with government contracts. Carlson and Lyman (1984) studied the influence of US government programs on Silicon Valley. They note that military procurement policies, which pressed for continual performance improvements and did not discriminate against start-ups, encouraged the formation of semiconductor start-ups. Although the government also financed the education of many entrepreneurs through fellowships, research training grants and the like, Carlson and Lyman conclude that the government's role in the success of Silicon Valley is limited primarily to its procurement actions. The other major role of government is in tax policy. As is widely known, the US has lower tax rates on capital gains and personal income than most developed countries. This favorable tax structure provides both more capital to start-ups as well as more incentive to entrepreneurs and investors.

On the surface, the availability of

financial resources plays an important role in the rate of technical entrepreneurship. At the same time, government policies and capital availability do not really explain why entrepreneurship is a relatively regional phenomenon. Pennings' (1980) study of technical entrepreneurship in the plastics, telecommunications and electronics industries is germane to this question. Pennings looked at entrepreneurship in these three industries in 79 metropolitan areas of the US. He examined a variety of variables including financial resources such as venture capital, the proportion of wealthy individuals, and the savings rate. While greater financial resources did increase the rate of entrepreneurship, that effect was modest. These conclusions are buttressed by Susbauer's (1972) study of Austin. In that study, financial resources were not a major factor in the large number of technical start-ups in Austin. Also, Landau (1984) notes that the old wealth of Boston (except for the Cabots) has not influenced entrepreneurship. Finally, banks have historically been poor sources of capital for start-ups in the US because of their preference for established firms with solid loan collateral (Venture, 1984).

The Role of The Universities

The proximity of universities with strong technical programs is often touted as a determinant of technical entrepreneurship (e.g., Vesper and Albaum 1979). The existence of a technically trained labor pool is also regarded by many as an essential ingredient (e.g., Vesper and Albaum 1979, Bruno and Tyjebee 1980). For example, Roberts and Wainer (1968) profile the technical entrepreneur as someone who is young and highly educated in the sciences. However, the US experience suggests that these are necessary, but not sufficient, conditions for high rates of technical entrepreneurship. In the case of universities, Stanford and MIT are generally regarded as having played modest roles in the growth of Silicon Valley and Route 128, respectively. However, there has been very little evidence of technical entrepreneurship near other major universities, most notably the land grant schools of the Midwest. In terms of labor pool, both

Silicon Valley and Route 128 regions employ many technical people. However, there are other areas in the US and throughout the world which have many technical people and low rates of technical entrepreneurship. The Pennings (1980) study examines the number of technical universities and technically trained people in 70 metropolitan areas. His results show that such factors have only very modest effects on the rate of technical start-ups in the electronics, plastics, and telecommunications industries.

The Role of Other Entrepreneurs

A more crucial resource appears to be the existence of incubator companies within a region. Technical entrepreneurs often obtain their work experience (usually in development, marketing, or general management) at particular incubator companies in the same industry in which they launch their start-up. Cooper's (1970) study of technical entrepreneurship in the Silicon Valley showed that more than 90% of all entrepreneurs started companies in the same industry or market as their previous employer. In their study of Route 128, Roberts and Wainer (1968) note a high rate of technology transfer from former employers to the start-up. Furthermore, several studies (e.g., Susbaur 1972, Roberts and Wainer 1968) have shown that most successful technical enterprises were started by two or more founders. In many cases, the co-founders met each other at their previous employer. In sum then, incubator companies provide role models, contacts with other potential founders, and knowledge of technology and markets to would-be entrepreneurs. If the incubators are themselves start-ups, the incubators often provide the seed capital for new ventures by paying their current employees in stock which they, in turn, can liquidate.

Private sector firms, where the entrepreneur is in contact with both potential markets and technology, constitute the most favorable incubator environments. A study by Cooper (1971) showed that small companies and small, autonomous divisions of large firms have proportionately higher spin-off rates. Scientists who work in big R & D labs at large companies, universities and in the public sector are apparently less commercially driven in their research. In such organizations, having one's innovation adopted or commercialized is not usually the most important performance measure. Moreover, in large organizations, would-be entrepreneurs have more difficulty obtaining general management exposure, particularly in finance and marketing, at early career stages.

The Role of Social and Technical Volatility

Both technical and social volatility play an important role in the high rate of technical start-ups in the US. Social revolutions and technological innovations create waves of organizational births. In the case of technology, volatility in products and/or process creates gaps which can be filled by new companies. For example, it is possible to link the wave of start-ups in the late 19th and early 20th centuries to changing technology. Brittain and Freeman (1980) linked the high number of semiconductor start-ups since World War II to specific changes in product and process technology. Software and biotechnology are other obvious examples of a rash of start-ups which followed technical innovation. Social volatility is important as well. In the US and throughout the world, immigrants and distinctive ethnic groups form a disproportionate share of entrepreneurial talent. Many entrepreneurs in West Germany came from East Germany, many Korean enterpreneurs came from North Korea, the Chinese are the major entrepreneurs in much of Southeast Asia, and so on. Other evidence comes from Pennings' study which demonstrates the importance of immigration, both foreign and domestic. Indeed, apart from Route 128, the major centers of technical entrepreneurship are located in the Sunbelt, the major destination of domestic migration. Diversity also contributes to social volatility. Occupational and industry diversity were the most important predictors of high rates of technical entrepreneurship in the Pennings study. Diversity is a more important predictor of entrepreneur-

ship than regional financial resources such as wealthy people and savings rates. Diversity is also a more important predictor than regional labor resources such as a large technical labor pool and university programs. Finally, population dynamics affect the rate of high technology start-ups. That is, start-ups beget start-ups. For example, Hewlett Packard has spawned Tandem, Apple, Ridge, and other firms. Fairchild spawned Intel, AMD, National Semiconductor, and others. There are several reasons for the fertility of start-ups. Recent start-ups are ideal incubator companies. They offer early general management exposure, role models, and contacts. They also often offer stock options which can be parlayed by employees into seed capital for their own start-ups.

In summary, the US experience suggests the importance of establishing a regenerative venture capital cycle in which successful ventures generate financial and human capital for new ventures. An active OTC market and tax policy play a crucial role in this cycle by permitting entrepreneurs and investors to "cash out" and thereby recycle their capital. Also, important are incubator firms, and technical and social volatility.

UNITED KINGDOM

The United Kingdom and the rest of Western Europe exhibit a lower rate of technical entrepreneurship than the US. For example, it is estimated that between 1950 and 1975 the UK had two hundred succesful technical start-ups while Silicon Valley alone had over 800 in the comparable period (Arthur D. Little 1977). The United Kingdom is an interesting case because while its rate of technical entrepreneurship has been roughly comparable (perhaps somewhat higher) to that of other Western European countries, changes are occurring which are accelerating its rate of technical entrepreneurship.

There are two important formal studies of technical entrepreneurship in the UK. One is the Arthur D. Little (1977) comparison of the UK and West Germany. The authors of that study concluded that capital

availability is a key restraint on entrepreneurship in the UK. There is substantial wealth within the UK, but this wealth is largely inherited, not self-made, and is not funneled to start-up firms. Wealth per se does not increase the rate of technical entrepreneurship. The other formal study was conducted at the Manchester Business School (Watkins 1977). This study showed that technical entrepreneurs in the UK start companies in the same industry and geographic area as their prior employer. The implication is that incubator companies may play an important role in technical entrepreneurship as they do in the US. However, the Watkins' study gives us no information about these incubators.

The Role of Taxes, Capital and The Securities Markets

The increasing activity in technical start-ups since the ADL and Manchester studies is the most striking change in the UK. Although there is little direct evidence, there is much indirect evidence about the factors which are apparently accelerating the rate of technical entrepreneurship. A major factor appears to be the tax structure which has been greatly changed in favor of investment in start-ups. The marginal personal and investment income tax rate has been reduced from 85%. The capital gains tax has been sharply reduced and capital losses may now be deducted for income tax purposes. There is a new tax credit on capital investments which has led to the formation of roughly twenty investment funds. Several new venture capital firms have been started and $200 million of venture capital is now committed (Fortune 1983). Two firms which were started in 1980 indicate the trend in the UK. One is Venture Founders Capital, a subsidiary of a US venture capital firm specializing in high technology investments, and the other is Rainford Venture Capital, which is backed by Pilkington Brothers. Pilkington's involvement is particularly noteworthy because it repeats the US model of a successful technical entrepreneur attempting to pick future technology "winners". These two venture capital firms have an average of $600,000 per investment (versus

34

$800,000 in the US), and a third of all investments are in start-ups. Thus changes in the tax structure have attracted would-be venture capitalists and have provided would-be entrepreneurs with seed capital and with incentives for future gain. A regenerative venture capital cycle may be beginning. As in the US, tax structure plays an important role in launching a regenerative venture capital cycle by providing an initial pool of capital to the would-be entrepreneur and by providing incentives for future gain to both entrepreneurs and investors.

A second factor which is apparently spurring current technical start-ups is the Unlisted Securities Market, which was launched in late 1980. By any measure, it has been a great success. By its third anniversary, the USM traded close to 200 stocks, has raised 250 million pounds in new equity, and has a long list of companies waiting to be listed. Thus, the USM provides a means of liquidating gains, some of which are recycled into new ventures. As in the US, an OTC market plays an important role in technical entrepreneurship.

The Role of the Universities

Other factors in the UK seem less related to the rate of entrepreneurship. As in the US case, universities and a large, scientifically trained labor pool play only a modest role. Many technical people in the UK work for research laboratories in universities, government institutes, and large companies. These organizations are often managed in a hierarchial and compartmentalized fashion, with little marketing orientation. In such organizations, individuals have little market contact and therefore, little awareness of how to fill market needs. They are poor incubators. Not surprisingly, British innovations are largely technology driven, not market driven. Thus, as in the US, British universities and the existence of a large scientific labor pool are not directly related to the rate of technical entrepreneurship. Many British technical people simply work in poor incubator environments.

The Role of the Government

The UK experience also suggests that direct government involvement is only modestly effective. Government organizations set up to promote technical start-ups—the National Research Development Corporation (NRDC) and the Technology Development Corporation (TDC)—have not been commercially successful. The Swedish experience is slightly better than that of the UK in this regard. The Swedish direct government loan program, the Regional Development Fund (RDF), was set-up with a restrictive risk premium of 25% added to the loan principal. The venture capital program, Svetab, has funded 13 investments out of 1,084 prospects with an average investment of $200,000. However, as in the US and UK, tax structure changes and the establishment of an OTC market seem more potent. The Swedish OTC market was begun in 1983, and the wealth tax assessment was lowered to 30% of the firm's book value. In the first 6 months of the OTC market, 10 companies were listed with another 20 to 40 waiting in the wings and a dozen venture capital pools were formed (Economist 1983).

The Role of Culture

The factor which is most difficult to assess is culture. In 1981 Martin Wiener published *English Culture and the Decline of the Industrial Spirit* in which he argued that industrial values are essentially antithetical to traditional English values. The middle-class industrialist soon succumbs to pseudo-aristocratic attitudes, retires to the country, educates his sons in the classics at "Oxbridge", and frowns on capitalist enterprise. British technical entrepreneurship in the purest sense—the formation of new companies for the express purpose of exploiting a technical innovation—unleashed the Industrial Revolution. Many observers argue that this spirit of enterprise later died.

Whether or not the British cultural values are antithetical to entrepreneurship is unclear, but what is clear is that until very recently the UK had no role models for technical entrepreneurship. Instead there were some

well-known failures such as the venture capital firm, Spey Investments. Furthermore, as mentioned above, the government organizations which were to promote start-ups and technical innovation, the NRDC and TDC, have not proven themselves commercial successes. There are thus no outstanding recent role models such as Hewlett-Packard, Tandem, Apple and DEC in the US. Things are beginning to change with technical entrepreneurial successes like Sinclair and Acorn Computer. Perhaps the fact that Clive Sinclair was recently knighted is a sign that technical entrepreneurship and, more importantly, continuing involvement in technical enterprise, has become entirely acceptable.

JAPAN

While large Japanese companies have enjoyed tremendous success, little technical entrepreneurship has taken place since World War II. Recently, several venture capital firms have started in Japan, and there have been entrepreneurial success stories such as SORD Computer. However, the overall level of technical entrepreneurial activity is low compared with the US and Western Europe. There are few high growth, high technology entrepreneurial firms. The large number of small Japanese businesses are predominantly subcontractors with weak technology bases and modest ambitions for growth (Riggs, 1984).

The Role of Taxation and Capital

Obviously this low level of technical entrepreneurship is not related to an absence of financial resources in Japan overall. As is well known, the Japanese have one of the highest savings rates in the world at almost 20% of GNP. Rather, a partial answer lies in the distribution of those resources. While venture capital is growing in Japan, it is embryonic and has not significantly affected entrepreneurship in the country. In his recent comparison of the US and Japan, Riggs (1984) notes that both banks and venture capital firms prefer to invest in lucrative, established firms and not start-ups. At the same time, the absence of employee equity participation implies the need for such external financing at the start-up stage. The OTC market has also been ineffective in providing financing to new firms, and liquidity to investors and entrepreneurs. In late 1983, Japan revamped this market, which had been hampered by restrictions such that OTC entrants had to be at least two years old, to have paid dividends, and to have pre-tax earnings of at least Y10 per share. While trading volume has increased, there has been no rush by companies to be listed. Finally, the lack of acquisition activity closes another potential source of liquidity. In sum, there are few available financial resources available to the technical start-up and little investment ljquidity.

The Role of the Other Technical Organizations

Limited financial sources and personal wealth opportunities are not the only factors which inhibit technical entrepreneurship. There are a paucity of good incubator organizations. Large Japanese companies, which hire the better science and engineering graduates, are poor incubator environments to an even greater extent than their US and UK counterparts. Obviously, the well-known Japanese practice of hiring only at entry levels and for a career position makes entrepreneurship personally risky. Employees rarely change companies, let alone spin off their own start-up. Finally, technical people gain the general management exposure, which is very important in the US experience, relatively late in their careers. By that time, they are often well past the US prime age for entrepreneuring (Riggs 1984).

The Role of Culture

Little social and structural volatility also contributes to the low rate of Japanese entrepreneurship. There is very little foreign or domestic immigration in Japan. Society in terms of ethnicity and values is relatively stable and homogeneous. Companies prefer long term, stable, and close relationships with suppliers and customers. Thus, there is a relatively fixed industrial structure. Finally, the Japanese culture itself inhibits entrepreneur-

ship. There is an emphasis on company loyalty. Furthermore, "individuals striking off on their own know that they will not be readily accepted by their families, social groups, and perhaps, most importantly, future employers should they fail" (Riggs 1984, pg. 29). As Riggs notes, the risk is particularly great for the best graduates who have the most to lose in a society which values status.

INDIA

The critical entrepreneurial functions in a developing country like India are often fundamentally different from the advanced countries such as the US. Starting a technical business in, for example the US, usually involves perceiving an economic opportunity and carrying through a technical innovation. In a developing country, the critical entrepreneurial tasks are different. Personal wealth, appropriate government connections, and improvising substitutes for often unavailable skills, especially in marketing and engineering, are usually crucial, while the actual product innovation may be new only to the country.

The Role of Social Stratification and Diversity

There have been studies done on entrepreneurship in four parts of India (Nafziger 1978, Tripathi 1981, Koppel and Peterson 1975): Punjab, a suburb of Calcutta, Madras, and the eastern coastal town of Visakhapatnam (known as Vizag). Although these studies do not deal with technical entrepreneurship, they are informative about India. When Pakistan was formed in 1947, Punjab was split in two, and there were mass migrations in both directions across the border. In the Punjab study, refugees were over-represented as entrepreneurs and were found to be more innovative. In the town of Howrah, a suburb of Calcutta, 65% of the entrepreneurs belonged to one subcaste (the Mahisijas). The companies were largely small-scale, and had developed as railway ancillaries (Howrah was the headquarters of the East Indian Railway). In a study of

the light engineering industry in Madras, access to capital and possession of business experience and technical knowledge were important. While sociological factors, notably caste, are highly correlated to these factors, the authors argue that the caste system per se is not a barrier to entrepreneurship. Indeed, traditional caste occupations are not even relevant to modern industry. Thus, while the Vizag study finds a disproportionately high percentage of entrepreneurs to be from high castes, this may have more to do with economic than social factors. Immigrant status was also a significant factor in Vizag.

Empirical studies of industrial entrepreneurs in other developing countries such as Lebanon, Greece, Nigeria, and Pakistan corroborate the Indian findings (Nafziger 1978). Entrepreneurs in these studies were usually from the socio-economic elite, had a business background, and had much mobility. Refugees again were often over-represented.

Despite some entrepreneurship, the overall number of start-ups growing to any significant size is very low. Partially, this is because in India as well as other developing countries, the overwhelming majority of the population is effectively excluded from entrepreneurship (Forbes, 1984). Entrepreneurship is the province of the socio-economic elite who have the personal financial resources and social contacts. The Indian tax structure, through a combination of income, wealth and capital-gains taxes, effectively blocks large monetary rewards to individuals. Correspondingly, compensation is increasingly made in kind through perquisites. While this allows a relatively comparable standard of living, it prevents the formation of large pools of capital. Less capital is fed back into the regenerative venture capital cycle of the kind found in the US. This lack of liquid capital is an important impediment to the Indian entrepreneur and explains in part why entrepreneurship is available only to the elite. Other prospective entrepreneurs rarely can save enough capital to seed their businesses. The other reason that entrepreneurship is blocked to those outside the elite is

36

that in India (as in many developing countries), access to bank funds is limited to those with connections and venture capital is principally available to those within relatively closed, homogeneous communities such as the Gujaratis. Finally, the cumbersome industrial licensing process (meant to do the opposite) perpetuates the concentration of business clout. It is one more barrier facing those outside of the elite.

In sum, India has a low level of technical entrepreneurship despite a relatively large, technical labor pool. A major reason is the Indian tax structure which blocks the opportunity for wealth necessary in a regenerative venture capital cycle. As in other countries, banks and the established wealthy elite have not spurred technical entrepreneurship. Finally, social volatility is associated with Indian entrepreneurship in which successful ventures provide the human and financial capital for new ventures.

CONCLUSIONS

A regenerative venture capital cycle is a key factor in high rates of technical entrepreneurship. This cycle is launched in part by a favorable tax climate. In Japan, for traders and those selling large amounts of stock, capital gains are taxed as ordinary income. In contrast, the US and UK saw a sharp rise in venture capital after the capital gains tax was reduced. Sweden's favorable wealth tax treatment of small companies has also spurred the creation of several venture capital firms. A favorable tax structure is an incentive to entrepreneurs and investors, and provides the wealth which is often partially returned to the venture capital cycle to spur creation of more companies. Moreover, the successful entrepreneur often contributes essential business experience as well as capital to later firms.

The other key to launching a regenerative venture capital cyle is an OTC market. Such a market allows venture capitalists, entrepreneurs, and would-be entrepreneurs with a means to liquidate their investments. Nasdaq in the US and London's USM are examples of the importance of such markets. On the other hand, the

Japanese OTC has been less successful since it has been saddled with numerous restrictions such as the requirements of history of dividend payouts.

While a regenerative venture capital cycle seems crucial, other financial resources seem to have less effect. High rates of wealth per se do not stimulate entrepreneurship. Banks throughout the world show preference for large, established clients. Experience with government programs (e.g., NRDC in the UK and VEC in Japan) suggests that while their charge is to help medium and small business, they, in fact, focus their resources on larger, more established businesses. They also base their investment decisions in part on sociopolitical criteria such as aid to depressed regions.

The second key factor in technical entrepreneurship is the presence of incubator companies. In the US, small companies and autonomous divisions of large companies make the best incubators. On the other hand, government and university research labs are not particularly good incubators. The role that incubators play is to provide would-be entrepreneurs with industry knowledge, managerial and/or development experience, contacts with potential entrepreneurial partners, role models, and sometimes even seed capital. The existence of incubator companies accounts for the high rate of entrepreneurship in the US overall as well as for regional US differences. In contrast, the Japanese have relatively poor incubator environments. The most talented people work in large organizations. From a government policy viewpoint, attracting numerous branches of technical firms, such as the Irish and Scots are doing, is likely to create an entrepreneurial environment. On the other hand, major universities and scientific labor pools are important for technical entrepreneurship, but they do not guarantee it.

The third key factor in stimulating entrepreneurship is volatility. Technological volatility creates the niches and gaps which can be exploited by start-ups. That volatility can also be social. Foreign and domestic immigration, as well as occupational and

social differentiation and interclass mobility are all associated with high rates of entrepreneurship throughout the world, and with differential rates of entrepreneurship in countries. The key idea is that technical and social instability create a fluid system, one with opportunities.

The cultural factor is the most difficult to assess. At the very least, one needs a receptive population that does not frown upon leaving a parent firm to start one's own firm. Perhaps the best concrete factor is the existence of role models. It is reasonably clear throughout the world that entrepreneurs are overrepresented as the children of entrepreneurs (Proctor 1980), and that entrepreneurs in a region or industry beget more entrepreneurs in that region or industry (Delacroix and Carroll 1983). Indeed, in some areas of the US, the technical entrepreneur has become a modern folk hero.

In summary, a regenerative venture capital cycle spurred by an OTC market and favorable tax policies, incubator companies, and social and technical volatility are the common denominators of high rates of technical entrepreneurship throughout the world. Moreover, it is amply clear that such entrepreneurship is enhanced by a supportive culture and stimulates innovation in an important way. However, there are some caveats. There appear to be limits to the effectiveness of a regenerative venture capital cycle as the number of start-ups outpaces the rate of technical innovation. There can be too much capital chasing too few ideas—as may well be the case in the US small computer disk drive industry today. There are also other paths to innovation such as the large company, process technology orientation of the Japanese. Finally, small companies, especially start-ups, take a heavy personal toll on many of their employees, including stress, low pay, and long working hours. Nonetheless, technical entrepreneurship remains a key path to innovation and economic vitality throughout the world.

We wish to thank our colleagues Robert Burgelman, Warren Hausman, Hank Riggs, and Bob Sutton for their comments on an earlier draft of this paper.

REFERENCES

Aldrich, Howard E., *Organizations and Environment*, Prentice-Hall, Englewood Cliffs, 1979.

Arthur D. Little, Inc., *New Technology-based Firms in the United Kingdom and the Federal Republic of Germany*, Wilton House, London, 1977.

Bollinger, Lynn, Katherine Hope and James M. Utterback, "A Review of Literature and Hypotheses on New Technology-based Firms", *Research Policy*, Vol. 12, No. 1, February, 1938.

Brittain, Jack W. and John H. Freeman, "Organizational Proliferation and Density Dependent Selection", in *The Organizational Life Cycle*, John R. Kimberly and Robert H. Miles, eds., Josey-Bass, San Francisco, 1980.

Bruno, Albert V. and Tyzoon T. Tyebjee, "The Environment for Entrepreneurship," in *Encyclopedia for Entrepreneurship*, Calvin Kent, Ed., 1980.

Carlson, Richard and Theodore Lyman, *U.S. Government Programs and Their Influence on Silicon Valley*, SRI Project 6654, 1984.

Cooper, Arnold C., "The Palo Alto Experience", *Industrial Research*, May, 1970.

Cooper, Arnold, "Spin-offs and Technical Entrepreneurship," *IEEE Transactions on Engineering Management*, Vol. EM-18, No. 1, February, 1971.

Cooper, Arnold C., "Technical Entrepreneurship: What Do We Know", *R&D Management* 3, No. 2, February, 1973.

Delacroix, Jacques and Glenn R. Carroll, "Organizational Foundings: An Ecological Study of the Newspaper Industries of Argentina and Japan," *Administrative Science Quarterly*, (23), 1983.

Economist, "Unlisted Securities Market—Now We are Three", November, 1983.

Forbes, "Counselor/Coach Syndrome", October, 1984.

Forbes, Naushad, *Entrepreneurship: Business Start-Ups in India and the United States*, Working Paper, Stanford University, 1984.

Fortune, "Europe Rediscovers the Entrepreneur,' October, 1983.

Koppel, Bruce and Richard Peterson, Industrial Entrepreneurship in India: A Reevaluation," *The Developing Economies*, September, 1975.

Landau, Ralph, personal communication, 1984.

Nafziger, E. Wayne, *Class, Caste and Entrepreneurship: A Study of Indian Industrialists*, University Press of Hawaii, Honolulu, 1978.

Pennings, Johannes M., "An Ecological Perspective on the Creation of Organizations", in *The Organizational Life Cycle*, John R. Kimberly and Robert H. Miles, eds., Josey-Bass, San Francisco, 1980.

Pennings, Johannes M., "Organizational Birth Frequencies", *Administrative Science Quarterly*, 27, 1982.

Proctor, Michael H., "Executive Summary", *New Innovative Companies in the Netherlands*, TNO-Staff Group Strategic Studies, September, 1980.

Riggs, Henry E., *Innovation: A U.S.-Japan Perspective*, Working Paper, Stanford University, 1984.

Roberts, Edward B., and H.A. Wainer, "New Enterprises on Route 128", *Science Journal*, December, 1968.

Schumpter, Joseph A., *The Theory of Economic Development*, Harvard University, Cambridge, 1934.

Shapero, Albert, "The Process of Technical Company Formation in a Local Area", in *Technical Entrepreneurship: A Symposium*, eds. L. Komives, Center for Venture Management, Milwaukee, 1972.

Susbauer, Jeffrey C., "The Technical Entrepreneurship Process in Austin, Texas", in *Technical Entrepreneurship: A Symposium*, eds. Arnold C. Cooper and John L. Komives, Center for Venture Management, Milwaukee, 1972.

Timmons, Jeffrey A., "New Venture Creation: Models and Methodologies," in *Encyclopedia of Entrepreneurship*, Calvin Kent, ed., 1982.

Tripathi, Dwigendra, "Occupational Mobility and Industrial Entrepreneurship in India: A Historical Analysis," *The Developing Economies* 19(1), 1981.

Venture, "The Loan That Launched a Start-Up," September, 1984.

Vesper, Karl H., *Frontiers of Entrepreneurship Research*, Babson College, Wellesley, Mass., 1983.

Vesper, Karl H. and Gerald Albaum, "The Role of Small Business in Research, Development, Technological Change and Innovation in Region 10," Working Paper, University of Washington, 1979.

Wainer, H.A., "The Spin-off of Technology from Government-sponsored Research Laboratories: Lincoln Laboratory, Unpublished M.S. thesis, MIT, 1965.

Watkins, David, "Entrepreneurship and Technical Innovation in the U.K.", *Proceedings of the Academy of Management*, Orlando, Florida, 1977.

[6]

Journal of Economic Perspectives—Volume 16, Number 3—Summer 2002—Pages 153–170

The Central Role of Entrepreneurs in Transition Economies

John McMillan and Christopher Woodruff

A ll sorts of small enterprises boomed in the countryside, as if a strange army appeared suddenly from nowhere," remarked Deng Xiaoping, reflecting in 1987 on the first eight years of China's economic reforms (Zhao, 1996, p. 106). These startup firms drove China's reform momentum; they were arguably the single main source of China's growth. But their rapid emergence, Deng said, "was not something I had thought about. Nor had the other comrades. This surprised us." The reformers had not foreseen the key to their own reforms. The other ex-communist economies had similar experiences. As in China, new firms were drivers of reform. They strengthened the budding market economy by creating jobs, supplying consumer goods, mobilizing savings and ending the state firms' monopoly. As in China, also, the reformers usually did not anticipate the force of entry.

Of the two routes to a private sector—privatizing the existing firms and creating new ones—the policy debates focused almost exclusively on the former. Little attention was given to what reform policies would foster entry. Dusan Triska, for example, the architect of Czechoslovakia's privatization program, said privatization "is not just one of the many items on the economic program. It is the transformation itself" (Nellis, 2001, p. 32). It is not surprising that those who had spent their lives under central planning did not foresee the impact of entrepreneurship, but few analysts from the West predicted it either.

The reason for underestimating entrepreneurship, perhaps, was a sense that setting up a business, risky anywhere, is especially risky in an economy undergoing

■ *John McMillan is Professor of Economics, Graduate School of Business, Stanford University, Stanford, California. Christopher Woodruff is Assistant Professor of Economics, Graduate School of International Relations and Pacific Studies, University of California at San Diego, La Jolla, California. Their e-mail addresses are ⟨mcmillan_john@gsb.stanford.edu⟩ and ⟨cwoodruff@ucsd.edu⟩.*

deep reform. With prices volatile as a result of the reforms, it is unclear which lines of business are going to be the most profitable. State firms, fearing competition, harass the new firms, and corrupt bureaucrats extort bribes. Without the normal market-supporting institutions, the new firms usually cannot rely on the courts to enforce their contracts; bank loans are unobtainable for most; and there is little legal or regulatory provision for shareholding.

These handicaps notwithstanding, large parts of the new market economy arose spontaneously, through the initiatives of entrepreneurs. They succeeded by self-help: they built for themselves substitutes for the missing institutions. Reputational incentives substituted for court enforcement of contracts. Trade credit (loans from firm to firm along the supply chain) substituted for bank credit. Reinvestment of profits substituted for outside equity.

In this paper, we summarize entrepreneurial patterns in the transition economies, particularly Russia, China, Poland and Vietnam.[1] Markets developed spontaneously in every transition country, but they were built at varying speeds. Some governments impeded the entrepreneurs' self-help by creating conditions that made it hard for informal contracting to work; others created an environment that was conducive to self-help. The spontaneous emergence of markets, furthermore, has its limits. As firms' activities became more complex, they came to need formal institutions. Some governments fostered entrepreneurship by building market-supporting infrastructure; others did not (Frye and Shleifer, 1997). We will argue that the success or failure of a transition economy can be traced in large part to the performance of its entrepreneurs.

The Environment for Entrepreneurship

All the transition economies, from the former Soviet Union and central and eastern Europe to China and Vietnam, were similar in one important respect: their planned economies had been dominated by large firms, producing few consumer goods. Small and medium-sized firms were almost nonexistent, although they are a large part of every market economy. Trade and services were also a much smaller part of the transition economies than is typical for a market economy. As reform led to greater flexibility in prices, wages and production decisions, the imbalances inherited from the planned economy created enormous profit opportunities for entrepreneurs. Entrepreneurs responded by starting enterprises at a rapid— though varying—rate in each of the transition countries.

Some governments actively made it hard for entrepreneurs to operate. Expropriation of profits through official corruption was the most conspicuous of such actions. Managers of startup manufacturing firms were asked in a survey whether "extralegal" payments were needed in order to receive government services or a

---

[1] Our focus will be on the state's role in encouraging startup firms, not on efforts to create a market sector by revamping the old state firms; on that issue, see Djankov and Murrell (2002), Megginson and Netter (2001) and Nellis (2001).

business license (Johnson, McMillan and Woodruff, 2002b). More than 90 percent of Russian managers said they were, compared with about 20 percent of Polish managers. Corruption deters investment. Those firms in the sample that were the most concerned about corruption invested nearly 40 percent less than those least concerned. The mafia is a further deterrent to entrepreneurship. Asked whether payments to private agencies were necessary for "protection" of their activities, more than 90 percent of Russian managers and 8 percent of Polish managers said they were.

Managers were asked in the same survey whether they would invest $100 today if they expected to receive $200 in two years (an implied annual rate of return of 40 percent). The responses to this question give an indication of both the opportunity cost of money and the security of property. A striking 99 percent of the Russian managers said they would not, compared with 22 percent of the Polish managers.

Illegitimate takings aside, official policies often make it expensive to set up firms. Entrepreneurs must apply for business licenses to establish that their company's name is unique and provide proof of their startup capital; then they must file with the tax and labor authorities. In Russia, setting up a new business takes an entrepreneur over two months and costs 38 percent of per capita GDP in official fees (Djankov et al., 2002). In Poland, it takes nearly a month and costs 28 percent of per capita GDP. In Vietnam, it takes nearly six months and costs a striking 150 percent of per capita GDP.

The government's decisions on privatizing state firms may also have affected the environment for new firms. Mass privatization could add to the general uncertainty, thus deterring entry. Across Russia's regions, more new firms have been formed where there was less privatization of small state enterprises, though more entry has occurred where there was more privatization of large-scale state enterprises (Berkowitz and Holland, 2001). The continued presence of state enterprises also raised barriers to entry. They absorbed scarce capital and received regulatory favors (as did the privatized firms). Anecdotes abound of state firms stifling new entrants to prevent them from becoming competitors.

Not only did governments impede entrepreneurship, formal institutions to underpin entrepreneurial activity developed only slowly. In Vietnam in the mid-1990s, for example, after a decade of reform, the market institutions were still inadequate. Banks almost exclusively served state-owned firms. There were no credit-reporting bureaus. Courts able to enforce contracts between private firms were just being created. Among manufacturers we surveyed between 1995 and 1997, less than 10 percent said that courts or the government could enforce a contract with a buyer or seller, and just 10 percent said that they had received credit from banks when they started their business (McMillan and Woodruff, 1999b). In another survey carried out in 1997, 74 percent of private firms reported having no debts to banks, and such debts represented only 20 percent of the capital among the 24 percent of the firms that did have them (Ronnås, 1998).

Profits and Entry

Four transition countries, Poland, Russia, China and Vietnam, span the range of entrepreneurship patterns. Poland was among the most successful in fostering new private firms. Russia was among the least successful, though entry occurred even there. China took a distinctive path with entry of competitive enterprises run by local governments. Vietnam offers an example of robust growth of private firms even with an almost total absence of formal institutions to facilitate business.

A telling measure of the success of a transition economy's reforms is the time path of entrants' profits. Figure 1 shows the path of profits in the five years following the start of transition in China (1979–1984) and in Poland and Russia (1990–1995). In China, at the start of the reform era in 1979, the average profits of nonstate firms were 28 percent of invested capital. This is very high in comparison to earnings in a mature market economy: small businesses in the United States typically earn returns between 9 percent and 15 percent of assets.[2] As China's transition proceeded, the new firms' profits declined steadily through the first decade of reform, falling to 15 percent of invested capital in 1984 and leveling out at 6 percent in 1991 (Naughton, 1995, p. 150).

In Poland, profit rates of manufacturing firms in their first year of operation fell from an average of 25 percent of invested capital for firms formed in 1990 to 6 percent for firms formed in 1995. In Russia, also, profits earned by entrants were high at the start of the reforms: firms established in 1990 earned an average profit of 17 percent on invested capital in their first year of operation. By contrast with China and Poland, however, profits did not decline over time: first-year profits for firms established in 1995, at 16 percent, were almost as high as those for the firms established in 1990 (Johnson, McMillan and Woodruff, 2002b).[3]

The high profits earned in all three countries early in the transition are easily explained. The starting point was a heavily distorted economy with unfilled market niches. Firms that were able to overcome the impediments to doing business and produce and sell goods and services were very profitable. In Poland and China, as market-supporting institutions developed, the impediments declined and so rents

---

[2] The U.S. data are from the National Survey of Small Business Finances (Federal Reserve Board of Governors, 1994). The NSSBF sampled 273 manufacturing firms with between 10 and 250 employees. The return on invested capital averages 15 percent. However, in the surveys of firms in the five eastern European countries, profits as a percentage of assets were obtained in categories, with the lowest category being "negative" and the highest category being "41 percent or greater." When these categories are used with the U.S. data, the average return on invested capital is 9 percent rather than 15 percent. It is likely, then, that the data from Poland and Russia discussed in this section understate somewhat the return to capital.

[3] A word of caution about comparing the profit data from China on the one hand and Russia and Poland on the other: The Polish and Russian data are from surveys of about 300 manufacturers in each country in 1997 (Johnson, McMillan and Woodruff, 2002b). Firms were asked about profits in their first year of operation. Figure 1 shows the average profit rate of firms beginning operation in each year. As such, they are subject to possible recall and selection bias. The China data were gathered contemporaneously from firms operating at the time.

Figure 1
Time Path of Profits

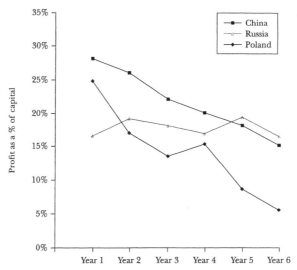

Notes: The horizontal axis shows the number of years into reform. For China, year 1 means 1979 and year 6 means 1984. For Poland and Russia, year 1 means 1990 and year 6 means 1995.
Sources: China: Naughton (1996, p. 150). Poland and Russia: Johnson, McMillan and Woodruff (2002b).

fell. Russia's stalled transition shows up in the absence of any decline in profit levels.

Data on the rate of entry of new firms are consistent with the profit paths shown in Figure 1. Entry occurred rapidly in China. Most of the new entrants there were not private firms, but rural enterprises run by local governments, called township and village enterprises. The share of China's industrial output accounted for by rural enterprises increased from 9 percent in 1978 to 30 percent in 1991 (Naughton, 1995, p. 164). Since none of the increase in output of rural firms in China came from privatized state firms, all of it is attributable to newly formed firms. The entry of these new enterprises was driven by the extraordinarily high rates of profit available early in the reforms. The competition engendered by rapid entry was the primary cause of the fall in profits.

Entry in Poland was also rapid. Industrial employment in Poland's private sector firms increased from 15 percent in 1991 to 37 percent in 1994, according to Konings, Lehmann and Schaffer (1996), using data collected by the Polish Central Statistical Office. The 21-percentage-point increase was apparently largely the result of new entrants, since privatized firms represented only 6 percent of industrial employment in 1994. At least one-sixth of industrial employment in Poland in 1994, then, was in de novo firms ("de novo" meaning started from scratch rather than being spun off from state-owned firms). The level of self-employment in Poland increased from 6 percent of the labor force in 1988 to 12 percent in 1993 (according to Earle and Sakova, 1999, using labor market surveys).[4] Although most of the firm-level studies in transition countries focus on manufacturing, entry may have been even more important in the service sector, given the underdevelopment of the service sector in the centrally planned economies. In Poland, the service sector grew from 40 percent of nonagricultural GDP in 1989 to 66 percent of GDP in 1997.

Russia, by contrast, saw less rapid entry. A 1995 study found that just 6 percent of manufacturing employment was in de novo firms (Richter and Shaffer, 1996). Self-employment in Russia in the early years of the transition increased only from 2 percent of the labor force in 1988 to 3 percent in 1993 (Earle and Sakova, 1999). Confirmation of the slowness of entry comes from data collected by Djankov and Nenova (2001) on employment in manufacturing firms with fewer than 50 employees in 1997. Since small firms were uncommon in the planned economy, small size is a rough proxy for de novo startups. They find that small firms represented 24 percent of manufacturing employment in Poland, but only 10 percent in Russia, and that the employment share of small firms in the Russian service sector more than doubled from 13 percent in 1989 to 30 percent in 1997.[5] All data on increasing shares in Russia need to be interpreted in the context of a shrinking economy. For example, Russia also saw services increase from 40 percent of the nonagricultural economy in 1989 to 62 percent in 1997. The share of services increased in spite of the fact that output of services actually declined by 1 percent per year during the 1990s; manufacturing declined much more rapidly.

The speed of entry in China, Poland and Russia was consistent with the time path of profits shown in Figure 1. Robust entry in China and Poland brought plummeting profits. In Russia, entry was slower, and profits remained high.

In Vietnam, also, the available data indicate that entry of private firms was robust (though we are unaware of any profit data there). Vietnam is an intriguing example, for it is an extreme case in its lack of formal market-supporting institutions. Yet Vietnam's private sector boomed. The number of registered private firms grew by 40 percent per year between 1993 and 1997. Private sector employment grew from 3.8 million to 10.2 million between 1988 and 1992, while employment in state firms fell from 4.1 million to 3.0 million and in cooperatives fell from 20.7 million to 18.6 million. In the following three years, from 1992 to 1995, private

---

[4] The labor survey data indicate that the majority of the self-employed work for their own account. These workers may represent not robust entry, but desperation in the face of unemployment (Earle and Sakova, 2000). Nevertheless, in 1993, over 4 percent of Poland's workforce were self-employed people who also hired others, a level much higher than in the other transition countries examined by Earle and Sakova.

[5] Djankov and Nenova (2001) data also show that employment in small firms grew rapidly in Poland during the 1990s, from an average of 8 percent in 1990–1992 to 23 percent in 1996–1998. (Comparable data for Russia are not available.) For Russia, small manufacturing firms are defined as those with fewer than 100 employees, rather than 50, as in Poland, hence the difference between Poland and Russia is understated. The service sector data for Russia and Poland are from the World Development Indicators database.

sector employment grew by more than 2.4 million, during which time state sector employment remained constant.[6] Substantially all of this private sector growth came from new entry or expansion of household enterprises, mostly retail and repair shops or small manufacturing enterprises. Vietnam has had no formal program of privatization. Though there were some ad hoc spin-offs from state-owned firms, these represent a minority of the private firms. For example, only 6 percent of firms we surveyed in 1995 said that more than half of their equipment came from state-owned firms (McMillan and Woodruff, 1999b).

Entry was robust, then, in Poland, Vietnam and, in its own way, in China, while it was comparatively weak in Russia. Other transition countries saw entry to varying degrees. Ukraine and the rest of the former Soviet Union were like Russia, for example, whereas Slovakia was more like Poland. Profits were high early in the transition because the inefficiencies of the planned economy left unsatisfied demands and unfilled market niches. Where reform was successful, it brought competitive markets, eroding profits. Where it was less successful, the entrants' profits remained high.

Entrepreneurs' Strategies

In the early years of economic transition, the absence of credit markets, courts and other market institutions created substantial impediments to entry. Potential entrants had to find money with which to purchase equipment and inputs. They had to identify reliable suppliers and customers when most firms were new and little information was available. The unusually high profit rates early in the transition provided a strong incentive for entrepreneurs. But what substituted for the missing formal institutions?

How did the entrepreneurs succeed in overcoming the lack of market-supporting institutions? Ongoing relationships among firms substituted for the missing institutions. Firms relied on the logic of the incentives to cooperate that arise in playing a repeated game. Where courts and laws are unreliable for settling disputes, firms trust their customers to pay their bills and their suppliers to deliver quality goods out of the prospect of future business. Interviews with Vietnamese managers, for example, indicate that they think quite consciously in terms of building relationships with specific customers and suppliers (McMillan and Woodruff, 1999a).[7]

Early in the process of transition, repeated game incentives work especially

---

[6] Registration data are from McKenzie (2000); employment data from Wolff (1999, p. 63). Joint ventures between state firms and foreign investors are included in the state sector. Beginning in 1993, statistics for collectives and private firms were combined. The increase of 2.4 million jobs is for private firms and collectives combined; however, it is reasonable to presume that collectives continued to decline (their output shrank from 2.7 percent of GDP in 1992 to 0.8 percent in 1998), meaning the employment increase is attributable to private firms.

[7] On the interaction between formal and informal contracting mechanisms, see Baker, Gibbons and Murphy (1994)

well. When it is hard to locate alternative trading partners, because firms are scarce or market information is inadequate or transport costs are high, firms make efforts to maintain their existing relationships. They recognize that they are to some extent locked in with their trading partners, which provides an incentive to behave cooperatively (Kranton, 1996; Ramey and Watson, 2001). The evidence we present in this section suggests that self-enforcing contracts are all that is needed to support a lot of entrepreneurship, especially at the start of the reforms.

Evidence from Vietnam is especially pertinent here, since formal institutions were almost nonexistent for some years after its transition began. Consider access to capital. Even in developed market economies, a major source of capital for small- and medium-sized firms is trade credit from suppliers. The lack of formal financial markets meant that credit from suppliers was even more important to private sector firms in transition countries. In 53 percent of the relationships between the manufactures we surveyed and their customers, some portion of the bill was paid on credit. That suppliers were willing to offer credit in the absence of formal enforce-ment of contracts is noteworthy. What gave the suppliers confidence that they would be paid? The willingness to sell goods on credit depended upon repeated interactions, according to the managers we surveyed (McMillan and Woodruff, 1999a). Trading relationships most often began with cash transactions, as the partners "tested" each other. Firms got contractual assurance by dealing with firms they knew through having dealt with them before.

Informally enforced trade rests on the shadow of the future. A firm lives up to its agreements because it wants to go on doing business with this trading partner. For the future to weigh heavily enough to induce cooperative behavior, the discounted value of the future profit stream must outweigh whatever immediate profits could be squeezed from the deal. Some of the conditions in the transition economies actually worked against cooperation. The scarcity of credit meant the opportunity cost of capital was high. With high discount rates, firms have an incentive to take current profits rather than wait for future profits. Moreover, as we saw, profits tended to decline over time. To the extent that this was predictable, the gains from forward-looking behavior were lowered. That firms were nevertheless able to operate mutually beneficial relationships is striking.

Other circumstances of the transition aided informal contracting. Cooperation is easier to sustain when severing the relationship results in higher costs. Early in the transition, trading partners were most often located in the same city or even the same neighborhood. There were usually few firms nearby producing any given product. When a supplier severed a relationship with a customer, the customer had to incur a high cost of searching for another trading partner. As a result, trading partners tended to be locked in with each other, inducing them to try to sustain their existing relationships (Kranton, 1996; Ramey and Watson, 2001).

Cooperation is more easily sustained, also, if punishment for malfeasance comes not only from the trading partner who has been cheated but also from other firms in the community. We found that gossip was important in Vietnam's manu-facturing community. Firms gathered information about potential or existing trading partners from other firms. Sometimes this information gathering was organized. Trade associations helped firms to work productively with each other, by spreading information about who had breached contracts and coordinating the sanctioning of them. This meant that reneging brought more severe consequences than merely losing the business of the offended party and thus increased the likelihood of cooperation (McMillan and Woodruff, 2000; Recanatini and Ryterman, 2000).

The self-help mechanisms evolved over time to support more complex transactions. Early in the transition, firms sold mostly to customers located in the same city or limited sales to customers about whom they had prior information from family members, friends or other firms with whom they did business. They were likely to inspect a customer's factory or store before selling to it. These are ways to reduce the risk of dealing with new trading partners, though they involve costs of exclusion or of time spent investigating trading partners. Relationships with firms located in distant cities are harder to manage than local sales, but limiting the circle of trading partners means passing up some opportunities for growth. Sales to customers located in other cities, and to customers about whom the manufacturer had no prior information, became more common as the transition progressed.

Table 1 illustrates these changes using data from surveys in three transition countries, Vietnam, Poland and Russia. The surveys asked firms about the characteristics of their oldest and newest customer relationships. The table splits relationships into those that began earlier and later in the transition. Relationships labeled "old" are those begun in the first six years of reform, before 1993 in Vietnam and before 1995 in Poland and Russia, while those labeled "new" were formed between 1994 and 1997 in Vietnam and between mid-1995 and 1997 in Poland and Russia. All of the variables shown on Table 1 are measured at the start of the relationship and, as such, are indicators of the formation of new relationships rather than the development of the specific bilateral relationships.

These data show statistically significant increases in transactions with customers from other cities, with customers about whom nothing was known at the start of the relationship, and in relationships that were initiated without the seller having visited the buyer's factory or store. In Poland, for example, 35 percent of the customer relationships started by surveyed firms between 1989 and mid-1995 involved customers from a different city, compared with 45 percent of relationships started in 1995 or after. About 39 percent of the newer customers in Poland were anonymous when the trading relationship began, compared with 27 percent of the older customers. Trading started in 38 percent of the new Polish relationships without the seller visiting the buyer's facility, compared with 29 percent of the older relationships.

The patterns in the other countries are similar, both for Vietnam and Russia, as shown in the table, and for Slovakia, Romania and Ukraine, which are not shown. Further evidence on the increase over time in the sophistication of dealings comes from Bulgaria, where quality incentives developed. Suppliers became increasingly willing to guarantee quality and to replace substandard goods based on their trading relationships (Koford and Miller, 1998).

These data suggest that the problems of governing more complex relationships

Table 1
Development of Relationships with Trading Partners

	Vietnam Relationships		Poland Relationships		Russia Relationships	
	Old	New	Old	New	Old	New
Located in a different city	28.8%	38.9% (2.27)	35.0%	45.0% (2.40)	14.5%	31.8% (3.44)
Previously unknown	57.6%	65.5% (1.74)	27.0%	38.9% (2.94)	n.a.	n.a.
Did not visit before first transaction	36.6%	50.5% (3.00)	28.8%	37.5% (2.16)	35.3%	30.8% (0.70)
Number of firms	191	281	226	342	344	66

Notes: Old relationships are those initiated prior to 1993 in Vietnam and prior to 1995 in Poland and Russia. In parentheses: *t*-values for differences between old and new relationships. The data on "previously unknown" for Vietnam and Poland are not directly comparable because of differences in the survey instrument. Entries marked "n.a." are not available in the survey used in the given country.
Sources: Johnson, McMillan and Woodruff (2000); McMillan and Woodruff (1999b).

can be overcome not only where courts work relatively well, as in Poland, but even where courts do not function at all, as in Vietnam. Receiving no help from the state, entrepreneurs made do for themselves, by relying on the incentives that arise in ongoing relationships. Repeated games substituted for the courts; trade credit and profit reinvestment substituted for financial markets. The mechanism of self-help supported increasingly sophisticated transactions—at least in the early years of transition.

State Support for Entrepreneurship

Self-help in creating market institutions is not a permanent solution for entrepreneurs. It faces a number of natural limits.

First, the development of the market as the transition proceeds lowers the costs of searching out new trading partners, which weakens a firm's threat to cut off dealings if a trading partner reneges on a deal. The cost of breaking a relationship falls. Firms then become less willing to cooperate with each other, and the need for workable laws of contract and courts able to enforce them becomes more pressing.

Second, repeated games entail personalized interfirm relationships. When firms are small, they need only deal with customers and suppliers with whom they have a particular connection: those located nearby, or managed by a friend or relative, or coming via personal recommendations. Firms were able to some extent to overcome these limitations, as noted above: even in Vietnam, they were able to trade at a distance. Such informal mechanisms are limited, however. To grow beyond a certain size, firms need to manage arms-length anonymous dealings: for example, to begin trading with firms in distant cities rather than just with geographically nearby firms. Anonymous trades need a greater extent of formal contractual assurance.

Third, as products become more complex, there is an increased need to order them, and to commit to buy them, in advance of production. Without the courts, suppliers may be unwilling to switch to producing complex goods and services.

Fourth, although firms can for a while grow incrementally by investing their retained earnings, they reach a point where, to take advantage of economies of scale, they must make big discrete jumps in their investments. Having a long-delayed return, such investments are unlikely to be made on the basis of ongoing relationships. Sunk costs tempt someone to renege: a purchaser after the costs are sunk may renegotiate the buying price, or the government after the costs are sunk may impose a specific tax. Large-scale investments require legal protection.

Finally, as profits decline through the process of economic transition, while investments often become larger and longer term, firms can rely less on retained earnings to grow and increasingly need access to external finance.

A role for the government, even early in the transition, is to set a stable platform for entrepreneurs' self-help. Macroeconomic instability, common at the beginning of a reform program, can undermine informal cooperation. Consider a trading relationship in which the seller allows the buyer to pay with a 30-day delay. In stable times, the ability to delay payment has a predictable value to the buyer and cost to the seller. The value of continuing the relationship is also predictable. The level of credit offered can be set in such a way that repayment is in the seller's interest. But now suppose that, after the goods are delivered by the seller, there is some unforeseen shock that increases the value to the buyer of not making the required payment and affects only the trading partners' current payoffs, not the stream of future gains from the relationship (such as a sharp decrease in bank credit or a rapid decline in the buyer's demand). If the shock makes the gains from reneging large enough, the buyer will not pay.[8]

Risks were inherent in any trading relationship in all of the transition countries, but the policies of some governments magnified them. Unstable macroeconomic conditions made it harder to predict the behavior of trading partners. High and variable rates of inflation and economic growth led to fluctuations in a trading partner's gain from breaking the cooperative relationship. Macroeconomic stability was conducive to the development of informal trading relationships. On this score, countries like Slovakia, where inflation peaked in 1991 at 35 percent, and Poland, where inflation peaked in 1990 at 75 percent, fared well. Russia and Ukraine, where price stability was longer in coming, fared worse. Of course, the lack of entry in Russia and Ukraine may have contributed to macroeconomic instability as well as the other way around. We know of no data that would allow us to separate the

---

[8] The situation we have in mind is similar to the Rotemberg and Saloner's (1986) model of price wars during economic booms. In their model, collusion is most likely to break down in a boom when the demand for the product is high, because that is when an individual seller's gain from undercutting the group-maximizing price is highest. Hence, collusion is harder to sustain in industries with more variable demand.

directions of causation. But given the importance of informal trading arrangements early in the transition, theory suggests that, by making relationships harder to establish, macroeconomic instability created a barrier to entry.

While contracting is mainly supported by informal relationships among firms, the courts also foster it. The courts in the transition economies are still inadequate; it takes a long time to build a well-functioning legal system. The evidence shows, however, that even these highly imperfect courts facilitate doing business. Managers of startup firms were asked in a 1997 survey whether they could appeal to the courts to enforce a contract with a trading partner. In Poland, 73 percent said they could, and in Russia, 56 percent said they could. Belief in the courts affects behavior. Those who say the courts are effective offer more trade credit and are more willing to take on new trading partners (Johnson, McMillan and Woodruff, 2002a; see also Frye and Shleifer, 1997; Hendley, Murrell and Ryterman, 1999). By making it easier for new firms to enter, workable courts improve on relational contracting and boost overall productivity. Even weak courts can be useful.

The absence of well-functioning credit markets matters less early in transition than later. In place of external funds, firms reinvest from their own profits. The high profits mean that entrepreneurs have the resources they need for expansion, without needing to borrow. Retained earnings has been the biggest single source of investible funds for startup firms in transition economies. In addition, where interfirm relationships are working well, firms receive trade credit from their suppliers. Trade credit was almost nonexistent among Russian firms as of 1997, but in Poland it was as large a source of firms' capital as bank loans (Johnson, McMillan and Woodruff, 2002b). As entry occurs and profit rates are driven downward, however, credit markets become more important. In Vietnam, there is some evidence that credit markets were beginning to reach new private firms: 24 percent of firms in a 1997 survey reported having bank credit, up from 8 percent in 1991 (Hemlin, Ramamurthy and Ronnås, 1998).

An alternative source of capital is equity markets. State support is needed for an equity market to develop. In Poland, a regulatory agency that intervened to protect minority shareholders from expropriation by insiders allowed the stock market to develop rapidly (Glaeser, Johnson and Shleifer, 2001). New issues were offered regularly. In the Czech Republic, by contrast, the absence of regulatory oversight meant people were, rightly, reluctant to invest in firms because they feared the managers would misuse their money, and so the stock market stayed inactive. Why is regulation needed for equity markets? Informal creation of share ownership is difficult. Fixed costs of issuing shares to a large group of investors prevent a slow buildup of the relationship, with investors testing entrepreneurs as trading partners in Vietnam reported doing. Because outside shareholders lack information on the firm's internal affairs, managers can easily expropriate the returns owed to the shareholders (Johnson and Shleifer, 2001). Prospective shareholders need legal and regulatory protection before they are willing to hand their money over to firms.

Entrepreneurs running de novo startups in Poland reported that an average of 25 percent of their equity capital was owned by private firms or people other than the top manager's family. This is a somewhat higher level of outside ownership than other countries for which such data are available: Vietnam, at 19 percent, Slovakia, 19 percent, and Romania, 14 percent (Johnson, McMillan and Woodruff, 2000; McMillan and Woodruff, 1999b). The lesson, once again, is that informal mechanisms work only up to a point. Investors are willing to entrust their money to managers they have some reason to believe in, perhaps because of ties of family or ethnicity or because the manager comes recommended by a trusted third party. Large firms with diversified shareholding cannot develop by such informal mechanisms, but some degree of outside ownership can.

Evidence that self-help mechanisms in financial markets have limits comes from Earle and Sakova's (2000) study of entrepreneurship in Poland, Russia and four other eastern European countries. Employers, as compared to wage workers, are more likely to have received property during posttransition restitution and to have had higher earnings in 1988. Also, the parents of those who became employers were more likely to have owned a business prior to communism and more likely to have had a university degree than are the parents of wage workers. These findings suggest that access to capital was a binding constraint on entry, one not entirely overcome by informal credit.

China did things differently with its new firms. Entry occurred in the non-standard form of the township and village enterprises (Che and Qian, 1998; Whiting, 1996). These firms were publicly owned, by communities of a few thousand people. They were managed by village government, and the profits were shared between villagers and local government by explicit rules. Around 60 percent of profits were reinvested, and the remainder was paid as bonuses to workers or used for local public goods such as education, roads and irrigation. Managerial discipline in the township and village enterprises came from the fact that these enterprises had no access to government subsidies to cover any losses and faced intensely competitive product markets.

The township and village enterprises received some benefits from having the village government as a partner. Access to state banks and to rationed inputs was eased. Public ownership helped remedy the lack of laws protecting against arbitrary expropriation by the state, as well as helping with contract enforcement. Moreover, China's local governments, arguably, did not sabotage their township and village enterprises by overtaxing them because they could see that if they did, the firms would fail and their own revenue source would be lost.

The township and village enterprise organizational form was a transitional device. After a decade and a half of growth, they began to be privatized. By the late 1990s, more than half of them were partially or fully privately owned (Li and Rozelle, 2000). By the turn of the century, the township and village enterprises were well on their way to becoming conventional firms.

Entrepreneurs require more from the state, in the medium and long run, than the absence of interference. If firms are to be able to grow to yield economies of scale, they need laws of contract so they can take on anonymous dealings and financial regulation so they can get bank loans and outside shareholding.

Welfare Effects of Entrepreneurship

The creation of jobs has been arguably the most important welfare benefit of the new entrants. Given the distortions and inefficiencies in the communist planned economy, the old firms had to shed jobs during the transition, and new entrants were needed to take up the slack. New firms have usually been the fastest-growing segment in transition economies. In Poland and in Russia, de novo manufacturing firms grew faster, invested at a higher rate and generated faster employment growth than did privatized firms (Belka et al., 1995; Richter and Schaffer, 1996; Johnson, McMillan and Woodruff, 2000). In Vietnam, the private sector created (in net terms) some 10 million jobs in the seven years from the start of reforms, while the state-owned and collective firms shed workers.

This pattern is repeated in most of the transition economies for which data exist. In Estonia, small privately owned firms—mostly startups—created almost all of the new jobs between 1989 and 1994 (Haltiwanger and Vodopivec, 2000). In Romania, 86 percent of de novo manufacturing firms created jobs between 1994 and 1996, while only 13 percent of privatized firms did so. In Slovakia, 79 percent of de novo firms grew, against 52 percent of privatized firms (Johnson, McMillan and Woodruff, 2000). De novo firms in Bulgaria, Hungary and Romania between 1990 and 1996 grew more quickly than did privatized or state-owned firms (Bilsen and Konings, 1998). Though de novo firms represented less than 3 percent of employment in the samples in Bulgaria and Romania, they created more than half of the new jobs. In a sample of firms from 25 transition countries, Carlin et al. (2001) find that sales and employment grow faster in de novo firms than in privatized or state firms; they also find that productivity gains are smaller, probably reflecting that new firms start at a higher level of efficiency than the state firms and thus have less room for productivity growth.

The key difference does not seem to be between state-owned and private firms, but rather that de novo firms outgrew all other firms. Many studies find little difference between the performance of state-owned firms and privatized firms. The finding that de novo firms perform better than privatized and state-owned firms is not quite universal, however. The Johnson, McMillan and Woodruff (2000) data show essentially no difference in the growth rates of startups and privatized firms in Russia and Ukraine. Lizal and Svejnar (2001) find that the rates of investment of private firms in the Czech Republic were somewhat lower on average than those of state-owned firms in the 1992–1998 time period and that small firms in the Czech Republic were credit constrained while large firms were not (which may explain in part their first finding). Taken as a whole, then, the evidence indicates that de novo firms were more dynamic than privatized state firms, except perhaps where the latter had favored access to capital.

Entrepreneurial firms provide other benefits. Small new firms are dynamic. They learn and change rapidly, and thus they provide a large number of independent experiments on how to do business. One measure of this dynamism is their job churning. In a study of Estonia, Haltiwanger and Vodopivec (2000) separate the net change in employment into the creation of new jobs by expanding firms and the destruction of existing jobs by shrinking firms. For state-owned firms, in the first half of the 1990s, job creation was small and job destruction among these enterprises was large. In the private sector, there was a lot of job creation. Yet, surprisingly, the private sector also had higher rates of job destruction than the state enterprise sector. These data indicate more flux in the private sector, with some firms expanding rapidly and others contracting. The simultaneous high rates of job creation and job destruction were especially pronounced among the smallest firms, those with fewer than 20 workers. This could be attributable to learning by the small firms, which is especially important in the transition setting, where costs and demands are subject to far wider uncertainty than in a stable economy.

New firms also provide competitive discipline for the pre-existing firms. State-owned and privatized firms in eastern Europe and the former Soviet Union are significantly more likely to have undergone restructuring if they faced competition (Carlin et al., 2001; Djankov and Murrell, 2002). In China through the 1980s, while the township and village enterprises burgeoned, the state firms' markup of price over marginal cost fell by 15 percent; the increased competitiveness of the output market was associated with an increased total factor productivity for the state firms (Li, 1997).

There is some evidence, also, that a transition economy's overall performance is correlated with entry. Comparing economic growth rates of the different regions of Russia, Berkowitz and DeJong (2001) find that the faster-growing regions have more entry of new firms.

Implications for Policy

In the early 1990s, a common view among those advising the reforming countries was that the overriding objective was to get the government out of the economy. Once the prohibitions on market activity were abolished, the argument went, the private sector would quickly take over. Later, in light of the grim performance of Russia and the rest of the former Soviet Union, this simple view was supplanted by a recognition that reforming an economy is exceedingly hard. Success requires a complex package of microeconomic reform, macroeconomic stability and institution building.

Our analysis speaks to both views. On the one hand, it says there is something in the leave-it-to-the-market view. Profit-driven entrepreneurs can do a remarkable amount, even to the extent of creating temporary replacements for the key social institutions of property rights and contract.

On the other hand, our analysis says getting the government out achieves its aim only in a narrow set of circumstances. The self-help substitutes for market-supporting institutions work well only for firms that are small. Larger firms, dealing with many suppliers and customers and trading at a distance, cannot rely solely on personalized relationships to undergird their transactions. Formal institutions are needed, therefore, both by privatized firms and, after a while, by startup firms if they are to grow to an efficient scale. Moreover, government policy does matter even at the level of the small startups, for the business environment must be reasonably stable and predictable if the shadow of the future is to give firms reason to be able to trust each other. If you keep your word only because of the prospect of future gains, you are more likely to renege when the business environment is very noisy. Corrupt bureaucrats and politicians, by extorting bribes, discourage entrepreneurs from investing (Johnson, McMillan and Woodruff, 2002b). High and volatile inflation could undermine firms' attempts at self-help contracting. Mass privatization, by adding to the uncertainty about which lines of business are going to be profitable, might disrupt the nascent interfirm relationships.

The same ambivalence between the force of informal mechanisms and their limits, by the way, is seen in many developing countries. In Africa and Latin America, firms lacking access to the courts engage in a remarkable range of productive activity (de Soto, 1989; Fafchamps, 2001; Woodruff, 1998). The lack of market-supporting institutions, however, makes it hard or impossible for these firms to grow into sophisticated corporations.

The economic transition has been far more painful in some ex-communist countries than in others. Relative success came in those countries where new market activities were quickly established. Ironically, and contrary to the leave-it-to-the-market view, markets arose faster where the government did not completely withdraw, but rather set a stable platform. New firms entered and grew more slowly in Russia, where the government abruptly ceased controlling prices and rapidly privatized the state firms, than in China, where the government mostly continued doing what it had been doing before. [9]

Conclusion

The importance of entrepreneurs in the transition economies is a reminder that the task of economic transition is not just a matter of government officials enacting certain policies or setting certain rules of operation for the new economy. Entrepreneurs acted as reformers, too. Indeed, much of the task of devising the new ways of doing business in transition economies has been taken on by entrepreneurs.

"By pursuing his own interest," Adam Smith (1776 [1976], volume 1, pp. 477–78) famously wrote of the merchant, "he frequently promotes that of society more effectually than when he really intends to promote it." The entrepreneurs in the transition countries exemplify Smith's dictum. By creating jobs, supplying consumer goods, constraining the market power of the state firms and building reform momentum, they have produced real welfare gains.

■ *We thank David Ahn, Simon Board, Simeon Djankov, Brad De Long, John Earle, Alan Krueger, Barry Naughton, Timothy Taylor and Michael Waldman for helpful comments. McMillan thanks the Stanford Graduate School of Business for research support.*

---

[9] On the parallel roles of bottom-up and top-down forces in developing market rules and procedures, see McMillan (2002).

References

Baker, George, Robert Gibbons and Kevin J. Murphy. 1994. "Subjective Performance Measures in Optimal Incentive Contracts." *Quarterly Journal of Economics.* 109:4, pp. 1125–156.

Belka, Marek et al. 1995. "Enterprise Adjustment in Poland: Evidence from a Survey of 200 Private, Privatized, and State-Owned Firms." Centre for Economic Performance Discussion Paper No. 233, April.

Berkowitz, Daniel and David DeJong. 2001. "Entrepreneurship and Post-Socialist Growth." William Davidson Institute Working Paper No. 406.

Berkowitz, Daniel and Jonathan Holland. 2001. "Does Privatization Enhance or Deter Small Enterprise Formation?" *Economics Letters.* 74:1, pp. 53–60.

Bilsen, Valentijn and Jozef Konings. 1998. "Job Creation, Job Destruction and Growth of Newly Established, Privatized and State-Owned Enterprises in Transition Economies: Survey Evidence from Bulgaria, Hungary and Romania." *Journal of Comparative Economics.* 26:3, pp. 429–45.

Brown, David and John Earle. 2001. "Privatization, Competition, and Reform Strategies: Theory and Evidence from Russian Enterprise Panel Data." SITE Working Paper No. 159, Stockholm School of Economics.

Carlin, Wendy et al. 2001. "Competition and Enterprise Performance in Transition Economies: Evidence from a Cross-Country Survey." CEPR Discussion Paper No. 2840.

Che, Jiahua and Yingyi Qian. 1998. "Institutional Environment, Community Government, and Corporate Governance: Understanding China's Township Village Enterprises." *Journal of Law, Economics, and Organization.* 14:1, pp.1–23.

de Soto, Hernando. 1989. *The Other Path.* New York: Harper and Row.

Djankov, Simeon and Peter Murrell. 2002. "Enterprise Restructuring in Transition: A Quantitative Survey." *Journal of Economic Literature.* 40:3, pp. 739–92.

Djankov, Simeon and Tatiana Nenova. 2001. "Constraints to Entrepreneurship in Kazakhstan." World Bank, March.

Djankov, Simeon et al. 2002. "The Regulation of Entry." *Quarterly Journal of Economics.* 117:1, pp. 1–37.

Earle, John and Zuzana Sakova. 1999. "Entrepreneurship from Scratch: Lessons on the Entry Decision into Self-Employment from Transition Economies." IZA Discussion Paper No. 79.

Earle, John and Zuzana Sakova. 2000. "Business Start-ups or Disguised Unemployment? Evidence on the Character of Self-Employment from Transition Countries." *Labour Economics.* 7:5, pp. 575–601.

Fafchamps, Marcel. 2001. "Networks, Communities and Markets in Sub-Saharan Africa: Implications for Firm Growth and Investment." *Journal of African Economies.* 10:0, pp. 109–42.

Federal Reserve Board of Governors. 1994. *National Survey of Small Business Finance.* Washington, D.C.: Board of Governor of the Federal Reserve and U.S. Small Business Administration.

Frye, Timothy and Andrei Shleifer. 1997. "The Invisible Hand and the Grabbing Hand." *American Economic Review.* Papers and Proceedings, 87:2, pp. 354–58.

Glaeser, Edward, Simon Johnson and Andrei Shleifer. 2001. "Coase versus the Coaseans." *Quarterly Journal of Economics.* 114:3, pp. 853–900.

Haltiwanger, John and Milan Vodopivec. 2000. "Gross Worker and Job Flows in a Transition Economy: An Analysis of Estonia." Mimeo, University of Maryland, November.

Hemlin, Maud, Bhargavi Ramamurthy and Per Ronnås. 1998. "The Anatomy and Dynamics of Small Scale Private Manufacturing in Vietnam." Mimeo, Stockholm School of Economics.

Hendley, Kathryn, Peter Murrell and Randi Ryterman. 1999. "Law, Relationships, and Private Enforcement: Transactional Strategies of Russian Enterprises." Mimeo, University of Wisconsin, January.

Johnson, Simon and Andrei Shleifer. 2001. "Privatization and Corporate Governance." Mimeo, MIT.

Johnson, Simon, John McMillan and Christopher Woodruff. 2000. "Entrepreneurs and the Ordering of Institutional Reform: Poland, Slovakia, Romania, Russia and Ukraine Compared." *Economics of Transition.* 8:1, pp. 1–36.

Johnson, Simon, John McMillan and Christopher Woodruff. 2002a. "Courts and Relational Contracts." *Journal of Law, Economics, and Organization.* 18:1, pp. 221–77.

Johnson, Simon, John McMillan and Christopher Woodruff. 2002b. "Property Rights and Finance." *American Economic Review.* Forthcoming.

Koford, Kenneth and Jeffrey B. Miller. 1998. "Contractual Enforcement in an Economy in Transition." Mimeo, Department of Economics, University of Delaware.

Konings, Jozef, Hartmut Lehmann and Mark E. Schaffer. 1996. "Job Creation and Job Destruction in a Transition Economy: Ownership, Firm Size and Gross Job Flows in Polish Manufacturing." *Labour Economics.* 3:2, pp. 299–317.

Kranton, Rachel E. 1996. "Reciprocal Exchange: A Self-Sustaining System." *American Economic Review.* 86:4, pp. 830–51.

Le, Wei. 1997. "The Impact of Economic Reform on the Performance of Chinese State Enterprises, 1980–1989." *Journal of Political Economy.* 105:5, pp. 1080–106.

Li, Hongbin and Scott Rozelle. 2000. "Saving or Stripping Rural Industry: An Analysis of Privatization and Efficiency in China." *Agricultural Economics.* 23:3, pp. 241–52.

Lizal, Lubomir and Jan Svejnar. 2001. "Investment, Credit Rationing, and the Soft Budget Constraint: Evidence from the Czech Republic." *Review of Economics and Statistics.* 83:1, pp. 92–99.

McKenzie, John. 2000. "Creating a Market in Management Training for Vietnam's Private Firms." International Labour Organization Working Paper.

McMillan, John. 2002. *Reinventing the Bazaar: A Natural History of Markets.* New York: Norton.

McMillan, John and Christopher Woodruff. 1999a. "Dispute Prevention Without Courts in Vietnam." *Journal of Law, Economics, and Organization.* 15:3, pp. 637–58.

McMillan, John and Christopher Woodruff. 1999b. "Interfirm Relationships and Informal Credit in Vietnam." *Quarterly Journal of Economics.* 114:4, pp. 1285–320.

McMillan, John and Christopher Woodruff. 2000. "Private Order under Dysfunctional Public Order." *Michigan Law Review.* 98:8, pp. 2421–458.

Megginson, William L. and Jeffry M. Netter. 2001. "From State to Market: A Survey of Empirical Studies on Privatization." *Journal of Economic Literature.* 39:2, pp. 321–89.

Naughton, Barry. 1995. *Growing Out of the Plan.* New York: Cambridge University Press.

Nellis, John. 2001. "The World Bank, Privatization, and Enterprise Reform in Transition Economies: A Retrospective Analysis." Mimeo, Operations Evaluation Department, World Bank.

Ramey, Garey and Joel Watson. 2001. "Bilateral Trade and Opportunism in a Matching Market." *Contributions to Theoretical Economics.* 1:1, ⟨http//www.bepress.com/bejte/contributions/vol1/iss1/art3/⟩.

Recanatini, Francesca and Randi Ryterman. 2000. "Disorganization or Self-Organization?" Mimeo, World Bank.

Richter, Andrea and Mark Schaffer. 1996. "The Performance of *De Novo* Private Firms in Russian Manufacturing," in *Enterprise Restructuring and Economic Policy in Russia.* Commander, Fan and Schaffer, eds. Washington, D.C.: World Bank, pp. 253–74.

Ronnås, Per. 1998. "The Transformation of the Private Manufacturing Sector in Vietnam in the 1990s." Stockholm School of Economics Working Paper No. 241.

Rotemberg, Julio and Garth Saloner. 1986. "A Supergame-Theoretic Model of Price Wars during Booms." *American Economic Review.* 76:3, pp. 390–407.

Smith, Adam. 1976 [1776]. *An Enquiry into the Nature and Causes of the Wealth of Nations.* Chicago: University of Chicago Press.

Whiting, Susan H. 1996. "Contract Incentives and Market Discipline in China's Rural Industrial Sector," in *Reforming Asian Socialism.* J. McMillan and B. Naughton, eds. Ann Arbor: University of Michigan Press, pp. 63–110.

Wolff, Peter. 1999. *Vietnam: The Incomplete Transformation.* London: Frank Cass Press.

Woodruff, Christopher. 1998. "Contract Enforcement and Trade Liberalization in Mexico's Footwear Industry." *World Development.* 26:6, pp. 979–91.

Zhou, Kate Xiao. 1996. *How the Farmers Changed China.* Boulder: Westview Press.

[7]

Pergamon

World Development Vol. 26, No. 5, pp. 897–911, 1998
© 1998 Elsevier Science Ltd
All rights reserved. Printed in Great Britain
0305-750X/98 $19.00+0.00

PII: S0305-750X(98)00013-8

Adaptive Entrepreneurship and the Economic Development of Hong Kong[1]

TONY FU-LAI YU

School of Economics and Management, The University of New South Wales, Canberra, Australia

Summary. — This paper examines the role of entrepreneurship in the economic development of Hong Kong. It argues that the dynamics of Hong Kong's economy are attributed largely to adaptive entrepreneurs who are alert to opportunities, maintain a high degree of flexibility in their production and respond rapidly to change. In the manufacturing sector, adaptive entrepreneurship is manifested in the forms of product imitation, small-scale enterprise, subcontracting and spatial arbitrage. Using these entrepreneurial strategies, Hong Kong manufacturers have learnt from foreign firms and imitated their products. By selling improved commodities at lower prices, they compete against the original suppliers from overseas. Furthermore, to exploit new profit opportunities, Hong Kong's entrepreneurs have shifted their production activities from one product to another, from one industry to another, from higher cost to lower cost regions, from traditional fishing and agriculture into manufacturing, and then to finance and other services. Their efforts have brought about structural transformation in the economy and have enabled Hong Kong to catch up with economically more advanced economies. © 1998 Elsevier Science Ltd. All rights reserved

Key words — East Asia, Hong Kong, entrepreneurship, economic development, catching up

1. HONG KONG'S ECONOMIC "MIRACLE"

When Hong Kong was ceded to the British in 1842, it was only a "barren island with hardly a house upon it" (Chan, 1991, p. 21). The colony in 1951 was described by a visiting American journalist as a "dying city" (Ho, 1992, p. 5). This changed, however, when Hong Kong embarked on its export-led industrialization in the early 1950s and experienced rapid growth in the 1960s. During 1968–71, the average growth rate in real terms was approximately 6.5% and by 1971, the per capita income reached HK$6,096, placing it second behind Japan in East Asia (Riedel, 1974, p. 11). Since the early 1970s it has further emerged as a major financial center in the Asia-Pacific region. By 1992, the GDP reached HK$742,582 million. After more than three decades of rapid growth, Hong Kong has emerged as one of the richest economies in Asia (Chau, 1993, p. 1).

This miraculous performance naturally has intrigued economists interested in economic development. However, most studies have utilized orthodox neoclassical theories, particularly the Cobb–Douglas production function and the theory of comparative advantage, to explain the economic success of Hong Kong (for example, see Riedel, 1974; Hsueh, 1976; Chen, 1979; Peebles, 1988). Unfortunately, these works have not critically examined the role of entrepreneurship and have therefore failed to yield a satisfactory explanation of the economic success of Hong Kong. In recent years, Chen (1988) acknowledges that entrepreneurship is one of important factors of production in the first stage of Hong Kong's industrialization. Integrating Schumpeter's entrepreneurship into his model, he explained the East Asian "miracles" in terms of Neo-Confucianism. Wu (1989) also employs Schumpeter's arguments to explain the economic activities in Hong Kong. However, the approach in both papers is inadequate.[2] As Nafziger (1986, p. 7) correctly argues, Schumpeter's concept of the entrepreneur is

somewhat limited in less developed countries, since the majority of indigenous Schumpeterian entrepreneurs are traders whose innovations are the opening of new markets. In light of the possibilities of technical transfer from advanced economies, no undue emphasis should be put on the development

Correspondence to: Tony Fu-Lai Yu, School of Economics and Management, University College, The University of New South Wales, Canberra, ACT 2600, Australia. E-mail: yutaaaaa@emnw2.arts.adfa.oz.au of entirely new combinations. People with technical, executive and organisational skills may be too scarce in less developed countries to use in developing new combinations in the Schumpeterian sense

Specifically in Hong Kong, Wong (1988, p. 166) notes that entrepreneurs in the cotton spinning industry did not fit into the theoretical mold constructed by Schumpeter. Reviewing the works on overseas Chinese entrepreneurship, Mackie (1992, p. 60) concluded that scholars need to go beyond the Schumpeterian concepts of entrepreneurship and take note of more recent thinking on the subject.[3] This study attempts to fill such a gap.

2. ADAPTIVE ENTREPRENEURSHIP AND ECONOMIC DEVELOPMENT IN LATECOMER ECONOMIES

This paper argues that Hong Kong's economic success is mainly attributable to the dynamics of adaptive entrepreneurs who are alert to opportunities and exploit them. Through their efforts, the tiny economy has been able to catch up with the economically more advanced economies. Such an adaptive response[4] is best explained by Kirzner's theory of entrepreneurship. In contrast to Schumpeter's argument, Kirzner contended that a unique feature of entrepreneurship lies in its alertness and opportunity exploitation. Building upon Mises' insight, Kirzner (1973, p. 33) noted:

> Human action, in the sense developed by Mises, involves the course of action taken by the human being to remove uneasiness and to make himself better off. Being broader than the notion of economizing, the concept of human action does not restrict analysis of the decision to the allocation problem posed by the juxtaposition of scarce means and multiple ends...but also the very perception of the ends-means framework within which allocation and economizing are to take place...Mises' homo agens...is endowed not only with the propensity to pursue goals efficiently, once ends and means are clearly identified, but also with the drive and alertness needed to identify which ends to strive for and which means are available.

In the market process, the opportunity that human agents are alert to, is monetary profit. The role of the entrepreneurs, as Kirzner (1973, pp. 39–41) argues, arises out of their "alertness to hitherto unnoticed opportunities". They proceed through their alertness to discover and exploit situations in which they are able to sell for high prices that which they can buy for low prices. Alertness implies that the actor possesses a superior perception of economic opportunity.

It is like an "antennae that permits recognition of gaps in the market that give little outward sign" (Gilad *et al.*, 1988, p. 483).

For Kirzner, alertness to profit opportunity implies arbitrage activities. Indeed, Kirzner has never distinguished arbitrageurship from entrepreneurship (White, 1976, p. 4).[5] With regard to the arbitrageurship function, Kirzner (1973) argues that the existence of disequilibrium situations in the market implies profit opportunity. The entrepreneur endeavors to exploit this opportunity, eliminate errors, and in the process moves the economy toward equilibrium.

Furthermore, it is the notion of entrepreneurial discovery that enhances economic progress. As Kirzner (1985, p. 162) has elaborated, entrepreneurial process consisted of

> the social integration of the innumerable scraps of existing information that are present in scattered form throughout society... Yet the same entrepreneurial spirit that stimulates the discovery in the market of the value of information now existing throughout the market also tends to stimulate the discovery or creation of entirely new information concerning ways to anticipate or to satisfy consumer preferences. The entrepreneurial process at this second level is what drives the capitalist system toward higher and higher standards of achievement.

Extending Kirzner's insights to the catching-up process, Cheah (1992, p. 466) has contended that entrepreneurs in latecomer economies "increase knowledge about the situation, reduce the general level of uncertainty over time and promote market processes which help to reduce or to eliminate the gap between leaders and followers". For Cheah, these entrepreneurial activities include "arbitrage, speculation, risk taking, adaptive innovation, imitation as well as planning and management efforts in response to market signals". In this sense, Kirzner's mode of entrepreneurship broadly encompasses the functions of a gap filler or routine entrepreneurship (Leibenstein, 1968, pp. 72–83), and imitative entrepreneurship (Baumol, 1988, pp. 85–94). In this study, all these activities are referred to as adaptive entrepreneurship. In the following sections, the industrial dynamics of Hong Kong will be explained by the concept of adaptive entrepreneurship based on small-scale enterprise, subcontracting, product imitation and spatial arbitrage.

This study will focus on Hong Kong's two leading manufacturing industries, namely, electronics and textile and garment manufacturing. The data required for the empirical analysis were collected by a questionnaire survey and case studies. The aim of the questionnaire survey was to obtain opinions on the choice of business strategies from a large group of entrepreneurs. The questionnaire was comprised mainly of structured responses. A total of 31 questions were asked.[6] The target respondents of this survey were the owners of the manufacturing firms. The Hong Kong Government Census and Statistics Department supplied a list of the names and addresses of a 20% sample of firms from each of the two industries. From this list, the author drew a sample of 50 companies. When requests for interviews were accepted, interviews were then conducted, guided by a questionnaire. This process was repeated until 50 firms were interviewed successfully. A pre-test was conducted in five factories and the questionnaire was subsequently modified before a formal survey was performed. Each survey interview took an average of 20 minutes. Because of the resource constraints in the field work, the sample does not constitute a random sample, and the small size of the sample (50 firms) does not justify the use of more sophisticated statistical techniques in the analysis of the collected information.

The materials for case studies were obtained from published documents, for example, a company handbook or a commercial directory, and from direct in-depth interviews. For each of the industries, five case studies were undertaken. The selection of the firms was guided by a prior understanding of the companies' backgrounds obtained from published sources, such as company directories and handbooks. The choice was unavoidably influenced by the willingness of the owners to cooperate. The selected firms were all local Chinese firms and had been established for at least 5 years. Each case study involved of an interview with the founder(s), (sometimes together with his/her assistants), and visits to the workshops (for most cases). Subsequent communications with the owners, their assistants or marketing managers were made to clarify some points that related to the company strategies or to request more information.[7] The empirical analysis is presented as below.

3. ADAPTIVE ENTREPRENEURSHIP AND HONG KONG'S INDUSTRIAL DYNAMICS: OPPORTUNITY EXPLOITATION, SMALL FIRMS AND FLEXIBILITY

In a small open economy and with a unique political structure such as Hong Kong's,[8] manufacturers have encountered an extremely volatile economic condition. They have tackled these problems by being alert to business opportunities, making quick decisions, acting promptly,

and maintaining a high degree of flexibility and adaptability. They have preferred family businesses and made informal or oral agreements based on trust. They have taken shortcuts to produce some non-capital-intensive and not too sophisticated commodities, with short gestation periods (Chau, 1993, p. 25). Their survival has relied largely on adaptive entrepreneurship manifested in the form of small-scale enterprise, subcontracting, product imitation and spatial arbitrage.

(a) *Opportunity exploitation*

Virtually without any government support in research and development (R&D), the technological level of Hong Kong's manufacturing industry has lagged behind South Korea and Taiwan (Chen and Wong, 1989, pp. 207–208). Hong Kong's entrepreneurs have survived by being alert to opportunities. The case of Luks Industrial Co. Ltd serves as a good illustration.[9] The growth of the company was largely because of its founder, Mr Luk King-Tin's ability to identify market opportunities.

According to Mr Luk, South Korea and Taiwan have been Hong Kong's two major rivals. Mr Luk utilized the insight of *Sun Tsu Bing-Fa* (a military strategy book in ancient China): "If you know thy enemies and know yourself, then you will win the battle" and avoided direct confrontation with the rivals. In the 1980s, the UK restricted the sale of South Korean and Taiwan-made black-and-white televisions, but imposed no restriction on those made in Hong Kong. Therefore, Luks Industrial Co. Ltd continued to produce and export black-and-white televisions to the UK, despite black-and-white televisions becoming a low value-added product, which many producers did not consider to be worthwhile.

Furthermore, colour televisions in the UK and certain European countries used Phase Alternation Line (PAL) system, but South Korea and Taiwan at that time were producing televisions that conformed to National Television System Committee (NTSC), which were mainly for the US markets. So Mr Luk bought the PAL patent from Telefunken and manufactured colour television and television kits that conformed to the PAL system, and which he then exported to European countries. In this way, Mr Luk avoided any direct encounters with South Korean and Taiwanese manufacturers. In 1986, the export of Luks' televisions to the UK represented approximately 30% of the company's total turnover

(Luks Industrial Co. Ltd: A Company Profile,
p. 10).

Prior to 1986, the import of televisions to
China was subject to high import duty, whereas
the import of television kits, a collection of
components for the assembly of a television, was
subject to duty at much lower rates. So Mr Luk
manufactured television kits in Hong Kong and
then sold them to Luks Shekou, or other
Chinese concerns for final assembly, and hence
enjoyed low custom duty. As a result, the
company's total turnover in television kits
increased from approximately HK$40.4 million
in 1981 to HK$205 million in 1985, a 500%
growth rate *(Luks Industrial Co. Ltd: A Company
Profile,* p. 9).

In response to this, in 1986, the European
Common Market began to critisize Hong Kong
television manufacturers. In 1989, a special sales
tax was imposed on colour televisions made in
mainland China by Hong Kong firms. As a
consequence of these events, the company
shifted its emphasis to supplying production
equipment and essential component kits, which
were supplemented by the sale of complete
television sets. Furthermore, in the early 1990s, it
had established an assembly arrangement
through the incorporation of a wholly owned
subsidiary in the United Kingdom to assemble
final television sets for export to Europe.

The above illustrations suggest that in facing
keen competition from South Korea and Taiwan
and trade restrictions from developed countries,
Hong Kong producers such as Mr Luk can still
survive because of their ability to identify profit
opportunities and exploit narrow profit margins.

(b) *Small scale enterprises and guerrilla capitalism*

A distinct feature of Hong Kong's industrial
structure is that each industry has a large
number of small concerns that are responsive to
buyers' orders, or to subcontracting orders from
either their larger counterparts or their peers
(Ho, 1992, p. 111). In 1950, there were 1,478
manufacturing establishments, who employed
more than 81,000 people. The average size of a
firm was approximately 55 persons per establishment. In 1992, the total number of establishments increased to 41,937, but the number of
persons employed had declined to 571,181. The
average size was 14 persons per establishments
(Hong Kong Government Industry Department,
1993, p. 17). In 1994, 72% of the textile and
garment firms and 62% of the electronics firms,
respectively, employed less than 50 people for

their plants in Hong Kong (Yu, 1995, pp. 152,
185). From this, Ho (1992, p. 112) commented
that "The average size of Hong Kong's industrial
undertakings, which was small already by international standards had actually become smaller
over a period of rising prosperity. The data
clearly shows that Hong Kong's manufacturing
sector has been dominated by small and medium
establishments. The argument that the
dominance of small and medium enterprises is
only a characteristic of an early stage of
industrialization, and that they are deemed to
decrease gradually as an economy industrializes
does not seem to apply in Hong Kong".

Small firms in Hong Kong survived by being
flexible, alert to economic change and by
responding rapidly to market needs (Youngson,
1982, p. 23; Sung, 1987, pp. 47–48; Chau, 1993,
p. 25). Cheng (1982, p. 50) noted that Hong
Kong's manufacturing firms are "capable of
accepting orders subject to widely differing
requirements as amount, date of delivery and
special specifications, and that there is a constant
attempt to develop new lines of products in
response to change in the world market". In
particular, they are able to handle small orders.
Woronoff (1980) observed that some factories
even managed a multiplicity of small jobs at the
same time. The jobs were so small that big
companies could not handle them profitably.
Especially during the recession, orders came only
in small quantities and only small firms could
manage this type of order within a very narrow
profit margin. For example, the only three
semiconductor firms in Hong Kong could take
advantage of their small size to produce shorter,
more customized chips. The firms in Japan such
as Toshiba would not consider small orders, but
Hong Kong producers may readily accept an
order as small as 20,000 chips (Wilson, 1991,
p.71). Sometimes, they received orders with
value as small as US$1,000 (Engardio and Gross,
1992, p. 64).

For small firms, with small overheads,
machinery and personnel costs, the opportunity
cost of shifting to other sectors is low. This
implies that small firms are more ready to close
down or switch to new kinds of production.
Kwok (1978, p. 72) reported that the cessation
rate of small firms in Hong Kong was seven
times higher than that of large ones. Speed is
essential in product development in Hong Kong
(Davies *et al.,* 1993, p. 12), and the small firms
are usually the first groups to get out of a
declining sector and move into new markets.

Sit and Wong (1989, p. 27) noted that "flexibility and diversity of products through minutes

changes in design, creating new variable products within the same industries and filling existing market niches are more significant elements behind the dynamism of Hong Kong manufacturing". Similarly, Ho (1992, p. 119) noted that "the economy in Hong Kong is extremely vulnerable to fluctuations in the world market. To survive, Hong Kong firms, large and small alike, must be ready to move into new lines, to vary their production plans and even to switch technologies at short notice. There is no room for inertia". Only by grasping new opportunities and making decisions quickly can small firms in Hong Kong continue to survive. In this respect, they can be regarded as vehicle for flexible adjustment.[10] Referring to this feature as guerrilla capitalism, Lam and Lee (1992, p. 109) remarked that small and medium family-sized Chinese-owned firms succeed by exploiting market opportunities that use the strategy of a guerrilla force: they seek out an opportunity for high profit margins for a particular merchandise, develop a formula, exploit it by rapidly flooding the market before the established firms can respond, make profits over the short term, and then leave the market for another before competition forces the prices down to the point where they are no longer profitable without large-scale investments in technology or infrastructure.

4. SUBCONTRACTING AND THE SIGNIFICANCE OF ORIGINAL EQUIPMENT MANUFACTURER (OEM) STRATEGY

During the early stage of Hong Kong's industrialization, many trading firms dispatched production contracts to small local factories. Some of them provided technical advice and assistance in the design and marketing of small factory's products, and helped small manufacturers to secure loans. In 1988, roughly one-third of small- and medium-sized manufacturing establishments were linked up with other local factories by subcontracting agreements (Sit and Wong, 1989, p. 153). In 1994, 72% of the textile and garment firms and 58% of the electronics firms, respectively, subcontracted some production processes to other firms (Yu, 1995, pp. 161, 189).

Under the subcontracting network, many small firms in Hong Kong undertake one production process or participate in the production of finished goods for large firms. Hence large firms

can gain flexibility. In some extreme cases, firms may have no production site at all; they simply have an office for administrative purposes and subcontract all jobs to others from the orders they receive. They exploit profit margins by providing their managerial and marketing knowledge to foreign buyers and sellers.

A form of international subcontracting in Hong Kong has been Original Equipment Manufacturer (OEM) business in which local manufacturers produce according to the requirements of the orders received from overseas companies. Products made by Hong Kong manufacturers are sold in overseas markets under the brand names of foreign companies. Despite the growth in the design skills of some local firms, OEM business still accounts for a large proportion of total electronics output in Hong Kong (Hobday, 1995, p. 1176). In 1994, about 66% of the electronics firm had been and would continue to be OEM suppliers (Yu, 1995, pp. 191).[11] For example, as a typical OEM, Termbray Electronics Co. in 1984 successfully secured its first order from AT & T to manufacture telephone sets and telephone answering machines designed by AT & T. Initially orders were only for basic models but the company later succeeded in obtaining contracts to manufacture upgraded and more complex products that offered many features, including memory functions, speaker phones, liquid crystal displays and two-way recording functions. In the same year, the company set up an additional factory to expand its productive capacity for OEM activities. In 1991, sales to AT & T accounted for approximately 84% of the company's OEM sales and 60% of the company's operating profit. In 1991, total turnover in the OEM business amounted to HK$601.9 million, with an operating profit of HK$97.2 million (Yu, 1995, pp. 338–343).

If a firm engages in OEM business, the firm does not need to be involved in marketing and promotions. The strategy of OEM business is best summarized by the statement: "We make it, you sell it" as made by Mr Lap Lee, the founder of Termbray Electronics Ltd. His insight is indeed the secret behind the success of most Hong Kong manufacturing exporters. This strategy shuns grand marketing plans and multi-million-dollar brand promotions. Instead, local producers let the overseas buyers bear the risk of the finished products. By producing for overseas companies, firms such as Termbray have contributed significantly to Hong Kong's export and created what development economists called export-led industrialization.

5. PRODUCT IMITATION STRATEGY: A LATECOMER'S TECHNOLOGY PATH

Hong Kong's manufacturers in general have been regarded as being followers and imitators rather than innovators (Sit *et al.*, 1979, p. 40; Hobday, 1995, pp. 1171–1193). Davies *et al.* (1993, p. 12) contended that "Hong Kong's manufacturing industries traditionally are oriented towards incremental, rather than radical change, technological followership rather than leadership and cost reduction rather than product differentiation". In 1994, about 42% of textile and garment firms simply exactly copied from other manufacturers, while 44% of them copied, but with some modifications. Furthermore, 88% of the respondents did not use patent protection. A similar situation was found in the electronics industry. About 62% of electronics manufacturers copied and modified other products in the market, while 18% of them copied exactly from other firms without any modification. In total, 80% of them pursued imitative strategies (Yu, 1995, pp. 156, 199). In an earlier study of Hong Kong's manufacturing industry, Espy's survey (Espy, 1970, p. 50) revealed that manufacturers in Hong Kong adopted product strategies that were labor intensive, and that they employed low level of technology that did not require any design skills and were aimed at mature products. These strategies enabled the firms to achieve high growth rates. They competed in world markets by their capacity to manufacture at low cost and their flexibility to meet changing patterns of demand at very short notice (Redding, 1994, pp. 81, 85). For this reason, most manufacturing firms in Hong Kong used mature or even obsolete production equipment and technologies to combine relatively cheap inputs to produce goods designed by overseas customers. The smallness of the firms and their low capitalization also mean that R&D was avoided (Redding, 1994, p. 81). A survey by the Hong Kong Government Industry Department and Census and Statistics Department (1991, pp. 84–88) revealed that 88% of manufacturing establishments in Hong Kong did not carry out R&D. In terms of R&D expense, only 36% of establishments spent 5% or more of their total annual revenue on R&D. About 42% of the establishments spent less than 5% of their annual revenue, and 22% of the establishments had no fixed R&D budget.

More importantly, a strong correlation between the kinds of entrepreneurial strategies adopted and the business performance of the

firms was found (Yu, 1995, p. 217). Firms that adopted imitative strategies were able to survive, although many of them relied on a narrow profit margins. Innovative strategies were rarely adopted. If they were adopted, the results were not impressive. Specifically, in 1994, only 6% of electronics firms and 4% of textile and garment firms adopted innovative strategies, and their business performance was reported as either poor or unsatisfactory, which shows that innovative strategies were not practical in the business environment of Hong Kong.

The success of imitative strategies can be illustrated from Vtech Co. in the production of educational toys and cordless phones. Vtech competed by improving product design, with new models that were more functional than the original products from overseas. In 1982, Texas Instruments in the USA successfully created three popular electronic educational toys that taught children spelling, pronunciation and numbers. Each sold for US$35. When they appeared on the market, Vtech soon imitated these products. More importantly, it combined all three functions in one toy, called "Play Tech", which sold for only US$30. The product soon undersold the Texas Instruments toys and in 1994 captured 60% of the US market. This case demonstrates how a latecomer capitalized on various advantages and challenged the pioneer and market leader. In the case of cordless telephones, before Vtech introduced its product, the market was dominated by 49 MHz units. Vtech improved the design and supplied the first digital 900 MHz cordless telephones with better sound quality and reliability. As a result, the company seized 70% of the US market. By 1990, the company manufactured cordless phones for Phillips and Alcatel in Europe, and AT & T in the US, as well as its own branded products (see Yu, 1995, pp. 331–337). In short, Vtech, like many other firms in Hong Kong, succeeded by pursuing a "follower strategy".[12]

6. ENTREPRENEURSHIP AND STRUCTURAL TRANSFORMATION

Entrepreneurship is not only confined to the manufacturing sector, but also operates in tertiary fields such as retailing, transport, finance and real estate (Chau, 1993, p. 26). It has been argued that while South Korea and Taiwan have sophisticated manufacturing bases, Hong Kong has diversified significantly into the service sector (Chen, 1989, p. 36).[13] The shift from one sector to another can be explained consistently by the

dynamic operations of adaptive entrepreneurship. When entrepreneurs perceive that other
activities such as finance or services in the
tertiary sector have higher growth potentials than
the manufacturing sector, they will attempt to
arbitrage. The following cases illustrate the
various directions in which Hong Kong's
manufacturing firms have shifted their activities.

(a) *From manufacturing to property development: the case of Cheung Kong Ltd*

Chau (1993, p. 26) remarked that, in Hong
Kong, it was in the property market that the
mentality of merchant entrepreneurs found their
fullest expression. Land in the Territory is a
scarce resource. Because of its physical attributes, land in Hong Kong can only be increased
through reclamation. Therefore, land has to be
used more intensively, by either moving to higher
value uses or by constructing multistorey buildings.[14] The changes in use of a piece of land
requires imagination and the alertness of entrepreneurs. This is made evident by a classic acquisition conducted by Cheung Kong holding Ltd.[15]
In the 1960s, Li Ka-Shing, the managing director
of Cheung Kong Holding Ltd, saw that the
supply of land in Hong Kong was limited,
whereas population growth was unlimited. As a
consequence he reduced his manufacturing
businesses and moved into property development
(Rafferty, 1991, p. 309). In the 1980s, he
perceived that the land owned by the British
firm, Green Island Cement Co., possessed
considerable development potential, for it is
located in Hungham, the city center. If the land
was developed into a residential estate it would
yield a huge profit. After acquiring a 25% stake
of Green Island and entering the managing
board of the company in the 1980s, Li successfully converted the land in Hungham into a
gigantic residential estate, namely Whampao
Gardens (Chen, 1983; Gue, 1990, p. 5). The
change in use of the land and its subsequent rise
in value was not automatic, but was made
possible by entrepreneurial insight. Otherwise
the opportunity would have remained
unexploited.

(b) *From a manufacturing factory to a trading firm: Victory Garment Factory Co.*

While some manufacturing firms have moved
into real estate business, others have evolved
into trading firms. For example, Victory

Garment Factory in 40 years of development,
have moved from one strategy to another (from
private-label garment to customer-label
garment), from one region to another (from
Hong Kong to Guangdong), and from one
product to another (underwear, shirts, dresses).
Its development path fully illustrates the adaptability and flexibility of Hong Kong's manufacturers. Currently, the company's office in Hong
Kong has no actual manufacturing activities. It
merely performs the functions of a headquarters,
and is involved in sourcing, receiving orders,
merchandising etc. In short, Victory Garment
Co. is now a trading firm rather than a manufacturing firm. The boundary between a secondary
industry and a tertiary industry is increasingly
blurred. The transformation of the company
mirrors the structural changes in the Hong Kong
economy.

(c) *Diversification in the tertiary sector: Tak Sun Alliance Co.*

Clothing production is a very labor-intensive
business. As labor costs in Hong Kong rise, profit
margins from garment manufacture decrease. By
being aware of this, Ma Kai-Tak, the founder
and the managing director of Tak Sun Alliance
Company Ltd, diversified his investments into
less labor-intensive businesses, namely trading,
real estate, and food and beverages, which have
been some of the Hong Kong's major tertiary
activities in the 1990s.

Through its subsidiary, the company has
engaged in trading a wide range of materials and
apparel including textiles, knitwear and finished
garments. These materials and apparel have
been sourced from Hong Kong, China and
South-East Asia for sale to Europe and South
Africa. In 1991, trading accounted for approximately 3% of the company's turnover. The
company intends to expand its retail networks by
setting up a more extensive retail chain and
more department store counters in major
shopping areas. Ma considers Hong Kong as a
stepping stone for expansion into other affluent
Asian countries.

Ho (1992, p. 169) argues that most garment
manufacturers in Hong Kong nowadays become
property developers, and transform their factory
sites into commercial complexes, or invest in real
estate. Tak Sun Co. has been no exception.
Apart from the property occupied by the
company, it has also held property investments
that have generated rental income. The portfolio

of property investments is comprised of commercial properties located in Kowloon with an aggregate floor area of approximately 1,600 square feet. For the year ending 31 March 1991, property investments generated approximately HK$344,000 of rental income for the company.

The company had been involved in the food and beverage industry since 1985 and has invested in Ginza Development Company and the Carrianna Chiu Chow Restaurant. Each of these companies owned directly or indirectly one of the well-known Carrianna Restaurants in Hong Kong. The restaurants were located in prime areas of Wanchai and Tsim Sha Tsui and specialize in Chiu Chow cuisine. In 1991, the two restaurants contributed to approximately 5% of the company's total profits. Ma plans to open more Chiu Chow restaurants in Hong Kong, China and South-East Asian countries where Chiu Chow cuisine is popular.

In summary, on the one hand, when entrepreneurs see opportunities in the service sector that give them higher returns, they move to this sector accordingly. On the other hand, some entrepreneurs heve relocated their production out of the economy in order to reduce the demand for the Territory's relatively scarce resources (Tan, 1992, p. 38). Each profitable move made by the entrepreneurs denotes an increase in the value of resources. This is the essence of the Kirznerian model of economic growth. As a result of entrepreneurial activities, Hong Kong's economy had been transformed in the 1950s and the 1960s from traditional fishing and agriculture to manufacturing, and then in the 1970s and 1980s to the finance and service sectors. It has evolved from a traditional entrepot into an international trade and financial center (Chau, 1993, p. 16). In the manufacturing sector, Hong Kong has been integrated into a new subregional division of labor, with Japan serving as the epicenter (Chee, 1991, p. 424).

7. CATCHING-UP IN WORLD DEVELOPMENT: DAVID VERSUS GOLIATH

It is well known that Japanese producers have not only been able to copy other nation's products, but also to change and perfect them in such a way that the replicated goods become typical Japanese models (Majumdar, 1982, p. 115). Hong Kong's manufacturing firms have followed a similar path, and the following examples illustrate this.

(a) *From customer label garment to own label garment: Tak Sun Alliance*

Ernst and O'Connor (1989, pp. 67, 88) have argued that firms in the Asian NIEs initially supplied finished products to foreign firms, and that later, they marketed the products under their own brand names. In the garment industry, local suppliers started out with simple products and gradually worked their way up to more sophisticated items, by moving from customer-label products to own-label products. Tak Sun Alliance Ltd is a typical example. It was traditionally involved in customer-label garments, which were made only against confirmed orders. Though the manufacture of customer-label garments had its advantages, its founder Ma Kai-Tak was well aware that in confining itself to that, the company was unduly exposed to the marketing ability of others. Ma wanted to reduce this exposure. Previous involvement in customer-label garments provided Ma with a sufficient technical knowledge in brand development. In 1977, the company created its own label garments, "Cherry", and distributed them in the US. The resulting sales encouraged the company to distribute its own label garments in The Netherlands. In 1991, approximately 90% of the company's products were sold in the US, and 71% of those sold in Europe were own-label garments. The own label garments business contributed to nearly 70% of the company's total turnover. The move away from customer-label garments to own-label garments reflects the improvement in the firm's capabilities. Ma's case also illustrates how firms in the Asian NIEs attempt to catch up with world fashions. In fact, Hong Kong garment manufacturers have moved up-markets into fashion garments (Tan, 1992, p. 143). They are now in the upper 30% of the price range for clothing on sale in the US. Clothing designed by Diane Freis, Judy Mann, Jenny Lewis, Ragence Lam, Eddie Lau and William Tang command a premium in world fashion markets. It is believed that local designs are as good as Japan's and much better than the United States (Rafferty, 1991, pp. 179–180).

(b) *The "no-brand-one-niche-product" strategy: the case of Termbray Electronics*

When caught in a squeeze between competitors from developing countries who give lower wages and the need to match the increasing technological sophistication of the industrialized economies, Hong Kong manufacturers have shifted their focus to higher valued specialty niche products that require quick responses to new fashions and market trends (Castells and Tyson, 1989, p. 64). They have tended to concentrate on one- or two-niche products that have enabled them to boost quality and trim costs to unbeatable levels. This is precisely the strategy of Termbray Electronics Company, which has not relied on the manufacture of a diverse range of branded products. On the contrary, it has focused on the strategy of producing no-brand one-niche products.

With years of experience in the production of printed circuit boards, Lee Lap, the owner of Termbray in 1981, decisively invested HK$5 million to relocate his entire manufacturing plant to Tsuen Wan, one of the Hong Kong's new industrial areas, to produce more complex printed circuit boards. The new plant occupied a total floor area of 30,000 square feet, employed 400 people, and produced high precision double-sided printed circuit boards for sale to a number of customers, including Atari and Commodore. In 1983, the company even ceased the production of its own brand name products in order to concentrate on printed circuit boards and OEM products.

In conjunction with the technological development in the computer industry, which demanded more sophisticated high precision printed circuit boards, the company in 1984 commenced the manufacture of multilayer printed circuit boards. On the success of its printed circuit board business, Lee remarked: "I can never make computers like Commodore or IBM, but I can make printed circuit boards for them better than many other producers". By 1991, the company's total turnover in printed circuit boards amounted to HK$165.85 million, with an operating profit of HK$26.8 million. By 1994, the more advanced printed circuit boards were manufactured in Hong Kong, while the more competitively priced printed circuit boards were made in mainland China. This case shows that Hong Kong manufacturers at first learnt to make niche products and later to produce them in low cost regions, to allow them to compete in international markets.

(c) *The catching-up process in the watch industry*

The catching-up process can be illustrated in Hong Kong's watch industry. Previously, Hong Kong's watch industry was only a small sector that produced watchbands, cases and some simple movement products. Making movements requires highly trained labor and very refined techniques. Some producers imported Swiss movements and combined them with locally made cases. It is generally admitted that Hong Kong at that time was far behind Switzerland and Japan in watch production. Then came the technological innovation in watch manufacturing. With the development of LEDs (light emitting diodes) and LCDs (liquid crystal displays), electronic digital quartz watches came on to the scene. Hong Kong producers seized these opportunities. The techniques were simpler and easier to learn. More importantly, production could be done in small factories, which fitted perfectly into the requirements of Hong Kong's industrial structure, namely, small business and flexibility. Since the innovation, Hong Kong's watch industry has never ceased to grow. A wide range of new designs and models have kept pouring into world markets. Later, by taking advantage of the lower production costs in Mainland China, the prices of watches fell to as little as HK$2 per unit. During this period, several major watch companies appeared. C.P Wong's Stelux became one of the largest watch companies in the world (Woronoff, 1980, p. 170). Hong Kong's export sales in watches rose from approximately 73 million units in 1979 to 329 million units in 1988, a 350% increase in 10 years. Hong Kong ranked number one in watch exports and was regarded as one of the three major watch production centers in the world (Economic Reporter, 1990, p. 6).[16]

Because of the dynamics of entrepreneurs, the economy has been able to catch up with the economically more advanced nations. The income gap between Hong Kong (latecomer) and Western developed nations (leaders) has been narrowed. Heitger (1993, p. 75) commented that for the decade 1960–70, relative per capita income in Hong Kong was about 24% of the per capita income of the US. By the 1970s, she was able to double her per capita income and on her way to catch up with the US. By the mid 1980s, the World Bank regarded Hong Kong as middle income economy. In fact, by 1988, Hong Kong's GDP per capita reached HK$75,969 (US$9,740), clearly in the lower reaches of the high income economies. Comparatively, in 1987, Hong Kong's per capita income amounted to about 78% of the UK equivalent (US$10,420) but higher than the three OECD nations, namely Spain (US$6,010), Ireland (US$6,120) and New Zealand (US$7,750). Her neighbor, Communist China, had a per capita income only about US$290 (Ho, 1992, p. 13). By 1992, the World Bank (1993, pp.

119–120) placed Hong Kong in the high income group, along with the US and other OECD nations. By 1995, Hong Kong's per capita income reached US$21,670. Among the OECD countries, only Japan (US$21,090) and Germany (US$20,165) showed comparable performance (Asiaweek, 1995, pp. 53–54).[17] Hong Kong has joined Japan and the other Asian NIEs, Singapore, Taiwan and South Korea as the most prosperous economies in Asia.[18]

8. POLICY IMPLICATIONS

Having explained and demonstrated the important role of adaptive entrepreneurship in the industrial development of Hong Kong, several implications can be drawn. Firstly, this study has highlighted the importance of the entrepreneurial approach to economic problems. It argues that any policy recommendation on economic development should be based on analysis that incorporates entrepreneurship, the engine of economic growth. For instance, in facing competition from other developing economies, most mainstream economists have advised latecomers in Asia to upgrade their technologies.[19] However, statistics show that in the late 1980s, ventures in Hong Kong were still in technologically simple areas such as backing retail clothing franchises, rather than sophisticated technological schemes (Rafferty, 1991, p. 191). These results are not surprising if we apply the entrepreneurial approach to economic problems. Apart from upgrading technologies, there are other measures that entrepreneurs can consider. As this study has already revealed, some manufacturers in Hong Kong still explore profit opportunities in certain low value-added products, which many foreign firms do not consider to be worthwhile. Other entrepreneurs have shifted towards the tertiary sector, or moved to other low costs countries, using unsophisticated technology.[20] This is how Hong Kong has maintained its impressive economic growth despite the fact that its export composition has remained at a relatively low value of added activities, with labor-intensive and technologically simple goods continuing to make up by far the largest share (Wade, 1990, p. 332). Yet we are not arguing that upgrading manufacturing technology is unproductive. In fact, Taiwan and South Korea, because of their governments' "directive" interventions,[21] were always further ahead with innovation than Hong Kong, and therefore gained a competitive edge. It can be seen that governments play different roles in the

development of the Asian NIEs. In Taiwan, South Korea and Singapore, their governments have acted as entrepreneurs and intervention in these economies was "directive". Specifically, these states took initiatives about what technologies should be encouraged and put public resources and influences behind these initiatives (Yu, 1997). In Hong Kong, the government intervention is "facilitative" in the sense that the government creates an environment for private entrepreneurs to exploit opportunities. Apart from building a legal, social and institutional framework necessary for the effective operation of markets, the government has demonstrated its entrepreneurship in maintaining social stability. A classic entrepreneurial intervention is in housing provision. Specifically, Hong Kong's public housing programme has accommodated more than 50% of the total population (Yu, 1997, p. 57). Castells (1992, p. 49) points out that the public housing programme has subsidized workers and allowed them to work long hours without putting too much pressure on their employers, most of them with little margin to afford salary increases. It has also provided a safety net for small entrepreneurs who took a chance in starting their businesses with small savings. Another entrepreneurial intervention in Hong Kong is in land development. The Hong Kong government has substantially intervened in land supply to the benefit of export competitiveness. It has used land revenue as a budgetary mechanism to allow the delivery of a relatively extensive welfare system while maintaining low corporate and personal taxation.[22] The economy's low tax rates in turn enable "money fructify in the pockets of taxpayer" through the exercise of private entrepreneurship.

In manufacturing development, the government had chosen to play a catalytic role by motivating the people to exercise their entrepreneurial spirit (Soon, 1994, p. 144). It had deliberately restrained itself from subsidising or protecting any industry and let private enterprises function on their own. The government has assisted entrepreneurs to pick the "right" industries by furnishing them only with limited amount of consultancy facilities, such as the Hong Kong Productivity Centre and The Trade Development Council. This policy was subtly coined by the Colony's former financial secretary, Sir Phillips Haddon-Cave, in 1978 as "positive non-interventionism". Paradoxically, this philosophy is by no means *laissez-faire*. Instead, the government would restrain its visible hand if it found that the private sector could do better than the government, such as has been illustrated in its manufacturing activities, but would interfere if it found it necessary, as is the case of housing provision.[23]

Secondly, this study casts some doubts on the validity of the arguments forwarded by the Dependency School. According to this school of thought, capitalist development is crucially dependent on the superexploitation of labor. Specifically, after the Second World War, transnational corporations have dominated the production and distribution of goods and services in developing countries. They have established assembly plants and utilized the cheap and unskilled labor of the developing countries. For the Dependency School, the ultimate objective of transnational corporations has been to exploit the economic "surplus" in the form of profits, interest, royalty payments and debt repayments from the developing areas. There was very little research and development or for the transfer of the appropriate technology to the developing countries. On the contrary, the introduction of capital intensive investment by transnational corporations in the developing countries has aggravated the acute unemployment in these countries. As a result, the developing countries lost control over their economies. The general consequence was that minimal benefit accrued to the developing economies while maximum advantage accrued to the transnational corporations (Bhattacharya, 1989, pp. 96–98).[24] The theory concludes that it is impossible for developing economies to industrialize under the capitalist system. However, the industrial success of Hong Kong has flatly contradicted these arguments (see also Deyo, 1987, p. 15; Wu and Tai, 1989, pp. 46–47). This study argues that relying on and learning from advanced capitalist nations can be a useful development strategy. More specifically, by employing entrepreneurial strategies such as OEM business, small scale enterprise, subcontracting and product imitation, which are largely dependent on foreign firms, manufacturing firms in developing economies can compete in world markets and catch up with the economically more developed nations.

Another attempt to explain the increasingly integrated world economy is the global commodity chains approach.[25] Similar to the theory of comparative advantage is the argument that industrialization is a process of adjustment in which countries move through different stages of comparative advantage, Gereffi and Wyman (1990, p. 92) note that developing countries are primarily export platforms that produce simple, low technology, labor-intensive goods by using low-wage, unskilled workers. These countries are later able to upgrade their industries, and shift from commodities such as textiles, apparel and footwear to higher value-added items that employ sophisticated technology and require a more extensively developed tightly integrated local industrial base.

Designating specific processes within a commodity chain as nodes, the global commodity chains framework enables us to pose questions about contemporary development issues that are not easily handled by the conventional Neoclassical paradigm. It is a network-centered and historical-centered approach that probes above and below the level of the nation-state to analyse the structure and change in the world-economy (Gereffi and Korzeniewicz, 1994, p. 2). It allows us to more adequately forge the macro–micro links between processes that are generally assumed to be discretely contained within global, national, and local units of analysis. Despite these merits, the global commodity chains approach focuses on spatial patterns of commodity chains, which is essentially commodity-based rather than human-agency based, and in which significant factors, such as entrepreneurial perception of the external environment, imitation and learning, are lacking.[26]

In this regard, this study advocates Porter's arguments in favor of using the concept of competitive advantage in analysing the growth performance of both firms and nations (Porter, 1990, p. 45). In Porter's view, the competitive advantage approach emphasizes organizational learning, knowledge, and creative thinking. It arises out of entrepreneurial perception or the discovery of better ways to compete in an industry. Accordingly, this approach fits into our entrepreneurial paradigm that focuses on imitation, learning and catching-up in the dynamic world economy.

Finally, our argument that the industrial success for latecomers hinges on the adaptive mode of entrepreneurship is not limited to Hong Kong or other Asian Newly Industrializing Economies,[27] though such entrepreneurship may appear in different form. The crucial point is whether latecomers can successfully develop adaptive entrepreneurship so as to exploit international market opportunities. Though the rise of international protectionism may restrict opportunities for international trade and transfer of technology, this study suggests that in the future, new NIEs will still emerge, because in the dynamic world development process, market opportunities, the result of the creative power of entrepreneurs, will never be exhausted. Whether

908   WORLD DEVELOPMENT

a developing nation can catch up with economically more advanced countries depends on whether it can promote entrepreneurship to identify and exploit these opportunities.

NOTES

1. An earlier version of this paper was presented at the 24th Conference of Economists held at the University of Adelaide, Australia, 24–27 September 1995. The author thanks H. B. Cheah, Paul L. Robertson and Paul A. McGavin for their encouragement, assistance and insightful criticisms in this research. They are not responsible for the deficiencies that remain. Final revision accepted December 5, 1997.

2. An exception is Chau (1993). Based on Kirzner's contribution, he argued that the economic dynamics of Hong Kong has been attributed to what he called 'merchant-entrepreneurs'. A crucial point he made is that the success of merchant entrepreneurs in Hong Kong is not confined only to manufacturing, but extends to the tertiary sector as well.

3. By means of "more recent thinking on the subject", Mackie referred to the works of Kirzner (1973, 1982), Casson (1982), Drucker (1985) and Nafziger (1986).

4. Schumpeter (1947, p. 150) identified two kinds of response in economic development, namely, creative response and adaptive response. See also Yu (1995, p. 48); Cheah and Yu (1995, p. 366).

5. Such an argument has raised a number of criticisms both from within and outside the Austrian camps. Specifically, White (1976) commented that Kirzner failed to recognize the highly important part played by entrepreneurial imagination. Defending his position, Kirzner (1982) subsequently accepted the elements of creativeness and imagination into his model, by introducing multi-period arbitrageurship. However, Kirzner, in a personal correspondence to the author (January 13, 1994), noted that he preferred to consider his entrepreneurship as a subset of entrepreneurship, and confined to those activities that take advantage of existing scattered knowledge.

6. For the content of the questionnaire, see Yu (1995, Appendix 1).

7. For a detail description of the methods of analysis in this research, see Yu (1995, pp. 83–94).

8. For a detail account of the economic and political setting of Hong Kong, see Ho (1992, pp. 1–43); Chau (1993, pp. 1–19) and Yu (1995, pp. 95–104).

9. This case is adopted from Yu (1995).

10. Using examples from developing countries, Jacobson (1992) has argued that flexibility is a critical strategic factor in the entrepreneurial discovery process.

11. In the textile and garment industry, international subcontracting was conducted through customer label garment business. My survey shows that in 1994, 78% of the textile and garment firms had been and would

continued to be involved in the customer label garment business (Yu, 1995, p. 165).

12. For an account of how Hong Kong's electronics firms such as RJP pursued imitative strategies, see Hobday (1995, pp. 1181–1182) and Yu (1993).

13. Rafferty (1991, p. 168) wrote: "Hong Kong today is much more diversified than a mere manufacturing centre…[it] is also a big financial centre involved in round-the-clock trading; has a strong service sector catering for tourists and business conferences, especially for people who want to see new ideas and a dynamic marketplace; and has an important communications role, keeping the Asia-Pacific region in touch with the rest of the world by means of air and shipping services and telecommunications".

14. The former Financial Secretary, Sir Philip Haddon-Cave, argued that the scarcity of land in Hong Kong had encouraged intensive development (Youngson, 1982, p. 80).

15. Acquisition can be regarded as a form of arbitrage of the difference in organizational advantages. The benefits are sought through the re-structuring of a company after takeover. When entrepreneurs discover that there are unused or underutilized assets in a company and that the value of its share is undervalued, they will acquire the company. After re-structuring, the assets are bought into a more efficient use, bringing impressive returns for acquirers. See Yu (1993).

16. For an excellent account of how the Hong Kong entrepreneur, Mr David C.W. Yeh developed his small toy factory, Universal Associated Co. into a multinational giant and eventually acquired the world famous British toy maker Lesney Group, see *Forbes*, 1993, October, pp. 68–70.

17. The process of catching-up involves more than just technological improvement or higher incomes. There are other factors that affect the gaps between the leaders and the followers and their ranks in the international income ladder. These factors are related to social capability (Abramovitz, 1988). Accordingly, a country's potential for rapid growth is strong when it is technologically backward but is socially advanced. Some determinants of social capability are educational level, communication networks, customs and institutions, to name a few.

18. Rafferty (1991, p. 170) wrote: "The Territory has almost no natural resources…. Yet today it can claim these achievements:

● Asia's leading financial center and the third in the world after New York and London.
● Asia's largest gold-trading center.
● World's largest exporter of garments, toys and plastic products.

- World's largest exporter in volume of watches, clocks and radios.
- 18th among the world's trading nations (now about 12th).
- 20th among the world's exporters of domestic manufactures.
- World's third busiest container port, after Rotterdam and New York [today the busiest container port in the world].
- World's biggest single air cargo terminal.
- Highest living standard in Asia outside Japan.
- World's largest public housing program.
- World's third largest diamond-trading center after New York and Antwerp."

19. For example, see Chen and Wong (1989, pp. 208, 223).

20. In particular, Wade (1990, p. 333) has argued that "Hong Kong's restructuring success has been in finance rather than in industry, led by the major banks".

21. Luedde-Neurath (1988, p. 103) distinguished two kinds of government intervention, namely promotional and directive. The former aims to restore markets to their proper function. It seeks to provide public goods such as infrastructure, education, etc., which cannot be supplied adequately in private markets. The latter aims to achieve predetermined results through conscious interference with market forces and selective application of incentives and/or controls. Following Luedde-Neurath, Yu (1997) refers to government policies that interfere on a large scale to make significant change in investment and production patterns in an industry as "directive" entrepreneurial intervention, and government policies that attempt to create an environment for private enterprises to pursue their interests as "facilitative" entrepreneurial intervention.

22. Hong Kong has maintained a standard income tax of 15% and profit taxes that range from 15.5% to 16.5% for many years.

23. For a detail discussion of the role of government in the economic development of the Asian NIEs, see Yu (1997).

24. Like the Dependency School, the global commodity chains approach also emphasizes on the relationship between core and peripheral nations. it argues that within a commodity chain, a relatively greater share of wealth generally accrues to core-like nodes than to peripheral ones. This is because, as this approach argues, enterprises and states in the core nations gain a competitive edge through innovations that transfer competitive pressure to peripheral areas of the world-economy (Gereffi and Korzeniewicz, 1994, p. 2). For the roles of innovation and imitation in the world development, see Cheah (1992) and Yu (1995).

25. According to Gereffi and Korzeniewicz (1994, p. 2), a commodity chain is a network of labor and production processes whose end result is a finished commodity. A global commodity chain consists of sets of interorganizational networks that are clustered around one commodity or product, and that link households, enterprises and states to one another within the world economy. Specific processes or segments within a commodity chain are represented as nodes that are linked together in networks. Each successive node within a commodity chain involves acquisition and/or organization of inputs, labor power and consumption. The analysis of a commodity chain shows how production, distribution and consumption are shaped by the social relations that characterize the sequential stages of input acquisition, manufacturing, distribution, marketing and consumption. The global commodity chains framework is said to be in many ways similar to Porter's value chain approach (see Gereffi and Korzeniewicz, 1994, pp. 6, 188).

26. Though scholars in the global commodity chains framework note the efforts of entrepreneurs in shaping the world trade patterns (see Gereffi and Korzeniewicz, 1994, p. 3), they have not carefully considered the role of entrepreneurship.

27. Some scholars such as Wu and Tai (1989) argue that the economic success of the Asian NIE is attributable to the Neo-Confucian culture.

REFERENCES

Abramovitz, M. (1988) Following and leading. In *Evolutionary Economics: Applications of Schumpeter's Ideas*, ed. H. Hannsch. pp. 323–341, Cambridge University Press, Cambridge.

Asiaweek (1995) Bottom line. 10 March, pp. 53–54.

Baumol, W. J. (1988) Is entrepreneurship always productive? In *Entrepreneurship and Economic Development*, eds H. Leibenstein and D. Ray. pp. 85–94, United Nations, New York.

Bhattacharya, D. (1989) *Economic Development and Underdevelopment*. Australian Professional Publications, Sydney.

Casson, M. (1982) *The Entrepreneur: An Economic Theory*. Blackwell, Oxford.

Castells, M. (1992) Four Asian tigers with a dragon head: a comparative analysis of the state, economy and society in the Asian Pacific rim. In *States and Development in the Asian Pacific Rim*, eds R. Appelbaum and J. Henderson. pp. 33–70 Sage Publications, London.

Castells, M. and Tyson, L. D'A. (1989) High technology and the changing international division of production. In *The Newly Industrialising Countries in the World Economy: Challenges for US Policy*, ed. R. P. Purcell. pp. 20–82, Lynne Rienner Publisher, Colorado.

Chan, W. K. (1991) *The Making of Hong Kong Society*. Clarendon Press, Oxford.

Chau, L. L. C. (1993) *Hong Kong: A Unique Case of Development*. A World Bank Publication, Washington, DC.

Cheah, H. B. (1992) Revolution and evolution in the entrepreneurial process. Proceedings of World Conference on Entrepreneurship, Aug 11–14, 1992, pp. 462–474, Singapore.

Cheah, H. B. and Yu, T. F. (1995) Adaptive response: entrepreneurship and competitiveness in the economic development of Hong Kong. Proceedings of the Sixth ENDEC World Conference on Entrepreneurship, Shanghai, China, pp. 366–377.

Chee, P. L. (1991) The changing pattern of foreign direct investment in the Asian Pacific Region: implications for Hong Kong. In *Industrial and Trade Development in Hong Kong*, eds Chen, E. *et al*. pp. 406–426, Centre of Asian Studies, Hong Kong.

Chen, E. K. Y. (1979) *Hyper-growth in Asian Economies*. The MacMillan Press, London.

Chen, E. K. Y. (1983) Multinationals from Hong Kong. In *The New Multinationals: The Spread of Third World Enterprises*, ed. S. Lall. pp. 89–136, John Wiley and Sons, Chichester.

Chen, E. K. Y. (1988) The economic and non-economics of Asia's four little dragons. An Inaugural Lecture, University of Hong Kong, *Gazette*, **35**(1 Suppl.), March 21.

Chen, E. K. Y. (1989) Hong Kong's role in Asian and Pacific economic development. *Asian Development Review* **7**(2), 26–47.

Chen, E. K. Y. and Wong T. (1989) The future direction of industrial development in the Asian newly industrialized economies (NIEs). Asian and Pacific Development Centre.

Cheng, T. Y. (1982) *The Economy of Hong Kong*. Far East Publications, rev. edn, Hong Kong.

Davies, H., Ling, J. and Cheung, F. (1993) Product design and the location of production: strategic choice in Hong Kong manufacturing. *Academy of International Business* **3**, 1–14.

Deyo, F. (1987) *The Political Economy of the New Asian Industrialism*. Cornell University Press, Ithaca.

Drucker, P. (1985) *Innovation and Entrepreneurship*. Heinemann, London.

Economic Reporter (1990) A profile of young industrialist. 5 March, p. 6 (text in Chinese).

Engardio, P. and Gross, N. (1992) Asia's high-tech quest. *International Business Week*, 30 November, pp. 64, 67.

Ernst, D. and O'Connor, D. (1989) *Technology and Global Competition: The Challenge for Newly Industrialising Economies*. OCED, Paris.

Espy, J. L. (1970) The strategies of Chinese enterprises in Hong Kong. Unpublished DBA Thesis, Harvard University, USA.

Forbes (1993) The future of Hong Kong's TV manufacturers. October, pp. 68–70 (text in Chinese).

Gereffi, G. and Korzeniewicz, M. (1994) *Commodity Chains and Global Capitalism*. Praeger, Westport, CT.

Gereffi, G. and Wyman D. L. (1990) *Manufacturing Miracles*. Princeton University Press, New Jersey.

Gilad, B., Kaish, S. and Ronen, J. (1988) The entrepreneurial way with information. In *Applied Behavioural Economics*, ed. S. Maital. pp. 481–503, Wheatsheaf, Vol. II, Somerset.

Gue, W.-F. (1990) Dang Dai Quang Tai Nan Yang Jing Ji Qiang Ren Lei Zhuan [An Annotated Bibliography of Contemporary Business people from Hong Kong, Taiwan and South East Asia]. *Economic Daily Press*, Beijing (text in Chinese).

Heitger, B. (1993) Comparative economic growth: catching up in East Asia. *ASEAN Economic Bulletin*, July, pp. 68–82.

Ho, Y. P. (1992) *Trade, Industrial Restructuring and Development in Hong Kong*. MacMillan, London.

Hobday, M. (1995) East Asian latecomer firms: learning the technology of electronics. *World Development* **23**(7), 1171–1193.

Hong Kong Government Census and Statistics Department, *Hong Kong Annual Digest of Statistics*, various issues, Hong Kong: Hong Kong Government Printer.

Hong Kong Government Industry Department (1993) *Hong Kong's Manufacturing Industries*. Hong Kong Government Printer.

Hong Kong Government Industry Department and Census and Statistics Department (1991) *Survey on the Future Development of Industry in Hong Kong: Statistical Survey of Manufacturers, 1984–1989*. pp. 84–89, Hong Kong Government Printer.

Hsueh, T.-T. (1976) The transforming economy of Hong Kong 1951–1973. *Hong Kong Economic Papers* **10**, 46–65.

Jacobson, R. (1992) The Austrian school of strategy. *Academy of Management Review* **17**(4), 782–807.

Kirzner, I. M. (1973) *Competition and Entrepreneurship*. University of Chicago Press, Chicago.

Kirzner, I. M. (1982) Uncertainty, discovery and human action. In *Method, Process and Austrian Economics*, ed. I. M.Kirzner. D. C. Heath, Canada.

Kirzner, I. M. (1985) *Discovery and the Capitalist Process*. University of Chicago press, Chicago.

Kwok, P. (1978) Small manufacturing business in Hong Kong. M.Phil. Thesis, University of Hong Kong.

Lam D. K.-K. and Lee I. (1992) Guerrilla capitalism and the limits of statist theory: comparing the Chinese NICs. In *The Evolving Pacific Basin in the Global Political Economy*, eds C. Clark and S. Chan. pp. 107–124, Lynne Rienner Publishers, London.

Leibenstein, H. (1968) Entrepreneurship and development. *American Economic Review* **58**, 72–83.

Luedde-Neurath, R. (1988) State intervention and export-oriented development in South Korea. In *Developmental States in East Asia*, ed. G. White. pp. 68–112, St Martin's Press, New York.

Mackie, J. A. C. (1992) Overseas Chinese entrepreneurship. *Asian-Pacific Economic Literature*, May, pp. 41–64.

Majumdar, B. A. (1982) *Innovations, Product Developments and Technology Transfers: An Empirical Study of Dynamic Competitive Advantage, The Case of Electronic Calculators*. University Press of America Inc, Washington, DC.

Nafziger, E. W. (1986) *Entrepreneurship, Equity, and Economic Development*. JAI Press, Conneticut.

Peebles, G. (1988) *Hong Kong's Economy*. Oxford University Press, Hong Kong.

Porter, M. E. (1990) *The Competitive Advantage of Nations*. Free Press, NY.

Rafferty, K. (1991) *City on the Rocks: Hong Kong's Uncertain Future*. Penguin Books, London.

Redding, S.G. (1994) Competitive advantage in the context of Hong Kong. *Journal of Far Eastern Business* **1**(1), 71–89.

Riedel, J. (1974) *The Industrialization of Hong Kong*. J. C. B. Mohr (Paul Siebeck), Tubingen.

Schumpeter, J. A. (1947) The creative response in economic history. In *Essays of J.A. Schumpeter*. Addison–Wesley, Cambridge, MA.

Sit, V. and Wong, S.-L. (1989), *Small and Medium Industries in an Export-Oriented Economy: The Case of Hong Kong*. Centre of Asian Studies, University of Hong Kong.

Sit, V., Wong, S.-L. and Kiang, T.-S. (1979) *Small Scale Industry in a Laissez-Faire Economy: A Hong Kong Case Study*, Centre of Asian Studies, University of Hong Kong.

Soon, C. (1994) Government and market in economic development. *Asian Development Review* **12**(2), 144–165.

Sung, Y.-W. (1987) Flexibility and Hong Kong's competitiveness. *Hong Kong Economic Journal Monthly*, February, No. 119. (text in Chinese).

Tan, G. (1992) *The Newly Industrialising Countries of Asia*. Times Academic Press, Singapore.

Wade, R. (1990) *Governing the Market*. Princeton University Press, New Jersey.

White, L. H. (1990) Entrepreneurship, imagination and the question of equilibrium. In *Austrian Economics*, Vol. III, ed. S. Littlechild. pp. 87–104, Edward Elgar, England.

Wilson, J. (1991) It's do or die for a struggling chip industry. *Electronics Business Asia*, July, p. 71.

Wong, S.-L. (1988) *Emigrant Entrepreneurs: Shanghai Industrialists in Hong Kong*. Oxford University Press, Hong Kong.

World Bank (1993) *The East Asian Miracle: Economic Growth and Public Policy*. Oxford University Press, Oxford.

Woronoff, J. (1980) *Hong Kong: Capitalist Paradise*. Heinemann Asia, Hong Kong.

Wu, J. S. K. (1989) Entrepreneurship. In *The Economic System of Hong Kong*, eds C. Y. Ho and L. C. Chau. Asia Research Service, Hong Kong.

Wu, Y.-L. and Tai, H.-C. (1989) Economic performance in five East Asian Countries: a comparative analysis. In *Confucianism and Economic Development: an Oriental Alternative*, ed. H. Tai. pp. 38–54, The Washington Institute for Values in Public Policy, Washington, DC.

Youngson, A. (1982) *Hong Kong; Economic Growth and Policy*. Oxford University Press, Hong Kong.

Yu, T. F. (1993) Entrepreneurship and the economic development of Hong Kong: an analytical framework, Paper presented at the international conference on Chinese and East Asian Economies in the 1990s organized by the Chinese Economic Association (Australia) held at The Australian National University, Canberra, November 30–December 1, 1993.

Yu, T. F. (1995) Adaptive response: Entrepreneurship and economic development in Hong Kong. PhD Thesis, School of Economics and Management, University College, The University of New South Wales.

Yu, T. F. (1997) Entrepreneurial states: the role of government in the economic development of the Asian Newly Industrialising Economies. *Development Policy Review* **15**(1), 47–64.

Part III
Innovation

[8]

The Tradeoff Between Firm Size and Diversity in the Pursuit of Technological Progress

Wesley M. Cohen
Steven Klepper

1. Introduction

Since the writings of Schumpeter, the role of firm size in promoting technical advance has preoccupied scholars of technological change. As international competitive pressures have intensified in recent years, the role of firm size has emerged as a central concern of policymakers and industrialists as well. In the United States, some argue that the small entrepreneurial firm is the primary vehicle through which new ideas are introduced into the marketplace and that the diversity of ideas and approaches flowing from small firms represents American manufacturing's key competitive advantage (e.g., Gilder, 1988; Rodgers, 1990; Shaffer, 1990). On the other side, it is argued that only large firms or consortia can command the resources necessary to field the large research efforts required to keep up with the large, often cooperatively organized research operations of Japan, and, more recently, Europe (e.g., Ferguson, 1988; Norris, 1983; Noyce, 1990). Over the course of his career, Schumpeter himself spanned the poles of this debate. In his earlier work, Schumpeter (1934) saw the small-scale entrepreneur as the key to capitalism's vitality. Later Schumpeter (1942) argued that the large scale enterprise was the principal engine of technological progress, although he feared that the bureaucratic character of the large modern corporation would undermine entrepreneurial initiative and eventually sap capitalism of its technological vitality.

Final version accepted on June 13, 1991

Carnegie-Mellon University
Department of Social & Decision Sciences
Pittsburgh, PA 15213-3890, U.S.A.

In recent years, this controversy has been dominated, with some exceptions (e.g., Jorde and Teece, 1990), by industrialists and policy analysts. Most of the arguments advanced by both sides are based upon specific industries, most notably the semiconductor and computer industries. These arguments have largely failed to galvanize economists. Not only have the arguments been casually developed, but there are strong counterarguments to each, leaving us with little a priori basis for favoring either position. For example, proponents of large scale enterprise often allude to scale economies and capital market imperfections to rationalize the need for large firms and consortia. Scale economies, however, bear only on the optimal size of the R&D effort and relate only indirectly to the optimal size of the firm. With regard to capital market imperfections, there is no consensus among economists as to the import of such imperfections for investment in general, much less R&D in particular. Those arguing in behalf of small size have claimed that small firms, unencumbered by bureaucracy, provide both the freedom and economic incentives that stimulate creativity and agility in response to economic opportunity. On the other hand, while large firms may be more bureaucratic, they provide a superior human and capital infrastructure to support innovative activity.

To the extent that economists have probed the relationship between firm size and innovative activity, the evidence for either side of the debate has also not been compelling. Indeed, the predominant finding from a voluminous literature on the subject is that in most industries, above a modest threshold firm size large firms are no more research intensive than smaller firms. This implies that consolidation of firms above the threshold would have no effect on total industry R&D

Small Business Economics **4**: 1—14, 1992.

expenditures, which has been widely interpreted to indicate that above a modest firm size neither small nor large firm size confers any advantage in R&D (e.g., Kamien and Schwartz, 1982; Scherer, 1980; Baldwin and Scott, 1987).

We propose that even if small and large firms are equally capable at R&D, there may nonetheless be important social advantages associated with *both* large and small firm size. We suggest that there is merit to both sides of the debate about the optimal firm size for R&D, but not for the reasons typically advanced. Our demonstration of the social advantages of small and large firm size proceeds in two stages. First, drawing heavily on prior work (Cohen and Klepper, 1990, 1991), we suggest that both firm size and technological diversity influence firm R&D expenditures within industries and we highlight evidence that supports this claim. In the second stage, we go beyond our earlier analysis, and, in a more speculative spirit, consider not only how firm size and diversity influence firm R&D expenditures, but also how they affect the technical advance generated by the expenditures. We argue there are virtues both to having a large number of small firms in an industry and to consolidating output in a few large firms.

The social advantages in our framework of an industry composed of numerous small firms rests on two notions suggested by Nelson's (1981) argument about the importance of competition and diversity for technological change. The first notion is that in the typical industry undergoing technological change, there are many productive ways of innovating. The other notion is that firms have different capabilities and perceptions which lead them to pursue different sets of approaches to innovation. In such a world, dividing up industry output over a greater number of small firms increases the chances that any given approach to innovation will be pursued, thereby increasing the diversity of technological efforts in the industry. While increasing the number of firms does not necessarily benefit individual firms in the industry, it promotes technical advance and, hence, benefits society by increasing the number of productive approaches to innovation that are collectively pursued in the industry. From this perspective, the source of the social advantage associated with small firm size is not smallness per se but the greater number of firms that small size implies given some industry demand.

Our argument about the social advantages of large firm size stems from the idea that large firms possess an advantage in appropriating the returns from innovation due, in part, to imperfections in the market for information (Arrow, 1962). This causes the returns to large firms from any given R&D effort to be greater than the returns to small firms, leading large firms to conduct more socially desirable R&D than smaller firms. Consequently, consolidating output over a smaller number of firms will result in the performance of more socially desirable R&D for each approach to innovation that is pursued. This benefit is realized independent of whether there are any economies of scale in the conduct of R&D or whether large firms have superior ability to finance R&D.

Given the social advantages associated with both large firm size and more numerous small firms, there will always be a tradeoff associated with changing the number of firms within an industry. Reducing the number of firms will increase the average firm size, which will increase the level of innovative effort applied to each approach to innovation that is pursued. This comes, however, at the cost of reducing the number of productive approaches to innovation that are collectively pursued in the industry. On the other hand, increasing the number of firms will increase the diversity of approaches that are pursued in the industry but reduce the level of effort for each approach. The optimal number of firms in each industry will depend on the relative importance of these two effects, which we argue will vary across industries.

We speculate that market forces alone are not likely to lead to the socially optimal average firm size and number of firms in each industry. For example, the eventual displacement of larger incumbent firms by smaller new firms will compromise the appropriability advantages of size. Alternatively, even when entry of new firms can enhance social welfare by increasing the diversity of approaches to innovation pursued within an industry, we argue that such entry will not necessarily be forthcoming. Although these opposing forces could conceivably balance out to yield some optimal number of firms, we have no reason to expect this to occur in the typical industry.

We discuss how the failure of private initiatives to lead to a socially optimal state will create a tension from a policy standpoint. Following recent trends, obstacles to cooperative R&D efforts within industries could be removed, which would encourage the development of larger scale innovating units. This will, however, reduce the diversity of technological approaches pursued. Alternatively, diversity could be stimulated by government subsidies to entrants. However, more entry will reduce average firm size, thereby compromising the advantages of size. We suggest that it may well be just this tension that, in part, has given rise to the recent policy debates. We argue that there are policies, however, that can to some degree preserve the benefits of size while at the same time maintain technological diversity.

The paper is organized as follows. In Section 2, we present our framework and briefly review the evidence that supports it. In Section 3, we suggest how larger firm size is tied to technical advance. In Section 4, we suggest how a larger number of firms may yield greater technological diversity and how that diversity, in turn, contributes to technical advance. In Section 5, we discuss the tradeoff implied by the existence of both an appropriability advantage of large firm size and a diversity-inducing advantage of having numerous small firms within an industry. In Section 6, we conclude by highlighting the limitations of our analysis and by suggesting issues for further research.

2. A model of R&D investment

In this section we consider how firms decide how much to spend on R&D. Our conception follows the model of R&D investment developed in Cohen and Klepper (1990, 1991). We discuss the basis for the model and provide a brief description of its implications. We refer the reader to Cohen and Klepper (1990, 1991) for the formal and more extensive development of the model.

The model is based on a distinctive conception of an industry. The industry is assumed to be subject to ongoing technological change. Following Nelson (1990) and others, it is assumed that technological advance can be achieved in many different ways. A distinction is commonly drawn, for example, between process and product innovations. Moreover, there are typically many different ways of improving technology within each of these categories. For example, a production process may be improved through automation and by increasing the scale of production. Similarly, a

product may be improved along a range of dimensions. For example, personal computers can be made more user-friendly and they can be made to work faster. These different approaches to enhancing product and process performance are often additive in their effect on technical advance; they do not represent competing or mutually exclusive approaches to satisfying the same performance objective. A firm in principle could pursue all of the approaches or any subset of them.

Firms are assumed to be uncertain about the profitability of pursuing any given approach to innovation, both in terms of the cost of the innovation and its gross returns. For simplicity, we assume that all approaches are profitable to pursue, although the firms do not know that in advance. The uncertainty concerning the profitability of the various approaches to innovation generates differences in firms' expectations about which approaches are worth pursuing. These differences are assumed to reflect the differences in the sorts of expertise possessed by each firm. The differing expectations cause the firms to make different bets on which approaches to pursue.

The firms that make the best bets will experience the greatest rate of innovation and technical advance. It is assumed that eventually all innovations (but not the approaches themselves) will be copied, so that ultimately all benefits from innovation will be passed on to buyers in the form of lower prices. In the interim, however, firms that innovate most will reap economic profits. They will grow at the fastest rates over time, although growth will tend to be incremental, reflecting, among other things, the impact of uncertainty on investment and convex adjustment costs. Those firms that innovate the least will find the price of their product falling below their costs and will eventually exit. Over time the expertise required to evaluate and exploit approaches to innovation will change as the industry's technology evolves. Firms will be limited in their ability to change their expertise,[1] and in the long run new firms with more suitable expertise will replace the industry leaders.

The consequence of this process is that at a given moment in each industry there will be an array of firms of different sizes and capabilities with different views about which approaches to innovation are worth pursuing. The model focuses on how these differences condition firm decisions

Entrepreneurship and Economic Growth

about which approaches to pursue and about how much to spend on R&D for each approach pursued. The number of firms and the output of each firm are taken as given, having been determined by the evolutionary process leading up to that moment in the industry's history. For simplicity, firms are also assumed to be price takers and to choose their R&D expenditures independent of the R&D expenditures of their rivals.

With regard to the approaches a firm decides to pursue, we assume this choice is determined exclusively by the expertise of the firm. A firm is assumed to pursue a particular approach if it possesses the expertise that would enable it to exploit and recognize the value of the approach. Consequently, in each industry the environment governing the endowment of firms with expertise will ultimately determine the approaches to innovation that are pursued by firms in the industry. We use a very simple model to represent this environment. First, we assume that in each industry the likelihood of a firm possessing the expertise that would lead it to pursue any given approach is independent of the likelihood of the firm possessing the expertise that would lead it to pursue any other approach. This implies that the probability of a firm pursuing any given approach is independent of the probability of it pursuing any other.[2] Second, we assume that in each industry the likelihood of a firm being endowed with the expertise that would lead it to pursue any given approach is independent of the size of the firm. This implies that the probability of a firm pursuing any given approach is independent of its size.

The choice about how much the firm should spend on each approach to innovation it pursues is conceived as follows. Each approach to innovation is assumed to be characterized by a range of projects with different marginal products, where the marginal product of a project is defined in terms of the technical advance (measured in standard units) generated from the project. Ordering the projects by their marginal products defines a diminishing marginal product schedule that relates the marginal product of R&D expenditures on an approach to the level of R&D expenditures on the approach, where it is assumed that the level of R&D expenditures is proportional to the number of projects pursued. All firms that pursue an approach are assumed to face the same marginal product of R&D schedule for the approach.

Although the marginal productivity schedules for all approaches are assumed identical across firms, the marginal revenue schedules associated with the approaches will differ across firms. The marginal revenue a firm earns from a project depends on the marginal product of the project and the level of output over which the innovations from the project are applied. It is assumed that firms will typically not sell their innovations in disembodied form either due to imperfections in the market for information (Arrow, 1962) or because the innovations are more valuable to the innovator than to other firms (Cohen and Klepper, 1990).[3] This implies that firms will appropriate the returns to their innovations primarily through their own output.[4] We also assume that the firm expects its growth due to innovation to be incremental and conditioned by its pre-innovation output level. This implies that the returns a firm earns from any given R&D project will be proportional to its sales prior to the R&D project, which we refer to as the firm's *ex ante* sales.

The assumptions governing the choice of approaches to innovation and the amount spent per approach form the basis for predictions about firm R&D expenditures in an industry. First, assuming no economies of scale in R&D, Cohen and Klepper (1991) demonstrate that the assumption that the firm's expected returns to innovation are scaled by its *ex ante* output implies that in each industry all firms pursuing a particular approach will spend an amount on R&D on the approach that is proportional to their *ex ante* sales. The simple intuition behind this result is that the greater the firm's sales then the larger the returns from any given R&D effort and thus the larger the optimal R&D expenditures of the firm. Furthermore, if the number of approaches to innovation pursued by the firm is uncorrelated with its sales, Cohen and Klepper (1990) show that the overall R&D intensity of the firm (i.e., the ratio of the firm's R&D expenditures on all approaches to its sales) will be independent of its *ex ante* sales. Alternatively expressed, in each industry total firm R&D expenditures will vary across firms proportionally with the *ex ante* sales of the firms.

Second, Cohen and Klepper (1991) demonstrate that if it is assumed that in each industry the marginal product schedule of each approach to innovation is the same and firms are equally likely to adopt each approach to innovation, then the number of approaches to innovation pursued by firms and their overall R&D intensity will be binomially distributed. Intuitively, given that firms will pursue different numbers of approaches, the adoption of each approach by a firm can be thought of as an independent Bernoulli trial. As a consequence, in each industry the number of approaches pursued by firms will be binomially distributed. It was noted above that firms' R&D expenditures on any given approach will be proportional to their sales. Coupled with the assumption that the marginal product schedules of the approaches do not differ, Cohen and Klepper (1991) show that this implies that in each industry firm R&D intensities will also be binomially distributed, with the firms that pursue the greatest number of approaches having the largest R&D intensities and the firms that pursue the smallest number of approaches having the smallest R&D intensities.

Both sets of predictions of the model are supported by evidence on how firm R&D expenditures vary within industries. Cohen and Klepper (1990) note how the predictions of the model concerning the independence of firm R&D intensities and firm sales accords with the large body of evidence about the proportional relationship within industries between R&D expenditures and firm sales noted in the introduction. The predictions of the model concerning the nature of the distribution within industries of firm R&D intensities are supported by the empirical regularities in industry R&D intensity distributions documented by Cohen and Klepper (1991) for a sample of business units[5] belonging largely to the 1,000 leading American manufacturing firms as of 1974–1977. These distributions tend to be unimodal, positively skewed, and to contain a substantial number of nonperformers of R&D, which is consistent with firm R&D intensity being binomially distributed. Moreover, across industries the moments of the distributions are correlated, which is also compatible with the binomial. Indeed, as Cohen and Klepper (1991) show, the model is capable of explaining not only the fact that the moments are correlated but also the signs of the correlations.

Thus, the model can explain a fairly exacting set of regularities that characterize the distribution of R&D intensities within industries. This provides indirect support for the two central tenets of the model: (1) returns to R&D are scaled by the size of the firm; and (2) differences in firm R&D intensities are attributable to differences across firms in the number of approaches to innovation pursued.

3. The advantages of large size

In this section we consider the implications of our framework for the advantages of large firm size, where size refers specifically to the level of output of a particular product. Our discussion is largely based on Cohen and Klepper (1990). Following our earlier work, we assume that the mechanisms within an industry for appropriating rents due to innovation, such as patents, are given. We focus on the welfare implications of the link in our framework between firm size and the appropriability of the returns to innovation.

Since, in our framework, the firm earns returns on its innovations through its own output and growth tends to be incremental, the returns to R&D are scaled by the firm's *ex ante* sales. As we noted, this is the key in our framework to explaining the proportional relationship between R&D effort and firm size. This argument also implies that large firms will have an advantage over smaller firms in R&D competition. To see this, consider two firms that produce the same product and pursue the same number of approaches to innovation. Suppose, for simplicity, that all R&D expenditures result in innovations which lower the average cost of production.[6] If the two firms spend the same amount on R&D then our framework implies that they would achieve the same unit cost reduction. The larger firm, however, would apply the unit cost reduction over a larger level of output, enabling it to earn greater profits from its R&D.[7] Moreover, our framework implies that if two firms pursue the same number of approaches, they will have the same R&D intensity, which implies that the bigger firm will actually perform more R&D than the smaller firm. This reflects the greater return it earns from any given level of R&D due to its greater size, which provides it with an incentive to perform a greater level of R&D than its smaller rival. Since it will earn positive profits from this additional R&D, this reinforces its advantage over its smaller rival.

Our interpretation of the relationship within industries between R&D effort and firm size is quite unconventional. The standard interpretation is that the proportional relationship between R&D effort and firm size suggests no advantage or disadvantage of large firms in R&D, although Fisher and Temin (1973) caution against making inferences about the advantages of firm size in R&D from the relationship between R&D effort and firm size. Of course, all we have shown is that the evidence is compatible with a theory in which there is an appropriability advantage to large firm size in R&D. There is, however, no competing explanation for why R&D effort should be proportional to firm sales.

Our framework implies that the private advantage accruing to large firm size also represents a social advantage. Perhaps the easiest way to see this is to consider the merger of two firms that produce the same product, are the same size, pursue the same approaches to innovation, and spend the same amount on R&D on the same projects within each approach to innovation. The merger would result in two social dividends. First, duplicative R&D would be eliminated, a point suggested by other researchers (e.g., Spence, 1984). Second, and more novel, for each approach to innovation pursued by the two firms, the merger will increase the profitability of R&D *at the margin*, thereby leading the merged firm to undertake socially efficient R&D projects that were not undertaken by either firm before the merger. In effect, the merged firm will be better able to appropriate the returns from its innovations than either firm alone was able to do, causing it to undertake a greater number of socially efficient R&D projects than were collectively undertaken by the two firms before the merger.

Much of the empirical literature in the Schumpeterian tradition assumes that if R&D effort rises proportionally with firm size, then the size distribution of firms would have no effect on the amount of technological change achieved in the industry. In this view, technical advance is solely a function of the total amount of R&D performed in the industry, notwithstanding who performs it. In contrast, Cohen and Klepper (1990) argue that if innovations cannot be sold and lead to incremental growth, then the total amount of technological change generated in an industry will be a function of not only the total amount of R&D performed by all firms but also

the distribution of R&D effort across firms. By redistributing sales and R&D expenditures from smaller to larger firms, total R&D expenditures would not change but a greater number of socially efficient R&D projects would be collectively undertaken, thereby increasing the amount of technological change generated per unit of industry R&D expenditure.

If large firms have an advantage in conducting R&D, as our framework implies, then the appropriability advantage of size would be fully realized under monopoly. We do not, however, commonly observe the emergence of monopoly in R&D intensive industries despite the appropriability advantage of size. An explanation for this is that even successful firms grow only slowly, and that over time technology typically evolves in ways that favor either new firms or firms that were formerly less successful. Indeed, in his development of the notion of creative destruction, Schumpeter (1942) suggested that even monopolists will be displaced in the long run for such reasons.

In the absence of monopoly, firms will have an incentive to cooperate in R&D if they can appropriate the returns to their innovations only through their own output. For any given approach to innovation, all firms pursuing the approach could benefit by pooling their efforts. They would avoid the costly duplication of effort that would otherwise occur. Moreover, because they could apply innovations to their joint output, the firms would collectively profit from R&D expenditures that none of the firms could profit from individually. This suggests that it may be efficient for government to allow cooperative R&D ventures among competing firms pursuing the same approaches to innovation. Indeed, since the 1984 passage of the National Cooperative Research Act, prohibitions against cooperative R&D ventures have been relaxed. A large fraction of the cooperative ventures formed since that time, however, have brought together firms with complementary capabilities rather than firms pursuing the same approaches to innovation (Scott, 1988). This suggests that firms have a range of incentives to cooperate in their R&D efforts, and the one we have identified may not, in practice, be paramount.[8] Moreover, cooperation among firms pursuing the same approaches to innovation may be impeded by difficulties in communication and concerns about competitive advantage. If so, then a more active role for government may be indicated.

It is important to stress that the advantage of size in our framework is based solely on the assumption that firms' returns to innovation are scaled by their *ex ante* output. To the extent that innovations can be sold in disembodied form and/or that firms can reap the returns to their innovations through rapid growth, the advantage of *ex ante* large firm size will be less significant. It is likely that both of these factors will vary across industries and perhaps types of innovations (e.g., product versus process innovations).[9] The greater the extent to which the returns to innovation do not depend on *ex ante* output, then the lower will be the social benefits from cooperation.

4. The advantages of diversity

In this section we consider the role of technological diversity in technical advance and the link between diversity and the number of competitors.

Diversity across firms is incorporated in our framework through the assumption that firms pursue different sets of approaches to innovation. This in turn gives rise to differences in firm R&D intensities that reflect differences in the total number of approaches to innovation pursued by each firm. As we discussed, this form of technological diversity allows us to explain regularities characterizing the nature of the distribution within industries of firm R&D intensities. Of course, this does not mean that diversity is actually an important determinant of R&D intensities within industries, but it does provide indirect support for this view.

In our framework, diversity across firms' innovative activities stems from the existence of different noncompeting approaches to innovation within an industry. We conceive of these different approaches not as substitute or parallel ways of achieving the same technological objective but as independent ways of achieving technological change.[10] The total number of approaches to innovation in an industry can be thought of as being determined by the science and technology underlying R&D in the industry. Which of these approaches are actually pursued by firms in the industry at any given moment will depend upon

the expectations and capabilities of firms in the industry. It is certainly possible that some subset of the approaches will not be pursued by any firm in the industry. Indeed, if there are X firms in the industry and the probability of any approach being pursued by any given firm is p, then the likelihood of any approach not being pursued by any firm in the industry is $(1 - p)^X$.

A simple measure of technological diversity in our framework is the number of distinct approaches to innovation that are actually pursued by the firms in the industry. This measure corresponds well to the notion of diversity implicit in the arguments of proponents of small scale enterprise who stress the greater breadth of ideas and types of innovations pursued in industries composed of numerous small firms (e.g., Rodgers, 1990). It follows directly from this measure of technological diversity that the extent of diversity will be directly related to the number of firms in the industry. Since the likelihood of a potential approach to innovation in an industry not being pursued by any firm is $(1 - p)^X$, the expected number of different approaches to innovation pursued in an industry will be an increasing function of the number of firms, X. This implies that on average industries composed of a greater number of firms will be characterized by a greater amount of technological diversity. Note that this greater diversity does not emerge from any superior creativity on the part of smaller firms. It is simply the result of having a greater number of firms in the industry choosing which approaches to innovation to pursue.

The predicted relationship between the number of firms and technological diversity depends upon a key assumption of our framework, namely that the likelihood of a firm pursuing any given approach is independent of the size of the firm. If, alternatively, the probability of a firm pursuing any given approach increased with the size of the firm, it would no longer follow that increasing the number of firms would necessarily increase the expected degree of diversity.[11] While there are undoubtedly industries where the probability of pursuing an approach is correlated with firm size, the evidence concerning the regularities in the industry R&D intensity distributions suggests that the number of such industries is limited. Otherwise, our framework implies that there would be a large number of industries for which the largest firms are characterized by above average R&D intensities,[12] which does not conform with the evidence. Moreover, if the probability of pursuing an approach were an increasing function of the size of the firm, then based on our framework the distribution of firm R&D intensities within an industry would depend on the size distribution of firms and would, in all likelihood, not conform to the regularities in the industry R&D intensity distributions documented by Cohen and Klepper (1991).

If the likelihood of pursuing an approach to innovation is independent of the size of the firm then two firms of equal size would together be expected to pursue a greater number of distinct approaches to innovation than one firm twice their size. Having more firms provides more "independent minds" to consider the alternatives, which results in greater technological diversity. There are a number of organizational factors that might explain why the likelihood of pursuing any approach is independent of firm size and, hence, why diversity is promoted by a greater number of firms. We suspect it has something to do with the way R&D proposals are processed within firms. Following the argument suggested by Sah and Stiglitz (1986, 1988), suppose that proposals are initiated by technical staff and then subsequently considered by higher level decision makers. If large firms have more hierarchical levels than small firms and a proposed approach can be rejected at any level, an approach will have a greater chance of being approved by a smaller firm. As long as the number of proposed approaches in the two firms combined and the one large firm are equal, the two smaller firms would then be expected to pursue a greater number of distinct approaches than the large firm. Alternatively, suppose the probability of an approach being rejected is independent of the size of the firm. Even in this case, if all approaches proposed in the large firm are proposed in at least one of the two smaller firms and some are proposed in both of the smaller firms,[13] then the two smaller firms combined will approve a greater number of distinct approaches than the larger firm.[14]

Suppose we are correct and the number of firms is an important determinant of the diversity of approaches to innovation pursued in an in-

dustry. In order for there to be an advantage associated with small firm size, there must be some benefit associated with the greater diversity brought about by a greater number of firms. Our framework highlights an obvious benefit from the greater diversity — the exploitation of beneficial approaches to innovation that otherwise would not have been pursued. Indeed, this advantage of diversity was suggested long ago by Alfred Marshall when he stated that, "The tendency to variation is a chief source of progress" (Marshall, 1920, p. 355). Even if diversity does promote progress, as Marshall suggests, this does not mean that social welfare is necessarily promoted by the greater diversity associated specifically with an increase in the number of firms. Holding the output of the industry constant, if the number of firms is increased then the average size of each firm will decline. In the prior section, we showed how in our framework the consolidation of firms would yield social benefits. It follows that reducing the average firm size would impose a social cost. Assuming that the returns to innovation are scaled by *ex ante* output, each firm will spend less on R&D on the approaches it pursues, and for some amount of time, the innovations developed by each firm will be applied over a smaller level of output. The net effect on social welfare of increasing the number of firms depends on the magnitude of these costs relative to the benefits of having additional approaches to innovation pursued. We consider this tradeoff further in the next section.

While it is not straightforward to establish the social advantage of diversity in our framework, it is possible to imagine circumstances in which the increase in diversity brought about by a greater number of firms unequivocally promotes social welfare. For instance, suppose that firms are fully able to sell their innovations and there is no duplication among firms in their R&D efforts. In such a world, all innovations will be applied immediately to the entire output of the industry, and a reduction in the size of each firm will not diminish its incentives to conduct R&D. Then the decrease in firm size associated with the increase in the number of firms will have no effect on the R&D expenditures of the incumbent firms nor on the output over which any innovations resulting from these expenditures are applied. Consequently, any increase in the number of approaches pursued resulting from an increase in the number of firms will provide a net benefit to society. Intuitively, having a greater number of different minds (i.e., firms) evaluate the possible approaches to innovation will diminish the chance that a beneficial approach to innovation will be overlooked.

Our claim that diversity within an industry will increase with the number of firms implicitly assumes that at any given moment there may be firms outside of an industry that would pursue an otherwise unpursued approach if they entered the industry. Stated more baldly, it assumes that there may be potential entrants who recognize an opportunity but who do not enter the industry to exploit it. One reason this could occur is if there is some cost to entering the industry that exceeds the gross profit the entrant could make from pursuing the unexploited opportunity. From a social welfare perspective, however, this cost should be counted against the technical advance generated by the increase in the number of firms. If the social benefit of this technical advance was solely limited to the producer surplus resulting from the entrant's pursuit of a new approach, the net change in social welfare from the increase in the number of firms would be negative since the cost of entry would exceed the gross profits the producer could make from entering. Thus, for the increase in diversity to bring about an increase in social welfare, there must be some kind of wedge between the private and social returns from the pursuit of a new approach.

Our analysis of innovative activity, like many others (e.g., Arrow, 1962; Scherer, 1979; Spence, 1984), provides the basis for such a wedge. In laying out the framework, we noted that eventually all innovations are imitated. To the extent that the costs of imitation are less than the benefits, the social returns to innovation will exceed the private returns.[15] Consequently, it is possible that the pursuit of new approaches to innovation by entrants could be socially beneficial but not profitable to the entrant. In that case, the social benefits from greater diversity would not be realized through private initiative.

Our arguments suggest that if policies to increase the number of firms in an industry were undertaken, diversity would be expected to increase, which, in turn, could increase social welfare. Such policies could include prohibitions on horizontal mergers, subsidies of failing firms, and/or subsidies of entrants. Note that none of these policies requires the government to have any special insights about the sort of innovations an industry should pursue. Indeed, there is no reason to expect the government to be any more enlightened than firms about the best innovations to pursue. The rationale for these policies is simply that by getting more firms in the industry, there will be less chance that beneficial opportunities for technical advance will be unexploited.

It is important to note that the diversity-inducing effect of the presence of many small firms clearly depends upon the vitality of the science and technology underlying technical advance in any given industry, which we take as given. If this science and technology base is moribund, then the number of approaches to innovation that could be pursued will be few. In this case, the relationship between the number of firms and technological diversity, and, in turn, technical advance, will be weaker.

5. The tradeoff

In the last section we argued that it is not possible to bring about an increase in diversity through an increase in the number of firms without compromising some of the benefits associated with large firm size. Not surprisingly, it is also not possible to reap the benefits of large firm size without compromising the advantages associated with greater diversity. In this section we consider further the nature of this tradeoff.

When diversity is promoted through a greater number of firms, average firm size is reduced, which compromises the advantages associated with large size firms. Consider, alternatively, the costs associated with promoting the advantages of large firm size through the consolidation of firms. By reducing the number of firms in the industry, the expected number of approaches to innovation collectively pursued in the industry will decline. Then, on average, a smaller fraction of the beneficial opportunities for innovation will be pursued, which will reduce social welfare. Thus, just as increasing diversity through an increase in the number of firms has offsetting costs, so does increasing firm size through the consolidation of firms.[16]

Thus, in our framework, there is a tradeoff between the advantages associated with small firms and those associated with large firms. In order to have more approaches to innovation pursued, it is necessary to sacrifice some intensity of effort for each approach, and *vice versa*. The nature of this tradeoff is complicated and will depend on a number of factors. Analyzing the optimal average firm size for any industry in our framework requires a formal model of this tradeoff, which is beyond the scope of the paper. We can, however, use our framework to speculate about the role of factors that would be expected to shape the nature of the tradeoff: the extent to which firms can either sell their innovations or grow rapidly due to innovation, and the vitality of an industry's technology, as represented by the number of different approaches to innovation potentially available in the industry. To the extent that firms can realize rents due to innovation via rapid growth, licensing, and other mechanisms that do not exploit the firm's *ex ante* output, the appropriability advantage of size will be limited. In that case, an industry composed of a greater number of firms will be desirable. To the extent that the science and technology base of an industry is such that the potential number of approaches to innovation available to the industry is small, the diversity advantage associated with numerous small firms will be limited. In that case, an industry composed of a smaller number of firms will be desirable.

Consider the case of an industry in which there are a large number of approaches to innovation and firms can appropriate the returns to innovation only through their own *ex ante* output, which is the case where the tradeoff between the advantages associated with large and small firm size is the most acute. We suspect a substantial number of technologically progressive industries will be characterized by just such an acute tradeoff. There is no reason to believe that in these types of industries market forces alone will result in an optimal number of firms. In any given industry, there likely will be either too little entry to promote sufficient diversity or entry may be so unencumbered that the appropriability advantage of larger firm size is excessively compromised.

If market forces cannot be expected to lead to the optimal number of firms, policy makers will be faced with the challenge of deciding whether the number of firms in each industry is too large or too small. This will require making extremely difficult judgments. It is possible, however, that we have overblown the challenge posed by the tradeoff and policies can be designed to achieve the benefits of both diversity and large size. Consider, for example, current proposals that government condone firm cooperation on "generic" research (e.g., Nelson, 1990). Such proposals can be interpreted as suggesting that firms pursue separately R&D on approaches which they do not pursue in common and pursue together R&D on approaches which they do pursue in common. In this fashion, cooperative agreements could be crafted that would permit the industry and society to benefit from the appropriability advantage of large firm size without compromising the benefits of diversity. Indeed, cooperation on something resembling what we call generic research is apparently one of the models for cooperative research employed in the Japanese manufacturing sector.

6. Conclusion

Our analysis lends support to both sides of the debate concerning the optimal firm size for achieving technical advance. It provides a basis for why industries composed of many small firms will tend to exhibit greater diversity in the approaches to innovation pursued, and why greater diversity will contribute to more rapid technological change. It also provides a basis for why industries populated by larger firms will achieve a more rapid rate of technical advance on the approaches to innovation that are pursued. These arguments together suggest that a tradeoff exists between the appropriability advantage of large size and the advantages of diversity that accrue from numerous small firms.[17]

Our analysis has been more appreciative than rigorous and, indeed, often explicitly speculative. While we attempted to raise important questions, our framework requires more structuring before we can be confident about any of our conclusions. Even in its inchoate form, however, our analysis demonstrates that much needs to be done before the current debate about firm size can seriously inform policy. If we accept the plausibility of our basic framework, it focuses attention on a range of issues and questions. The fundamental premise of our analysis is that firm capabilities and perceptions differ within industries. This premise is not, however, widely reflected in analyses of industry behavior and performance, which typically take some representative firm as their starting point. Indeed, the analytic utility of our particular premise deserves scrutiny. Are differences in firm capabilities and perceptions as critical to explaining the industry patterns in innovative activity and performance as we suggest? Do these differences persist? Is our abstract characterization of these differences and their effects on innovative activity up to the task of providing a basis for policy?

These intraindustry differences in capabilities and perceptions underpin the hypothesized relationship in our framework between the number of firms within an industry and the number of distinct technological activities pursued by the industry as a whole. Surely this hypothesis should be tested. To establish the relationship between numbers of firms and technological diversity, we also made two important assumptions, which themselves should be examined. First, we assumed that firms independently decide upon which approaches to innovation to pursue. This assumption precludes the clustering of firms around innovative activities due to imitation, a phenomenon highlighted by Nelson (1981) and Scott (1991). To the degree that innovative activities yield relatively fast, public results, the assumption may be suspect. While our evidence indirectly suggests that such clustering may not be critical for explaining innovative activity in a wide range of industries, more research would be helpful. Second, we assumed that the number of approaches to innovation pursued by firms is independent of their size, implying large and small firms will tend to pursue the same number of approaches. This assumption probably does not apply to the smallest firms within an industry, particularly to the extent that such firms are often not full line manufacturing firms. Does it apply, however, to the medium to large firms that account for the preponderance of R&D and economic activity in the manufacturing sector? While our evidence again provides indirect support for this claim, more empirical and theoretical research is indicated.

We also made other claims and assumptions that deserve further attention. For example, we argued that greater technological diversity stimulates technical advance and provides gross increments to social welfare. Assuming it exists, the mechanism linking diversity and technical advance has never been examined empirically and is not obvious. Our assumption that expected firm growth due to innovation is incremental played an important role in permitting us to hypothesize an appropriability advantage of large size. Again, both the assumption and its alleged effect on innovative activity are worth examining. Finally, we also need to test whether the relationship between R&D and firm size within industries depends upon appropriability conditions, particularly upon the extent to which firms can sell their innovations or grow rapidly due to innovation.[18] In conclusion, this litany of reasonable but unsubstantiated assumptions and arguments should make clear that this paper is only a modest beginning of a daunting research agenda.

Acknowledgements

We are indebted to Mark Kamlet, Jonathan Leland and F. M. Scherer for their suggestions.

Notes

[1] An important theme of the work on industry evolution is that it is difficult for a firm to change deliberately its core expertise (e.g., Nelson and Winter, 1982; Klepper and Graddy, 1990). The corporate strategy literature also implicitly makes this point when arguing that firms should exploit their "core competences" (e.g., Andrews, 1971; Porter, 1980), suggesting that it is difficult for firms to transform their capabilities.

[2] This is a strong assumption which we plan to relax in subsequent development of our model. It can be rationalized, however, by simply defining two approaches as distinct if the likelihood of the approaches being pursued by any given firm are independent.

[3] In recent years, it has been recognized that many innovations are most valued by the innovators themselves because they are either idiosyncratic to the innovator (Nelson, 1989) or require idiosyncratic expertise for their exploitation that is only generated in the course of the innovation process itself (Cohen and Levinthal, 1989, 1990).

[4] The survey results of Levin *et al.* (1987) provide a strong empirical basis for the claim. They find that the most effective mechanism for appropriating rents due to innovation are first-mover advantages, secrecy, and complementary sales and service, all of which are implemented via the firm's own sales.

[5] A business unit represents a firm's activity in a given industry.

[6] The following argument applies equally to product innovations (Cohen and Klepper, 1990).

[7] Cf. Nelson, Peck and Kalachek (1967) and Scherer (1970), who also note this potential advantage of size.

[8] See Scott (1988), Link and Bauer (1989), and Katz and Ordover (1990) for a discussion of the range of factors that may affect the benefits and costs of R&D cooperation.

[9] For example, the ability of firms to sell their innovations in disembodied form will vary across industries according to the ease of defining and enforcing property rights over innovations.

[10] To make the idea of different, noncompeting approaches to technological change within an industry more concrete, consider the semiconductor industry. Historically, research in semiconductors has been conducted in many areas, including silicon manufacture, low-cost methods for semiconductor manufacture, and the design of various devices such as MOS, bipolar, integrated circuit, and memory devices. Each of these can be thought of as different but complementary approaches to innovation in semiconductors. Also, consistent with our general framework, semiconductor firms have differed considerably in the sets of these approaches that they pursued. Texas Instruments, for example, possessed a broad range of expertise in solid state physics, materials properties. and preparation, production process chemistry, advanced photolithographic processes, semiconductor device and design technologies, and pursued a broad range of approaches to innovation. In contrast, companies such as Mostek, American Micro-Systems and SEMI possessed more circumscribed expertise in device design technologies, and pursued a narrower range of approaches to innovation that focused on the design of MOS, bipolar, or memory devices.

Our characterization of approaches as noncompeting contrasts with others' conceptualization of different approaches to innovation. For example, in the analyses of Evenson and Kislev (1976) and Nelson (1982), different approaches represent distinct, competing ways of achieving the same technological end. Differentiating approaches in this way is relevant when there is uncertainty about how best to achieve a particular technological objective. In our framework, however, we abstracted from this kind of uncertainty. Our firms differ, in contrast, in the objectives (i.e., approaches) they pursue, reflecting differences in their expertise. While there is often uncertainty about how best to achieve a particular technological objective, we have abstracted from this kind of uncertainty because it would not readily explain the regularities in industry R&D intensity distributions. Indeed, it does not readily explain why R&D intensities of firms in an industry should differ at all in any systematic way (Cohen and Klepper, 1991).

[11] Holding industry output constant, an increase in the number of firms will reduce the average firm size. If the probability of a firm pursuing an approach were positively related to its size, then the increase in the number of firms would decrease the probability of any firm pursuing any given approach. Then the probability of any given approach not being pursued by any firm in the industry could fall with an increase in the number of firms, which would cause the expected amount of diversity to fall.

[12] In our framework, if the probability of pursuing an approach were positively related to the size of the firm, then larger firms would be expected to pursue a greater number of approaches to innovation, causing them to have above average R&D intensities.

[13] This is plausible if some of the approaches proposed in the large firm are proposed by multiple individuals. In that case, if the larger firm were broken into two firms, there would be some probability that the technical personnel in each of the smaller firms would propose the same approach.

[14] Another reason firms of equal size might pursue a greater number of distinct approaches than one firm twice their size is that most firms tend to funnel control over their R&D operations for a given industry through one individual, and that individual will naturally reflect his/her own expertise and perceptions in the decisions that are made. Thus, regardless of the firm's size, the approaches that are pursued will tend to reflect one individual's judgment. Indeed, a recent article in the *The Wall Street Journal* (Rigdon, 1991) about Kodak's research on filmless cameras highlighted the importance — and difficulty — of decentralizing high-level R&D decision-making authority when a firm becomes aware of a distinct and viable new approach to innovation within an industry. It noted that while the research team working on new filmless camera technology has been given its own budget and autonomy over hiring decisions, the same individual who oversees research on more conventional film technologies also oversees this research, which may ultimately inhibit Kodak's willingness or ability to pursue the new technology.

[15] In a static setting, imitation reinforces the gross social benefits accruing from greater diversity because the benefits from the pursuit of new approaches will be reaped by more than just the firms pursuing the new approaches. Imitation may also yield dynamic dividends. As noted by Marshall (1920, p. 271), ". . . if one man starts a new idea, it is taken up by others and combined with suggestions of their own; and thus it becomes the source of further new ideas . . ." Thus, pursuing a given approach may stimulate other firms "to improve it, variegate it, more generally contribute to its further advance," (Nelson, 1989, p. 6) even in ways that cannot be anticipated when the approach is first pursued. Von Weizsacker (1980) also recognized this point when he explored the implications of "sequential innovations" for the welfare effects of entry barriers.

[16] We managed to sidestep this cost in the example we used earlier to illustrate the benefits of large firm size by focusing on the merger of two firms that pursued the same approaches to innovation. This insured that the merger of the firms did not reduce the diversity of approaches pursued in the industry. However, firms generally will not pursue the identical set of approaches to innovation, so that consolidations will be expected to compromise the collective number of approaches to innovation pursued in the industry.

[17] Others, such as Nelson (1981), have also recognized a tradeoff between the diversity-inducing advantage of more competitive industry structures and advantages of large firm size, but not the particular tradeoff we have identified.

[18] Cohen and Klepper (1990) demonstrate that if firms can sell some fraction of their innovations in disembodied form or

if growth due to innovation is unconditioned by existing output levels, then large firm size will confer less of an advantage and R&D effort should rise less than proportionally with firm size.

References

Andrews, K. R., 1971, *The Concept of Corporate Strategy*, Homewood, Illinois: Dow Jones-Irwin.

Arrow, K., 1962, 'Economic Welfare and the Allocation of Resources for Inventions', in R. R. Nelson (ed.), *The Rate and Direction of Inventive Activity*, Princeton, NJ: Princeton University Press for the National Bureau of Economic Research.

Baldwin, W. L. and J. T. Scott, 1987, *Market Structure and Technological Change*, Chur: Harwood Academic Publishers.

Cohen, W. M. and S. Klepper, 1990, 'A Reprise of Size and R&D', mimeo, Carnegie Mellon University.

Cohen, W. M. and S. Klepper, 1991, 'The Anatomy of Industry R&D Intensity Distributions', *American Economic Review*, forthcoming.

Cohen, W. M. and D. Levinthal, 1989, 'Innovation and Learning: The Two Faces of R&D', *Economic Journal* **99**, 569—596.

Cohen, W. M. and D. Levinthal, 1990, 'Absorptive Capacity: A New Perspective on Innovation and Learning', *Administrative Science Quarterly* **35**, 128—152.

Evenson, R. E. and Y. Kislev, 1976, 'A Stochastic Model of Applied Research', *Journal of Political Economy* **84**, 265—281.

Ferguson, C. H., 1988, 'From the People Who Brought You Voodoo Economics', *Harvard Business Review* (May—June), 55—62.

Fisher, F. M. and P. Temin, 1973, 'Returns to Scale in Research and Development: What Does the Schumpeterian Hypothesis Imply?', *Journal of Political Economy* **81**, 56—70.

Gilder, G., 1988, 'The Revitalization of Everything: The Law of the Microcosm', *Harvard Business Review* (March—April), 49—61.

Jorde, T. M. and D. J. Teece, 1990, 'Innovation and Cooperation: Implications for Competition and Antitrust', *The Journal of Economic Perspectives* **4**, 75—96.

Kamien, M. I. and N. L. Schwartz, 1982, *Market Structure and Innovation*, Cambridge: Cambridge University Press.

Katz, M. L. and J. A. Ordover, 1990, 'R&D Cooperation and Competition', *Brookings Papers on Economic Activity, Microeconomics*, 137—203.

Klepper, S. and E. Graddy, 1990, 'The Evolution of New Industries and the Determinants of Market Structure', *The Rand Journal of Economics* **21**, 27—44.

Levin, R. C., A. Klevorick, R. Nelson and S. Winter, 1987, 'Appropriating the Returns from Industrial Research and Development', *Brookings Papers on Economic Activity* **3**, 783—820.

Link, A. N. and L. L. Bauer, 1989, *Cooperative Research in U.S. Manufacturing — Assessing Policy Initiatives and*

Corporate Strategies, Lexington, Mass.: Lexington Books.

Marshall, A., 1961, *Principles of Economics*, New York: The Macmillan Company, 9th (variorum) edition, Vol. 1, with annotations by C. W. Guillebaud (based on New York: The Macmillan Company, 8th edition, 1920).

Nelson, R. R., 1981, 'Assessing Private Enterprise: An Exegesis of Tangled Doctrine', *The Bell Journal of Economics* **12**, 93—111.

Nelson, R. R., 1982, 'The Role of Knowledge in R&D Efficiency', *Quarterly Journal of Economics* **97**, 453—470.

Nelson, R. R., 1989, 'What Is 'Commercial' and What Is 'Public' About Technology, and What Should Be?', mimeo, presented at the Conference on Economic Growth and the Commercialization of New Technologies, Stanford University, September 11—12, 1989.

Nelson, R. R., 1990, 'Capitalism as an Engine of Progress', *Research Policy* **19**, 193—214.

Nelson, R. R. and S. G. Winter, 1982, *An Evolutionary Theory of Economic Change*, Cambridge: Harvard University Press.

Nelson, R. R., M. J. Peck and E. D. Kalachek, 1967, *Technology, Economic Growth, and Public Policy*, Washington: Brookings Institution.

Norris, W. C., 1983, 'How to Expand R&D Cooperation', *Business Week*, April 11, p. 21.

Noyce, R. N., 1990, 'Cooperation Is the Best Way to Beat Japan', *New York Times*, July 9, Section 3, p. 2.

Porter, M. E., 1980, *Competitive Strategy: Techniques for Analyzing a Business, Industry and Competitors*, New York: Free Press.

Rigdon, J. E., 1991, 'Kodak Tries to Prepare for Filmless Era Without Inviting Demise of Core Business', *The Wall Street Journal*, April 18, 1991, B1, B5.

Rogers, T. J., 1990, 'Landmark Messages from the Microcosm', *Harvard Business Review* (January—February), 24—30.

Sah, R. J. and J. E. Stiglitz, 1986, 'The Architecture of Economic Systems: Hierarchies and Polyarchies', *American Economic Review* **76**, 716—727.

Sah, R. J. and J. E. Stiglitz, 1988, 'Committees, Hierarchies and Polyarchies', *Economic Journal* **98**, 451—470.

Scherer, F. M., 1970, *Industrial Market Structure and Economic Performance*, 1st edition, Chicago: Rand McNally College Publishing Company.

Scherer, F. M., 1979, 'The Welfare Economics of Product Variety: An Application to the Ready-to-Eat Cereals Industry', *Journal of Industrial Economics* **28**, 113—134.

Scherer, F. M., 1980, *Industrial Market Structure and Economic Performance*, 2nd edition, Chicago: Rand McNally College Publishing Company.

Scherer, F. M. and D. Ross, 1990, *Industrial Market Structure and Economic Performance*, 3rd edition, Boston: Houghton Mifflin.

Schumpeter, J. A., 1934, *The Theory of Economic Development*, Cambridge: Harvard University Press.

Schumpeter, J. A., 1942, *Capitalism, Socialism, and Democracy*, New York: Harper.

Scott, J. T., 1988, 'Diversification Versus Cooperation in

R&D Investment', *Managerial and Decision Economics* **9**, 173—186.

Scott, J., 1991, 'Research Diversity and Technical Change', in Z. Acs and D. Audretsch (eds.), *Innovation and Technical Change*, Ann Arbor: University of Michigan Press, pp. 132—151.

Shaffer, R. A., 1990, 'Let a Thousand Companies Fight', *New York Times*, July 9, Section 3, p. 2.

Spence, A. M., 1984, 'Cost Reduction, Competition, and Industry Performance', *Econometrica* **52**, 101—121.

Von Weizsacker, C. C., 1980, *Barriers to Entry*, New York: Springer-Verlag.

[9]

Limited Entrepreneurial Attention
and Economic Development

Sharon Gifford

ABSTRACT. Economic development depends on the allocation of entrepreneurial resources to efforts to discover new
profit opportunities. Limited entrepreneurial attention is allocated between maintaining current activities and starting new
activities. This paper addresses the problem of allocating
limited entrepreneurial attention in a variety of contexts. The
issues that are addressed are product improvement and
new product development; the choice of career as an innovative entrepreneur, a managerial entrepreneur or a salaried
employee; the venture capitalist's attention to current and new
ventures and funds; the writing of internal contracts and
market contracts and the supervising of current employees and
hiring additional employees.

> If we seek to explain the success of those
> economies that have managed to grow signifi-
> cantly, compared with those that have remained
> relatively stagnant, we find it difficult to do so
> without taking into consideration differences in
> the availability of entrepreneurial talent and in
> the motivational mechanisms that drive them on.
> (Baumol, 1993, p. 5)

> In my speaking to women's business groups, my
> favorite metaphor of the business owner is the
> man on "The Ed Sullivan Show" who balanced
> spinning dinner plates on the ends of tall sticks.
> Just as he had fifteen spinning, one would start
> to wobble and then another and then another.
> (Anita F. Battina, *Inc.* May, 1993.)

1. Introduction

William Baumol argues in his new book that the
amount of entrepreneurial activity in an economy
during any period of time depends on two characteristics of the economy: the amount of entrepreneurial resources that exist and how those

Final version accepted on July 22, 1996

Graduate School of Management
Rutgers University
Newark, NJ

resources are allocated among productive and
unproductive activities. The allocation of entrepreneurial resources, as with any resources, is
affected by the relative rewards to the various
possible activities. These rewards themselves are
dependent on the "rules of the game", such as
property rights, patent protection, legal institutions, etc.

All entrepreneurial activity, productive and
unproductive, involves the recombination of
resources. However, productive activities generate
new products and services. It is the creation of
these new products and services which creates new
jobs and promotes economic development. The
more productive entrepreneurial activity there is,
the faster the economy develops. However, one
of the difficulties in analyzing the role of entrepreneurs in economic development is understanding what it is that entrepreneurs do and how
to encourage more productive entrepreneurial
activity.

As Baumol argues, not all entrepreneurial
activity is virtuous, in the sense of being good for
the economy as a whole. Some activities merely
reallocate wealth. Entrepreneurs, however, will
allocate their resources to those activities which
reward them the most. Some of these activities
may actually reduce the growth of the economy.
It is not always obvious which activities are productive and which are unproductive. For example,
consider efforts by the management of a public
corporation to prevent hostile takeovers which
threaten their positions. Golden parachutes, which
are compensation packages for current management in the event of a hostile takeover, appear to
be nothing more than a wealth transfer from stockholders to management. If this is true, then this
in and of itself is not inefficient, but all resources
expended in obtaining these contractual arrangements are wasted resources since they are diverted

from productive activities. However, as Baumol points out, the golden parachute may not be inefficient if it elicits more investment of management's entrepreneurial human capital in the firm because there is a guaranteed return to this investment. Therefore, the golden parachutes may or may not be productive.

Before we can promote productive entrepreneurial activity we must also ask how entrepreneurial resources are allocated. But what are these entrepreneurial resources that make these new products possible and promote the development of an economy? How much of these resources are there and what determines their allocation? Israel Kirzner (1979) argues that the essence of entrepreneurship is alertness to new profit opportunities. But to be alert to new opportunities requires that the entrepreneur allocate attention away from other matters in order to observe a new profit opportunity. A person who is completely absorbed in dealing with current activities may not notice a twenty dollar bill lying on the ground. Opportunities do not often just fall in a person's lap.

But this diversion of attention away from other matters implies that entrepreneurial activity has an opportunity cost: the neglect of other, perhaps more routine, activities. It is this opportunity cost and the entrepreneur's belief that there are profit opportunities to be alert to which determine the amount of entrepreneurial resources forthcoming, the amount of entrepreneurial activity, and the rate of development of the economy. And, as Baumol argues, it is the payoff structure of these new opportunities which determine how entrepreneurial attention is allocated among them.

Therefore, it is imperative to analyze the ways in which institutional arrangements and payoff structures affect the allocation of entrepreneurial resources. The thesis of this paper is that to analyze economic development, we must take into account the payoffs to and opportunity costs of limited entrepreneurial attention. My research has focused on the optimal allocation of limited entrepreneurial attention between current, routine activities and innovative activities, with a variety of applications. In this paper I will describe how I think this research relates to Kirzner's theory of entrepreneurial alertness and Baumol's theory concerning the allocation of entrepreneurial resources among productive and unproductive activities.

The importance of limited entrepreneurial attention has been recognized among economists for some time.[1] When Adam Smith writes, in 1776, about the incentive problems arising from the separation of management from ownership, he describes the attention requirements of overseeing a joint stock company. He provides a very graphic description of the demands on the attention of the primary decision-maker of any firm. Nicholas Kaldor in 1934 points out that limited attention implies a fixed input into the problem of coordinating activities, which includes the choice of which activities to engage in. John Commons observes in 1934 that a decision maker cannot do everything at once, but must devote his limited attention to the most important issue at any moment. Friedrick von Hayek argues in 1945 that the limits of attention, combined with the dispersion of knowledge, result in a limit to the feasibility of central planning. Kenneth Arrow points out in 1974 that the limited capacity for acquiring and using information implies a bottleneck in information processing and diminishing returns to increasing information resources. All of this implies that there is no such thing as free information. All information must be processed before it can be useful and the attention required for information processing has an opportunity cost.

Organization theorists have analyzed the implications of limited attention under the heading of 'span of control'. Chester Barnard, in 1938, following Commons, argues that one of the roles of organizations is to focus the attention of employees among alternative current operations to maintain coordination. The role of attention in gathering information is addressed by James March and Herbert Simon in 1958 when they describe the decision-maker who can do only one or a few things at a time and can attend to only some of the information available. Alfred Chandler points out in 1977 that, as firms grew during the industrial revolution, the limits to the span of control led to the development of professional management to routinize activities in order to maintain control as the firm increased in size.

My research has focused on developing an analytical (read, mathematical) model that captures the issues addressed in this more descriptive literature. This allows us to draw out more specific and detailed implications of limited attention. The allocation of limited time has been modeled mathematically by others, starting with Gary Becker in 1965. However, in these models, the number of targets for attention is fixed. In my model, the number of targets among which attention is to be allocated is determined by the allocation of attention itself. This is because limited entrepreneurial attention can be allocated to acquiring additional activities. The issues that have been addressed by my research are the choice between current product improvement and new product development; the choice of career as an innovative entrepreneur, a managerial entrepreneur or a salaried employee; the allocation of a venture capitalist's attention between current and new ventures and funds; the choice between writing internal contracts with employees and writing market contracts with other firms and the choice between supervising current employees and hiring additional employees. The last topic concerns the optimal completeness of employment contracts, the internalization of transactions, monitoring intensity, performance standards, efficiency wages and promotions.

The quote at the beginning of this paper provides an analogy which makes the structure of the problem intuitively clear.[2] Imagine a juggler on the "Ed Sullivan Show" who is rewarded according to the number of plates she can spin on the tips of long sticks on a table. The plates are the targets of attention and the juggler allocates limited attention between respinning old plates and setting up new plates. Assume that there is an unlimited supply of plates and sticks (and table top). As soon as one plate is spinning, she can set up another one. However, as she continues to set up additional spinning plates, the first one starts to wobble, threatening to fall.

The choice the juggler faces is to either continue to set up new plates or to go back and try to respin old plates. The best course of action depends on two characteristics of these plates: their balance and their tendency to break if dropped. A balanced plate is easy to set spinning while an unbalanced plate cannot be spun successfully. Only a fraction of new plates, however, are balanced and spin successfully. The probability that a new plate is balanced affects the expected value of trying to spin a new plate. Plates that have already been spun successfully are balanced and

so can be easily respun. However, plates that have fallen may be cracked or even broken and no longer spinnable. The tendency of plates to break affects the expected value of trying to respin old plates. If plates break easily then the expected value of trying to respin old plates is low.

It turns out that there are two optimal plans of action. One is to continue to set up new plates and let the old ones fall and be freely discarded. This is optimal if most new plates are balanced and the breakage rate is high. The other alternative is to respin each old plate periodically and then try to set up a new plate when not respinning an old plate. This is the best course of action if few new plates are balanced and old plates do not easily crack or break. This reflects Kirzner's concept of entrepreneurial alertness. An entrepreneur who already has many activities (plates) to which to attend will not be alert to new opportunities because all attention is focused on current activities.

With this analogy we can now discuss the entrepreneurial problems to which this model has been applied and the implications of limited entrepreneurial attention. These applications include the innovation of entrepreneurial firms, the choice of career for entrepreneurs, the relationship between the entrepreneur and the venture capitalist and the hiring and monitoring of employees. I will close with a discussion of the allocation of entrepreneurial attention between productive and unproductive activities. All of these applications consider entrepreneurial firms and so assume that the entrepreneur's responsibilities are not delegated to employees. This effectively limits the amount of attention which can be devoted to the entrepreneurial activities. However, each application requires some modification of the basic model in order to more accurately represent the unique nature of each of these specific problems.

2. Innovation versus product improvement

In Gifford (1992a) the model is applied to the problem of allocating entrepreneurial attention between innovating new products and using product improvement to maintain the profitability of current product lines. Product lines represent the plates. In both cases the entrepreneur is actively involved in the decision-making and does not delegate these decisions to others. The implication of the optimal allocation is that there are two best courses of action. The first is that the entrepreneur constantly attempts to innovate new products and discontinues products lines which are no longer profitable. The second is to improve each current product periodically and innovate only if no current product is being improved. The model has implications for the innovativeness of entrepreneurial firms and its dependence on monopoly profits and firm size, and the optimal firm size and rate of growth of the entrepreneurial firm.

In this model, the balance and breakage of plates represent two characteristics of innovation: opportunities for new inventions and opportunities for product improvement or process innovation. The first is called technological opportunity since it is usually technological breakthroughs which generate opportunities for innovation. The second has no common expression so I have adopted the term "durability" to reflect the current product's resistance to economic obsolescence.

The first implication of the optimal allocation of attention is that the entrepreneur conducts product improvement only if the durability of current products is sufficiently high relative to the degree of technological opportunity. This means that greater economic obsolescence, resulting in less durable products, increases the amount of entrepreneurial activity devoted to new product innovation. This obsolescence may be due to innovations from competitors which make successful improvements in the current product difficult. This can have a ripple effect through other firms. For example, the automobile made the horse-drawn buggy obsolete which in turn made the buggy whip obsolete.

Another implication is that the rate of new product innovation is dependent on firm size and monopoly profits only if the firm conducts product improvement as well as new product innovation. In this case, each current product line is improved periodically and as firm size grows, there is less time to devote to new product innovation. In addition, if current products are periodically improved, then greater monopoly profits means that current product lines do not have to be improved as frequently and so the firm can maintain a greater number of them. This implies

that new product innovation is increasing in monopoly profits. However, if the firm makes no attempt at improving current product lines, then all attention is focused on innovating new products and the rate of innovation is constant, independent of firm size and monopoly profits. In addition to the dependence of firm size on monopoly profits, the model also implies that, if current product lines are periodically improved, then the maximum firm size is less than if the entrepreneur conducts only new product improvement.

Therefore, improving current products because economic obsolescence is low diverts attention from innovating new products, which is the source of firm growth. In Acs and Gifford (1996), empirical tests of the results of this paper offer support for the effect of economic obsolescence of current product lines on new product innovation and its dependence on firm size and monopoly profits. However, new product innovation is not an end in itself. The generation of permanent jobs through the maintenance of product lines which are not subject to obsolescence also fosters economic wellbeing. The implication here is that growth has a cost: the neglect of other activities.

3. Innovator or manager

Gifford (1993) applies the model to the problem of the individual's choice of career between being an innovative entrepreneur, a managerial entrepreneur or a salaried employee. This choice will depend upon two characteristics of the individual: innovative ability and managerial ability. Innovative ability is the ability to recognize a new profit opportunity once attention has been focused on it. Managerial ability determines the entrepreneur's ability to manage the production of a product line once it has been introduced. A career as an innovative entrepreneur implies constant innovation while a managerial entrepreneur also allocates attention to managing current operations.

A career as an innovative entrepreneur is best if innovative ability is high and managerial ability is sufficiently low. A career as a managerial entrepreneur is optimal if managerial ability is high and innovative ability is low. This all appears perfectly obvious. However, as the wage rate of salaried employees rises, innovative entrepreneurs disappear but there will always be managerial entrepreneurs for any wage rate. Notice that this is not socially suboptimal, since entrepreneurs are allocating their resources to the highest valued use, and there are no information or market imperfections which might result in inefficiencies.

However, one might want to extend this analysis and ask how entrepreneurial ability might be increased through training. Most business schools in the U.S. focus primarily on managerial training, as opposed to training entrepreneurs. Until now, with increasing numbers of middle management jobs available, this appears to have been the appropriate balance. However, a shift in focus may be advisable now that firms are downsizing and reducing the ranks of middle management. Most of the displaced middle managers will be looking at self-employment as an alternative.

In addition to predicting career choices, the model also predicts a diversity of the composition of R&D effort. The composition of R&D comes from the fact that innovating new products carries an opportunity cost embodied in the neglect of current operations. Firms with high entrepreneurial ability conduct only new product innovation, independent of monopoly profits and firm size. Firms with high managerial ability, facing the same technological opportunity and entry of competition, conduct both new product innovation and process innovation (or product improvement). For these latter firms, the new product innovation will be increasing in monopoly profits and decreasing in firm size and process innovation will increase with firm size. In addition, for these firms new product innovation and process innovation are inversely related.

Finally, this application reverses the direction of causation between innovation and firm size from that proposed in Schumpeter (1934). As Dosi (1988, p. 1153) states: "Big firms happen to grow big because they innovated successfully in the past and continue to do so in the present without, however, finding a differential advantage in 'bigness' as such." Rather than taking the size of the firm as exogenous and asking how that determines innovativeness, the model of limited entrepreneurial attention lets the size of the firm be determined by the entrepreneur's ability to increase its size through new product innovation.

4. The entrepreneur and the venture capitalist

Another important determinant of economic development is the availability of venture capital for high technology startup firms. However, financial capital is not the only resource required by venture capitalists. They also invest a great deal of time searching for and incubating new ventures. Gifford (forthcoming) models the allocation of a venture capitalist's limited attention between current ventures and acquiring new ventures. A venture capitalist (general partner) allocates limited attention (time) between evaluating new ventures and supervising and consulting with current portfolio ventures. The optimal allocation determines the optimal frequency of meetings with the entrepreneur and the optimal termination date at which the venture goes public. The opportunity cost of attending to an incubating venture is the foregone evaluation of new ventures. This opportunity cost implies that the venture capitalist wants to have fewer and less frequent consultations with the entrepreneur than is required to maximize the entrepreneur's return. This explains Bill Sahlman's observation that "[t]he seemingly irrational act of shutting down an economically viable entity is rational when viewed from the perspective of the venture capitalist confronted with allocating *time* and capital among various projects" (Sahlman, 1990, p. 507, footnote 12, emphasis added).

Since the model implies that the value of the venture to the entrepreneur can be increased with more attention from the venture capitalist, it is natural to ask if the entry of additional venture capitalists would supply these additional consultation services. However, the assumption of free entry does not mitigate the incentive problem between the venture capitalist and the entrepreneur but increases it. Entry of additional venture capitalists occurs when the price paid for venture capital services is greater than the zero profit price. Entry then reduces this price, increases the number of ventures held by any one venture capital fund but reduces the frequency and number of consultations which each venture receives. Therefore, we have a further divergence of interests with the entry of additional venture capitalists. However, entry does increase the average fund size and the upper bound on firm size and so the number of funded ventures.

Since the assumption of free entry does not remove the divergence of interests between the venture capitalist and the entrepreneur, but in fact increases it, we must ask whether this outcome is not, in fact, socially optimal. I show that maximizing the value of the firm to the entrepreneur is not socially optimal, while maximizing the venture capitalist's value is socially optimal. This is because the entrepreneur bears none of the opportunity costs of the venture capitalist, so these profits do not reflect net social gains. In addition, if investors have information costs and the venture capitalist is compensated for the operating costs of the venture fund through the carried interest and management fees paid by the limited partners, then the outcome above may be Pareto preferred to the outcome which results when there are no venture capitalists playing the role of financial intermediary.

The model implies that we should see contracts between venture capitalists and entrepreneurs which stipulate the venture capitalist's allocation of time to the venture or the date of the initial public offering (IPO). A possible explanation for the lack of such contracts is the inability to specify in advance what the appropriate amount of time and IPO date would be. As suggested in Holmstrom and Milgrom (1990), for multi-task agents, providing incentives for some measurable task, such as the number and frequency of the venture capitalist's consultations with the entrepreneur, can divert attention away from other, unmeasurable tasks, such as the quality of these meetings.

With the timing of the IPO, the decision to go public depends strongly on market conditions, so this decision cannot be made years in advance, either. Although market considerations are not included in the model above, they would only add a stochastic element to the IPO timing. In addition, if the venture capitalist remains actively involved in the venture past the date of the IPO, then the date of the IPO is not relevant to the analysis above.

There are several other implications of this model when ventures are homogeneous ex ante. As expected, increased opportunities for new ventures decrease the frequency and number of consultations between the venture capitalist and the entrepreneur. An increase in the share of the

venture going to the venture capitalist increases the frequency and number of consultations. In addition, an increase in the opportunities for new ventures increases the upper bound on the size of the venture capital firm and the long run expected firm size.

However, when we consider ventures with different rates of decline in profits, we find that a venture with a lower rate of decline in profits has less frequent consultations and a fewer number of consultations. In addition, the venture with the lower rate of decline pays a lower share of the venture's value to the venture capitalist in order to be funded. This implies that the venture capitalist's compensation is increasing in the amount of attention the venture receives.

If the venture capitalist manages several different venture funds then the limited partners of any one fund are in the same predicament as the entrepreneur of a single venture. The venture capitalist allocates limited attention between managing the existing funds and raising financial capital for new funds. Each fund's limited partners do not share all the consultation costs, just as the entrepreneur does not, and so the venture capitalist does not maximize the income of the limited partners. However, as before, this is not inefficient. It only means that the venture capitalist should be rewarded by each fund according to the amount of consultation resources it uses. This hypothesis is supported by Gompers and Lerner (1994) where they find that compensation based on asset value is being replace with compensation based on consultation costs. In the latter case, venture funds with higher effort requirements to monitor the ventures also have higher compensation.

Recent research has shown that venture capital investments have tended toward later stages in the ventures' development. This results in safer investments with more rapid returns. An increase in investments in late-stage ventures and LBO's and a decrease in investments in start-ups between 1983 and 1987 suggest that the investment-based fee is diverting venture capitalists away from their proper role, "building companies" (Schilit, 1991, p. 59). This shift of investment capital has been attributed to the need to economize on the general partner's attention because these ventures require less of the general partner's assistance (Timmons and Sapienza, 1992). These later stage investments include leveraged buyouts in which the company and its management are well established and the only service provided by the venture capitalist is financing.

If a more mature venture means that its deterioration rate is less, then this implies the venture receives less frequent attention and a fewer number of evaluations from the general partner. However, if mature ventures are less responsive to the general partner's efforts, then this also implies that attention is allocated to this venture less frequently and a fewer number of times. In either case, more mature ventures receive less attention. I show that if the limited partners prefer less mature investments to more mature investments and the general partner's share of the fund is small relative to the opportunity cost of time, then the general partner prefers more mature investments than the limited partners do. This is because the more mature investments receive less attention, the cost of which is born by the general partner but not the limited partners.

This analysis explains the complaints of entrepreneurs that venture capitalists are out for a fast buck. However, it also shows that this is not necessarily a bad thing. When the costs of the venture capitalist's time is taken into account, we see that it is socially optimal to refuse to maximize either the limited partners' or the entrepreneur's profits by allocating attention to other funds or ventures.

5. In-house or out-source

Since it is common to define entrepreneurial activity as any reallocation of resources which produces new products or service, we can apply the model to problems which are not as obviously entrepreneurial as the last three. One part of the process of innovation is the decision of what to create. Another part of this process is the decision of how to produce it. We turn next to the decision of whether to produce a product or service oneself, by hiring the necessary employees, or buy it from another firm through a market contract. And if produced in-house, then how are the employees to be monitored, motivated and compensated? These questions are not traditional questions of entrepreneurship. However, these questions must be

answered before a new product or service can be introduced and in each of these cases, attention is allocated between current activities and acquiring new activities. Since the definition of entrepreneurial activity covers the allocation of attention to acquiring any kind of new activity, writing contracts and hiring employees are also entrepreneurial activities. This section considers the problem of whether to produce oneself or to purchase goods over markets. Section 6 turns to the question of how to motivate employees if one chooses to produce in-house.

In Gifford (1994a) and (1994b), limited attention is allocated between writing new contracts with other firms and writing and directing internal employment contracts. In the first case, the entrepreneur interviews and negotiates new contracts which are carried out by other firms while in the second case, the entrepreneur hires employees who carry out the contract but also are monitored by and receive direction from the entrepreneur. This monitoring and directing of employees diverts attention away from writing new contracts.

There are two primary issues addressed by these papers: 1) which transactions should take place between firms (over markets) and which should take place within the firm, and 2) how much time should be spent writing these contracts, whether market or internal, in an effort to make them more complete. Following Coase (1937), internal transactions are those which are directed by the entrepreneur. Transactions within the firm are distinguished from those over markets by the coordination mechanism: "co-ordination is the work of the price mechanism in one case and of the entrepreneur in another" (Coase (1937, p. 389). Market transactions, once entered into, receive no further attention from the entrepreneur since they are directed by the price system. As noted by Hayek (1945), the advantage of transacting across markets is that markets allow us to "extend the span of our utilization of resources beyond the span of control of any one mind" and to "provide inducements which will make the individuals do the desirable things without anyone having to tell them what to do."

The model is extended here to determine the amount of time spent writing contracts. The performance of a contract, whether internal or market, depends on the completeness with which it is written. The completeness of a contract depends on how much time is spent writing contingencies. Much of the economic literature on contracts assumes that comprehensive contracts which specify the required performance and compensation for all contingencies are impossible to write. The justification for this assumption is based on the combinatoric problem of listing all possible contingencies, the possibility of unforeseen circumstances, the imprecision of language, and the opportunity cost of time spent writing contracts. My model endogenizes the costs of writing more complete contracts, which is embedded in the neglect of other current contracts. This essentially formalizes the combinatoric problem of listing contingencies.

Both the type of contract and its completeness are shown to depend upon the entrepreneur's abilities to find new trading partners and to direct internal contracts. Think of contracts as the spinning plates. Then the ability to direct a contract is reflected by the ability of the juggler to respin old plates (resistance of the plates to breakage) and the ability to find new trading partners is reflected in the ability to spin new plates (proportion of new plates that are balanced). The completeness of a contract determines the rate at which profits from a neglected contract decline over time. This is reflected in the initial spin that a plate receives. The more time spent spinning the plate (writing the contract) the faster it spins (more complete the contract). The faster the initial spin (more complete contract), the longer the plate continues to spin unattended (better performance).

The two best courses of action are to either write only internal employment contracts and direct each employee's activities periodically or write only market contracts with other firms and let the other entrepreneur direct his or her employees. With this model I am able to show that the completeness of internal contracts is decreasing in the ability of the entrepreneur to direct the contract and increasing in the ability to find new trading partners. A higher ability to direct the employee as contingencies arise implies that they need not be included in the initial contract. The negative effect of the ability to direct the contract is intuitively appealing. If contingencies can be dealt with later as they arise then this reduces the need to consider all contingencies in the initial contract.

The result that an increased ability to find new trading partners increases the completeness of the contract is counter-intuitive, since writing new contracts with other parties is an opportunity cost of spending more time on any one contract. Since this opportunity cost increases with an increase in the ability to find new trading partners, one would expect that the entrepreneur would spend less time writing any particular contract if this opportunity cost is higher. However, a more complete internal contract receives less frequent direction and so allows the entrepreneur to allocate more attention to the search for new trading partners which has a high probability of success. Thus the opportunity cost of attending to current contracts implied by the probability of writing a new contract manifests itself in more complete internal contracts and a reduced frequency of attending to them.

Optimal internal contracts are found to be less complete than optimal long term market transactions because contingencies can be dealt with as they arise. That is, market contracts take longer to write and are more complete, ex ante, than internal contracts. The intuition of this is that internal contracts can be less complete because they can be directed at future dates, whereas long-term market contracts are not directed at future dates and so more contingencies are included in the initial contract.

Internal contracts are optimal if the internal governance power (ability to direct contracts) of firms is sufficiently high relative to the governance power of the price system (ability to find new trading partners). This reflects Coase's argument that internal transactions are preferred if it is sufficiently difficult to "find the relevant prices" for market transactions. If prices are not posted or quality is not observable or enforceable, for example, finding suitable trading partners over markets may be sufficiently difficult to make internal contracts optimal.

Also, transactions are internalized if the number of market transactions which are replaced by the internal contract is not too large. Therefore, even if the entrepreneur's ability to direct an internal contract is greater than the ability to find another trading partner, market transactions are optimal if the number of market transactions that would be replaced by the internal contract is large enough. This depends on the optimal amount of time to spent writing both internal and market contracts.

Transaction-specific investments introduce the other source of market transaction costs: opportunistic behavior by one party to extract quasi-rents from the party which has made transaction-specific investments. Limited attention implies that, if opportunism increases with transaction-specific investments, then the critical governance power of hierarchies above which transactions are internalized decreases. Internal contracts are preferred to long-term market contracts at a lower governance power of internal contracts if there are transaction-specific investments.

The another issue of the internalization of transactions addressed in my research is the size of the firm, as measured by the number of employees. As before, the bound on firm size, that is, the maximum number of internal contracts that can be directed by the entrepreneur, is bounded away from a larger firm size which would be more valuable if it could be attained instantaneously, that is, without allocating the entrepreneur's attention to writing the contract. Therefore, as hypothesized by Kaldor (1934), limited entrepreneurial attention implies a bound on firm size because it limits the number of contracts which can be acquired and coordinated.

This result of this analysis of contracts contradicts the accepted wisdom of the effect of transaction costs on the internalization of transactions. I show that the bound on firm size is increasing in the governance power of markets and is decreasing in governance power of internal contracts. If the governance power of markets is inversely related to transaction costs and the governance power of internal contracts is inversely related to what Demsetz (1988) calls management costs, then this implies that the bound on firm size decreases with transaction costs and increases with management costs, contrary to intuition and the assertion by Demsetz (1988) that an increase in transaction costs increases firm size. The negative effect of transaction costs on firm size is due to the fact that to internalize operations, say by acquiring another firm, requires one more transaction across markets: the purchase of the other firm. The positive effect of management costs on

the bound on firm size is due to the fact that the high management costs of maintaining operations implies a low opportunity cost of attending to writing new internal contracts. These counter-intuitive results arise again when I consider average firm size. I find that the average firm size is decreasing in market transaction costs; however, the number of firms is increasing in transaction costs. Therefore, transaction costs may increase or decrease both types of trades, internal and market. The number of market transactions is also decreasing in market transaction costs.

When I allow transaction costs to be determined by the allocation of attention, I can trace the evolution of the economy. Assuming that the governance power of markets increases with the number of market transactions, I find that there are two conditions which must be satisfied for economies to convert to markets. The exogenous increase in market governance power must be sufficiently large to increase the number of market transactions and to motivate the marginal firm to convert to markets and the market governance power must be sufficiently responsive to an increase in the number of market transactions to continue the process. Under these conditions, this exogenous increase in market governance power will lead to an purely market economy with no internal transactions. In addition, an economy with more entrepreneurs converts more easily to market transactions.

The hope is that this analysis can be applied to the problem of the transition from a command economy to a market system. If an economy lacks the kind of legal institutions that result in low transaction costs, then efforts to transform the economy to a market system may fail because transaction costs result in little trade over markets and so there are continued high transaction costs.

6. Employee monitoring, performance standards and compensation

Once an entrepreneur has decided to produce a new product or service, the next problem is to organize the production process. This requires acquiring all the necessary resources and hiring the necessary employees. The final application of the model of limited attention which I will discuss is the problem of hiring, monitoring and compensating employees. This work explicitly models the entrepreneur's performance evaluations of employees when the cost of these observations is the opportunity cost of the entrepreneur's time, which is embodied in the neglect of potential new employees. This monitoring cost determines the optimal monitoring intensity, performance standard, and the existence of an efficiency wage.

The role of monitoring is critical to the literature on efficiency wages. The efficiency wage hypothesis (Leibenstein, 1957) states that the services rendered by a worker are a function of the wage received. This is used to explain the paradox of the coexistence of unemployment and a positive wage. Unemployment exists only if wages do not fall to clear labor markets and this can be due to imperfect monitoring. Firms pay more than the "going wage" to prevent shirking. However, if all firms pay wages above workers' opportunity costs, then the quantity of labor demanded is less than that supplied and unemployment is the result.

However, Carmichael (1990) suggests that the puzzle of wage rigidity remains unsolved by the efficiency wage models since most either assume rigid wages or imply wage inflexibility. Lang and Kahn (1990) assert that the assumption of monitoring costs implies efficiency wages. In the literature on efficiency wages, the independence of pay from performance is taken as exogenous and rationalized by the assumption of exogenous monitoring costs. To economize on these costs, performance evaluations are infrequent and a premium is paid to employees to motivate high performance between evaluations.

This payment of a "premium" (rent) generated by a wage higher than the opportunity cost to prevent shirking was first formally analyzed in Shapiro and Stiglitz (1984) but was suggested earlier in Klein, Crawford and Alchian (1978) as a method of preventing systematic opportunistic behavior. Krueger (1991) provides empirical evidence that monitoring costs affect compensation timing and generosity. Where monitoring is more difficult (company owned outlets) salaries are higher and rise more steeply with tenure than where monitoring is easier (franchisee-owned outlets).

The unique characteristic of the model of limited attention is that the monitoring costs are

endogenous. Preliminary results indicate that the optimal monitoring intensity, performance standard, and efficiency wage are chosen by the entrepreneur so that the employee's actual performance is above the performance standard, is increasing in the performance standard and is increasing in the wage rate. However, this requires a high measurement error and so infrequent monitoring and so efficiency wages. The high performance as a hedge against imperfect monitoring is an additional benefit of economizing on monitoring resources.

The main contribution of the model is the determination of the optimal monitoring frequency and wage and their dependence on the endogenous opportunity costs of attention. The frequency of monitoring has two implications. Less frequent monitoring delays the future date of performance evaluation and the consequences of effort and reduces the variance of the measurement error. Therefore, more frequent monitoring results in increased effort. This application is still in the development stage. However, earlier research on contracts implies that monitoring frequency is decreasing in the ability to hire new employees and is increasing in the ability of the entrepreneur to observe shirking. This implies that the wage is increasing in the ability to hire new employees and decreasing in the ability to observe shirking. This provides empirically testable hypotheses concerning the efficiency wage.

One issue to be addressed with this model of employee monitoring is the choice of compensation packages between performance pay, efficiency wages and promotions. Another issue is the effect of monitoring technology and employee skill on the choice of compensation package, firm size and the level of employment. These issues are all critical to economic development.

7. Productive and unproductive entrepreneurial activities

From the previous discussion, it is clear that the model of limited entrepreneurial attention is applicable to a wide variety of economic issues. The model addresses the question of whether to pursue a career as an entrepreneur, what type of innovation policy to follow, financing high tech startups, whether to produce in-house or out-source and if in-house, how to monitor and motivate employees. Each of these issues concerns allocating attention between previously acquired activities and acquiring additional activities, making the number of available activities endogenous.

Another issue which also fits in this category is the allocation of entrepreneurial resources among productive and unproductive activities. As suggested in Baumol (1993), this allocation should depend on the structure of rewards from these two types of activities. However, Baumol criticizes mathematical models for being "mechanistic and automatic" and for displaying no "entrepreneurial imagination and initiative." (p. 14) But purely descriptive models also seem to be lacking because of a version of the Heisenberg Uncertainty Principle: "description of such activities going beyond the sort of generalities that have already been offered here may be all but impossible. ... The very process of describing them can transmute pioneering entrepreneurial undertakings into routine managerial activities" (p. 15).

There seems some hope in satisfying Baumol's criteria for properly modeling entrepreneurial activity. It is not necessarily maximization models per se which preclude entrepreneurial activity, but static maximization. Since entrepreneurs do allocate a scarce resource, it seems plausible that "much of the standard theoretical apparatus remains pertinent" (p. 18). However, it is imperative that, since entrepreneurs create new activities, the choice set itself is endogenous and so the model must be dynamic. That is, these activities "affect productivity growth, but productivity growth, in turn, itself influences" these activities (p. 260).

The theory of the allocation of entrepreneurial attention satisfies these criteria: it is a stochastic discounted dynamic programming model which makes no attempt to nail down what exactly it is that entrepreneurs do with their entrepreneurial resources, but only analyzes how incentives affect the allocation of these resources. The discussion above implies that this allocation should depend not only on rewards but also upon the opportunity costs of these resources. In addition, although entrepreneurial activities can affect productivity, either positively or negatively, an increasing number of activities can strain entrepreneurial

resources. Therefore, productivity growth has a cost embodied in the need to continue to allocate entrepreneurial resources among a growing number of activities.

In Baumol's suggested preliminary model of economic growth, he focuses on how entrepreneurial activity can be incorporated in a feedback model along with other ancillary variables, such as equipment investment and education, which directly affect productivity growth. Although this model is to be analyzed further in a forthcoming book, it appears to yield implications for the role of entrepreneurial innovation and transfer of technology (imitation) and the convergence of productivity growth. Entrepreneurial innovation enters into the model as the most developed country's "autonomous rate of technological change" (p. 266). Entrepreneurial technology transfer is reflected in the dependence of a less developed country's future income gap on its current income gap, relative to the most developed country. Depending on the relative sizes of the parameters, this model can generate a convergence of incomes across countries.

The model of limited entrepreneurial attention can contribute to this feedback model of development by analyzing how the autonomous rate of technological change and the rate of technology transfer depend on the entrepreneurs' allocation of attention. Since the task of acquiring new activities can be accomplished through either innovation or imitation, the model can be used to show how these depend upon the parameters of the entrepreneur's environment. Specifically, new product innovation (or imitation) is increasing in the level of technological progress, as suggested by Baumol. However, the rate of economic obsolescence and the level of technological opportunity are both low, then entrepreneurs also allocate attention to maintaining the profitability of these new products, and innovation is decreasing in firm size and increasing in monopoly profits. This in itself would generate a convergence of incomes in any one country, even the leader. If economic obsolescence and technological opportunity are high, then the rate of innovation is constant.

The model of limited entrepreneurial attention also sheds light on the number of innovative, as opposed to managerial, entrepreneurs that are available and how the supply of these two types of entrepreneurs depends on their innovative and managerial ability and the wage rate. Innovative and managerial ability may themselves be influenced by education, one of the ancillary variables of empirical research in this area. A population of individuals trained in business schools may be especially capable managers, but perhaps untalented innovators. Training in engineering and science may generate more innovative entrepreneurs.

Much of our current productivity increases are due to firms in high tech industries which got their start as ventures in a venture capitalist's fund. My research has shown that there is indeed a divergence of interests between the venture capitalist and the entrepreneur in that the venture capitalist does not maximize the entrepreneur's profits. However, since the venture capitalist chooses the socially optimal amount of attention for each venture, this does not result in any inefficiencies. In addition, increased opportunities to fund successful new ventures increases the average size and the upper bound on the size of the venture capital firm and the venture capitalist's long run equilibrium share of each venture's value but also reduces the number and frequency of consultations between the venture capitalist and the funded entrepreneurs. Therefore, the divergence of interests of the venture capitalist and entrepreneur increases. However, this remains the socially optimal allocation of the venture capitalist's attention.

The last two applications of the model of limited entrepreneurial attention are apparently unrelated to the problem of development through innovation and technological transfers. However, both of these applications deal with problems faced by entrepreneurs in carrying out their roles in economic development. The contract papers illustrate the entrepreneur's dilemma of producing an intermediate product, say, or farming it out to another firm. The advantage of producing the input in-house is that the entrepreneur can oversee the production process to make sure it is done correctly. It is this ability to deal with contingencies as they arise that eliminates the need to write complete contracts initially. The disadvantage of in-house production is that it distracts the entrepreneur from other activities.

The advantage of out-sourcing the production of the intermediate product is that the responsibility for overseeing production is delegated to another firm, freeing the entrepreneur to devote time to other, possibly more important matters. The disadvantage of delegating this responsibility is that the other firm may not supply the exact same input as the entrepreneur would have produced himself. However, if the desired specifications of the input can be spelled out in advance this may not be a problem. But for many inputs, especially when the final product is still in the development stage, a considerable amount of learning goes on during production and adjustments are made in the input specifications. These advantages and disadvantages are reflected in the governance power of internal contracts and the governance power of markets. It is these two characteristics which determine whether production is via internal employment contracts or external market contracts.

The model can also be interpreted to illustrate the importance of Baumol's "rules of the game". Internal contracts may be preferred to market transactions because of the costs of opportunism in market transactions. Opportunism is basically a practice of not fulfilling the understood terms of the deal and getting away with it. The other firm may succeed in either producing an inferior product or charging higher prices because the "rules of the game" allow it or are too costly to enforce. These rules of the game include the ability to enforce the contract through the court system and the protection of property rights, including patents and copyrights. The ability of markets to provide trades which are not subject to opportunism is reflected in the parameter measuring the governance power of markets or the ability to find new (trustworthy or compliant) trading partners. Since both market and internal contracts must be written initially over markets, the "rules of the game" determine how much trade can actually take place and so affect the development of the economy.

We saw how the model of limited entrepreneurial attention can be used to explain the existence of efficiency wages and how they depend on the endogenous costs of monitoring due to limited attention. Since the existence of efficiency wages implies equilibrium unemployment, they have apparent significance for economic development. The resulting unemployment may not be inefficient if it is due only to these monitoring costs. However, these monitoring costs are due to the principal-agent problem between the entrepreneur and employees which exists as a result of the inability of the entrepreneur to freely and perfectly monitor performance. These monitoring costs are wasted resources in the welfare sense because they are incurred only to prevent shirking or opportunism on the part of employees.

In this application, the "rules of the game" appear again as the ability to hire new (trustworthy or compliant) employees. As in the contract papers, this has an effect on the allocation of attention. Market institutions which make market transactions easily enforceable result in less attention allocated to monitoring employees and more to hiring additional employees. Greater ability to accurately monitor employees and enforce contracts also reduces monitoring and increases employment. Thus, in these last two applications we can see that improving the effectiveness of our court system and the protection of property rights can lead to greater production and employment.

Notes

[1] For a more detailed review, see Gifford (1992b).
[2] The model is formally developed in Gifford and Wilson (1995).

References

Acs, Zoltan and Sharon Gifford, 1996, 'Innovation of Entrepreneurial Firms', *Small Business Economics*, special issue, 203–218.

Arrow Kenneth J., 1974, *The Limits of Organization*, New York: W. W. Norton & Company.

Barnard, Chester I., 1938, *The Functions of the Executive*, Cambridge, MA: Harvard University Press.

Baumol, William J., 1993, *Entrepreneurship, Management, and the Structure of Payoffs*, Cambridge, MA: MIT Press.

Becker, Gary S., 1965, 'A Theory of the Allocation of Time', *Economic Journal* **75**, 493–517.

Chandler, Alfred. D., 1977, *The Visible Hand: The Managerial Revolution in American Business*, Cambridge, MA: Harvard University Press.

Carmichael, H. Lorne, 1990, 'Efficiency Wage Models of Unemployment – One View', *Economic Inquiry* **28**(2), 269–295.

Coase, Ronald H., 1937, 'The Nature of the Firm', *Economica* **4**, 386–405.

Commons, John. R., 1934, *Institutional Economics*, New York: Macmillan Company.

Demsetz, Harold, 1988, 'The Theory of the Firm Revisited', *Journal of Law, Economics and Organization* **4**, 141–161.

Dosi, Giovanni, 1988, 'Sources, Procedures, and Microeconomic Effects of Innovation', *Journal of Economic Literature* **26**, 1120–1171.

Gifford, Sharon, 1992a, 'Innovation, Firm Size and Growth in a Centralized Organization', *The Rand Journal of Economics* **23**, 284–298.

Gifford, Sharon, 1992b, 'Allocation of Entrepreneurial Attention', *Journal of Economic Behavior and Organization* **19**, 265–284.

Gifford, Sharon, 1993, 'Heterogeneous Ability, Career Choice and Firm Size', *Small Business Economics* **5**, 249–259.

Gifford, Sharon, 1994a, 'Limited Entrepreneurial Attention and the Optimal Completeness of Contracts', Working Paper, Rutgers University.

Gifford, Sharon, 1994b, 'Limited Entrepreneurial Attention and the Internalization of Transactions', Working Paper, Rutgers University.

Gifford, Sharon, forthcoming, 'On the Role of the Venture Capitalist', *Journal of Business Venturing*.

Gifford, Sharon and Charles A. Wilson, 1995, 'A Model of Project Evaluation With Limited Attention', *Economic Theory* **5**, 67–78.

Gompers, Paul and Joshua Lerner, 1994, 'An Analysis of Compensation in the U.S. Venture Capital Partnership', Working paper, Harvard Business School.

Hayek, Fredrick von, 1945, 'The Use of Knowledge in Society', *American Economic Review* **35**, 519–530.

Holmstrom, B. and P. Milgrom, 1990, 'Incentive Contracts, Asset Ownership and Job Design', Working Paper Series D #45, Yale School of Organization and Management.

Kaldor, Nicholas, 1934, 'The Equilibrium of the Firm', *Economic Journal* **44**, 60–76.

Kirzner, Israel M., 1979, *Perception, Opportunity and Profit*, Chicago: University of Chicago Press.

Klein, Benjamin, Robert A. Crawford and Armen A. Alchian, 1978, 'Vertical Integration, Appropriable Rents, and the Competitive Contracting Process', *Journal of Law and Economics* **21**, 297–326

Krueger, Alan, 1991, 'Ownership, Agency and Wages: An Examination of Franchising in the Fast Foods Industry', *Quarterly Journal of Economics*: 75–101.

Lang, Kevin and Shulamit Kahn, 1990, 'Efficiency Wage Models of Unemployment: A Second View', *Economic Inquiry* **28**, 296–306.

Leibenstein, H., 1957, *Economic Backwardness and Economic Growth*, New York: Wiley.

March, James G. and Herbert A. Simon, 1958, *Organizations*, New York: John Wiley & Sons.

30   *Sharon Gifford*

Sahlman, William A., 1990, 'The Structure and Governance of Venture-Capital Organizations', *Journal of Financial Economics* **27**, 473–521.

Schilit, W. Keith, 1991, *Inside the Venture Capital Industry*, Englewood Cliffs, NJ: Prentice Hall.

Schumpeter, Joseph A., 1934, *The Theory of Economic Development*, Cambridge, MA: Harvard College.

Shapiro, Carl and Joseph E. Stiglitz, 1984, 'Equilibrium Unemployment as a Worker Discipline Device' *American Economic Review* **74**, 433–444.

Timmons, Jeffrey A. and Harry J. Sapienza, 1992, 'Venture Capital: The Decade Ahead', in Donald L. Sexton and John D. Kasarda (eds.), *The State of the Art of Entrepreneurship*, Boston: PWS-Kent Publishing.

[10]

Economics Letters 35 (1991) 339–342
North-Holland

339

Are new firms an important source of innovation?

Evidence from the PC software industry

Thomas J. Prusa and James A. Schmitz, Jr.

State University of New York, Stony Brook, NY 11794, USA

Received 25 June 1990
Accepted 13 August 1990

We examine data from the PC software industry to determine if new forms play an important role in the advance of technology in this industry over the period 1982–1987. We find that new firms have a comparative advantage (over established firms) in *creating* new software categories, while established firms have a comparative advantage in developing subsequent improvements in *existing* categories.

1. Introduction

In their important book, Jewkes, Sawers and Stillerman (1958) (henceforth, JSS) studied the sources of the important inventions of the 19th and 20th centuries. A primary goal was to determine the importance of the small, independent entrepeneur relative to the large industrial research laboratory in developing these inventions. They found, contrary to the popular wisdom of the day, that the small, independent entrepeneur continued to play an important role in technological change during the 20th century. The purpose of this paper is to examine some of the same issues studied by JSS but for a more recent experience. In particular, we examine the importance of 'new' versus 'established' firms in generating innovations in the PC software industry. Similar to JSS, we find that new firms contribute a very large share of industry innovation.

The question of whether new (or small) firms play an important role in technological progress is an issue which has attracted considerable theoretical attention [see e.g. Holmstrom (1989), Williamson (1985) and Aron and Lazear (1990)]. Clearly more empirical evidence is needed on this issue. While this paper explores only a single industry, data similar to ours should be available for many more, from sources such as trade groups and for-profit firms (the source of our data).

2. Description of data

The data was obtained from Dataquest, Inc., an information services company. For each of 206 software products we have the following information:

(1) the introduction date of the program (month, year),
(2) the software category of the program (Dataquest has defined 17 categories which will be given below),

(3) the operating system on which the program runs,

(4) the firm marketing the program, and

(5) the annual unit sales of the program for the years 1982–1987.

Of course, most programs were introduced sometime during the period 1982–1987 and for those programs sales figures are available for the introduction year and beyond. Dataquest obtains its estimates for unit sales by surveying industry vendors (i.e. wholesalers and retailers) [1].

There were obviously many more software programs over this period than the ones in the data set. While the data set has only a few of the many programs available in this period (all programs in the data set sell at least 1000 units annually), the program in the data set account for a large majority of industry sales. In particular, the Software Publishers Association, the industry trade group, estimates that industry revenue was $2.7 billion in 1987. The revenue from the sales of programs on the data set in 1987 was $2.5 billion. [2]

3. New and established firms' share of category innovations

We define a firm to be 'new' at date *t* if the firm first appears on the data set at time *t*, while a firm is said to be an 'established' firm if it has appeared on the data set prior to time *t*. We also need a means to rank innovations. Ideally, we would like to use the social surplus created by a product as the means to rank innovations [as done by Trajtenberg (1989)]. Social surplus created by a program cannot be calculated from the data set but two reasonable proxies can be employed. Let us initially say a program is an important innovation if the program is the first program in a category. There is good reason to define a program which creates a new category as an important innovation. By showing the possibility of a new type of software, the program will obviously generate large 'spillovers'.

There are a total of seventeen software categories as defined by Dataquest (see table 1). In fifteen of these categories there is a unique firm which 'opened up' the software category. In two categories there was more than one firm; in one category four firms introduced programs 'simultaneously' (i.e., same month and year), while in the other category two firms introduced programs simultaneously. There are therefore a total of 21 products which introduced software categories. Of these 21 products, 18 (or 86%) were introduced by new firms and 3 were introduced by established firms. The type of firm introducing the first product in each category are given in the first column of table 1. The fourth column presents the number of established software firms in the data set at the time a category was introduced. This column defines the set of established firms which could have developed the category-opening product. The third column reports the total number of programs in each category, which might be thought of as a measure of the 'spillover' created by the first product.

These numbers do not imply, however, that established firms are not innovating. They are. First, of the 206 products introduced over this period, 108 (52%) were introduced by established firms, while 98 were introduced by new firms. Second, of the 108 products introduced by established firms, 47 (44%) were in categories in which the firm did not have a previous product. So nearly half the products introduced by established firms are in 'new' (for the firm) software categories. Third, these firms have developed a more equal share of important innovations under the second proxy for social surplus created.

---

[1] The reader might be interested in how the results below depend on the influence of the 'industry standard' operating systems, Microsoft DOS, Apple DOS, Apple Macintosh DOS, and Digital CP/M. The 206 programs actually do not include these programs which are bundled with hardware; if we had included them none of the results below would change.

[2] Dataquest does not report revenue data by program but by firm (from software sales). We use this firm revenue data in the comparison above.

Table 1
Software category innovators.

Category	Type of firm introducing first program [a]	Type of firm introducing category's product with greatest cumulative sales [a]	Total number of programs in category	Number of firms in existence prior to category's opening
Database management	(1,0)	(1,0)	23	0
Accounting	(1,0)	(1,0)	17	1
Word processing	(1,0)	(1,0)	26	1
Spreadsheets	(0,1)	(1,0)	14	6
File management	(1,0)	(1,0)	11	8
Graphics	(0,1)	(0,1)	33	8
Integrated	(1,0)	(0,1)	12	8
CAD	(1,0)	(1,0)	8	13
Languages	(1,0)	(1,0)	3	18
Personal finance	(4,0)	(1,0)	4	19
Utilities and accessories	(1,0)	(0,1)	23	19
Project management	(1,0)	(0,1)	4	29
Communications	(1,0)	(1,0)	8	30
Desktop publishing	(1,0)	(1,0)	8	47
Operating environments and operating systems	(1,0)	(0,1)	3	47
Development tools	(1,0)	(0,1)	7	53
Information Management	(1,1)	(0,1)	2	88
Total	(18,3)	(10,7)	206	

[a] The pair (x, y) in parentheses are defined as follows: x denotes the number of firms new firms while y denotes the number of established firms.

As the second proxy for the important innovation in a category we use the program which has the greatest cumulative sales in the category. Under some reasonable conditions (e.g., development costs approximately equal across programs), sales should also be a decent proxy for social surplus created by a program. We find that new and established firms provided roughly the same number of programs which had the greatest cumulative sales in each category (column 2, table 1). Comparing columns 1 and 2 of table 1 suggests that new firms have a comparative advantage in developing *new* categories, while established firms have a comparative advantage in developing subsequent improvements within existing categories.

In table 2 we consider the possibility that many firms were developing category-opening programs independently and introduced them a few months apart. If this were the case then we would want to count these other products as category 'openers'. In particular, suppose it takes k months to imitate a new program. Then all programs which were introduced within k months of a category-opening product were developed independently of the first program and should also be judged as *creating* the new category. In table 2 we present the types of firms which independently developed category-opening products based on different assumptions of how long it takes to imitate a program. We see that the result in column 1 of table 1 does not change much for the different imitation lags. The result that new firms provide a large share of category opening products is a robust one.

Table 2
Alternative specifications for 'limitation lag'.

Imitation lag value (months)	Type of firm introducing first program [a] (Total)
0	(18,3)
3	(20,4)
6	(22,6)
9	(22,6)
12	(23,10)

[a] The pair (x, y) in parentheses are defined as follows: x denotes the number of new firms while y denotes the number of established firms.

References

Aron, Debra and E. Lazear, 1990, The introduction of new products, American Economic Review Paper and Proceedings 80, 421–426.
Holmstrom, B., 1989, Agency costs and innovation, Journal of Economic Behavior and Organization, 305–327.
Jewkes, J. and D. Sawers and R. Stillerman, 1958, The sources of invention, (Macmillan, London).
Trajtenberg, M., 1989, The welfare analysis of product innovation, with an application to computed tomography scanners 97.
Williamson, O., 1985, The economic institutions of capitalism (The Free Press, New York).

Part IV
Growth Models

[11]

Imitation, Entrepreneurship, and Long-Run Growth

James A. Schmitz, Jr.

State University of New York at Stony Brook

Despite the widespread belief that entrepreneurship is a key factor in economic development, there have been few attempts to develop formal models to analyze the phenomenon. This paper presents a model in which endogenous entrepreneurial activity is a key determinant of economic growth. The theory also differs from standard models in that growth is driven by the imitative activities of entrepreneurs. Previous theories have focused on the direct production of knowledge, underemphasizing the importance of imitation in the growth process. The paper also examines external effects arising from these entrepreneurial activities—effects distinct from those studied by Paul Romer.

I. Introduction

Entrepreneurship is generally recognized to be a key factor in economic growth. The entrepreneur plays a central role in prominent descriptive theories of economic development as well, such as that developed by Schumpeter (1934). Yet despite this recognition and early descriptive theories, there have been very few attempts to construct formal models to analyze the phenomenon. This paper presents a formal model of entrepreneurship, in particular, a model of

I am indebted to my advisor Edward Prescott. I thank Paul Romer for his helpful comments as a discussant at the summer Econometric Society meetings. This paper was originally titled "Growth and New Product Development" and benefited from the comments of Pat Kehoe, Nobu Kiyotaki, Luis Locay, Ramon Marimon, Ariel Pakes, Robert Porter, and Nancy Stokey. I am very grateful to a referee whose detailed comments greatly improved this paper, and to Sam Peltzman for his help in focusing my ideas.

[*Journal of Political Economy*, 1989, vol. 97, no. 3]

economic growth in which endogenous entrepreneurial activity is a key determinant of productivity growth.

While the theory presented here focuses on the entrepreneur, the entrepreneur's role in promoting growth differs from that emphasized by Schumpeter and others. In the Schumpeterian model, the innovating entrepreneur plays the key role, with imitators assigned a minor part in the growth process. In contrast, the theory below focuses on the role of imitation—the act of transferring and implementing a new technology—in promoting growth. Rather than the Schumpeterian innovating entrepreneur, it is the activities of imitating entrepreneurs that drive growth below. This emphasis on imitation is motivated by the historical research of Baumol (1986, 1988) on entrepreneurship and productivity growth. One of the main conclusions from his work is that this type of entrepreneurship has contributed a significant amount to the growth of most economies. Though the historical record indicates its importance, theoretical research on growth has underemphasized the importance of imitation.

The predictions of the theory are consistent with the widely held, intuitive view that entrepreneurship is important for growth. That is, in the model, economies with a high proportion of entrepreneurs will grow persistently faster than economies with a smaller proportion. The theory also yields implications for the determinants of entrepreneurial activity. For example, the extent of entrepreneurship is shown to be positively related to the economy's communication infrastructure. The theory therefore relates such variables as entrepreneurship, imitation, the communication infrastructure, and the pace of economic growth. In this regard, the paper should help in future efforts to measure the contributions of entrepreneurship. At the same time, the model can be used for normative purposes, for evaluating the impact of policies on entrepreneurial activity and ultimately growth.

II. Relation to Previous Literature and Brief Description of the Model

This paper develops a model of endogenous economic growth motivated by the notable contribution of Romer (1986*b*). However, the theory differs in three important respects from Romer's model and most other growth models. Each of these differences will be described in turn, with the discussion also serving as a means to introduce the model. A formal description is provided in the next section.

Starting with the treatments of Cass (1965) and Koopmans (1965), the literature on economic growth has studied how the optimal (equilibrium) allocation of resources between consumption and investment each period should be (is) determined. From the onset, these models have been highly aggregative in the sense that the institutional context in which these investment and consumption decisions are made is usually kept in the background. For example, in the decentralization of the models, the number of firms is usually unimportant for the results (e.g., if production occurs under constant returns), or if it is important (e.g., if there are decreasing returns), then the number of firms is taken as given. Since there is generally no analysis of how these institutional arrangements (i.e., the number of firms) arose, the models are of limited use for addressing such questions as what determines the number of individuals (firms) engaged in entrepreneurial activity. In contrast, in the model below the determination of the underlying institutional arrangements in which the aggregate investment and consumption decisions are made is brought into the foreground. Admittedly, the institutional details are simple: each period each individual decides to work as an employee for an entrepreneur or to pursue entrepreneurial activity. Individuals can change their occupations over time. Being an entrepreneur means imitating the existing industry knowledge and, together with employee time, implementing the knowledge to produce output of the single consumption good. The model therefore predicts the underlying industrial organization of the economy at each date, that is, the fraction of employees and entrepreneurs. This first difference then distinguishes the model from both the standard growth model and most of the recent endogenous growth theories as well. However, the work of Prescott and Boyd (1987) is an exception since they also introduce institutional details into a growth context. Rather than determining the extent of individual entrepreneurship, their paper studies the formation of coalitions of individuals. Another exception is Holmes and Schmitz (1988), who study the determinants of individual entrepreneurship in a vintage capital type model.

The second difference distinguishes the model from theories of growth that are driven by the development and diffusion of knowledge. In most of these theories, such as Romer's, the emphasis is on the direct production of knowledge. For example, in Romer's model firms decide what resources to devote toward knowledge creation, with newly developed knowledge completely and costlessly diffusing to the other firms in the economy. As mentioned, the theory here begins a more detailed examination of this latter activity: of the act of imitation and implementation by which technology diffuses. Rather than having imitation a passive activity, the model assumes that resources must be devoted to the activity. In order to keep matters simple, I analyze the polar case to Romer's model. That is, in the model entrepreneurs decide whether or not to imitate and implement current knowledge, with new knowledge creation occurring as a by-product in a learning-by-doing fashion. Specifically, at each date there is a stock of industry knowledge. Those individuals deciding to be entrepreneurs imitate this knowledge. In the process of implementing the current industry technique, entrepreneurs augment the existing stock of industry knowledge in a learning-by-doing fashion. Note in this formulation that there is no individual-specific knowledge, only industry knowledge. Knowledge is a common property resource, and no one earns a return from creating new knowledge. An entrepreneur's compensation comes entirely from imitating existing activities and putting them to use. However, in the process, entrepreneurs create knowledge in a learning-by-implementing or learning-by-imitating fashion.

This emphasis on the role of imitation in the growth process is motivated by the growth experiences of numerous economies: growth records that are difficult to understand in the context of standard models that focus on the direct production of knowledge. For example, Baumol (1988) provides historical descriptions of economies in which important inventions were made, yet sustained growth did not follow. Though there was direct production of knowledge in these economies, there was very little effort devoted to imitating and implementing the ideas. Often the social systems in these economies discouraged these efforts. Perhaps the most persuasive example is the economy of ancient China. Though there were numerous important inventions (e.g., gunpowder) in early China, the most substantial rewards in wealth and prestige were conferred on the scholar-bureaucrat; business enterprise was frowned on. For a current example, consider explaining the difference in growth performance between mainland China and Hong Kong. Models emphasizing direct knowledge production would focus on such things as the analogue of the National Science Foundation budget in the two economies and the funding of basic research by firms. But as with ancient China, this would miss the essential difference between these economies, which seems to be the extent of entrepreneurial activity directed at implementing knowledge.

The third difference distinguishes the model from those examining external effects in knowledge creation. In most of these models, such as Romer's, the term representing external effects from research enters as an argument of the production function, influencing the productivity of producing current output. The theory below examines a different specification for external effects, one in which these effects enter the accumulation technology, influencing the productivity in developing new knowledge. The motivation for examining an additional formulation for external effects is provided by the historical research on technology by Nathan Rosenberg and also recent empirical work on research spillovers.

From his study of economic growth during the nineteenth and twentieth centuries, Rosenberg (1976, 1982) has concluded that an important source of the phenomenal growth during this period was the process of "technological convergence." By technological convergence Rosenberg means the fact that "industrialization was characterized by the introduction of a relatively small number of broadly similar productive processes to a large number of industries" (1976, p. 15). As a consequence of this convergence, a new technique developed in one industry could readily be modified for use in other industries. Rosenberg provides numerous examples of such cross-industry effects during the nineteenth century. As argued in Rosenberg (1982), this phenomenon continues to play an important role in the twentieth century. The chemical industry developing synthetic fibers used by the textile industry, and lubricants and coatings used by the electrical industry, is just one example. An important message that emerges from this work is that productivity in developing new products, for example new types of clothes, depends on innovation efforts in other industries. Put differently, an important lesson is the critical role of external effects in the accumulation of knowledge. Recent attempts at measuring the external effects in knowledge accumulation have supported the conclusions of Rosenberg (see, e.g., Griliches 1979; Jaffe 1986). In the paper by Jaffe, it is demonstrated that the R & D productivity of firms is increased by the R & D of "technological neighbors." For example, it is estimated that a doubling of a firm's own R & D would double the patents it receives, while if the firm and its technological neighbors doubled their R & D, the firm's patents would increase by a factor of four, the spillover accounting for half the increase.

With the historical work of Rosenberg and the recent empirical analysis as motivation, this paper examines external effects in the accumulation of knowledge. In particular, in order to study Rosenberg's idea of technological convergence and cross-industry effects, the model below will consist of a "large" number of industries. Each industry produces the same consumption good but uses a different technology. Different technologies are employed since individual skills are assumed to be technology specific. (I have chosen a single consumption good for notational convenience; see the discussion below.) The new knowledge that results from the imitative activities of entrepreneurs in a particular industry will spill over to industries that are technologically "close" to the industry in question. The magnitude of spillover to other industries will depend in part on the number of individuals who decide to be entrepreneurs in the industry that period. It will also depend on the degree of technological convergence, that is, how "similar" the technologies are to each other. The effect of the spillover to other industries is to increase the productivity of entrepreneurs in creating knowledge in those industries and, ultimately, to increase per capita growth rates.

The parameter indexing technological convergence can also be interpreted as a measure of the communication infrastructure. Consequently, there is a direct relationship between the extent of the economy's communication infrastructure and the pace of economic growth, a result similar in spirit to Townsend (1983), where an (exogenous) increase in the degree of financial integration is shown to increase the level of the economy's income. There have been some historical analyses, as well as very preliminary empirical work, concerning the relationship between communication and growth. For example, in his discussion of the role communication played in U.S. economic growth, Cole (1959, pp. 85–88) distinguishes three eras since the country gained its independence. According to him, "over the first fifty or seventy-five years there was precious little business literature," while the next period, from about 1825 to 1885, witnessed a growth in industry literature. However, it "was an era when knowledge was, in a sense, partitioned off by industry." During the last period, "speculative thinkers, and engineers in particular, began to grasp the notion that there were uniformities in business, maybe 'laws' of a sort," and these ideas were incorporated into the business literature. "In this period came also the institutions which could serve as vehicles for the cross-industrial transmission of thought . . . the professional associations and the schools of business." It is interesting to note that average per capita growth rates increased in each of these three successive periods. As for more quantitative studies, communication and other infrastructure data have been collected in Europe for the study of regional development. In particular, in Nijkamp's (1986) study of the Netherlands regional infrastructure, data for 11 Dutch provinces for two time periods (1970–75 and 1976–80) were collected. A significant positive correlation was found between the communication infrastructure and average regional product.

The remainder of the paper proceeds as follows. In Section III a formal description of the model is presented. The model is embedded into a growth context in Section IV, where the competitive equilibrium and social optimum are defined. Rather than characterize the solutions to these problems, which is done in the Appendix, an example is studied in this section. Section V presents ideas for future research.

III. Formal Description of the Model

The model is composed of a "large" number of industries, say N, each producing the same consumption good but using a different technology. Industries are modeled as lying, equally spaced from one another, on a circle of unit length. They will be indexed by their position $j \in [0, 1]$ on the circle, and the closer are their positions, the more "similar" are their technologies. There are also N individual types indexed by j. What defines an individual as being of type j is that he or she must work (as an employee or entrepreneur) in industry j. Let there be M individuals per industry (type) so that $MN = \bar{N}$ is the total population. Define $E(j, t)$ to be the number of entrepreneurs in industry j at time t—so $M - E(j, t)$ is the number of employees—and $e(j, t)$ to be the fraction of entrepreneurs, or $E(j, t)/M$. It will be convenient to define a sequence of economies and to study the economy that is the limit of this sequence. Consider then the sequence of economies in which the number of equally spaced industries N increases, while the total population and the fraction of entrepreneurs in each industry remain fixed. In the limit, there will be an industry for each real number in the unit interval, while $\bar{N}$ will be the total population and $e(j, t)$ the fraction of entrepreneurs in industry j. We will consider the case of symmetric industries, so $e(t)$ will denote the fraction of entrepreneurs in a representative industry. The fraction of entrepreneurs in the total population is the total number of entrepreneurs $e(t)\bar{N}$ divided by $\bar{N}$ and is also $e(t)$. For simplicity, we shall choose $\bar{N} = 1$ so that there will be no distinction between aggregate and per capita quantities.

Consider individuals in a representative industry. Each individual is endowed with a unit of time each period, which can be used in one of two roles: (1) as an entrepreneur or (2) as an employee working for another entrepreneur. Note that individuals can change occupations through time. Employees simply supply their time to entrepreneurs for a wage. Entrepreneurs imitate the existing stock of knowledge. Using this knowledge together with employee time, the entrepreneur produces output. Entrepreneurial compensation, the excess of production over wages, comes entirely from imitating existing activities and putting them to use. However, in the process, entrepreneurs (as a group) create new knowledge in a learning-by-doing fashion, where here it is learning by imitating and implementing, not learning by producing. And as described, the productivity of this learning-by-implementing technology will depend on the extent of knowledge and entrepreneurial activity in other industries. The production and knowledge creation technologies are now described.

Since $e(t)$ is the fraction of entrepreneurs in the representative industry at time t, $1 - e(t)$ is the fraction of employees and $[1 - e(t)]/e(t)$ is employee labor input per entrepreneur. If the current stock of knowledge in the industry is denoted by $k(t)$, the output $y(t)$ produced by a representative entrepreneur will be given by $y(t) = F(k(t), [1 - e(t)]/e(t))$. The new knowledge created by entrepreneurs in industry j as they implement current techniques will depend on the stock of knowledge in industry j and the fraction of individuals imitating in j. It will also depend on the spillover to the industry from other industries, which will be a function of the stock of knowledge and the fraction of entrepreneurs in those industries. Formally, the law of motion for $k(j, t)$ will be $\dot{k}(j, t) = G(h(j, t), H(j, t))$, where $h(j, t) = \bar{h}(e(j, t), k(j, t))$ is the own industry effect and $H(j, t)$ is the spillover effect on knowledge creation. The function $\bar{h}$ is assumed increasing in both arguments. As mentioned, the spillover $H(j, t)$ is assumed to depend on the stock of knowledge $k(i, t)$ and the fraction of entrepreneurs $e(i, t)$ for industries i in some set I. For notational simplicity, assume that I is some subset of the unit interval. Viewing the set I as the unit interval would downplay the costs associated with both the gathering and assimilating of knowledge. Though these costs are not formally modeled here, a more appropriate measure would be the set of industries that are "close," in a technological sense, to the industry in question. Closeness will have as a determinant the communication infrastructure of the economy, this influencing the costs just described. Improved communication will expand the range of technologies that an entrepreneur is familiar with and can learn from. Therefore, let s denote the value of the economy's communication infrastructure and assume that I is a function of s, $I(s)$. Define the spillover to industry j to be $H(j, t) = \int_{I(s)} \bar{h}(e(i, t), k(i, t)) di$. For simplicity, assume that $\bar{h}$ takes the form $\bar{h}(e, k) = ek$ and that $I(s) = [j - (s/2), j + (s/2)]$, with $s < 1$. Then we have $H(j, t) = se(t)k(t)$ using symmetry. Therefore, spillover will depend on entrepreneurial density, which will be determined in the model, and on communication infrastructure, which is given exogenously. The parameter s can also be interpreted as the degree of technological convergence, the concept introduced by Rosenberg and discussed above. Since industries lie on a circle, each industry receives the same spillover from other industries, and $H(j, t)$ need not be indexed by j. Finally, note that in the G function there is no argument for individual effort. This reflects the fact that all knowledge is a common property resource and no one earns a return from creating new knowledge, only from imitating it.

   Before we proceed to the growth model, the roles of the assumptions above are discussed. First, since industries produce the same consumption good, individual abilities in innovating and working as employees are assumed to be industry or technology specific. This prevents "bunching" of effort around a single technology type in order to "capture" all the spillover and achieve total integration. Actually, with the continuum of technology types an optimal solution would not exist without these specificities. An alternative approach would be to assume that each industry produces a different consumption good and that each good is produced with a different technology. Bunching of effort around a single technology type would not be optimal here because of a presumed desire for product diversity. Though models of growth with many products have been constructed (see, e.g., Judd 1985; Lucas 1985; Schmitz 1986; Romer 1987; Stokey 1988), adding product diversity would add notation without changing the nature of the conclusions. It would be of interest in future work to examine environments in which there is bunching of effort in equilibrium since firms in particular industries often tend to be located close to each other geographically. The formal model here suggests one potential reason for this bunching, reduction in communication costs. Second, the decision to examine the polar case of Romer's model enables the analysis to proceed using a single state variable. That is, this formulation permits the study of a representative entrepreneur, even as $e(t)$ fluctuates through time. To see this, suppose that more individuals in an industry decide to become entrepreneurs at date t. Then "next" period how can these individuals have the same level of $k(t)$ as those who were entrepreneurs previously? Precisely under the assumption that $k(t)$ is knowledge and can be imitated by new entrepreneurs. If it had been assumed that some knowledge could be kept private, then a distinction would need to be made between "new" and "old" entrepreneurs. If this were the case, the dimensionality of the state variable would necessarily increase.

IV. The Growth Model

A. Description of Dynamic Competitive Equilibrium

The growth model is constructed in continuous time. For the description of the competitive equilibrium the consumption good is chosen to be numeraire, with $w(t)$ denoting the wage of employees in units of the consumption good at time t. Individuals in a representative industry j must decide each period whether to be employees or entrepreneurs. The payoff to an employee is simply $w(t)$, while the payoff $\pi(j, t)$ to imitating and implementing the existing stock of knowledge $k(j, t)$ is $\pi(j, t) = \max_z F(k(j, t), z) - w(t)z$, where z is the employment choice of the entrepreneur. Note that the individual decision problem is essentially a "sequence" of static decision problems. To make the best occupational decision at time t requires knowing only $w(t)$ and

$k(j, t)$ since individuals can costlessly change occupations each period. Again, this is a consequence of the assumption that knowledge is a common property resource that can be fully imitated. If, for example, there was a fixed cost of changing occupations (so that in effect knowledge was no longer a common property resource), then in addition to the paths $w(t)$ and $k(j, t)$, individuals would need to forecast the paths $e(i, t)$ and $k(i, t)$ for $i \in [j - (s/2), j + (s/2)]$ and for $t \in [0, \infty)$ since these paths would determine the paths $h(j, t)$ and $H(j, t)$ and therefore $\dot{k}$ and hence the profits to entrepreneurship over a fixed period. In order to define equilibrium, let $d(j, t)$ be a decision rule, $d = 1$ ($d = 0$) meaning that individuals decide to be entrepreneurs (employees), and $z(j, t)$ the employment level entrepreneurs choose. Then if the industry index is dropped, a dynamic competitive equilibrium is a set of functions $(w^*(t), k^*(t), d^*(t), z^*(t))$, where w^* and k^* are forecasts for wages and industry knowledge while d^* and z^* are decisions, that satisfy the following conditions: (1) entrepreneurs choose their employment levels optimally; that is, $z^* = \text{argmax } F(k^*, z) - w^*z$; (2) the labor market clears; that is, $z^* = (1 - e^*)/e^*$, where $e^* = \int d^*$; (3) individuals are indifferent about being employees or entrepreneurs each period; that is, $w^* = F(k^*, z^*) - w^*z^*$; and (4) the individual decisions, based on the forecast k^*, generate k^* as the equilibrium outcome. A critical aspect of this construction is that each individual ignores the impact of his or her entrepreneur/employee choice on the aggregate spillover. This will lead to a divergence between the equilibrium and optimal rates of imitation activity.

B. The Equilibrium and Social Optimization Problems

Rather than proceeding to calculate a competitive equilibrium in the usual fashion, I present a maximization problem with the property that solutions, satisfying a fixed-point property, will correspond to competitive equilibrium quantities. This maximization problem is a myopic planner's problem, that is, a planner who makes entrepreneur/employee assignments ignoring their impact on the aggregate spillover. This method for analyzing equilibrium closely follows the work of Romer (1986*b*). This "equilibrium" optimization problem and the usual social optimization problem are now presented.

    The accumulation technology is assumed to be homogeneous of degree one and will be expressed as $\dot{k} = G(h, H) = hg(H/h)$, where $g(H/h) = G(1, H/h)$. It is assumed that g is twice continuously differentiable, increasing, and strictly concave with $g(0) = 0$. The production technology is also taken to be homogeneous of degree one, so output of the representative entrepreneur can be written as $y = F(k, (1 - e)/e) = kf((1 - e)/ek)$, where $f((1 - e)/ek) = F(1, (1 - e)/ek)$ and f

has the same properties as g. Total production in the economy is ey, which is also per capita consumption $c(t)$ since $\bar{N} = 1$. As a function of e, $c = ekf((1 - e)/ek)$ equals zero at $e = 1$ since $f(0) = 0$. Further, it is assumed that it equals zero when $e = 0$ and that it is a twice continuously differentiable and strictly concave function over $[0, 1]$. Hence there is a unique $e' \in (0, 1)$ that maximizes per capita consumption at each date. Since k is increasing in e, it is clear that the equilibrium and optimal solutions will always entail a fraction of entrepreneurs at least as large as e'. Preferences over the infinite horizon are assumed to take the form $\int_0^\infty u(c(t))e^{-\delta t}dt$, with $\delta > 0$ and u satisfying the assumptions of f and g. The social optimization problem, denoted PS, and the "equilibrium" optimization problem referred to above, denoted $P(h, H)$, are

$$PS: \quad \max \int_0^\infty e^{-\delta t} u(c(t))dt$$

$$\text{subject to } c(t) = e(t)k(t)f\left(\frac{1 - e(t)}{e(t)k(t)}\right),$$

$$\dot{k}(t) = e(t)k(t)g(s);$$

$$P(h, H): \quad \max \int_0^\infty e^{-\delta t} u(c(t))dt$$

$$\text{subject to } c(t) = e(t)k(t)f\left(\frac{1 - e(t)}{e(t)k(t)}\right),$$

$$\dot{k}(t) = h(t)g\left(\frac{H(t)}{h(t)}\right).$$

Note that in both these problems, the control variable $e(t)$ is constrained by $e(t) \in [0, 1]$ and the state variable $k(t)$ has an initial condition $k(0) = k_0$. The only difference between the two problems lies in the specification of the accumulation technology. In the social optimization problem, the planner recognizes the external effect entrepreneurs have on each other's productivity in imitative activity. Therefore, the substitutions $h(t) = e(t)k(t)$ and $H(t) = se(t)k(t)$ are made in this problem. In the second problem, the external effects on productivity are not considered in entrepreneur/employee assignment. Therefore, the paths $h(t)$ and $H(t)$ are taken parametrically in this problem. The general procedure for finding equilibria from problem $P(h, H)$ is as follows. For given paths h^* and H^*, there will be a solution to $P(h^*, H^*)$ consisting of paths e and k. If the solution (e, k) satisfies $ek = h^*$ and $sek = H^*$, then the paths are also equilibrium quantities (see Romer 1986*b*).

Conditions ensuring the existence of solutions to PS and $P(h, H)$ can be derived using the methods in Romer (1986a) and will not be discussed in detail here. Given the assumptions above, the continuity and concavity conditions of Romer's theorem are satisfied. Then a solution to PS will exist if a bound on the rate of growth of k can be found that ensures finiteness of the objective function. A sufficient condition for this is $\delta > g(s)$. Note that in the problem $P(h, H)$ the control e does not enter the law of motion for k. Therefore, continuity of $ekf((1 - e)/ek)$ in e on $[0, 1]$ guarantees that a solution to $P(h, H)$ exists. Assumptions about the paths $h(t)$ and $H(t)$ are not needed to prove existence.

The equilibrium and optimal solutions are characterized in Appendix A. The details of the Hamiltonian dynamics are presented there so as not to obscure the simplicity with which the equilibrium can be calculated for this model, as illustrated by the following example.

C. An Example and Discussion of Competitive Equilibrium

Consider the example given by $u(c) = c$, $f(x) = x^{1-\beta}$, and $g(x) = x^{1-\sigma}$ (so $F(w, v) = w^{\beta}v^{1-\beta}$ and $G(w, v) = w^{\sigma}v^{1-\sigma}$), these functions satisfying the assumptions above. Since in the market solution entrepreneurs ignore the impact of their activities on the evolution of industry knowledge, the equilibrium fraction of entrepreneurs at each date is simply the fraction that maximizes current output. That is, the equilibrium fraction, denoted e_m (m for market), is given by e_m = argmax $ekf((1 - e)/ek)$. Note that e_m corresponds to e' defined above and for this example $e_m = \beta$. What makes this example particularly simple is that the maximizer of $ekf((1 - e)/ek)$ is independent of k, so that the fraction of entrepreneurs is constant through time. The growth rates of knowledge and consumption in equilibrium are therefore $\dot{k}/k = e_m g(s)$ and $\dot{c}/c = \beta e_m g(s)$. Before we discuss the equilibrium further, the social optimum for the example is presented. Since its calculation requires the use of Hamiltonian techniques, the details are presented in Appendix B, which draws on the results in Appendix A. The fraction of entrepreneurs in the optimal solution, denoted e_p (p for planner), is given by $e_p = \delta\beta[\delta - g(s)\beta(1 - \beta)]^{-1}$, with growth rates determined by replacing e_m with e_p above. A direct comparison shows $e_p > e_m$ for this example. The Appendix shows that this intuitive result is true in general.

Let us turn to the implications of the competitive equilibrium analysis. The communication infrastructure (or the degree of technological integration) matters for growth, as does the level of entrepreneurial activity. Each of these predictions suggests reasons why growth rates differ across countries and through time. As for the level of entrepreneurial activity, countries certainly differ in the incentives they provide for entrepreneurship and imitation. Tax systems, or legal and social systems, that penalize the returns to these activities may have large impacts on growth. A tax on entrepreneurial earnings in the model will lead to a reduction in both the fraction of individuals pursuing the activity and growth. For example, suppose that entrepreneurs are taxed a percentage $1 - \tau$ of their earnings. Assume that tax receipts are returned lump-sum to all individuals. The equilibrium fraction of entrepreneurs is no longer the fraction that maximizes current output. For this example, the equilibrium can be calculated using only the first three conditions in the definition of equilibrium. The reason is that the first three conditions are independent of k^*, so they determine the path for knowledge. With the tax, these conditions are (1) $z^* = $ argmax $\tau(F(k^*, z) - w^*z)$ or (dropping the asterisks) $(1 - \beta)k^\beta z^{-\beta} = w$, (2) $z = (1 - e)/e$, and (3) $w = \tau(k^\beta z^{1-\beta} - wz)$. Substituting into (3) from (1) for w, then multiplying both sides of (1) by z, and substituting into (3) for wz determines $z = (1 - \beta)/\tau\beta$. Using equation (2) determines the equilibrium fraction of entrepreneurs $e = \tau\beta/[\beta(\tau - 1) + 1]$ and growth rate $\dot{k}/k = eg(s)$. It is easy to verify that the tax reduces the equilibrium fraction of entrepreneurs and growth rate. This exercise captures what seems to be the essential difference between such economies as mainland China and Hong Kong. Rather than differences in the direct production of knowledge, the crucial distinction between these economies lies in the entrepreneurial rewards, here τ, accruing to imitating and implementing knowledge. While this analysis does capture an essential aspect of these economies, it is incomplete along one dimension. In particular, some of the imitative effort in Hong Kong is directed at implementing knowledge from countries in the West. This too is an important feature of the growth record, and extensions incorporating it are discussed in the conclusion.

Countries also differ in the extent of their integration into the world technology pool. The reasons for this are that countries differ in their industrial compositions, while the ease with which a technology diffuses internationally depends on the industry in which the innovation was developed. For example, experience has shown that agricultural R & D is highly location specific and must be conducted in environments approximating those in which the innovation will be employed (Solo 1966). Consequently, countries that are primarily agricultural have difficulty benefiting from agricultural research conducted in other countries. As another example, differences in the ease of international diffusion were found in a comparison of construction and manufacturing innovations (Strassmann 1972). Given

differences in industrial composition, and hence technological integration, the model predicts that the growth performance of countries
should vary accordingly. For example, everything else equal, countries that are primarily agricultural should grow slower than those in
which manufacturing is more important. This discussion is admittedly using the model liberally since the model was constructed with
symmetric industries, each receiving the same spillover. However, it
should be clear that these predictions would emerge from an extension of the model that incorporated industry differences.

The discussion thus far has centered on the model's potential
usefulness in understanding observed differences in growth rates
across countries. The model has normative implications as well. While
improvements in communication (and the extent of technological
convergence) are best treated as exogenous, the endogeneity of entrepreneurial activity certainly has important policy implications. If the
government has access to lump-sum taxation, then a subsidy to entrepreneurial earnings (such as a percentage subsidy with $\tau > 1$ above)
financed by a lump-sum tax on all individuals can support the social
optimum (see Rebelo [1987] and Jones and Manuelli [1988] for interesting discussions of tax/subsidy schemes in growth contexts).

D. Further Discussion of Model Assumptions

This section is concluded with a few additional comments on the
model's ingredients. Examining the accumulation technology for the
problems PS and $P(h, H)$ above shows that growth will depend on
the size measure s. Such a dependence of growth on size will result
in any model in which external effects are in the accumulation technology and in which the technology is linear in the state. There are
other interesting implications of such a specification. For example,
consider a model with individual state k and spillover K with $\dot{k} =
k^\sigma K^{1-\sigma} m(\ )$, $m(\ )$ capturing the effect of other inputs in fixed supply.
Suppose that $K = sk$ for some size measure s. The equation $\dot{k} =
k^\sigma K^{1-\sigma} m = s^{1-\sigma} km$ has diminishing returns at the private level, and
constant returns at the social level, to the accumulation of k. However,
there are increasing returns at the social level when s is treated as a
separate input. That is, there are increasing returns in k and s together, an effect distinct from conventional increasing returns. It is a
kind of increasing returns at the level of combining economies if in
combining two economies there is an increase in the size measure s.[1]

----

[1] I thank the referee for suggesting this interpretation, as well as how to present this
effect.

For example, consider two countries that, in the absence of trade, have relevant size measures s_1 and s_2. By introducing trade between the countries, which is widely viewed as important for knowledge flows, each country's relevant size measure may well increase.

V. Conclusion

Previous theories of economic growth have for the most part been highly aggregative in nature, keeping in the background institutional details such as the number of firms and how the number is determined. Hence the models are of limited use for addressing such issues as what determines the extent of entrepreneurial activity in an economy. Also, the recent theories of endogenous growth have focused primarily on the direct production of knowledge and its role in the growth process. These models have underemphasized the importance of imitation and implementation of knowledge in promoting growth.

The model developed here provides a simple framework to discuss both these phenomena, entrepreneurship and imitation. The analysis has been simplified considerably by examining the polar case of Romer's model, in which decisions are made concerning imitation, with direct knowledge production occurring in a learning-by-doing fashion. In future research, it will be important to consider models in which resources are devoted to both imitation and the direct production of knowledge. In such a model, individuals would earn some private benefit from accumulating new knowledge. However, in time their knowledge would be imitated as other individuals devote resources to the activity. Such a model would be an intermediate case to the Romer model and that developed here. With it many questions could be addressed. For example, as compared with the optimal solution, does the equilibrium entail a greater fraction of the research budget (resources devoted to direct knowledge production plus those devoted to imitation) devoted to imitation activities? These ideas can be studied in a model with a representative individual who divides his research time between creation of new knowledge and imitation of others. However, there are other issues in this area that must necessarily be examined in a model with asymmetric individuals (or countries). For example, such a model is needed to address the questions of what determines whether a country is a "leader" (engaged primarily in direct knowledge production) or a "follower" (engaged primarily in imitation and implementation of knowledge), and what causes a country to move from one role to the other, as happened with the Netherlands and Britain.

Appendix A

Characterization of Equilibrium and Social Optimum

For the analysis of problem *PS*, define the current-valued Hamiltonian

$$H(e, k, \lambda) = u\left[ekf\left(\frac{1 - e}{ek}\right)\right] + \lambda ekg(s).$$

As part of the first-order necessary conditions for paths $(e(t), k(t))$ to be an interior $(e(t) > 0)$ solution to *PS*, there must be a path $\lambda(t)$ such that the following equations are satisfied:

$$Du(c)\left[f(x) - Df(x)\,\frac{1}{ek}\right] = -\lambda g(s), \tag{A1}$$

$$\dot{\lambda} = \delta\lambda - \left\{ Du(c)\left[ef(x) - \frac{1 - e}{k}\,Df(x)\right] + \lambda eg(s)\right\}, \tag{A2}$$

and $\dot{k} = ekg(s)$, where *D* denotes derivative and $x = (1 - e)/ek$. To analyze the types of paths that can be solutions, the phase diagram is constructed in figure A1. The $\dot{k} = 0$ locus is defined by the condition $e = 0$. Clearly if $e = 0$, then $\lambda = 0$ since $e = 0$ means that there is no entrepreneur producing output and the value of additional knowledge is zero. To calculate the $\dot{\lambda} = 0$ locus when $e(t) > 0$, use the $\dot{\lambda}$ equation to solve $\dot{\lambda} = 0$ for

$$\lambda = [\delta - eg(s)]^{-1}\left\{ Du(c)\left[ef(x) - \frac{1 - e}{k}\,Df(x)\right]\right\}.$$

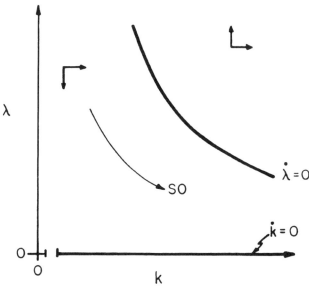

FIG. A1

This expresses λ as a function of e and k. Substituting for $Du(c)$ from equation (A1) into this equation, defining $\theta = Df(x)/[f(x)/x] < 1$, and rearranging yields

$$[\delta - eg(s)]^{-1}g(s)e(1 - e)\left[\frac{1 - \theta}{\theta - (1 - e)}\right] = 1. \tag{A3}$$

This gives e as a function of k, call it $\hat{e}(k)$. An examination of equation (A3) shows the solution $\hat{e} > 1 - \theta > 0$. Substituting $\hat{e}$ for e in the original equation gives the $\lambda = 0$ locus $\hat{\lambda}(k)$:

$$\hat{\lambda} = [\delta - \hat{e}g(s)]^{-1}[Du(c)\hat{e}f(x)(1 - \theta)]. \tag{A4}$$

For each k, $\hat{\lambda}(k) > 0$; that is, this locus lies everywhere above the $\dot{k} = 0$ locus, which is $\lambda = 0$. The case in which $\hat{\lambda}$ is downward sloping is illustrated in figure A1. The optimal trajectory is denoted SO, with $k(t)$ growing without bound along this path.

The analysis of $P(h, H)$ proceeds using the current-valued Hamiltonian

$$\bar{H}(e, k, \lambda, h, H) = u\left[ekf\left(\frac{1 - e}{ek}\right)\right] + \lambda hg\left(\frac{H}{h}\right).$$

As part of the first-order necessary conditions for paths $(e(t), k(t))$ to be an interior $(e(t) > 0)$ solution, there must be a path $\lambda(t)$ such that the following equations are satisfied:

$$Du(c)\left[f(x) - Df(x)\frac{1}{ek}\right] = 0, \tag{A5}$$

$$\dot{\lambda} = \delta\lambda - \left\{Du(c)\left[ef(x) - \frac{1 - e}{k}Df(x)\right]\right\}, \tag{A6}$$

and $\dot{k} = hg(H/h)$. As described above, solutions to $P(h, H)$ are equilibrium quantities if the solutions based on the forecasts (h, H) give rise to the forecasted series. Therefore, to find the competitive equilibrium, substitute $se(t)k(t)$ for $H(t)$ and $e(t)k(t)$ for $h(t)$ in the equations above. This substitution imposes the fixed-point property that equilibrium quantities satisfy. The $\dot{k} = 0$ locus is defined by $e = 0$, so that this locus is again $\lambda = 0$. The $\dot{\lambda} = 0$ locus is calculated to be

$$\bar{\lambda} = \delta^{-1}[Du(c)\bar{e}f(x)(1 - \theta)], \tag{A7}$$

where from equation (A5) $\bar{e}(k)$ satisfies $f(x) = Df(x)(\bar{e}k)^{-1}$, which can be expressed as $1 - \bar{e} = \theta(\bar{e})$. From equation (A1) the optimal solution $\hat{e}$ satisfies $1 - \hat{e} < \theta(\hat{e})$. Given the assumptions above, this implies $\hat{e} > \bar{e}$, so the fraction of entrepreneurs (as well as growth rates $\dot{k}/k$) in the optimal solution is always larger. To see this, note that the first derivative of $ekf((1 - e)/ek)$ with respect to e can be expressed as

$$\frac{f(x)k}{1 - e}\{1 - [\theta(e) + e]\},$$

so that this is negative evaluated at $\hat{e}$. The claim follows from the assumed concavity of the function.

Appendix B

Calculation of the Social Optimum for the Example

The analysis of the social optimization problem for this example will employ the results from Appendix A. The $\dot{k} = 0$ locus is defined by the condition $e = 0$ and is therefore given by $\lambda = 0$. The $\dot{\lambda} = 0$ locus is defined by equations (A3) and (A4) above. For this f technology $\theta = 1 - \beta$, so that $\hat{e}$ defined by equation (A3) is independent of k. Therefore, equation (A4) can be written as $\dot{\lambda} = (\text{constant})k^{\beta-1}$. The phase diagram is therefore as pictured in figure A1. For this example, it is possible to calculate explicit solutions for the steady-state constants $\dot{k}/k$, $\dot{\lambda}/\lambda$, and e. Equation (A1) can be written as $k^{\beta-1} = \lambda$ (constant), remembering e is constant in the steady state. Differentiating this with respect to time gives $\dot{\lambda}/\lambda = -(1 - \beta)(\dot{k}/k)$. Dividing equation (A2) by λ, using $\dot{\lambda}/\lambda = -(1 - \beta)eg(s)$, gives

$$-(1 - \beta)eg(s) = \delta - eg(s) - \lambda^{-1}\left[ef'(x) - \frac{1-e}{k}Df(x)\right].$$

Solving equation (A1) for λ^{-1}, substituting into the last equation, and using $\theta = 1 - \beta$ produces an equation determining e,

$$\beta eg(s) = \delta + g(s)e(1 - e)\beta(\beta - e)^{-1}.$$

Solving for e yields the optimal fraction of entrepreneurs e_p (p for planner),

$$e_p = \delta\beta[\delta - g(s)\beta(1 - \beta)]^{-1}.$$

References

Baumol, William J. "Entrepreneurship and the Long Run Productivity Record." Manuscript. New York: New York Univ., 1986.

———. "Entrepreneurship: Productive, Unproductive and Imitative; or the Rule of the Rules of the Game." Manuscript. New York: New York Univ., 1988.

Cass, David. "Optimum Growth in an Aggregative Model of Capital Accumulation." *Rev. Econ. Studies* 32 (July 1965): 233–40.

Cole, Arthur H. *Business Enterprise in Its Social Setting.* Cambridge, Mass.: Harvard Univ. Press, 1959.

Griliches, Zvi. "Issues in Assessing the Contribution of Research and Development to Productivity Growth." *Bell J. Econ.* 10 (Spring 1979): 92–116.

Holmes, Thomas, and Schmitz, James A., Jr. "How Economies Pursue Opportunities: The Role of Specialization in Entrepreneurial and Managerial Tasks." Manuscript. Madison: Univ. Wisconsin, 1988.

Jaffe, Adam B. "Technological Opportunity and Spillovers of R & D: Evidence from Firms' Patents, Profits, and Market Value." *A.E.R.* 76 (December 1986): 984–1001.

Jones, Larry, and Manuelli, Rodolfo. "A Model of Optimal Equilibrium Growth." Manuscript. Stanford, Calif.: Stanford Univ., 1988.

Judd, Kenneth L. "On the Performance of Patents." *Econometrica* 53 (May 1985): 567–85.

Koopmans, Tjalling C. "On the Concept of Optimal Economic Growth." In *Study Week on the Econometric Approach to Development Planning.* Amsterdam: North-Holland, 1965.

Lucas, Robert E., Jr. "On the Mechanics of Economic Development." Manuscript. Chicago: Univ. Chicago, 1985.

Nijkamp, Peter. "Infrastructure and Regional Development: A Multidimensional Policy Analysis." *Empirical Econ.* 11, no. 1 (1986): 1–21.

Prescott, Edward C., and Boyd, John H. "Dynamic Coalitions: Engines of Growth." *A.E.R. Papers and Proc.* 77 (May 1987): 63–67.

Rebelo, Sergio. "Long Run Policy Analysis and Long Run Growth." Manuscript. Rochester, N.Y.: Univ. Rochester, 1987.

Romer, Paul M. "Cake Eating, Chattering, and Jumps: Existence Results for Variational Problems." *Econometrica* 54 (July 1986): 897–908. (*a*)

———. "Increasing Returns and Long-Run Growth." *J.P.E.* 94 (October 1986): 1002–37. (*b*)

———. "Growth Based on Increasing Returns Due to Specialization." *A.E.R. Papers and Proc.* 77 (May 1987): 56–62.

Rosenberg, Nathan. *Perspectives on Technology.* New York: Cambridge Univ. Press, 1976.

———. *Inside the Black Box: Technology and Economics.* New York: Cambridge Univ. Press, 1982.

Schmitz, James A., Jr. "Growth and New Product Development." Manuscript. Madison: Univ. Wisconsin, 1986.

Schumpeter, Joseph A. *The Theory of Economic Development.* Cambridge, Mass.: Harvard Univ. Press, 1934.

Solo, Robert A. "The Capacity to Assimilate an Advanced Technology." *A.E.R. Papers and Proc.* 56 (May 1966): 91–97.

Stokey, Nancy. "Learning by Doing and the Introduction of New Goods." *J.P.E.* 96 (August 1988): 701–17.

Strassmann, W. Paul. "International Transfer of Technology in Construction and in Manufacturing: A Comparison." In *Inducing Technological Change for Economic Growth and Development,* edited by Robert A. Solo and Everett M. Rogers. East Lansing: Michigan State Univ. Press, 1972.

Townsend, Robert M. "Financial Structure and Economic Activity." *A.E.R.* 73 (December 1983): 895–911.

[12]

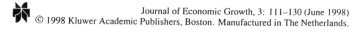

Journal of Economic Growth, 3: 111–130 (June 1998)
© 1998 Kluwer Academic Publishers, Boston. Manufactured in The Netherlands.

Capital Accumulation and Innovation as Complementary Factors in Long-Run Growth

PETER HOWITT

The Ohio State University, Department of Economics, 410 Arps Hall, 1945 North High Street, Columbus, OH 43210-1172 USA

PHILIPPE AGHION

University College, London and EBRD, Department of Economics, Gower Street, London WC1E 6BT, United Kingdom

We study capital accumulation and innovation as determinants of long-run growth by adding capital to our earlier model of creative destruction. No special functional forms are imposed on the aggregate production function. The equations describing perfect foresight equilibrium are identical to those of the augmented Ramsey-Cass-Koopmans model, except that the rate of technological change is a function of the stock of capital per effective worker. Contrary to previous models, a subsidy to capital accumulation will raise the long-run growth rate. The key assumption is that capital is used in R&D. Some evidence is presented on the capital intensity of R&D.

Keywords: economic growth, capital accumulation, innovation, creative destruction

JEL classification: 040, 030, E22

1. Introduction

Is growth ultimately attributable to the accumulation of capital or to the accumulation of knowledge (technological progress)? It is commonly argued that while both of these forces contribute positively to growth in the short run, only the rate of technological progress matters in the long run. According to this common view, capital accumulation plays at best a passive, supporting role, affecting only the level of output, not its rate of growth. Although the growth rate of an economy's output will ultimately be the same as that of the capital stock, the ultimate driving force determining both growth rates is technological progress.

Although this common view has not been maintained by all who have written on economic growth,[1] it is a logical implication of almost all the widely used growth models that make explicit the distinction between capital accumulation and technological progress. In the neoclassical growth model of Solow and Swan, diminishing returns to capital accumulation would eventually make any growth in excess of the rate of technological progress self-limiting. Endogenous growth models that include capital as well as innovation (e.g., Romer, 1990; Grossman and Helpman, 1991, ch. 5) come to the same conclusion. For in these models, the incentive to innovate determines the rate of technological progress, which in turn determines the economy's long-run growth rate, independently of the amount of capital in the economy.[2]

The view that technological progress reigns supreme in the long run is also the consensus view of mainstream textbooks. For example, Blanchard (1997, pp. 461, 496) asserts, in a discussion of the sources of growth, that "growth must ultimately be due to technological progress" and, in summary of a chapter on technological progress and growth, that "the rate of output growth in steady state is independent of the saving rate." David Romer (1996, p. 95) states that, in knowledge-based endogenous growth models, "the driving force of growth is the accumulation of knowledge . . . capital accumulation is not central to growth."

We believe that this common view is mistaken. Capital and knowledge are two state variables determining the level of output at any point of time. Only under special conditions would a subsidy to the activities driving one of those state variables have no effect on the long-run growth rate. In the general case, capital accumulation and innovation should be complementary processes, both playing a critical role.

More specifically, just as capital accumulation cannot be sustained indefinitely without technological progress to offset diminishing returns, so too technological progress cannot be sustained indefinitely without the accumulation of capital to be used in the R&D process that creates innovations and in the production process that implements them. This would be true even in the absence of embodied technical progress and learning by doing, two channels sometimes thought to provide a link between capital accumulation and long-run growth.

In this article we formalize the argument of the preceding paragraphs by developing a simple endogenous growth model that combines elements of the Solow-Swan neoclassical model of capital accumulation and the Aghion-Howitt (1992) model of creative destruction. The steady-state growth rate in the model is determined by the same factors as in our earlier model of creative destruction and in addition by the incentive to accumulate capital, as parametrized by a subsidy rate to the holding of capital. An increase in the capital-subsidy rate will raise the incentive not only to accumulate capital but also to innovate, through two channels. First, the increase in the capital stock will induce higher R&D through a "scale effect." That is, it will raise national income and hence raise the demand for the products created by successful innovators, thus raising the reward to innovation. Second, the increase in capital stock will reduce the cost of capital in the long run, and thus it will reduce the capital component of the cost of R&D.

We argue (in Sections 4.1 to 4.3 below) that the absence of such an effect from previous endogenous growth models with innovation and capital accumulation is a consequence of a special and unrealistic assumption made in those models, to the effect that capital is not used in the R&D technology that produces innovations.[3]

We also argue that the embodiment of new technologies in capital goods, important though it might be as an empirical phenomenon, is not crucial to the main channel through which capital accumulation affects growth. For most of our analysis we abstract from embodiment by assuming that capital is perfectly malleable and can be transferred costlessly from one use to another. When we take embodiment into account (in Section 4.4 below), it turns out, somewhat paradoxically, that the effect of a capital subsidy on long-run growth, while still positive, is *reduced* by this modification of the model.

The significance of our main result is threefold. First, it suggests that recent evidence[4] to the effect that investment is an empirically important determinant of long-run growth does not in any way refute innovation-based endogenous growth theory. On the contrary, the simple Schumpeterian endogenous growth theory developed below implies that capital accumulation has a crucial role to play in promoting economic growth. For although R&D is the *proximate* determinant of long-run growth, the level of R&D is an endogenous variable that will be affected, even in the long run, by the incentive to accumulate capital. In the extreme case where a prohibitive tax eliminated the incentive to accumulate capital, it would also eliminate the incentive to perform R&D, and hence it would eliminate long-run growth.

Second, our main result offers hope to governments that have been faced by seemingly insoluble agency problems when trying to increase growth by subsidizing R&D directly. For it implies that direct subsidies to R&D are not needed to stimulate technological progress and growth in the long run. A subsidy to capital accumulation in general can have the same qualitative effect, while being less subject to agency problems because the production of physical capital goods is generally easier to monitor and verify than the production of intangible knowledge.

Third, the embodiment of new technologies in physical capital, which some have seen as a possible reason for capital accumulation to affect the rate of technological progress, may be less important than a hitherto unsuspected aspect of capital—namely, its role as an input to R&D.

2. The Basic Model

The basic model is similar to the model of endogenous growth with capital presented in Aghion and Howitt (1996), which in turn is a straightforward extension of our earlier model without capital (Aghion and Howitt 1992), except that here we deal with out-of-steady-state behavior, and we assume that intermediate products are produced by capital alone rather than by capital and labor.[5]

2.1. Production Relations

There is a single final output, produced under perfect competition by labor and a continuum of intermediate products, according to the production function

$$Y_t = \int_0^1 A_{it} F(x_{it}, L)di, \tag{1}$$

where Y_t is gross output at date t, L is the flow amount of labor used in producing the final output,[6] x_{it} is the flow output of intermediate product $i \in [0, 1]$, A_{it} is a productivity parameter attached to the latest version of intermediate product i, and $F()$ is a smooth, concave, constant-returns production function. Assume that intermediate products are necessary factors $F(0, L) \equiv 0$ and that

$$2F_{11}(x, L) + x F_{111}(x, L) < 0 \text{ for all } x, L > 0. \tag{2}$$

114   PETER HOWITT AND PHILIPPE AGHION

Condition (2) makes the marginal revenue of each intermediate producer a strictly de-creasing function of that good's output, which guarantees that the second-order conditions for profit maximization are always satisfied. It holds in the special Cobb-Douglas case $F(x, L) \equiv x^{\alpha} L^{1-\alpha}$, $0 < \alpha < 1$, which we refer to from time to time. Unlike previous attempts to integrate capital into Schumpeterian growth theory, however, our approach is not restricted to any such special case.

Final output can be used interchangeably as a consumption or capital good or as an input to R&D. Each intermediate product is produced using capital, according to the production function

$$x_{it} = K_{it}/A_{it}, \tag{3}$$

where K_{it} is the input of capital in sector i. We divide K_{it} by A_{it} in (3) to indicate that successive vintages of the intermediate product are produced by increasingly capital-intensive techniques.[7]

Innovations are targeted at specific intermediate products. Each innovation creates an improved version of the existing product, which allows the innovator to replace the incum-bent monopolist until the next innovation in that sector.[8] The incumbent monopolist of each good produces with a cost function equal to $\zeta_t K_{it} = \zeta_t A_{it} x_{it}$, where the cost of capital ζ_t is the rate of interest (r_t) plus the rate of depreciation (δ) minus the subsidy rate to the holding of capital (β_k):

$$\zeta_t = r_t + \delta - \beta_k.$$

The price schedule facing the monopolist is the marginal product schedule $p_{it} = A_{it} F_1(x_{it}, L)$.

Since each intermediate firm's marginal revenue and marginal cost schedule are both proportional to A_{it}, and since the firms differ only in their value of A_{it}, they will all choose to supply the same quantity of intermediate product $x_t = x_{it}$ for all i. Putting this common quantity into (3) and taking into account that the total demand for capital must equal the given supply K_t, we find

$$x_{it} = x_t = k_t L, \tag{4}$$

where k_t is the capital stock per "effective worker" $k_t \equiv K_t/A_t L$, and A_t is the average productivity parameter across all sectors.[9]

Substituting from (4) into (1) shows that output per effective worker is given by the familiar intensive-form production function

$$Y_t/A_t L \equiv y_t = F(k_t, 1) \equiv f(k_t), f' > 0.$$

Substituting from (4) into the profit-maximization condition of each intermediate firm, and taking into account that F is homogenous of degree one, we find that the interest rate must satisfy the equilibrium condition[10]

$$r_t = R(k_t) - \delta + \beta_k, R' < 0, \tag{5}$$

CAPITAL ACCUMULATION AND INNOVATION IN LONG-RUN GROWTH

where $R()$ is each intermediate firm's marginal revenue product function,[11] which according to (2) is strictly decreasing in k_t. We also find that each local monopolist will earn a flow of profits proportional to its productivity parameter A_{it}—namely,[12]

$$\pi_{it} = A_{it}\pi_t(k_t)L, \pi' > 0.$$

The fact that profits are increasing in capital-intensity k_t is crucial for understanding why capital accumulation matters as well as innovation in determining the economy's long-run growth rate. It is an example of the sort of scale effect now common in Schumpeterian growth models. As capital per efficiency unit rises, so does output per efficiency unit, and so do profits. In the special Cobb-Douglas case, profits are a constant fraction of output $\pi(k) = \alpha(1-\alpha)f(k)$.

2.2. Innovations

Improvements in the productivity parameters come from R&D activities that use final output as the only hired input.[13] The Poisson arrival rate ϕ_t of innovations in each sector is

$$\phi_t = \lambda n_t, \lambda > 0, \tag{6}$$

where λ is a parameter indicating the productivity of R&D, and n_t is the productivity-adjusted quantity of final output devoted to R&D in each sector—that is, R&D expenditure divided by the "leading-edge technology parameter" $A_t^{max} \equiv \max\{A_{it} \mid i \in [0, 1]\}$. We deflate expenditures by A_t^{max} to take into account the force of increasing complexity; as technology advances, the resource cost of further advances increases proportionally.[14] This assumption prevents growth from exploding as the capital used in producing R&D grows without bound.

The same amount of input n_t (adjusted for the leading-edge productivity parameter) will be used in R&D in each intermediate sector because the prospective payoff is the same in each sector. Specifically, each innovation at date t results in a new generation of that intermediate sector's product, which embodies the leading-edge productivity parameter A_t^{max}.

Assume that R&D expenditures are subsidized at the rate β_n. Then the arbitrage condition governing the equilibrium level of R&D is that the marginal net cost of a unit of R&D expenditure equal the expected marginal gain. Since a unit of *R&D* expenditure raises the Poisson arrival rate by λ/A_t^{max}, this yields

$$1 - \beta_n = \lambda \int_t^\infty e^{-\int_t^\tau (r_s + \phi_s)ds} \pi(k_\tau)Ld\tau, \tag{7}$$

where r_s is the instantaneous rate of interest at date s. The instantaneous discount rate applied in (7) is the rate of interest plus the rate of creative destruction ϕ_s; the latter is the instantaneous flow probability of being displaced by an innovation.[15]

Setting the time derivative of the right-hand side of (7) equal to zero and using (6) yields the more familiar arbitrage equation

$$1 - \beta_n = \lambda \frac{\pi(k_t)L}{r_t + \lambda n_t},$$

which can be solved, using (5), for the R&D intensity n_t as an increasing function of the capital intensity k_t:

$$n_t = \tilde{n}(k_t), \tilde{n}' > 0. \tag{8}$$

The R&D function $\tilde{n}$ is increasing because as capital increases, the flow of profits $\pi(k)$ earned by a successful innovator rises, and the rate of interest $R(k) - \delta + \beta_k$ at which those profits are discounted decreases. On both counts the prospective reward to R&D increases, which induces a rise in the intensity of R&D.

2.3.   Technological Progress and Capital Accumulation

Growth in the leading-edge parameter $A_t^{\max}$ occurs as a result of the knowledge spillovers produced by innovations.[16] That is, we follow Caballero and Jaffe (1993) in assuming that at any moment of time the leading-edge technology is available to any successful innovator, and this publicly available (but not costless) knowledge grows at a rate proportional to the aggregate rate of innovations. The factor of proportionality, which is a measure of the marginal aggregate impact of each innovation on the stock of public knowledge, is $\sigma > 0$. Thus the rate of technological progress at each date equals

$$g_t \equiv \dot{A}_t^{\max} / A_t^{\max} = \sigma \lambda n_t. \tag{9}$$

One can show that the ratio of the leading edge $A_t^{\max}$ to the average productivity parameter A_t will converge monotonically to the constant[17] $1 + \sigma$. Thus we assume that $A_t^{\max} = A_t(1 + \sigma)$ for all t, so that the rate of growth of the average productivity parameter A_t will also be given by (9).

The rate of change of the capital stock per efficiency unit k_t is given by

$$\dot{k}_t = f(k_t) - c_t - n_t(1 + \sigma)/L - (\delta + g_t)k_t, \tag{10}$$

where δ is the rate of capital depreciation and c_t is consumption per efficiency unit of labor. The first three terms on the right-hand side of (10) represent gross capital accumulation per efficiency unit, which is GDP minus consumption minus the resources used up in R&D, all expressed in efficiency units.[18] The remaining terms represent the reduction in the capital stock per efficiency unit that takes place through depreciation and the increase in the number of efficiency units.

2.4.   Equations of Motion

We make the conventional assumption that saving is determined by intertemporal utility maximization on the part of a representative consumer, who has intertemporally additive preferences over consumption, a constant rate of time preference ρ and a constant elasticity of marginal utility ε. As usual this implies that c_t must obey the Euler equation[19]

$$\frac{d}{dt}(A_t c_t)^{-\varepsilon} = (\rho - r_t)(A_t c_t)^{-\varepsilon},$$

which can be rewritten, using (9), as

$$\dot{c}_t = c_t[(r_t - \rho)/\varepsilon - g_t]. \tag{11}$$

Equations (10) and (11) are the usual equations of the Cass-Koopmans-Ramsey model of optimal growth, modified to include labor-augmenting technological progress. The only novelty is that the rate of technological progress g_t is no longer an exogenous constant but depends on the R&D intensity n_t. These equations can be reduced, with the aid of (5), (8), and (9), to the two-dimensional system in capital intensity k_t and consumption intensity c_t:

$$\dot{k}_t = f(k_t) - c_t - \tilde{n}(k_t)(1+\sigma)/L - [\delta + \sigma\lambda\tilde{n}(k_t)]k_t$$
$$\dot{c}_t = c_t[(R(k_t) - \delta + \beta_k - \rho)/\varepsilon - \sigma\lambda\tilde{n}(k_t)].$$

The system's rest point $(\hat{k}, \hat{c})$ is a steady-state equilibrium with balanced growth in the usual sense. The steady state is locally stable, in the sense that for any initial capital intensity in a neighborhood of $\hat{k}$ there is a unique initial value of c that puts the system on a stable trajectory converging monotonically to the steady state.[20]

3. Steady-State Analysis

The steady-state values of capital intensity (k), R&D intensity (n), the rate of interest (r), and the rate of growth of output per person (g) are defined by the following equations:

$$R(k) = r + \delta - \beta_k \tag{K}$$
$$1 - \beta_n = \lambda \frac{\pi(k)L}{r+\lambda n}. \tag{N}$$
$$r = \rho + \varepsilon g \tag{R}$$
$$g = \sigma\lambda n. \tag{G}$$

Equation (K) equates the cost of capital to its marginal revenue product. Equation (N) is the same equation that defines the steady-state R&D intensity in the Aghion-Howitt (1992) model. It equates the marginal cost of R&D (which was a productivity-adjusted wage in Aghion-Howitt model where labor was the only R&D input) to the expected discounted marginal benefit. Equation (R) is the familiar Fisher equation showing how the rate of interest depends on the growth rate of consumption. Equation (G) is the spillover equation determining the rate of technological progress and hence the steady-state rate of growth. Straightforward comparative-statics techniques yield the following proposition:

Proposition 1: *The steady-state growth rate g depends positively on the two subsidy rates* (β_k, β_n)*, the productivity of R&D* (λ)*, and the size of innovations* (σ)*; and negatively on the*

118   PETER HOWITT AND PHILIPPE AGHION

elasticity of marginal utility (ε), *the rate of time preference* (ρ), *and the rate of depreciation* (δ).

Most of the specific results of Proposition 1 are unremarkable, except for the positive effect of the capital subsidy rate. To see more clearly how this works, use equations (R) and (G) to eliminate r from the first two equations. This leaves the two-dimensional system illustrated in Figure 1. The capital curve (K) is downward sloping because higher R&D intensity raises the rate of growth, which raises the interest rate through the Fisher relation, which reduces the steady-state demand for capital. The R&D curve (N) is upward sloping because more capital raises the flow of profits $\pi(k)L$ to a successful innovator.[21] An increase in the subsidy rate on capital shifts the capital curve to the right, raising the steady-state R&D intensity. The steady-state growth rate increases according to the growth equation (G).

In addition to having a positive marginal effect on growth, capital accumulation is necessary for growth to be sustained in the long run. Suppose that the capital tax were continually raised in such a way as to ensure that the capital stock per worker K_t/L were frozen. Then positive long-run technological progress would imply a capital stock per effective worker k_t that approached zero in the long run. Since capital is assumed to be a necessary factor of production, this would drive output per effective worker, and hence profit per effective worker $\pi(k_t)$, to zero in the long run. (In addition, if we had imposed an Inada condition on the production function F the rate of interest would have been driven to infinity.) Thus the reward to innovation on the right-hand side of the steady-state equation (N) would be driven to zero, making it impossible for the condition to be satisfied. In this way, a prohibitive tax on capital accumulation would eventually choke off long-run growth, just as a prohibitive tax on R&D would.

4. Capital Accumulation and Growth

The result that a subsidy to capital can permanently raise growth runs counter to the conventional belief that the long-run rate of growth is unaffected by capital accumulation, a belief that is supported by the neoclassical growth model of Solow and Swan, in which technical progress drives long-run growth independently of capital accumulation, and by the endogenous growth models of Romer (1990) and Grossman and Helpman (1991, ch. 5), in which the incentive to perform R&D determines the long-run growth rate independently of the stock of capital.

4.1. Capital as an Input to R&D

The key difference between the model we have just presented and these other endogenous growth models is that we assume R&D uses the same mix of inputs as does the production of capital and consumption goods, whereas these other models assume that the only input to R&D is a factor that is fixed in supply, independently of its rate of remuneration. Although the factor is often referred to as "human capital," the fact that it cannot be accumulated even

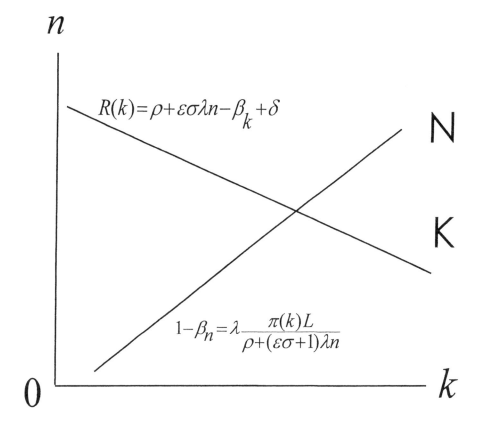

Figure 1. Determination of steady-state values of R&D (n) and capital per effective worker (k).

temporarily in response to a change in its price makes it just like the labor in the present model.

The reason that this difference is so important can be seen by provisionally modifying the above model to make labor the only R&D input. In this modified model the flow of aggregate output would be determined by equation (1) above, except that the labor input to manufacturing would be $L - n$ instead of L, where n is the labor used in R&D. The flow of innovations would be, as before, λn. By exactly the same reasoning as before, the steady-state arbitrage equation would be

$$(1 - \beta_n)\omega(k) = \lambda \frac{\pi(k)(L - n)}{r + \lambda n},$$

where $k \equiv K_t / A_t(L - n)$ is now the ratio of capital to manufacturing labor in efficiency

120   PETER HOWITT AND PHILIPPE AGHION

units, and $\omega(k) \equiv \frac{1}{1+\sigma} F_2(k, 1)$ is the real wage divided by $A^{\max}$ under our assumption of perfect competition in the final goods sector. The rest of the equations defining a steady state would be unaffected by this change.

Thus, restricting labor to be the only input to R&D would give an offset to the positive effect of capital on innovation. For an increase in capital would raise the marginal product of labor in manufacturing, thus raising the cost $\omega(k)$ of the only input to R&D. This would tend to counteract the rise in profits to a successful innovator. In fact, in the special case of a Cobb-Douglas technology, the two effects would exactly cancel because $\omega(k)$ and $\pi(k)$ would both be proportional to output per effective worker $f(k)$. In this special case the R&D curve (N) in Figure 1 would be horizontal, so a change in the capital subsidy that shifted the capital curve (K) would not affect the steady-state R&D intensity.

However, as long as R&D used any capital at all this conclusion would not be valid. The general result in the Cobb-Douglas case is that when capital intensity increases, the cost of R&D rises less than in proportion to the equilibrium flow of profit, and hence R&D and growth both increase. Suppose, for example, that R&D used capital and labor according to a standard constant-returns production function

$$n = G^n(K^n / A^{\max}, L^n),$$

where n is now the intensity of R&D, and K^n, L^n are the amounts of capital and labor used in R&D in each sector. Then the R&D equation (N) would be

$$(1 - \beta_n) c^n(R(k), \omega(k)) = \lambda \frac{\pi(k) \left[L - na_L^n \left(\frac{\omega(k)}{R(k)} \right) \right]}{r + \lambda n}, \tag{12}$$

where c^n is the unit cost function[22] associated with the production function G^n, and a_L^n is the unit demand function for labor in R&D. If R&D uses any labor at all, then the elasticity of c^n with respect to ω is less than unity. Thus in the Cobb-Douglas case where ω and π are proportional to each other, when k increases, the resulting increase in the cost of R&D that works through the wage rate will be less than proportional to the rise in profit. The overall effect will be a net stimulus to R&D.

In addition, equation (12) indicates two further effects that will each give a stimulus to R&D. First, the cost of capital used in R&D ($\zeta = R(k)$) will fall. Second, the rise in the wage-rental ratio will induce R&D firms to economize on their use of labor, which would leave more in the manufacturing sector if R&D intensity were not to increase. The resulting increase in output per product would raise the flow of profit per product, thus inducing R&D intensity to increase.

Moreover, even if labor were the only R&D input, a subsidy to capital accumulation would raise growth in the Cobb-Douglas case if there were any positive elasticity at all to the supply of labor because while the rise in profits per effective worker would raise the reward to labor as much in manufacturing as in R&D, the overall rise in the wage would induce an increased supply.

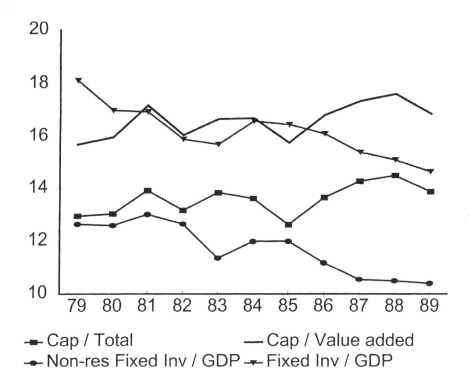

Figure 2. Capital expenditures on R&D in higher education as a percentage of total higher education R&D expenditures.

4.2. Some Evidence

In fact, neither of the assumptions needed to avoid the positive effect of a capital subsidy on long-run growth is very plausible. R&D actually uses a great deal of physical capital, in the form of laboratories, offices, plant, and equipment needed for constructing and testing pilot models and prototypes, computers and other scientific instruments, particle accelerators, observatories, space vehicles, and so forth. Direct evidence on capital intensity in U.S. R&D is almost nonexistent, but at least two bits of indirect evidence exist. First, in assembling satellite R&D, the U.S. Department of Commerce (Carson et al, 1994, p. 56) estimated that depreciation of equipment and structures constituted 6.5 percent of the value added (total expenditure minus the cost of materials and supplies) by Industrial R&D in 1987, which was 52.4 percent of the national depreciation/GDP ratio for that year.

Second, as Figure 2 shows, between 1979 and 1989 the ratio of capital R&D expenditures to total R&D expenditures in higher education in the United States was 0.136.[23] If materials

Table 1. Components of U.K. BERD (percentage).

	1969	1978	1981	1985	1989
Capital spending	10	10	9	10	11
Wages and salaries	50	48	44	42	42
Materials	21	21	23	22	21
Other	19	21	24	26	27

Source: Cameron (1996).

and supplies constituted the same percent of total R&D expenditure each year in higher education as in industry[24] then the average ratio of gross investment to value added was 0.166. This ratio is actually larger than the national average; the ratio of gross fixed investment to GDP during these years was 0.162, while the ratio of gross fixed nonresidential investment to GDP was 0.117. These observations, tenuous though they might be, suggest that, if anything, the assumption of a capital intensity in R&D equal to that of the rest of the economy is probably closer to the truth than the assumption of a zero R&D capital intensity.

This evidence is corroborated by data on business enterprise R&D in the United Kingdom, as shown in Table 1. These data show that capital expenditures have constituted about 10 percent of total R&D expenditures since the late 1960s, or about 12.5 percent of value added (ie of total expenditures minus materials expenditures).

Also, although there may not be a significant long-run elasticity to the supply of unskilled labor, there is no reason to doubt that a rise in the skill premium would induce a significant supply response of the skilled labor used intensively in R&D. People would remain in school for longer periods, demand a higher quality of education, and engage in more training and other skill-acquisition activities. The resulting increase in the supply of skills would dampen the rise in the cost of R&D without dampening the rise in the payoff to a successful innovator. To be more precise, if skilled and unskilled wages were to rise by equal proportions when the capital stock rose, as they would if both skilled and unskilled labor worked with capital in a Cobb-Douglas aggregate production function, the rate of return to investing in skills would increase with the capital stock unless labor were the only factor of production used in acquiring skills. But, in fact, labor is not the only input to skill acquisition. Higher education uses a lot of physical capital in the form of buildings, computers, and other facilities. In addition, the experience of working with modern capital equipment is one of the most important inputs to acquiring skills through learning by doing.

4.3. The Role of Human Capital

In order to see more clearly the role of human capital in R&D, we now briefly consider a disaggregated model that distinguishes explicitly between physical and human capital. Suppose first that both types of capital are produced by the same technology as consumption and R&D and that intermediate products are produced according to a constant-returns production function

$$x_{it} = G(K_{it}, H_{it})/A_{it}.$$

Then the same reasoning as before leads to the steady-state equations

$$R_k(k, h) = r + \delta_k - \beta_k \qquad\qquad (K')$$

$$R_h(k, h) = r + \delta_h - \beta_h \qquad\qquad (H')$$

$$1 - \beta_n = \lambda \frac{\pi(k, h)L}{r + \lambda n} \qquad\qquad (N')$$

$$r = \rho + \varepsilon g \qquad\qquad (R)$$

$$g = \sigma \lambda n, \qquad\qquad (G)$$

where β_h is the subsidy rate to human capital, h is human capital per effective worker, R_k is the marginal revenue product of physical capital, defined as

$$R_k(k, h) \equiv [F_1(G(k, h), 1) + G(k, h)F_{11}(G(k, h), 1)]G_1(k, h),$$

R_h is the (analogously defined) marginal revenue product of human capital, and π is profit per effective worker

$$\pi(k, h) \equiv -G(k, h)^2 F_{11}(G(k, h), 1).$$

It is straightforward to solve equations (K') and (H') and substitute into the profit function π to get the indirect profit function $\tilde{\pi}(r + \delta_k - \beta_k, r + \delta_h - \beta_h)$, $\tilde{\pi}_1, \tilde{\pi}_2 < 0$. Substituting this into (N') and using (R) and (G) to eliminate r and n yields the growth equation

$$1 - \beta_n = \lambda \frac{\tilde{\pi}(\rho + \varepsilon g + \delta_k - \beta_k, \rho + \varepsilon g + \delta_h - \beta_h)L}{\rho + \varepsilon g + g/\sigma}.$$

Using this equation it is straightforward to verify that all the comparative-statics results of Proposition 1 above go through in this disaggregated model and that, in addition, an increase in the human-capital subsidy rate (β_h) raises the steady-state growth rate.

Even if human capital were the only factor of production used in R&D, the only difference this would make would be to the arbitrage equation (N'), which would become

$$(1 - \beta_n)(r + \delta - \beta_h) = \lambda \frac{\pi(k, h)L}{r + \lambda n},$$

where now h and k represent the ratios of human and physical capital to effective workers in manufacturing. Again, Proposition 1 would be valid. In this case, any tendency for the cost of R&D to be driven up by a subsidy to physical capital would be offset completely by an infinitely elastic supply response of human capital.

4.4. The Embodiment Hypothesis

It is sometimes argued that subsidizing capital accumulation can affect long-run growth because it accelerates the rate at which technological progress is embodied in new capital goods. We are convinced by the arguments in Scott (1989) and others that capital does indeed embody new technologies and that this fact renders almost meaningless accounting exercises designed to measure the relative importance of capital and technology. However, we have ignored embodiment up to this point in the interest of simplicity. For although we have assumed that capital is needed to produce new intermediate products, the capital goods themselves have not been assumed to be specific to any particular technology. That is, implicit in our derivation of the cost of capital was the assumption that when a new innovation displaces an incumbent in an intermediate sector, the capital that the incumbent has been using can be reconstituted at no cost and used to produce the new generation of intermediate product. (That is, we were assuming putty-putty.)

The results of the previous sections show clearly that the embodiment hypothesis is not crucial for the result that a capital subsidy will affect long-run growth. What we show in the present section is that incorporating embodiment actually has the paradoxical effect of weakening the result, although not overturning it. For the fact that capital embodies a particular technology increases the positive effect of R&D on the cost of capital. This is because it increases the expected rate of obsolescence, which must be added to the rate of depreciation in computing that cost. This obsolescence effect will dampen the effect on R&D of a capital subsidy because as R&D increases in response to the subsidy, it raises the cost of capital, thus counteracting the original stimulus.

To see how this works we now go to the other extreme (putty-clay) and assume that each new innovator must use entirely new capital goods.[25] The only difference this makes to the steady-state equations of Section 3 is to add the expected rate of depreciation λn to the cost of capital. That is, equation (K) is replaced by

$$R(k) = r + \delta - \beta_k + \lambda n.$$

It is easily verified that with this modified system of equations, the capital curve in Figure 1 will be shallower than before. An increase in the subsidy rate β_k will shift the shallower curve to the right by the same amount as before. Thus the resulting increases in both k and n will be less than before.

If in addition to embodiment we assumed that the rate of technological progress depends on the rate of learning by doing, which in turn depends on the rate of investment, then we would have an additional channel through which capital accumulation affects long-run growth. But without this extra learning-by-doing dimension, embodiment by itself does not provide such a channel. For a speed up of investment may just result in more capital goods of each technological vintage rather than a faster rate of improvement of the capital goods, with no stimulus to the rate of technological progress that proximately determines the long-run growth rate.

5. Conclusions

In summary, we have presented a Schumpeterian growth theory that treats capital accumulation and innovation as equal partners in the growth process. The model incorporates in a simple framework the essential elements of the Solow model of capital accumulation and the Aghion-Howitt model of creative destruction. Contrary to the consensus view of neoclassical growth theory and other endogenous growth theories, a subsidy to capital accumulation, either physical or human, will have a permanent effect on the economy's growth rate. The key to this result is the recognition of capital as an input to R&D.

These results offer hope to governments that have been faced by seemingly insoluble incentive problems when trying to subsidize R&D directly. For they imply that a broad subsidy to capital accumulation in general may be just as effective a means of stimulating technological progress and growth in the long run as a direct subsidy to R&D. Such a subsidy might work not by inducing a higher rate of technological progress through learning by doing or through increasing the rate at which new technologies are embodied in new capital goods, but rather by raising the reward to innovations that need capital for their production and implementation.[26]

Moreover, the results show that Schumpeterian endogenous growth theory is not refuted by recent evidence to the effect that investment is an empirically important determinant of long-run growth. Indeed, the Schumpeterian theory developed above is more consistent with this evidence than is the neoclassical theory of Solow and Swan, in which long-run growth is driven by exogenous technological progress that takes place independently of the incentive to accumulate capital. Our model provides a simple vehicle for exploring the relative roles of capital accumulation and innovation in long-run growth, without eliminating one of them a priori as does neoclassical growth theory.

Appendix: Allowing Previous Innovators to Compete

This appendix modifies the assumption concerning competition between the latest innovator in a product and previous innovators in the same product. In the text we assumed that once the previous innovators had left, they were unable to reenter. Thus the latest innovator was never threatened by a competitive fringe. Here we make the opposite assumption—namely, that the previous innovator is always able to reenter at no cost.

This means that if someone innovates in a product where the previous innovation took place very recently, then the difference in quality between the latest generation of the product and the previous one will not be large enough for the latest innovator to ignore the threat of competition from the previous innovator. In the language of the patent race literature (Tirole, 1988, ch. 10), the innovation will be nondrastic.

More specifically, suppose that the latest innovator in intermediate product i has a productivity parameter A_i, while the previous innovator has $\bar{A}_i$. Suppose that the innovations in all other sectors are drastic. Then the price charged by each local monopolist will be the marginal product

$$p_j = A_j F_1(x_j, L) = A_j F_1(k, 1), \tag{13}$$

where we have made use of (4) and of the linear homogeneity of the production function F.

The latest innovation in intermediate product i will be drastic if and only if no final-good producer will buy the previous generation of the product in a situation where the latest innovator is charging a price given by (13) and the previous innovator is charging a price $\bar{p}_i$ equal to marginal cost

$$\bar{p}_i = \bar{A}_i \zeta. \tag{14}$$

A final-good producer will buy from the previous innovator at this price if and only if the variable profit it makes using that version of intermediate product i is larger, per worker employed, than if it used the latest version. In that case the producer will buy the quantity $\bar{x}_i$ per worker employed, such that the marginal product equals the price (14)

$$F_1(\bar{x}_i, 1) = \zeta. \tag{15}$$

Making use of Euler's theorem, (4), and (13) to (15), we can express the variable profit per worker employed in the two cases as

$$\pi_i \equiv \frac{A_i F(x, L) - p_i x}{L} = A_i[F(k, 1) - k F_1(k, 1)] = A_i F_2(k, 1)$$

and

$$\bar{\pi} \equiv \bar{A}_i F(\bar{x}_i, 1) - \bar{p}_i \bar{x}_i = \bar{A}_i[F(\bar{x}_i, 1) - \bar{x}_i F_1(\bar{x}_i, 1)] = \bar{A}_i F_2(\bar{x}_i, 1).$$

So the innovation will be drastic if and only if $\pi_i \geq \bar{\pi}_i$—that is, if and only if

$$A_i F_2(k, 1) \geq \bar{A}_i F_2(\bar{x}_i, 1), \tag{16}$$

where $\bar{x}_i$ is determined by

$$F_1(\bar{x}_i, 1) = F_1(k, 1) + k F_{11}(k, 1). \tag{17}$$

Equation (17) follows from (15), the equilibrium condition (5) and the definition of the cost of capital ζ_t.

Consider now the Cobb-Douglas case $F(x, L) \equiv x^\alpha L^{1-\alpha}$. It follows in this case from (16) and (17) that the innovation will be drastic if and only if

$$A_i(1 - \alpha)k^\alpha \geq \bar{A}_i(1 - \alpha)\bar{x}_i^\alpha,$$

where $\bar{x}_i$ is determined by

$$\alpha \bar{x}_i^{\alpha-1} = \alpha^2 k^{\alpha-1}.$$

That is, if and only if

$$A_i/\bar{A}_i \geq \alpha^{\frac{\alpha}{\alpha-1}}. \tag{18}$$

In this Cobb-Douglas case there will exist a stationary equilibrium in which all innovations are drastic, under the condition that

$$\frac{\alpha}{\alpha - 1} \frac{\ln \alpha}{\sigma} < 1. \tag{19}$$

To construct such an equilibrium, note that given the linear R&D technology, no R&D at date t will be targeted at sectors whose technological vintage is later than $t - T$, where T is determined by the conditions that (18) hold with equality

$$e^{gT} = \alpha^{\frac{\alpha}{\alpha - 1}}, \text{ or } T = \frac{\alpha}{\alpha - 1} \frac{\ln \alpha}{g}. \tag{20}$$

If older sectors are targeted, any resulting innovation will be drastic, resulting in a profit flow of $\pi(k)$ until the next innovation, whereas if a newer sector was targeted, the resulting innovation would be nondrastic, resulting in a lower profit flow. Since the value of innovating in the newer sectors will be less than in the older sectors, only the older sectors will be targeted.

Let n again be the economywide R&D intensity in a steady-state equilibrium. Let f denote the fraction of all sectors that are targeted by R&D—that is, the fraction that are at least as old as T. The flow of new untargeted sectors is the flow of innovations λn. Each one remains untargeted for a period of length T. Thus at any date in a steady-state equilibrium, the mass $1 - f$ of untargeted sectors is the cumulative flow of new ones over the past T units of time

$$1 - f = \lambda n T. \tag{21}$$

According to (20), (21), and the growth equation $g = \sigma \lambda n$, condition (19) is necessary for f to be positive.

The productivity-adjusted value of an innovation v at any date is the flow of expected discounted profits $\pi(k)$. The discounting must now take into account that for the first T units of time after the innovation there is no risk of creative destruction; the innovator will be untargeted. After T, the innovator will be subject to a Poisson destruction rate of

$$\phi = \lambda n / f, \tag{22}$$

since there will be a flow of λn innovations per unit of time spread over a mass f of products. Hence

$$v = \pi(k) \left(\int_0^T e^{-rs} ds + e^{-rT} \int_0^\infty e^{-(r+\phi)s} ds \right) = \frac{\pi(k)}{r + \phi} \left[1 + (1 - e^{-rT}) \phi / r \right]. \tag{23}$$

As before, the steady-state capital intensity k will be determined by equation (K) above, and the rate of interest by the Fisher equation (R). Hence, we can write the flow of profit as

$$\pi(k) = \tilde{\pi}(\rho + \varepsilon g + \delta - \beta_k), \tilde{\pi}' < 0. \tag{24}$$

Combining equations (20), (22), (23), and (24) and the arbitrage condition $1 - \beta_n = \lambda v$, we get the final equation determining the steady-state growth rate in the Cobb-Douglas case:

$$1 - \beta_n = \lambda \frac{\tilde{\pi}(\rho + \varepsilon g + \delta - \beta_k)}{\rho + \varepsilon g + g / \sigma f} \left[1 + \left(1 - \alpha^{\frac{\alpha(\rho + \varepsilon g)}{(1 - \alpha)g}} \right) g / \sigma f (\rho + \varepsilon g) \right], \tag{25}$$

where by (20), (21), and the growth equation (G), f is given by

$$f = 1 - \frac{\alpha}{\alpha - 1} \frac{\ln \alpha}{\sigma}.$$

Since the right-hand side of (25) is increasing in β_k and the left-hand side is decreasing in β_n, once again a subsidy to either innovation or capital accumulation will raise the steady-state growth rate, provided that the right-hand side of (25) is decreasing in g. To show this, note that the effects of g working through the argument of the indirect profit function $\tilde{\pi}$ and through the exponent of α are both negative. The remaining effects have the same sign as the effect of g on

$$\frac{1}{\rho + \varepsilon g + g/\sigma f}[1 + \xi g/\sigma f(\rho + \varepsilon g)], \tag{26}$$

where $\xi(= 1 - \alpha^{\frac{\alpha(\rho+\varepsilon g)}{(1-\alpha)g}})$ is held constant. Note that (26) can be rewritten as

$$\frac{(\rho + \varepsilon g + \xi g/\sigma f)}{(\rho + \varepsilon g + g/\sigma f)} \frac{1}{(\rho + \varepsilon g)},$$

which is decreasing in g because $\xi < 1$.

Acknowledgments

This article is part of a broader project on growth theory, the results of which are described at length in our recent book (Aghion and Howitt, 1998). We have benefited from comments of seminar participants at the Canadian Institute for Advanced Research, the Ohio State University, and the European Science Foundation conference on growth theory in Castelvecchio Pascoli, especially Gavin Cameron.

Notes

1. For example, it is not supported by the AK version of endogenous growth theory, according to which technological progress and capital accumulation do not constitute independent causal forces in the growth process.
2. Barro and Sala-i-Martin (1995) do not consider models with both capital accumulation and innovation. The only model we have found in the literature that does not imply the common result is the "lab-equipment" model of Rivera-Batiz and Romer (1991), who do not, however, discuss the issue of capital accumulation versus innovation.
3. One way to see what is at issue is to suppose that output (Y) is determined by capital (K) and technological knowledge (A) according to $y = K^\alpha A^{1-\alpha}$ and that the accumulation of capital and knowledge are governed by fixed savings rates $\dot{K} = s_K Y$, $\dot{A} = s_A Y$. The steady-state growth rate $g = s_K^\alpha s_A^{1-\alpha}$ depends positively on s_K, holding s_A constant. The above-mentioned endogenous growth models imply however that s_K and s_A are not independent of each other and that an increase in s_K would cause an exactly offsetting decrease in s_A, with no overall effect on the growth rate. What we argue below is that this exact offset is a polar case.
4. For example, DeLong and Summers (1991) and Mankiw, Romer, and Weil (1992). In Aghion and Howitt (1998, ch. 12) we argue that innovation-based growth theory is also consistent with the growth accounting evidence of Jorgenson (1995) and Young (1995), with evidence on conditional convergence and with Jones's (1995) evidence on the absence of a scale effect in postwar data.

5. This same simplifying assumption was made by Romer (1990). A detailed analysis of the present model in the case where both labor and capital enter the production function for intermediate products is contained in Howitt (1997, app. A).

6. We abstract in this article from population growth and labor supply by assuming L to be an exogenous constant. See Howitt (1997) for a treatment of population growth in a similar model.

7. In the special case of a Cobb-Douglas technology this has no substantive implications.

8. No innovations are done by incumbents because of the Arrow or replacement effect (see Aghion and Howitt, 1992).

9. From (3), the definition of A_t and the adding up condition, we have $K_t = \int_0^1 A_{it} x_t di = A_t x_t$.

10. After substitution from (4), the first-order condition is $\zeta_t = F_1(k_t L, L) + k_t L F_{11}(k_t L, L)$. By Euler's theorem, F_1 is homogeneous of degree zero and F_{11} is homogeneous of degree -1. Hence $\zeta_t = F_1(k_t, 1) + k_t F_{11}(k_t, 1)$. Equation (5) follows from this and the definitions of ζ_t and $R(k_t)$.

11. That is, $R(k_t) \equiv F_1(k_t, 1) + k_t F_{11}(k_t, 1)$

12. Specifically, $\pi(k_t) \equiv -k_t^2 F_{11}(k_t, 1)$, which according to (2) is strictly increasing in k_t.

13. Or, equivalently, they use intermediate products and labor according to the same technology as in the final goods sector. Barro and Sala-i-Martin (1995, chs. 6, 7) make the same assumption.

14. Howitt (1997) shows that the analysis can easily be generalized to the case in which $\phi_t = \lambda\phi(n_t)$, where the function ϕ exhibits the decreasing returns found empirically by Arroyo, Dinopoulos, and Donald (1994) and Kortum (1993).

15. We assume that each innovator enters into Bertrand competition with the previous incumbent in that sector, who by definition produces an inferior product. Rather than face a price war with a superior rival, the incumbent exits. Having exited, the former incumbent cannot threaten to reenter. This is why the local monopolist can always charge the unconstrained monopolist price without worrying about competition from earlier vintages of the product (see the appendix for the generalization to the case where the previous incumbent can always reenter at no cost).

16. See, for example, the historical analysis of Rosenberg (1963) or Griliches's (1992) survey of econometric work.

17. Each innovation replaces a randomly chosen A_{it} with the leading edge A_t^{max}. Since innovations occur at the rate ϕ_t per product and the average change across innovating sectors is $A_t^{\text{max}} - A_t$, we have

$$\frac{dA_t}{dt} = \phi_t(A_t^{\text{max}} - A_t).$$

This and equation (9) imply that the ratio $\Omega_t = A_t^{\text{max}}/A_t$ evolves according to

$$\frac{1}{\Omega_t}\frac{d\Omega_t}{dt} = \phi_t\sigma - \phi_t(\Omega_t - 1).$$

It follows that as long as ϕ_t is bounded above zero, Ω_t will converge asymptotically to $1 + \sigma$, as asserted in the text.

18. Because n_t is R&D input per product divided by A_t^{max}, it must be multiplied by $\frac{1+\sigma}{L}$.

19. Since there is a continuum of sectors with independent risks of creative destruction, investing in R&D involves only diversifiable risk. Hence r_t is a risk-free rate.

20. That is, the rest point exhibits saddle-point stability. This can be demonstrated by showing that the Jacobian matrix

$$J \equiv \begin{bmatrix} \partial\dot{k}/\partial k & \partial\dot{k}/\partial c \\ \partial\dot{c}/\partial k & \partial\dot{c}/\partial c \end{bmatrix}_{(k,c)=(\hat{k},\hat{c})} = \begin{bmatrix} f'(\hat{k}) - \delta - g - \bar{n}'(\hat{k})\left(\frac{1+\sigma}{L} + \sigma\lambda\hat{k}\right) & -1 \\ \hat{c}\left[\frac{R'(\hat{k})}{\varepsilon} - \sigma\lambda\bar{n}'(\hat{k})\right] & 0 \end{bmatrix}$$

has a negative determinant, which follows from direct calculation, since $R'(k) < 0$ and $\bar{n}'(k) > 0$.

21. The fact that these two curves have opposite signed slopes guarantees uniqueness of the steady state.

22. That is, $c^n(\zeta, \omega) \equiv \text{Min } \zeta\kappa + \omega\eta$ subject to $G^n(\kappa, \eta) = 1$.

23. These data come from the National Science Foundation's annual survey of research and development expenditures at universities and colleges, as presented in the NSF data retrieval system WebCaspar.
24. The ratios for industry are taken from Jankowski (1990).
25. Thus each innovation can be thought of as a new intermediate product, combined with a new capital good to produce it.
26. If, however, we took into account some of the agency problems involved in managing firms we would find that, at least in some cases, subsidizing capital accumulation can retard innovation by giving non-profit-maximizing managers financial relief from the competitive pressure to innovate. For more details, see Aghion and Howitt (1998, ch. 7).

References

Aghion, P., and P. Howitt. (1992). "A Model of Growth Through Creative Destruction," *Econometrica* 60, 323–351.

Aghion, P., and P. Howitt. (1996). "The Observational Implications of Schumpeterian Growth Theory," *Empirical Economics* 21, 13–25.

Aghion, P., and P. Howitt. (1998). *Endogenous Growth Theory*. Cambridge, MA: MIT Press.

Arroyo, C. R., E. Dinopoulos, and S. G. Donald. (1994). "Schumpeterian Growth and Capital Accumulation: Theory and Evidence." Unpublished manuscript.

Barro, R. J., and X. Sala-i-Martin. (1995). *Economic Growth*. New York: McGraw-Hill.

Blanchard, O. J. (1997). *Macroeconomics*. New York: Prentice-Hall.

Caballero, R. J., and A. B. Jaffe. (1993). "How High Are the Giants' Shoulders: An Empirical Assessment of Knowledge Spillovers and Creative Destruction in a Model of Economic Growth." In *NBER Macroeconomics Annual, 1993*. Cambridge, MA: MIT Press.

Cameron, G. (1996). "On the Measurement of Real R&D: Divisia Price Indices for UK Business Enterprise R&D," *Research Evaluation* 6, 215–219.

Carson, C. S., et al, U.S. Department of Commerce. (1994). "A Satellite Account for Research and Development," *Survey of Current Business*, 74, 37–71.

De Long, J. B., and L. H. Summers. (1991). "Equipment Investment and Economic Growth." *Quarterly Journal of Economics* 106, 445–502.

Griliches, Z. (1992). "The Search for R&D Spillovers," *Scandinavian Journal of Economics* 94, 29–47.

Grossman, G. M., and E. Helpman. (1991). *Innovation and Growth in the Global Economy*. Cambridge, MA: MIT Press.

Howitt, P. (1997). "Capital Accumulation and Innovation in Endogenous Growth: Confronting the Facts." Mimeo, Ohio State University.

Jankowski, J. E. (1990). "Construction of a Price Index for Industrial R&D Inputs." NSF Working Paper.

Jones, C. I. (1995). "R&D-Based Models of Economic Growth," *Journal of Political Economy* 103, 759–784.

Jorgenson, D. W. (1995). *Productivity*. Cambridge, MA: MIT Press.

Kortum, S. (1993). "Equilibrium R&D and the Patent-R&D Ratio: U.S. Evidence," *American Economic Review Proceedings* 83, 450–457.

Mankiw, N. G., D. Romer, and D. N. Weil. (1992). "A Contribution to the Empirics of Economic Growth," *Quarterly Journal of Economics* 107, 407–438.

Rivera-Batiz, L. A., and P. M. Romer. (1991). "Economic Integration and Endogenous Growth," *Quarterly Journal of Economics* 106, 531–555.

Romer, D. (1996). *Advanced Macroeconomics*. New York: McGraw-Hill.

Romer, P. M. (1990). "Endogenous Technological Change," *Journal of Political Economy* 98, S71–S102.

Rosenberg, N. (1963). "Technological Change in the Machine Tool Industry, 1840–1910," *Journal of Economic History*, 23, 414–443.

Scott, M. F. (1989). *A New View of Economic Growth*. Oxford: Clarendon Press.

Tirole, J. (1988). *The Theory of Industrial Organization*. Cambridge, MA: MIT Press.

Young, A. (1995). "The Tyranny of Numbers: Confronting the Statistical Realities of the East Asian Growth Experience," *Quarterly Journal of Economics* 110, 641–680.

[13]

The Economic Journal, **113** (*January*), 207–225. © Royal Economic Society 2003. Published by Blackwell Publishing, 9600 Garsington Road, Oxford OX4 2DQ, UK and 350 Main Street, Malden, MA 02148, USA.

LOW RETURNS IN R&D DUE TO THE LACK OF ENTREPRENEURIAL SKILLS*

Claudio Michelacci

This paper proposes a model of endogenous growth where innovating requires both researchers, who produce inventions, and entrepreneurs who implement them. As research and entrepreneurship compete in the allocation of aggregate resources, the relation between growth and research effort is hump-shaped. When entrepreneurs appropriate too little rents from innovation, too few resources are allocated to entrepreneurship and returns to R&D are low because of this lack of entrepreneurial skills. When so, innovation should be promoted by encouraging entrepreneurship rather than research.

Since the Malthusian (1986 [1798]) and Ricardian (1951 [1817]) prophecies of the eventual coming of a stationary state, the spectre of diminishing returns has hovered over economics. Arguably, such diminishing returns may arise because of the progressive exhaustion of investment opportunities which makes the returns to R&D effort decrease over time.[1] According to Schumpeter (1943, 1946) this is, however, just one of two competing explanations of the 'state of decay' of the 'capitalist society'. A 'more plausible' one is that 'the individual leadership of the entrepreneur tends to lose importance'.

According to this view, entrepreneurial ability is as important as research ability in determining the growth rate of an economy. Indeed, Schumpeter (1947) stresses the distinction between the inventor and the entrepreneur: 'The inventor produces ideas, the entrepreneur "gets things done" [...] an idea or scientific principle is not, by itself, of any importance for economic practice'. Hence, in order to grow, an economy requires both researchers who produce inventions and entrepreneurs who implement them.[2] Scientific knowledge has no economic impact unless some effort is made to spread it.[3]

---

* I would like to thank Philippe Aghion, Samuel Bentolila, Chris Pissarides and Javier Suarez for very helpful discussions and suggestions at different stages of the project. I am also particularly indebted to Christopher Bliss, another Editor and two anonymous referees for valuable and thoughtful comments on previous versions of the paper. The usual disclaimer applies.

[1] Recent empirical evidence seems to support some form of diminishing returns in research over time. For example, Griliches (1990) and Kortum (1993) note that, in the US, the ratio of the number of patent applications to the scientists and engineers involved in R&D has fallen over time in the post-war period, while Jones (1995*a*, *b*) points out that the economy growth rates have remained constant and even declined despite an increase in the amount of R&D effort. Indeed, Griliches (1979) concludes that 'the exhaustion of inventive and technological opportunities remains a major suspect for the productivity slow-down in the 70's'.

[2] The history of innovation is full of examples of successful inventor-entrepreneur partnerships. For example, Mokyr (1990) notices that even James Watt would have hardly succeeded in the implementation of the steam engine without the help of his partner, Matthew Boulton.

[3] Economists are well aware of the importance of allocating resources to both research and entrepreneurial activities. They must allocate their time between the studying required to write new papers and teaching students, talking with colleagues, presenting work at the NBER meetings, etc.

[207]

In order to model the aggregate trade off between allocating resources to research and entrepreneurship, I consider an endogenous growth model where an innovation requires the matching of an entrepreneur with a successful invention. In the model, individuals face the choice of whether to become researchers, who produce inventions, or entrepreneurs who implement them.[4] Hence an economy that allocates too many individuals to the research sector produces too many inventions which will be wasted because there will not be enough entrepreneurs to implement them. Thus the relationship between productivity growth and research effort is hump-shaped.

The existence of search frictions in the process whereby entrepreneurs and researchers are matched produces a natural incompleteness of contracts. Hence, the share of the rents from innovation appropriated by either researchers or entrepreneurs does not necessarily reflect their contribution to innovation. In general equilibrium, however, such rents determine whether individuals choose to become researchers or entrepreneurs. Consequently, the allocation of skill sustained in equilibrium might depart substantially from the socially efficient one. Interestingly, any point on the growth-research effort technological frontier can be sustained as a decentralised equilibrium of the economy.

One of the key results of the paper is that the innovation process can suffer because of the lack of either research effort or entrepreneurial skills. Economic history may provide examples of either case. Islamic civilisation at the end of the twelfth century may be an example of the former. Indeed Mokyr (1990) argues that it declined because it 'was not capable of adding much new to the existing stock of ideas it retrieved and applied so brilliantly'. Mokyr also discusses notorious examples of societies, such as the Greeks and the Romans, that suffered because of the lack of entrepreneurial skills. Such a deficit may also well explain the economic decline of the late Victorian Britain usually attributed to the inability of British entrepreneurship in promoting the diffusion of new and advanced production methods.[5]

Some relation to the literature. By positing that innovation requires the random matching of entrepreneurs with valuable inventions, my model borrows elements from the standard search model, e.g. Pissarides (1990). This setting is, however, extended to capture two important features of the innovation process. First, I introduce a technological externality generated by firm creation that leads to endogenous growth. Second, I allow the skill allocation to be endogenous by

---

[4] Schumpeter (1949) was concerned that his model resembled a model of 'exogenous' technological growth: 'a stumbling block' of the theory 'may be expressed by saying that the entrepreneur simply does nothing but take advantage of technological progress, which therefore appears, implicitly or explicitly as something that goes along entirely independently of entrepreneurial activity [...] It is perhaps not difficult to understand that technological progress, so obvious in some societies and so nearly absent in others, is a phenomenon that needs to be explained'. My model stresses the role of the entrepreneurial function in an endogenous growth framework.

[5] The 1998 White Paper by the British Government argues that the UK is still lacking in entrepreneurial skills. The recent experience of 'Silicon Fen' – the cluster of over 1,600 high tech firms that have grown up around Cambridge University – is sometimes perceived as a successful attempt to reverse this secular deficit in entrepreneurship.

permitting agents to decide on whether to become an entrepreneur or a researcher.[6] In this context I generalise earlier results, originally due to Diamond (1982) and Hosios (1990), on the efficiency of economies subject to search frictions. In particular I show that restoring efficiency under the presence of technological externalities requires research to have more bargaining power relative to the Hosios's benchmark.

The paper also relates to those strands of the growth literature that have analysed the relation between growth and R&D effort. It shares with Helpman and Trajtenberg (1994) the premise that inventions have widespread economic consequences only if implemented. The finding that research effort can be excessive arises also in Tirole (1988, p.399), in Aghion and Howitt (1992), and in Aghion and Howitt (1998, ch. 6), while the emphasis on the allocation of talent is shared with Baumol (1990) and Murphy *et al.* (1991). It is the interaction between these strands of the literature that is new here.

The model has also some implications for the recent literature which has analysed the relation between growth and the scale of the economy.[7] Jones (1995*b*), Kortum (1997), Young (1998) and Howitt (1999) propose a theoretical solution to the observed absence of relation between the scale of R&D effort and growth. Their models have in common the assumption that the output cost of an innovation is increasing with the level of development. Due to this form of exhaustion of investment opportunities, the amount of research effort increases over time to keep growth constant. Importantly such decreasing returns to R&D arise as the efficient response of a competitive economy to the increase in its scale.[8]

The paper might propose a complementary reading of the same empirical facts. I show theoretically that the returns to R&D might be decreasing if they are the result of an inefficient equilibrium shift that increases the amount of research effort to the detriment of more socially useful entrepreneurial skills. Furthermore, I show that the data are consistent with the existence of a constant-returns-to-scale matching function that links a measure of innovation (number of patent applications) to a measure of research effort (number of scientists involved in R&D) and entrepreneurship (population of self-employed). This implies that, at the optimal allocation, the returns to R&D never decrease since well-balanced increases in the amount of research and entrepreneurial effort always exhibit a constant marginal effect on the innovation rate.

Section 1 expounds the general set-up while Section 2 solves for the steady state equilibrium. Section 3 deals with efficiency. Section 4 carries out some exercises of comparative statics. Section 5 discusses some empirical implications. The conclusions are in Section 6. The Appendix contains some technical derivations.

---

[6] See Acemoglu (1996, 1997) for an analysis of workers' decisions to accumulate human capital in a labour market subject to search frictions.

[7] See Jones (1999) for a survey.

[8] For example, both in Jones (1995*b*) and Kortum (1997) the economy growth rate is the socially optimal one, while in Young (1998) the total amount of R&D effort is optimal even if its allocation among different dimensions of innovation might not be.

1. The Model

The economy is populated by a continuum of agents of size C. Each agent is infinitely lived, risk-neutral and maximises expected returns in output units discounted at rate $r > 0$. At each point in time agents can choose either to become researchers or entrepreneurs. I indicate with f_t the time-t fraction of researchers in the population and I refer to it as the level of *research effort* in the economy.

A researcher discovers *inventions* according to a Poisson process with intensity λ. When he makes a discovery, he starts searching for entrepreneurs able to implement it. Keeping the invention up-to-date requires a flow cost of χx_t per unit of time, where x_t represents the leading technology in the economy at time t and $\chi \geq 0$. I assume that the opportunity of transforming an invention into an innovation vanishes according to a Poisson process with rate of arrival v. This implies that at each point in time the stock of scientific knowledge, k_t, measured by the number of inventions suitable for economic exploitation, increases in response to the discovery of new inventions, while it tends to fall as the old ones become obsolete. This allows one to capture some key characteristics of the process of accumulating scientific knowledge; see Adams (1990). First, the stock of scientific knowledge is *fundamental* in that its applicability is not immediate. Secondly, it recognises that the stock of knowledge is made up of *heterogenous* pieces of information since the implementation of an invention requires a costly search for a suitable entrepreneurs. Thirdly, the use of the stock of knowledge is *repetitive*, as an invention can give rise to a 'cluster' of innovations concentrated 'in certain sectors and their surroundings' (Schumpeter, 1939, pp. 100–1). Finally it recognises its *time specificity*, as scientific knowledge becomes obsolete as time goes by.[9]

An *innovation* requires an invention discovered by a researcher and an entrepreneur. Once they match, a new firm run by the entrepreneur is created. A firm created at time t accesses the leading technology of that date x_t. A firm can produce, at each point in time t, a flow of goods equal to Px_t and is shut down according to a Poisson process with rate of arrival δ.[10]

The entrepreneur can be either running a firm or working at home; see Benhabib *et al.* (1991). When the entrepreneur runs a firm, he receives a profit flow π_t. Profits of the entrepreneur are chosen, so as to share with the researcher the gains from running the firm, by using a generalised Nash bargaining solution. The bargaining powers of the entrepreneur and the researcher are β and $1 - \beta$, respectively. When the entrepreneur works at home, he produces a flow of goods equal to hx_t where $h \geq 0$ measures the level of human capital of the entrepreneur who uses it according to the technology available at time t. In equilibrium an entrepreneur running a firm has no incentive to search. Hence only entrepreneurs

---

[9] The model could be extended by assuming that the rate v at which inventions become obsolete, depends on the rate of growth of the leading technology of the economy x_t so that technological progress causes the obsolescence of scientific knowledge – an effect reminiscent of Schumpeter's idea of creative destruction. The main implications of the model would remain however unchanged.

[10] I model firms in this way for analytical convenience. In fact the results of the paper would remain qualitatively unchanged if either a firm's death probability or output were assumed to be a function of its age, as they arguably are in reality.

working at home are 'available' for innovating. I will denote their number at time t by s_t and I will refer to it as the amount of *entrepreneurial slackness* available in the economy.

The rate at which free entrepreneurs find suitable inventions is determined by the homogeneous-of-degree-one matching function $m(k_t, s_t)$; see Pissarides (1990). This function is increasing and concave in each of its arguments. The matching function allows one to represent in a parsimonious fashion two key characteristics of the innovation process: the fact that both entrepreneurial skills and inventions are heterogenous, so that the search for viable partnerships is time consuming, and the fact that entrepreneurial skills are a scarce resource for which different researchers compete. The probability that an invention matches with an entrepreneur is given by $q(\theta_t) = m(k_t, s_t)/k_t$ where $\theta_t = k_t/s_t$ will be referred to as the level of *knowledge intensity* in the economy. By analogous considerations it follows that $p(\theta_t) = \theta_t q(\theta_t)$ is the instantaneous probability that a free entrepreneur finds a valuable invention. I also assume that

$$p(0) = q(\infty) = m(0, s_t) = m(k_t, 0) = 0, \quad \text{and} \quad p(\infty) = q(0) = \infty \qquad (A1)$$

so as to avoid dealing with uninteresting corner solutions.

Vertical innovations are the only source of growth in this economy. I follow Caballero and Jaffe (1993) and Aghion and Howitt (1998), among others, in assuming that the rate of growth of the technological parameter x_t is given by the product of the size of the innovation, σ, and the frequency of innovation. With the above assumptions, this frequency coincides with the number of innovations introduced in the economy at time t, $\theta_t q(\theta_t) s_t$. Hence the growth rate of the technological parameter x_t is given by $g_t = \sigma \theta_t q(\theta_t) s_t$.[11]

A sufficient condition to assure finite present values is $\sigma C\delta < r$ since it will imply that in steady state equilibrium $g_t < r$. Whereas obtaining a positive equilibrium level of research requires that $(\lambda/v)(1 - \beta)(P - h) > 0$. As in Romer (1990), in order to sustain growth we must assign a strictly positive capacity of rent appropriation to researchers, $\beta < 1$, since future rents are the only compensation for the sunk investment in research necessary to produce an invention.

The endogenous variables of the model are the level of knowledge intensity θ, the level of research effort f and the steady state growth rate g.

2. Equilibrium

In this section, I first write down value functions and characterise individual behaviour. I then analyse the level of research effort and the growth rate that arise in a steady state equilibrium.

---

[11] A natural interpretation is that there is a continuum of increasingly productive techniques indexed by a real number which corresponds to the log of its productivity parameter. Creation of a new firm means that the entrepreneur has succeeded in discovering a new technique and all entrepreneurs can thereafter search for the next technique in the continuum. So, at any point in time, the rate of technological progress is proportional to the flow of newly created firms.

2.1. *The Value of Research and Entrepreneurship*

The value of doing research at time t, R_t, solves

$$R_t = E_{\tau \geq 0}\{[(L_{t+\tau} + \sup(R_{t+\tau}, H_{t+\tau})]e^{-r\tau}\}, \qquad (1)$$

where L_t and H_t are the time-t value of an invention and of being an entrepreneur working at home, respectively. $t + \tau$ is the arrival date of the first invention whose arrival rate is λ, while the second term in the right-hand side captures the option a researcher has of becoming an entrepreneur at a later date.

Since an invention becomes obsolete at rate v and requires a cost of χx_t to remain up-to-date, it has a value L_t to the researcher which follows the asset-type equation

$$(r + v)L_t = -\chi x_t + q(\theta)I_t + \dot{L}_t. \qquad (2)$$

I_t measures the time-t value to a researcher of an innovation, $\dot{L}_t$ is the time derivative of L_t while $q(\theta)$ is the probability that an invention matches with an entrepreneur. As a firm produces a flow of goods equal to Px_t and entrepreneurs' profits are equal to π_t, I_t can be obtained by solving

$$(r + \delta)I_t = Px_t - \pi_t + \dot{I}_t, \qquad (3)$$

where $\dot{I}_t$ represents the time derivative of I_t while δ is the firm's death probability.

Analogously, the value to an entrepreneur of working at home at time t, H_t, solves the asset equation

$$rH_t = hx_t + \theta q(\theta)(E_t - H_t) + \dot{H}_t, \qquad (4)$$

where hx_t, E_t and $\dot{H}_t$ are respectively the real flow of goods produced by an entrepreneur working at home, the entrepreneur's value of running a firm and the time derivative of H_t. $\theta q(\theta)$ is the instantaneous probability that a free entrepreneur finds an invention that he can implement. Analogously E_t solves

$$rE_t = \pi_t + \delta[\sup(R_t, H_t) - E_t] + \dot{E}_t, \qquad (5)$$

where the above equation embodies the option entrepreneurs have of becoming researchers.

Profits are the outcome of bilateral bargaining between the researcher with the invention and the entrepreneur. Hence they maximise the weighted product of the researcher's and entrepreneur's net return from the creation of a new firm equal to I_t and $E_t - H_t$, respectively. Hence

$$\pi_t = \arg\max(I_t)^{1-\beta}(E_t - H_t)^{\beta},$$

where H_t is the entrepreneur's outside option which from the point of view of the maximisation is taken as constant. As a result, profits are such that

$$I_t = (1 - \beta)(I_t + E_t - H_t) = (1 - \beta)S_t, \qquad (6)$$

where $S_t = I_t + E_t - H_t$ is the private net surplus generated by the creation of a new firm. Of this surplus, researchers and entrepreneurs appropriate fractions $1 - \beta$ and β respectively.

2.2. *Free Entry Condition*

In steady state, each variable is growing at the same rate g as the economy so

$$R_t = Rx_t, \quad I_t = Ix_t, \quad L_t = Lx_t, \quad H_t = Hx_t, \quad E_t = Ex_t. \tag{7}$$

From making use of (7) to rewrite (2), (3), (4) and (5) it follows that

$$L = \frac{1}{r - g + v}[-\chi + q(\theta)(1 - \beta)S], \tag{2'}$$

$$I = (1 - \beta)S, \tag{3'}$$

$$H = \frac{1}{r - g}[h + \theta q(\theta)\beta S], \tag{4'}$$

$$E = H + \beta S \tag{5'}$$

where $S = I + E - H$ measures (once divided by x_t) the private net surplus associated with the creation of a new firm and is equal to

$$S = \frac{P - h}{r - g + \delta + \theta q(\theta)\beta}. \tag{8}$$

In equilibrium, agents must be indifferent between becoming a researcher or an entrepreneur, so that the *free entry condition* $R_t = H_t$ must hold at each point in time. But then, from using this condition, the fact that $R_t = Rx_t$ and then substituting into (1) it follows that

$$R = \frac{\lambda L}{r - g}.$$

Together with (2') and (4') this implies that the condition $R_t = H_t$ reads as

$$h + \theta q(\theta)\beta S = \frac{\lambda[-\chi + q(\theta)(1 - \beta)S]}{r - g + v}. \tag{9}$$

The left-hand side of (9) represents the relative profitability of being an entrepreneur as an increasing function of the amount of knowledge intensity θ: the larger the stock of scientific knowledge available per entrepreneur, the more profitable is entrepreneurship. Analogously, an increase in θ reduces the profitability of being a researcher because the implementation of inventions becomes progressively more difficult. As a result the right-hand side of (9), which measures the relative profitability of being a researcher, is decreasing in θ. Hence, for any given level of the steady state growth rate g, there exists a unique value of knowledge intensity θ such that the right-hand side equals the left-hand side. At such value individuals are indifferent between becoming researchers or entrepreneurs.[12]

---

[12] One can also check that steady state profits π_t are equal to πx_t, where, from substituting (3), (4), (5) into (6), it follows that $\pi = \beta P + (1 - \beta)h + \theta q(0)\beta I$.

2.3. Technological Frontier

Since firms are closed at rate δ, entrepreneurial slackness, s_t, evolves according to the differential equation

$$\dot{s}_t = \delta[C(l - f) - s_t] - \theta q(\theta)s_t, \tag{10}$$

so that in steady state it is equal to

$$s_t = s = \frac{\delta C(1 - f)}{\delta + \theta q(\theta)}. \tag{11}$$

Analogously, the dynamics of the stock of knowledge, k_t, is governed by

$$\dot{k}_t = \lambda Cf - vk_t. \tag{12}$$

so that in steady state $k_t = k = (\lambda/v)Cf$.

From the assumption that the frequency of innovation is equal to the number of successful matches between k_t and s_t, it follows that the steady state growth rate g of the technological parameter x_t is equal to

$$g = \sigma\theta q(\theta)s = \sigma Cm\left[\frac{\lambda}{v}f, \frac{\delta(1 - f)}{\delta + \theta q(\theta)}\right], \tag{13}$$

where $\theta = k/s$ solves the simple non-linear equation

$$\theta = \theta(f) = \frac{\lambda}{v}\frac{[\delta + \theta q(\theta)]f}{\delta(1 - f)}. \tag{14}$$

Equation (14) merely expresses knowledge intensity as the ratio of the steady state amount of scientific knowledge to the amount of slackness given by (11). Notice that (14) defines an function $\theta(f)$ that associates to each f the corresponding value of θ that solves the equation. Such function is increasing since a larger f associates with a larger k and a lower s. But then, after substituting $\theta(f)$ for θ in (13), one can define a function $g = g(f)$ which relates the level of research effort, f, to the steady state growth rate of the economy. Since the function $g(f)$ determines the frontier of technological possibilities of the economy, I refer to it as the *TE-schedule*. Such a schedule is hump-shaped and it satisfies the property that no growth can be the outcome of either too much or too little research effort, $g(0) - g(1) = 0$ (see Propositions 1 and 2 in the Appendix for a formal proof).[13] As both research and entrepreneurial skills are required to innovate, an over-allocation to either factor harms technological process.

2.4. Equilibrium

Equations (9) and (13), given the constraint imposed by (14), completely solve the model in the research effort, f, growth rate, g, space. Equation (9) determines, for

---

[13] Denote by $0 < \eta < 1$ the elasticity of the matching function with respect to the level of entrepreneurial slackness. Then one can show that $g(f)$ is globally strictly concave if, for example, η is weakly increasing in θ. One can also show that $g(f)$ has a unique maximum under the milder condition: $-d\eta/d\theta < \eta^2$. For example, both conditions would obviously be satisfied in the case of a Cobb–Douglas matching function.

any given level of the growth rate, the relative amount of resources that the econ-omy will end up devoting to research. Given (14) and the associated function $\theta(f)$, (9) allows to define the function $g = e(f)$ which relates the level of research effort that solves the free-entry condition to the given level of the growth rate. Hereafter I will refer to the function $e(f)$ as the *FE-schedule*. Such function maps the zero one interval onto the whole real line (see Proposition 3 in the Appendix). Furthermore $e(f)$ is increasing. To understand why it is so, notice that research requires a longer time than entrepreneurship to become productive and yield some (positive) rev-enue. Also notice that in the model an increase in the growth rate, g, affects indi-vidual decisions through a capitalisation effect that reduces the effective discount rate of agents. But a change in the discount factor always tends to have a greater effect on the investment with the longer time horizon so, as a result of the increase in g, the value of both research and entrepreneurship increase but the value of research increases relatively more so f must rise to restore the free entry condition.

The steady-state equilibrium is defined by the point at which the *FE*-schedule, $e(f)$, crosses the *TE*-schedule, $g(f)$, like at point A in Figure 1. At such a point no researcher has an incentive to become an entrepreneur (or *vice-versa*) and the economy grows at the constant steady state growth rate determined by the tech-nological frontier.

3. Welfare Analysis

In this section, I compare the equilibrium to the constrained social optimum. I define social welfare $\bar{W}$ as the net present discounted value of the aggregate income flows produced by entrepreneurs and researchers. The social planner

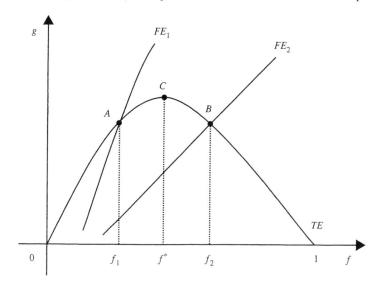

Fig. 1. *Steady State Equilibrium*

takes as given the search frictions involved in the innovation process. At any point in time, the state of the economy is fully summarised by the quantities k_t and n_t that represent the time-t stock of scientific knowledge and total number of firms, respectively. Given the focus on steady state equilibria, I consider time invariant allocations described by a fixed amount of research effort f.

3.1. *The Social Planner Problem*

Once multiplied by x_t,

$$y(k_t, n_t; f) = Pn_t + h[C(1 - f) - n_t] - \chi k_t$$

denotes the net income flow produced by the economy at time t. Also notice that the evolution of the number of firms in the economy is governed by

$$\dot{n}_t = m[k_t, C(1 - f) - n_t] - \delta n_t \tag{15}$$

while the stock of scientific knowledge grows at a rate $\dot{k}_t$ given by (12). Hence one can implicitly define social welfare as the product of x_t and the function $W(k, n, f)$ which solves

$$rW(k_t, n_t; f) = y(k_t, n_t; f) + W_k \dot{k}_t + W_n \dot{n}_t + g_t W(k_t, n_t; f) \tag{16}$$

where $g_t = \sigma m(k_t, s_t)$ while $W_k = \partial W / \partial k_t$ and $W_n = \partial W / \partial n_t$ measure the social shadow value of an invention and of an additional firm, respectively. Three components account for social welfare in (16): the first is current income, the second is the capital gain associated with changes in the state of the system – the second and third term in (16) – and last the capitalisation effect associated with technological progress, the fourth term in (16).

To characterise the constrained socially optimum allocation, denote by g and n the economy's steady state value of the growth rate and number of firms, respectively. Furthermore let

$$\bar{W} = \frac{Pn + h[C(1 - f) - n] - \chi k}{r - g} \tag{17}$$

denote (once divided by x_t) the steady state level of social welfare which is equal to the present discounted value of the level of output net of research costs. Finally let η indicate the elasticity of the matching function with respect to entrepreneurial slackness.[14] Then differentiating (16) with respect to f and after some algebra, the Appendix shows that

$$\frac{dW}{df} = -\frac{C}{r - g} \left\{ h + \theta q(\theta) \eta S^E - \frac{\lambda[-\chi + q(\theta)(1 - \eta)S^E]}{r - g + v} \right\} \tag{18}$$

where

$$S^E = W_n + \sigma \bar{W} = \frac{P - h + \sigma(r - g + \delta)\bar{W}}{r - g + \delta + \theta q(\theta) \eta} \tag{19}$$

[14] Notice that η is in general a function of θ.

is the net social surplus associated with the creation of a new firm. Such surplus is equal to the sum of the shadow value of a new firm W_n plus the gains associated with the technological externality generated by innovation, which have value $\sigma \bar{W}$.

3.2. *Results*

I can now state my first result on efficiency: the social optimum always lies on the positively sloped arm of the *TE*-schedule, $g(f)$. To prove this result, the Appendix first shows that the steady state growth rate g is maximised at the 'golden rule' level of research effort f^* such that the level of knowledge intensity $\theta^* = \theta(f^*)$ solves

$$\theta^* = \frac{\lambda}{\nu}\frac{1-\eta}{\eta}. \tag{20}$$

Then the Appendix shows that the derivative of W with respect to f evaluated at f^* is negative which indeed implies that at the growth maximising allocation the level of research effort in the economy is too large.

The economic intuition of the result is pretty simple. Given the objective of maximising the present discounted value of output, the central planner must equate the marginal benefit of increasing research effort to its marginal cost. Notice that (13) and (15) imply that the value of f that maximises the steady state number of operating firms, n, also maximises the steady state growth rate, g. So the sign of the social marginal benefits of research coincides with that of the derivative of the *TE*-schedule, $g(f)$. But then, since increasing research always involves a strictly positive marginal cost (relative to increasing entrepreneurship), the social optimum must be at a point where the marginal benefits from increasing f are also strictly positive and this is so only on the strictly increasing arm of *TE*-schedule.

It is interesting to compare the level of research effort sustained by the decentralised economy to the social optimal one. This can be done by comparing (9) with (18) and checking when the decentralised economy implements a level of research effort which induces $dW/df = 0$. One can immediately see that the two conditions associate with the same level of research effort only if the private and social net-surplus from the creation of a new firm coincide, $S = S^E$. In the absence of technological externalities, $\sigma = 0$, this occurs when entrepreneurs' bargaining power is such that $\beta = \eta$ so that (8) and (19) are identical. Hosios (1990) first proved that, in an economy with search frictions, a constrained efficient allocation of resources requires bargaining power to reflect each side's contribution to the creation of net surplus as measured by the elasticity of the matching function. Here I have generalised this result to an environment where the allocation of skill is endogenous.

When technological externalities are present, $\sigma > 0$, however, the Appendix shows that entrepreneurs' bargaining power (β must be smaller than η for the decentralised economy to implement the socially efficient allocation. To understand the result, notice that search frictions simultaneously induce a negative externality to agents on the same side of the market (congestion externalities) and a positive one to agents on the other side of the market (thin market externalities). At ($\beta = \eta$ the congestion and thin-market externalities balance exactly. Yet, at this point, technological externalities are still operating and tend to discourage activities, namely research, characterised by a longer time horizon and larger initial investment. Hence restoring efficiency requires $\beta < \eta$. There is only one case where the Hosios's rule $\beta = \eta$ still applies even in the presence of technological externalities. This occurs when the type of investment required to specialise in different activities is the same, that is when the instantaneous return from becoming a researcher or an entrepreneur are equal $h = \chi = 0$, (see Appendix).

4. Comparative Statics

Proposition 4 in the Appendix states that, depending on the parameters of the model, any point on the *TE*-schedule, $g(f)$, can be sustained as an equilibrium of the economy, including those situated on the negatively sloped arm of the *TE*-schedule, like point *B* in Figure 1. A point like *B* is associated with a Pareto dominated equilibrium since a reduction in research effort would simultaneously lead to an increase in the output level and in the growth rate (both over the transition path and in the new steady state). These types of equilibria can be sustained for reasons similar to those analysed by Hosios (1990) and Caballero and Hammour (1996). An economy characterised by *ex-ante* competitive relationships but *ex-post* bilateral monopolies has no compelling tendency to coordinate itself towards the social optimum, since there is no reason why the amount of rents appropriated by each party should reflect his contribution to the creation of social surplus.

In equilibria like point *B* in Figure 1, research effort crowds out more socially useful entrepreneurial skills and the growth process stagnates precisely because of this *lack of entrepreneurial skills*. Indeed, as the amount of research effort rises, the stock of scientific knowledge increases, but it also becomes progressively more difficult to implement inventions both because more researchers are competing for the same resources (congestion externalities) and because an increase in research effort crowds out useful entrepreneurial skills (thin market externalities). When the stock of scientific knowledge is already large while the amount of entrepreneurial skills is low, an increase in research effort reduces the growth rate of the economy, because it misallocates socially useful resources. For example, an increase in research effort can be translated into stagnant or declining growth rates, if the equilibrium of the economy shifts from point *A* to point *B* in Figure 1.

Such shifts in the equilibrium can occur, for example, in response to a fall in the bargaining power of entrepreneurs β. A fall in β makes research relatively more profitable for any given level of the growth rate so that the *FE*-schedule shifts to the right while it has no effect on the *TE*-schedule. Such a fall in β might relate to the Schumpeterian (1943, 1946) claim that cultural and sociological shifts tend to destroy the 'protective strata' able to sustain the entrepreneurial function.[15] Since β measures the outcome of a bilateral bargaining problem here specified

[15] Culture, understood as prevailing values and beliefs, is often perceived as an important determinant of the level of entrepreneurship in the economy, see Davidson and Wilklund (1997). In terms of the model, a cultural environment more favourable to entrepreneurship may translate into a larger either β or h. This last case may correspond to societies that reward more (in terms of social status) entrepreneurial 'success' and 'leadership'.

parsimoniously, one can also argue that, in the presence of some asymmetric information that favours researchers, β might be affected by the technological content of the innovation: innovations that are more technological advanced might associate with a greater ability of the researcher to appropriate rents and therefore with a lower β.

Particularly interesting are the consequences of a change in the firms' destruction rate δ. A change in δ has generally ambiguous effects on the *FE*-schedule. To see this notice that, a fall in δ requires an increase in the level of knowledge intensity, θ, to restore the free entry condition (9). However, (14) implies that for given f, a lower δ associate with a larger value of θ, since the amount of entrepreneurial slack is reduced. If this last effect is sufficiently strong the *FE*-schedule, $e(f)$, shifts to the left, otherwise f must rise to restore the free entry condition and $e(f)$ shifts to the right.

What is not ambiguous is the impact of a change in δ on the technological frontier of the economy. A fall in δ implies a downward shift of the *TE*-schedule, with the hump of the schedule moving leftward. To prove the downward movement, notice that for given f a fall in δ reduces the steady state level of entrepreneurial slack given by (11) both directly through δ and indirectly through the induced positive effect on θ, see (14). The leftward movement of the hump follows from the fact that entrepreneurial slack falls for any given level of f, so the constraint imposed by the number of free entrepreneurs on the innovation process becomes progressively more binding as f increases. In other words, an economy that liquidates more often (i.e. with a larger δ) has more frequent opportunity to rebuild its productive stock at a higher technological level and grows faster thanks to the intertemporal spill-overs typical of standard endogenous growth models. Thus the model suggests a channel whereby an increase in the pace of reallocation promotes growth by increasing the amount of resources available for innovating.[16]

5. Empirical Implications

I next discuss some empirical implications of the model. The analysis is simply meant to be illustrative of some of the theoretical properties of the model.

If one assumes that the matching function is Cobb–Douglas,

$$m(k_t, s_t) = A(k_t)^{\alpha}(s_t)^{\gamma}, 0 < \alpha, \gamma < 1, \tag{21}$$

then (13) suggests running the following regression

$$\ln(g_t) = \alpha \ln(f_t C_t) + \gamma \ln(s_t) + \alpha \ln\left(\frac{\lambda}{\nu}\right) + \ln \sigma + \ln(A). \tag{22}$$

The model has two important testable implications. First, the parameters α and γ must both be positive numbers strictly between zero and one. Indeed this would imply that both entrepreneurial and research skills affect the innovation rate of

---

[16] See Mortensen and Pissarides (1998) for a model where the causality between reallocation and growth reverses. In their model an increase in the rate of exogenous technological progress raises the job reallocation rate in the economy.

the economy. Second, the matching function (21) exhibits constant returns to scale, that is $\alpha + \gamma = 1$. This would imply that, at the optimal allocation, the returns to R&D can never be decreasing since well-balanced increases in the amount of research and entrepreneurial effort have constant marginal effects on the innovation rate.

To illustrate the methodology, I estimate (22) for the US over the period 1950–90.[17] I follow Griliches (1979, 1990) in taking the total number of patent applications as an index of innovative activity in order to proxy for g_t,[18] and Jones (1995b) in considering the ratio of scientists and engineers involved in R&D over the population if working age as a measure of (relative) research effort f_t. As a proxy for the scale of the economy C_t in (22) I take the population if working age. Identifying entrepreneurship is more problematic. According to Schumpeter (1949) the entrepreneurial function can be identified only *a posteriori*.[19] In fact, Evans and Jovanovic (1989) note how, in their sample, 20% of the individuals who switched into self-employment formed incorporated businesses. That is why I follow Evans and Jovanovic (1989), Evans and Leighton (1989) and Blanchflower and Oswald (1998) in using as a proxy of the amount of entrepreneurship, s_t, the population of self-employed.

To control for cyclical disturbances, I also consider some additional specifications with the unemployment rate, the growth rate of *per capita* GDP and an index of the number of vacancies as independent variables.[20] The unemployment rate together with the other cyclical indicators could correct for that part of the population of self employed that does not represent real entrepreneurship but simply people that moved into self-employment from unemployment to find a job.[21]

Table 1 reports the estimates obtained by running the regression (22), allowing for different lags in the relation between research effort, entrepreneurship and innovation. The table shows that, in these data, both implications of the model tends to receive empirical support. In fact, α and γ are both positive and significantly different from zero with α ranging between 0.47 and 0.54 while γ ranges

---

[17] Data before 1970 are taken from *Historical Statistics of the United States: Colonial Times to 1970*; after 1970 they are from various issues of *The Statistical Abstract of the United States*.

[18] Whether a patent corresponds more to the notion of invention or innovation, is a topic beyond the scope of this paper. The Patents Laws-United State Code, U.S.C. 101, states that 'whoever invents or discovers any new and useful process, machine, manufacture, or composition of matter, or any new and useful improvement thereof, may obtain a patent'. The UK Patents Act 1977 states that the invention to be patented must be 'capable of industrial application'. More generally Cornish (1989) states that 'a patent cannot be granted for a thing or process which however interesting or suggestive it might be to scientists, has no known practical application at the priority date'. The requisite of 'industrial applicability' is not contained in the US law. It seems however, that the requisite of 'usefulness' roughly coincides with that of 'industrial applicability', so that even if a patent still represents something between an invention and an innovation as defined in this paper, it seems to be closer to the latter.

[19] Indeed, he writes: 'our definitions of entrepreneur, entrepreneurial function and so on can only grow out of it *a posteriori*' and again 'when we speak of the entrepreneur we do not mean so much a physical person as we do a function, but even if we look at individuals who at least at some juncture in their lives fill the entrepreneurial function it should be added that these individuals do not form a social class. They hail from all the corners of the social universe'.

[20] Data on the unemployment rate, growth rate of GDP *per capita* and the number of vacancies are taken from the OECD-CEP data set, see Bagliano *et al.* (1991).

[21] Blanchflower and Oswald (1998) document that flows from unemployment into self-employment are large.

Table 1

Results from Running Regression (22) in the Text

Indep. variable:	Lagged $\ln(f_t C_t)$	Lagged $\ln(s_t)$	Unempl. rate	GDP per cap. growth rate	Vacancy index	R^2	Wald test (p-value) $\alpha + \gamma = 1$
1lag	0.47 (0.03)	0.24 (0.10)	–	–	–	0.84	0.005
2lags	0.49 (0.03)	0.29 (0.10)	–	–	–	0.86	0.03
3lags	0.50 (0.04)	0.37 (0.10)	–	–	–	0.86	0.24
4lags	0.52 (0.04)	0.48 (0.10)	–	–	–	0.86	0.94
1lag	0.50 (0.04)	0.30 (0.10)	−0.02 (0.008)	–	–	0.86	0.06
2lags	0.53 (0.04)	0.37 (0.10)	−0.02 (0.008)	–	–	0.88	0.36
3lags	0.54 (0.04)	0.45 (0.10)	−0.02 (0.009)	–	–	0.88	0.97
4lags	0.54 (0.05)	0.53 (0.11)	−0.01 (0.009)	–	–	0.87	0.62
1lag	0.51 (0.04)	0.33 (0.10)	−0.02 (0.009)	−0.53 (0.45)	–	0.88	0.15
2lags	0.54 (0.04)	0.39 (0.10)	−0.02 (0.009)	−0.33 (0.42)	–	0.89	0.56
3lags	0.54 (0.04)	0.44 (0.11)	−0.02 (0.009)	0.10 (0.43)	–	0.88	0.92
1lag	0.46 (0.07)	0.32 (0.10)	−0.02 (0.009)	−0.54 (0.45)	0.08 (0.08)	0.88	0.10
2lags	0.47 (0.07)	0.39 (0.10)	−0.02 (0.009)	−0.34 (0.41)	0.10 (0.08)	0.89	0.25
3lags	0.46 (0.07)	0.44 (0.11)	−0.01 (0.01)	0.09 (0.42)	0.10 (0.07)	0.89	0.48

The regression was run using OLS, the dependent variable being the (logged) number of patent applications. Similar results are obtained when allowing for first-order auto-correlation in the residuals and a non-scalar auto-covariance matrix.

from a value of 0.24 to 0.48. This implies that the relation between the number of innovations and research effort $f_t C_t$ turns out to be concave and hump-shaped. Furthermore, Table 1 documents that, if we consider reasonable a lag of over two years before research effort shows up in a patent application, the hypothesis that the matching function (21) exhibits constant returns to scale cannot be rejected even at a 10% level of significance. Moreover, in the specification with the unemployment rate as independent variable, this hypothesis cannot be rejected whatever the number of lags considered.

6. Conclusions

This paper has shown how an increase in the amount of resources devoted to research does not necessarily increase the growth rate of the economy. In a world with rent sharing and inter-temporal spill-overs, an increase in research effort can crowd out more socially useful entrepreneurial skills, reduce the growth rate and ultimately lead to an allocation of skills which is Pareto dominated. Thus, the model might provide some foundations to the Schumpeterian warning that the 'state of decay of the capitalist society' can ultimately be driven by the lack of entrepreneurial skills.

The question on whether the economy's skill allocation is optimal for growth is likely to be particularly relevant in advanced economies where innovation is so *complex* that a single agent fails to possess both the scientific knowledge and the entrepreneurial ability required to innovate. When this is so, individuals must specialise and innovation requires the contribution of different, highly specialised agents. Consequently, the allocation of skills to different tasks changes from being internal to the *individual* to being internal to the *market* and the amount of rents from innovating appropriated by each task may become a crucial determinant of the economy's skill allocation. For instance, the division of rents could affect the choice between allocating resources to accumulating either education or experience as well as any occupational choice, especially among those occupations that are likely to participate to the sharing of the rents from innovation – say, whether to become a manager, a politician, a financier or an entrepreneur.

Investigating whether the actual skill allocation tends to depart from the optimal one as the economy develops and gets more specialised, remains however a question for further research that requires more careful micro-based empirical investigation. Looking at the skill composition either by occupations or along the experience-schooling dimension could be a promising avenue to address this question.

CEMFI, Madrid

Date of receipt of first submission: August 2000
Date of receipt of final typescript: January 2002

Dataset is available for this paper: www.res.org.uk

Appendix

In this Appendix I derive some technical results discussed in the text. Before proceeding, notice that the derivatives of $m(k,s)$ with respect to k and s can be computed as

$$\frac{\mathrm{d}m}{\mathrm{d}k} = (1-\eta)q(\theta) \quad \text{and} \quad \frac{\mathrm{d}m}{\mathrm{d}s} = \eta\theta q(\theta),$$

respectively.

Properties of the function $\theta(f)$

PROPOSITION 1: *Equation (14) defines the level of knowledge intensity θ as an increasing function of f, $\theta = \theta(f)$, with the property that $\theta(0) = 0$ and $\theta(1) = \infty$.*

Proof: By using $\mathrm{d}\theta q(\theta)/\mathrm{d}\theta = (1-\eta)q(\theta)$, total differentiating (14) with respect to θ and f yields

$$\frac{\mathrm{d}\theta}{\mathrm{d}f} = \frac{\delta + \theta q(\theta)}{\delta + \eta\theta q(\theta)} \frac{(\lambda/v)[\delta + \theta q(\theta)] + \delta\theta}{\delta(1-f)} \tag{23}$$

which proves monotonicity. The properties of the function $\theta(f)$ at the boundary follow directly from (14) and (A1) together with the fact that the elasticity of the right hand side of (14) with respect to θ is less than one.

Properties of the TE-schedule

PROPOSITION 2: *Given (14), (13) determines the growth rate g, as a function of f, $g = g(f)$ with the property that $g(0) = g(1) = 0$. Steady state growth is maximised at an allocation such that (20) is satisfied.*

Proof: Note that (11) together with proposition 1 allow to define entrepreneurial slackness as a decreasing function of f, $s = s(f)$. After substituting in (13), one obtains that

$$g = g(f) = \sigma m\left[\frac{\lambda}{v}Cf, s(f)\right],$$

which explicitly defines the function $g(f)$.

To conclude the proof, notice that from (23), it follows that

$$\frac{\mathrm{d}s(f)}{\mathrm{d}f} = \frac{\mathrm{d}}{\mathrm{d}f}\left[\frac{\delta(1-f)}{\delta + \theta q(\theta)}\right] = -\frac{\delta + (\lambda/v)(1-\eta)q(\theta)}{\delta + \eta\theta q(\theta)},$$

thus the derivative of $g(f)$ reads as

$$\frac{\mathrm{d}g(f)}{\mathrm{d}f} = \frac{\sigma C\delta q(\theta)[(\lambda/v)(1-\eta) - \eta\theta]}{\delta + \eta\theta q(\theta)},$$

which proves (20).

Properties of the FE-schedule

PROPOSITION 3: *Given (14) and the associated function $\theta = \theta(f)$, (9) defines the growth rate of the economy g as an increasing function of f, $g = e(f)$, with the properties that $e(0) = -\infty$ and $e(1) = \infty$.*

Proof: Multiply the left and right hand side of (9) by $[r - g + \delta + \theta q(\theta)\beta]$. The resulting left hand side of the equation is strictly increasing in θ and equal to $h(r + \delta - g)$ when $\theta = 0$, while the resulting right hand side is strictly decreasing in θ and it approaches infinity when θ goes to zero since $(\lambda/v)(1 - \beta)(P - h) > 0$ by assumption. This implies that, for given g, a θ that solves (9) always exists. Furthermore, an increase in g causes a downward (upward) shift in the left (right) hand side so that θ unequivocally increases. As $\theta = \theta(f)$ is increasing, $e(f)$ is also increasing. The properties of the function $e(f)$ at the boundary follow immediately from condition (A1) and the properties of $\theta(f)$ established in Proposition 1.

PROPOSITION 4: *There exist values of the parameters such that any point on the TE-schedule, $g(f)$, can be sustained as an equilibrium.*

Proof: Note that, for a given level of g, changes in P, h, χ and β modify the value of θ that solves (9) without affecting the function $\theta(f)$. Hence, one can find a combination of parameters such that arbitrary given values of f and g are on the FE-schedule. Since changes in these parameters do not affect the TE-schedule, any point along $g(f)$ can possibly be sustained as an equilibrium.

Efficiency Results

The derivative of W with respect to f. Partially differentiating (16) with respect to k_t and n_t and after using the fact that in steady state $\dot{k}_t = \dot{n}_t = 0$ yields

$$W_k = \frac{-\chi + (1-\eta)q(\theta)(W_n + \sigma\bar{W})}{r - g + v} \tag{24}$$

and

$$W_n = \frac{P - h - \sigma\eta\theta q(\theta)\bar{W}}{r - g + \delta + \eta\theta q(\theta)}. \tag{25}$$

Differentiating (16) with respect to f and evaluating this derivative in steady state yields

$$\frac{\mathrm{d}W}{\mathrm{d}f} = \frac{C}{r - g}[-h - \eta\theta q(\theta)(W_n + \sigma\bar{W}) + \lambda W_h]$$

which after using (24) immediately leads to expression (18) in the main text.

Relation between θ^* and the social optimum. To prove that the social optimum always lies on the positively sloped arm of the *TE*-schedule, evaluate (18) at $\theta^* = [\lambda(l - \eta)]/v\eta$. This immediately yields

$$\frac{\mathrm{d}W}{\mathrm{d}f} = -\frac{C}{r - g}\left[h + \frac{\lambda\chi}{r - g + v} + \frac{(r - g)\eta\theta^* q(\theta^*) S^E}{r - g + v} \right]$$

which is negative.

The efficient sharing rule. I now prove that it exists $\beta < \eta$ such that the decentralised economy implements the optimal allocation. From (9) it follows that

$$h + \frac{\lambda\chi}{r - g + v} = \left[\frac{\lambda(1 - \beta)}{r - g + v} - \beta\theta \right] q(\theta)S, \qquad (26)$$

which substituted into (18) and after using the definition of S^E in (19) yields

$$\frac{\mathrm{d}W}{\mathrm{d}f} = \frac{C(\beta - \eta)q(\theta)\{\theta(r - g + \delta) - \lambda[r - g + \delta + \theta q(\theta)]/(r - g + v)\}S}{(r - g)[r - g + \delta + \eta\theta q(\theta)]}$$
$$+ \frac{\sigma Cq(\theta)(r - g + \delta)[\lambda(1 - \eta)/(r - g + v) - \eta\theta]\bar{W}}{(r - g)[r - g + \delta + \eta\theta q(\theta)]}.$$

Evaluating this derivatives at $\beta = \eta$, one can see that the first term is equal to zero while (26) implies that the second term is strictly positive, so that, at this level of β, research effort is too low. Now note that (9) implies that f is negatively related to β, so that β must fall below η for the economy to reach efficiency. There are two exceptions where at $\beta = \eta$, $\mathrm{d}W/\mathrm{d}f = 0$. The former arises when $\sigma = 0$, the latter when $h + \lambda\chi/(r - g + v) = 0$ so that, by (26), $[\lambda(1 - \eta)]/(r - g + v) - \eta\theta = 0$.

References

Acemoglu, D. (1996). 'A micro-foundation for social increasing returns in human capital accumulation', *Quarterly Journal of Economics*, vol. 111(3), pp. 779–804.
Acemoglu, D. (1997). 'Training and innovation in an imperfect labour market', *Review of Economic Studies*, vol. 64, pp. 445–64.
Adams, J. (1990). 'Fundamental stocks of knowledge and productivity growth', *Journal of Political Economy*, vol. 98, pp. 673–702.
Aghion, P. and Howitt, P. (1992). 'A model of growth through creative destruction', *Econometrica*, vol. 60, pp. 323–51.
Aghion, P. and Howitt, P. (1998). *Endogenous Growth Theory*, Cambridge, MA: MIT Press.
Bagliano, F., Brandolini A. and Dalmazzo, A. (1991). 'The OECD-CEP data set', Centre for Economic Performance Working Paper No. 118, June.
Baumol, W. (1990). 'Entrepreneurship: productive, unproductive, and destructive', *Journal of Political Economy*, vol. 98(5), pp. 893–921.
Benhabib, J., Rogerson, R. and Wright, R. (1991). 'Homework in macroeconomics: household production and aggregate fluctuations', *Journal of Political Economy*, vol. 99(6), pp. 1166–87.
Blanchflower, D. G. and Oswald, A. (1998). 'What makes an entrepreneur?', *Journal of Labour Economics*, vol. 16, pp. 26–60.
Caballero, R. and Hammour, M. (1996). 'The fundamental transformation in macroeconomics', *American Economic Review, Papers and Proceedings*, vol. 86(2), pp. 181–6.
Caballero, R. and Jaffe, A. (1993). 'How high are the giants shoulders: an empirical assessment of knowledge spillovers and creative destruction in a model of economic growth', in (O. Blanchard, and S. Fischer, eds), *NBER Macroeconomics Annual 1993*, Cambridge MA: MIT Press, pp. 15–74.
Cornish, W. R. (1989). *Intellectual Property: Patents, Copyright, Trade Marks and Allied Rights*, 2nd edn, London: Sweet & Maxwell.
Davidson, P. and Wilklund, J. (1997). 'Values, beliefs and regional variations in new firm formation rates', *Journal of Economic Psychology*, vol. 18, pp. 179–99.

Diamond, P. (1982). 'Wage determination and efficiency in search equilibrium', *Review of Economic Studies*, vol. 49, pp. 217–27.

Evans, D. and Jovanovic, B. (1989). 'An estimated model of entrepreneurial choice under liquidity constraints', *Journal of Political Economy*, vol. 97(4), pp. 808–27.

Evans, D. and Leighton, L. (1989). 'Some empirical aspects of entrepreneurship', *American Economic Review*, vol. 79(3) (June), pp. 519–35.

Griliches, Z. (1979). 'Patents: recent trends and puzzles', *Brookings Papers on Economic Activity, Micro-economics*, pp. 291–330.

Griliches, Z. (1990). 'Patent statistics as economic indicators: a survey', *Journal of Economic Literature*, vol. 28 (December), pp. 1661–707.

Helpman, E. and Trajtenberg, M. (1994). 'A time to sow and a time to reap: growth based on general purpose technologies', NBER Working Paper Series, No 4854, September.

Hosios, A. (1990). 'On the efficiency of matching and related models of search and unemployment', *Review of Economic Studies*, vol. 57, pp. 279–98.

Howitt, P. (1999). 'Steady endogenous growth with population and R&D inputs growing', *Journal of Political Economy*, vol. 107(4), pp. 715–30.

Jones, C. (1995a). 'Time series tests of endogenous growth models', *Quarterly Journal of Economics*, vol. 110, pp. 495–525.

Jones, C. (1995b). 'R&D based models of economic growth', *Journal of Political Economy*, vol. 103(4), pp. 759–83.

Jones, C. (1999). 'Growth: with or without scale effects', *American Economic Review Papers and Proceedings*, vol. 89(2), pp. 139–44.

Kortum, S. (1993). 'Equilibrium R&D and the decline in the patent-R&D ratio', *American Economic Review: Papers and Proceedings*, vol. 83(2), pp. 450–7.

Kortum, S. (1997). 'A model of research, patenting and productivity growth', *Econometrica*, vol. 65(6), pp. 1389–419.

Malthus, T. R. (1986 [1798]). *An Essay on the Principle of Population*, London: W.Pickering.

Mokyr, J. (1990). *The Lever of Riches: Technological Creativity and Economic Progress*, Oxford: Oxford University Press.

Mortensen, D. T. and Pissarides, C. (1998). 'Technological progress, job creation, and job destruction', *Review of Economic Dynamics*, vol. 1(4), pp. 733–53.

Murphy, K., Shleifer, A. and Vishny, R. (1991). 'The allocation of talent: implications for growth', *Quarterly Journal of Economics*, vol. 56, pp. 503–30.

Pissarides, C. A. (1990). *Equilibrium Unemployment Theory*, Oxford: Basil Blackwell.

Ricardo, D. (1951 [1817]). *On the Principles of Political Economy and Taxation*, Cambridge: Cambridge University Press.

Romer, P. (1990). 'Endogenous technological change', *Journal of Political Economy*, vol. 98(5), pp. 71–102.

Schumpeter, J. A. (1939). *Business Cycles: a Theoretical, Historical and Statistical Analysis of the Capitalist Process*, New York: McGraw-Hill.

Schumpeter, J. A. (1943). 'Capitalism in the postwar world', in (S. E. Harris, ed.), *Postwar Economic Problems*, New York: McGraw-Hill, pp. 113–26.

Schumpeter, J. A. (1946). 'Capitalism', in *Encyclopaedia Britannica*, vol. IV, Encyclopaedia Britannica Inc., pp. 801–7.

Schumpeter, J. A. (1947). 'The creative response in economic history', *Journal of Economic History*, vol. 7 (November), pp. 149–59.

Schumpeter, J. A. (1949). 'Economic theory and entrepreneurial history', in (Research Center in Entrepreneurial History, Harvard University) *Change and the Entrepreneur*, Cambridge, MA: Harvard University Press, pp. 63–84.

Tirole, J. (1988). *The Theory of Industrial Organization*, Cambridge, MA: MIT Press.

Young, A. (1998). 'Growth without scale effects', *Journal of Political Economy*, vol. 106(1), pp. 41–63.

[14]

Journal of Economic Growth, 4: 213—232 (June 1999)
© 1999 Kluwer Academic Publishers, Boston.

Entrepreneurs, Professionals, and Growth

MURAT F. IYIGUN

Board of Governors of the Federal Reserve System

ANN L. OWEN

Hamilton College

We examine the implications for growth and development of the existence of two types of human capital: entrepreneurial and professional. Entrepreneurs accumulate human capital through a work-experience intensive process, whereas professionals' human capital accumulation is education-intensive. Moreover, the return to entrepreneurship is uncertain. We show how skill-biased technological progress leads to changes in the composition of aggregate human capital; as technology improves, individuals devote less time to the accumulation of human capital through work experience and more to the accumulation of human capital through professional training. Thus, our model explains why entrepreneurs play a relatively more important role in intermediate-income countries and professionals are relatively more abundant in richer economies. It also shows that those countries that initially have too little of either entrepreneurial or professional human capital may end up in a development trap.

Keywords: education, work experience, self-employment, growth

JEL classification: J24, O11, O40

1. Introduction

Both entrepreneurial and professional skills are important components of an economy's human capital stock, but they influence the level of technology and aggregate production in potentially different ways. Entrepreneurial skills generate new ideas, innovations, and products, while professional skills help to facilitate economic transactions. Both skills are important for the process of development. Yet while professional and entrepreneurial skills can complement each other in aggregate production, they can compete for an individual's time in their accumulation. This article explores the implications for growth of the existence of more than one type of human capital, showing how the choice between entrepreneurship and professional employment evolves as an economy develops and examining how individuals' decisions to accumulate different types of human capital affect the economy's long-run potential.

There are two main results. First, entrepreneurial human capital plays a relatively more important role in intermediate income countries, whereas professional human capital is relatively more important in richer economies. We demonstrate that as an economy develops, individuals choose to invest more time accumulating professional skills through schooling than accumulating entrepreneurial human capital. The resulting change in the relative stocks of entrepreneurial and professional human capital is a direct consequence of our assumption that providing professional services is a relatively safe activity and providing entrepreneurial skills is risky. As per capita income grows and the payoff to being a professional increases, individuals are less willing to gamble on entrepreneurial ventures. This phenomenon occurs even though the expected value of entrepreneurship rises with per capita income. While entrepreneurs in a more developed economy face a clearly better lottery than entrepreneurs in a less developed economy, the price of the lottery ticket—foregone professional earnings—is higher in the developed economy, making individuals less willing to take the bet. Second, we find that, in an economy where both entrepreneurial and professional human capital affect the future level of technology, the initial stocks of both types of human capital are important for the process of development.

Our approach is related to that of Banerjee and Newman (1993), who show how the distribution of wealth and credit market imperfections influence occupational choice. In their model, there is a fixed cost to becoming an entrepreneur and the distribution of wealth determines the percent of the population that undertakes such a venture.[1] We take a slightly different view on the defining characteristic of entrepreneurship, choosing to focus on the element of risk inherent in the concept rather than the financial requirements. Thus, while both models generate the result that high-income economies will have more employer-employee relationships, our model focuses particularly on how the incentives to accumulate professional and entrepreneurial human capital change as an economy grows. Specifically, while Banerjee and Newman (1993) demonstrate that economic development may foster entrepreneurial investment, our model shows that, as economies develop, the increasing relative return to professional employment has an offsetting negative effect on resources devoted to entrepreneurship relative to that devoted to professional activities. Our use of more than one type of human capital also ties into recent work such as Galor and Tsiddon (1997), who study the interaction between technological progress and the return to different dimensions of skills (i.e., specific human capital and ability).

Another idea that has been discussed in recent literature that is relevant to our article is that the risk associated with economic activity evolves with development. Acemoglu and Zilibotti (1997) show that when there are indivisible investment projects, in the early stages of development, diversification is not possible. As wealth accumulates, however, diversification becomes possible, and investment risk is reduced. In the same vein, Levine and Zervos (1998) show that stock market liquidity and banking development are associated with higher growth rates, suggesting that the more developed financial markets associated with higher levels of income reduce the disincentive for investment by reducing liquidity risk. We also examine investment risk in our model. However, there is an important distinction: we look at the risk of human capital investment and not physical capital investment. In our model, as per capita income increases, the variability of payoffs to the uncertain activity (entrepreneurship) increases, raising the risk of some kinds of human capital investment. In response to the increased variability of payoffs to entrepreneurial skills and the increase in the certain payoff to professionalism, individuals in the more developed economies reallocate their time toward the safer activity. Thus, although development is associated with increased risk for some types of human capital investment, it also provides individuals with better opportunities to reduce their investment in risky activities.

In what follows, we present a two-period overlapping-generations model in which aggregate human capital is the sum of both professional and entrepreneurial human capital. Individuals of differing abilities choose to accumulate human capital when their wages as human capital providers would be greater than their wages as laborers. They accumulate professional human capital by investing time in schooling and entrepreneurial human capital by investing time working as an entrepreneur. A key difference between the two types of human capital is that the reward paid to professional human capital is certain but the payoff to entrepreneurial human capital is not.

The level of technology employed by any one generation of workers is determined by the level of professional and entrepreneurial human capital of the previous generation. Thus, in an environment where technological change is skill-biased, the compensation to professional human capital and the expected compensation to entrepreneurial human capital increase as the stock of professional and entrepreneurial skills grow. For fixed factor prices, this raises the incentive to become a human capital provider, lowers the threshold level of ability above which individuals accumulate skills, and increases the number of individuals who invest in human capital. However, when individuals are compensated for their manual labor as well as their aggregate human capital input, skill-biased technological change induces more variability in the entrepreneurial payoff. Thus, as the return to the safe activity increases and the payoffs to the risky activity become more variable, human capital accumulators devote more time to schooling and less time to gaining entrepreneurial experience. In essence, individuals in high-income economies with higher wages to professionals have more to lose by gambling on an entrepreneurial venture. In contrast, individuals in low-income countries face less variable payoffs to entrepreneurship and a lower return to their investment in professional skills and are therefore more willing to invest in entrepreneurial skills.

In our model, entrepreneurial activities are more risky than professional activities. Entrepreneurial skills are accumulated through a more work-experience-intensive process and, as a result, are distinct from those accumulated through an education-intensive process. These unique skills contribute to the development or adoption of the economywide technology in a way that is potentially different from skills accumulated through education. While some entrepreneurial skills may be employed in the R&D sector, it is not necessary for all of them to be for the average level of entrepreneurial skills to influence the level of technology. Entrepreneurs may also indirectly influence the level of technology by starting new businesses that put competitive pressures on existing businesses to innovate. Thus, even if an entrepreneurial venture serves only to increase the variety of goods produced and does not directly enhance current technology, its existence spurs others to invent. At the same time, professionals are also capable of creating improvements in the level of technology. Some professionals may be directly employed with the invention of new technology (such as an engineer who works for a large company) or may aid with the administration of that new technology (such as a corporate lawyer who helps a company obtain patents for its inventions). In either case, we assume that because professional skills are accumulated in a different way than entrepreneurial skills, the skills of the professional and the skills of the entrepreneur are different and may contribute in a different way to the level of technology.

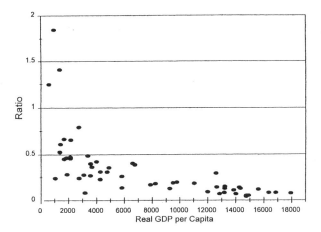

Figure 1. Real GDP per capita and the employers and self-employed to employees ratio (excluding agricultural workers). Data source: Summers and Heston (1991); *Mark 5.6*; International Labour Office (1993). Note: One observation per country is reported within the period 1986 to 1992.

If the way professional and entrepreneurial human capital are combined in output production is different from the way the two types of human capital are combined to determine the level of technology, then time devoted to schooling will be inefficient. In other words, if developing the technology utilizes the two types of human capital in a different way than implementing the technology, individuals, whose compensation is based on their contribution to output production, will not choose the socially optimal combination of schooling and entrepreneurial investment. In particular, if entrepreneurial ventures are more important in determining the level of technology and less important in its utilization, then the steady-state level of education will be too high, and per capita income would be higher with more entrepreneurial skills and fewer professional skills.[2]

These results are developed in the following: Section 2 presents some supporting empirical evidence, Section 3 describes the basic model, Section 4 discusses its dynamic behavior, and Section 5 concludes.

2. Empirical Evidence

This article is motivated, in part, by a stylized fact: in economies with higher per capita income, fewer individuals are employers compared to the number of individuals who work for others (see Figure 1).[3] Moreover, the fraction of workers classified in managerial and professional occupations increases with per capita income (see Figure 2).[4] This pattern of occupational change is also evident when examining individual countries over time; Bregger (1996) shows that the percentage of self-employed workers in nonagricultural industries steadily decreased in the United States from 12 percent in 1948 to 7.5 percent in 1994.

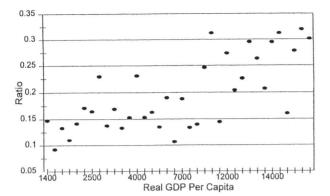

Figure 2. Real GDP per capita and managers and professionals as a share of nonagricultural workers. Data source: Summers and Heston (1991); *Mark 5.6*; International Labour Office (1993). Note: One observation per country is reported for either 1989 or 1990.

Table 1. Average age, education, and experience of self-employed and salaried workers.

	Respondent's Occupational Choice	
	Self-Employed	Salaried
Age	47.5	40.8
Education	13.8	13.5
Job tenure	13.2	8.2

Data source: Federal Reserve (1995).
Note: All variables measured in years. Individuals not working at the time of the survey are excluded from the sample.

Other empirical regularities also shed light on how occupational choice and the process of human capital accumulation might be related. First, the channels of human capital accumulation for entrepreneurs are more work-experience intensive than for wage and salary workers. Summary statistics from the *1995 Survey of Consumer Finances* show that self-employed workers are on average older and have longer job tenures than those who work for others, suggesting that experience gained with age may be an important component of entrepreneurial human capital (see Table 1).[5] These results are supported by Evans and Leighton (1989) and Evans and Jovanovich (1989), who show that the probability of being self-employed increases with labor-market experience but not with education.[6]

The second empirical observation that bears on our analysis is that both entrepreneurs and professionals contribute to the process of technological change. They contribute directly by being the inventors of new technology: the U.S. patent office reports that 22 percent of the patents for inventions granted over the period 1963 to 1984 were awarded to independent inventors and 75 percent were awarded to organizations.[7] In addition, people in both types of occupations contribute indirectly to the development of new technology. Entrepreneurs start new businesses that help to increase competitive pressures on existing businesses to innovate, and professionals help to administer an economic system that fosters invention.

Finally, education and work experience do not seem to be perfect substitutes in the accumulation of human capital. Evans and Leighton (1989) show that the probability of being an entrepreneur depends positively on previous business experience but not on education, suggesting that work experience may be an avenue of human capital accumulation particularly suited for the self-employed. Anecdotal evidence of entrepreneurs who did not receive degrees from traditional four-year college help this claim ring true.[8]

3. The Model

3.1. Production

Consider a small open company that operates in a perfectly competitive world in which economic activity extends over an infinite discrete time. The output of the economy Y_t is a single homogeneous good that can be produced by two technologies—one that uses physical capital K_t and efficiency units of skilled labor (or human capital) H_t and another that uses an unskilled labor aggregate L_t only. The output produced at time t in the skilled sector Y_t^h and the unskilled sector Y_t^l are given by

$$Y_t^h = F(K_t, \lambda_t H_t), \quad \text{and} \quad Y_t^l = \phi L_t, \quad \phi > 0; \qquad Y_t = Y_t^h + Y_t^l, \tag{1}$$

where F is a concave production function with constant returns to scale (CRS), and the endogenously determined technology level, denoted by λ_t, complements human capital H_t. The latter indicates that technological change in this economy is skill-biased.[9]

We assume that markets are competitive, which implies that factor inputs earn their marginal products:

$$r_t = F_K(K_t, \lambda_t H_t), \quad w_t^h = \lambda_t F_{\lambda H}(K_t, \lambda_t H_t), \quad \text{and} \quad w^l = \phi, \tag{2}$$

where r_t is the rental rate of physical capital, and w_t^h, w^l, respectively, denote the returns to human capital and unskilled labor.

Suppose that the world interest rate is constant at $\bar{r}$. Since the small open economy permits unrestricted physical capital mobility, its interest rate is constant at $\bar{r}$ as well. Given that F exhibits CRS, this implies that the ratio $K_t/\lambda_t H_t$ as well as $F_{\lambda H}(K_t, \lambda_t H_t)$ are also constant. Thus, with $F_{\lambda H}(K_t, \lambda_t H_t)$ normalized to one, factor payments are given by the following:

$$r_t = \bar{r} = F_K(K_t, \lambda_t H_t) \quad \Rightarrow \quad F_{\lambda H}(K_t, \lambda_t H_t) = \bar{w} \equiv 1 \quad \Rightarrow \quad w_t^h = \lambda_t. \tag{3}$$

3.2. *Individuals*

Individuals, who live for two periods in overlapping generations, are endowed with one unit of time in every period. At birth, they are also endowed with an innate mental ability level a_i, which we assume to be drawn from a uniform distribution. That is,

$$\int_{\underline{a}}^{\bar{a}} \frac{1}{\bar{a} - \underline{a}} da = 1, \tag{4}$$

where $\bar{a}$, $\underline{a}$ respectively denote the upper and lower bounds of the support of the ability distribution. Individuals' innate mental ability levels a_i augment their human capital and labor input.

In the first period, individuals decide whether they will be labor or human capital suppliers during their lifetime. If they choose to become labor providers, they devote all of their time endowment in the first and second periods to work, saving their first-period income in the world capital market. If they choose to become human capital suppliers, they also decide what fraction of their time in the first period to devote to accumulating professional human capital through education and to acquiring entrepreneurial human capital by working in a business venture. In the second period, individuals supply their total human capital and labor endowment and they consume. The size of the population is normalized to one, and there is no population growth.

Regardless of individuals' choice of occupation, we assume that their innate abilities are unobservable without any schooling or work experience. More specifically, because employers cannot observe the ability of young workers, they pay these workers an unskilled wage that is proportional to the expected innate ability level of unskilled labor in that period. In contrast, employers pay old unskilled workers a wage that is dependent on their specific innate ability, as old workers' experience in the previous period reveals their type.[10] Therefore, individual i's income from being a lifetime labor provider in both periods is given by

$$(I^i)^u = \begin{cases} w^l \alpha_t & \text{when young,} \\ w^l a_i & \text{when old,} \end{cases} \tag{5}$$

where α_t denotes the expected ability of unskilled workers in period t. Note that when all individuals choose to become labor providers in any given period t, the expected ability of unskilled workers α_t will equal $\frac{\bar{a} + \underline{a}}{2} \equiv 1$.

For those individuals who choose to become human capital providers, skills require time to develop, and thus, these individuals earn no income when they are young. We assume that the time devoted to education in the first period s_t^i increases an individual's stock of professional capital in the second period p_{t+1}^i, whereas time devoted to work x_t^i increases his entrepreneurial capital e_{t+1}^i:

$$e_{t+1}^i = a_i f(x_t^i), \tag{6}$$

and

$$p_{t+1}^i = a_i f(s_t^i), \tag{7}$$

where $x_t^i + s_t^i \leq 1$, the standard Inada conditions hold, and $\forall\, x_t^i, s_t^i \geq 0$, $f' > 0$, $f'' < 0$. One can think of the initial time devoted to augment entrepreneurial human capital as a startup cost for entrepreneurial ventures.

As the above specification implies, we have chosen to allow a single individual to supply both entrepreneurial and professional human capital even though individuals tend to be classified empirically as either entrepreneurs or professionals. We believe this formulation to be quite plausible to the extent that performing any job requires some combination of each type of human capital and markets reward each of those potentially differently. That noted, one can reconcile the results of our model with the empirical classification of occupations by interpreting the percentage of time human capital providers allocate to each activity as the percent of the skilled labor force involved in each occupation. More realistically, if we incorporated another dimension of ability into our model so that some individuals had a comparative advantage in supplying entrepreneurial human capital while others had a comparative advantage in supplying professional human capital, we could classify individuals as either entrepreneurs or professionals based on how they accumulated the majority of their human capital.

We assume that there is uncertainty in the return to entrepreneurial ventures but that the return to education (which generates professional human capital in the following period) is not subject to any uncertainty. Specifically, individual i's income from becoming an entrepreneur, $(I_{t+1}^i)^e$, is

$$(I_{t+1}^i)^e = \begin{cases} w_{t+1}^h e_{t+1}^i = \lambda_{t+1} e_{t+1}^i & \text{with probability } q \\ 0 & \text{with probability } 1-q, \end{cases} \tag{8}$$

and his income from professional activities $(I_{t+1}^i)^p$ is

$$(I_{t+1}^i)^p = w_{t+1}^h p_{t+1}^i = \lambda_{t+1} p_{t+1}^i, \tag{9}$$

where $0 < q \leq 1$. In equation (8), the probabilities q and $1-q$ are the odds of success and failure faced by each entrepreneur. In aggregate, given a sufficiently large number of entrepreneurs, q percent will succeed and $1-q$ percent will fail.

Finally, we assume that the level of technology in period $t+1$, λ_{t+1}, is determined by the average levels of the entrepreneurial and professional human capital in the previous period.[11] Specifically,

$$\lambda_{t+1} = \lambda(e_t, p_t), \tag{10}$$

where $\frac{\partial \lambda_{t+1}}{\partial e_t}$, $\frac{\partial \lambda_{t+1}}{\partial p_t} > 0$, $\frac{\partial^2 \lambda_{t+1}}{\partial e_t^2}$, $\frac{\partial^2 \lambda_{t+1}}{\partial p_t^2} < 0$ and $\frac{\partial^2 \lambda_{t+1}}{\partial e_t \partial p_t}$, $\frac{\partial^2 \lambda_{t+1}}{\partial p_t \partial e_t} > 0$.

Individuals maximize expected utility from consumption in the second period and their rate of time preference is zero. The expected utility of individual i of generation t takes the following specific form:

$$E\left[u(c_{t+1}^i) \mid t\right] = q \ln(c_{t+1,q}^i) + (1-q) \ln(c_{t+1,1-q}^i), \tag{11}$$

where $c_{t+1,q}^i$ and $c_{t+1,1-q}^i$, respectively, denote the consumption of individual i in the good and bad states.[12]

In addition to $s_t^i + x_t^i \leq 1$, individual i is subject to the budget constraint below:

$$
I_{t+1}^i = \begin{cases} [(1+\bar{r})\alpha_t + a_i]\phi & \text{if } i \text{ is a labor provider} \\ \phi a_i + (I_{t+1}^i)^e + (I_{t+1}^i)^p & \text{if } i \text{ is a human capital provider,} \end{cases} \tag{12}
$$

where $(I_{t+1}^i)^e$ and $(I_{t+1}^i)^p$ are given by equations (8) and (9).[13]

Given the problem specified above, there exists a threshold innate ability level for every period t—that, henceforth we will denote by $\tilde{a}_t$—below which individual i will choose to be a labor supplier. Combining equations (6) to (9), (11), and (12), we can show that $\tilde{a}_t$ satisfies the following equality:

$$
q \ln \{\phi\tilde{a}_t + \lambda_{t+1}\tilde{a}_t[f(s_t^i) + f(1 - s_t^i)]\} + \{(1-q)\ln\{\phi\tilde{a}_t + \lambda_{t+1}\tilde{a}_t f(s_t^i)\}\}
$$
$$
= \ln\{[(1+\bar{r})\alpha_t + \tilde{a}_t]\phi\}. \tag{13}
$$

If individual i's innate mental ability level is such that $a_i > \tilde{a}_t$, individual i—while young—chooses to accumulate human capital instead of supplying labor. In that case, the optimal amount of time allocated to education by the individual s_t^i satisfies

$$
\frac{q}{1-q} = -\frac{\phi + \lambda_{t+1}[f(s_t^i) + f(1 - s_t^i)]}{\phi + \lambda_{t+1}f(s_t^i)} \frac{f'(s_t^i)}{f'(s_t^i) - f'(1 - s_t^i)}. \tag{14}
$$

Note that the first-order condition above implies that the amount of time individual i devotes to schooling is independent of his innate ability level a_i. Put differently, $s_t^i = s_t \; \forall i$ such that $a_i > \tilde{a}_t$.

Equations (13) and (14) lead to the propositions below:

Proposition 1: $\forall t \geq 0$ *such that $\tilde{a}_t < \bar{a}$, the threshold innate ability level in period t, $\tilde{a}_t$, is a decreasing function of average levels of entrepreneurial and professional human capital in the same period, e_t and p_t. Namely,*

$$
\frac{\partial \tilde{a}_t}{\partial e_t}; \frac{\partial \tilde{a}_t}{\partial p_t} < 0. \tag{15}
$$

Proof: Using equation (13) and the implicit function theorem, it is straightforward to show

$$
\frac{\partial \tilde{a}_t}{\partial e_t} = -\frac{\tilde{a}_t(3\tilde{a}_t + \underline{a})}{\underline{a}} \left[\frac{q[f(s_t) + f(1 - s_t)]}{\phi + \lambda_{t+1}[f(s_t) + f(1 - s_t)]} + \frac{(1-q)f(s_t)}{\phi + \lambda_{t+1}f(s_t)} \right] \frac{\partial \lambda_{t+1}}{\partial e_t}
$$
$$
< 0, \tag{16}
$$

and

$$
\frac{\partial \tilde{a}_t}{\partial p_t} = -\frac{\tilde{a}_t(3\tilde{a}_t + \underline{a})}{\underline{a}} \left[\frac{q[f(s_t) + f(1 - s_t)]}{\phi + \lambda_{t+1}[f(s_t) + f(1 - s_t)]} + \frac{(1-q)f(s_t)}{\phi + \lambda_{t+1}f(s_t)} \right] \frac{\partial \lambda_{t+1}}{\partial p_t}
$$
$$
< 0. \tag{17}
$$

■

The above proposition shows that, in the early stages of development when the returns to both types of human capital input are relatively small, only those with the highest ability levels choose to supply human capital, whereas a majority of the population chooses to supply labor. As improvements in technology raise the relative return to human capital, however, a larger fraction of the population chooses to accumulate human capital while young by allocating time to education and working as entrepreneurs.[14]

Proposition 2: *(i)* $\forall q$, $0 < q \leq 1$, and $\forall t \geq 0$ such that $\tilde{a}_t < \bar{a}$, the optimal amount of time individual i chooses to devote to education s_t is such that $s_t \geq \frac{1}{2}$. *(ii)* $\forall q$, $0 < q < 1$, and $\forall t \geq 0$ such that $\tilde{a}_t < \bar{a}$, the amount of time individual i chooses to devote to education in period t, s_t, is an increasing function of average levels of entrepreneurial and professional human capital in the same period, e_t and p_t. Namely,

$$\frac{\partial s_t}{\partial e_t}, \quad \frac{\partial s_t}{\partial p_t} \quad > 0. \tag{18}$$

Proof: (i) Given that the lhs and the first term on the rhs of equation (14) are positive, we establish that the term $\frac{f'(s_t)}{f'(s_t)-f'(1-s_t)}$ on the rhs needs to be nonpositive. Thus, $f'(s_t) - f'(1 - s_t) \leq 0 \Leftrightarrow s_t \geq \frac{1}{2} \ \forall i$ such that $a_i > \tilde{a}_t$.

(ii) Using the first-order condition given by (14) and invoking—once again—the implicit function theorem, we get

$$\frac{\partial s_t}{\partial e_t} = -\frac{1}{\eta} \frac{\phi f(1-s_t) f'(s_t)}{\phi + \lambda_{t+1} f(s_t)} \frac{\partial \lambda_{t+1}}{\partial e_t} > 0, \tag{19}$$

where

$$\eta = \left\{ \begin{array}{c} -\frac{\phi\lambda_{t+1}f'(s_t)f'(1-s_t)+\lambda_{t+1}^2 f(s_t)f'(1-s_t)+\lambda_{t+1}^2 f(1-s_t)f'(s_t)}{\phi+\lambda_{t+1}f(s_t)} \\ -\{\phi + \lambda_{t+1}[f(s_t) + f(1-s_t)]\}\frac{f''(s_t)f'(1-s_t)+f''(1-s_t)f'(s_t)}{f'(s_t)-f'(1-s_t)} \end{array} \right\} < 0.$$

$\frac{\partial s_t}{\partial p_t}$ is equal to an expression almost identical to (19), where $\frac{\partial \lambda_{t+1}}{\partial e_t}$ is replaced by $\frac{\partial \lambda_{t+1}}{\partial p_t}$. ∎

Proposition 2 shows how increases in the human capital stock, which raise the level of technology and per capita income, affect the accumulation of the two different types of human capital. Specifically, it demonstrates that technological change, by inducing human capital suppliers to devote more time to schooling, leads to a shift away from entrepreneurial human capital accumulation.[15] The reason is that technological change not only raises the relative return to human capital, but it also increases the *risk* of time invested in entrepreneurial human capital accumulation in the sense that the discrepancy between the payoffs in the good and bad states increases as the economy develops.[16] As a result, those individuals who find it optimal to become human capital suppliers choose to stay in school longer and develop a higher ratio of professional to entrepreneurial skills. As will be seen in the next section, the change in the ratio of professional to entrepreneurial skills does not necessarily imply a reduction in aggregate entrepreneurial skills because the aggregate value is also affected by decreases in $\tilde{a}_t$ which cause more individuals to become human capital providers.

One can see from equation (14) that, besides the inherent risk in the payoff to entrepreneurial skills, there are two key elements in generating the dynamics discussed above. First, individuals get paid for their raw labor ($\phi \neq 0$) even when they are human capital providers. Second, technological progress is skill-biased. The implications of both of these assumptions, taken together, is that the variability of payoffs in the good and bad states increases with development. If either human capital providers were not compensated for their raw labor ($\phi = 0$) or if the payment to raw labor increased proportionally with λ_{t+1} (for example, the return to raw labor was equal to $\phi\lambda_{t+1}$), then λ_{t+1} would drop out of the first-order condition and individuals would not reallocate their time away from investing in entrepreneurial skills. When all individuals get paid for their raw labor ($\phi \neq 0$), however, skill-biased technological change induces higher variability in the payoffs in the good and bad states. Thus, as an optimal response to this increased variability of payoffs, individuals increase their level of schooling s_t.

4. The Evolution of the Economy

Given (13) and the specification of the technology parameter λ_{t+1} in (10), we identify that there exists a minimum level of technology below which all individuals choose to work as labor and no one allocates time to activities that foster human capital accumulation. Let

$$\mu = \left\{ (e_t, p_t) \left| \begin{array}{l} q\ln\{\phi\bar{a} + \lambda_{t+1}\bar{a}[f(s_t) + f(1 - s_t)]\} \\ + (1 - q)\ln\{\phi\bar{a} + \lambda_{t+1}\bar{a}f(s_t)]\} \le \ln((1 - \bar{r} + \bar{a})\phi) \end{array} \right. \right\}. \quad (20)$$

Thus, when $(e_t, p_t) \in \mu$, $\bar{a} \le \tilde{a}_t$, not even the highest-ability individuals choose to devote time to education or work experience and $e_{t+1} = p_{t+1} = 0$.

In contrast, for all pairs of entrepreneurial and professional human capital in any given period t, $(e_t, p_t) \notin \mu$, the dynamical system is characterized by the two equations that govern the evolution of entrepreneurial and professional human capital stocks. Namely,

$$e_{t+1} = \begin{cases} \int_{\tilde{a}_t}^{\bar{a}} \frac{1}{\bar{a}-\underline{a}} f(x_t^i) da_i = \frac{\bar{a}-\tilde{a}_t}{\bar{a}-\underline{a}} f(x_t) = \frac{\bar{a}-\tilde{a}_t}{\bar{a}-\underline{a}} f(1 - s_t) & \text{when } \bar{a} > \tilde{a}_t > \underline{a} \\ f(1 - s_t) & \text{when } \tilde{a}_t \le \underline{a} \end{cases}$$

$$p_{t+1} = \begin{cases} \int_{\tilde{a}_t}^{\bar{a}} \frac{1}{\bar{a}-\underline{a}} f(s_t^i) da_i = \frac{\bar{a}-\tilde{a}_t}{\bar{a}-\underline{a}} f(s_t) & \text{when } \bar{a} > \tilde{a}_t > \underline{a} \\ f(s_t) & \text{when } \tilde{a}_t \le \underline{a}. \end{cases} \quad (21)$$

Given that both $\tilde{a}_t$ and s_t are functions of the technology level in period $t + 1$, λ_{t+1}, which in turn is a function of the entrepreneurial and professional human capital in the previous period, e_t and p_t,

$$e_{t+1} = \Gamma(e_t, p_t) \quad \text{and} \quad p_{t+1} = \psi(e_t, p_t). \quad (22)$$

In this economy, a steady-state is characterized by $(\bar{e}, \bar{p})$ such that, $\forall t \ge T$, $\bar{e} = \Gamma(\bar{e}, \bar{p})$ and $\bar{p} = \Psi(\bar{e}, \bar{p})$.

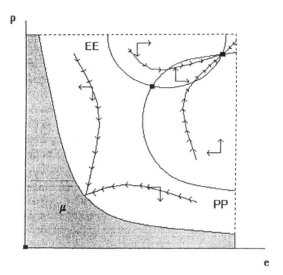

Figure 3. Entrepreneurial and professional human capital accumulation dynamics.

Proposition 3: $\forall q,\ \tilde{q} \le q \le 1$ *and* $(e_0, p_0) \notin \mu,\ \exists$ *a nontrivial, stable, steady-state equilibrium for the dynamical system specified in (22) if*

(i) the technology of human capital production f is sufficiently productive,

(ii) ϕ is sufficiently small.

Proof: See Appendix for the derivation of the dynamical system.

The reason for the first condition in Proposition 3 is intuitive: the technology of human capital production must be effective enough to induce individuals to accumulate entrepreneurial and professional skills. The reason for the second condition is intuitive as well: because ϕ is the opportunity cost of providing human capital, when it is too large, individuals will not invest in either professional or entrepreneurial skills, and a nontrivial steady state will not exist.

Figure 3 presents the phase diagram of the dynamical system. As shown, only when the initial stocks of entrepreneurial *and* professional human capital, $(e_0, p_0) \notin \mu$, are sufficiently large, does the system converge to a nontrivial, stable steady-state, $(\bar{e}, \bar{p}) \gg 0$. In that case, the production technology used in the skilled sector continually improves along with increases in fraction of individuals who become human capital providers. Until the system reaches its steady-state, such individuals allocate an increasing share of their time to formal education in order to accumulate relatively more professional human capital. However, when $(e_0, p_0) \ll (\bar{e}, \bar{p})$, the stock of entrepreneurial human capital may still increase during some part of the transition to the steady-state despite the fact that human capital providers allocate a decreasing fraction of their time to entrepreneurial activities during the transition. The reason is that, throughout the transition, more individuals are choosing to become human capital providers instead of remaining unskilled. Otherwise, if the initial stocks of entrepreneurial *and* professional human capital, (e_0, p_0), are not sufficiently large, then the initial level of technology is not sophisticated enough to guarantee that an increasing fraction of individuals become human capital providers. As a result, fewer and fewer individuals allocate their time to augmenting their human capital, and the system converges to a steady-state in which production is carried out solely in the unskilled sector.

There are several important implications of the dynamics of our model. First, entrepreneurial human capital plays a relatively (but not absolutely) more important role in intermediate income countries, whereas professional human capital is relatively (and absolutely) more abundant in richer economies. For those countries that start off with a sufficiently high combination of entrepreneurs and professionals, an increasing fraction of the population chooses to invest in both skills during the transition to the steady state. Moreover, those who choose to do so devote an increasing amount of time to the accumulation of professional human capital and a decreasing amount of time to entrepreneurial human capital. The reason, as we have stated earlier, is that as per capita income grows and the payoff to being a professional increases, individuals are less willing to gamble on enterpreneurial ventures. Of course, higher probabilities of entrepreneurial success (higher values of q) generate higher stocks of entrepreneurial skills.

The key mechanism that generates the decline in the relative importance of entrepreneurial skills as an economy grows is that the opportunity cost of being self-employed increases faster than its expected return. While the major conclusions of our model would hold if either the probability of a successful venture or the payoff to a failed entrepreneur increased as an economy develops, these increases must not be too large. If they are too large, then the expected benefit of self-employment would increase more than its opportunity cost, and individuals would allocate more time to it as per capita income grows.

A second important implication of the dynamics of our model is that the initial stock of *both* entrepreneurial and professional human capital are important for the process of development. Notably, those countries that start off with too little entrepreneurial or professional human capital end up in a development trap in which production is carried out in the unskilled sector only and there is no human capital investment of any type. This result obtains because both entrepreneurial and professional human capital play a role in the determination of the level of technology. Therefore, when either type of human capital is relatively small initially, the level of technology and the return to human capital investment relative to the labor input are also small. As a result, an increasing fraction of individuals choose to become labor suppliers instead of becoming human capital providers.[17]

A relevant example of the importance of this second point may be found in the former east-bloc countries. As some have pointed out (e.g., Overland and Spagat, 1996), these economies have a highly educated labor force and may be primed for an economic takeoff. However, our model highlights the possibility that these economies, if short on entrepreneurs, may be further away from the high-income steady state than education levels alone would indicate. In fact, some of them may even be unable to reach it.

A third implication of our model is that because the social marginal returns to work and education may differ from the private marginal returns, it is likely that even the steady state with positive human capital investment is inefficient. However, because in our model the alternative to education is also a productive activity, the source of the inefficiency is not standard: there may be too much investment in education in the steady state. Specifically, when entrepreneurs are more important in determining the level of technology than professionals, the high-income steady state may be characterized by overinvestment in education. Similarly, when professional human capital has greater influence on the technology in use, the high-income steady state has too little education. The key feature of the model that produces these unique inefficiencies is that entrepreneurial and professional human capital may be combined in different ways in production and in the formation of the technology of production. Therefore, it is important to note that inefficiencies may result not from too much human capital but from a misallocation of the existing human capital stock between professional and entrepreneurial skills. In fact, a more socially efficient ratio of professionals to entrepreneurs will raise the steady-state level of technology and increase the wages paid to human capital providers and the economy's human capital stock.

5. Conclusion

The model we present above demonstrates why both entrepreneurial and professional skills are important for development. It shows that the private incentives to accumulate entrepreneurial relative to professional skills are greater in intermediate income countries and that—due to the inherent riskiness of entrepreneurial ventures—those incentives decline relative to the incentives to become a professional as countries grow richer. Nonetheless, the initial stock of *both* types of human capital matter because together they determine the return to human capital relative to raw labor. Thus, the initial conditions are important in determining whether countries converge to an equilibrium in which, for a larger fraction of the population, investing time in human capital accumulation will be more profitable relative to labor provision.

Our model also demonstrates that when more than one type of human capital exists, individuals may not allocate their time in a socially efficient way to the accumulation of these different skills. More generally, our results indicate that a thorough macroeconomic investigation of all channels of human capital accumulation is necessary to formulate the appropriate tests of the role of human capital in development and to effectively design and implement the most successful policies. This is a fruitful area for further research.

Appendix

Proof of Proposition 3:   We prove this proposition in three steps:

- *Step 1:* We assume that the *EE* and *PP* loci do not lie within μ (i.e., $\tilde{a}_t < \bar{a} \, \forall \, t$ and equation (20) holds) and demonstrate that they have the form shown in Figure 3.

- *Step 2:* We then show that when $q = 1$, the *EE* and *PP* loci intersect when $f(\frac{1}{2})$ is large enough. We relax the assumption that the entire *EE* and *PP* loci derived in step 1 lie outside of μ, but show that the intersection of the two loci is still outside of μ.

- *Step 3:* Finally, we show that decreases in q shift the *EE* and *PP* loci continuously, guaranteeing that the *EE* and *PP* loci intersect for $\forall q, \tilde{q} \leq q \leq 1$.

Step 1 Let

$$EE = \{(e_t, p_t) \mid e_{t+1} - e_t = \Delta e = 0\} \tag{23}$$

and

$$PP = \{(e_t, p_t) \mid p_{t+1} - p_t = \Delta p = 0\}. \tag{24}$$

Assume that $\tilde{a}_t < \bar{a} \; \forall \; t$. Then, using the implicit function theorem, we are able to show that

$$\left.\frac{\partial p_t}{\partial e_t}\right|_{EE} = -\frac{\Gamma_e - 1}{\Gamma_p} = -\frac{\left(\frac{\bar{a}-\tilde{a}_t}{\bar{a}-\underline{a}}\right) f'(1-s_t)\frac{\partial s_t}{\partial e_t} + \left(\frac{1}{\bar{a}-\underline{a}}\right) f(1-s_t)\frac{\partial \tilde{a}_t}{\partial e_t} + 1}{\left(\frac{1}{\bar{a}-\underline{a}}\right) f(1-s_t)\frac{\partial \tilde{a}_t}{\partial p_t} + \left(\frac{\bar{a}-\tilde{a}_t}{\bar{a}-\underline{a}}\right) f'(1-s_t)\frac{\partial s_t}{\partial p_t}}, \tag{25}$$

where Γ_e and Γ_p respectively denote $\frac{\partial \Gamma}{\partial e_t}$ and $\frac{\partial \Gamma}{\partial p_t}$. Similarly,

$$\left.\frac{\partial p_t}{\partial e_t}\right|_{PP} = -\frac{\psi_e}{\psi_p - 1} = -\frac{\left(\frac{\bar{a}-\tilde{a}_t}{\bar{a}-\underline{a}}\right) f'(s_t)\frac{\partial s_t}{\partial e_t} - \left(\frac{1}{\bar{a}-\underline{a}}\right) f(s_t)\frac{\partial \tilde{a}_t}{\partial e_t}}{\left(\frac{\bar{a}-\tilde{a}_t}{\bar{a}-\underline{a}}\right) f'(s_t)\frac{\partial s_t}{\partial p_t} - \left(\frac{1}{\bar{a}-\underline{a}}\right) f(s_t)\frac{\partial \tilde{a}_t}{\partial p_t} - 1} \tag{26}$$

where ψ_e and ψ_p respectively denote $\frac{\partial \psi}{\partial e_t}$ and $\frac{\partial \psi}{\partial p_t}$. By combining (16) and (19) with (25), we find that if ϕ is relatively small then $\frac{\partial s_t}{\partial e_t}$ and $\frac{\partial s_t}{\partial p_t}$ are also small and $\Gamma_e, \Gamma_p \geq 0 \; \forall \; (e_t, p_t) \notin \mu$. Thus,

$$\left.\frac{\partial p_t}{\partial e_t}\right|_{EE} \begin{cases} \leq 0 & \text{when} \quad \Gamma_e \geq 1 \\ > 0 & \text{when} \quad \Gamma_e < 1, \end{cases} \tag{27}$$

and, since $\Psi_e, \Psi_p \geq 0 \; \forall \; (e_t, p_t) \notin \mu$, for all parameter specifications,

$$\left.\frac{\partial p_t}{\partial e_t}\right|_{PP} \begin{cases} \leq 0 & \text{when} \quad \Psi_p \geq 1 \\ > 0 & \text{when} \quad \Psi_p < 1. \end{cases} \tag{28}$$

Let e^* and p^*, respectively, denote (for given values of p_t and e_t) the values of e_t and p_t that set $q \ln\{\lambda_{t+1}\bar{a}[f(s_t) + f(1-s_t)]\} + (1-q) \ln\{\bar{a}[\phi + \lambda_{t+1}f(s_t)]\} = \ln[(1+\bar{r}+\bar{a})\phi]$. Given that $\tilde{a}_t < \bar{a}$, $\frac{\partial^2 \tilde{a}_t}{\partial e_t^2}$, $\frac{\partial^2 \tilde{a}_t}{\partial p_t^2}$ are positive, and $\frac{\partial^2 s_t}{\partial e_t^2}$, $\frac{\partial^2 s_t}{\partial p_t^2}$ are negative—as can be verified from (16) (17), and (19)—we determine that

$$\lim_{e_t \to e^*} \left(\left.\frac{\partial p_t}{\partial e_t}\right|_{EE}\right) < 0 \quad \text{and} \quad \lim_{e_t \to \infty} \left(\left.\frac{\partial p_t}{\partial e_t}\right|_{EE}\right) > 0 \tag{29}$$

and that

$$\lim_{p_t \to p^*} \left(\frac{\partial p_t}{\partial e_t} \bigg|_{PP} \right) < 0 \quad \text{and} \quad \lim_{p_t \to \infty} \left(\frac{\partial p_t}{\partial e_t} \bigg|_{PP} \right) > 0. \tag{30}$$

Moreover, given that s_t and $\tilde{a}_t$ are continuous in e_t and p_t—as implied by Propositions 1 and 2—along the EE locus $\exists \, (e', p') \notin \mu$ such that

$$\frac{\partial p_t}{\partial e_t} \bigg|_{EE} = 0 \tag{31}$$

and that, along the PP locus $\exists \, (e'', p'') \notin \mu$ such that

$$\frac{\partial p_t}{\partial e_t} \bigg|_{PP} = 0. \tag{32}$$

Thus, we establish the general forms of the EE and PP loci on the (e, p) map as shown in Figure 3.

Step 2   Next, we need to demonstrate that, for a nontrivial, stable steady-state to exist, $\exists \, (\bar{e}, \bar{p}) \notin \mu$.

First consider the case in which $q = 1$. When $q = 1$, $s_t = \frac{1}{2}$ and $f(s_t) = f(1 - s_t) = f(\frac{1}{2}) \equiv \tilde{f} \, \forall \, t$. Moreover, $\frac{\partial s_t}{\partial e_t} = \frac{\partial s_t}{\partial p_t} = 0$. Thus, (21) simplifies to

$$e_{t+1} = p_{t+1} = \begin{cases} \tilde{f} \int_{\tilde{a}_t}^{\bar{a}} \frac{1}{\bar{a}-\underline{a}} da_i = \frac{\bar{a}-\tilde{a}_t}{\bar{a}-\underline{a}} \tilde{f} & \text{when } \tilde{a}_t > \underline{a} \\ \tilde{f} & \text{when } \tilde{a}_t \leq \underline{a}. \end{cases} \tag{33}$$

Under this case, if a nontrivial steady state equilibrium $(\bar{e}, \bar{p}) \notin \mu$ exists, it satisfies $\bar{e} = \bar{p}$. It also follows directly from (33) that if $\exists \, (\hat{e}, \hat{p}) \in EE$ such that $\hat{e} = \hat{p}$ and $\exists \, (\tilde{e}, \tilde{p}) \in PP$ such that $\tilde{e} = \tilde{p}$, then $\hat{e} = \tilde{e} = \bar{e}$ and $\hat{p} = \tilde{p} = \bar{p}$ (that is, if the EE and PP loci cross the 45 degree line, they must cross at the same place).

Suppose that, there does not exist $(\bar{e}, \bar{p}) \notin \mu$. This implies that $\forall \, e_t = p_t$, $(e_t, p_t) \notin \mu$, Δp and Δe are both negative. However, (33) indicates that, for a large enough value of $\tilde{f}$, $\exists \, (e_t, p_t) \notin \mu$ s.t. $e_t = p_t$ and Δp and Δe are both positive. Thus, we can ensure that $\exists \, (e_t, p_t) \notin \mu$ s.t. $e_t = p_t$ and $\Delta p = \Delta e = 0$.

Step 3   We now show that as q is reduced, $\exists \, (\bar{e}, \bar{p}) \notin \mu$. First note that, when $q = 1$,

$$\frac{\partial p_t}{\partial e_t} \bigg|_{EE} \neq \frac{\partial p_t}{\partial e_t} \bigg|_{PP}, \tag{34}$$

when evaluated at $(\bar{e}, \bar{p})$. Thus, we can rule out a tangency at $(\bar{e}, \bar{p})$ when $q = 1$.

Using (21), (23), and (24) and the fact that s_t and $\tilde{a}_t$ are continuous in q, we can also establish that the EE and the PP locus shift continuously in response to changes in q. Taken together with the fact that *EE* and *PP* are not tangent at $(\bar{e}, \bar{p})$ when $q = 1$, we conclude that $\exists\, q, \tilde{q} \le q < 1$, such that $(\bar{e}, \bar{p}) \notin \mu$ (with $\bar{e} < \bar{p}$) exists.

Remark. Note that increases in the effectiveness of education and experience in human capital accumulation—as given by the function f—shift *EE* and *PP* in the opposite direction as decreases in q. Thus, the more effective f is in converting education and experience into human capital, the lower is $\tilde{q}$. ■

Acknowledgments

John M. Heitkemper provided valuable research assistance. We are grateful to Gerhard Glomm, Lant Pritchett, two anonymous referees, and the editor, Oded Galor, for useful comments and suggestions. All remaining errors are, of course, our own. This article represents the views of the authors and should not be interpreted as reflecting those of the Board of Governors of the Federal Reserve System or other members of its staff.

Notes

1. Evans and Jovanovich (1989) and Holtz-Eakin, Joulfaian, and Rosen (1994) provide some empirical support for the role that credit constraints play in shaping occupational choice by showing that wealthier people are more likely to become entrepreneurs and Holtz-Eakin, Joulfaian, and Rosen (1994) find that individuals who receive inheritances are more likely to remain entrepreneurs. Holtz-Eakin and Dunn (1995), however, show that financial assets influence the probability of being self-employed only modestly among a sample of young men and not at all in sample of young women, placing some doubt on the importance of credit market imperfections.
2. In fact, Murphy, Shleifer, and Vishny (1991) find some evidence that individuals may not choose to accumulate their human capital in a socially optimal way: countries with more students concentrating in legal studies grow slower. McGoldrick and Robst (1996) also report some evidence on this point by noting that a significant fraction of the U.S. labor force may be overeducated. They compare estimates of required schooling for each occupation as reported in the *Dictionary of Occupational Titles* to actual levels of schooling reported by the respondents to the *1985 Panel Study of Income Dynamics* and find that over half of the sample is overeducated. When they compare actual levels of education to individuals' own estimates of the educational requirements of their jobs, that fraction falls but remains substantial.
3. Following Evans and Jovanovich (1989), Evans and Leighton (1989), and Holtz-Eakin, Joulfaian, and Rosen (1994), we empirically associate entrepreneurship with self-employment and use the terms *entrepreneur* and *self-employed* interchangeably in this section. Clearly, not all self-employed individuals are entrepreneurs, particularly if we define entrepreneurs to be only those engaged in R&D (see Knight, 1921; Schumpeter, 1950, or even Baumel, 1990, for competing views on the definition of entrepreneurship). However, the self-employed do share an important characteristic with entrepreneurs: they face more uncertain returns to their labor than wage and salary workers. It is this common characteristic that we choose to highlight in our model.
   In addition, we should point out that, although individuals tend to be classified empirically as either entrepreneurs or professionals, our model takes a broader view of the process of human capital accumulation and allows a single individual to accumulate both entrepreneurial and professional skills.
4. Obviously, being self-employed and being a professional are not mutually exclusive activities. However, taken together, Figures 1 and 2 illustrate our major point: more developed economies have more people working for others and more people engaged in professional and managerial activities.

5. Even though both groups of workers have about the same level of education, self-employed workers' higher levels of job tenure and age suggest that these workers have accumulated their human capital through a more experience-intensive process.

6. More support for the idea that the human capital of the self-employed is more experience intensive can be found in Bregger (1996), who uses data from the Current Population Survey to show that workers are more likely to become self-employed as they become older. In addition, Fujii and Hawley (1991) show that self-employed workers have more work experience and a higher return to experience than wage and salary workers. Finally, LaFerrere and McEntee (1995), using French data, show that individuals are less likely to be self-employed if they have a third-level education.

7. The remaining patents were awarded to the U.S. and foreign governments.

8. Michael Dell, CEO of Dell Computers and Inc. Magazine's 1989 entrepreneur of the year, attended University of Texas at Austin but never finished. Bill Gates, cofounder of Microsoft, dropped out of Harvard in his junior year, and Ross Perot, founder of the multimillion-dollar corporation, Electronic Data Systems (EDS), attended Texarkana Junior College.

9. Skill-biased technological change is not essential for our results. Rather, what is crucial for the dynamics we describe below is a positive link between educated labor and skill-biased technological change. Put differently, the basic model we lay out below could easily accommodate directed technological change along the lines proposed by Acemoglu (1998). In his model, increases in the number of skilled workers generate economywide incentives for investment in skill-biased technological change. Extending that reasoning to cover our model, coefficients on human capital and raw labor in equation (1) could be modified so that they respectively depend positively and negatively on the ratio of skilled to unskilled labor. The thrust of our qualitative conclusions would not change under such a modification.

10. The results we present below are not dependent on this specification either. Under a technically more complicated alternative, for example, labor income could be fixed and independent of innate ability throughout the lifetime.

11. As will become clear in what follows, the dynamics of the model depend on the lag with which the existing stock of human capital affects the *level* of technology. Alternatively, we could have chosen to follow Romer (1990) and adopt what is by now a more conventional approach where the *rate* of technological progress or adoption depends on the existing stock of human capital. Our main arguments would go through unaffected under such a modification as well.

    Note also that this general form does not require us to make the assumption that both entrepreneurs and professionals are required—only that entrepreneurs and professionals are both capable of contributing to the level of technology or to its adoption. As we state in the introduction, both independent inventors and corporations are responsible for a significant portion of patent applications in the United States, suggesting that both entrepreneurs and professionals play a role in fostering innovation. We are, of course, implicitly assuming that the marginal contribution of each new entrepreneur to the level of technology is the same regardless of whether or not this entrepreneur works in the R&D sector. This would occur if we assume that the fraction of entrepreneurs in the R&D sector remains constant over time or if entrepreneurial skills applied in the non-R&D sector are just as effective in improving the technology.

12. We have chosen logarithmic preferences to demonstrate that increasing relative risk aversion is not necessary to generate the declining willingness to gamble on entrepreneurship as per capita income grows. Clearly, this result could be generated with any utility function that features increasing relative risk aversion, and some, but not all, utility functions that feature decreasing relative risk aversion.

13. In our setup, individuals are compensated for each of the three types of labor they provide. This is similar to the specification used in Galor and Weil (1996) in which individuals are compensated for both their physical and mental abilities. See the discussion at the end of this section for the implications of alternative schemes in which human capital providers are not compensated for their physical abilities (that is, $\phi = 0$ for human capital providers).

14. In our model, individuals must pass the innate-ability threshold in order to become human capital providers. As mentioned in the introduction, there may also be a threshold level of wealth required of entrepreneurs in the absence of perfect capital markets. One could adapt our model to other rationing rules such as one that takes into account both parental wealth and ability (similar to that found in Owen and Weil, 1998) without altering its major conclusions.

15. Our formulation abstracts from how the magnitude of improvements in the level of technology—due to higher human capital—might affect relative returns to different components of the human capital stock. For a relevant discussion on this issue, see Galor and Tsiddon (1997).

16. It is relatively straightforward to demonstrate that the risk of an entrepreneurial venture increases with technological change. In addition, if abilities were perfectly observable and we were to allow competitive insurance companies to provide coverage, the insurance premium an entrepreneur would pay to insure against potential loss π_t^i would equal

$$\pi_t^i = (1-q)\lambda_{t+1}a_t^i f(1-s_t^i).$$

For a fixed level of schooling, a higher level of technology λ implies that this premium is greater. In the absence of insurance against entrepreneurial loss, it is clear that raising the time devoted to schooling s_t^i is an optimal response to improvements in technology.

17. Obviously, the existence of a development trap in this model is not a consequence of having two types of human capital but is rather related to whether human capital accumulation has an opportunity cost (that is, labor wage income). That noted, however, the model presented above demonstrates that when a development trap exists, the initial stocks of both types of human capital need to be taken into account in assessing the potential evolution of the economy.

References

Acemoglu, D. (1998). "Why Do New Technologies Complement Skills? Directed Technical Change and Wage Inequality," *Quarterly Journal of Economics* 113, 1055–89.

Acemoglu, D., and F. Zilibotti. (1997). "Was Prometheus Unbound by Chance? Risk, Diversification and Growth," *Journal of Political Economy* 105, 709–751.

Azariadis, C., and A. Drazen. (1990). "Threshold Externalities in Economic Development," *Quarterly Journal of Economics* 105, 501–526.

Banerjee, A., and A. Newman. (1993). "Occupational Choice and the Process of Economic Development," *Journal of Political Economy* 101, 274–298.

Baumol, W. J. (1990). "Entrepreneurship: Productive, Unproductive, and Destructive," *Journal of Political Economy* 98, 893–921.

Becker, G. S. (1993). *Human Capital: A Theoretical and Empirical Analysis, with Special Reference to Education.* Chicago: University of Chicago Press.

Bregger, J. E. (1996). "Measuring Self-Employment in the United States," *Monthly Labor Review* 119, 3–9.

Evans, D. S., and B. Jovanovic. (1989). "An Estimated Model of Entrepreneurial Choice Under Liquidity Constraints." *Journal of Political Economy* 97, 808–827.

Evans, D. S., and L. S. Leighton. (1989). "Some Empirical Aspects of Entrepreneurship." *American Economic Review* 79, 519–535.

Federal Reserve Board of Governors. (1995). *1995 Survey of Consumer Finances.* http://www.federalreserve.gov/pubs/oss.

Fujii, E. T., and C. B. Hawley. (1991). "Empirical Aspects of Self-Employment." *Economics Letters* 36, 323–329.

Galor, O., and D. Tsiddon. (1997). "Technological Progress, Mobility and Economic Growth." *American Economic Review* 87, 363–382.

Galor, O., and D. N. Weil. (1996). "The Gender Gap, Fertility and Growth." *American Economic Review* 86, 374–387.

Holtz-Eakin, D., and T. Dunn. (1995). "Capital Market Constraints, Parental Wealth and Transition to Self-Employment Among Men and Women." Bureau of Labor Statistics, NLS Discussion Paper, 96-29.

Holtz-Eakin, D., D. Joulfaian, and H. S. Rosen. (1994). "Sticking It Out: Entrepreneurial Survival and Liquidity Constraints." *Journal of Political Economy* 102, 53–75.

International Labour Office. (1993). *1993 Year Book of Labour Statistics.* Geneva: International Labour Office.

Knight, F. (1921). *Risk, Uncertainty, and Profit.* New York: Houghton Mifflin.

LaFerrerre, A., and P. McEntee. (1995). "Self-Employment and Intergenerational Transfers of Physical and Human Capital: An Empirical Analysis of French Data." *Economic and Social Review* 27, 43–54.

Levine, R., and S. Zervos. (1998). "Stock Markets, Banks and Economic Growth." *American Economic Review* 88, 537–558.

Lucas, R. E. (1988). "On the Mechanics of Economic Development." *Journal of Monetary Economics* 22, 3–42.

Lucas, R. E. (1993). "Making a Miracle." *Econometrica* 61, 251–272.

McGoldrick, K. M., and J. Robst. (1996). "Gender Differences in Overeducation: A Test of the Theory of Differential Overqualification." *American Economic Review, Papers and Proceedings* 86, 280–284.

Mincer, J. (1993). *Studies in Human Capital: Collected Essays of Jacob Mincer* (vol. 1). Brookfield, VT: Edward Elgar.

Mincer, J. (1996). "Economic Development, Growth of Human Capital and the Dynamics of the Wage Structure." *Journal of Economic Growth* 1, 29–48.

Murphy, K. M., A. Shleifer, and R. Vishny. (1991). "The Allocation of Talent: Implications for Growth." *Quarterly Journal of Economics* 106, 503–530.

Overland, J., and M. Spagat. (1996). "Human Capital and Russia's Economic Transformation." *Transition* 2, 12–15.

Owen, A. L., and D. N. Weil. (1998). "Intergenerational Earnings Mobility, Inequality and Growth." *Journal of Monetary Economics* 41, 71–104.

Romer, P. M. (1990). "Endogenous Technological Change." *Journal of Political Economy* 98, 571–602.

Schumpeter, J. (1950). *Capitalism, Socialism, and Democracy* (3rd ed.) New York: Harper & Row.

Stokey, N. L. (1988). "Learning by Doing and the Introduction of New Goods." *Journal of Political Economy* 96, 701–717.

Summers, Robert, and Alan Heston. (1991). "The Penn World Table: An Expanded Set of International Comparisons, 1950–1988." *Quarterly Journal of Economics* 106, 327–443 Mark 5.6.

U.S. Patent Office. (19). *Historic Data: All Technologies Report.* Washington, DC: U.S. Government Printing Office. http://www.uspto.gov/web/offices/ac/ido/ocip/taf.

[15]

Review of Economic Studies (2000) **67**, 147–168

0034-6527/00/00080147$02.00

Enterprise, Inequality and Economic Development

HUW LLOYD-ELLIS
University of Toronto

and

DAN BERNHARDT
University of Illinois Urbana–Champaign

First version received November 1995; *final version accepted February* 1999 (*Eds.*)

We characterize an equilibrium development process driven by the interaction of the distribution of wealth with credit constraints and the distribution of entrepreneurial skills. When efficient entrepreneurs are relatively abundant, a "traditional" development process emerges in which the evolution of macroeconomic variables accord with empirical regularities and income inequality traces out a Kuznets curve. If, instead, efficient entrepreneurs are relatively scarce, the model generates long-run "distributional cycles" driven by the endogenous interaction between credit constraints, entrepreneurial efficiency and equilibrium wages.

1. INTRODUCTION

Research in developing economies typically identifies two key obstacles to the creation and expansion of small and medium sized enterprises: a lack of access to credit, especially to finance working capital, and a relative scarcity of entrepreneurial skills.[1] This paper characterizes an equilibrium development process driven by the interaction of the distribution of wealth with credit constraints and the distribution of entrepreneurial efficiency. When efficient entrepreneurs are relatively abundant, a "traditional" development process emerges (*e.g.* Lewis (1954) and Fei and Ranis (1966)), in which the evolution of macroeconomic variables accord with key empirical regularities and income inequality traces out a Kuznets curve. If, instead, efficient entrepreneurs are relatively scarce, our model generates long-run "distributional cycles" driven by the endogenous interaction between credit constraints, entrepreneurial efficiency and equilibrium wages.

Our model features single-period lived agents who value both consumption and bequests to their children. Individuals, who differ in both entrepreneurial efficiency and inherited wealth, choose whether to work as entrepreneurs, as wage labourers in industry or in subsistence agriculture. An entrepreneur uses his inherited wealth as collateral in return for a loan to pay for start-up costs and working capital. Potential moral hazard in debt repayment limits borrowing. He hires labour at the prevailing equilibrium wage, which he pays out of earned revenues, receiving the balance as profit.

Initially, few agents are efficient enough to become entrepreneurs and those who do operate on a small scale. With little competition for labour, the equilibrium wage is just sufficient to entice workers away from the rural sector. Over time, the distribution of

---

1. See Levy (1993) and Fidler and Webster (1996).

wealth grows in the *first-order stochastic sense*, permitting the extent and scale of entrepreneurial activity to expand, so that profits rise and income inequality worsens. When wages are low, even relatively inefficient projects are worth undertaking if sufficient capital can be employed—wealth rather than entrepreneurial efficiency is the primary determinant of economic activity. Consequently, even though entrepreneurial efficiency is uncorrelated across generations, wealth inequality persists.

Eventually, competition amongst entrepreneurs for workers bids up the equilibrium wage, so that profits eventually fall, and income and wealth inequality start to decline. At this point, the skewness of the efficiency distribution is crucial in determining whether growth continues unabated, or whether cycles appear as the economy matures. With decreasing returns to scale, past wage increases effectively transfer wealth from the rich with low marginal products to the poor with high marginal products, (the "productivity effect"). However, if entrepreneurial efficiency is skewed so that low cost entrepreneurs are scarce, then this transfer reduces the supply of entrepreneurs coming from the rich by more than it increases that coming from the poor (the "enterprise effect").

If the productivity effect dominates, the supply of entrepreneurs and their demand for labour still rise. Wages are bid up further, output expands and the distributions of wealth and income grow in the *second-order sense*. As wages rise, less efficient agents prefer to enter the labour force (though they could profitably become entrepreneurs) and production becomes increasingly efficient. Gradually, entrepreneurial efficiency replaces wealth as the primary determinant of occupational choice, so that wealth becomes less persistent along family lineages. This benchmark process matches several empirical regularities associated with development:

- Market-clearing wages remain low initially, but then rise monotonically;
- There is continuous rural–urban migration and increasing participation in manufacturing;[2]
- The labour share of GNP and of value-added in manufacturing rises with *per capita* GNP;[3]
- The capital–output ratio initially rises, but levels off and may decline as wages rise;[4]
- Average firm size grows and then declines. The dispersion in firm sizes also grows and then falls;
- Equilibrium growth rates are high in early stages, decline as workers leave the rural sector, then increase after all workers leave subsistence, before declining again as the economy matures;
- Income inequality rises in the Lorentz dominance sense during the early phases of development, then gradually falls as the economy matures.[5]

If, instead, the enterprise effect dominates, then the redistribution of inheritances caused by past wage increases actually causes the supply of entrepreneurs and their

2. Young (1993) finds that the recent rapid growth of East Asian NICs was largely due to the accumulation of capital and increased participation in the manufacturing sector rather than total factor productivity growth.
3. The prediction holds for a cross-section of countries (Lloyd-Ellis and Bernhardt (1998)) and for the industrial revolution in Europe (Mathias and Postan (1978)). Labour share of GNP also rose in the U.S. but labour share of manufacturing value-added has been constant for the last 100 years.
4. See Maddison (1989) and Kim and Lau (1994) for related evidence.
5. This Kuznets relationship holds for a cross-section of market economies (Paukert (1973), Ahluwalia (1976), Lydall (1979), Summers, Kravis and Heston (1984)). Although inequality declined in most developed countries during the twentieth century (Fields and Jakubsen (1994)), studies of the U.K. and U.S. that include nineteenth century data find support for Kuznets' hypothesis (*e.g.* Lindert and Williamson (1980)).

demand for labour to *decline*. Wages fall and aggregate output contracts. The resulting redistribution towards the rich increases the supply of entrepreneurs and their demand for labour, so that the economy's decline is reversed. The process continues in this fashion, generating endogenous "distributional cycles" in economic activity which persist into the long run. Wages evolve procyclically so that income inequality worsens during recessions and improves during economic booms.

Our model is most closely related to those of Banerjee and Newman (1993), and Aghion and Bolton (1997).[6] Both models feature one-period lived, risk-neutral agents who *ex ante* differ *only* in their inheritances but not their efficiency, and whose entrepreneurs face *ex post* production risk. Banerjee and Newman have the same moral hazard problem in credit markets as we do, and consider an environment in which entrepreneurs employ workers and capital in one of two exogenously-specified combinations. Their analysis focuses on how the long-run distribution of wealth is related to technology parameters: they find that because of the non-convexities in the feasible technology choices of entrepreneurs, the long-run distributions of wealth may depend on initial conditions. In Aghion and Bolton, agents either invest in a fixed-size, risky project, lending any remaining wealth or borrowing if necessary; or they earn a safe, low income and lend. Limited liability and the dependence of the success probability on non-contractable effort induces credit-rationing based on inherited wealth. Equilibrium between borrowers and lenders determines a market interest rate which, in contrast to ours, varies with the distribution of wealth. As wealth accumulates, demand for credit declines and supply rises, so that interest rates fall and, although it may initially rise, wealth inequality eventually falls. Neither model features a fully-specified labour market, *ex ante* differences in entrepreneurial efficiency or working capital, so they are silent with respect to the evolution of key macroeconomic aggregates.

A crucial distinction between our model and theirs is the timing of the revelation of information regarding entrepreneurial efficiency. In our economy, agents learn their potential efficiency *before* choosing occupations, and we abstract from *ex post* production risk.[7] This timing captures, to some extent, the feature that if there were multiple production periods within a lifetime, agents would condition actions on their revealed efficiency. As a result of this timing, both potential efficiency and inherited wealth affect agent decision-making—occupational choice, capital employed and labour hired—and consequently the paths of macroeconomic aggregates. The impacts of inherited wealth and efficiency are distinct and vary as the economy develops. While in initial stages, wealth is the primary determinant of occupation because wealthy agents can invest in capital and profitably exploit cheap labour on a grander scale; in later stages, entrepreneurial efficiency matters more both because fewer agents are wealth constrained and because higher wages reduce the profitability of large scale production. The consequence for the dynamics of income and wealth inequality is that they first rise and persist along family lineages, and then fall and are less persistent along lineages. If the efficiency distribution is skewed, the importance of entrepreneurial efficiency relative to wealth is cyclical; rising during booms and falling during recessions.

Section 2 of our paper lays out the economic environment and characterizes the periodic equilibrium of the economy. Section 3 details the mechanisms driving the economy through each phase of the development cycle and characterizes the movements of

---

6. Other related contributions to the literature include Greenwood and Jovanovic (1990), Galor and Zeira (1993) and Piketty (1997).

7. Production risk would play no real role if, as in Banerjee and Newman, it is bounded in such a way that default never occurs (see Lloyd-Ellis and Bernhardt (1998)). In contrast, production risk plays a central role in Aghion and Bolton because of the possibility of default.

key macroeconomic variables and the evolution of inequality over this cycle. Section 4 shows how a highly skewed distribution of entrepreneurial efficiency can lead to endogenous cycles. All proofs are in the Appendix.

2. THE MODEL

There are countably many times periods, $t = 0, 1, 2, \ldots$. The economy is populated by a continuum of family lineages of measure one. Each agent is active for one period, then reproduces one agent. An agent's endowment consists of a bequest inherited from his parent. Agents have identical preferences over consumption, C_t, and bequests to their children, B_{t+1}, represented by

$$u(C_t, B_{t+1}). \tag{1}$$

The utility function is homogeneous of degree one, strictly increasing in both arguments and strictly quasi-concave. The assumption that the preference is for the bequest itself, not for the offspring's utility, simplifies the analysis and captures the idea of a tradition for bequest-giving (see Andreoni (1989)). Homegeneity can be relaxed considerably without changing the results.

At time $t = 0$ a new production technology comes into existence. Entrepreneurs who pay the necessary start-up costs (discussed below), combine labour, l_t, and capital, k_t, to produce a single consumption good according to the common production function,

$$f(k_t, l_t). \tag{2}$$

The production function is strictly increasing in both arguments, strictly concave and quasi-homothetic. Capital and labour are complements and third-order derivatives are negligible, so the product function is well approximated by a second-order Taylor series expansion.

Agents are distinguished by two characteristics: their initial wealth inheritances, b, and their personal costs of undertaking a project, x. Project start-up costs are drawn from a time-invariant distribution, $H(x)$, with support $[0, 1]$ and a linear density

$$h(x) = mx + 1 - \frac{m}{2}, \tag{3}$$

where $m \in [-2, 2]$. Start-up costs reflects innate entrepreneurial efficiency and are uncorrelated with inherited wealth. Linearity can be relaxed considerably without changing our results.

Entrepreneurs can borrow to finance their investments. However, the capital market is limited by a moral hazard problem as in Sappington (1983) and Banerjee and Newman (1993). Specifically, there exists an alternative activity which yields a safe gross return of $r \geq 1$. Competition amongst lenders then drives the interest on loans down to r. Entrepreneurs can borrow L, but they must put up their inheritance b as collateral. After production they can abscond, losing rb, but escaping the repayment obligation, rL. If absconders are apprehended, which they are with probability p, they can hide their income from the authorities, but they receive a punishment which imposes on them an additive disutility of d. With homogeneous preferences, borrowers would renege if $\beta rb + pd < \beta rL$, where β is a positive preference parameter. Recognizing this, lenders only make loans that satisfy $L \leq b + \Delta$, where $\Delta = pd/\beta r$. The scale of the project is therefore limited by an agent's inheritance, start-up cost and the degree of market completeness summarized by Δ.

LLOYD-ELLIS & BERNHARDT   ENTERPRISE AND INEQUALITY 151

Given his type (b, x), each agent chooses his occupation taking the equilibrium wage and his own potential profits as given. If his inheritance is large enough, he can become an entrepreneur in the manufacturing sector. Both project set-up costs and productive capital employed must be financed out of bank loans. Alternatively, agents can work in the manufacturing sector at the prevailing equilibrium wage rate, w_t, and invest their inheritance in the alternative activity, earning rb. Finally, agents may prefer to remain in rural areas and receive the subsistence income, γ. The manufacturing sector is located in urban areas, where agents incur a cost of living equal to $v \geq 0$. With homogeneous preferences, one can interpret this cost as a disutility of labour incurred by entrepreneurs and workers, but not by subsisters.

The occupational choice of an agent of type (b, x) determines his lifetime income given the equilibrium obtaining that period, $y(b, x, w_t)$. His total lifetime wealth equals

$$W_t = W(b, x, \iota_t, w_t) = y(b, x, w_t) - \iota_t v + rb, \tag{4}$$

where $\iota_t = 1$ if the agent lives in an urban area and $\iota_t = 0$ otherwise.

2.1. *Optimal behaviour*

An agent with wealth W_t maximizes $u(C_t, B_{t+1})$ subject to $C_t + B_{t+1} = W_t$, yielding optimal linear consumption and bequest policies, $C(W_t)$ and $B(W_t)$. We assume that the pre-industrial economy has reached a steady state with constant bequests defined by $b^0 = B(\gamma + rb^0)$.

Agents who are efficient enough become entrepreneurs. Wages are paid out of end-of-period revenues. After paying the start-up cost, x, an entrepreneur chooses capital to maximize profits subject to the constraint that capital must be financed out of the remainder of his loan, $b + \Delta - x$. Thus, the net profits earned by a type (b, x) entrepreneur equal

$$\pi(b, x, w_t) = \max_{k_t, l_t} \{f(k_t, l_t) - w_t l_t - r(k_t + x) \text{ s.t. } 0 \leq k_t \leq b + \Delta - x\}. \tag{5}$$

Profit maximization yields capital and labour demand functions, $k(b, x, w_t) \leq k^u(w_t)$ and $l(b, x, w_t) \leq l^u(w_t)$, where u denotes unconstrained levels.[8] We assume that most agents are initially borrowing constrained, *i.e.* $\Delta < k^u(\underline{w}) + x^* - b^0$, where x^* is sufficiently small, and $\underline{W} = \gamma + v$ is the reservation wage below which potential workers prefer to remain in subsistence.

For an agent with inherited wealth b to undertake a project, he must draw a start-up cost that is less than $b + \Delta$. Even if such an agent can afford to become an entrepreneur there may still exist a marginal set-up cost level, $x^m(b, w_t)$, defined implicitly by $\pi(b, x^m, w_t) = w_t$, at which the agent would be indifferent between working and becoming an entrepreneur. We assume that $\pi(b^0, \underline{x}, \underline{w}) > \underline{w}$ so that some projects are always undertaken.[9] The start-up cost of an agent with inherited wealth b who is just willing and able to undertake a project at time t is given by

$$z(b, w_t) = \min[b + \Delta, x^m(b, w_t)]. \tag{6}$$

Lemma 1. $z(b, w)$ *is increasing and also concave in* b, *decreasing in* w *and* $\lim_{b \to \infty} z_b(b, w) = 0$.

---

8. The assumption of quasi-homotheticity implies that the demand for labour by a constrained entrepreneur increases linearly with firm size.
9. This condition is sufficient for the limiting distribution to be ergodic.

2.2. Macroeconomic equilibrium

Let $G_t(\cdot)$ denote the time t distribution of inheritances. Then, integrating the optimal decisions of agents over their types, (b, x), yields the following aggregates:

Enterprise: $\quad E_t(w_t) \quad = \int H(z(b, w_t))G_t(db);$ \hfill (7)

Start-up costs: $\quad X_t(w_t) \quad = \int \int_0^{z(b,w_t)} xH(dx)G_t(db);$ \hfill (8)

Labour force: $\quad L_t(w_t) \quad = \int \int_0^{z(b,w_t)} l(b, x, w_t)H(dx)G_t(db);$ \hfill (9)

Capital invested: $\quad K_t(w_t) = \int \int_0^{z(b,w_t)} k(b, x, w_t)H(dx)G_t(db);$ \hfill (10)

Output: $\quad Q_t(w_t) \quad = \int \int_0^{z(b,w_t)} f(k(b, x, w_t), l(b, x, w_t))H(dx)G_t(db);$ \hfill (11)

Net income: $\quad Y_t(w_t) \quad = \int \left(\int_0^{z(b,w_t)} \pi(b, x, w_t)H(dx) \right) G_t(db) + w_t L_t(w_t).$ \hfill (12)

Aggregate subsistence is given by $S_t(w_t) = 1 - E_t(w_t) - L_t(w_t)$. These aggregates are time-varying functions of the wage because they also depend on the distribution of inherited wealth.

A *competitive equilibrium* for an economy with inheritance distribution $G_t(\cdot)$ is a tuple $\{w_t^e, E_t^e, L_t^e, S_t^e\}$ such that:

- Given the wage w_t^e, an agent of type (b, x) selects his occupation to maximize utility;
- Type (b, x) entrepreneurs choose capital and labour to maximize profits subject to $k \leq b + \Delta - x$;
- Markets clear: $E_t^e(w_t^e) + L_t^e(w_t^e) + S_t^e(w_t^e) = 1$, where $S_t^e(w_t^e) = 0$ if $w_t^e > \underline{w}$.

Two kinds of equilibria can arise. In a *dual economy* equilibrium, the supply of entrepreneurs and their labour is insufficient to draw all agents out of subsistence and the wage settles at its reservation level, $\underline{w}$. In an *advanced economy* equilibrium the supply of entrepreneurs and their labour demand are high enough that the surplus labour is exhausted and the wage is bid up above $\underline{w}$. The following lemma is useful for understanding how the economy evolves in such an equilibrium:

Lemma 2. *Aggregate income, Y_t, is equal to the area below the upper envelope generated by the supply and demand curves for labour.*

At time t, a fraction $S_t^e/G_t(b^0)$ of agents that inherit b^0 remain in subsistence. A proportion $z(b, w_t)$ of agents with inheritance b realize a low enough start-up cost, $x < z(b, w_t)$, to undertake their projects. Let $\bar{x}(y^*, b, w_t)$ be the value of x such that $\pi(b, x, w_t) = y^*$. Then the distribution of income conditional on inherited wealth and the

LLOYD-ELLIS & BERNHARDT   ENTERPRISE AND INEQUALITY 153

equilibrium obtaining at time t can be represented by the cumulative distribution function

$$\Phi(y|b, w_t) = \begin{cases} 0, & \text{if } y < \gamma \text{ or } y < w_t, b > b^0, \\ S_t/G_t(b^0), & \text{if } \gamma \le y < w_t, b = b^0, \\ 1 - H(z(b, w_t)), & \text{if } w_t \le y < \underline{\pi}(b, w_t), \\ 1 - H(\tilde{x}(y, b, w_t)), & \text{if } \underline{\pi}(b, w_t) \le y \le \bar{\pi}(b, w_t), \\ 1, & \text{otherwise.} \end{cases}$$ (13)

Here $\underline{\pi}(b, w_t) = \max[w_t, \pi(b, b+\Delta, w_t)]$ is the lower support on profits and $\bar{\pi}(b, w_t) = \pi(b, \underline{x}, w_t)$ is the upper support. The unconditional distribution of incomes is therefore $\Phi_t(y) = \int \Phi(y|b, w_t)G_t(db)$.

An agent's final wealth is simply the sum of the return on his inheritance and his lifetime income, net of any urban living costs. An agent of type (b_t, x_t) bequeaths $b_{t+1} = B(y(b_t, x_t, w_t) - t_t v + rb_t)$. Note that an agent's inheritance depends not only on his parent's inheritance and cost realization, but also on the past distribution of wealth via its effect on the equilibrium wage. The distribution of wealth evolves according to an endogenous non-stationary probability transition function, so the unconditional distribution of bequests is

$$G_{t+1}(b') = \int P(b'|b, w_t)G_t(db),$$ (14)

where $P(b'|b, w_t) = \Phi(B^{-1}(b') + t_t v - rb|b, w_t)$.

A firm's "size" corresponds to the amount of capital it employs. The distribution of firm size conditional on inherited wealth b is

$$J(k|b, w_t) = \begin{cases} 0, & \text{if } b > \hat{b}(w_t), k < k^u(w_t), \\ \dfrac{H(z(b, w_t)) - H(b+\Delta-k)}{H(z(b, w_t))}, & \text{if } b < \hat{b}(w_t), k < k^u(w_t), \\ 1, & \text{otherwise,} \end{cases}$$ (15)

where $\hat{b}(w_t)$ is the inheritance level such that all wealthier entrepreneurs are unconstrained. Thus, the time t distribution of firm sizes is $J_t(k) = \int J(k|b, w_t)G_t(db)$.

3. A LEWIS–KUZNETS DEVELOPMENT PROCESS

In this section we detail the dynamic evolution of the economy when entrepreneurial ability is uniformly distributed ($m = 0$). The results hold more generally as long as the distribution is not too skewed towards high start-up costs (*i.e.* m is not too large). The implications of more skewed distributions for the development process are discussed in Section 4.

3.1. *The phases of economic development*

Proposition 1. *Following the time $t = 0$ introduction of a new production technology to the long-run pre-industrial economy, the economy passes through four distinct phases of development:*

Phase 1 (*The Dual Economy,* $0 \leq t < \tau_1$): *Wages remain at $\underline{w}$. Incomes and wealths grow in the first-order stochastic sense.*

Phase 2 (*The Transition,* $\tau_1 \leq t < \tau_2$): *Wages begin to rise, but incomes and wealths continue to grow in the first-order stochastic sense.*

Phase 3 (*Advanced Economic Development,* $t > \tau_2$): *Wages rise, and incomes and wealths grow in the second-order stochastic sense.*

Phase 4 (*Long Run*): *Wages converge and the distributions of incomes and wealths converge to unique limiting distributions,* $\Phi^*(\cdot)$ *and* $G^*(\cdot)$*, which are independent of the initial distribution.*

At $t = 0$, agents with sufficiently low start-up costs migrate to urban areas to become entrepreneurs. They employ additional agents at the prevailing wage. If b^0 is sufficiently low, a dual economy equilibrium obtains: Surplus labour remains in the rural sector earning the subsistence income, γ, and the equilibrium wage settles at $\underline{w}$. At the end of their lives, workers and farmers bequeath b^0. However, entrepreneurs bequeath more than b^0, so that the distribution of inheritances at $t = 1$, $G_1(\cdot)$, dominates $G_0(\cdot)$ in the first-order stochastic sense.

The stochastic increase in wealth encourages more generation $t = 1$ agents to engage in entrepreneurial activities and on a greater scale. The associated increase in labour demand draws migrants from the rural sector, output rises and the distribution of income at $t = 1$, dominates that at $t = 0$ in the first-order stochastic sense. Although most agents still receive $\underline{w}$ or less, entrepreneurial profits increase in the first-order stochastic sense. The development process continues in this fashion as long as there is surplus labour in the economy and the wage remains at $\underline{w}$.

Eventually, the supply of subsistence labour is exhausted. At some date τ_1, an advanced economy equilibrium obtains: increased competition for workers by entrepreneurs bids the wage rate above $\underline{w}$.[10] Although wages rise, profits may still rise due to the relaxation of financing constraints. So long as the bequests of the richest lineages do not decline, the distribution of inheritances continues to grow in the first-order stochastic sense for several periods after τ_1. During this transitional phase, labour demand rises and supply declines, so that both wage and aggregate income rise. However, with strict concavity in production, the largest entrepreneurs eventually achieve the optimal scale so their incomes start to decline. Eventually, this declining income offsets the rising lineage wealth, so that at some time $\tau^2 \geq \tau^1$, $\bar{b}_{\tau^2+1} > \bar{b}_{\tau^2}$, and the next phase of development begins.

To understand how the economy evolves in the advanced phase, suppose the distribution of inheritances at date $t \geq \tau^2$, $G_t(\cdot)$, dominates $G_{t-1}(\cdot)$ in the second-order stochastic sense. Since the production function is strictly concave and quasi-homothetic, a unit transfer of wealth from rich to poor entrepreneurs raises labour demand. Although some high cost projects become undesirable, the uniform distribution of entrepreneurial efficiencies ensures that the redistribution of wealth does not reduce the supply of entrepreneurs. Hence, the equilibrium wage and aggregate incomes rise.

The children of entrepreneurs are more likely to be entrepreneurs themselves, but receive lower profits than their parents. Conversely, the children of workers are predominantly workers and experience an increase in income. As a result, the distribution of income evolves in the manner illustrated in Figure 1. Formally, there exists a y^* such that

---

10. A sufficient condition for $\tau_1 < \infty$, is given in the Appendix in Lemma A4.

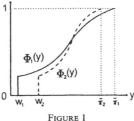

$0 < \Phi_t(y^*) < 1$ and $0 < \Phi_{t-1}(y^*) < 1$ and

$$\Phi_t(y) \geq \Phi_{t-1}(y) \quad \forall y < y^*,$$
$$\Phi_t(y) \leq \Phi_{t-1}(y) \quad \forall y \geq y^*,$$

(16)

where the inequality is strict on an interval of positive measure. We say that distribution $\Phi_t(\cdot)$ is more *X-Dispersed* than distribution $\Phi_{t-1}(\cdot)$.

Since average income also increases, the distribution of income must grow in the second-order stochastic sense. Similar results hold for wealth so that the distribution of inheritances, $G_{t+1}(\cdot)$, dominates $G_t(\cdot)$ in the second-order stochastic dominance, the result follows by induction from period $t = \tau^2$.

The economy cannot grow without bound. In particular, there exists an efficient state in which all agents who wish to become entrepreneurs can do so at the unconstrained optimum scale given the equilibrium wage rate. The associated market clearing condition, $[1 + l''(\bar{w})]x'''(\bar{w}) = 1$, implicitly defines an upper bound for the equilibrium wage, $\bar{w}$. Since the wage increases monotonically with time and is bounded, it must converge to some long-run value $w^* \in [\underline{w}, \bar{w}]$. It follows that the transitional dynamics governing the distribution of wealth converge to a stationary Markov process, $P(\cdot | b, w^*)$. This process satisfies the Monotone Mixing Condition (Hopenhayn and Prescott (1992)), so that the distributions of wealth and income converge to unique limiting distributions.

The limiting distributions are non-degenerate: wealth disparities continue to exist, *but do not persist forever between lineages*. Since the limiting distributions are independent of the initial distribution of inheritances, $G_0(\cdot)$, economies that start out with more unequal distributions, while they may not follow the same cycle of development, will end up with the same long-run distribution.

If the share of wealth bequeathed is sufficiently high, then the efficient state is eventually reached. In this case, the conditional distribution of income is independent of inherited wealth: $\Phi(y | b, \bar{w}) = \Phi(y | \bar{w})$, $\forall b$, and inequality is low because the wage is at its highest possible level, $\bar{w}$. If the share of wealth bequeathed is very low, the economy never achieves enough momentum to leave the dual economy phase (*i.e.* $\tau^1 = \infty$). Consequently, the wage remains at $\underline{w}$, production is inefficient because most entrepreneurs are constrained, wealth and income inequality remain very high and even though the economy satisfies the mixing condition, wealth is very persistent along lineages.

3.2. *The macrodynamics of development*

We now detail the evolution of key macroeconomic variables over the economy's development cycle. We illustrate the results using the following specifications for preferences and technology

$$u(C_t, B_{t+1}) = C_t^{1-\omega} B_{t+1}^{\omega}, \tag{17}$$

$$f(k_t, l_t) = \alpha k_t - \beta k_t^2 + \xi l_t - \rho l_t^2 + \sigma l_t k_t. \tag{18}$$

To emphasize the robustness of the results, we allow for some skewness in the distribution of start-up costs (*i.e. m* > 0). Figure 2 illustrates the time paths for key aggregate variables.[11]

Growth rates of wages and aggregate income are non-monotonic. After leaving the dual economy phase, wage growth first accelerates because, with decreasing returns to scale, the demand for labour from low wealth entrepreneurs expands more rapidly than the reduction in demand from high wealth entrepreneurs. In general, the growth rate in aggregate income first rises then declines gradually in the dual phase, rises again when the wage starts to increase, and then declines as the economy develops further. The first growth spurt occurs because as some lineages become wealthy, the supply of entrepreneurs increases rapidly, offsetting the decline in the marginal return to wealth. The growth rate then declines as agents become less constrained and the marginal return to their wealth falls. Output growth rises again when wages rise due to the effective redistribution of wealth towards poorer agents who are more productive on the margin. As the economy develops further, because there is no engine for long-run growth, wage increases decline and growth rates fall.

Proposition 2 (Occupations). *During the dual phase the rate of enterprise,* $E_t(\underline{w})$ *and labour force participation,* $L_t(\underline{w})$, *grow over time. There exists a* $\theta > |f_{kl}^2/f_{kk}|$ *such that if the slope of the marginal product curve for labour is sufficiently small,* $|f_{ll}| < \theta$, *then during later phases the rate of enterprise,* $E_t(w_t)$, *still increases but wage labouring,* $L_t(w_t)$, *declines.*

We have already described the mechanism driving the increase in enterprise and labour force participation in the early phases of the cycle. In the advanced phase, second-order stochastic growth is sufficient to cause labour supply to fall and labour demand to rise. In general, whether the equilibrium number of labourers rises or falls depends on the wage elasticities of supply and demand. If the wage elasticity of demand is sufficiently high ($|f_{ll}|$ sufficiently small), then the number of entrepreneurs increases over time.[12]

Proposition 3 (Factor Shares). *There exists a* $\delta > 0$ *and a* $\theta > |f_{kl}^2/f_{kk}|$ *such that if the optimal firm-level demand for labour is sufficiently great,* $l(\underline{w}) > \delta$, *and the slope of the marginal product of labour curve is sufficiently small,* $|f_{ll}| < \theta$, *then the labour share of value-added in manufacturing rises monotonically throughout the development cycle.*

During the dual phase, the manufacturing labour force expands and the wage is constant. If the wage elasticities of supply and demand are high enough (*e.g.* when the sufficient conditions on primitives in Proposition 3 hold), then the labour share of value-added rises as the manufacturing sector expands. In the advanced phase, when the equilibrium labour force may decline, continued growth in the labour share requires that the equilibrium wage, w_t, rises sufficiently rapidly relative to aggregate income, Y_t. Again, if

---

11. Parameter values are $m = 0.5, \omega = 0.2, \gamma = 0.12, \nu = 0.08, \alpha = 1.1, \beta = 50, \xi = 3.2, \rho = 0.5, \sigma = 4, r = 1, b^0 = 0.03, \Delta = 0.01$. The numerical example tracks the entire distribution of wealth on a discretized support. The associated code is available from the authors.

12. The qualitative implications for the wage rate, aggregate income and inequality do not depend on this elasticity.

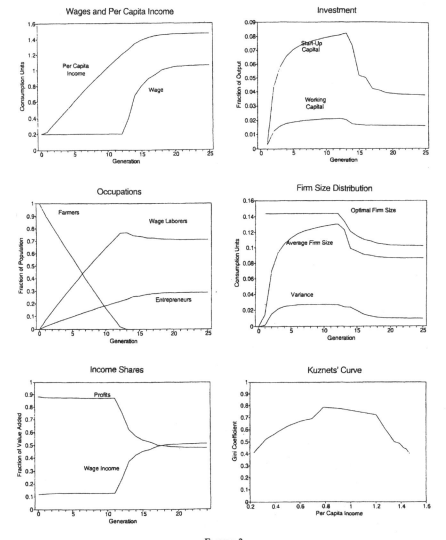

FIGURE 2
The macrodynamics of development

the wage elasticities of labour demand and supply are sufficiently high, the increments to aggregate profits are always proportionately less than the increments in the aggregate wage bill.

Proposition 4 (Investment).   *During the early phases both aggregate working capital, K_t, and aggregate start-up capital, X_t, grow monotonically. However, during the advanced phase these variables may evolve non-monotonically.*

In the dual phase, first-order stochastic growth in wealth causes both aggregate working capital, $K_t(w_t)$, and aggregate start-up costs, $X_t(w_t)$, to grow. Later in the development cycle, the time paths of these aggregates depend on the net effect of two opposing forces: the second-order stochastic increase in inheritances causes the demand for start-up and working capital to rise for a given wage, however, the rising wage induces less efficient agents to become workers, causing the equilibrium level of capital to fall. If the wage elasticity of demand for capital is high enough,[13] then the aggregate working capital stock falls (see Figure 2). Similarly, aggregate start-up costs, $X_t(\cdot)$, decline as long as the wage elasticity of the supply of entrepreneurs is sufficiently high.

Proposition 5.   *The distribution of firm sizes, $J_t(\cdot)$, becomes increasingly X-Dispersed during phases 1 and 2, before becoming gradually less X-Dispersed in the advanced phase.*

During the dual phase, the wealth of agents drawing a particular cost level, stochastically increases with each generation. Hence, the level of capital employed by them (firm size) also stochastically increases. Although during later phases, the rising wage implies that average firm size eventually falls, the dispersion of firm sizes evolves in a way similar to that of incomes and wealths. Figure 2 depicts the time paths of the average and variance of firm sizes for the parameterized economy. Recall that the rate of enterprise, E_t, increases throughout the process, but that the aggregate capital stock first falls and then rises during the advanced stages. The evolution of the average firm size reflects this. The variance rises, reaching a peak during the dual stage and then declining throughout the advanced stage. If maximum efficiency is attained, the variance falls to zero because all entrepreneurs produce at the optimal scale, $k^u(\bar{w})$. Otherwise, the limiting distribution of firm sizes is non-degenerate and the variance converges to a positive value.

Proposition 6 (The Lorentz Curve).

(a) *There exists a time period $t^* < \tau^1$, such that for all $t < t^*$, income inequality increases in the Lorentz dominance sense.*

(b) *There exists a $\delta > 0$ and a $\theta > |f_{kl}^2/f_{kk}|$ such that if the optimal firm level demand for labour is sufficiently great, $l^u(\bar{w}) > \delta$ and the slope of the marginal product of labour curve is sufficiently small, $|f_{ll}| < \theta$, then for all $t > \tau^2$, income inequality declines in the Lorentz dominance sense.*

The first panel of Figure 3 depicts a typical Lorentz curve, $Z_t(p)$, during the dual stage of development.[14] The linear segment OA corresponds to the traditional sector, the linear segment AB corresponds to wage labourers and the convex segment BC corresponds to entrepreneurs. Inequality increases in the *Lorentz dominance* sense if the entire Lorentz curve shifts to the right (*i.e.* the curve shifts from $OABC$ to $OA'B'C$). Sufficient conditions are that (1) the growth rate in *per capita* income exceeds the growth rate in the income of migrating agents; and, (2) the largest entrepreneur's profit, $\pi_t(\bar{b}_t, \underline{x}, \underline{w})$, increases faster than mean income, Y_t. Both conditions are trivially true in the first period and hold subsequently as long as the marginal product of capital is sufficiently high and $\underline{w}$ is sufficiently low.

---

13. That is, if labour and capital are sufficiently strong complements, the supply of entrepreneurs is sufficiently wage elastic and the fraction of constrained entrepreneurs is small enough.

14. The Lorentz curve is $Z_t(p) = 1/Y_t \int_0^{\hat{y}_t(p)} y\Phi(dy)$, where $\Phi_t(\hat{y}_t) = p$. Our analysis here is influenced by Bourguignon (1990).

LLOYD-ELLIS & BERNHARDT   ENTERPRISE AND INEQUALITY 159

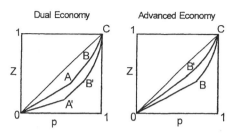

FIGURE 3

Evolution of Lorenz curves

During the advanced stages of economic development, the Lorentz curve no longer includes the segment corresponding to the traditional sector. The maximum income in the economy falls and the mean rises, so the slope at C declines. For inequality to decline unambiguously, the wage must grow more quickly than *per capita* income. This will be the case if the elasticities of the demand for, and supply of, labour are sufficiently large (*i.e.* the sufficient conditions in Proposition 6(b) apply), because this ensures that a wage increase has a large negative impact on aggregate profits. Figure 3 illustrates the implied relationship between the Gini coefficient[15] and *per capita* income.

A key factor driving these development dynamics is that an agent's ability to borrow is limited by his inherited wealth. As the value of Δ is increased (see Figure 4), the development cycle occurs more rapidly, but its nature remains much the same. Income inequality rises to a high value much more rapidly before declining. As the borrowing constraint is relaxed further the economy reaches the efficient state. For $\Delta \geq k''(\underline{w}) + \bar{x} - b^0$, the economy jumps immediately to the efficient state and the degree of income inequality reflects only variations in entrepreneurial efficiency.

4. ECONOMIC DEVELOPMENT WHEN EFFICIENT ENTREPRENEURS ARE SCARCE

A key problem facing developing economies is the relative scarcity of high skilled entrepreneurs. As Fidler and Webster (p. 25, 1996) point out "Poorly developed business skills

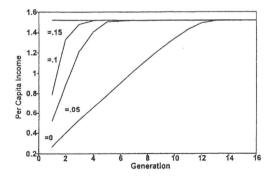

FIGURE 4

Relaxing the collateral requirement

15. Twice the area between the Lorenz curve and the 45° line.

are a binding constraint to enterprise growth, even more than lack of access to credit in many cases. Entrepreneurs' complaints about lack of access to credit often mask technical and managerial inadequacies . . .". This section considers the implications for the development process when we incorporate the feature that efficient entrepreneurs are a relatively scarce resource—*i.e.* the distribution of entrepreneurial efficiency is skewed towards high cost entrepreneurs: $m > 0$.

During the dual-economy phase, the qualitative nature of our results are independent of the shape of the distribution of entrepreneurial efficiency. However, in later phases, when the wage rate is endogenous, the nature of the development path is sensitive to the skewness of this distribution:

If the distribution of entrepreneurial efficiency is sufficiently skewed towards high cost projects, then the economy exhibits endogenous long-run cycles in production. Wages evolve pro-cyclically so that income inequality falls during booms and rises during recessions.

To understand the mechanism driving this result, consider the special case where no working capital is used in production and the skill density is highly skewed ($m = 2$). Then the relationship between the rate of enterprise and wealth for any given wage w is

$$\psi(b, w) = H(z(b, w)) = \min [b^2, x_m^2(w)]. \qquad (19)$$

Consider two wealth levels b^l and b^h and the agents who inherit them (see Figure 5). If $b^l < x_m(w) < b^h$, then a unit transfer of wealth from the rich agents to the poor agents unambiguously increases the supply of entrepreneurs. If, however, $b^l < b^h < x_m(w)$ (*i.e.* both wealth levels lie on the convex segment) then such a transfer decreases the supply of entrepreneurs from the high wealth group by more than it increases the supply from the low wealth group.

Past wage increases result in many such transfers from rich to poor agents. If the support of the distribution of inheritances is such that the measure of agents with wealth greater than $x_m(w)$ is small and if the increase in mean inheritance is sufficiently small, then a second-order stochastic increase in the distribution of inherited wealth, can cause the aggregate supply of entrepreneurs at the wage w, to *decline*. If this is the case at each and every wage, the supply curve for labour must shift inward.

With no capital in production and $m = 2$, the demand for labour from entrepreneurs with wealth b is proportional to the supply of entrepreneurs:

$$\lambda(b, w) = l(w) \min [b^2, x_m^2(w)]. \qquad (20)$$

Hence, a second-order stochastic increase in the distribution of wealth reduces the aggregate demand for labour at each wage. From Lemma 2, both the wage and aggregate income must decline in equilibrium as a consequence of this "enterprise effect".

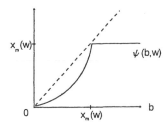

FIGURE 5

Occupational choice with a skewed distribution of skills

LLOYD-ELLIS & BERNHARDT   ENTERPRISE AND INEQUALITY 161

As the wage falls, wealth starts to be redistributed away from poorer lineages and back towards richer lineages. By a converse argument to that given above, this causes an increase in the supply of entrepreneurs and an increase in their demand for labour, even if the inheritances fall slightly. By Lemma 2, the equilibrium wage and aggregate income rise and the economy's decline is reversed. As wages rise, wealth is redistributed towards the centre and the process begins all over again.

When the production function exhibits decreasing returns to working capital, the wealth transfer due to rising wages in the past represents a transfer from agents with low marginal products to those with high marginal products. This "productivity effect" tends to increase the supply of entrepreneurs and the demand for labour. However, so long as the enterprise effect dominates, which it will if m is large enough, the redistribution of wealth resulting from past wage increases can still cause a decline in the equilibrium wage and reduce aggregate income. The economy continues to evolve in this fashion so that the long run path exhibits recurrent "distributional cycles" in economic activity.

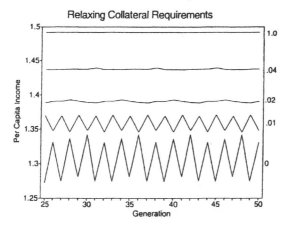

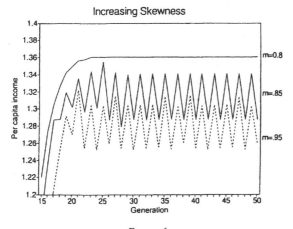

FIGURE 6
Endogenous cycles

These cycles are intimately related to the interaction between capital market imperfections, the skewness of the distribution of entrepreneurial efficiency and the labour market equilibrium. As m is increased, so that relatively efficient entrepreneurs become increasingly scarce, the economy moves from no cycles, to cycles of gradually increasing amplitude relative to the mean. Eventually, efficient entrepreneurs become so scarce that the economy cannot escape from the first development phase. Relaxing the borrowing constraints (*i.e.* raising Δ, holding m constant) causes the cycles to decline and eventually disappear.

Thus, both the severity of capital market imperfections and the skewness of entrepreneurial efficiency offer a potential explanation for differences in the amplitude and persistence of long-run cycles across economies. Moreover, these factors may help us to understand differences in the long run variability of factor shares and income inequality across economies. For example, as Blanchard (1997) documents, factor shares have been more variable in European than in Anglo-Saxon economies (the U.S., the U.K. and Canada); one potential explanation is that credit-market imperfections are more severe in Europe. Cross-country evidence on cyclical movements in income inequality is mixed (Deninger and Squire (1996)). However, Beach (1976) finds that U.S. Income inequality tends to fall during booms and rise during recessions.

5. CONCLUDING REMARKS

In the model described here, the distribution of entrepreneurial efficiency is time invariant so the only source of economic growth comes from the reduced importance of borrowing constraints as agents accumulate wealth. If the distribution of start-up costs were to improve over time, this would reinforce the results of Section 3. As Figure 6 suggests, in the long-run cyclical economy, an improving distribution of skills would eventually eliminate the cycles.

Our analysis could be extended in several directions. The impacts of the shocks of the mid-1970s varied considerably across economies according to their stage of development. Some economies have yet to recover to their 1973 levels of *per capita* income and many have experienced large increases in inequality. When such shocks are incorporated into our model, the time taken to recover depends crucially on the interaction between the distribution of entrepreneurial efficiency and the extent of credit market imperfections. Relatedly, the recent financial crisis in Asia can be represented by an increase in potential entrepreneurial moral hazard leading to a decline in the ratio of lending to wealth. Our model can be used to trace out the consequences. Models such as that described here can also be used to study and evaluate the impacts of macroeconomic policy. Townsend (1997) argues that such models are crucial to the systematic formation of development policies.

APPENDIX

Lemma A1. *For constrained firms:* $k_b(b,x,w)=-k_x(b,x,w)=1$, $l_b(b,x,w)=-l_x(b,x,w)=-(f_{kl}/f_{ll})$, $k_w(b,x,w)=0$, $l_w(b,x,w)=1/f_{ll}$. *For unconstrained firms* $k_b(b,x,w)=k_x(b,x,w)=l_b(b,x,w)=l_x(b,x,w)=0$, $k_w(b,x,w)=-f_{kl}/(f_{kk}f_{ll}-f_{kl}^2)<0$, $l_w(b,x,w)=f_{kk}/(f_{kk}f_{ll}-f_{kl}^2)<0$.

Lemma A2. $\pi_b(\cdot)=f_k-r\geq 0$; $\pi_x(\cdot)=-f_k\leq -r$; $\pi_w(\cdot)=-l(b,x,w)<0$.

Lemma A3. *Let* $\tilde{x}$ *be implicitly defined by* $\pi(b,\tilde{x},w)=y$. *Total differentiation reveals that* $\tilde{x}_y<0$, $\tilde{x}_b\geq 0$, $\tilde{x}_w<0$. *Also* $\tilde{x}_{yy}=\tilde{x}_{bb}=\tilde{x}_{yb}<0$, $\tilde{x}_{bw}=\tilde{x}_{yw}<0$ *and* $\tilde{x}_{ybb}>0$.

LLOYD-ELLIS & BERNHARDT   ENTERPRISE AND INEQUALITY 163

Proof of Lemma 1. Let $\tilde{b}(w_t)$ denote the inheritance below which the marginal entrepreneur is constrained on the extensive margin, so that $x'''(\tilde{b}, w_t) = \tilde{b} + \Delta$. Let $\hat{b}(w_t)$ denote the inheritance level above which marginal entrepreneurs are unconstrained, so that $x'''(\hat{b}, w_t) = \hat{x}'''(w_t)$. Then if

$$b \in [0, \tilde{b}(w_t)]: z_w(b, w_t) = 0, \qquad z_b(b, w_t) = 1, \qquad z_{bb} = 0;$$

$$b \in [\tilde{b}(w_t), \hat{b}(w_t)]: z_w(b, w_t) = -\frac{1 + l(b, z(b, w_t), w_t)}{f_k} < 0, \qquad z_b(b, w_t) = \frac{f_k - r}{f_k} > 0, \qquad z_{bb} = \frac{f_{kk}f_{ll} - f_{kl}^2}{f_{ll}f_k^3} < 0;$$

$$b \in [\hat{b}(w_t), \infty): z_w(b, w_t) = -(1 + l''(w_t)), \qquad z_b(b, w_t) = z_{bb} = 0.$$

Since $z_b(b, w) = 0$ for all $\underline{b} > \hat{b}(w)$, it follows that $\lim_{b \to \infty} z_b(b, w) = 0.$ ||

Proof of Lemma 2. Aggregate income is given in (12). This can be written as

$$Y_t(w_t) = \int_b \int_{w_t}^{\infty} \left[-\int_0^{z(b,w)} \pi_w(b, x, w) H(dx) - wh(z) z_w(b, w) \right] dw G_t(db) + w_t L_t(w_t). \tag{A1}$$

From Lemma A2, $\pi_w(b, x, w) = -l(b, x, w)$, so that this can be reduced to

$$Y_t(w_t) = \int_b \int_{w_t}^{\infty} \left[\int_0^{z(b,w)} l(b, x, w) H(dx) - wh(z) z_w(b, w) \right] dw G_t(db) + w_t L_t(w_t). \tag{A2}$$

But $(d/dw)[wH(z(b, w))] = wh(z) z_w(b, w) + Hz(b, w))$, and so

$$Y_t(w_t) = \int_b \int_{w_t}^{\infty} \left(\int_0^{z(b,w)} [1 + l(b, x, w)] H(dx) \right.$$

$$\left. - \frac{d}{dw}[wH(z(b, w))] \right) dw G_t(db) + w_t L_t(w_t). \tag{A3}$$

However,

$$-\int_{w_t}^{\infty} \frac{d[wH(z(b, w))]}{dw} dw = w_t H(z(b, w_t)),$$

and so

$$Y_t(w_t) = \int_b \int_{w_t}^{\infty} \int_0^{z(b,w)} [1 + l(b, x, w)] H(dx) dw G_t(db) + w_t E_t(w_t) + w_t L_t(w_t), \tag{A4}$$

which is the area under the upper envelope created by the supply and demand curves. ||

Theorem 1 (Hadar and Russell (1971)). *Let $M_t = \int \mu(b) G_t(db)$, where $\mu_b(b) \geq 0, \forall b; \mu_b(b) > 0$ on an interval. If $G_t(b)$ FSD (first-order stochastically dominates) $G_{t-1}(b)$ then $M_t > M_{t-1}$.*

Theorem 2 (Hadar and Russell (1971)). *Let $M_t = \int \mu(b) G_t(db)$, where $\mu_{bb}(b) \leq 0, \mu_{bb}(b) < 0$ for some b and $\lim_{b \to \infty} \mu_b(b) = 0$. If $G_t(\cdot)$ SSD (second-order stochastically dominates) $G_{t-1}(\cdot)$ then $M_t > M_{t-1}$.*

Lemma A4. *Suppose that the increase in the urban population between time $t = 0$ and $t = 1$ is sufficient to absorb all immigrant entrepreneurs,*

$$E_1(\underline{w}) + L_1(\underline{w}) - E_0(\underline{w}) - L_0(\underline{w}) > E_0(\underline{w})(1 - E_0(\underline{w})). \tag{A5}$$

Then if the distribution of wealth grows in the first-order stochastic sense, migration occurs in the rural-to-urban direction only.

Proof. See Lloyd-Ellis and Bernhardt (1998). ||

Proof of Proposition 1.

Phase 1 (*The Dual Economy*). Suppose that for some $t, G_t(\cdot)$ FSD $G_{t-1}(\cdot)$ and $w_t = \underline{w}$. The resulting change in the distribution of income for any y equals

$$\Phi_t(y) - \Phi_{t-1}(y) = \int \Phi_b(y | b, \underline{w}) [G_{t-1}(b) - G_t(b)] db. \tag{A6}$$

But $\Phi_b(y|b,\underline{w}) = -\tilde{x}_b \leq 0$, from Lemma A3. Hence, from Theorem 1, $\Phi_t(b)$ FSD $\Phi_{t-1}(b)$. Analogous results hold for the distribution of final wealth and, hence, bequests: $G_{t+1}(\cdot)$ FSD $G_t(\cdot)$. Since $G_1(\cdot)$ FSD $G_0(\cdot)$, the first part of Proposition 1 follows by induction.

Phase 2 (The Transition). Suppose that for some period t, $w_t > w_{t-1}$, $\bar{b}_{t+1} > \bar{b}_t$ and $G_t(\cdot)$ FSD $G_{t-1}(\cdot)$. Since $\Phi_t(y) = 0$ and $\Phi_{t-1}(y) \geq 0$, $\forall y < w_t$, it must be that $\Phi_t(y) \leq \Phi_{t-1}(y)$ $\forall y < w_{st}$. For incomes $y > w_t$, decompose the change in the distribution of income as follows:

$$\Phi_t(y) - \Phi_{t-1}(y) = \int_b \Phi(y|b,w_t)G_t(db) - \int_b \Phi(y|b,w_{t-1})G_{t-1}(db)$$

$$= \int_b \Phi(y|b,w_t)G_t(db) - \int_b \Phi(y|b,w_t)G_{t-1}(db)$$

$$+ \int_b \Phi(y|b,w_t)G_{t-1}(db) - \int_b \Phi(y|b,w_{t-1})G_{t-1}(db)$$

$$= \int_b [G_{t-1}(b) - G_t(b)]\Phi_b(y|b,w_t)db + \int_b \int_{w_{t-1}}^{w_t} \Phi_w(y|b,w)dwG_{t-1}(db). \tag{A7}$$

Since $\Phi_b(y|b,\underline{w}) = \tilde{x}_b \leq 0$ and $G_t(\cdot)$ FSD $G_{t-1}(\cdot)$, the first term must be negative. Since $w_t > w_{t-1}$ and $\Phi_w(y|b,w) = -\tilde{x}_w > 0$, from Lemma A3, the second term is positive. Hence, the sign of the expression is, in general, ambiguous. However, differentiating with respect to y, for $y \in (w_t, \bar{\pi}_t]$ the change in the slope of the distribution function is

$$\phi_t(y) - \phi_{t-1}(y) = \int [G_{t-1}(b) - G_t(b)]\Phi_{yb}(y|b,w_t)db + \int \int_{w_{t-1}}^{w_t} \Phi_{yw}(y|b,w)dwG_{t-1}(db). \tag{A8}$$

From Lemma A3, $\Phi_{yb}(y|b,w_t) = -\tilde{x}_{yb} > 0$ and $\Phi_{yw}(y|b,w) = -\tilde{x}_{yw} > 0$. Hence, using Theorem 1, $\Phi_t(y) - \Phi_{t-1}(y)$ must increase with y on $(w_t, \bar{\pi}_t]$. If $\bar{\pi}_t > \bar{\pi}_{t-1}$, this implies that the cumulative distribution functions do not intersect. It follows that $\Phi_t(\cdot)$ FSD $\Phi_{t-1}(\cdot)$. A similar decomposition can be carried out for the distribution of inheritances:

$$G_{t+1}(b') - G_t(b') = \int [G_{t-1}(b) - G_t(b)]P_b(b'|b,w_t)db + \int \int_{w_{t-1}}^{w_t} P_w(b'|b,w)dwG_{t-1}(db). \tag{A9}$$

Since $P_{bb'} > 0$ and $P_{wb'} > 0$ it follows that $G_{t+1}(b') - G_t(b')$ increases with b'. Hence, $\bar{b}_{t+1} > \bar{b}_t$ implies $G_{t+1}(b')$ FSD $G_t(b')$. Since $G_{\tau^1}(\cdot)$ FSD $G_{\tau^1-1}(\cdot)$, the proposition follows by induction.

Phase 3 (Advanced Economic Development). Suppose that for some t, $G_t(\cdot)$ SSD $G_{t-1}(\cdot)$. Since, from Lemma A4, $\lim_{b\to\infty} z_b(b,w) = 0$, the change in the supply of entrepreneurs equals

$$E_t(w) - E_{t-1}(w) = \int z_{bb}(b,w) \int_0^b [G_t(\hat{b}) - G_{t-1}(\hat{b})]d\hat{b}db. \tag{A10}$$

Since $z_{bb}(b,w) \leq 0$, where the inequality is strict on a set of positive measure, Theorem 2 implies that the supply of entrepreneurs increases for a given wage. In turn, the increase in the supply of entrepreneurs implies that the supply of labour must fall. Since $\lim_{b\to\infty} z_b(b,w) = 0$, the shift in the demand schedule for labour equals

$$L_t(w) - L_{t-1}(w) = \int \frac{d^2}{db^2}\left(\int_0^{z(b,w)} l(b,x,w)dx\right)\int_0^b [G_t(\hat{b}) - G_{t-1}(\hat{b})]d\hat{b}db, \tag{A11}$$

where (d^2/db^2) $(\int_0^{z(b,w)} l(b,x,w)dx) = -(1 - z_b(b,w))^2 l_k(w) + z_{bb}(b,w)l(b,z(b,w),w) \leq 0$. By Theorem 2, the demand for labour rises, so that $w_t > w_{t-1}$ and $Y_t > Y_{t-1}$ (Lemma 2). The change in the slope of the income distribution function is given by (A8). Since $w_t > w_{t-1}$, the second term is positive. Since $G_t(\cdot)$ SSD $G_{t-1}(\cdot)$ and, from Lemma A3, $\Phi_{ybb} = -\tilde{x}_{ybb} < 0$, Theorem 2 implies that the first term is also positive. Hence, $\Phi_t(y) - \Phi_{t-1}(y)$ increases with $y \in (w_t, \bar{\pi}_t]$. Hence, $\bar{\pi}_t < \bar{\pi}_{t-1}$ implies the c.d.f.'s intersect only once:

$$\Phi_t(y) \leq \Phi_{t-1}(y) \quad \text{if } y < y_t^*,$$
$$\Phi_t(y) \geq \Phi_{t-1}(y) \quad \text{if } y \geq y_t^*. \tag{A12}$$

Since $Y_t > Y_{t-1}$, it follows that $\Phi_t(\cdot)$ SSD $\Phi_{t-1}(\cdot)$. An analogous argument establishes that $G_{t+1}(\cdot)$ SSD $G_t(\cdot)$. Since $G_{\tau^2}(\cdot)$ SSD $G_{\tau^2-1}(\cdot)$, the proposition follows by induction.

Phase 4 (*The Long Run*). The wage increases monotonically and is bounded above by $\bar{w}$. Hence, it must converge to some $w^* \in [\underline{w}, \bar{w}]$. In particular, for all $\varepsilon > 0$ there must exist a T such that

$$w^* - w_T < \frac{\varepsilon}{l''(w_T)}. \tag{A13}$$

Since the L.H.S. decreases over time and the R.H.S. increases, if this inequality holds for $t = T$ it must hold for all $t > T$. Using the differentiability of $\Phi(y|b, w)$ in w, we have

$$\Phi(y|b, w^*) - \Phi(y|b, w_t) = \int_{w_t}^{w^*} \Phi_w(y|b, w)dw, \quad \forall y, b. \tag{A14}$$

Using Lemma A4 this can be expressed as

$$\Phi(y|b, w^*) - \Phi(y|b, w_t) = \int_{w_t}^{w^*} \frac{l(b, \tilde{x}(y, b, w), w)}{f_k(b, \tilde{x}(y, b, w), w)}dw. \tag{A15}$$

But $l(b, \tilde{x}(y, b, w), w) \leq l''(w_t), \forall w > w_t$ and $f_k(b, \tilde{x}(y, b, w), w) \geq 1$, and so

$$\Phi(y|b, w^*) - \Phi(y|b, w_t) \leq (w^* - w_t)l''(w_t). \tag{A16}$$

Hence, for all $t \geq T$, $\Phi(y|b, w^*) - \Phi(y|b, w_t) < \varepsilon, \forall y, b$. The same analysis holds for the distribution of inherited wealth, so that the evolution of the distribution of inheritances converges to a stationary, monotone Markov process, $P(\cdot|b, w^*)$. Hopenhayn and Prescott (1992) detail conditions for this class of Markov processes that ensure the limiting distribution is unique and invariant. Thus, given any initial distribution at time $t \geq T$, $G_t(\cdot)$, the associated sequence converges:

$$\lim_{n \to \infty} G_{t+n}(\cdot) = \int \lim_{n \to \infty} P^n(\cdot|b)G_t(db) = P^*(\cdot). \quad || \tag{A17}$$

Proof of Proposition 2. $E_t(\underline{w})$ and $L_t(w)$ are both expected values of increasing functions of b and, hence, by Theorem 1, grow monotonically during the dual economy phase. In the later phases, when the wage rises, decompose the equilibrium change in the labour force into

$$L_t(w_t) - L_{t-1}(w_{t-1}) = \int \frac{d}{db}\left(\int_0^{z(b, w_t)} l(b, x, w_t)dx\right)[G_{t-1}(b) - G_t(b)]db$$

$$+ \int \int_{w_{t-1}}^{w_t}\left(\int_0^{z(b,w)} l_w(b, x, w)dx + l(b, z(b, w), w)z_w(b, w)\right)dwG_{t-1}(db). \tag{A18}$$

The slope of the individual firm's labour demand curve, l_w, increases with $|f_{ll}|$ (see Lemma A1). A value of f_{ll} that is sufficiently close to f_{kl}^2/f_{kk}, (thus preserving the concavity of the production function) ensures that $L_t < L_{t-1}$. ||

Proof of Proposition 3. The slope of labour supply is equal to minus the slope of entrepreneurial supply: $-E_w = -\int_b z_w(b, w)G_t(db)$. Using Lemma A2, the greater is $l''(w)$, the greater is the slope of the labour supply curve. From Lemma A1, as $(f_{ll} \to (f_{kl}^2/f_{kk})$, $l_w \to -\infty$. *Ceteris paribus*, if these slopes are sufficiently large, then the increment in the equilibrium wage proportionately exceeds the increment in *per capita* income. ||

Proof of Proposition 4. $X_t(\underline{w})$, $K_t(\underline{w})$ and $Q_t(\underline{w})$ are all expected values of increasing functions of b and, hence, by Theorem 1, must grow monotonically during the dual economy phase. ||

Proof of Proposition 5. During the dual phase, the change in the distribution of firm sizes is

$$J_t(k) - J_{t-1}(k) = \int_b J_b(k|b)[G_{t-1}(b) - G_t(b)]db, \tag{A19}$$

where

$$J_b(k|b, w_t) = \frac{b + \Delta - k}{z(b, w_t)}\left[\frac{z_b(b, w_t)}{z(b, w_t)} - \frac{1}{b + \Delta - k}\right]. \tag{A20}$$

Since $z_b(b, w) \leq 1$ and $z(b, w) > b + \Delta - k, \forall k < k''(w_t)$, this expression is negative. Thus, by Theorem 1, $G_t(\cdot)$ FSD $G_{t-1}(\cdot)$ implies that $J_t(\cdot)$ FSD $J_{t-1}(\cdot)$. Since the lower support on firm sizes is fixed at $\underline{k}(b^0, \underline{w}) = b^0 + \Delta - z(b^0, \underline{w})$

and a strictly positive measure of firms are of this size, the distribution of firm sizes must exhibit increasing X-Dispersion throughout this phase.

During the later phases, the upper support on firm size is $k''(w_t)$. Since the wage increases over time, the upper support on firm size falls. The lower support on firm size is $\underline{k}_t = \underline{b}_t + \Delta - z(\underline{b}_t, w_t)$. Both $\underline{b}_t$, and w_t rise, so $\underline{k}_t$ must also rise over time. The c.d.f. for the distribution of firm sizes for $k \in [\underline{k}_t, k''(w_t)]$ is given by

$$J_t(k) = \int_{\underline{b}} \left[1 - \frac{b + \Delta - k}{z(b, w_t)} \right] G_t(db), \tag{A21}$$

which is linear in k. Hence, the distributions $j_t(\cdot)$ and $J_{t-1}(\cdot)$ intersect only once on $[\underline{k}_t, k''(w_t)]$. ||

Proof of Proposition 6(a).   Since migration is strictly positive and Y_t increases, A' lies above and to the left of A. The horizontal component of $A'B'$ exceeds that of AB because L_t increases and its slope is lower since Y_t rises. The slope of $A'A$ exceeds the slope of $A'B'$ if

$$\frac{Y_t - Y_{t-1}}{Y_{t-1}} > \frac{v}{\gamma} \left(\frac{S_{t-1} - S_t}{S_{t-1}} \right). \tag{A22}$$

Since E_t increases, the horizontal component of $B'C$ exceeds that of BC. Hence, if (A22) holds, the fact that AB is steeper than $A'B'$ implies that B' must lie below and to the left of B.

Now consider the change in the convexity of the Lorentz curve segment BC

$$Z_t''(p) - Z_{t-1}''(p) = \frac{\hat{y}_t'(p)}{Y_t} - \frac{\hat{y}_{t-1}'(p)}{Y_{t-1}} = \frac{1}{\phi_t(\hat{y}_t(p))Y_t} - \frac{1}{\phi_{t-1}(\hat{y}_{t-1}(p))Y_{t-1}}. \tag{A23}$$

During the dual economy stage of development, if $\Phi_t(\cdot)$ FSD $\Phi_{t-1}(\cdot)$ then $\hat{y}_t(p) \geq \hat{y}_{t-1}(p)$. Now

$$\phi_t(\hat{y}_t) - \phi_{t-1}(\hat{y}_{t-1}) = \int \phi(\hat{y}_t | b, \underline{w}) G_t(db) - \int \phi(\hat{y}_{t-1} | b, \underline{w}) G_{t-1}(db)$$

$$= \int \phi_b(\hat{y}_t | b, \underline{w})[G_{t-1}(b) - G_t(b)]db + \int [\phi(\hat{y}_t | b, \underline{w}) - \phi(\hat{y}_{t-1} | b, \underline{w})] G_{t-1}(db). \tag{A24}$$

Now $\phi_b(y | b) = -\tilde{x}_{yb}(y, b, \underline{w}) \geq 0$ and so, since $G_t(\cdot)$ FSD $G_{t-1}(\cdot)$, the first term is positive. Also, since $\hat{y}_t(p) > \hat{y}_{t-1}(p)$ and $\tilde{x}_{yy} < 0$,

$$\phi(\hat{y}_t | b) - \phi(\hat{y}_{t-1} | b) = \tilde{x}_y(\hat{y}_{t-1}, b, \underline{w}) - \tilde{x}_y(\hat{y}_t, b, \underline{w}) \geq 0. \tag{A25}$$

Hence, the second term is positive, so that $\phi_t(\hat{y}_t) > \phi_{t-1}(\hat{y}_t)$. Since $Y_t > Y_{t-1}$,

$$Z_t''(p) < Z_{t-1}''(p), \qquad \forall p \geq 1 - E_{t-1}. \tag{A26}$$

It follows that if the slope at C is increasing, the Lorentz curves cannot intersect on this segment. This is the case if

$$\frac{\pi(\bar{b}_t, \underline{x}, \underline{w})}{Y_t} \geq \frac{\pi(\bar{b}_{t-1}, \underline{x}, \underline{w})}{Y_{t-1}}. \tag{A27}$$

If this holds throughout the dual phase, then t^* is the period in which the profit of the richest entrepreneur ceases to grow faster than mean income. Hence, for all $t > t^*$, the slope of the Lorentz curve at C must decline. ||

Proof of Proposition 6(b).   Consider the percentile–income combination (p^*, y^*) at which $\Phi_t(\cdot)$ and $\Phi_{t-1}(\cdot)$ intersect: $p^* = \Phi_t(y^*) = \Phi_{t-1}(y^*)$. Since $\Phi_t(y) > \Phi_{t-1}(y)$ for all $y > y^*$, it must be true that for any $p > p^*$, $\hat{y}_t(p) < \hat{y}_{t-1}(p)$. Given that $Y_t(w_t) > Y_{t-1}(w_{t-1})$, this implies that

$$\frac{\hat{y}_t(p)}{Y_t} < \frac{\hat{y}_{t-1}(p)}{Y_{t-1}}, \qquad \forall p > p^*. \tag{A28}$$

But this says that the slope of the Lorentz curve must be less at time t than at time $t-1$ for all $p > p^*$. Since the Lorentz curves meet at $p = 1$, it follows that

$$Z_t(p) > Z_{t-1}(p), \qquad \forall p > p^*. \tag{A29}$$

LLOYD-ELLIS & BERNHARDT   ENTERPRISE AND INEQUALITY   167

For $p < p^*$ we know that $\hat{y}_t(p) > \hat{y}_{t-1}(p)$, so the above argument cannot hold. Consider, now, the change in the density function for any $p < p^*$. This can be decomposed into

$$\phi_t(\hat{y}_t) - \phi_{t-1}(\hat{y}_{t-1}) = \int \phi_b(\hat{y}_t(p)|b, w_t)[G_{t-1}(b) - G_t(b)]db$$

$$+ \int \int_{w_{t-1}}^{w_t} \phi_w(\hat{y}_t(p)|b, w)dwG_{t-1}(db) + \int [\phi(\hat{y}_t|b, w_t) - \phi(\hat{y}_{t-1}|b, w_t)]G_{t-1}(db). \quad (A30)$$

As in Lemma A3, the first two terms must be positive and, as in Proposition 6(a), the third term must also be positive. Hence, the Lorentz curve at t must be less convex than at $t-1$

$$Z_t''(p) < Z_{t-1}''(p), \qquad \forall p \in [1 - E_{t-1}, p^*]. \quad (A31)$$

Thus, the Lorentz curves intersect at most once. If the supply and demand curves for labour are so wage elastic that $(w_t/Y_t) > (w_{t-1}/Y_{t-1})$, then the Lorentz curves cannot intersect at all. ||

Acknowledgements. This paper has benefitted from the comments of David Andolfatto, Charles Beach, Jim Bergin, V. V. Chari, Mick Devereux, Burton Hollifield, Arthur Hosios, Tom McCurdy, Aloysius Siow, Robert Townsend, Dan Usher, and seminar participants at Brock, Cornell, Minnesota, Northwestern, Pennsylvania, Queen's, Rutgers, Toronto, UBC, and Waterloo. All remaining errors and omissions are our own. Funding from the Social Sciences and Humanities Research Council of Canada is gratefully acknowledged.

REFERENCES

ADREONI, J. (1989), "Giving with Impure Altruism: Applications to Charity and Ricardian Equivalence", *Journal of Political Economy*, **97**, 1447–1458.

AGHION, P. and BOLTON, P. (1997), "A Theory of Trickle-Down Growth and Development", *Review of Economic Studies*, **64**, 151–172.

AHLUWALIA, M. S. (1974), "Income Distribution and Development: Some Stylized Facts", *American Economic Review*, **66**, 128–135.

BANERJEE, A. V. and NEWMAN, A. F. (1993), "Occupational Choice and the Process of Development", *Journal of Political Economy*, **101**, 274–298.

BEACH, C. M. (1976), "Cyclical Impacts on the Personal Distribution of Income", *Annals of Economic and Social Measurement*, **5**, 29–52.

BLANCHARD, O., (1997) "The Medium Run", *Brookings Papers on Economic Activity* (Macroeconomics), **??**, ???–???.

BOURGIGNON, F. (1990), "Growth and Inequality in the Dual Model of Development: The Role of Demand Factors", *Review of Economic Studies*, **57**, 215–228.

FEI, J. C. H. and RANIS, G. (1966), "Agrarianism, Dualism and Economic Development", in I. Adelman and E. Thorbecke (eds.), *The Theory and Design of Economic Development* (Baltimore: Johns Hopkins Press), 3–44.

FIDLER, L. and WEBSTER, R. P. (eds.) *The Informal Sector and Microfinance Institutions in West Africa*, World Bank Regional and Sectoral Studies, 1996.

FIELDS, G. and JAKUBSEN, G. H. (1994), "New Evidence on the Kuznets Curve" (Mimeo, Cornell University).

GALOR, O. and ZEIRA, J. (1993), "Income Distribution and Macroeconomics", *Review of Economic Studies*, **60**, 35–52.

GREENWOOD, J. and JOVANOVIC, B. (1990), "Financial Development, Growth and the Distribution of Income", *Journal of Political Economy*, **5**, 1076–1107.

HADAR, J. and RUSSELL, W. (1971), "Stochastic Dominance and Diversification", *Journal of Economic Theory*, **3**, 288–305.

HOPENHAYN, H. and PRESCOTT, E. C. (1992), "Stochastic Monotonicity for Dynamic Economies", *Econometrica*, **60**, 1387–1406.

KIM, J.-I. and LAU, L. J. (1994), "The Sources of Economic Growth of the East Asian Newly Industrialized Countries", *Journal of the Japanese and International Economies*, **8**, 235–271.

KUZNETS, S. (1955), "Economic Growth and Income Inequality", *American Economic Review*, **45**, 1–28.

LLOYD-ELLIS, H. and BERNHARDT, D. (1998), "Enterprise, Inequality and Economic Development" (Mimeo, University of Toronto).

LEVY, B. (1993), "Obstacles to Developing Indigenous Small and Medium Enterprises: An Empirical Assessment", *The World Bank Economic Review*, **7**, 65–83.

LEWIS, A. W. (1954), "Economic Development with Unlimited Supplies of Labour", *Manchester School of Economics and Social Studies*, **22**, 139–151.

LINDERT, P. H. and WILLIAMSON, J. G. (1985), "Growth, Equality and History", *Explorations in Economic History*, **22**, 341–377.

168   REVIEW OF ECONOMIC STUDIES

LYDALL, H. (1979) *A Theory of Income Distribution* (Oxford: Clarendon Press).

MADDISON, A. (1989) *The World Economy in the 20th Century* (Paris: Development Centre of the Organization for Economic Co-operation and Development).

PAUKERT, F. (1973), "Income Distribution at Different Levels of Development: A Survey of Evidence", *International Labor Review*, **108**, ???–???.

PIKETTY, T. (1997), "The Dynamics of the Wealth Distribution and the Interest Rate with Credit Rationing", *Review of Economic Studies*, **64**, 173–191.

RODRIK, D. (1994), "Getting Interventions Right: How South Korea and Taiwan Grew Rich" (NBER Working Paper No. 4964).

SAPPINGTON, D. (1983), "Limited Liability Contracts between Principal and Agent", *Journal of Economic Theory*, **29**, 1–21.

SCHUMPETER, J. A. (1934) *The Theory of Economic Development* (Cambridge: Harvard University Press).

SUMMERS, R., KRAVIS, I. B. and HESTON, A. (1984), "Changes in the World Income Distribution", *Journal of Policy Modeling*, **6**, 237–269.

TODARO, M. P. (1994), *Economic Development in the Third World* New York: Longman.

TOWNSEND, R. M. (1997), "Microenterprise and Macropolicy", in D. M. Kreps and K. F. Wallis (eds.), *Advances in Economics and Econometrics: Theory and Applications*, **2** (Cambridge: Cambridge University Press).

WILLIAMSON, J. G. (1985) *Did British Capitalism Breed Inequality?* (Boston: Allen & Unwin).

YOUNG, A. (1993), "Lessons from the East Asian NICs: A Contrarian View" (NBER Working Paper No. 4482).

[16]

Journal of Economic Growth, 3: 53–80 (March 1998)
© 1998 Kluwer Academic Publishers, Boston. Manufactured in The Netherlands.

Technological Change, Market Rivalry, and the Evolution of the Capitalist Engine of Growth

PIETRO F. PERETTO

Department of Economics, Duke University, Durham, NC 27708

In the early stages of Western industrialization, innovation was the domain of individuals who devoted their entrepreneurial talents to the development of a new product or process, typically setting up a new firm in order to take the innovation to the market. Today, commercial R&D is almost exclusively carried out by corporate laboratories affiliated with manufacturing firms. The corporate R&D lab, however, did not exist in its modern form until the late nineteenth century. The history of Western industrialization, thus, suggests that a fundamental change in the structure of incentives, and consequently in the nature and the organization of the R&D process, occurred around the turn of the century. Three questions arise. What is the nature of this change? What economic forces caused it? What are its implications? To answer these questions, I construct a model where this change is endogenous to the evolution of the economy toward industrial maturity. The change in the locus of innovation—from R&D undertaken by intventor-entrepreneurs, to R&D undertaken within established firms in close proximity to the production line—results from the interaction of market structure and technological change. This interaction captures the essence of the evolution of the capitalist engine of growth and provides an economic explanation of a "stylized fact" that has received no attention in the theoretical literature. The endogenous market structure generates dynamic feedbacks that shape the growth path of the economy and determine the structural change it undergoes, including the endogenous formation of corporate R&D labs. The evolution of market rivalry explains when and how established firms become the major locus of R&D activity.

Keywords: industrialization, R&D, technological change, long-run growth, entry, market structure

JEL classification: E10, L16, O31, O40

1. Introduction

In this article, I study a fact that has not received the attention it deserves in the literature on endogenous technological change. Namely, the nature of industrial capitalism has changed quite radically in the course of time. The best illustration of this "stylized fact" is Schumpeter's discussion (1928) of the shift of focus in his own work, from the inventor-entrepreneurs of his model of competitive capitalism to the professional R&D managers that characterize his model of trustified capitalism.

In the period that economic historians label the first Industrial Revolution, innovation was the domain of individuals who, spurred by the expectation of substantial economic returns, devoted their entrepreneurial talents to the development of new goods and processes. Often, taking the new product and the new process to the market required these entrepreneurs to start up a new firm (Mowery and Rosenberg, 1989, chs. 2–3). Many historical accounts of the development of major innovations, like the Watt steam engine (Scherer, 1984, ch. 2) or the Bessemer steel process (Temin, 1964), emphasize the effort of the individual inventors who devoted their time and resources to developing the innovation.[1] In time, this picture changed. Maddison (1982, pp. 56–57) reports that 82 percent of patents granted in the United States in 1901 were granted to individuals. In 1970, in contrast, only 21 percent of patents were granted to individuals. Today, commercial R&D is almost exclusively carried out by corporate laboratories affiliated with manufacturing firms.[2] Mowery and Rosenberg (1989, ch. 6) report that in the United States in 1985, 73 percent of total industrial R&D was performed by the private, corporate sector (although only 50 percent was financed by it, the rest being financed primarily by the federal government). In a survey study conducted between 1982 and 1984, managers of R&D labs were asked to rank the contribution of various sources of technological advance in their industries. They ranked "firms in the industry" as the most important and "individual independent inventors" as the least important (Levin, Klevorick, Nelson, and Winter, 1987; Klevorick, Levin, Nelson, and Winter, 1995). Similar results emerge from work on USPO and EPO data showing that in a majority of technological classes most patents are granted to established firms (Malerba and Orsenigo, 1995, 1996; Malerba, Orsenigo, and Peretto, 1997).[3]

The corporate R&D lab, however, did not exist in the modern form until the late nineteenth century. Scherer and Ross (1990, ch. 17), for example, report that in the 1770s and 1780s the firm of Boulton and Watt had the equivalent of an R&D lab for work on steam engines, although the scale and type of activity was not exactly what one sees today (see Scherer, 1984, ch. 2, for details). They trace the genesis of the modern corporate R&D lab in the United States to 1876, when Thomas Edison opened his R&D lab in Menlo Park and Alexander Graham Bell established a similar facility in Boston. Mowery and Rosenberg (1989, pp. 38–39) have an example that, for the purposes of this article, is rather illuminating. They report that the first Bessemer steel was made in the United States in Wyandotte, Michigan, in 1864 and that in anticipation of the problems associated with chemical variations in inputs, a chemical lab was established in Wyandotte in 1863. This was the first chemical lab established in the metallurgical sector in the United States and one of the first attached to an industrial firm. Steel users made similar decisions. Railroad companies, like the Burlington Railroad in 1876 and the Pennsylvania Railroad in 1874, established their own central testing labs to make sure that the steel met appropriate specifications. Similar stories can be told about many other manufacturing sectors in the United States and in European countries (see Mowery and Rosenberg, 1989, chs. 3–4, and the references cited therein).

According to Baumol (1993, ch. 6), the most important characteristic of corporate R&D is that it is systematic, incremental, and cumulative.[4] In addition, it implies intertemporal decision-making of the type that is typically used in economic theory to characterize the accumulation of physical capital but that does not apply to R&D decisions in the standard models of endogenous technological change (see, in particular, pp. 117–119). This different type of decision-making has important implications. In one of his most cited passages, Schumpeter (1942, p. 132) remarks that "[the entrepreneur's] social function is already losing importance and is bound to lose it at an accelerating rate . . . innovation itself is being reduced to routine. Technological progress is increasingly becoming the business of teams of trained specialists who turn out what is required and make it work in predictable ways. The romance of earlier commercial adventure is rapidly wearing away." Commenting on this passage, Mowery and Rosenberg (1989, pp. 61–62) claim: "Although a number of major manufacturing firms had emerged during the late nineteenth century from the innovations of such individual inventor-entrepreneurs as Eastman, Edison, Bell, and Westinghouse, in the twentieth century innovation became too important to be left to the whims of the market and the wiles of the individual inventor.... The growth of research within the U.S. industry was primarily an increase in research within the firm. Independent research organizations not affiliated with manufacturing firms declined in importance during the first decades of this century."[5] Similarly, Baumol (1993, p. 115) writes: "Observation appears to confirm that in reality the innovation process has veered toward becoming yet another humdrum activity of the firm, with corporate R&D taking over a substantial portion of the field and transforming it into a preprogrammed activity."

History, therefore, suggests that a fundamental change in the structure of R&D incentives, and consequently in the nature and organization of the R&D process, occurred at the turn of the century. Three questions arise. What is the nature of this change? What economic forces caused it? What are its implications?

Recently, Thompson and Waldo (1994), Smulders and van de Klundert (1995), van de Klundert and Smulders (1997), and Peretto (1994, 1995, 1996a, 1996b) have developed a number of models of endogenous innovation that focus on corporate R&D and study its macroeconomic implications.[6] These contributions can be related to the previous literature in order to understand the historical change in the locus of innovation—from R&D undertaken by outside inventors-entrepreneurs, to R&D undertaken within established firms in close proximity to the production line. In this article, I construct a model where this change is endogenous to the evolution of the economy toward industrial maturity.

Imagine a one-sector economy where oligopolistic firms sell differentiated consumption goods to households. When profitable, firms establish in-house R&D facilities to produce a continuous flow of innovations. In symmetric equilibrium, the number of firms summarizes two dimensions of the notion of market structure—concentration and relative firm size (relative to the size of the market). This property allows use of only one variable to characterize market structure. The dynamics of the number of firms are determined by the free-entry condition that the present value of profits, net of R&D costs, equal sunk entry costs. In this environment, market structure and technological change are interdependent. At a moment in time, market structure determines market rivalry and, therefore, the returns to innovation and the R&D behavior of profit-seeking firms. In addition, the number of firms changes in response to demand and technology conditions. Market structure, therefore, is endogenous and generates dynamic feedbacks that shape the growth path of the economy and determine the structural change it undergoes, including the formation of corporate R&D labs. This setup, in my view, captures the essence of the evolution of the capitalist system and provides an interpretation of the "stylized fact" that emerges from the history of Western industrialization. Namely, the evolution of the structure of the market for manufacturing goods, in particular the endogenous change in market rivalry, drives the change in the incentives faced by economic agents and thereby explains when and how established firms become the major locus of R&D activity.

The article is organized as follows. In Section 2, I present technology and preferences. In Section 3, I define and construct the Nash equilibrium (NE) with free entry for the manufacturing sector of the economy. In Section 4, I analyze the GE dynamics of the

56

model and discuss the transition from one form of R&D to the other. In particular, I show that the economy converges to a stable industrial structure where entrepreneurial R&D and the formation of new firms peter out, while growth is driven by corporate R&D undertaken by established oligopolists. I then discuss the properties of this steady state and provide some comparative statics results. I conclude the section with a critical review of the setup of the model and a comparison to alternative specifications that yield similar results. This comparison highlights the fundamental insight provided by the article and suggests directions for future research.

2. The Model

I consider a closed economy with a fixed population L of identical households who supply labor services and consumption loans in competitive labor and capital markets. Each household is endowed with one unit of labor that it supplies inelastically.

2.1. Households

The typical household maximizes lifetime utility

$$U(t) = \int_t^\infty e^{-\rho(\tau-t)} \log C(\tau)\, d\tau, \tag{1}$$

subject to the intertemporal budget constraint that the present discounted value of expenditure, cannot be greater than the present discounted value of labor and dividend income plus initial wealth,

$$\int_t^\infty R(\tau)E(\tau)\, d\tau \le \int_t^\infty R(\tau)[W(\tau) + D(\tau)]\, d\tau + B(t),$$

where $\rho > 0$ is the individual discount rate, $R(\tau) \equiv e^{-\int_t^\tau r(s)\, ds}$ is the cumulative discount factor, E is per capita expenditure, B is asset holding, W is the wage rate, and D is dividends (profits are distributed in equal shares to households). Households have symmetric preferences over a range of differentiated goods

$$C = \left[\sum_{i=1}^N C_i^{(\varepsilon-1)/\varepsilon}\right]^{\varepsilon/(\varepsilon-1)}, \tag{2}$$

where $\varepsilon > 1$ is the elasticity of product substitution, C_i is the household's purchase of each differentiated good, and $N > 1$ is the number goods (the number of firms).

The solution for the optimal expenditure plan is well known. Households set

$$\dot{E}/E = r - \rho \tag{3}$$

and, taking as given this time-path of expenditure, maximize (2) subject to $E = \sum_{i=1}^N P_i C_i$.

This yields the demand schedule faced by firm i

$$X_i = LE \cdot \left[P_i^{-\varepsilon} / \sum_{j=1}^{N} P_j^{1-\varepsilon} \right],$$ (4)

where $X_i = L \cdot C_i$ is output of firm i since there are L identical households. It is useful for future reference to define the market share of firm i. Multiplying (4) by firm i's price yields

$$S_i \equiv P_i^{1-\varepsilon} / \sum_{j=1}^{N} P_j^{1-\varepsilon},$$

which is the value of firm i's sales divided by the value of the industry's sales.

2.2. Firms

The typical firm produces one differentiated consumption good with the technology

$$L_{Xi} = h(Z_i) \cdot X_i,$$ (5)

where X_i is output and L_{Xi} is labor employment. Unit production costs $h(Z_i) \equiv Z_i^{-\theta}$, where $0 < \theta < 1$, are an isoelastic function of the firm's knowledge stock Z_i. When profitable, firms establish in-house R&D facilities to produce a continuous flow of innovations. Corporate R&D is described by

$$\dot{Z}_i = \alpha K \cdot \left[L_{Zi} + \gamma \sum_{j \neq i}^{N} L_{Zj} \right],$$ (6)

where $\dot{Z}_i$ is the flow of innovations generated by an R&D project employing L_{Zi} units of labor for an interval of time dt and αK is the productivity of labor in R&D as determined by the exogenous parameter $\alpha > 0$ and by the stock of public knowledge K. The latter captures firms' intertemporal interaction in R&D. Equation (6), in addition, allows for contemporaneous interaction in R&D. The idea is that firms affect each other not only via the standard channel of intertemporal spillovers, but also through contemporaneous interaction between researchers working on different projects at different firms. In a more general setup, this interaction may be modeled as endogenous. In this article, however, I assume it to be a characteristic of the R&D technology and represent it with the "interaction" parameter $0 \leq \gamma \leq 1$. For $\gamma = 0$ the firm's technology advances only as a function of the its own R&D effort. For $\gamma = 1$ it advances as a function of the collective effort of all firms in the industry.

2.3. Knowledge

This economy accumulates two types of knowledge—private and public. When one firm generates a new idea to improve its own production process, it also generates general-purpose knowledge that other firms exploit in their own research efforts. Firms appropriate the returns from R&D through a variety of means (Levin, Klevorick, Nelson, and Winter, 1987) but cannot prevent others from using the general-purpose knowledge that spills into the public domain. The productivity of R&D is determined by some combination of all these different sources of knowledge. A simple way of capturing these notions is to posit that an R&D project that produces $\dot{Z}_i$ units of private knowledge also generates $\dot{Z}_i$ units of public knowledge and to write

$$K = \sum_{i=1}^{N} S_i Z_i$$

stating that the technological frontier is given by the weighted average of the knowledge of all firms, with weights given by the market shares. Overall, the R&D technology (6) exhibits increasing returns to scale to public knowledge and labor, and constant returns to scale to public knowledge, the accumulated factor. This property makes a steady state with constant growth feasible.

The key to this setup is that innovations are nontrivial at the firm level but not at the industry level. It is often argued that, by its own nature, technology is nonrival across firms as well as within the firm (Romer, 1990). This is true if by *technology* one means disembodied knowledge of a general nature that can be codified and transmitted at low (possibly zero) cost. In reality, industrial technology is both excludable and rival, often to a substantial degree, due to patent laws, intellectual property rights, secrecy, tacitness, and the firm-specificity of most innovations (Levin, Klevorick, Nelson, and Winter, 1987; Dosi, 1988; Malerba, 1992; Klevorick, Levin, Nelson, and Winter, 1995). Moreover, R&D is most effective when institutionally linked with production and marketing operations. Independent research firms have access to much less detailed knowledge of the production process and the characteristics of the product and cannot develop innovations of the same quality or at the same cost as in-house R&D labs. There are, therefore, strong incentives for firms to integrate the R&D function in-house and increasing returns due to the nonrival nature of technology are largely internal to the firm, the institution where innovations are developed and applied. To the extent that R&D generates general-purpose public knowledge, in addition, there are increasing returns external to the firm in the R&D process that complement those internal to the firm.

2.4. *Entrepreneurs*

An entrepreneur can create a new firm by running an R&D project that takes as input the public knowledge K, generated by incumbents' R&D activity, and develops a new differentiated product and its manufacturing process (Hence, entry implies *both* product and process innovation.). Since this operation requires labor, it entails a sunk, entry cost. Because of this cost, entrepreneurs *must* develop new differentiated products since entering an existing product line in Bertrand competition with the incumbent would lead to losses. The entrepreneur who incurs the entry cost becomes an entrant and joins the industry with some initial level of productivity. In this setup, entrants are net creators of knowledge: they create a new product and the knowledge necessary to run manufacturing operations. It is reasonable to assume that the cost of creating the new firm is proportional to the initial level of productivity and that this level is proportional to the average productivity level in the industry, Z.

These assumptions capture two ideas. First, entrants face escalating entry costs because of the industry's ongoing technological advance. Second, the public knowledge stock K raises the productivity of both incumbents' in-house R&D and entrants' efforts to create new product lines. The key is that the same stock of public knowledge provides spillovers in both the vertical and the horizontal dimensions. Entrepreneurs can enter the industry at the average level of productivity, but they do not compensate incumbents for the services derived from the stock of public knowledge. This fact ties the two dimensions of technological advance in one and only one stock of knowledge in the economy. This suggests that the cost of entry should be modeled as proportional to the ratio between the entrant's target level of productivity Z and the public knowledge stock K. Since in this setup the two effects of knowledge accumulation by incumbents cancel out, I can write the entry cost in units of labor as a constant, $1/\beta$.

2.5. Discussion

I should emphasize some aspects of my conceptual setup that, if misunderstood, might lead to a misinterpretation of the model and its relation to the literature. The type of cost reduction discussed above can be reinterpreted as quality improvement and therefore as product innovation. Hence, it is not useful to interpret entry costs as product R&D and say that firms (incumbents) do process R&D while entrepreneurs (entrants) do product R&D. Similarly, it is not useful to say that firms do vertical product innovation (a higher-quality version of an existing product) while entrepreneurs do horizontal product innovation (a totally new product). In a model with multiproduct firms, for example, horizontal product innovation could occur without creation of new firms (the extreme case being one monopolist supplying all products). As a matter of fact, the notion of corporate R&D discussed above applies to all three types of innovation—horizontal product innovation, vertical product innovation, and process innovation. The characterization of corporate innovation versus entrepreneurial innovation does not hinge on the distinction between vertical and horizontal innovation or between product and process innovation. These distinctions are misleading because they focus on the "innovation" as opposed to the "institution" that brings the innovation to the market. The focus of this article is on the interaction between the systematic innovative activity undertaken in-house by established firms, what I call *corporate R&D*, and the creation of new independent firms that bring to the market new products and processes, what I call *entrepreneural innovation*. Regardless of what firms and entrepreneurs bring to the market—a new product, a new process, both—the focus of the article is on the historical evolution of the "institutional arrangement" through which innovations are brought to the market.[7] Despite its formal similarity, therefore, my setup is conceptually very different from the existing literature and needs to be interpreted with some flexibility. This implies a potential cost for my choice of using the Dixit and Stiglitz (1977) framework of product differentiation and formalizing corporate R&D as cost-reduction. In my judgment, however, this cost is largely offset by three benefits: first, this setup is simple and analytically tractable;

second, the notation is already familiar to most readers; third, this specific application generalizes the implications, and thereby expands the scope, of the theory of technological change and industrial dynamics that I have developed in my previous work (Peretto 1994, 1995, 1996a, 1996b). I discuss these issues in more detail in Section 4.

3.   Equilibrium of the Manufacturing Sector

In this section, I construct the symmetric, noncooperative equilibrium with free entry and exit for the manufacturing sector of the economy. Firms face identical production and R&D technologies and demand schedules and maximize the value of their shares.

3.1.   Definition of Equilibrium

$$V_i = \int_t^\infty R(\tau)\Pi_i(\tau)\,d\tau. \tag{7}$$

Using the cost function (5), instantaneous profits are $\Pi_i = [P_i - h(Z_i)] \cdot X_i - L_{Zi}$, where, taking the wage rate as the numeraire, L_{Zi} is R&D expenditure. With perfect foresight, V_i is the stock market value of the firm, the price of the ownership share of an equity holder.

I consider a symmetric Nash equilibrium (NE) in open-loop strategies. Let $a_i = [P_i(\tau), L_{Zi}(\tau)]$ for $\tau \geq t$ be firm i's strategy, where $P_i(\tau)$ and $L_{Zi}(\tau)$ are the time-paths of price and R&D. This price and R&D strategy induces time-paths of production, sales, and innovation. At time t, firms commit to time-paths of price and R&D, taking as given the time-path of the number of firms.[8] Similarly, entrants take as given the incumbents' time-paths of price and R&D. Let $V_i(N, a_1, \ldots, a_N)$ be the value of the firm when there are N firms playing strategies $(a_1, \ldots, a_N)$. At time t, $[N, a_1, \ldots, a_N]$ is an instantaneous equilibrium with free entry and free exit if for all i

$$V_i[N, a_1, \ldots, a_i, \ldots, a_N] \geq V_i[N, a_1, \ldots, a_i', \ldots, a_N] \geq 0 \tag{8}$$

and for all N

$$V_i[N+1, a_1, \ldots, a_{N+1}] \leq 1/\beta, \tag{9}$$

where a_i' denotes that firm i deviates from the optimal time-paths of price and R&D while the other firms do not deviate (see Dasgupta and Stiglitz, 1980). Condition (8) requires that the active firm maximizes the present value of net cash flow, taking as given the other firms' strategies, and that this maximized value be nonnegative. The latter inequality is the free-exit condition since the scrapping value of the active firm, the opportunity cost of incumbency, is zero. Equation (9) is the free-entry condition that the value of the entrants, net of sunk entry costs, be nonpositive.

3.2. Pricing and Research

The intertemporal problem of the firm is to maximize value (7), subject to the production and R&D technologies (5) and (6), the demand schedule (4), $Z_i(t) > 0$ (the initial knowledge stock is given), $Z_j(\tau)$ for $\tau \geq t$ and $j \neq i$ (the firm takes as given the rivals' innovation paths), and $\dot{Z}_i(\tau) \geq 0$ for $\tau \geq t$ (innovation is irreversible). The current value Hamiltonian is

$$CVH_i = [P_i - h(Z_i)] \cdot X_i - L_{Zi} + q_i \cdot \alpha K \cdot \left[L_{Zi} + \gamma \sum_{j \neq i}^{N} L_{Zj} \right],$$

where the costate variable q_i is the value of the patent. The firm's knowledge stock Z_i is the state variable, and R&D investment L_{Zi} and the product's price P_i are the control variables.

Irreversibility of research and the finite labor supply impose bounds on R&D investment in this problem, $0 \leq \int_0^N (L_{Zi} + L_{Xi}) \, di \leq L$. The linear Hamiltonian yields

$$L_{Zi} = \begin{cases} 0 & \text{for } 1 > q_i \cdot \alpha K \\ L_Z/N & \text{for } 1 = q_i \cdot \alpha K, \\ \infty & \text{for } 1 < q_i \cdot \alpha K, \end{cases}$$

where L_Z/N is a finite value to be specified below. The case $1 > q_i \cdot \alpha K$ implies that the value of the innovation is lower than its cost and the firm does not invest. The case $1 < q_i \cdot \alpha K$ implies that the value of the innovation is higher than its cost. This case violates the GE conditions and is ruled out. The first-order conditions for the interior solution are given by equality between the marginal benefit and marginal cost of the innovation, $1 = q_i \cdot \alpha K$, the transversality condition, $\lim_{t \to \infty} R(t) \cdot q_i(t) \cdot Z_i(t) = 0$, the constraint on the state variable, $\dot{Z}_i = L_{Zi} \cdot \alpha K$, and a differential equation in the costate variable,

$$r = \frac{\dot{q}_i}{q_i} - \frac{h'(Z_i) \cdot X_i}{q_i}, \tag{10}$$

that defines the rate of return to R&D as the ratio between revenues from the innovation and its (shadow) price plus (minus) the appreciation (depreciation) in the value of the knowledge stock. Revenues from the innovation are given by the cost reduction it yields times the scale of production to which it applies. The optimal Bertrand-Nash price strategy is

$$\frac{P_i}{h(Z_i)} = \frac{\eta_i}{\eta_i - 1}, \tag{11}$$

where $\eta_i \equiv \varepsilon - (\varepsilon - 1) \cdot S_i$ is the price elasticity of demand that firm i faces and the market share S_i has been defined in Section 2.[9] A Bertrand-Nash equilibrium exists only if the price elasticity of demand is larger than one. In symmetric equilibrium, this requires $N > 1$.

Consider now the interior solution where the condition $1 = q_i \cdot \alpha K$ holds, and let $g_K \equiv \dot{K}/K$ be the rate of growth of public knowledge. One can reduce the first-order conditions to

$$r + g_K = \frac{LE\alpha\theta(\eta_i - 1)S_i}{\eta_i} \cdot \frac{K}{Z_i}. \tag{12}$$

This is a perfect-foresight, no-arbitrage condition that defines the rate of to R&D for firm i. Specifically, revenues from the innovation must equal the cost of R&D financed by borrowing at the market interest rate (direct cost), and this must equal the return on a riskless loan, at the market rate, of the resources spent on R&D (opportunity cost). The rate of return to R&D is the market interest rate r plus the term g_K because the cost of R&D falls with the accumulation of public knowledge.

The NE of this symmetric knowledge accumulation game is given by the first-order conditions for all firms. The following proposition establishes a property that turns out to be very useful.

Proposition 1: *Assume* $\theta(\varepsilon - 1) < 1$. *The NE has a symmetric steady state.*

Proof. See the appendix.

This result allows study of the dynamics of the model by focusing on the symmetric steady state of the NE.[10] This requires some additional assumptions, discussed in the appendix, but it simplifies the analysis because it reduces the space-state of the model to only two variables (see below).

In symmetric equilibrium, (12) yields the rate of innovation

$$g_Z = g_K = \alpha \cdot [1 + \gamma(N - 1)] \cdot \frac{L_Z}{N}, \tag{13}$$

where L_Z is aggregate employment in R&D ("aggregate R&D") and L_Z/N is average employment in R&D ("average R&D"). Using (12), the rate of return to R&D becomes

$$r_{R\&D} = \alpha \cdot \left[\frac{LE\theta(\eta - 1)}{N\eta} - \frac{L_Z}{N} \cdot [1 + \gamma(N - 1)] \right], \tag{14}$$

where $\eta = \varepsilon - (\varepsilon - 1)/N$. Below, I refer to this equation as the R&D locus.

The terms $LE/N\eta$ and $\theta(\eta - 1)$ are, respectively, the *gross-profit* and the *business-stealing* effects. These arise from firms' market interaction. Intuitively, the returns to R&D are given by the gross profits earned on a given market share and by the increase in market share achieved by the R&D project. The gross-profit effect has two components—a *scale* effect, captured by the firm's sales LE/N; and a *markup* effect, captured by the profit margin $1/\eta$. The gross-profit effect is decreasing in the number of firms because both the market share and the oligopoly markup are lower the larger is N. In contrast, the business-stealing effect is increasing in the number of firms because the potential gain of market share is proportional to the rivals' total market share. To see this, note that $\theta(\eta - 1) = \theta(\varepsilon - 1)(N - 1)/N$, where $(N - 1)/N$ is the rivals' market share. Overall, the rate of return to R&D is hump-shaped in the number of firms because the business-stealing effect, which depends on the rivals' market share, and the gross-profit effect, which depends on the firm's market share, work in opposite directions.

The term $-L_Z[1 + \gamma(N - 1)]/N$ is the *intertemporal-spillover* effect. Firms do not include in the value of innovations their contribution to reducing future R&D costs. This includes the contemporaneous interaction in R&D. Intuitively, the larger the contemporaneous interaction, the larger the intertemporal spillovers since at any moment in time more knowledge is created for a given level of R&D effort.

3.3. *Entry*

The discussion in Section 2 allows me to posit the aggregate entry technology $\dot{N} = \beta \cdot L_N$, where $\beta > 0$ is the productivity of labor in entry and L_N is the amount of labor devoted to starting up $\dot{N}$ new firms for an interval of time dt. Note the change of notation. I defined preferences (2) over a range of differentiated goods where the number of goods N is discrete. It is, however, convenient in the following analysis to treat N as a continuous variable. I could have defined preferences over a continuum of goods and used integrals, thus eliminating the need to change notation. However, the assumptions discussed in Section 2 and the definition of equilibrium given in Section 3 are much more transparent if one treats the number of firms as discrete. Thus, I chose to discuss the setup of the model with a discrete N and switch now to treating it as a continuous variable.

Entry costs $1/\beta$ and produces value V_i. The case $V_i > 1/\beta$ yields an unbounded demand for labor in entry and is ruled out. A free-entry equilibrium requires $V_i \leq 1/\beta$, with equality whenever $\dot{N} > 0$ and strict inequality whenever $\dot{N} = 0$. This implies that in an equilibrium with entry the exit condition is not binding. This is intuitive: entry costs lead to different thresholds for entry and exit. Here the threshold value for exit, zero, is never binding since firms have the option of setting R&D to zero and the value of the firms is strictly positive.

Taking logs and time-derivatives of (7) and rearranging terms yields

$$r = \frac{\Pi_i}{V_i} + \frac{\dot{V}_i}{V_i},$$

which is a perfect-foresight, no-arbitrage condition for the equilibrium of the capital market. It requires that the rate of return to firm ownership equal the rate of return to a riskless loan of size V_i. The rate of return to firm ownership is the ratio between profits and the firm's stock market value plus the capital gain (loss) from the stock appreciation (depreciation).

In an equilibrium with entry, $V_i = 1/\beta$ implies $\dot{V}_i = 0$, and one obtains the instantaneous free-entry condition $r = \beta \Pi_i$. Imposing symmetry yields the rate of return to entry,

$$r_{\text{entry}} = \beta \cdot \left[\frac{LE}{\eta N} - \frac{L_Z}{N} \right]. \tag{15}$$

The condition $V_i = 1/\beta$ implies that in an equilibrium with entry, the rate of return to entry is equal to the rate of return to firm ownership. The former is equal to the ratio between net revenues and entry costs. Alternatively, if profits are distributed to shareholders, the rate of return to firm ownership is equal to the ratio between dividends and the value of the firm. Below, I refer to this equation as the entry locus.

The terms $LE/\eta N$ and L_Z/N are, respectively, the gross-profit and the *R&D-cost* effects. In equilibrium, gross profits equal entry costs. These have two components—R&D expenditures and interest payments on exogenous entry costs. The former are the costs that the entrant pays to keep the pace of progress of the industry. The latter are the costs that he pays to write off the initial start-up investment.

3.4. The Free-Entry Equilibrium

I have discussed two types of investments—in-house R&D and start-up of new firms. No-arbitrage in the capital market requires that they yield equal rates of return.

Proposition 2: *Assume* $\beta < \alpha\theta(\varepsilon - 1) < \alpha$. *The following free-entry equilibrium exist:*

$$
L_Z = \begin{cases} 0 & \text{for } 1 < N \le N_0 \\ \dfrac{LE}{\eta} \cdot \dfrac{\alpha\theta(\eta - 1) - \beta}{\alpha[1 + \gamma(N - 1)] - \beta} & \text{for } N > N_0 \end{cases} , \tag{16}
$$

where $N_0 \equiv \alpha\theta(\varepsilon - 1) - \beta]$.

Proof. See the appendix

In order to keep the exposition from becoming taxonomic, and to address the issues that motivate this article, I focus on this equilibrium. (A full characterization of the set of possible equilibria is available on request.) Equation (16) expresses aggregate R&D L_Z as a percentage of aggregate gross profits LE/η. There is a critical number of firms N_0 that identifies a no-R&D region. Let $g \equiv \theta \cdot g_Z$ be the average rate of cost reduction. This is the rate of growth of labor productivity ("growth"). Equations (13) and (16) yield

$$
g = \begin{cases} 0 & \text{for } 1 < N \le N_0 \\ \alpha\theta \cdot \dfrac{1 + \gamma(N - 1)}{N} \cdot \dfrac{LE}{\eta} \cdot \dfrac{\alpha\theta(\eta - 1) - \beta}{\alpha[1 + \gamma(N - 1)] - \beta} & \text{for } N > N_0 \end{cases} . \tag{17}
$$

The equilibrium rate of return to investment (R&D and entry) is

$$
r = \begin{cases} \beta \cdot \dfrac{LE}{\eta N} & \text{for } 1 < N \le N_0 \\ \beta \cdot \dfrac{LE}{\eta N} \cdot \dfrac{\alpha[1 + \gamma(N - 1) - \theta(\eta - 1)]}{\alpha[1 + \gamma(N - 1)] - \beta} & \text{for } N > N_0 \end{cases} \tag{18}
$$

It is useful to emphasize the relation between the growth rate and the state variables of the model.

Result 1: *In free-entry equilibrium, growth g is hump-shaped in the number of firms N and increasing in aggregate consumption expenditure LE.*

These properties are explained by the *rivalry*, *dispersion*, and *scale* effects. These effects play a central role in this model, and it is worth discussing them in detail.

The rivalry effect—the effect of an increase in the number of firms on aggregate R&D—is captured by the slope of (16). Consider Figure 1 and recall that firms take as given the time-paths of consumption and the number of firms. At a moment in time, therefore, the only variable that adjusts to ensure equality of the rates of return to R&D and entry is aggregate

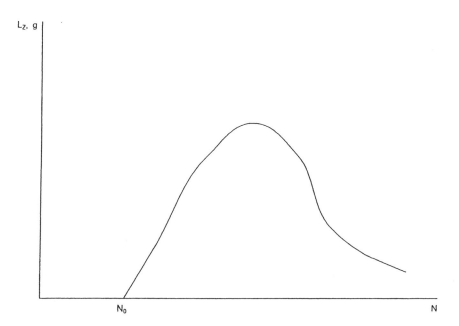

Figure 1.

R&D. Consider an increase in the number of firms. The rate of return to entry falls. The rate of return to R&D may fall or rise since it is hump-shaped in the number of firms. In Figure 1, the rivalry effect is initially positive and then negative. The intuition is simple. Consider Figure 2, which plots the two rate-of-return schedules in (N, r) space, and recall that the condition $\alpha > \beta$ implies that labor is more productive in R&D than in entry. Let equilibrium be at the crossing of the two loci on the upward sloping portion of the R&D locus. Suppose an increase in the number of firms. The rate of return to entry is now lower than the rate of return to R&D. An increase in aggregate R&D lowers the rate of return to R&D faster than the rate of return to entry, thereby closing the gap between them and restoring equilibrium. Suppose, in contrast, that equilibrium is initially on the downward sloping portion of the R&D locus. A reduction in aggregate R&D raises the rate of return to R&D faster than the rate of return to entry and restores equilibrium.

The dispersion effect—the effect of an increase in the number of firms on growth for a given level of aggregate R&D—captures the notion that firm size and concentration of R&D resources determine the rate of productivity growth of this economy. In this model, the rate of cost reduction depends on the scale of the R&D program of the individual firm. Growth, accordingly, depends on average R&D, not aggregate R&D. The dispersion effect can be compensated by contemporaneous interaction in R&D. One can see in (17) that for $\gamma = 1$ there is no dispersion affect at all.

66

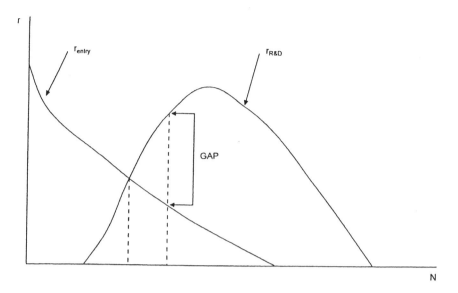

Figure 2.

Finally, consider an increase in aggregate demand LE. Both rates of return increase, but the rate of return to R&D increases more than the rate of return to entry. Hence, restoring equilibrium requires an increase in aggregate R&D. This is the standard scale effect of R&D models with increasing returns. As the size of the market increases, the rents available to innovators increase and aggregate R&D increases.

4. General Equilibrium, Dynamics, and the Evolution of the Capitalist Engine of Growth

In this section I characterize the transitional dynamics of the model and discuss the main results of the article. The fundamental insight is that he endogenous evolution of market structure, in particular the increase in market rivalry, drives the change in incentives that ·leads from a regime where growth comes from entry of new firms that bring to the market new goods and processes, to a regime where growth comes from in-house R&D that established firms undertake in order to reduce production costs and increase product quality. I conclude the section with a critical review of the setup of the model and a comparison of the formulation adopted in this article to alternative specifications that yield similar results.

4.1. General Equilibrium

To determine the aggregate dynamics of the economy, I impose two GE conditions—labor market clearing and equality between the rate of return to investment and the rate of return to saving. Substituting the price strategy (11) into the cost function (5), using (4), and summing across firms yields aggregate employment in production ("aggregate production")

$$L_X = \frac{LE(\eta - 1)}{\eta}. \tag{19}$$

Labor market clearing requires $L = L_X + L_Z + L_N$, where $L_N = \dot{N}/\beta$ is aggregate employment in entry. In an equilibrium with entry, employment in all activities must be positive and $L > L_X + L_Z$ must hold. Substituting (16) and (19) into the labor market clearing condition yields

$$\dot{N} = \beta \cdot \begin{cases} L - \dfrac{LE(\eta - 1)}{\eta} & \text{for } E < E_0(N) \text{ and } 1 < N \leq N_0 \\[2ex] L - \dfrac{LE}{\eta} \cdot \left[(\eta - 1) + \dfrac{\alpha\theta(\eta - 1) - \beta}{\alpha[1 + \gamma(N - 1)] - \beta} \right] & \text{for } E < E_0(N) \text{ and } N > N_0 \\[2ex] 0 & \text{for } E \geq E_0(N) \text{ and } N > 1 \end{cases} \tag{20}$$

where

$$E_0(N) = \begin{cases} \dfrac{\eta}{\eta - 1} & \text{for } 1 < N \leq N_0 \\[2ex] \eta \cdot \left[\dfrac{\eta - 1}{\eta} + \dfrac{\alpha\theta(\eta - 1) - \beta}{\alpha[1 + \gamma(N - 1)] - \beta} \right]^{-1} & \text{for } N > N_0 \end{cases}$$

The rate of return to investment is given by (18). The expenditure plan (3) yields

$$\frac{\dot{E}}{E} = \begin{cases} \beta \cdot \dfrac{LE}{\eta N} - \rho & 1 < N \leq N_0 \\[2ex] \beta \cdot \dfrac{LE}{\eta N} \cdot \dfrac{\alpha[1 + \gamma(N - 1) - \theta(\eta - 1)]}{\alpha[1 + \gamma(N - 1)] - \beta} - \rho & N > N_0 \end{cases} \tag{21}$$

The GE of the economy is thus described by a system of two differential equations in (N, E) space.

4.2. Transitional Dynamics

Consider the phase diagram in Figure 3. The constraint $0 \leq L_X \leq L$ defines the feasible region of the phase plane. Using (19), this can be written

$$0 \leq E \leq \overline{E}(N) \equiv \frac{\eta}{\eta - 1}.$$

Above this locus labor demand exceeds the finite labor supply. The $E_0(N)$ locus defined in (20) splits the phase plane in two regions: above the locus, entry is not profitable; below it, entry is profitable. These are, respectively, the blockaded-entry and the free-entry region. Setting $\dot{E} = 0$ yields

$$E = \begin{cases} \dfrac{\rho \eta N}{L\beta} & \text{for } 1 < N \le N_0 \\[2ex] \dfrac{\rho \eta N}{L\beta} \cdot \dfrac{\alpha[1 + \gamma(N-1)] - \beta}{\alpha[1 + \gamma(N-1) - \theta(\eta-1)]} & \text{for } N > N_0 \end{cases}. \tag{22}$$

Expenditure increases above this locus and decreases below it. Crossing of the $\dot{E} = 0$ and $E_0(N)$ loci identifies the free-entry steady state (N_{FE}, E_{FE}). In the entry region to the right of (N_{FE}, E_{FE}) there is a saddle path leading to that point.

Proposition 3: *There is a unique perfect-foresight GE. If the initial number of firms is smaller than N_{FE}, the economy jumps on the saddle path and converges to (N_{FE}, E_{FE}). If the initial number of firms is larger than N_{FE}, the economy enters a steady state with no entry.*

Proof. See the appendix.

The free-entry steady state can occur to the left or to the right of N_0. In the former case I have a free-entry steady state with zero R&D; in the latter, I have a free-entry steady state with positive R&D. Inspection of Figure 3 suggests that the steady state (N_{FE}, E_{FE}) is in the R&D region if the $\dot{E} = 0$ locus evaluated at N_0 is below the $E_0(N)$ locus evaluated at the same point. Recalling that the definition of N_0 implies $\alpha\theta(\eta - 1) = \beta$, one can show that this condition reduces to

$$L > \frac{\rho}{\alpha\theta} \cdot \frac{\alpha\theta(\varepsilon - 1)}{\alpha\theta(\varepsilon - 1) - \beta}.$$

Intuitively, the free-entry steady state is inside the R&D region if population is sufficiently large.

4.3. Steady-State Comparative Statics

It is useful to describe the steady states of this model as follows. First, I construct the locus *FF* of the full-employment, value-maximizing labor allocations. This locus describes equilibria where entry is blockaded and the number of firms does not adjust endogenously to changes in parameters. (Thus, it describes the equilibrium of a model with an exogenous number of firms.) Consider the rate of return to R&D in (14). In steady state, this must equal the discount rate ρ. Using (19), the labor market clearing condition, and (13) yields

$$g = \begin{cases} \dfrac{\theta[1 + \gamma(N-1)]}{\theta + 1 + \gamma(N-1)} \cdot \left[\dfrac{L\alpha\theta}{N} - \rho\right] & \text{for } 1 < N < \overline{N} \\[2ex] 0 & \text{for } N \ge \overline{N} \end{cases}. \tag{23}$$

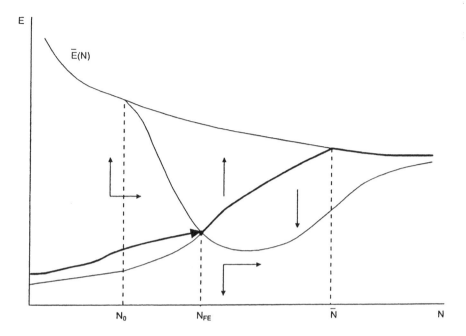

Figure 3.

Next, I construct the locus *NN* of the no-arbitrage, value-maximizing labor allocations. This locus describes equilibria where the number of firms adjusts endogenously to changes in parameters. The no-arbitrage condition for the rates of return to R&D and entry yields the R&D equation (16). Using (22) and (13) yields

$$g = \begin{cases} 0 & \text{for } 1 < N \le N_0 \\ \dfrac{\theta\rho}{\beta} \cdot \dfrac{[1+\gamma(N-1)] \cdot [\alpha\theta(\eta-1)-\beta]}{1+\gamma(N-1)-\theta(\eta-1)} & \text{for } N > N_0 \end{cases} \tag{24}$$

These equations, depicted in Figure 4, give two loci in (N, g) space.

The *NN* locus is hump-shaped, initially increasing, then decreasing, but bounded from below. The *FF* locus is everywhere decreasing. The key to these loci is that for a given allocation of labor to R&D there is a tradeoff between the number of firms and growth. The *FF* locus identifies this tradeoff in the labor market. Suppose an increase in the number of firms. Equation (14) implies that the rate of return to R&D stays equal to ρ if aggregate production rises. This implies a fall in aggregate R&D and, because the number of firms has risen, an even larger fall in average R&D. As a consequence, growth falls. The *NN* locus identifies the tradeoff in the capital market. When the number of firms rises, (22) and (19) require that aggregate production rise to keep the rate of return to R&D and entry equal

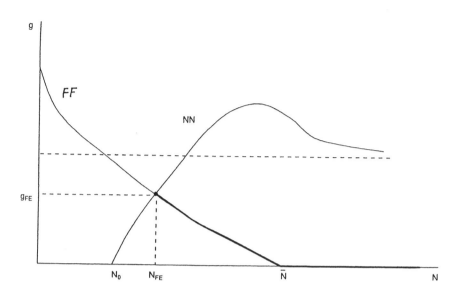

Figure 4.

to ρ. Equation (16), on the other hand, implies that aggregate R&D rises when aggregate production rises. In addition, the rivalry effect implies that the initial increase in the number of firms leads to an increase in aggregate R&D. Initially, these two effects are more than sufficient to make up for the fall in average R&D caused by the larger number of firms, and, therefore, growth rises with the number of firms. Eventually, the dispersion effect dominates, and further increases in the number of firms lead to lower growth.

A discussion of the comparative statics effects of the parameters is beyond the scope of this article. (Results are available on request.) It is, however, useful to discuss in some detail an example. Consider the effects of the opportunity parameter α. Equation (3.10) states that the increase in the productivity of labor in R&D leads to an increase in aggregate R&D. Labor market clearing implies that aggregate production falls, and to keep all rates of return equal to ρ the number of firms must fall. The intuition for the fall in the number of firms is the *escalation* effect (Sutton, 1991): better technological opportunity leads firms to spend more on R&D, but R&D expenditures are sunk costs that make entry and incumbency more costly and labor more scarce for production. These forces explain the reduction in the number of firms.[11] The effect on growth depends on the balance between the first-order effect of α, which increases growth for any level of aggregate R&D, and the second-order effect, the endogenous adjustment in the number of firms and in the allocation of labor to R&D. Here, aggregate R&D increases and the number of firms falls. Hence, average R&D increases and growth rises.

This mechanism leads to the even more interesting results on population size L.

Result 2: *Population size has a threshold effect on growth, when the number of firms becomes sufficiently large to "trigger" R&D spending. Beyond that point, population size has a positive effect on growth. As the number of firms becomes very large, population size has a negative effect on growth that vanishes asymptotically.*

To see the global effect of population size, it is sufficient to notice that the *NN* locus does not depend on L so that as population increase the *FF* locus shifts out and traces the *NN* locus. An increase in population implies that the resource base of the economy is larger. One expects both aggregate R&D and production to rise. Suppose that the extra labor force initially goes into production and that the number of firms rises. Although both these changes drive up aggregate R&D, via the rivalry and the scale effects, the dispersion effect might be so strong that growth falls. This *crowding-in* effect is the intuition for the downward-sloping portion of the NN locus: in an already crowded market a further enlargement leads to a dominant dispersion effect and a fall in growth. As the number of firms becomes very large, these effects cancel out, and growth is asymptotically independent of population size.[12]

4.4. Interpreting the Transition: Industrial Structure and the Nature of R&D Competition

The phase diagram in Figure 3 allows me to address the issues raised by the historical evidence discussed in the introduction.

Result 3: *The economy starts out in the no-R&D region where existing firms do not undertake in-house R&D. When a critical number of firms have entered the market, established firms begin investing in R&D. The economy then converges to a steady state where no new firms are created but where productivity grows at a constant rate due to the R&D activity of established firms.*

What happens to the economy's rate of growth along this transition? At a moment in time, the behavior of the growth rate g is given by (17). Along the transition, aggregate demand LE and the number of firms N increase. The behavior of the growth rate, therefore, depends on the interaction of the rivalry, dispersion, and scale effects. Decomposing (17), growth depends on aggregate demand LE and a term that summarizes the effects of the number of firms,

$$f(N) \equiv \alpha\theta \cdot \frac{1 + \gamma(N-1)}{N} \cdot \frac{\alpha\theta(\eta-1) - \beta}{\alpha[1 + \gamma(N-1)] - \beta}.$$

This term is hump-shaped because the rivalry effect is positive and initially dominates over the dispersion effect. Eventually, the rivalry effect turns negative and $f(N)$ goes to zero as the number of firms grows large. The two cases represented in Figure 5 are possible. In the first case, the scale effect is very strong and dominates over the rivalry and dispersion affects. The rate of growth is initially zero. It then increases throughout the transition and approaches the steady-state value from below. In the second case, the rivalry and dispersion effects, whose balance eventually turns negative, dominate over the scale effect. The rate of

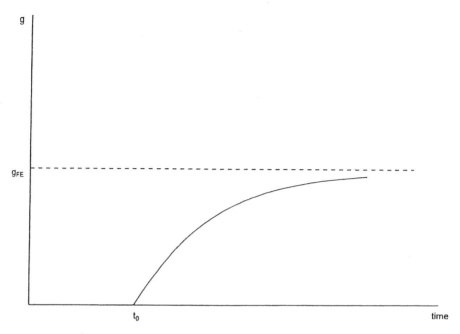

Figure 5a.

growth is initially zero and then increases for a while, overshooting the steady-state level. Eventually, it starts to decrease and approaches the steady-state value from above.

The key to these dynamics is the following mechanism. The R&D behavior of forward-looking firms depends on expected market rivalry because this determines the future returns to innovation. Market rivalry, on the other hand, is endogenous. In particular, the entry behavior of forward-looking firms depends on the expected R&D behavior in the post-entry equilibrium. In an environment where firms live forever and develop innovations in-house, R&D expenditure is one component of the firm's total cost and increases the cost of incumbency. It is useful to be specific here. Incumbents take as given the time-path of entry, and entrants take as given incumbents' time-paths of price and R&D. Incumbents and entrants have rational expectations and, with perfect foresight, correctly anticipate these time-paths. The symmetric free-entry equilibrium, then, can be represented with the simple feedback rule (16) that yields aggregate R&D as a function of aggregate demand and the number of firms in the market. This rule describes how, at a moment in time, current demand and market structure determine the rate of growth of the economy and its response to changes in the fundamentals and policy variables. To assess the long-run effects of these changes, one needs to track the endogenous evolution of aggregate demand and the number of firms. This point leads to the main results discussed in this section. In the long run, the number of firms, productivity growth, aggregate demand, and the interest rate

EVOLUTION OF THE CAPITALIST ENGINE OF GROWTH   73

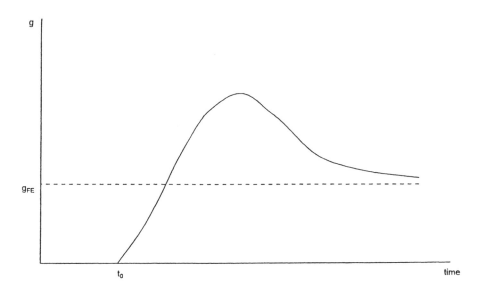

Figure 5b.

are endogenous and jointly determined. The number of firms, in particular, is a sufficient statistic for the state of competition and therefore for the relation between returns to R&D and returns to entry. The time-path of the number of firms, thus, predicts the timing and the shape of the transition from growth led by entrepreneurial R&D to growth led by corporate R&D.

This analytical structure allows me to tell the following story. The economy starts out with a small range of consumption goods, each one supplied by a single firm. Households like variety and buy all available consumption goods. There are, therefore, high returns from bringing new goods to the market. Entry is costly, and entrepreneurs compare the present value of profits from introducing a new good to the entry cost. Once in the market, firms live forever and engage in price competition. When profitable, they establish in-house R&D facilities. This event occurs when a sufficiently large number of firms have entered the market and rivalry has become sufficiently tough. The business-stealing effect is critical here: only when the number of firms in the market is large, it pays off for incumbents to invest in R&D in order to reduce costs, offer lower prices, and steal market share. The economy, therefore, undergoes a change in the structure of incentives. Differently from entry, in addition, I have assumed that the process of in-house innovation is self-sustaining. As firms invest in R&D, they contribute to the pool of public knowledge and reduce the cost of future R&D. These intertemporal spillovers allow the economy to grow at a constant rate in steady state. This is reached when entry peters out and the economy settles into a stable industrial structure.[13]

74

4.5. Alternative Specifications

It is useful to compare the specification that I adopted in this article with two alternative ones that yield qualitatively similar results. The first one is straightforward. Although I tell the story in terms of consumption goods, nothing substantial changes if my oligopolistic firms do not sell differentiated consumption goods to consumers but supply specialized inputs to producers of consumption goods. Formally, one simply defines the utility index (2) as the production function for a final good that is sold by a competitive firm. This production function is thus defined over a range of nondurable intermediate inputs supplied by a number of specialized suppliers. One advantage of this formulation, one might argue, is that the expansion of the range of specialized good affects the output of the final good that grows even in the absence of in-house cost-reducing R&D in the intermediate sector. Allowing for this additional source of growth is surely interesting, above all if one wants to check the aggregate empirical implications of the model. It is not necessary, however, to make the main point of this article. Again, the key to my story is the endogenous evolution of market structure and its effects on the incentives to entry and in-house R&D. Whether entry leads only to growth of utility or also to growth of physical output is irrelevant since the main mechanism remains the same.

Similarly, nothing substantial changes if my oligopolistic firms—whether sellers of consumption goods or suppliers of intermediate goods—do not engage in cost-reducing R&D but in quality-improving R&D. Quality improvement and cost reduction are formally equivalent when one considers the quality of the good as determining the cost at which the good delivers its services (Spence, 1984; Tirole, 1988). Thus, although I focus on cost reduction, I can rewrite the model in terms of quality improvement and interpret it as a smooth version (quality being a continuous variable) of the quality-ladder model with an endogenous variety of goods (number of firms). One advantage of this formulation, one might argue, is that it makes clear that it is not the switch from product innovation to process innovation that matters in this article. Whether growth comes from innovations that improve labor productivity in the same sector where they are originated or in some downstream sector is irrelevant to my story (see Scherer, 1984, for an empirical definition of product and process R&D along these lines). What really matters is whether innovations are carried out by established producers or by outsiders that set up new firms in order to bring the innovations to the market. Established firms make decisions based on the marginal value of knowledge.[14] Entrants, in contrast, base their decisions on the value of the firm. In particular, they do so by taking into account that once they join the industry, they have to keep improving the product, or reduce the cost, in order to keep up with the competition. This is a crucial point because R&D expenditure is a sunk cost that increases the cost of incumbency. It is the interaction between incentives to entry and incentives to in-house R&D that shapes the transition path depicted in Figure 3. As argued, this interaction is captured by the endogenous evolution of market structure.

5. Conclusion

History suggests that new industries are borne out of radical innovations that come about in a crude form and whose arrival is driven by events outside the domain of economic forces. Crafts (1996), for example, argues that *macroinventions*, like the invention of the internal combustion engine, the light bulb, the transistor, or the personal computer, all inventions that started some of today's major "technologies" or "industries," should be described as unpredictable events that to a large extent originate from outside the economic system. Once the basic invention appears, however, economic forces take over and drive the development of the technology through the systematic implementation of *microinventions*. If one imagines that the model developed in this article describes industries that at some moment in time start out under similar conditions, then each industry goes through a *life cycle* described by the dynamics discussed in the previous section. To the extent that industries are similar, their life cycles are synchronized.

In many industrial sectors a major change in the locus of innovation occurred at the turn of the nineteenth century and in the early twentieth century. In those years, a large number of basic inventions appeared that either started entirely new industries or revolutionized existing ones. These macroinventions appeared as an *artifact* and a *technique*, a specific product and the process to make it, and a *knowledge base* that provided the framework for further development of the technology through minor but systematic improvements (see Mowery and Rosenberg, 1989, chs. 3–4, and the references cited therein for a number of examples). When the basic idea of a truly new good appears—say, the idea of the personal computer or of the integrated circuit—a revolution occurs: something fundamentally new has been invented. Technologically, much of the development of the original idea is just a refinement of the original version of the product or process. According to Rosenberg (1982, ch. 3), however, this is where the contribution of the new idea to productivity and living standards comes from. Economically, the microinventions that perfect the original macroinvention are crucial (although they might be, and often are, perceived as technologically marginal). The question, then, is where do these microinventions come from and at what rate do they arrive. This article provides an answer. The profit, often phenomenal, made by the original monopolist attracts entry. As more and more entrepreneurs enter the market, the industry becomes more competitive. As market rivalry becomes tougher, established producers find it profitable to start exploring the technology through in-house R&D. The economy, then, experiences a transition from entrepreneurial to corporate R&D.

It is straightforward to generalize this story to interpret the evidence discussed in the introduction. The cluster of macroinventions that occurred in the late nineteenth century and early twentieth century gave birth to industries whose dynamics are similar and synchronized because the basic economic mechanism driving their development is the same. This suggests the next question on the research agenda. Why did these macroinventions appear in a cluster? To the extent that macroinventions are not events that can be entirely explained or predicted by looking at strictly economic forces, answering this question requires a careful analysis of the history of each technology in order to identify the scientific and technological forces that determined its appearance in the first place. Perhaps it would help to think of macroinventions as the solutions to some critical problems that constrain determined human activities, needs or desires (like the desire of flying and the consequent invention of the airplane). A better understanding of the technological and economic problem that each macroinvention solved, together with a better understanding of the basic motivation that spurred the inventor and of the basic constraints he had to face, would help explain the clustering of major inventions that appeared at the turn of the century and that originated many of today's industries.

Appendix: Proofs of Propositions

Proof of Proposition 1

Substituting (11) into (10) and integrating forward yields

$$q_i(t) = \int_t^\infty R(\tau)[LE\theta(\eta_i - 1)S_i/\eta_i Z_i]\, d\tau,$$

which defines the value of the innovation as the present discounted value of its contribution to current and future profits. The price strategy (11) yields a downward-sloping relationship between the product's price P_i and the firm's knowledge stock Z_i. Holding constant the knowledge stocks of all firms other than i, as the knowledge of firm i goes to infinity, the firm's price goes to zero and the market share S_i goes to one. This yields $\eta_i = 1$, and the value of the innovation goes to zero. In contrast, as the knowledge stock of firm i goes to zero, the firm's price goes to infinity and the firm's market share goes to zero. This yields $\eta_i = \varepsilon$ and the value of the innovation depends on the ratio between the market share and the knowledge stock,

$$\lim_{Z_i \to 0} \frac{S_i}{Z_i} = \lim_{Z_i \to 0} \frac{Z_i^{\theta(\varepsilon-1)-1}}{\sum_{i=1}^N Z_i^{\theta(\varepsilon-1)}} = \begin{cases} +\infty & \text{for } \theta(\varepsilon-1) < 1 \\ 0 & \text{for } \theta(\varepsilon-1) > 1 \end{cases}.$$

If the value of the innovation is decreasing in the firm's knowledge stock, the NE is symmetric and stable in the sense that if firms start out with different knowledge stocks, they converge to symmetry. Hence, a sufficient condition for stability is that the market share as a function of the knowledge stock satisfies the Inada-type condition that the marginal gain of market share is infinite when the firm's knowledge stock is close to zero. This intuition explains why the value of the innovation goes to zero when the knowledge stock is infinite: the firm becomes a global monopolist, and, as its market share approaches one, the marginal gain in market share approaches zero. The condition $\theta(\varepsilon - 1) < 1$, therefore, is sufficient for stability because it rules out situations where the firm's market share exhibits increasing returns to the knowledge stock. Now, there are two ways to support a symmetric NE at all times:

• Suppose that innovations are not firm-specific and can be traded in the patent market. Like in partial equilibrium models of investment in physical capital, this property implies that the firm's knowledge stock can change discretely at a point in time. This, however, does not mean that the aggregate knowledge stock can do so. Increases in the aggregate knowledge stock can be achieved only by allocating labor to R&D, and this activity is always constrained by the finite labor endowment. Since firms can trade knowledge, the industry-level transitional dynamics reduce to a jump to the steady state.

- Suppose that innovations are firm specific or cannot be traded in the patent market. Since innovations have to be produced in-house, the firm's knowledge stock cannot change discretely since there is an upper bound on R&D implied by the given labor supply. If firms have different initial knowledge stocks, there is convergence in time to the symmetric steady state. In order to have symmetry at all times one needs to assume identical initial conditions. This assumption and the characterization of entry discussed in Section 2 yield that the industry is always in symmetric equilibrium.

Proof of Proposition 2

The free-entry equilibrium can be represented in a diagram with the rate of return r on the vertical axis and aggregate R&D L_Z on the horizontal axis. The restriction $\theta(\varepsilon - 1) < 1$ implies that $\theta(\eta - 1) < 1$ for all $N > 1$. This implies that the R&D locus cuts the horizontal axis at a point to the left of that where the entry locus cuts it. The parameters α and β determine the slopes of the R&D and entry loci. A sufficient condition of the two loci to cross for positive values of the rate of return r is $\alpha > \beta$, which implies that the productivity of labor in R&D is higher than the productivity of labor in entry. This implies that the R&D locus is steeper than the entry locus since $\alpha[1 + \gamma(N - 1)] > \beta$ for all $N > 1$. To have an equilibrium with positive R&D, the R&D locus must have a higher intercept than the entry locus. This requires $\alpha\theta(\eta - 1) > \beta$. If this condition is violated, the two loci cross for a negative value of aggregate R&D, the nonnegativity constraint on R&D is binding, and $L_Z = 0$. Hence, the condition $\alpha\theta(\varepsilon - 1) > \beta$ must hold, otherwise R&D is always zero. Therefore, an equilibrium with entry and R&D (possibly zero) exists if $\beta < \alpha\theta(\varepsilon - 1) < \alpha$.

Proof of Proposition 3

All points on the $\dot{E} = 0$ locus in the blockaded-entry region are steady states. These are the blockaded-entry steady states with positive R&D. Crossing of the $\dot{E} = 0$ and $\bar{E}(N)$ loci identifies the point $(\bar{N}, \bar{E})$, where $\bar{N} \equiv L\alpha\theta/\rho$. All points on the $\bar{E}(N)$ bound to the right of $(\bar{N}, \bar{E})$ are blockaded-entry steady states with zero R&D since they imply that all labor is employed in production. The stable manifold of the system is the union of the saddle path in the entry region, the portion of the $\dot{E} = 0$ locus in the blockaded-entry region below the $\bar{E}(N)$ bound, and the portion of the $\bar{E}(N)$ bound to the right of $(\bar{N}, \bar{E})$. Paths below the stable manifold eventually yield zero production. In this case, the rate of return in (18) falls to zero and the transversality condition for firms' optimal R&D plans is violated (see Section 3). Paths above the stable manifold eventually yield that demand for labor exceeds labor supply. Stopping on the labor supply constraint is not feasible since it violates the Euler's equation (21).

78

Acknowledgment

I thank an anonymous referee for valuable comments.

Notes

1. Cardwell (1995) provides a detailed account of the development of technology from ancient times to today. Over so long a period of time, it is impressive to see the change in the way technology progresses. Mowery and Rosenberg (1989) argue that what characterizes the post-1859 period, which they suggest be called the "second Industrial Revolution," is the different nature of the advance of technology—in particular, its increasing scientific content and its organization.

2. Scherer (1984, ch. 3) constructs an input-output matrix of interindustry technology flows in the U.S. economy based on 1974 data. He finds that the manufacturing sector, which accounts for 95 percent of all company-financed R&D, exports to nonmanufacturing half of the R&D it originates. Of the half that it does not export, 57 percent is process R&D—that is, R&D performed in the same industry of use. In contrast, the amount of R&D originated, financed, and used within the nonmanufacturing sector is only 7 percent of the amount imported from manufacturing. Scherer concludes: "Evidently, if one has comparative advantage at doing industrial R&D, as most larger manufacturing enterprises have, there is a tendency toward considerable self-sufficiency in developing one's own specialized production technology" (p. 51).

3. In addition, in most cases when a new innovator appears on the scene of a technological class, it is a case of lateral innovation—that is, an established firm active in a neighboring class that diversifies into the class in question (Malerba and Orsenigo, 1995, 1996).

4. It is also, most of the time, rather unglamorous, as the numerous anecdotes and the systematic evidence discussed by Mowery and Rosenberg (1989, chs. 2–4) suggest. For example, the lab established at Wyandotte had the primary task of testing the quality of inputs, not inventing new ones.

5. For example, they report that the share of employment of scientific professionals in independent R&D organizations was 15.2 percent of the total in 1921 and 6.9 percent in 1946 (Mowery and Rosenberg, 1989, p. 83, Table 4.7).

6. These papers incorporate into general equilibrium (GE) growth models the market structure and innovation approach of the industrial organization (IO) literature. See Peretto (1996a, 1996b) for a detailed discussion. Kamien and Schwartz (1982), Baldwin and Scott (1987), Cohen and Levin (1989), and Scherer and Ross (1990, ch. 17) review the IO literature, theoretical, and empirical.

7. A corollary to this discussion is that it is important to interpret N as the number of firms, not the number of industries, like it is common place in the literature that uses the Dixit and Stiglitz (1977) framework to generate models of monopolistic competition.

8. One might argue that this degree of commitment is unrealistic. However, choosing open-loop strategies is necessary to solve the model in closed form and study its aggregate properties. Feedback strategies are more realistic because they are subgame perfect, but I cannot solve the model in that case.

9. Note that the price elasticity of demand is not equal to the elasticity of product substitution. This approximation, regularly used in the literature, is based on the assumption that firms are atomistic and take the industry price index as given. Here firms take into account their effect on the industry price index. Thus, there is oligopolistic rivalry. This generates the additional term that captures the fact that the demand curve faced by each firm becomes more elastic the smaller the firm's market share (see Beath and Katsoulacos, 1991, ch. 3). The industry becomes more competitive as more firms enter. Monopolistic competition emerges as the limit for a number of firms that tends to infinity.

10. This is the steady state of the partial equilibrium model only, not the steady state of the general equilibrium model. The latter is studied in Section 4. For a discussion of the properties of this class of capital accumulation games, see Spence (1984), Fershtman and Meuller (1984), Tirole (1988, ch. 8), and Fudenberg and Tirole (1991, ch. 13).

11. This is a comparative statics result only and does not take into account the dynamics of the model. Economies with different parameter α converge to different free-entry steady states characterized by different numbers of firms. Thus, in the case discussed in the text, the economy with the larger α converges to the free-entry steady state with the smaller number of firms. The same economy's response to a change in the parameter

α is a different question. The model, in fact, exhibits hysterisis: temporary changes in parameters can have permanent effects, since in free-entry equilibrium the exit condition is never binding (see Section 3). Thus, an increase in α that calls for a reduction in the steady state number of firms does not lead to firms exiting the market. Rather, the economy enters immediately a steady state with no entry and adjusts its growth rate only.

12. I should emphasize one implication of this result: the sign and magnitude of the scale effect depend on the specific stage of industrialization. That is, they depend on market structure. In Peretto (1996a, 1996c), I study in detail the scale effect and the role of population growth in models of this class.

13. The model allows for entrepreneurial innovation in the long run only in population grows. This empirical prediction fits two well-established facts in IO: larger countries have a larger number of firms; entry rates are positively correlated to the rates of expansion of markets. In Peretto (1996c), I show that if population grows at a constant rate, the steady-state rate of entry is equal to the growth rate of the labor force, while the rate of cost reduction does not depend on the size or the growth rate of the labor force. Asymptotically, this result obtains in this model as well.

14. If one interprets in-house product innovation as bringing to the market the next generation of a good that replaces the old one, as in quality-ladder models, it is immediate to see that established firms internalize the creative-destruction effect discussed by Grossman and Helpman (1991) and Aghion and Howitt (1992). In the deterministic environment of this article, this is just the Arrow replacement effect since all vertical innovations are carried out by incumbents (see Tirole, 1988, ch. 10). Thus, my setup does not rule out product obsolescence. It just internalizes within the firm the decision about the rate at which products are replaced (see Thompson and Waldo, 1994, for a good discussion of this point).

References

Aghion, P., and P. Howitt. (1992). "A Model of Growth Through Creative Destruction." *Econometrica* 60, 323–351.

Baldwin, W., and J. Scott. (1987). *Market Structure and Technological Change*. New York: Harwood Academy.

Baumol, W. (1993). *Entrepreneurship, Management, and the Structure of Payoffs*. Cambridge: MIT Press.

Beath, J., and Y. Katsoulacos. (1991). *The Economic Theory of Product Differentiation*. Cambridge: Cambridge University Press.

Cardwell, D. (1995). *The Norton History of Technology*. New York: Norton.

Cohen, W., and R. Levin. (1989). "Empirical Studies of Market Structure and Innovation." In Richard Schmalensee and Robert Willig (eds.), *Handbook of Industrial Organization*. Amsterdam: North Holland.

Crafts, N. (1996). "The First Industrial Revolution: A Guided Tour for Growth Economists." *American Economic Review Papers and Proceedings* 86, 197–201.

Dasgupta, P., and J. Stiglitz. (1980). "Industrial Structure and the Nature of Innovative Activity." *Economic Journal* 90, 266–293.

Dixit, A., and J. Stiglitz. (1977). "Monopolistic Competition and Optimal Product Diversity." *American Economic Review* 67, 297–308.

Dosi, G. (1988). "Sources, Procedures, and Microeconomic Effects of Innovation." *Journal of Economic Literature* 36, 1120–1171.

Fershtman, C., and E. Mueller. (1984). "Capital Accumulation Games of Infinite Duration." *Journal of Economic Theory* 33, 322–339.

Fudenberg, D., and J. Tirole. (1991). *Game Theory*. Cambridge: MIT University Press.

Grossman, G., and E. Helpman. (1991). *Innovation and Growth in the Global Economy*. Cambridge: MIT University Press.

Kamien, M., and A. Schwartz. (1982). *Market Structure and Innovation*. Cambridge: Cambridge University Press.

Klevorick, A., R. Levin, R. Nelson, and S. Winter. (1995). "On the Sources and Significance of Interindustry Differences in Technological Opportunities." *Research Policy* 24, 185–205.

Levin, R., A. Klevorick, R. Nelson, and S. Winter. (1987). "Appropriating the Returns from Industrial R&D." *Brookings Papers on Economic Activity* 3, 783–820.

Maddison, A. (1982). *Phases of Capitalist Development*. Oxford: Oxford University Press.

Malerba, F. (1992). "Learning by Firms and Incremental Technical Change." *Economic Journal* 102, 845–859.

Entrepreneurship and Economic Growth

                                                    PIETRO F. PERETTO

Malerba, F., and L. Orsenigo. (1995). "Schumpeterian Patterns of Innovation." *Cambridge Journal of Economics* 19, 47–65.

Malerba, F., and L. Orsenigo. (1996). "On New Innovators and Ex Innovators: An Empirical Analysis of the Patterns of Innovative Natality and Mortality." Manuscript, Bocconi University.

Malerba, F., L. Orsenigo, and P. Peretto. (1997). "Persistence of Innovative Activities, Sectoral Patterns of Innovation, and International Technological Specialization." *International Journal of Industrial Organization* 15, 801–826.

Mowery, D., and N. Rosenberg. (1989). *Technology and the Pursuit of Economic Growth.* Cambridge: Cambridge University Press.

Peretto, P. (1994). "Essays on Market Structure and Economic Growth." Ph.D. dissertation, Yale University.

Peretto, P. (1995). "Cost Reduction, Entry, and the Dynamics of Market Structure and Economic Growth." Working Paper 95/48, Department of Economics, Duke University.

Peretto, P. (1996a). "Industrialization, Technological Change, and Long-Run Growth." Working Paper 96/22, Department of Economics, Duke University.

Peretto, P. (1996b). "Sunk Costs, Market Structure and Growth." *International Economic Review* 37, 895–923.

Peretto, P. (1996c). "Technological Change and Population Growth." Working Paper 96/28, Department of Economics, Duke University.

Romer, P. (1990). "Endogenous Technological Change." *Journal of Political Economy* 98, S71–S102.

Romer, P. (1996). "Why, Indeed, in America? Theory, History, and the Origins of Modern Economic Growth." *American Economic Review Papers and Proceedings* 86, 202–206.

Rosenberg, N. (1982). *Inside the Black Box.* Cambridge: Cambridge University Press.

Rosenberg, N. (1994). *Exploring the Black Box.* Cambridge: Cambridge University Press.

Scherer, F. (1984). *Innovation and Growth: Schumpeterian Perspectives.* Cambridge: MIT University Press.

Scherer, F., and D. Ross. (1990). *Industrial Market Structure and Economic Performance.* Boston: Houghton Mifflin.

Schumpeter, J. (1928). "The Instability of Capitalism." *Economic Journal* 38, 361–386.

Schumpeter, J. (1942). *Capitalism, Socialism, and Democracy.* New York: Harper & Row.

Smulders, S., and T. van de Klundert. (1995). "Imperfect Competition, Concentration and Growth with Firm-Specific R&D." *European Economic Review* 39, 139–160.

Spence, M. (1984). "Cost Reduction, Competition, and Industry Performance." *Econometrica* 52, 101–121.

Sutton, J. (1991). *Sunk Costs and Market Structure.* Cambridge: MIT University Press.

Temin, P. (1964). *Iron and steel in Nineteenth-Century America.* Cambridge: MIT Press.

Thompson, P., and D. Waldo. (1994). "Growth and Trustified Capitalism." *Journal of Monetary Economics* 34, 445–462.

Tirole, J. (1988). *The Theory of Industrial Organization.* Cambridge: MIT Press.

van de Klundert, T., and S. Smulders. (1997). "Growth, Competition and Welfare." *Scandinavian Journal of Economics* 99, 99–118.

Part V
Competition

[17]

Competition and Corporate Performance

Stephen J. Nickell

Institute of Economics and Statistics, University of Oxford

Are people right to think that competition improves corporate performance? My investigations indicate first that there are some theoretical reasons for believing this hypothesis to be correct, but they are not overwhelming. Furthermore, the existing empirical evidence on this question is weak. However, the results reported here, based on an analysis of around 670 U.K. companies, do provide some support for this view. Most important, I present evidence that competition, as measured by increased numbers of competitors or by lower levels of rents, is associated with a significantly higher rate of total factor productivity *growth*.

I. Introduction

Most people believe that competition is a good thing. From Adam Smith, who commented that "monopoly . . . is a great enemy to good management" (1976, bk. 1, chap. 11, p. 165; cited in Vickers [1994]), to Richard Caves, who remarked that economists have a "vague suspicion that competition is the enemy of sloth" (1980, p. 88), this theme has been ever present in the writings of both economists and men of affairs. Furthermore, as these quotes indicate, this belief does not simply reflect the well-known result that a competitive economy generates an efficient allocation of resources. It is far more general. It is a belief that competition exerts downward pressure on costs, reduces

This work was funded by the Leverhulme Trust. I am most grateful to Giovanni Urga and Daphne Nicolitsas for their professional research assistance and to John Vickers for his generous help and ideas. Comments from Stephen Bond, Mike Devereux, Donald Hay, and a referee are much appreciated. The research is part of the Corporate Performance Programme of the Economic and Social Research Council Centre for Economic Performance.

[*Journal of Political Economy*, 1996, vol. 104, no. 4]

slack, provides incentives for the efficient organization of production, and even drives innovation forward. Furthermore, this belief has widespread consequences. It is the driving force behind numerous important policy changes ranging from the deregulation of numerous sectors in the OECD economies to *many* of the economic reforms in Eastern Europe.

However, this general belief in the efficacy of competition exists despite the fact that it is not supported either by any strong theoretical foundation or by a large corpus of hard empirical evidence in its favor. It is my purpose, therefore, to add a little to the rather meager body of knowledge in this area. I analyze the productivity performance of a large number of U.K. manufacturing companies, looking particularly at the impact of competition on both the level and the growth of total factor productivity. In what follows, I first give the theoretical and empirical background and then present my empirical model and results.

II. The Theoretical Background

I take an industry to be more competitive if there are fewer monopoly rents. The question I am directly concerned with here is the impact of competition on the efficiency and productivity growth rates of companies. Despite being in the currently rather passé structure, conduct, performance tradition, this is both a legitimate and an interesting issue to investigate. Two points are worth noting. First, it is a question that is very rarely pursued, much greater attention having been paid to profitability, which competition probably reduces, rather than to efficiency and productivity growth, which, it is hypothesized, competition increases. Since it is productivity growth that is the cause of the "wealth of nations," this emphasis on profitability is rather curious. Second, care must be exercised in any investigation of questions of this type because the degree of competition is not, in the long run, independent of company behavior. Thus, for example, high-performing companies may, eventually, gain a position of market power. This makes the interpretation of cross-section correlations very tricky,[1] particularly those at the industry level.

With this in mind, why should competition influence company performance? An obvious answer is that the existence of monopoly rents gives the company stakeholders, in particular managers and workers, the potential to capture these rents in the form of slack or lack of effort. But this is simplistic. The owners of monopolistic firms will be just as keen to prevent slacking by managers and workers as the

---

[1] This is closely related to the discussion in Demsetz (1973).

owners of competitive firms. However, it may be argued that the latter are in a better position to do so, at least under the uncontroversial assumption that managers know more about what is going on than owners. Concerning managerial effort, the work of Holmstrom (1982b), Nalebuff and Stiglitz (1983), and Mookherjee (1984) suggests that explicit incentive schemes will generate sharper incentives the greater the number of players involved. This arises because of the greater opportunities for comparison of performance. Hart (1983) provides a model of managerial incentives that demonstrates explicitly how competition between firms may sharpen incentives. He supposes there to be two types of firm in an industry, "managerial" (M), where there is a principal-agent problem, and "entrepreneurial" (E), where the "principal" runs the firm. All firms face common cost shocks. When (marginal) costs are low, E firms expand output whereas M firms have managers who take advantage of the good times to slack. This is consistent with the optimal incentive scheme under the condition that managers are not "too responsive" to monetary incentives. If the proportion of E firms is higher, industry output in good times (low cost) is higher, industry prices are lower, and the potential for managerial slack in the M firms is lower. This might be interpreted as an increase in competition leading to less slack. However, this is not a robust result. Scharfstein (1988) notes that the position is reversed if managers are highly responsive to monetary incentives. Then "competition" leads to more slack.

An alternative analysis is based on an idea in Meyer and Vickers (1995, sec. 2.1), which utilizes a model of *implicit* rewards due to Holmstrom (1982a). The idea is that while current managerial effort does not influence current earnings, it may influence future market-based rewards via its impact on the market's estimate of the manager's ability. The market cannot observe either effort or ability directly, but in future periods it can use knowledge of managerial output, which depends on effort, ability, and unobserved productivity shocks. The manager, therefore, has an incentive to raise effort early in her career because this will tend to increase future market estimates of her ability and, hence, future rewards.

What is the role of competition in all this? The notion is that the existence of other firms in the industry leads to a sharpening of effort incentives because the unobserved productivity shocks are likely to be correlated across firms operating in the same industry. In Meyer and Vickers (1995), it is shown that in a two-period model, first-period effort incentives are greater when there are two firms if both productivity shocks and managerial abilities are nonnegatively correlated, with the former correlation being larger than the latter, a not unlikely scenario. In fact this result extends to n firms, with manage-

CORPORATE PERFORMANCE   **727**

rial effort incentives increasing in n (see Nickell 1994). If a rise in n corresponds to an increase in competition, this implies that competition can tend to raise managerial effort and, hence, company performance.

An alternative framework relies not on the possibility that competition may give more precision to incentives based on relative performance but on the fact that competitive forces in the product market may raise the sensitivity of profits to the actions of managers. So if competition makes profits more responsive to managerial effort, for example, then owners have a greater incentive to ensure that managerial effort is kept high and inefficiency will be lower. Willig (1987) presents a model along these lines in which he demonstrates that in the context of a simple principal-agent framework, a ceteris paribus increase in the firm's product demand elasticity causes the firm's owners to induce the manager to raise her effort. However, a ceteris paribus fall in demand will have the opposite effect, so increased competition will raise effort and efficiency only if the demand elasticity effect dominates the demand reduction effect. Since an increase in competition may both raise the demand elasticity and reduce demand for the individual firm, the effort outcome is ambiguous. Some ambiguity also arises in the model due to Hermalin (1992), but no such ambiguity arises in similar models constructed by Martin (1993) and Horn, Lang, and Lundgren (1994). In both cases, they find that increased competition tends to be associated with *reduced* managerial effort! Schmidt (1994), however, points to a force in the opposite direction arising from the fact that competition raises the probability of bankruptcy and thereby generates strong incentives for managers to avoid this fate by improving efficiency.

As well as managerial effort, competition may also influence the effort of workers. This follows naturally from the notion that product market rents may be shared with workers. Such sharing occurs because this makes the life of managers more comfortable (expense preference; e.g., Smirlock and Marshall 1983), it enables unions to be kept out (e.g., Dickens and Katz 1987), or already entrenched unions use their bargaining strength to enforce it (e.g., Stewart 1990). Since rents may be captured in the form of higher wages or reduced effort, there is a direct connection between the degree of competition and the level of workers' effort. Since the majority of U.K. companies considered here are unionized, it is natural to focus on a union bargaining framework. In this context, it may be shown that, in a world in which unions and firms bargain over both wages and effort,[2] in-

---

[2] The proof of this result may be found in Nickell (1994). Incidentally, the majority of union-firm wage bargains in the United Kingdom also cover staffing ratios and

creases in product market competition lead directly to increases in bargained effort.

While the main argument in favor of a positive relationship between competition and productivity performance rests on the opportunities for slack introduced by monopoly power, there are alternatives. For example, consider the impact of competition on incentives for research and development. It is generally the case that cost-reducing improvements in productivity will generate larger increases in profit in a more competitive environment, thereby raising the incentives for R & D expenditure. However, following Schumpeter (1943), it has also been argued that more monopolistic firms can more readily fund R & D expenditure because they face less market uncertainty and have a larger, more stable cash flow (Levin, Cohen, and Mowery [1985] provide a useful summary of the arguments). Finally, it may be argued that in oligopolistic industries, resources may be spent on deterring rivals, and this can lead directly to production inefficiency. The use of excess capacity (too high capital intensity) to make entry deterrence credible is an example of this.

Overall, therefore, there is some theoretical basis for the belief that competition drives productivity improvements forward. But the basis is not, as yet, a strong one.

III. The Empirical Background

Perhaps the most compelling evidence on the power of competition to generate productivity growth is the most broad-brush. Three simple examples follow. First, the low level of productivity in Eastern Europe relative to that in Western Europe is an impressive example of what can be achieved by repressing the forces of market competition. Second, Porter (1990) demonstrates clearly the key role of domestic competition in generating world-beating industries. For example, the Japanese success stories (e.g., cars, motorcycles, cameras, video recorders, and musical instruments) are precisely those industries in which domestic competition is intense. Those Japanese industries in which domestic competition is feeble have little or no international success (e.g., construction, commodity chemicals, and paper). Third, deregulation is generally followed by significant productivity gains (see, e.g., Graham, Kaplan, and Sibley [1983] on the U.S. airline industry).

What of more "scientific" evidence? Here I consider a number of areas in turn.

---

other effort-related variables (see Daniel and Millward 1983, pp. 197, 182; Millward and Stevens 1986, p. 248). So the notion that firms and unions bargain over wages and effort is quite consistent with the facts.

Competition and R & D.—Expenditure on R & D has an impact on productivity growth (see, e.g., Griliches 1986). Much effort has been devoted to analyzing the relationship between competition and R & D expenditure. Studies usually take the form of investigating industry cross-section partial correlations between market structure and R & D intensity. Unfortunately, these studies are typically uninformative because they control inadequately for technological opportunities, which differ substantially across industries and tend to be correlated with market concentration.[3] One study that avoids this problem is Geroski (1990), which uses panel data. This enables Geroski to control for technological opportunities by using industry fixed effects, and the evidence then suggests that concentration and other measures of monopoly power tend to *reduce* the rate of innovation and, hence, productivity growth.

Competition and technical efficiency.—In recent years there have been a number of comprehensive studies of technical efficiency, which are reported in Caves and Barton (1990), Green and Mayes (1991), and Caves et al. (1992). These studies make use of frontier production function techniques to estimate technical efficiency indices and relate them to variables of interest. The relevant finding is that an increase in market concentration above a certain threshold tends to reduce technical efficiency. This result emerges in a number of countries and is consistent with the finding in the management literature, discussed in Caves (1980, pp. 85–86), that competition leads to companies' employment of more efficient decision-making structures.

Competition, productivity, and productivity growth.—The Caves and Green/Mayes studies are cross-section based, but similar competition effects on the level of productivity are confirmed with panel data on industries (Haskel 1990) or firms (Nickell, Wadhwani, and Wall 1992; Hay and Liu 1994). In both examples, a fixed-effects framework is used to discover that market concentration or market share has an adverse effect on the *level* of (total factor) productivity. By the nature of the fixed-effects estimation procedure, what this means in practice is that an increase in market concentration or market share is followed by a ceteris paribus fall in productivity. This view relates the result to the observation by the Massachusetts Institute of Technology commission in the United States (Dertouzos, Lester, and Solow 1989) that plants at the top of the productivity distribution rest on their laurels and lose their competitive advantage.[4]

---

[3] For example, in the simple Dasgupta and Stiglitz (1980) framework, technological opportunities, as captured by the elasticity of cost reduction with respect to R & D expenditure, are positively correlated with both R & D intensity and market concentration.

[4] This result is not, however, confirmed by Baily, Hulten, and Campbell (1992).

With regard to productivity *growth* effects, Nickell et al. (1992) find that firms with high market share tend to have *higher* productivity *growth*, the reverse of the productivity level effect previously mentioned. This growth effect is, however, a cross-section result and therefore suffers from the problem that, in the long run, firms with relatively high productivity growth will tend to grow faster and gain market share. So one cannot interpret it as a genuine competition effect. More informative is the evidence presented in the study by Van Wijnbergen and Venables (1993), who find that the trade liberalization and deregulation undertaken by Mexico during 1986–88 led directly to an increase in competition and a significant increase in productivity growth.

To summarize, there is some evidence that competition is good for technical efficiency, total factor productivity, and innovation. Formal evidence is, however, very thin, and, in particular, there is very little useful econometric evidence on the more interesting relationship between competition and productivity *growth*.

IV. The Empirical Formulation

I intend to use panel data on U.K. manufacturing sector companies to shed further light on the relationship between competition and productivity performance. In this section, I consider the basic model and data, measurement, and estimation problems.

The Productivity Equation

My framework utilizes a constant-returns, Cobb-Douglas production function, although I shall consider the effects of relaxing both the constant-returns and the Cobb-Douglas constraints. My basic model has the log-linear form

$$
\begin{aligned}
y_{it} = \beta_i + \beta_t + \lambda y_{it-1} + (1 - \lambda)\alpha_i n_{it} + (1 - \lambda)(1 - \alpha_i)k_{it} \\
+ \alpha_1 h_{it} + c_{it} + c_i t + \epsilon_{it},
\end{aligned}
\tag{1}
$$

where y_{it} is log real (value-added) output, n_{it} is log employment, k_{it} is log capital stock, h_{it} is a cyclical component, c_{it} reflects all factors capturing the impact of competition on the *level* of productivity, c_i reflects those factors that cover the impact of competition on productivity *growth*, i is the firm subscript, t is the time subscript, and β_i and β_t are firm effects and time effects. The former covers all unobserved company-specific factors influencing the level of productivity, and the latter captures shocks common to all firms. Finally, ϵ_{it} captures all other shocks to company productivity, and I suppose this error to be serially uncorrelated. Absence of serial correlation is assisted by the inclusion of dynamics in the form of a lagged dependent variable. This is the simplest way of capturing the fact that, whenever factors of production are changed, it typically takes some time for output to reach its new long-run level. For example, if new capital goods are purchased, it may take a considerable time before the new machines are fully operational.

Estimation

Before I discuss how I measure competition effects, it is useful to see how I intend to estimate the parameters of this model. To eliminate the firm effects, β_i, I simply difference the production equation (1) to obtain, after some rearrangement,

$$\Delta(y_{it} - k_{it}) = \Delta\beta_t + \lambda\Delta(y_{it-1} - k_{it}) + (1 - \lambda)\alpha_i\Delta(n_{it} - k_{it})$$
$$+ \alpha_1\Delta h_{it} + \Delta c_{it} + c_i + \Delta\epsilon_{it}. \tag{2}$$

In order to see the implications of this, note first that important components of the error term are those productivity shocks that are directly related to employment or capital intensity.[5] For example, autonomous shocks to effort (e.g., increasing the speed of the production line) may induce a rise in output and a possible fall in employment. In order to avoid the corruption of the parameter estimates caused by possible correlations between n_{it} or k_{it} and ϵ_{it}, I treat both employment and capital as endogenous. Furthermore, note that, after differencing, y_{it-1} is correlated with the equation error. As long as the basic error, ϵ_{it}, is serially uncorrelated, all lags on y, n, and k beyond $t - 1$ are valid instruments. Instrumental variable estimators based on this fact are essentially generalized method of moments estimators, making use of the moment restrictions generated by the serially uncorrelated error. This technique is due to Arellano and Bond (1991) and, of course, depends crucially on the absence of serial correlation in ϵ_{it}. This may be investigated using serial correlation tests developed by Arellano and Bond as well as via standard instrument validity tests.

Data Definitions and Measurement Issues

My data source is the published accounts of around 700 U.K. manufacturing companies over the period 1972–86. These data are aug-

---

[5] The other important component of the error is the skill composition of the workforce. Of course, only variations in this matter since the fixed effects deal with the remainder. Any cyclical components of skill variation will be captured by h_{it}, and there seems no obvious reason why noncyclical variations should be correlated with any of the included variables.

mented by a postal survey of a subset of the companies carried out by me and Sushil Wadhwani in 1989. From this, I obtain usable data from 147 companies. There is an unbalanced panel, with the sample peaking in 1977. The rapid decline in the sample size after 1981 does not reflect sample attrition but simply the fact that, because of changes in the reporting of employment in company accounts in 1982, consistent employment series are not available for the majority of companies across that date.

Data definitions for some of the variables are worth discussing here because they have important implications for the interpretation of the results. Complete definitions are available in the Data Appendix.

Output, y_{it}.—I use two alternatives to capture log value-added: (1) the value of sales deflated by a three-digit industry-specific price deflator and (2) value-added deflated in the same way. The reason why I use sales at all is that the value-added data are not quite as accurate. To generate the latter, I use accounting data on the wage bill plus pretax profits plus interest payments and depreciation. Unfortunately, accounting data on profits may differ somewhat from the true numbers, which causes the problem with value-added estimates.[6]

Employment elasticity, α_i.—This coefficient may vary across companies, so I either treat it as a constant, allowing the random elements to revert to the error term (incidentally producing another reason for the endogeneity of n and k), or suppose that $\alpha_i = \Sigma_j \, \alpha_j d_j$, where d_j are two-digit industry dummies.

Cycle measure, h_{it}.—Here I follow Muellbauer (1984) and use $\alpha_{11}(H_{ojt}/H_{njt}) + \alpha_{12}(H_{ojt}/H_{njt})^{-1}$, where H_o measures overtime hours per worker in industry j and H_n measures standard hours per worker. This form captures the asymmetry due to the fact that, in slumps, measured hours tend to overstate hours actually worked.

Competition measures, c_{it}, c_i.—The following relevant data are available: measures of market share at the firm level ($mksh_{it}$), measures of concentration ($conc_{jt}$) and import penetration (imp_{jt}) at the three-digit industry level, a survey-based measure of competition at the firm level for one time period only ($comp_i$), and a measure of average rents normalized on value-added ($rents_i$). These last two are important variables, so it is worth indicating how they are defined. The first of these (comp) is a dummy taking the value one if the management of the company answers yes to the question "Have you more than five competitors in the market for your product(s)?" and zero if the management answers yes to the question "Have you five or fewer competitors in the market for your product(s)?" The evidence pro-

---

[6] For example, bad debts are taken out of profits, realized gains on quoted investments are included, and some firms write off R & D expenditures against profits.

Entrepreneurship and Economic Growth

vided by Stewart (1990) indicates that this variable has considerable discriminatory power. For example, union wage effects are considerably smaller in "competitive" firms.[7] The second variable (rents) is an average over the sample period of profits less capital costs, normalized on value-added. Because I have no information on skill levels, I make no attempt to take account of worker rent capture by using alternative wages, instead of actual wages, as the measure of labor costs. So my rents measure reflects the ex post rents available to shareholders rather than the theoretically preferable ex ante rents that are potentially available to all stakeholders and may be dissipated in the form of higher pay and lower effort. However, it seems likely that the ex post rents, although lower, are highly correlated with ex ante potential rents.

Before I go into these measures in detail, it is worth noting that, because of the use of the fixed-effects panel data framework, the attempt to isolate the impact of competition on the *level* of productivity is essentially a search for a time-series effect. Indeed, it is clear from (2) that we are concerned with the impact of changes in the level of competition (Δc_{it}) on changes in productivity. This contrasts starkly with the investigation of the impact of competition on productivity *growth*. From equation (2) again, it is clear that this involves looking at the cross-section correlation between competition (c_i) and productivity growth. This distinction is very important for the specification of the model, as we shall see.

The role of market share.—There are a number of problems associated with the use of market share as a measure of market power (an inverse measure of competition). (i) Collusion depends not only on the size of the various firms involved relative to the market but also on other factors that are hard to control. They include asymmetries in cost and the ability of companies to "hide" their price changes, for example. (ii) Potential as well as actual competition influences market power. (iii) My measure of market share does not fully reflect foreign competitors. (iv) My measure of market share uses three-digit industry sales as the denominator. This is far from the correct measure because the three-digit industry does not represent anything like the "market." More particularly, the ratio of the true market size to the measured market size could vary enormously from firm to firm, even within an "industry."

These problems suggest that my estimate of market share has little value as a cross-section measure of market power. However, if it is

----

[7] Somewhat fortuitously, the number five appears to be quite important according to the evidence in Bresnahan and Reiss (1991). They find that increases in the number of firms operating in a market up to around five have significant effects in reducing market power.

used as a time-series measure of market power, the problems above are less serious. The omitted and unobservable factors are likely to be relatively stable over time, which implies that one might expect there to be some correlation between changes in the measure of market share and changes in a true measure of market power. Thus it is worth using Δmksh_{it} as an inverse measure of changes in the extent of competition. Furthermore, to eliminate reverse causality (high productivity growth leading to improvements in market share), I shall lag the variable two years and use Δmksh_{it-2}.

Turning now to the impact of competition on productivity *growth*, here I intend to focus on the survey measure of competition (comp_i) and on the ex post measure of the absence of competition (rents_i). With regard to the survey measure, since the managers of a company are more aware than anybody of the identity of their competitors, one can argue that problems iii and iv do not apply to this variable. Furthermore, it seems likely that the most significant cross-section variation in the omitted factors noted under problems i and ii occurs *between* industries, so the use of industry dummies would deal with much of this problem. Concerning the rents measure, we see the rents as being generated by lack of competition, and because it is an ex post measure, it can be viewed as complementary to the survey-based variable. Finally, we must note the reverse causality problem. Firms with relatively high productivity growth may, in the long run, become dominant in their market. Since we are looking at a cross-section correlation here, this problem is hard to avoid. We can attempt an instrumental variables approach, but this is rarely persuasive in a cross-section context because of the lack of good instruments. Luckily, however, reverse causality yields the opposite sign. High productivity growth in a company strengthens its market position and *reduces* the effective competition it faces. So if we find a *positive* relationship between productivity growth and competition, we might argue that the true relationship is even stronger.

To summarize, therefore, I shall specify the competition effect on the level of productivity, c_{it}, as

$$c_{it} = \alpha_2 \text{mksh}_{it-2} \tag{3}$$

and the productivity growth effect, c_i, as

$$c_i = \alpha_3 \text{comp}_i + \alpha_4 \text{rents}_i + \sum_j \alpha_4^j d_j + \alpha_{51} \text{size}_i$$
$$+ \alpha_{52} \text{conc}_{j.} + \alpha_{53} \text{imp}_{j.}. \tag{4}$$

In the latter formulation, I include two-digit industry dummies and averages of firm size, industry concentration, and industry import penetration simply as additional cross-section controls. The impact of industry concentration and import penetration on productivity growth may be of some interest, although the effects of comp and rents are the keys, as I have already indicated. In conclusion, the equation I estimate has the form

$$y_{it} = \beta_i + \beta_t + \lambda y_{it-1} + (1 - \lambda)\alpha_i n_{it} + (1 - \lambda)(1 - \alpha_i)k_{it}$$

$$+ \alpha_{11}\left(\frac{H_{ojt}}{H_{njt}}\right) + \alpha_{12}\left(\frac{H_{ojt}}{H_{njt}}\right)^{-1} + \alpha_2 \mathrm{mksh}_{it-2}$$

$$\hspace{6cm} (5)$$

$$+ \left(\alpha_3 \mathrm{comp}_i + \alpha_4 \mathrm{rents}_i + \sum_j \alpha_4^j d_j + \alpha_{51}\mathrm{size}_i\right.$$

$$\left. + \alpha_{52}\mathrm{conc}_{j.} + \alpha_{53}\mathrm{imp}_{j.}\right)t + \epsilon_{it}.$$

The results of the investigation are reported in the next section.

V. Results

The main results are presented in tables 1 and 2. I have a sequence of estimated equations to investigate the robustness of the key results, with regard to both changes in the equation specification and changes in the data sample. In table 1, I use an unbalanced panel of 147 companies for which I possess management survey data on the number of competitors. In columns 1–5, I compare the impact of the survey-based measure of competition and the rents-based measure, using a number of different measures of rent. Then in column 6 I allow the output-employment elasticity to vary across industries, and in column 7 I relax the Cobb-Douglas restriction. In column 8, I restrict the instruments to those dated $t - 3$ or before, and then in columns 9 and 10 I replace sales as the output variable by a measure of value-added. In table 2, I report results from a much larger sample of 676 companies that does not contain management survey information on the number of competitors. All the equations have company effects and time effects as well as two-digit industry-specific time trends.[8] They control for fixed company-specific and aggregate effects on the level of productivity and fixed industry effects on productivity growth.

Returning to the results in table 1, we see first that the rents measure dominates the survey-based competition measure (see col. 2),

---

[8] The industry-specific time trends simply reflect industry dummies in the estimated first-difference model.

TABLE 1

ESTIMATES OF THE PRODUCTION FUNCTION (Eq. [5]), 1975–86

Dependent Variable: y_{it}

| INDEPENDENT VARIABLE | BASIC EQUATION (1) | INCLUDES COMPETITION (2) | EXCLUDES RENT (3) | INCLUDES ALTERNATIVE MEASURES OF RENT | | EMPLOYMENT INTERACTED WITH INDUSTRY DUMMIES† (6) | ADDS CES TERM (7) | INSTRUMENTS DATED $t-3$ (8) | VALUE-ADDED AS DEPENDENT VARIABLE | |
				(4)	(5)				Basic Equation (9)	Includes Competition (10)
*y_{it-1}	.28 (3.2)	.26 (3.0)	.34 (4.0)	.29 (3.3)	.28 (3.1)	.21 (2.6)	.28 (3.1)	.07 (.6)	.06 (.6)	.15 (1.5)
*n_{it}	.41 (3.0)	.45 (3.8)	.52 (4.2)	.43 (3.0)	.38 (2.7)		.53 (3.0)	.57 (3.1)	.51 (3.6)	.60 (4.7)
*k_{it}	.31 (3.0)	.29 (2.4)	.14 (2.7)	.28 (2.3)	.34 (2.4)		.19	.36 (1.7)	.43 (1.6)	.25 (1.9)
H_{ojt}/H_{njt}	1.53 (2.4)	1.54 (2.4)	1.84 (2.7)	1.48 (2.3)	1.58 (2.4)	1.13 (1.4)	1.71 (2.7)	1.15 (1.7)	1.60 (1.6)	1.95 (1.9)
$10^{-3}(H_{ojt}/H_{njt})^{-1}$	.63 (1.5)	.61 (1.4)	.48 (1.0)	.67 (1.6)	.56 (1.3)	.79 (1.3)	.47 (1.2)	.60 (1.1)	.088 (.1)	.12 (.1)
$mksh_{it-2}$	-3.49 (2.1)	-3.42 (2.0)	-3.17 (2.1)	-3.41 (2.0)	-3.72 (2.2)	-2.02 (1.1)	-3.34 (1.8)	-4.46 (2.2)	-4.38 (1.8)	-4.19 (1.8)
$(conc_j)t$	-.12 (2.1)	-.14 (1.9)	-.11 (2.0)	-.097 (1.8)	-.13 (2.3)	-.13 (1.8)	-.13 (2.3)	-.16 (2.3)	-.17 (1.9)	-.17 (2.2)

	(1)	(2)	(3)	(4)	(5)	(6)	(7)	(8)	(9)	(10)
$(imp_j)t$	.084 (1.6)	.11 (1.4)	.11 (1.5)	.073 (1.3)	.079 (1.4)	.086 (1.1)	.083 (1.5)	.12 (1.7)	.13 (1.3)	.17 (1.8)
*$(size_j)t$	.40 (1.3)	.53 (1.4)	.84 (1.9)	.39 (1.3)	.30 (1.0)	-.13 (.3)	.29 (.9)	.59 (1.7)	.39 (1.0)	.39 (.8)
*$(comp_j)t$		.026 (.6)	.065 (2.0)							.071 (1.8)
*$(rent_{1i})t$	-.13 (2.9)	-.11 (2.2)				-.15 (2.7)	-.13 (3.0)	-.18 (3.7)	-.12 (2.3)	
*$(rent_{2i})t$				-.16 (2.7)						
*$(rent_{3i})t$					-.13 (3.0)					
*$(n_{it} - k_{it})^2$							.046 (1.3)			
Serial correlation [$N(0, 1)$]	.70	.70	.73	.74	.78	.20	.76	.67	-1.15	-.99
Instrument validity	$\chi^2(68) = 73.4$	$\chi^2(67) = 74.4$	$\chi^2(68) = 78.9$	$\chi^2(68) = 74.8$	$\chi^2(68) = 72.5$	$\chi^2(56) = 60.4$	$\chi^2(67) = 73.0$	$\chi^2(65) = 74.5$	$\chi^2(68) = 78.2$	$\chi^2(68) = 78.5$
Standard error	.094	.092	.095	.094	.094	.107	.095	.092	.126	.123

NOTE.—The number of firms is 147, and the number of observations is 978. The dependent variable is log(real sales) except in cols. 9 and 10, where it is log(real value-added). All equations are estimated in first differences and include both time dummies and two-digit industry dummies. Long-run constant returns is imposed in all equations by estimating the equation in the form of (2) in the text. Firm size is measured by $10^{-2}(n_{it})$. Instruments include $y_j(t-2, t-3)$, $k_j(t-2, t-3)$, and $n_i(t-2, t-3)$. In col. 8, instruments dated $t-2$ are omitted and those dated $t-4$ are included. The equations are estimated using the Dynamic Panel Data package, written and described by Arellano and Bond (1991). All columns report a consistent one-step estimator, where the minimized criterion takes no account of heteroskedasticity but the standard errors are robust to heteroskedasticity of general form. Results based on a two-step estimator, which is fully efficient, are much the same but with very much lower standard errors. However, these results are not reported because Monte Carlo experiments reported in Arellano and Bond indicate that the computed standard errors appear to overstate the efficiency gains, so the t-ratios are likewise oversated.

* Variables that are treated as endogenous.
† Col. 6 interacts the employment term with 13 two-digit industry dummies.

TABLE 2

Estimates of the Production Function Using Alternative Sample, 1975–86

Dependent Variable: y_{it}

Independent Variable	(1)		(2)		(3)	
*y_{it-1}	.11	(1.7)	.16	(2.7)	.10	(1.6)
*n_{it}	.77	(9.0)	.84	(10.4)	.73	(8.3)
*k_{it}	.13		.0		.17	
H_{ojt}/H_{njt}	.97	(2.9)	1.00	(3.0)	.96	(2.9)
$10^{-3}(H_{ojt}/H_{njt})^{-1}$	.097	(.4)	.16	(.6)	.072	(.3)
$mksh_{it-2}$	−1.25	(2.4)	−1.13	(2.0)	−1.30	(2.5)
$(conc_j.)t$	−.053	(1.8)	−.024	(.8)	−.061	(2.0)
$(imp_j.)t$	−.018	(.6)	−.028	(1.0)	−.023	(.8)
*$(size_i)t$	.48	(3.1)	.49	(3.3)	.39	(2.5)
*$(rent_{1i})t$	−.16	(4.7)				
*$(rent_{2i})t$			−.17	(4.8)		
*$(rent_{3i})t$					−.17	(4.7)
Serial correlation [$N(0, 1)$]	1.04		.43		1.42	
Instrument validity	$\chi^2(68) = 137.8$		$\chi^2(68) = 137.0$		$\chi^2(68) = 138.3$	
Standard error	.092		.094		.092	

Note.—The number of firms is 676, and the number of observations is 4,423. See also notes to table 1.

although they are jointly significant ($\chi^2(2) = 7.4$) and the survey-based measure is significant when the rents measure is dropped (see col. 3). This indicates some degree of collinearity but, nevertheless, reveals a strong impact of competition on productivity growth (i.e., a positive effect of number of competitors and a negative effect of rents). In columns 4 and 5, we see that the results are robust to the use of alternative measures of rents, the variation being in their treatment of the risk premium in the measure of the cost of capital (see the Data Appendix).

If we allow the output-employment elasticity to vary across industries (col. 6), there is no impact on the rents coefficient.[9] The same applies if we relax the Cobb-Douglas restriction (col. 7) or use deeper lags in the instruments (col. 8), thereby making them less susceptible to serial correlation in the errors. Furthermore, if we replace sales by value-added as the dependent variable (cols. 9 and 10), we again see

[9] It is also worth reporting that this remains true if we relax the constant-returns constraint. The key coefficients are

$$-3.92\,mksh_{it-2} - 0.12(rent_{1i})t.$$
$$(2.3) \qquad\qquad (2.4)$$

Freely estimated, the data push us rather strongly toward *diminishing* returns, which is not unusual in a dynamic time-series context. In my view, this is inherently most unlikely and probably arises because of inadequately controlled measurement error in n and k, strongly accentuated by differencing. For the purposes of investigating total factor productivity effects, it is better simply to impose constant returns.

CORPORATE PERFORMANCE   739

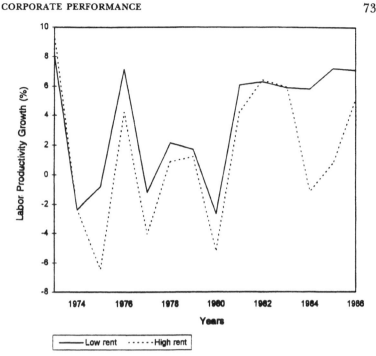

FIG. 1.—Labor productivity growth in high- and low-rent firms. The sample is divided into "low" and "high" at the median.

little change in the overall structure of the equation. So the overall conclusion from this sample is that we observe a robust and significant effect of the measures of competition on productivity *growth,* controlling for two-digit industry effects and firm size as well as concentration and import penetration in the three-digit industry in which the firm is located. Furthermore, even if a reverse causality problem remains after the relevant variables are treated as endogenous, the results still imply a significant effect for competition because reverse causality would tend to *reduce* its measured impact (higher productivity growth in a firm would tend to increase its market power and rents, reduce competition, and make the firm more dominant).

Next, we can ask whether or not the rents effect on productivity growth remains if the sample is expanded to include those firms for which there is no survey information on the number of competitors. This sample has over four times the number of firms, but, as we can see from table 2, the negative impact of rents on productivity growth is much the same and is highly significant. In order to confirm that this result does not follow from any econometric trickery, we see in figure 1 that if the sample is divided into high- and low-rent firms,

JOURNAL OF POLITICAL ECONOMY

TABLE 3

PERCENTAGE POINT TFP GROWTH RATE DIFFERENTIALS GENERATED BY DIFFERENCES
IN COMPETITION

Food, drink, and tobacco	−.2	Metal goods (other)	.8
Chemicals	−.8	Textiles	.9
Metal manufacture	−1.7	Clothing and footwear	1.0
Mechanical engineering	1.0	Bricks, pottery, and glass	2.0
Instrument engineering	−.6	Timber and furniture	1.6
Electrical engineering	−2.4	Paper, printing, and publishing	1.9
Vehicles	−1.3	Other manufacturing	−2.2

NOTE.—These are differentials from the unweighted mean.

the high-rent firms have *lower* labor productivity growth, on average, than the low-rent firms in almost every year of the sample period. Finally, it is worth remarking on the systematic negative effect of (three-digit) industry concentration, which hints that firms in less concentrated industries tend to have higher total factor productivity (TFP) growth rates, ceteris paribus.

Now that we have discovered that increased competition appears to be associated with higher TFP growth, it is worth trying to pin down the size of this important effect. If we take all the companies and rank them on the basis of rents ($rent_1$ is the measure used; see the Data Appendix), at the eightieth percentile, rents normalized on value-added are 0.29. At the twentieth percentile, the corresponding value is zero. When the $rent_1$ coefficients in table 1 and table 2 (col. 1) are used, this spread generates a ceteris paribus difference in TFP growth of between 3.8 and 4.6 percentage points in favor of the firm generating lower rents and, therefore, operating in the more competitive environment. This is clearly a significant effect, suggesting that competition can have an important role in influencing TFP growth.

Alternatively, we may use the rent and concentration ratio coefficients in column 1 of table 2 to generate a competition index equal to $-0.053 conc_j - 0.16 rent_1$. This measures the ceteris paribus impact of increases in rents and concentration in the firm's industrial sector on TFP growth. In table 3, I present the ceteris paribus industry TFP growth differentials generated by the differences in the average value of the competition index across industries. They capture differences in industry TFP growth rates caused by differences in the degree of competition. Again, these differences are quite substantial and are broadly consistent with other evidence on the extent of competition in various industries. It is, of course, important to recognize that these are differences in TFP growth generated by competition.

Technological opportunities will also differ substantially across industries and will have an important impact on the final outcome.

Let us now look at the impact of lagged market share on the *level* of productivity. This is essentially a time-series effect, where we attempt to detect falls in productivity two years after increases in market share. In all samples and all variants the effect is present, although sometimes only on the borders of significance.[10] However, its size differs systematically across the two samples (cf. table 1 with table 2). I pursued this last issue further by replacing absolute changes in market share by proportional changes. Now there are long-run effects that are closer in scale across the two samples, namely -0.042 and -0.028. This suggests that a 25 percent increase in market share leads to a 1 percent fall in total factor productivity in the *long run*.

VI. Summary and Conclusions

Are people right to think that competition improves corporate performance? Here I find that there are some theoretical reasons for thinking that competition might improve performance, but they are not overwhelming. I also see that there exists some empirical evidence in favor of this view, but again it is not overwhelming. Indeed, the broad-brush evidence from Eastern Europe and Japan is, if anything, more persuasive than any detailed econometric evidence. However, there is support for the general thesis in the empirical results. First, I find that market power, as captured by market share, generates reduced levels of productivity. Second and much more important, I present evidence that competition, measured either by increased numbers of competitors or by lower levels of rents, is associated with higher rates of total factor productivity growth. This is one of the first available pieces of systematic evidence that competition enhances growth rates.

Finally, it is worth entertaining the thought that we are barking up the wrong tree. Perhaps competition works not by forcing efficiency on individual firms but by letting many flowers bloom and ensuring that only the best survive (see, e.g., Jovanovic 1982). If there are lots of ways of doing things, competition allows many to be tried and then selects the best, something a monopoly finds hard to replicate. Focusing on the firms, as I have done, will not allow one to detect

---

[10] It has been suggested that because the numerator of the market share variable is the dependent variable, its second lag is simply picking up a negative second-order autoregression in output. If the second lag in output is included in the basic equation, it does indeed have a negative sign, but it is not significant ($t = 0.4$) and the coefficient on lagged market share is -3.94 (2.5), much the same as in the basic equation.

this kind of phenomenon. How to detect it in any general way is a problem awaiting a solution.

Data Appendix

The data are taken from the EXSTAT company database, which is based on the published accounts of U.K. quoted companies and is available from Extel Financial. The data take the form of an unbalanced panel, and the numbers of observations are given in table A1. Firms are selected from the EXSTAT data file of quoted companies in the manufacturing sector according to the following criteria: (i) they answered a postal questionnaire concerning the number of competitors (sample 1); (ii) there was enough information present to make an estimate of value-added; (iii) the number of consecutive periods for which data are held is at least six; and (iv) the accounts are prepared in a standard way; that is, the accounts marker is not relevant (item C25). The falloff in the numbers from 1982 corresponds to a change in the legal requirements concerning the reporting of employment in company reports, and only a small number of companies continued to report employment after July 1982 on a basis that was consistent with that used prior to that date.

Firm-Specific Variables

Output (y): Sales/turnover (EXSTAT item C31). This is normalized on an industry-specific price index (see below).

Value-added (y): Cost of employees (C16 + C18 + C72) + profits before tax (C34) + depreciation (C52) + interest payments (C53 + C54). This is normalized on an industry-specific price index (see below).

Employment (n): Number of employees (C15). This variable is recorded by EXSTAT as domestic employment. However, I have good reason to believe

TABLE A1

NUMBER OF OBSERVATIONS BY YEAR

	Sample 1	Sample 2
1972	92	423
1973	94	436
1974	98	451
1975	105	495
1976	143	650
1977	146	670
1978	145	665
1979	145	666
1980	144	662
1981	139	622
1982	72	309
1983	29	126
1984	26	103
1985	21	89
1986	20	84

that even in the small minority of firms in the sample that have overseas employees (around 14), this variable mostly reflects total employment.

Capital (k): This is based on transforming net tangible assets at historic cost into the same variable at current replacement cost and then normalizing on the price index for plant and machinery. This is an extremely complex calculation, and full details are provided in Wadhwani and Wall (1986).

Market share (mksh): Total sales in each industry (TSALS) is calculated as $TSALS_{jt} = N_j AVSALS_{jt}$, where $AVSALS_{jt}$ is the average sales of a firm in industry j at year t and N_j is the number of firms in industry j in a chosen base year (1980). The number of firms is kept constant over years to correct for the changing firm base of the sample. (The sample used to obtain these data includes about 1,200 firms, including all the major quoted companies in the industry.) The market share is obtained as sales in firm in year t (EXSTAT item C31) ÷ $TSALS_{jt}$.

Competition dummy (comp): This takes the value one if the managers of the firm answer yes to the question "Have you more than five competitors in the market for your product(s)?" and zero if the managers answer yes to either "Is your organization the main supplier of your product(s)?" or "Have you only a few (≤ 5) competitors?" This is dated 1989. I also have this variable dated 1984. The values it takes are the same for all but a handful of firms, and if this is used instead of the 1989 variable, the results are much the same.

Rents nomalized on value-added (rents): Rents are defined as profits before tax (C34) + depreciation (C52) + interest payments (C53 + C54) − cost of capital × capital stock. The capital stock is the replacement cost capital stock at current prices (see above under capital). The cost of capital is equal to $rr + \delta + \lambda\rho$, where rr is the real interest rate, δ is the rate of depreciation, ρ is the risk premium, and λ is a weight ($0 \leq \lambda \leq 1$). The real interest rate is equal to the annual real gross redemption yield on 2 percent Treasury index linked 1996 securities. They were issued in 1981. Prior to this date, the real interest rate is assumed to be constant at its 1981 level. It is worth noting that the real interest rate measured in this way fluctuates very little. Between 1981 and 1986, the minimum is 2.81 percent and the maximum is 3.94 percent. The depreciation rate is assumed to be constant at 4 percent. The risk premium is equal to the firm's average stock market return over the period 1972–86 less the average short-term interest rate over the same period. The three rent variables used in the paper correspond to three different values of λ. The variable $rent_1$ has λ = shareholders' funds (C132) ÷ [shareholders' funds (C132) + debentures (C136 + C137) + bank loans (C140) + other loans (C141) + bank overdrafts (C148) + acceptance credits (C149) + short-term borrowings (C150)]. That is, λ ≈ equity/(equity + debt). The variable $rent_2$ has $\lambda = 0$, and $rent_3$ has $\lambda = 1$. The rents variable is normalized on nominal value-added defined above. Note that since the cost of capital depends on the stock market return and rents are decreasing in the cost of capital, this suggests that there will be a negative relationship between rents and stock market returns. If firms with market power have higher returns, this will generate an unfortunate negative correlation between rents and market power. Fortunately, the efficiency of the stock market ensures that firms with market power do not have higher returns, on average.

Industry-Specific Variables

Prices: Producers' price indices for three-digit industries taken from *British Business* (*Trade and Industry* until 1979) and unpublished data from the Business Statistics Office.

Concentration ratio (five firms) (conc): Source is the *Census of Production*, summary tables PA1002, table 13.

Import penetration (imp): Ratio of imports to home sales. Source is the *Census of Production*, summary tables.

Overtime hours (H_o): Weekly overtime hours per operative on overtime times the fraction of operatives on overtime.

Standard hours (H_n): Normal weekly hours. Both H_o and H_n are taken from the *Employment Gazette*.

References

Arellano, Manuel, and Bond, Stephen. "Some Tests of Specification for Panel Data: Monte Carlo Evidence and an Application to Employment Equations." *Rev. Econ. Studies* 58 (April 1991): 277–97.

Baily, Martin N.; Hulten, Charles; and Campbell, David. "Productivity Dynamics in Manufacturing Plants." *Brookings Papers Econ. Activity: Microeconomics* (1992), pp. 187–249.

Bresnahan, Timothy F., and Reiss, Peter C. "Entry and Competition in Concentrated Markets." *J.P.E.* 99 (October 1991): 977–1009.

Caves, Richard E. "Industrial Organization, Corporate Strategy and Structure." *J. Econ. Literature* 18 (March 1980): 64–92.

Caves, Richard E., and Barton, David R. *Efficiency in US Manufacturing Industries.* Cambridge, Mass.: MIT Press, 1990.

Caves, Richard E., et al. *Industrial Efficiency in Six Nations.* Cambridge, Mass.: MIT Press, 1992.

Daniel, William W., and Millward, Neil. *Workplace Industrial Relations in Britain: The DE/PSI/SSRC Survey.* London: Heinemann, 1983.

Dasgupta, Partha, and Stiglitz, Joseph E. "Industrial Structure and the Nature of Innovative Activity." *Econ. J.* 90 (June 1980): 266–93.

Demsetz, Harold. "Industry Structure, Market Rivalry, and Public Policy." *J. Law and Econ.* 16 (April 1973): 1–9.

Dertouzos, Michael L.; Lester, R. K.; and Solow, Robert M. *Made in America: Regaining the Productive Edge.* Cambridge, Mass.: MIT Press, 1989.

Dickens, William T., and Katz, Lawrence F. "Inter-industry Wage Differences and Industry Characteristics." In *Unemployment and the Structure of Labor Markets*, edited by Kevin Lang and Jonathan S. Leonard. New York: Blackwell, 1987.

Geroski, Paul A. "Innovation, Technological Opportunity, and Market Structure." *Oxford Econ. Papers* 42 (July 1990): 586–602.

Graham, David R.; Kaplan, Daniel P.; and Sibley, David S. "Efficiency and Competition in the Airline Industry." *Bell J. Econ.* 14 (Spring 1983): 118–38.

Green, Alison, and Mayes, David G. "Technical Inefficiency in Manufacturing Industries." *Econ. J.* 101 (May 1991): 523–38.

CORPORATE PERFORMANCE   **745**

Griliches, Zvi. "Productivity, R & D, and the Basic Research at the Firm Level in the 1970's." *A.E.R.* 76 (March 1986): 141–54.

Hart, Oliver D. "The Market Mechanism as an Incentive Scheme." *Bell J. Econ.* 14 (Autumn 1983): 366–82.

Haskel, Jonathan. "Imperfect Competition, Work Practices and Productivity Growth." Manuscript. London: Queen Mary and Westfield Coll., Dept. Econ., 1990.

Hay, Donald A., and Liu, G. S. "The Efficiency of Firms: What Difference Does Competition Make?" Manuscript. Oxford: Univ. Oxford, Inst. Econ. and Statis., 1994.

Hermalin, Benjamin E. "The Effects of Competition on Executive Behavior." *Rand J. Econ.* 23 (Autumn 1992): 350–65.

Holmstrom, Bengt. "Managerial Incentive Problems—a Dynamic Perspective." In *Essays in Economics and Management in Honor of Lars Wahlbeck.* Helsinki: Swedish School Econ., 1982. (a)

———. "Moral Hazard in Teams." *Bell J. Econ.* 13 (Autumn 1982): 324–40. (b)

Horn, Henrik; Lang, Harald; and Lundgren, Stefan. "Competition, Long Run Contracts and Internal Inefficiencies in Firms." *European Econ. Rev.* 38 (February 1994): 213–33.

Jovanovic, Boyan. "Selection and the Evolution of Industry." *Econometrica* 50 (May 1982): 649–70.

Levin, Richard C.; Cohen, Wesley M.; and Mowery, David C. "R & D Appropriability, Opportunity, and Market Structure: New Evidence on Some Schumpeterian Hypotheses." *A.E.R. Papers and Proc.* 75 (May 1985): 20–24.

Martin, Stephen. "Endogenous Firm Efficiency in a Cournot Principal-Agent Model." *J. Econ. Theory* 59 (April 1993): 445–50.

Meyer, M. A., and Vickers, John. "Performance Comparisons and Dynamic Incentives." Discussion Paper no. 1107. London: Centre Econ. Policy Res., 1995.

Millward, Neil, and Stevens, Mark. *British Workplace Industrial Relations, 1980–1984: The DE/ESRC/PSI/ACAS Survey.* Aldershot, U.K.: Gower, 1986.

Mookherjee, Dilip. "Optimal Incentive Schemes with Many Agents." *Rev. Econ. Studies* 51 (July 1984): 433–46.

Muellbauer, John. "Aggregate Production Functions and Productivity Measurements: A New Look." Discussion Paper no. 33. London: Centre Econ. Policy Res., 1984.

Nalebuff, Barry J., and Stiglitz, Joseph E. "Prizes and Incentives: Towards a General Theory of Compensation and Competition." *Bell J. Econ.* 14 (Spring 1983): 21–43.

Nickell, Stephen J. "Competition and Corporate Performance." Discussion Paper no. 182. London: London School Econ., Centre Econ. Performance, 1994.

Nickell, Stephen J.; Wadhwani, Sushil B.; and Wall, Martin. "Productivity Growth in U.K. Companies, 1975–1986." *European Econ. Rev.* 36 (June 1992): 1055–85.

Porter, Michael E. *The Competitive Advantage of Nations.* London: Macmillan, 1990.

Scharfstein, David S. "Product-Market Competition and Managerial Slack." *Rand J. Econ.* 19 (Spring 1988): 147–55.

Schmidt, Klaus M. "Managerial Incentives and Product Market Competition." Discussion paper no. A-430. Bonn: Univ. Bonn, Wirtschaftspolitische Abteilung, 1994.

Schumpeter, Joseph A. *Capitalism, Socialism, and Democracy.* London: Allen and Unwin, 1943.

Smirlock, Michael L., and Marshall, William J. "Monopoly Power and Expense-Preference Behavior: Theory and Evidence to the Contrary." *Bell J. Econ.* 14 (Spring 1983): 166–78.

Smith, Adam. *An Inquiry into the Nature and Causes of the Wealth of Nations.* 1776. Reprint. Edited by Edwin Cannan. Chicago: Univ. Chicago Press, 1976.

Stewart, Mark B. "Union Wage Differentials, Product Market Influences and the Division of Rents." *Econ. J.* 100 (December 1990): 1122–37.

Van Wijnbergen, Sweder, and Venables, Anthony J. "Trade Liberalization, Productivity and Competition: The Mexican Experience." Manuscript. London: London School Econ., Centre Econ. Performance, 1993.

Vickers, John. *Concepts of Competition.* Oxford: Clarendon, 1994.

Wadhwani, Sushil B., and Wall, Martin. "The UK Capital Stock—New Estimates of Premature Scrapping." *Oxford Rev. Econ. Policy* 2 (Autumn 1986): 44–55.

Willig, Robert D. "Corporate Governance and Market Structure." In *Economic Policy in Theory and Practice,* edited by Assaf Razin and Efraim Sadka. London: Macmillan, 1987.

[18]

COMPETITION AND PRODUCTIVITY GROWTH: THE CASE OF THE U.S. TELEPHONE INDUSTRY

MICHAEL GORT and NAKIL SUNG*

The article focuses on the relation of competition to changes in productivity. Specifically, it compares the experience of AT&T Long Lines, operating in an increasingly competitive market, with that of eight local telephone monopolies. Both the estimation of total factor productivity growth and the analysis of shifts in cost functions show a markedly faster change in efficiency in the effectively competitive market than for the local monopolies. The article also examines three channels through which competition produces differential changes in efficiency. The results support, by implication, a policy of permitting entry and increasing competition in local telephone markets. (JEL L11, L96)

I. INTRODUCTION

There are few empirical studies on the relative performance of firms in competitive and monopolistic markets. This contrasts with the large body of literature that compares the performance of privately owned and governmental firms. One reason for the scarcity of studies of the former type is that competitive and monopolistic firms rarely coexist in the same industry and country.[1] This makes it difficult to distinguish between industry and market structure effects. On the other hand, relying on intercountry comparisons as, for example, Caves, Christensen, and Swanson [1981] do for U.S. and Canadian railroads, renders the analysis potentially sensitive to country effects.

The telephone industry in the United States offers one of the best opportunities for empirical analysis of the consequences of competition and monopoly. Some new entry in the long-distance telephone market was allowed by the early 1960s, while entry and competition in the local telephone market had yet to materialize by the beginning of the 1990s. Hence, it is appropriate to focus on differences in performance between AT&T Long Lines and the regional monopolies.[2] Since there may be differences in initial conditions between the local-service and long-distance markets, comparisons of performance should control for such differences. Both markets, however, clearly employ very similar technology. This, holding other relevant conditions constant, should lead to similar changes in productivity. To sharpen the analysis, we focus on differences in the annual *rate* of productivity growth and not the *level*.

While local exchange carriers (LECs) still largely maintain their monopolistic position, rapid technological advance in telecommunications is changing the established market structure in the local telephone industry. The recent U.S. Telecommunications Act of 1996 was aimed at eliminating legal barriers that

* We wish to thank two anonymous referees for valuable comments.

Gort: Professor, State University of New York at Buffalo, Buffalo, Phone 1-716-645-2121 x 42
Fax 1-716-645-2127, E-mail gort@acsu.buffalo.edu
Sung: Senior Researcher, Korea Telecom, Sungnam, Korea, Phone 82-342-727-0440, Fax 82-342-727-0493
E-mail nisung@kt.co.kr

1. There exist several interindustry studies on the impact of competition on the level or the growth of productivity. A recent example is Nickell [1996].

2. Data on long-distance companies, except those for AT&T, were not available. In contrast, even when AT&T Long Lines was a component of the Bell system, its operations were independent of other arms of AT&T and it filed financial and operating data with the FCC as a separate entity.

ABBREVIATIONS

LECs Local exchange carriers
TFP: Total factor productivity
FCC: Federal Communications Commission
RBOCs: Regional Bell operating companies
IXCs: Interexchange carriers
BLS: Bureau of Labor Statistics
PPI: Producer Price index

678

Economic Inquiry
(ISSN 0095-2583)
Vol. 37, No. 4, October 1999, 678–691

have suppressed technically feasible local competition. Certainly some competition in local telephone markets is under way. Is such competition socially justified and an appropriate objective of public policy? The effect of competition on productivity growth holds at least part of the answer. We need to know whether competitive markets are likely to raise efficiency in assessing how much effort should go into reducing entry barriers and increasing competition in the local telephone markets. Still another policy issue on which our study has a bearing is the relation of firm scale to costs. For example, in the context of recent mergers of regional telecommunication companies, are reductions in costs and increases in productivity a plausible expectation?

Competitive effects in the telephone industry have been examined mainly through aggregate time series data. Thus, Oum [1990], using Chessler's competition index for long-distance service, concludes there have been positive effects of competition on productivity, whereas Crandall [1991], using a time dummy, finds the results inconclusive.[3] At the firm level, Denny, Fuss, and Waverman [1981] and Kiss [1983] decompose total factor productivity(TFP) growth for Bell Canada through estimated cost functions. Nadiri and Prucha [1989] measure productivity growth for the U.S. Bell system with several alternative cost models. But none of these careful firm level studies focuses on competitive effects. Ying and Shin [1993], on the other hand, do examine the spillover effect of the AT&T divestiture on cost saving by the regional companies. Their interesting study, which shows positive spillover effects, does not, however, permit strong conclusions because of the shortness of the period examined (1976–87).

II. THE STATE OF COMPETITION IN THE U.S. TELEPHONE INDUSTRY

Before the divestiture of AT&T, the U.S. telephone industry consisted of several vertically integrated common carriers. AT&T ac-

counted for about 80% of industry revenues through a group of 22 operating companies plus the AT&T Long Lines. The Bell operating companies offered both local and intrastate toll services, while AT&T Long Lines provided interstate toll services. Even before divestiture, however, rapid technological change began to erode the monopoly position of AT&T and to induce the Federal Communications Commission (FCC) to modify the regulatory support it gave to monopoly.

For example, the development of microwave communications led the FCC in 1959 to authorize private firms to operate microwave facilities for their own use. In 1969, also, MCI was granted authority to build the microwave relay system for long-distance private-line services to subscribers and, thus, to compete with AT&T in a limited way. But it was not until the Execunet decision in 1977 that competition in message toll services, as distinct from private line services, commenced and effective competitive rivalry was firmly established.[4] Thus, 1977 is one of the key transition years.

Another factor commonly believed to have impeded entry into the industry was high vertical integration. After a seven-year antitrust suit initiated by the Justice Department with the objective of reducing vertical integration, AT&T and the Justice Department reached a settlement in 1982. It obliged AT&T to divest its 22 regional Bell operating companies (RBOCs) in 1984, and they were regrouped into seven regional holding companies. The market boundary between long distance and other services was also redrawn so that the surviving AT&T company was double the size of the previous long-lines component, measured in terms of gross plant, and almost seven times as large in terms of revenue. Thus, 1984 is another key transition year.

Since 1984, AT&T's market share in long-distance markets has declined from 90% in 1984 to 62% in 1991. By the end of our sample period (1951–91), most telephone lines nationwide were connected with equal access, which implies that consumers could access any long-distance carrier without dialing additional digits.

3. Chessler's index, as presented in Oum [1990], is based on the ratio of (a) connection charges paid by long-distance carriers other than AT&T plus resale carriers' lease payments to (b) total industry toll revenues.

4. In 1977, AT&T's revenues from message toll services were $11.1 billion while its private line service revenues were only $1.18 billion.

Entrepreneurship and Economic Growth

Notwithstanding these facts, substantial differences of opinion exist among economists regarding the intensity of competition in long-distance markets.[5] One group of economists concludes that actual rivalry between interexchange carriers (IXCs) has served to produce competitive outcomes, while the other argues that AT&T's competitors have often been involved in tacit collusion with AT&T. Two recent studies provide econometric evidence on the extent of AT&T's market power. Both Ward [1995] and Kahai, Kaserman, and Mayo [1996] , based on an estimate of the price elasticity of AT&T's demand curve, strongly support the conclusion that the postdivestiture long-distance markets are largely competitive. The time spans encompassed by the two studies are 1986–93 and 1984–93, respectively, which overlap our sample period.

The question of how competitive the long-distance market has been since divestiture has also been examined in the context of price behavior. The Bureau of Labor Statistics (BLS) Producer Price index for interstate message services dropped from 153 in 1983 to 105.6 in 1991. Even this decline, however, understates the true drop in prices since the BLS index does not account for the effect of discount plans that developed with competition in the industry. Complicating the implications of this change from the standpoint of price-cost relations have been (a) a sharp reduction in access charges paid to local telephone companies (a reduction strongly supported by the FCC), (b) economies attributable to changes in TFP, and (c) rises in input prices for long-distance telephone services.

AT&T estimated, as reported by Taylor and Zona [1997], that average revenue per minute, net of access charges, fell by roughly 5% per year, in real terms (deflated by the GDP-PI), in the period 1984–94. This is less than our estimate of changes in real costs as reflected in total factor productivity in the 1984–91 period (which rose roughly 6.8% per year). However, even if our estimate of productivity change were applicable to the longer interval,

no conclusions with respect to how competitive the market was could be drawn from such comparisons.

First, we do not know if the base-year return to capital was at a competitive equilibrium level. Second, the continued change in the market in terms of competition raised market risks and, as a consequence, should have raised the cost of capital. Third, the shift by the FCC (and some state commissions) from rate of return to price-cap regulation, which began to take effect in 1989, had as one of its objective generating incentives for cost reduction by the industry. This, in turn, implied that the industry would capture at least initially a part of the benefits of cost reduction.[6] And finally, it is not clear to what extent the drop in access charges, even with FCC support for it, was not itself partly a consequence of industry support for it in the context of a competitive environment for long-distance service. This raises the complex question in the theory of regulation of the reciprocal effects of company initiatives and regulatory decisions. These effects flow in both directions and not simply from the latter to the former.

Turning to market share, through most of the interval studied, AT&T continued to have a large share of the long-distance market. However, market share at a point in time is a far weaker indicator of competitive pressures than change in market share. It is the latter that indicates whether a market is at least potentially contestable. Judged by the steady increases in competition reflected in the erosion of AT&T's share, it is reasonable to hypothesize that potential competition was sufficient to have exerted strong pressures on managerial decisions in the long-distance market.

Accordingly, notwithstanding high market shares in the long-distance sector at individual points in time, the difference in competition between this sector and that of the regional monopolies should be both real and significant. This difference may prove to be a transitory episode in the industry's history as regional companies providing local service begin to face competition from cable companies and from multimodal wireless communi-

---

5. Kahai, Kaserman, and Mayo [1996] present a list of studies on the state of competition in long distance markets while Sappington and Weisman [1996] offer a brief summary of a debate on the issue sparked by the prospective entry of RBOC's into long-distance markets.

6. Taylor and Zona [1997] conclude from evidence that some of the reduction in costs was not passed forward into prices that the market was not competitive. For reasons given above, such a conclusion is not warranted.

cations providers. For the period we examined, however, the distinction between competition in the two markets is valid.

III. HYPOTHESES ABOUT THE RELATION OF COMPETITION AND PRODUCTIVITY

Productivity growth, which is often identified with technical change or technological progress, implies shifts in production or cost functions. We use both of these alternative measures of productivity growth, since the effects of competition on a firm's efficiency may be revealed in either measure.[7]

There are conflicting hypotheses in economic literature about the effect of competition on productivity growth. A priori reasoning does not lead to an unequivocal answer and the importance of alternative influences can only be ascertained empirically.[8] Even though there is no clear theoretical consensus on competition effects, some of the key channels through which competition may have an influence on a firm's performance can be ascertained. The existence of competitors can affect a firm's efficiency in at least four ways.

First, competition induces a firm to choose the profit-maximizing level and composition of output. This increases sales and the size of the market. As an aspect of this, competition induces rivals to search for segments of the market not previously served and to increase demand from existing customers by offering a greater variety of services. As an illustration, competition in the long-distance telephone market has led to a wide variety of services and discount plans. Even though an increase in demand may not directly induce shifts in a cost function, it often leads to an increase in productivity.

Second, the quality of physical capital and of labor affects productivity growth. Embodied technical change may result from rapid

capital turnover, i.e., modernization of plant and equipment or from capital additions to serve new demand. If both a monopolist and a competitive firm have equal access to perfectly competitive input markets, it is uncertain, a priori, which will employ higher input quality.[9] However, a firm which faces faster output growth tends to employ more recent capital goods and hence to improve the quality of its capital stocks. Since lower competitive prices should lead to faster growth in demand, this argues for a positive effect of competition on the quality of capital inputs.

The third and most frequently cited benefit from actual rivalry is its impact on the use and accumulation of firm-specific organizational capital. Organizational capital may take the form of managerial effort, matching tasks with the attributes of individual employees, the sorting of employees by competence, and other aspects of firm-specific learning-by-doing. Monitoring costs of a modern corporation are frequently associated with supervising this organizational capital. It is costly for shareholders to monitor and reward managers' decisions on the use of organizational capital in a monopolistic market because a monopoly lacks examples for comparison. A competitive market provides more information and, in this way, keeps monitoring costs down thereby forcing managers to reduce nonoptimizing use of organizational capital. The efficient use and accumulation of organizational capital may lead to shifts in a cost function, even when there is no embodied technical change.

Still another force relates to Schumpeterian hypotheses.[10] While rivalry may provide incentives for innovations, monopoly may offer a greater incentive to innovate to the extent that it permits capture of a larger fraction of the total returns to innovation. Monopolistic firms, it is also alleged, have greater financial resources to invest in innovation.

It is not our objective to identify the role of all variables that, a priori, may affect the relation of competition to productivity

---

7. The two measures should yield largely equivalent results assuming perfect competition equilibrium. In particular, the following three conditions are necessary for equivalence: (1) production is measured at the frontier, (2) there are constant returns to scale and (3) there is consistent optimization with respect to the combinations of inputs that firms choose to use.

8. Nickell [1996] surveys theoretical and empirical studies on competition and corporate performance in addition to providing his evidence on the effects of competition on a firm's efficiency. He concludes that the theoretical basis for the relation is not strong and that earlier econometric studies are inconclusive.

9. A competitive profit-maximizing firm chooses an optimal input quality/quantity mix for its survival, while a monopolistic firm has room for managerial slack. Managerial slack may, in turn, lead to either over- or underinvestment.

10. For a comprehensive survey of empirical studies on the Schumpeterian hypotheses, see Cohen and Levin [1989]. They conclude that the empirical evidence bearing on Schumpeterian hypotheses is inconclusive.

change. Rather our focus is on the direction of the net effect as revealed by empirical evidence. In the process of measuring this net effect, however, we are able to identify the role of both growth in output and of changes in the quality of inputs on productivity change. Since both growth in output (via price changes) and input quality can be shown to have been related to competition in the telecommunications industry, this permits us to isolate at least a part of the mechanism through which competition has affected productivity.

In contrast to output growth and input quality, we have no direct measure of organizational capital. However, once the effects of changes in demand and in the quality of capital and labor inputs have been identified, any residual effect of competition on productivity growth, whether positive or negative, can be imputed to either the quantity and use of organizational capital or, alternatively, to the class of variables captured by the Schumpeterian hypotheses. That is, the residual effect of competition on productivity should be positive to the extent that our hypotheses on the positive relation of competition and the effective use of organizational capital are valid. Conversely, the residual effect should be negative to the extent that hypotheses about the greater investment of monopolistic firms in innovation, or about the greater incentives to innovate in monopoly markets, are important characterizations of reality.

IV. GROWTH IN TOTAL FACTOR PRODUCTIVITY

Our empirical analysis is carried out with pooled cross-section and time-series data for the AT&T Long Lines and eight regional companies (six of them part of the Bell system before 1983 and independent following divestiture). The identity of the eight companies and the method used to measure inputs and output are briefly given in the Appendix.

For measuring TFP, we first aggregate (as described in the Appendix) three outputs (local, toll, and miscellaneous services). Three inputs (labor, capital, and materials) are also aggregated. For the capital input, we use alternatively net stock (in the conventional perpetual inventory version) and gross stock. Use of the latter permits an estimate of the

effects on TFP of changes in the quality of capital inputs as measured by vintage. A translog multilateral index of productivity is then calculated using a modification of the method of Caves, Christensen, and Diewert [1982].[11]

Table I shows the average annual rate of productivity growth for each of the firms in several stages defined by the evolution of competition as discussed earlier. The key results are as follows: (1) For both the gross and net capital versions of capital stock, AT&T Long Lines experienced a higher growth rate in TFP than the regional companies. The difference in growth rates appears in all periods after 1968 but is especially large for the 1985–91 interval when it is 7–14 times larger for AT&T than for the regionals (depending on whether gross or net stocks are used).[12] (2) The TFP growth rate of AT&T Long Lines rises systematically from stage to stage, while that for the regional companies shows a level growth rate as competition evolves only in the long-distance market. The very high average rate for AT&T Long Lines follows divestiture. We observe no spillover effects of divestiture for the regional companies, almost all of which show a decline in productivity growth in the 1985–91 period.

To examine whether the distribution of the observed TFP growth rate for the regionals has the same location parameter as that for AT&T Long Lines in the pre- and postdivestiture period, we conducted the following nonparametric tests: Wilcoxon rank sum test, Median test, Savage test, Van der Waerden test, and Fisher's exact test. The tests consistently show that the TFP growth rates of the two groups were sampled from an identical continuous population for the period 1952–83, but not for the period 1984–91.

Table II, which shows the growth rate in

---

11. For each firm, its aggregate output and input in 1951 was used as the initial year value for constructing a translog multilateral index of productivity. This implicitly assumes that initial year productivity was equal across all firms. AT&T Long Lines did not produce local services. Hence, the above modification to the Caves, Christensen and Diewert formula was necessary.

12. For the entire interval 1952–91, the 4.2%–4.3% annual rate for AT&T and the 2.5% rate for the regional companies may be compared with a rate of 4.0% for the Bell system for 1947–76 obtained by Nadiri and Schankerman [1981], a 2.9% rate for the U.S. telephone industry for 1951–87 obtained by Oum [1990] and a 3.5% rate for the industry for 1961–88 by Crandall [1991].

TABLE I
Average Annual Growth Rate in Total Factor Productivity for AT&T Long Lines
and 8 Regional Companies, 1952–91

Firm	Type of Capital Stock	No Competition (1952–68)	Transition Period (1969–76)	Competition (1977–91)	After Divestiture (1985–91)	Entire Period (1952–91)
AT&T	Gross	2.8%	4.7%	5.7%	6.8%	4.2%
Long Lines	Net	2.8%	4.9%	5.9%	8.5%	4.3%
R₁	Gross	2.0%	2.0%	2.5%	0.9%	2.2%
	Net	2.5%	2.5%	2.3%	0.3%	2.4%
R₂	Gross	1.9%	1.7%	2.3%	–0.2%	2.0%
	Net	2.1%	2.3%	1.9%	–1.1%	2.1%
R₃	Gross	2.0%	2.2%	2.8%	1.1%	2.3%
	Net	2.2%	2.5%	2.8%	0.4%	2.5%
R₄	Gross	2.0%	2.2%	2.3%	1.1%	2.2%
	Net	2.4%	2.4%	2.4%	1.0%	2.4%
R₅	Gross	3.0%	0.9%	2.5%	1.0%	2.4%
	Net	3.5%	1.2%	2.4%	0.6%	2.7%
R₆	Gross	2.2%	1.7%	2.2%	–0.7%	2.1%
	Net	2.6%	2.0%	1.8%	–1.8%	2.2%
R₇	Gross	3.3%	4.7%	3.5%	4.5%	3.7%
	Net	2.6%	4.1%	3.6%	4.7%	3.4%
R₈	Gross	4.5%	2.4%	2.3%	0.5%	3.0%
	Net	3.3%	2.3%	2.4%	0.9%	2.7%
Eight Regional	Gross	2.5%	2.2%	2.5%	1.0%	2.5%
Companies	Net	2.6%	2.4%	2.5%	0.6%	2.5%

Notes: Gross and net refer to average annual percentage changes in the TFP based on gross and net capital stock, respectively. R₁–R₈ denote regional companies. For sources and methods of deriving the data, see the Appendix.

output and in the quality of labor and capital inputs (with quality of capital proxied by the average vintage of all capital inputs) casts additional light on the TFP growth estimates. Two labor quality indexes are used. The first index, suggested by Gort, Bahk, and Wall [1993], is simply real wage rate. This measure of average labor quality has intuitive appeal because it allows for the effect of any attribute of labor that increases the productivity of labor.[13] Within the context of a cost function, we develop another index, which is defined as the ratio of the weighted sum to the simple sum of working hours with the weights being the ratio of each occupational group's hourly

13. If the assumption of a perfectly competitive labor market is violated, a high wage may not reflect high labor quality. Nevertheless, for cross-section analysis, using wages as an index of labor quality is valid insofar as the market for labor inputs was substantially the same across all companies.

earnings to average wages in the private sector.

The large spread in productivity growth between AT&T and the regional companies in the 1985–91 period was accompanied by a very large difference in the constant dollar growth in revenues, with AT&T showing annual growth of 10.1% as compared with 2.1% for the toll services of the regionals. A plausible inference is that the differential growth in output is at least partly causally related to rapid drop in long-distance prices, whatever its explanation. However, competition has also led to an increase in marketing efforts, especially through various customer-oriented services and discount plans.

The differential growth in output probably contributed to the sharper reduction in the vintage of physical capital in 1985–91 for AT&T, since it led to higher investment for AT&T than for the regionals in that period. For the

TABLE II
Average Annual Percentage Changes in Revenue and in the Quality of Inputs
for AT&T and 8 Regional Companies, 1952–91

Period	Current-Dollar Revenue			Constant-Dollar Revenue		
	Regionals		AT&T Long Lines	Regionals		AT&T Long Lines
	Local Services	Toll Services	Toll Services	Local Services	Toll Services	Toll Services
1952–1968	7.4%	9.7%	9.7%	6.0%	9.6%	9.8%
1969–1976	8.9%	11.8%	9.4%	4.8%	7.7%	7.5%
1977–1991	6.3%	7.5%	8.0%	1.6%	5.5%	8.7%
1977–1983	10.0%	12.1%	10.8%	4.7%	8.9%	7.3%
1985–1991	2.6%	2.9%	5.2%	−1.5%	2.1%	10.1%
1952–1991	7.3%	9.4%	9.0%	4.1%	7.6%	8.9%

Period	Real Wage		Labor Quality		Vintage of Capital	
	Regionals	AT&T Long Lines	Regionals	AT&T Long Lines	Regionals	AT&T Long Lines
1952–1968	2.8%	2.5%	0.4%	0.6%	−3.0%	−3.1%
1969–1976	3.1%	3.7%	2.7%	3.2%	−3.8%	−2.9%
1977–1991	0.6%	0.0%	1.5%	0.7%	−5.6%	−6.9%
1977–1983	1.2%	−0.7%	1.2%	0.4%	−5.2%	−5.4%
1985–1991	−0.1%	0.7%	1.7%	1.0%	−6.1%	−8.3%
1952–1991	2.0%	1.9%	1.3%	1.2%	−4.1%	−4.4%

Notes: For sources and measures of all variables, see the Appendix. The year 1984 is excluded because the transfer of assets and revenue to the new AT&T long-distance service may distort the measure of change. Lower vintage means higher quality of capital.

post-1984 period, average annual growth in AT&T real investment was roughly 9% as compared with 0.4% for the regionals. This, as is seen in the more formal analysis of relations among the variables in Table III, contributed to the higher growth in productivity.

The basic estimating equation for Table III is:

$$(1) \quad \ln TFP + \beta_0 + \beta_u\, U + \beta_t t + \beta_l \ln QL$$

$$+ \beta_K \ln QK + \beta_{ATT} ATT + \beta_c\, CD$$

$$+ \beta_{ATT,c}\, ATT \cdot CD$$

$$+ \beta_{t,ATT}\, t \cdot ATT + \beta_{t,c}\, t \cdot CD$$

$$+ \beta_{t,ATT,c}\, t \cdot ATT \cdot CD + \varepsilon,$$

where U refers to the rate of capacity utilization, QL to real wage rate measuring labor quality, QK to average vintage as a proxy for capital quality, t to the time trend, and e is the error term. ATT is a dummy variable that equals 1 for AT&T Long Lines and 0 for the regionals. The dummy variable (CD) for 1977 or 1984 is used to divide the interval into periods before and after 1977 or 1984, on the assumption that competition in the long-distance market changed after 1977 or 1984. In an alternative specification, we use the competition index of Chessler, transformed into logs, to proxy the degree of competition.[14]

The rate of capacity utilization (U) has a positive effect on TFP in the short run. U is proxied by actual minus predicted output level,

14. Chessler's competition index is extended by us to 1991 using market share data. The index rose from 1.7 in 1971 to 100 in 1983 and to 485 5 in 1991.

TABLE III
Total Factor Productivity Regressions

Explanatory Variable	(1) CORC/OLS	(2) CORC/OLS	(3) CORC/OLS	(4) CORC/OLS
Constant	0.367* (0.008)	−0.208* (0.007)	1.572* (0.123)	2.723* (0.047)
Capacity Utilization	0.503* (0.029)	0.270* (0.031)	0.270* (0.032)	0.509* (0.031)
Time	0.008* (0.003)	0.030* (0.002)	0.017* (0.005)	
Real Wage			0.131* (0.040)	0.205* (0.052)
Capital Vintage			−0.236** (0.121)	−0.347* (0.079)
Chessler's Index				−0.032* (0.015)
AT&T	−1.077* (0.327)	−0.297 (0.181)	−0.218* (0.077)	−0.007 (0.091)
1984		0.683* (0.170)	0.745* (0.171)	
AT&T*1984		−0.641 (0.499)	−0.505 (0.415)	
Time*AT&T	0.048* (0.009)	0.020* (0.007)	0.018* (0.003)	
Time*1984		−0.027* (0.005)	−0.029* (0.005)	
Time*AT&T*1984		0.028** (0.015)	0.024* (0.012)	
AT&T*Chessler's Index				0.133* (0.021)
D.W.	0.198	0.300	0.521	0.401
Adjusted R^2	0.533	0.756	0.849	0.586

Notes: CORC denotes a Cochrane-Orcutt procedure and OLS an ordinary least squares estimator. ATT = 1 for AT&T Long Lines Department and 0 for regional companies. For the period 1984–1991, 1984 = 1 and 0 for the period 1952–1983. All variables except dummy variables and time are in log form. Standard errors are in parentheses. * and ** signify significant at the 5% and 10% level, respectively. The number of observations is 348.

with the latter being obtained from the estimation of a production function. t measures residual or unidentified technical change, whether industry-wide or firm-specific, while QL and QK are firm-specific measures of the quality of labor and capital. The coefficient for the last interaction term captures the relative shift in the productivity of AT&T Long Lines compared to the regionals after competition (controlling for output and technical advance).

Differentiating the TFP level equation with respect to time trend produces the following TFP growth rate equation:

$$(2) \quad \dot{TFP} = \beta_t + \beta_u \dot{U} + \beta_l \dot{QL} + \beta_k \dot{QK}$$

$$+ \beta_{t,ATT} ATT + \beta_{t,c} CD + \beta_{t,ATT,c} ATT \cdot CD + \varepsilon'.$$

In the above equation, dots imply growth rate. In particular, productivity growth varies with two variables, ATT and CD. The coefficient of $t*ATT*CD$ in Table III therefore reflects differences in the productivity growth of AT&T and the regionals, before and after 1977 or 1984. The principal results of Table III follow:

1. An increase in capacity utilization shows a positive relation to TFP growth in every equation. Its coefficients, which range from 0.270 to 0.509, have the expected signs and are highly significant. High capacity utilization leads to an increase in TFP in the short run.

2. When due account is taken of the quality of inputs, the coefficient of time decreases from 0.030 in model (2) to 0.017 in model (3). This indicates that input quality (particularly the vintage of capital) accounts for a large fraction of technical change.

3. Both the coefficients of vintage and those of real wage rate are statistically significant and have the expected signs. This implies that improvements in labor and capital qualities contribute to TFP growth.

4. The coefficient for $t*ATT$ is always positive and statistically significant and implies that AT&T experienced higher productivity growth over time (by 1.8%–4.8% annually) than did the regionals. Moreover, as the coefficient of $t*ATT*1984$ shows, the higher productivity growth of AT&T is associated with a larger difference between the productivity growth of AT&T and the regionals following (than before) the rise in competition after 1984. Substituting 1977 for 1984 as a dummy variable results in similar estimates.[15] The total effect of competition on productivity in the 1980s is, moreover, greater than that captured by the dummy variable. This is because the change in the vintage of capital is accelerated by new investment and investment, in turn, responds to growth in demand. To the extent that growth in demand resulted from increased competition, some of the effect of competition is captured by the quality of capital variable.

The negative sign of $t*1984$ indicates that regionals suffer from a drop in productivity after 1984. While the coefficient for AT&T, without interaction with time, is negative, this

may reflect a low productivity level for AT&T at the outset of the period, that is, in 1952.

V. COMPETITION AND SHIFTS IN COST FUNCTIONS

We now examine the effects of competition on shifts in the cost functions for AT&T Long Lines and the regionals. The cost functions are estimated simultaneously with two factor-cost-share equations subject to the relevant cross-equation constraints. The differences in competition effects are tested by introducing competition variables as additional regressors in the cost functions. A single-product cost function is adopted because AT&T produces only toll services.

Specifically, we estimate the following four cost functions:

(3) (Model 1)

$$\ln C = g(\ln P_L, \ln P_M, \ln P_K, \ln Y, t; ATT),$$

(4) (Model 2)

$$\ln C = g(\ln P_L, \ln P_M, \ln P_K, \ln Y, t; ATT, CD),$$

(5) (Model 3)

$$\ln C = g(\ln P_L / QL, \ln P_M, \ln P_K, \ln Y,$$

$$\ln QK, t; ATT, CD),$$

(6) (Model 4)

$$\ln C = g(\ln P_L / QL, \ln P_M, \ln P_K,$$

$$\ln Y, \ln QK, \ln CI; ATT),$$

where Y refers to aggregate output, P_L to the wage rate, P_M to materials price, P_K to the user cost of capital, t is the time variable, QL the second labor quality index, QK capital quality as proxied by vintage, and CI is Chessler's competition index. Dummy variables are used, as before, for AT&T and for the period variable (that is, before and after 1977 or 1984). Models (1) and (2) represent the conventional specification of a cost func-

---

15. The coefficient for $t*ATT*1977$ is 0.036 in model (2) and 0.031 in model (3). Both are statistically significant at the 1% level.

tion with a time variable as a proxy for the state of technology, while models (3) and (4) use input quality indexes. From the definition of QL, the quality-adjusted wage is equal to quality-unadjusted wage (P_L) divided by QL.

It is assumed that $g(\cdot)$ is twice-differentiable and can be well approximated by a second-order Taylor series expansion, that is, translog flexible cost function. To illustrate, a translog cost function for model (3) is given by:

$$(7) \quad \ln C = \alpha_0 + \alpha_y \ln Y + \sum_{i=L,M,K} \alpha_i \ln P_i - \alpha_L \ln QL +$$

$$\alpha_K \ln QK + \alpha_t t + \frac{1}{2}\beta_{YY}(\ln Y)^2 + \frac{1}{2}\sum_{i=L,M,K}$$

$$\sum_{j=L,M,K} \beta_{ij} \ln P_i \ln P_j + \frac{1}{2}\beta_{LL}(\ln QL)^2 +$$

$$\frac{1}{2}\beta_{KK}(\ln QK)^2 + \frac{1}{2}\beta_{tt} t^2 + \sum_{i=L,M,K} \beta_{Yi} \ln Y \ln P_i -$$

$$\beta_{YL} \ln QL \ln Y + \beta_{YK} \ln QK \ln Y + \beta_{Yt} t \ln Y -$$

$$\sum_{i=L,M,K} \beta_{Li} \ln QL \ln P_i + \sum_{i=L,M,K} \beta_{Ki} \ln QK \ln P_i +$$

$$\sum_{i=L,M,K} \beta_{ti} t \ln P_i - \beta_{Lt} t \ln QL + \beta_{Kt} t \ln QK -$$

$$\beta_{LK} \ln QL \ln QK + \gamma_{ATT} ATT + \gamma_C CD +$$

$$\gamma_{ATT,C} ATT \cdot CD + \gamma_{t,ATT} t \cdot ATT +$$

$$\gamma_{t,C} t \cdot CD + \gamma_{t,ATT,C} t \cdot ATT \cdot CD + \varepsilon.$$

For translog estimates, normalization of all variables by sample means permits the first-order terms to be interpreted as the elasticities at the sample means. Conditions of linear homogeneity and symmetry are imposed, while monotonicity and concavity conditions are investigated after estimation.

Assuming cost minimization given the regular constraints, Shepard's lemma can be applied to obtain the following cost share equation.

$$(8) \quad s_j = \alpha_j + \sum_{i=L,M,K} \beta_{ji} \ln P_i + \beta_{Yj} \ln Y + \beta_{tj} t$$

$$- \beta_{Lj} \ln QL + \beta_{Kj} \ln QK + \varepsilon_j,$$

where ε_j is the disturbance term.

The first-order serial correlation in error terms is assumed, due to the time-series property of the data set. For the proper identification of autoregressive coefficients, we impose the restriction that all share equations have the same autoregressive parameter. Then we jointly estimate the cost function and the two cost share equations by iterating Zellner's nonlinear seemingly unrelated regression method. One of the cost share equations is deleted to obtain a nonsingular covariance matrix.

After the cost functions are estimated, the effects of competition on productivity growth are examined. In model (2), productivity growth, i.e. an annual time-dependent shift in the cost function, is calculated as follows.

$$(9) \quad \partial \ln C / \partial t = \beta_t + \beta_{Yt} \ln Y +$$

$$\sum_{i=L,M,K} \beta_{ti} \ln P_i + \beta_{tt} t + \gamma_{t,c} CD$$

$$+ \gamma_{t,ATT,C} ATT \cdot CD.$$

A negative sign of $\gamma_{t,ATT,C}$ indicates that AT&T experienced a larger increase in productivity growth after 1977 or 1984 than did the regionals. Similarly, in model (4) the effect of Chessler's competition index on cost decline is captured as follows.

$$(10) \quad \partial \ln C / \partial \ln CI = \alpha_c + \beta_{yc} \ln Y +$$

$$\sum_{i=L,M,K} \beta_{ic} \ln P_i - \beta_{lc} \ln QL$$

$$+ \beta_{kc} \ln QK + \beta_{cc} \ln CI + \gamma_{ATT,C} ATT.$$

If $\gamma_{ATT,C} = 0$, the hypothesis that AT&T experienced greater effects of competition would have been rejected.

Entrepreneurship and Economic Growth

Table IV presents the results of the cost functions. Most of the parameter estimates are significant at the 1% level and all the first-order terms for the explanatory variables proved statistically significant at the 5% level for all models except model (3). The second-order terms for all models are small. This implies stable elasticities. The principal conclusions are:

1. All models produce very similar estimates of output cost elasticity. These range, at the sample means, from 1.138 for model (3) to 0.890 for model (4). Thus, telephone companies appear to exhibit nearly constant returns to scale. This confirms Shin and Ying [1992]'s finding that the regionals are not natural monopolies any more.

2. All elasticities of cost with respect to input prices, that is, factor shares, are positive at the sample means.

3. The coefficients of all variables intended to capture the effects of technology change were significant and had the expected signs except for model (3). This implies significant downward percentage shifts in the cost functions attributed to technical advance. Model (1) points to a downward shift in the cost function of 2.9% per year at the sample mean. For model (2) it is 1.4%. Model (4) shows that a 1% increase in QL leads to a 0.39% downward shift in the cost function at the sample mean and, also, a 0.94% shift for QK. On average, capital and labor quality improvements result in 0.9% and 0.5% increases in productivity, respectively, so that the two account for more than two-thirds of total productivity growth. The time variable and QK (vintage of capital) largely capture the same phenomenon and when both are introduced, as in model (3), their coefficients become nonsignificant or under/over-estimated.

4. In models (2) and (3), the negative sign of the coefficient for $\ln PL*t$ indicates that labor share declines over time. In models (3) and (4), the sign of $\ln PL*\ln QK$ is positive and implies that capital quality improvements are labor-saving.

5. In model (1), the coefficient of $t*ATT$ is highly significant and has a negative sign. It shows that over the 1951–91 time span, AT&T experienced a 1.8% higher annual percentage shift in the cost function (at the sample mean) than did the regionals. In models (2) and (3), the coefficient of $t*ATT*1984$ is significant,

negative and large. These results reflect the fact that AT&T, but not the regionals, experienced a large rise in productivity growth after 1984.[16]

6. In model (4), the sign of $\ln CI*ATT$ is negative and reflects the relevance of competition to productivity growth for AT&T, with competition measured by Chessler's index.

VI. CONCLUSIONS

For both of the measures of capital stock used in the analysis, AT&T experienced a higher TFP growth rate than did any of the eight regional monopolies. Moreover, the average annual TFP growth rate for AT&T rose over time, while that for the regionals shows nearly no change.

The average rate of growth in TFP was particularly high for AT&T following divestiture. This was associated with high growth in output—a result attributed partly to the effect of competition on marketing efforts arising from rivalry over market shares. There also was a concurrent marked drop in the vintage of capital for AT&T. However, even after controlling for growth in demand and for the change in the vintage of capital (both partly attributable to competition), there still remains a positive net effect of competition on efficiency. We attribute this residual effect to the impact of competition on the effectiveness with which organizational capital is used.

The cost functions strongly confirm the conclusions of total factor productivity analysis. In addition, the results indicate that telephone companies exhibit nearly constant returns to scale. Thus, scale economies do not explain the differences in productivity growth and mere increases in size of regional monopolies through merger seem unlikely to generate net reductions in costs. The cost models yield the same relationships between input qualities and changes in costs as found with TFP growth rate regressions. That is, changes in the vintage of capital contribute significantly to explaining both differences in TFP growth and changes in costs.

16. When 1977 is adopted instead of 1984 as a dummy variable, the competition effect becomes a little unclear. While the coefficient of $t*ATT*1977$ is significant and has the expected sign in model (3), it becomes insignificant in model (2).

TABLE IV
Total Cost Functions

Explanatory Variable	(1) ITSUR/AR(1)	(2) ITSUR/AR(1)	(3) ITSUR/AR(1)	(4) ITSUR/AR(1)
Output	1.118* (0.046)	1.118* (0.036)	1.138* (0.082)	0.890* (0.041)
Labor Price	0.542* (0.015)	0.540* (0.015)	0.451* (0.030)	0.387* (0.017)
Capital Price	0.299* (0.018)	0.294* (0.018)	0.233* (0.035)	0.381* (0.020)
Time	−0.029* (0.006)	−0.014* (0.005)	−0.150 (0.079)	
Labor Quality			−0.451* (0.030)	−0.387* (0.017)
Capital Vintage			−3.371 (1.754)	0.942* (0.295)
Labor Price*Time	−0.008* (0.000)	−0.008* (0.000)	−0.002 (0.002)	
Labor Price*Capital Vintage			0.132* (0.040)	0.213* (0.016)
Chessler's Index				−0.032 (0.062)
AT&T	−0.377* (0.101)	−0.467* (0.060)	−0.338* (0.060)	−0.348* (0.087)
1984		−1.191* (0.285)	−1.324* (0.393)	
AT&T*1984		1.500* (0.557)	3.033* (0.948)	
Time*AT&T	−0.018* (0.004)	−0.017* (0.004)	−0.018* (0.004)	
Time*1984		0.045* (0.009)	0.049* (0.012)	
Time*AT&T*1984		−0.047* (0.016)	−0.094* (0.028)	
AT&T*Chessler's Index				−0.084* (0.027)
δ_c	0.951* (0.018)	0.908* (0.023)	0.886* (0.028)	0.918* (0.025)
δ_s	0.976* (0.009)	0.970* (0.010)	0.959* (0.011)	0.967* (0.011)

Notes: ITSUR denotes Zellner's iterative seemingly unrelated regression method and AR(1) the first-order autoregressive errors. ATT = 1 for AT&T Long Lines Department and 0 for regional companies. For the period 1984–1991, 1984 = 1 and 0 for the period 1952–1983. δ_c and δ_s are the first-order autocorrelation coefficients of the error terms in the cost and share equations, respectively. The translog regressions include all the second-order terms of the first-order terms reported in this table. All variables except dummy variables and time are in log form. Standard errors are in parentheses. * and ** signify signicant at the 1% and 5% level, respectively. The number of observations is 348.

Entrepreneurship and Economic Growth

The analysis of costs indicates that AT&T experienced a larger annual percentage shift in cost functions than did the regionals. Moreover, for AT&T, unlike the regionals, there was marked acceleration in the shift in cost functions after 1984 (or 1977)—a result we attribute to the rise in competition in the long-distance market. The fact that the difference in costs occurred mainly after competition had developed in AT&T's market, rather than for earlier periods, and is observable after controlling for the vintage of capital is noteworthy. That is, once again there remains a residual effect of competition even after due account is taken of its indirect effect via the change in the quality of capital inputs. In sum, the results consistently support the conclusion of positive net effects of competition on efficiency for the U.S. telephone industry. Thus, by implication, a policy of permitting entry and increasing competition in local telephone markets is likely to have similar effects in the form of raising the productivity growth of regional monopolies.

APPENDIX

Data Construction

The Appendix describes the details of data construction. The primary sources of company data were the *Statistics of Communications Common Carriers* of the FCC and the *Form M* reports in which reporting telephone companies file financial and operating data to the FCC. Annual data for AT&T Long Lines and for eight regional companies were collected for the period 1951–91. The sample of eight companies was composed of two very large producers, five medium-sized ones, and one that was fairly small. Six of the companies were part of the Bell system before divestiture. The companies were Chesapeake and Potomac of Virginia, Michigan Bell, Ohio Bell, Pacific Bell, Southwestern Bell, Wisconsin Bell, GTE California, and Lincoln Telecommunications.

Output. The output index was generated by deflating revenues by an appropriate price index. The revenues of a telephone company are composed of local service, toll service, and a miscellaneous category. The deflators were the Bell system price indexes for the period 1951–71 and the relevant BLS Producers' Price Indexes (PPI) for the period 1972–91. Miscellaneous revenues were deflated by a price index for directory advertising.

Constant dollar local, toll, and miscellaneous revenues were aggregated to create a translog index of aggregate output using revenue shares as weights. To create consistent output and cost data before and after divestiture, we subtracted access expenses of AT&T Long Lines from both the AT&T toll revenues and operating expenses.

Labor and Labor Quality. The *Form M* reports provide annual data for total number of employees, average weekly hours, and average hourly earnings of 34 occupational groups. Two aggregates of working hours were calculated; the simple sum and the weighted sum of working hours of each group. In computing the latter, the ratio of each group's hourly earnings to average wages in the private sector was used as a weight. The quantity of labor input is the simple sum of working hours of all occupational groups, while the index of labor quality in the estimation of a cost function is defined as the ratio of the weighted sum to the simple sum of working hours . Labor quality indexes had to be extrapolated for the period 1981–91, because of lack of data for this period. The current dollar wage rate (actual compensation per working hour) is divided by the average wage rate in the private sector to obtain a constant-dollar wage rate.

Materials. Expenses for materials are defined as a catch-all category that includes all operating expenses not attributable to labor and capital. Materials expenses are computed by subtracting total compensation plus depreciation charges from operating expenses. The PPI for intermediate inputs is used as a proxy for the price of materials inputs.

Capital, User Costs, and Capital Quality. We use two types of capital stock; net stock and gross stock. Net capital stock is constructed by the commonly used perpetual inventory method. The depreciation rates are obtained from Jorgenson, Gollop, and Fraumeni [1987]. We create gross capital stock series based on Gort, Bahk. and Wall [1993]. The pattern of retirements from the stock, however, is based on an assumed distribution of retirements while Gort, Bahk, and Wall assumed the simultaneous exit of investment goods of the same vintage.

To construct gross or net capital stock, we first classify telephone plant into five categories: land and buildings, furniture and office equipment, vehicles and other work equipment, communications equipment, and cable and wire. Next, yearly dollar amounts for each category are deflated by an appropriate price index to derive real investment for a specific year. Thus, the gross real capital stock of each category of telephone plant is the sum of real gross investment flows for that category cumulated over the service life of the investment. The aggregate capital stock is the weighted sum of the five types of real capital stock in which capital expense shares are used as weights. To compute net stocks, capital consumption estimates are subtracted from gross stocks by the conventional perpetual inventory method.

Price indexes and service lives were obtained from the Bureau of Labor Statistics and the Bureau of Economic Analysis. Benchmark capital stocks of each category of plant were the constant-dollar gross or net plant in 1950 for each category. Transferred assets due to the breakup of the Bell system are deflated using 1984 price indexes. While this inevitably arbitrary procedure may cause some measurement error, experimenting with price indexes of alternative years produced nearly the same results. The user cost of each type of plant consists of a constant rate of return (0.035) plus the depreciation rate for that class of plant.

For capital quality, we used weighted average vintage, with weights based on annual investment expenditure flows. Base-year (benchmark) capital stocks were assumed to be half their service lives. 1984 transferred assets of AT&T were omitted from the calculation of vintage, since there was no relevant information about them.

REFERENCES

Caves, Douglas W., Laurits R. Christensen, and Joseph A. Swanson. "Economic Performance in Regulated and Unregulated Environments: A Comparison of U.S. and Canadian Railroads." *Quarterly Journal of Economics*, November 1981, 559–81.

Caves, Douglas W., Laurits R. Christensen, and W. Erwin Diewert. "Multilateral Comparisons of Output, Input, and Productivity Using Superlative Index Numbers." *Economic Journal*, March 1982, 73–86.

Cohen, Wesley M., and Richard C. Levin. "Empirical Studies of Innovation and Market Structure," in *Handbook of Industrial Organization*, edited by Richard Schmalensee, and Robert D. Willig. Amsterdam: North Holland, 1989, 1059–107.

Crandall, Robert W. *After the Breakup*. Washington, D.C.: Brookings Institution, 1991.

Denny, Michael, Melvyn Fuss, and Leonard Waverman. "The Measurement and Interpretation of Total Factor Productivity in Regulated Industries, with an Application to Canadian Telecommunications," in *Productivity Measurement in Regulated Industries*, edited by Thomas G. Cowing, and Rodney Stevenson. New York: Academic Press, 1981, 179–218.

Gort, Michael, Byoung H. Bahk, and Richard A. Wall. "Decomposing Technical Change." *Southern Economic Journal*, July 1993, 220–34.

Jorgenson, Dale W., Frank M. Gollop, and Barbara M. Fraumeni. *Productivity and U.S. Economic Growth*. Cambridge: Harvard University Press, 1987.

Kahai, Simran K., David L. Kaserman, and John W. Mayo. "Is the 'Dominant Firm' Dominant? An Empirical Analysis of AT&T's Market Power." *Journal of Law and Economics*, October 1996, 499–517.

Kiss, Ferenc. "Productivity Gains in Bell Canada," in *Economic Analysis of Telecommunications*, edited by Leon Courville, Alain D. E. Fontenay, and Rodney Dobell. Amsterdam: North-Holland, 1983, 85–113.

Nadiri, M. Ishaq, and Ingmar R. Prucha. "Dynamic Factor Models, Productivity Measurement, and Rates of Return: Theory and an Empirical Application to the U.S. Bell System." National Bureau of Economic Research Working Paper No. 3041, 1989.

Nadiri, M. Ishaq, and Mark A. Schankerman. "The Structure of Production, Technological Change, and the Rate of Growth of Total Factor Productivity in the U.S. Bell System," in *Productivity Measurement in Regulated Industries*, edited by Thomas G. Cowing, and Rodney Stevenson. New York: Academic Press, 1981, 219–47.

Nickell, Stephen J. "Competition and Corporate Performance." *Journal of Political Economy*, August 1996, 724–46.

Oum, Tae Hoon. "The Effects of Competition in the Public Long-Distance Telephone Market on the Productivity of the U.S. Telephone Industry." Unitel Evidence Part 11, Testimony before the Canadian Radio-Television and Telecommunications Commission, Ottawa, Canada, August 1990.

Oum, Tae Hoon, and Yimin Zhang. "Competition and Allocative Efficiency: The case of the U.S. Telephone Industry." *Review of Economics and Statistics*, February 1995, 82–96.

Sappington, David E. M., and Dennis L. Weisman. *Designing Incentive Regulation for the Telecommunications Industry*. Cambridge, Mass.: MIT Press and Washington, D.C.: American Enterprise Press, 1996.

Shin, Richard T., and John S. Ying. "Unnatural Monopolies in Local Telephone." *Rand Journal of Economics*, Summer 1992, 171–83.

Taylor, William E., and J. Douglas Zona. "An Analysis of the State of Competition in Long-Distance Markets." *Journal of Regulatory Economics*, May 1997, 227–55.

Ward, Michael. "Measurement of Market Power in Long Distance Telecommunications." Federal Trade Commissions Staff Report, Washington, D.C., 1995.

Ying, John S., and Richard T. Shin. "Costly Gains to Breaking Up: LECs and the Baby Bells." *Review of Economics and Statistics*, May 1993, 357–61.

Part VI
Empirical Contributions

[19]

Economic Development and Business Ownership: An Analysis Using Data of 23 OECD Countries in the Period 1976–1996

Martin Carree
André van Stel
Roy Thurik
Sander Wennekers

ABSTRACT. In the present paper we address the relationship between business ownership and economic development. We will focus upon three issues. First, how is the equilibrium rate of business ownership related to the stage of economic development? Second, what is the speed of convergence towards the equilibrium rate when the rate of business ownership is out-of-equilibrium? Third, to what extent does deviating from the equilibrium rate of business ownership hamper economic growth? Hypotheses concerning all three issues are formulated in the framework of a new two-equation model. We find confirmation for the hypothesized economic growth penalty on deviations from the equilibrium rate of business ownership using a data panel of 23 OECD countries. An important policy implication of our exercises is that low barriers to entry and exit of businesses are necessary conditions for the equilibrium seeking mechanisms that are vital for a sound economic development.

1. Introduction

Joseph Schumpeter's contribution to our understanding of the mechanisms of technological progress and economic development is widely recognized. In *The Theory of Economic Development* he emphasizes the role of the entre-

Final version accepted on February 1, 2001

Martin Carree
Erasmus University Rotterdam and Maastricht University

André van Stel and Roy Thurik
Erasmus University Rotterdam and EIM Business and Policy Research

Sander Wennekers
EIM Business and Policy Research
P.O. Box 7001
2701 AA Zoetermeer
The Netherlands
E-mail: awe@eim.nl

preneur as prime cause of economic development. He describes how the innovating entrepreneur challenges incumbent firms by introducing new inventions that make current technologies and products obsolete. This process of *creative destruction* is the main characteristic of what has been called the Schumpeter Mark I regime. In *Capitalism, Socialism and Democracy*, Schumpeter focuses on innovative activities by large and established firms. He describes how large firms outperform their smaller counterparts in the innovation and appropriation process through a strong positive feedback loop from innovation to increased R&D activities. This process of *creative accumulation* is the main characteristic of what has been called the Schumpeter Mark II regime.

The extent to which either of the two Schumpeterian technological regimes prevails in a certain period and industry varies. It may depend upon the nature of knowledge required to innovate, the opportunities of appropriability, the degree of scale (dis)economies, the institutional environment, the importance of absorptive capacity, demand variety, etc. Industries in a Schumpeter Mark II regime are likely to develop a more concentrated market structure in contrast to industries in a Schumpeter Mark I regime where small firms will proliferate.

Most of the 20th century can be described as a period of accumulation. From the Second Industrial Revolution till the 1970s the large firm share was on the rise in most industries and the economy as a whole. It was the period of "scale and scope" (Chandler, 1990). It was the era of the hierarchical industrial firm growing progressively larger through exploiting economies of scale and scope in areas like production, distribution, marketing and R&D. The conglomerate merger wave of the late 1960s seemed to have set the case. The period has the characteristics of the Schumpeter Mark II regime. However, from the 1970s onwards times have changed. There is ample evidence that the share of small businesses in manufacturing in Western economies has started to rise (Acs and Audretsch, 1993; Thurik, 1999). Large firms have been downsizing and restructuring in order to concentrate on "core business" again. In the meantime the entrepreneur has risen from the dead. High-technology innovative small firms have come at the forefront of technological development in many (new) industries. Piore and Sabel (1984) claim that an "Industrial Divide" has taken place. Jensen (1993, p. 835) considers it the period of the "Third Industrial Revolution". The last quarter of the 20th century may therefore be characterized as a period of creative destruction in the sense of the Schumpeter Mark I regime. Audretsch and Thurik (2001) refer to a change from "a managed to an entrepreneurial economy".

In the present paper we discuss why this change happened and what its consequences have been for economic progress and the rate of business ownership. We develop a model relating the regime switch to economic development and present empirical evidence. In Section 2 we discuss a variety of theoretical considerations on the relation between business ownership rates and economic development. It is followed by Section 3 where we present our two-equation model. The first equation explains the change in the business ownership rate while the second equation explains economic growth. The notion of an equilibrium business ownership rate, being a function of the level of economic development, is crucial in the analysis. In Section 4 we present the data of 23 OECD countries and in Section 5 we present the estimation results. The final section is used for discussion.

2. Theory

In this section we will discuss how business ownership rates and economic development are interrelated. We will pay attention to the role that the "Schumpeterian regime switch" has played in this relationship. We discuss the pre-1970s era of

declining self-employment rates and the period thereafter in which the rates have risen in most Western economies. Next we discuss how the business ownership rate at the economy-wide level can be used to determine the extent of structural transformation.

The first three quarters of the 20th century can be characterized as a period of declining small firm presence in most industries. In many Western countries and industries this decline has ended and even reversed. Many old and large firms have been losing ground to their small, new and more entrepreneurial counterparts. It suggests a switch from a (more) Schumpeter Mark II type of regime towards a (more) Schumpeter Mark I type of regime. Audretsch and Thurik (2001) label this as a regime switch from "a managed to an entrepreneurial economy". We note that the regime labels are rough approximations as the industrial landscape shows a far too great variety to claim that in each and every industry one of the Schumpeter regimes is prevailing. A further complication is that business ownership and entrepreneurship are not synonymous for at least two reasons (see also Amit et al., 1993).

First, entrepreneurial energy is not limited to self-employed individuals. Large companies promote "intrapreneurship" within business units to achieve more flexibility and innovativeness (Stopford and Baden-Fuller, 1994). Second, business owners serve many roles and functions. Many researchers distinguish between Schumpeterian (or real) entrepreneurs and managerial business owners (Wennekers and Thurik, 1999). Entrepreneurs are a small fraction of the business owners. They own and direct independent firms that are innovative and "creatively destroy" existing market structures. After realizing their goals Schumpeterian entrepreneurs often develop into managerial business owners, but some may start new ventures. Managerial business owners dominate in the large majority of small firms. They include many franchisees, shopkeepers and people in professional occupations. They belong to what Kirchhoff (1996) calls "the economic core". Occasionally, entrepreneurial ventures grow out of them. In an empirical context it is difficult to discriminate between managerial business owners and entrepreneurs. Profiles of individual business owners would be required. Moreover, the discrimination is a theoretical one since most business owners are neither pure "Schumpeterians" nor pure "shopkeepers" but share the attitudes associated with these extremes in a varying degree (Audretsch and Thurik, 1998).

Despite these conceptual problems we argue that the secular trend of the business ownership rate declining and afterwards starting to rise again presents a fair indication of the general development of the level of entrepreneurship, at least in modern economies. It shows how the (secular) decline of "mom-and-pop" businesses in traditional sectors like retailing and craft has tended to become compensated for by a rise in new ventures in services and high-tech industries in the period from the 1970s onwards.

The impact of economic development on business ownership

The proportion of the labor force that is self-employed has decreased in most Western countries until the mid-1970s. Since then the self-employment rate has started to rise again in several of these economies. Blau (1987) observes that the proportions of both male and female self-employed in the nonagricultural U.S. labor force declined during most of this century. He also observes that this decline bottomed out in the early 1970s and started to rise until at least 1982. The data used in the present paper show that the business ownership rate in the U.S. has continued to rise in the 1980s while stabilizing in the 1990s.[1] More recently business ownership increased in several other countries as well. We will first discuss the period of decline of business ownership (Mark II regime) followed by a discussion of the period of reversal of this trend (Mark I regime).

Decline of business ownership

Several authors (Kuznets, 1971; Schultz, 1990; Yamada, 1996) have reported a negative relationship between economic development and the business ownership (self-employment) rate. Their studies use a large cross-section of countries with a wide variety in the stage of economic development.

There are a series of reasons for the decline of self-employment, and of small business presence in general. Lucas (1978) shows how rising real wages may raise the opportunity cost of self-employment relative to the return. Given an underlying "managerial" talent distribution this induces marginal entrepreneurs (in this context Lucas refers to managers) to become employees. This pushes up the average size of firms. Schaffner (1993) takes a different approach. She points out that "over the course of economic development the advantages firm owners derive from being less risk averse (better diversified) than self-employed producers are likely to rise relative to the disadvantages caused by the costliness of circumventing asymmetric information problems" (p. 435). Iyigun and Owen (1998) develop a model implying that economic development is associated with a decline in the number of entrepreneurs relative to the total number of employees. They argue that fewer individuals are willing to run the risk associated with becoming an entrepreneur as the "safe" professional earnings rise with economic development.

Chandler (1990) stresses the importance of investment in production, distribution, and management needed to exploit economies of scale and scope during the period after the second industrial revolution of the second half of the 19th century. It was a period of relatively well-defined technological trajectories, of stable demand and of seemingly clear advantages of diversification.[2]

Reversal of the trend

Several authors have provided evidence of a reversal of the trend towards less self-employment. Acs et al. (1994) report that of 23 OECD-countries, 15 experienced an increase in the self-employment rate during the 1970s and 1980s. They show that the weighted average of the self-employment rate in OECD-countries rose slightly from 8.4% in 1978 to 8.9% in 1987. Closely related to the development of the self-employment rate is the development of small business presence in general. Some of the other sources showing that the growing importance of large business has come to a halt in Western countries include Carlsson (1989), Loveman and Sengenberger (1991), Acs and Audretsch (1993), Acs (1996) and Thurik (1999).[3]

There are several reasons for the revival of small business and self-employment in Western economies.[4] First, the last 25 years of the 20th century may be seen as a period of creative destruction. Piore and Sabel (1984) use the term "Industrial Divide", Jensen (1993) prefers the term "Third Industrial Revolution", while Freeman and Perez (1988) talk about the transition from the fourth to the fifth Kondratiev wave. Audretsch and Thurik (2000) stress the effects of globalization and the information revolution leading to the demise of the comparative advantage of Europe in many of the traditional industries, such as machine tools, metalworking, textiles and automobile production. The most obvious evidence is the emergence of new industries like the software and biotechnology industries. Small firms play an important role in these new industries. Acs and Audretsch (1987) provide empirical evidence that small firms have a relative innovative advantage over their larger counterparts in such highly innovative industries. Evidence for the comparative advantage of small firms in inventing radically new products is also given in Prusa and Schmitz (1991) and Rothwell (1983, 1984).

Second, new technologies have reduced the importance of scale economies in many sectors. Small technology-based firms started to challenge large companies that still had every confidence in mass production techniques (Carlsson, 1989). Meredith (1987) argues that small firms are just as well, or better, equipped to implement technological advances and predicts the factory of the future to be a small factory. Jensen argues that "It is far less valuable for people to be in the same geographical location to work together effectively, and this is encouraging smaller, more efficient, entrepreneurial organizing units that cooperate through technology" (Jensen, 1993, p. 842). This is supported by Jovanovic claiming that: "recent advances in information technology have made market-based coordination cheaper relative to internal coordination and have partially caused the recent decline in firm size and diversification" (Jovanovic, 1993, p. 221). Others, like Rothwell (1983, 1984), stress that large and small firms complement and succeed each other in the innovation and diffusion process. See also Nooteboom (1994) for an account of this concept of "dynamic complementarity".

Third, deregulation and privatization movements have swept the world. In countries like Australia, Finland, Italy and Sweden there have been strong tendencies to deregulate and privatise (OECD, 1995, pp. 39–49). Phillips (1985) reports that small firms have dominated in both the creation of new businesses and new jobs in deregulated industry sectors in the U.S. in the early 1980s. This confirms some preliminary empirical evidence as provided by Shepherd (1982). Governments have also begun to acknowledge and promote the vital role of small (start-up) firms in achieving economic growth and development. See Storey and Tether (1998), OECD (1998) and EIM/ENSR (1994, 1996).

Fourth, there has been a tendency of large firms to concentrate on "core competences" (Carlsson, 1989). Jovanovic (1993) reports that the 1980s were characterized by corporate spin-offs and divestment. Aiginger and Tichy (1991) blame much of the "back-to-basics" and downsizing (or rightsizing) tendencies on the opportunistic conglomerate merger wave of the late 1960s.

Fifth, the increasing incomes and wealth have enabled individuals to strive for "higher" needs. As a result the demand for variety increases (Jackson, 1984). Cross-cultural influences have also enlarged the demand for variety. Small firms are often the most obvious suppliers of new and specialized products. The decrease in diversification as reported by Jovanovic (1993) suggests that large firms have not been capable of entering into such market niches.

Sixth, self-employment is more highly valued as an occupational choice than before. Roughly one out of four young U.S. workers pursue self-employment according to Schiller and Crewson (1997). Kirchhoff (1996) argues that self-employment is not characterized anymore as underemployment or as mom-and-pop establishments, but as a way to achieve a variety of personal goals. Also, as hypothesized in the social psychology there is a Maslowian hierarchy of human motivations, with physical needs at the bottom and self-realization at the top (Maslow, 1970). A higher level of prosperity will induce a higher need for self-realization and may stimulate entrepreneurship.[5]

Finally, the employment share of the services sector has been well documented to increase with per capita income (Inman, 1985). Given the relatively small average firm size of most services (barring airlines, shipping and some business and financial services) this creates more opportunities for business ownership.

Obviously, some of these factors may have a temporary effect only. For example, it is not unlikely for the outsourcing and deregulation waves to dry up. On the other hand, there are more permanent effects like the impact of new technologies. We refer again to Freeman and Perez (1988). They claim that in the new techno-economic paradigm (fifth Kondratiev wave) the organization of firms will be "networks" of large and small firms. See also Oughton and Whittam (1997) who emphasize the role of external economies of scale when explaining the viability of small firms. Moreover, the introduction of these new technologies is also positively related to the stage of economic development because they cannot be made effective without the necessary skills and other investments. This structural influence of economic development is reinforced by the increasing variety of demand for specialized goods and services and the enhanced valuation of self-realization which are also dependent on the level of prosperity.

An equilibrium rate of business ownership

In the present paper we investigate whether countries that deviate from the "equilibrium" business ownership rate for comparable levels of economic development suffer in terms of economic growth.[6] For this we develop an error-correction model to determine the "equilibrium" rate of business ownership as a function of GDP per capita. The notion of "equilibrium" appears more akin to neo-classical economic theory than to a Schumpeterian framework. However, in our empirical application the "equilibrium" concerns the labor market and not the product market.

Equilibrium rates of self-employment in the neo-classical framework can be derived by making assumptions about (1) the aggregate production function combining the efforts of business owners and wage-employed individuals and (2) their rational occupational choice between self- and wage-employment. Differences in the assumptions about which factors influence the choice for self-

employment lead to different equilibrium models. Two early contributions are Lucas (1978) and Kihlstrom and Laffont (1979). Lucas assumes individuals to have different managerial abilities while Kihlstrom and Laffont assume individuals to differ with respect to their risk attitudes. Calvo and Wellisz (1980) extend the Lucas model by introducing a learning process through which managers acquire the necessary knowledge. In a recent paper, Peretto (1999) presents a model in which "development and growth are subsequent stages of the process of structural transformation that economies undergo as they advance from poverty to affluence" (p. 390). This model as well as related models (see for example Lloyd-Ellis and Bernhardt, 2000) suggest that the stage of economic development is the driving force of "equilibrium".

We hypothesize an "equilibrium" relationship between the rate of business ownership and per capita income that is U-shaped.[7] The U-shaped pattern has the property that there is a level of economic development with a "minimum" business ownership rate.[8] Many forces may cause the actual number of business owners to deviate from the long-term equilibrium rate. Such a "disequilibrium" may result from cultural forces, institutional settings (regulation of entry, incentive structures, functioning of the capital market) and economic forces (unemployment, profitability of private enterprise). See Kirzner (1997), Davis and Henrekson (1999) and Henrekson and Johansson (1999).

There are several forces in market economies that contribute to a process of adapting towards the equilibrium. An example may illustrate this. A high labor income share and a structurally low number of enterprises have contributed to structural unemployment in the late 1970s and 1980s in many Western economies. Such high levels of unemployment may have various consequences. First, unemployment may have a direct effect on self-employment, as unemployed are claimed to be more likely to become self-employed than employees. See for instance Storey (1991) and Evans and Leighton (1989).[9] Second, structural unemployment gradually results in wage moderation helping to restore profitability of private enterprise (lower labor income share). In addition, a perceived shortage of business ownership will induce policies fostering entrepreneurship, ranging from better access to financing to competition policies. See OECD (1998). The overall impact of these equilibrating processes are hard to observe directly and may therefore be modelled best using an error correction mechanism.

The effect of business ownership on economic growth

There is some evidence on the relation between size class distributions and economic performance. For instance, see Nickell (1996), Nickell et al. (1997) and Lever and Nieuwenhuijsen (1999) who present evidence that competition, as measured by increased number of competitors, has a positive effect on the rate of total factor productivity growth.[10] Carree and Thurik (1998, 1999) show that the share of small firms in manufacturing industries in European countries has a positive effect on the industry output growth. Thurik (1996) reports that the excess growth of small firms[11] has had a positive influence on percentage change in gross national product for a sample of 16 European countries in the period 1988 through 1993.[12]

A theoretical endogenous growth model was developed by Schmitz (1989). His model predicts that an increase of the proportion of entrepreneurs in the working force leads to an increase in long-run economic growth. See also Holmes and Schmitz (1990) who develop a model of entrepreneurship in the spirit of T. W. Schultz. They show how specialization in managerial tasks and entrepreneurship – responding to opportunities for creating new products and production processes – may affect economic development. Finally, some evidence of a well-established historical (long-term) relationship between fluctuations in entrepreneurship and the rise and fall of nations has been assembled by Wennekers and Thurik (1999). Also the work of Eliasson (1995) on economic growth through competitive selection is of relevance. He shows (for the Swedish economy) how a lack of industry dynamics affects economic progress not so much on the short term but very strongly so on the long term (from about two decades on).

Another source of evidence on the relation between self-employment and progress is the economic history of the formerly centralized planned economies. A characteristic of these economies was the almost complete absence of small firms (and private ownership of the means of production), and this extreme monopolization constituted one of the major factors leading to the collapse of state socialism (Acs, 1996). The development of small enterprises is considered a vital part of the current transition process in Eastern Europe.[13]

In the present paper we investigate whether deviations between the actual and the equilibrium rate of business ownership will diminish the growth potential of an economy in the medium term. A shortage of business owners is likely to diminish competition with detrimental effects for static efficiency and competitiveness of the national economy. It will also diminish variety, learning and selection and thereby harm dynamic efficiency (innovation). On the other hand, a glut of self-employment will cause the average scale of operations to remain below optimum. It will result in large numbers of marginal entrepreneurs, absorbing capital and human energy that could have been allocated more productively elsewhere.

Iyigun and Owen (1998) show in a dynamic model with two types of human capital (professional and entrepreneurial) that a misallocation of the existing human capital stock between professional and entrepreneurial activities may occur. The nature of the inefficiency, however, is not clear-cut. There may be too much entrepreneurship or too little, depending on how entrepreneurial and professional skills contribute to the level of technology. They find that "a more efficient ratio of professional and entrepreneurial skills will raise the steady state of technology, the wages paid to human capital providers, and therefore, the economy's human capital stock" (p. 457). Their model supports our notion that deviations from the level of "equilibrium" entrepreneurial activity come at a cost of lower economic performance. See also Peretto (1999) who derives a hump-shaped relation between the number of firms and returns to investment and R&D.

3. Model

The object of this section is to develop a model of the interrelationship between business ownership and economic development at the macro level. The model consists of two main equations. The first equation deals with the causes of changes in the rate of business ownership whereas the second deals with its consequences. From the first equation we derive the equilibrium rate of business ownership as a function of the stage of economic development. In the second equation we estimate the effect on economic growth of deviating from this equilibrium rate.

The first equation of the model relates the change in the rate of business ownership E_{it} in country i in year t to the extent to which this rate deviated from the equilibrium rate E_{it}^*, to the unemployment rate U_{it} and to the labor income share LIQ_{it}. The second equation of the model relates the extent of economic growth to the (absolute) deviation of the actual business ownership rate from the equilibrium rate. Economic growth is measured as the relative change in the variable $YCAP_{it}$, the per capita gross domestic product in purchasing power parities per U.S. dollar in 1990 prices in country i and period t. We correct for catching-up effects by including the level of economic development. The equations use the notation $\Delta_4 X_t = X_t - X_{t-4}$. The third equation presents the equation relating the equilibrium business ownership rate to the level of economic development. It is assumed to be a quadratic function of $\ln(YCAP_{it} + 1)$.[14] The model reads as follows:

$$\Delta_4 E_{it} = b_1(E_{i,t-4}^* - E_{i,t-4}) + b_2(U_{i,t-6} - \overline{U}) + b_3(LIQ_{i,t-6} - \overline{LIQ}) + \varepsilon_{1it}, \tag{1}$$

$$\frac{\Delta_4 YCAP_{it}}{YCAP_{i,t-4}} = c_0 + c_1 |E_{i,t-4}^* - E_{i,t-4}| + c_2 YCAP_{i,t-4} + \varepsilon_{2it}, \tag{2}$$

$$E_{it}^* = \alpha + \beta\ln(YCAP_{it} + 1) + \gamma\ln^2(YCAP_{it} + 1). \tag{3}$$

The symbols stand for the following variables:

E: number of business owners per labor force;

E^*:   equilibrium number of business owners per labor force;

$YCAP$: per capita GDP in purchasing power parities per U.S. $ in 1990 prices;

U: unemployment rate;

$\overline{U}$:   sample average of unemployment rate;

LIQ: labor income share;

$\overline{LIQ}$:   sample average of labor income share;

$\varepsilon_1, \varepsilon_2$:   disturbance terms in equations (1) and (2), respectively.

Business ownership

In Equation (1), the variable to be explained is the growth in the number of business owners per labor force in a period of four years. The first explanatory variable in the equation, which has the parameter b_1 assigned to it, is an error correction variable describing the difference between the equilibrium and the actual rate of business ownership at the start of the period. The parameter b_1 is expected to have a positive sign. In this version of our model the equilibrium function is U-shaped with respect to per capita income (Equation (3) has a quadratic form). Because the parabola should first drop and then rise, we expect the parameter γ to be positive and the parameter β to be negative. In case of absence of economic development ($YCAP_{it} = 0$) the equilibrium function equals α. Since the relative number of business owners cannot be negative or in excess of one, the parameter α should lie between zero and one.

As a second explanatory variable we use lagged unemployment acting as a push factor for business ownership.[15] The expected sign of the parameter b_2 is positive. We choose a lag of six years instead of four for this variable because mental preparation, practical procedures and legal requirements are involved in starting a new enterprise.

As a third explanatory variable we use labor income share. This variable is a pragmatic proxy for the earning differentials between expected profits of business owners and wage earnings. We assume that a relatively high business profitability (as compared to wage earnings) acts as a pull factor for business ownership. The labor income share is defined as the share of labor income (including the "calculated" compensation of the self-employed for their labor contribution) in the net national income. The expected sign of the parameter b_3 is negative. As with the unemployment variable, a time lag has been included.

Economic growth

In Equation (2), the variable to be explained is economic growth in a four-year period, measured as the relative change in gross domestic product per capita. The first determinant of growth is the (absolute) deviation of the actual number of self-employed (business owners) from the equilibrium rate of business ownership at the start of the period. As explained in a previous section, the deviation variable is expected to have a negative impact on growth.[16]

Next to this deviation variable, we use the level of per capita income at the start of the period as a control variable. It allows to correct for the convergence hypothesis of countries: countries which are lagging behind in economic development grow more easily than other countries because they can profit from modern technologies developed in other countries. The expected sign of the parameter c_2 is negative.

4. Data and estimation technique

We use data of 23 OECD countries including the fifteen countries of the EU-15, Australia, Canada, Iceland, Japan, New Zealand, Norway, Switzerland and the U.S. and for the period 1976 through 1996.[17] Data are made available for the even years only. The main data sources are the *OECD Labour Force Statistics* and the *OECD National Accounts*. In Table I some summary statistics values are given for the first and last year of the sample and the mid year 1988 (due to lags only the period 1980–1996 will be used in the estimation procedure).

From Table I we see that Australia, Greece and

TABLE I
Summary statistics for the 23 OECD countries

Country	E_{1976}	E_{1988}	E_{1996}	$YCAP_{1988}$	E^*_{1988}
Austria	0.077	0.069	0.074	15,651	0.112
Belgium	0.098	0.109	0.119	15,326	0.113
Denmark	0.081	0.056	0.064	16,263	0.110
Finland	0.059	0.076	0.080	15,456	0.112
France	0.105	0.099	0.088	16,421	0.110
Germany (West)	0.070	0.070	0.082	17,245	0.109
Greece	0.179	0.186	0.196	7,274	0.180
Ireland	0.074	0.091	0.100	9,735	0.145
Italy	0.142	0.169	0.183	15,289	0.113
Luxembourg	0.093	0.075	0.062	21,103	0.107
The Netherlands	0.092	0.082	0.102	14,867	0.114
Portugal	0.110	0.116	0.160	8,424	0.161
Spain	0.109	0.122	0.130	10,886	0.135
Sweden	0.068	0.064	0.081	16,632	0.110
United Kingdom	0.074	0.101	0.109	15,590	0.112
Iceland	0.099	0.101	0.130	17,368	0.109
Norway	0.089	0.084	0.071	17,301	0.109
Switzerland	0.069	0.071	0.085	20,133	0.107
United States	0.081	0.107	0.104	21,543	0.107
Japan	0.126	0.123	0.101	16,328	0.110
Canada	0.078	0.106	0.128	18,573	0.107
Australia	0.147	0.164	0.154	16,154	0.111
New Zealand	0.098	0.116	0.133	13,532	0.119
Average	0.096	0.102	0.110	15,526	0.118

Note: The business ownership rates E are per labor force. The business ownership figures are exclusive of the business owners in the agricultural sector. The unit of GDP per capita (YCAP) is purchasing power parities per U.S. $ at 1990 prices. In the last column the estimated equilibrium business ownership rates for 1988 are given, using the estimates of α, β and γ from the "Two yearly" case from Table III. Germany refers to West-Germany for 1976 and 1988. This business ownership data set is referred to as COMPENDIA 2000.1.

Italy have the highest levels of self-employment (business ownership) in 1988: more than 15% of the labor force. The unweighted sample average level of self-employment in that year is 10%. The countries with the lowest levels of self-employment in 1988 are Denmark and Sweden: six percent of the labor force. Looking at the GDP per capita in 1988, we see that the United States, Switzerland and Luxembourg are the most affluent countries while Greece, Ireland, Portugal and Spain are the least affluent countries in the sample. The unemployment rates are not given in the table but they were highest in the 1980s in Ireland and Spain. Low unemployment rates were found in Japan, Norway, Sweden, Switzerland, Iceland and Luxembourg in that period.

Variables and sources

The variable definitions and their main sources are given below.

E: Self-employment or business ownership. This variable is defined as the number of business owners (in all sectors excluding the agricultural sector), expressed as a fraction of the labor force. Data sources include the OECD Labour Force Statistics 1976–1996 and 1978–1998. EIM completed the missing data by using ratios derived from various other sources. Furthermore, EIM made a unified data set of business owners as the definitions of business owners or self-employed (we use these terms interchangeably) in the OECD statistics are not fully compatible between countries. In some countries business owners are defined as individuals owning a business that is not legally incorporated. In other countries, owner/managers of an incorporated business (OMIBs) who enjoy profits as well as a salary are considered owners too. There are also countries who classify a part of the OMIBs as self-employed and another part as employee. This results from a different set-up of labor force surveys in different countries.[18] By and large, Australia, Japan, Norway and U.S. use a narrow business ownership definition (excluding OMIBs or excluding most OMIBs), while the other countries apply a broader characterization (including OMIBs or including most OMIBs). Business owners in the present report are defined to include OMIBs. For the countries not following this definition, EIM

made an estimation of the number of OMIBs using information derived from *The European Observatory for SMEs* (KPMG/ENSR, 2000), or using information from domestic sources for the non-European countries.[19] Another difference in definition is that for some countries unpaid family workers are included in the self-employment data as well, mostly for early years. For these years, the unpaid family workers were removed from the data by using ratios from more recent years for which separate data on unpaid family workers *are* available. Finally, for countries where important unclarified trend breaks occur, these trend breaks were corrected for. Data on the labor force are also from the OECD Labour Force Statistics. Again, some missing data have been filled up from various other sources.[20]

YCAP: Gross domestic product per capita. The underlying variables gross domestic product and total population are from OECD National Accounts 1960–1996, Detailed Tables, and from the OECD Labour Force Statistics 1976–1996 and 1978–1998, respectively. GDP is measured in constant prices. Furthermore, purchasing power parities of 1990 are used to make the monetary units comparable between countries.

U: (standardized) unemployment rate. This variable measures the number of unemployed as a fraction of the total labor force. The labor force consists of employees, self-employed persons, unpaid family workers, people employed by the Army and unemployed persons. The main source for this variable is *OECD Main Economic Indicators*. Some missing data on the number of unemployed have been filled up with help of data from the OECD Labour Force Statistics and the *Yearbook of Labour Statistics* from the International Labour Office.

LIQ: labor income share. Total compensation of employees is multiplied by (total employment/number of employees) to correct for the imputed wage income for the self-employed persons. Next, the number obtained is divided by total income (compensation of employees plus other income). The data on the separate variables are from the OECD National Accounts 1960–1996, Detailed Tables. Some missing data have been filled up with help of data from the OECD Labour Force Statistics.

When estimating the model, we weight the

observations with population. We consider larger countries such as the U.S. and Japan to be more important in establishing the relationship between business ownership and economic growth than small countries. When the data of, for example, Luxembourg or Iceland would call for a different relation, we would not want this to have a big impact on the estimation results.

5. Estimation results

To estimate the model (1)–(3) we substitute equation (3) into equation (1):

$$\Delta_4 E_{it} = a_0 - b_1 E_{i, t-4} + b_2 U_{i, t-6} + b_3 \text{LIQ}_{i, t-6}$$
$$+ a_4 \ln(\text{YCAP}_{i, t-4} + 1)$$
$$+ a_5 \ln^2(\text{YCAP}_{i, t-4} + 1) + \varepsilon_{1it} \qquad (4)$$

We apply (weighted) least squares to this equation and then find estimates for the equilibrium relation parameters through:

$$\hat{\alpha} = \frac{a_0 + b_2 \bar{U} + b_3 \overline{\text{LIQ}}}{b_1},$$
$$\hat{\beta} = \frac{a_4}{b_1}, \qquad \hat{\gamma} = \frac{a_5}{b_1}. \qquad (5)$$

These coefficients are substituted into Equation (3) so that we can calculate E^*. This variable is incor-

porated into Equation (2). This equation is then also estimated using (weighted) least squares.

We consider two samples. The first is the "Two yearly" case in which data for all the even years are used (1980, 1982, 1984, 1986, 1988, 1990, 1992, 1994 and 1996). The total number of observations then equals 207. As an alternative we use the "Four yearly" case in which data for the years 1980, 1984, 1988, 1992 and 1996 are used. The total number of observations then equals 115. The reason for removing observations from the sample is that the observation periods for two consecutive even years overlap. This may lead to a downward bias in the estimated standard errors of the coefficients.

Weighting with population (in the year $t-4$) implies that all variables (including constants and dummies) are multiplied with the square root of population before the least squares procedure is run. A more detailed description of the weighting of observations can be found in the Appendix to this paper.

The estimation results of model (1)–(5) are given in Table II.

From Table II we see that most coefficients are significant with the expected signs: unemployment has a positive effect on self-employment and the effect of labor income share is negative (coeffi-

TABLE II
Estimation results of model (1)–(5)

Parameter	Two yearly	Four yearly	Parameter	Two yearly	Four yearly
a_0	0.049 (1.1)	0.038 (0.6)	α	0.538 (0.6)	0.254 (0.2)
b_1	0.050 (2.8)	0.049 (1.8)	β	−0.127 (0.2)	0.104 (0.1)
b_2	0.066 (4.5)	0.057 (2.8)	γ	−0.004 (0.0)	−0.050 (0.3)
b_3	−0.030 (2.2)	−0.034 (1.8)	c_0	0.222 (7.5)	0.205 (5.6)
a_4	−0.006 (0.2)	0.005 (0.1)	c_1	−0.488 (3.0)	−0.349 (1.9)
a_5	−0.000 (0.0)	−0.002 (0.3)	c_2	−0.008 (5.3)	−0.007 (3.8)
R_1^2	0.224	0.197	R_2^2	0.504	0.569
N	207	115	N	207	115

Note: Absolute t-values are between brackets.

cients b_2 and b_3, respectively). Furthermore, the hypothesized error-correction process and the negative impact on growth of deviating from equilibrium also seem to be supported: coefficients b_1 and c_1 are significantly positive and negative, respectively. The speed of adjustment is low: 5%. However, the results on the error-correction process and the growth penalty should be interpreted with caution, since the estimated equilibrium relation between the business ownership rate and per capita income appears not well determined: coefficients α, β and γ have very low t-values.

Special position of Italy

The low t-values for the equilibrium relation coefficients may be caused by the existence of certain (large) countries with specific developments in the business ownership rate not covered by our model. This could influence the estimates towards implausible results. The country we suspect may deviate most from the other countries is Italy. Looking at Table I, we see that Italy combines a high level of self-employment with a near average level of per capita income. This is not in accordance with what we would expect: the countries with a high rate of self-employment (business ownership) are generally in a less advanced stage of economic development (for example Greece). Italy can be divided in two different economies: a well-developed economy (Northern Italy) and a less developed economy (Southern Italy or the Mezzogiorno). Italy might not fit well in our model because it basically consists of two different economies. A closer inspection of the data for Northern and Southern Italy[21] shows that Northern Italy in particular deviates from the expected pattern, i.e., the U-shaped trend of the relative number of business owners set out against per capita income. Here, a high self-employment rate is combined with a relatively high value of GDP per capita. Small and medium-sized firms seem to play a bigger role in (Northern) Italian manufacturing than in other industrialized countries.[22] A notable feature of the organization of Italian small and medium-sized firm production is its high geographical concentration in small areas or industrial districts (Piore and Sabel, 1984). The geographical distribution

also shows that the majority of small and medium-sized manufacturing firms is located in Northern and Central Italy (Acs and Audretsch, 1993). They often have a strong family component.

The Italian model of extensive small and medium-sized firm production differs from that in other countries in similar stages of development. It may have positive and/or negative effects on economic growth. Many of the Italian firms are highly specialized and are organized on a flexible basis, so as to meet specific customer needs, and produce well designed and fashionable goods, aimed at the richest segments of the market. Another characteristic of the Italian model is that Italian R&D expenditures as a percentage of GNP are by far the lowest among the largest OECD-countries. They amount to only half of that in Germany, the U.S. and Japan over a long period (Klomp and Pronk, 1998, p. 167). Hence, the number of business owners in Northern Italy is higher than one would expect on the basis of the advanced stage of economic development. The data for Southern Italy seem to be in conformity with the general pattern: there is also a high level of self-employment but combined with a low value of the GDP per capita.

Looking again at the Italian data in Table I, we see that Italy not only has a relatively high self-employment rate but also that self-employment in Italy continues to rise. Therefore we suspect that the hypothesized error-correction process does not apply to the Italian economy. We approach this problem by introducing a dummy variable D_{ITA} that is 1 for the Italian observations and 0 elsewhere. That is, we have the error term in Equation (1) equal to $\varepsilon_{1it} = a_{0,\,ITA}D_{ITA} + \eta_{it}$.

The estimation results of the model including the "Italy-dummy" are given in Table III.

We see that the t-values of the estimated coefficients of the hypothesized U-shape of the equilibrium rate of business ownership in Table III are higher than those presented in Table II. Also, the coefficients are in accordance with our expectations. The estimates of β and γ have the predicted signs and that of α lies between zero and one. However, the t-values of β and γ are still not high. This is not surprising, considering the high correlation between the linear and the quadratic $\ln(YCAP_{it} + 1)$ variables. Indeed, the Wald test for the hypothesis that β and γ are jointly zero is

TABLE III
Estimation results of model (1)–(5), including dummy for Italy in (4)

Parameter	Two yearly	Four yearly	Parameter	Two yearly	Four yearly
a_0	0.109 (2.5)	0.098 (1.5)	α	0.863 (2.5)	0.743 (1.5)
b_1	0.120 (5.4)	0.120 (3.6)	β	−0.494 (2.0)	−0.398 (1.1)
b_2	0.063 (4.5)	0.055 (2.8)	γ	0.081 (1.7)	0.062 (0.9)
b_3	−0.011 (0.8)	−0.014 (0.7)	c_0	0.182 (8.9)	0.183 (7.6)
a_4	−0.059 (1.9)	−0.048 (1.0)	c_1	−0.571 (2.7)	−0.576 (2.4)
a_5	0.010 (1.6)	0.007 (0.9)	c_2	−0.006 (5.3)	−0.006 (4.5)
$a_{0,\,ITA}$	0.011 (4.9)	0.011 (3.4)			
P-value of Wald test on $\beta = \gamma = 0$				0.002	0.042
Minimum value of E^* at $-\beta/2\gamma$				3.06 (12.5)	3.22 (5.2)
R_1^2	0.307	0.274	R_2^2	0.500	0.575
N	207	115	N	207	115

Note: Absolute *t*-values are between brackets.

rejected. Furthermore, an analysis of $-\beta/2\gamma$ (which is the minimum of the parabola in terms of $\ln(YCAP_{it} + 1)$) shows that this expression does have a high *t*-value, implying that the log-quadratic specification performs reasonably well. Further investigation of the parabola shows that for the "Two yearly" case the minimum value is reached for a level of per capita income of 20,398 U.S. dollar (in purchasing power parities) at 1990 prices. The minimum level of equilibrium business ownership is 10.7% of the labor force. In Figure 1 we show the equilibrium curve and the actual data for the G7-countries. In this figure also the (YCAP; E) combinations for the "out-of-sample" years 1972, 1974 and 1998 are incorporated. For the "Four yearly" case the value of the minimum is 0.103 and it is attained at a level of 23,930 U.S. dollar. We will concentrate on the results of the "Two yearly" case as they are similar to the "Four yearly" one.

The last column of Table I presents the equilibrium business ownership rates in the year 1988. Greece has the highest equilibrium rate, 0.180. Most of the countries are close to the minimum

of the curve, though. The two richest countries, Luxembourg and the United States, have an equilibrium rate which is close to the minimum of the curve. These countries have reached a level of per capita income in 1988 which just exceeds the GDP per capita level at which the equilibrium rate reaches its minimum. For the interpretation of this parabola describing the equilibrium rate of business ownership given a certain stage of economic development, it should be noted that the relation is based upon a limited range of values of GDP per capita. For values of per capita income far outside our sample range – for example less developed countries or GDP per capita levels twice as high as attained in the richest countries in our sample – the equilibrium rate of business ownership may not be described properly by the quadratic function. Furthermore, U-shaped equilibrium functions cannot be distinguished from L-shaped functions in a statistical sense, because the majority of the GDP per capita values in our sample lie below the level associated with the minimum of the parabola.

As before, we find that the hypothesized error-

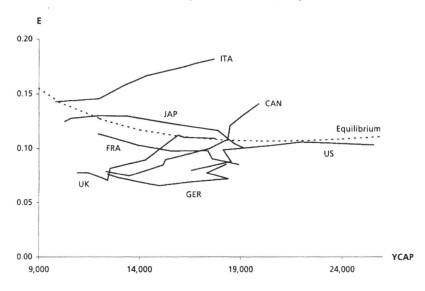

Figure 1. The actual and equilibrium rate of business ownership for G7-countries, 1972–1998.

correction process of the number of business owners towards the equilibrium rate is supported: the estimate of b_1 is significantly positive. The speed of adjustment is not high: the deviation from equilibrium at a certain point in time decreases with 12 percent in a period of four years. The low value of the speed of adjustment is not surprising. The convergence process of the actual business ownership rate towards the equilibrium rate is intrinsically slow because it involves structural changes on the supply side (setting up enterprises, investments in physical and human capital, divestments, etc.) as well as cultural and institutional changes. Note that the estimate of b_1 is higher than in Table II, in which the "Italy-dummy" was excluded from the model. It shows that Italy is an exception to the general pattern of the business ownership rate adjusting towards the equilibrium level. The lack of error-correction for Italian self-employment is also clear from Figure 1.[23]

The estimate of b_2 points at a positive impact of unemployment on self-employment: every percent point rise in the unemployment rate leads to a rise of 0.06 percent point in the self-employment rate in the succeeding six years. This is in accordance with evidence in some earlier studies:

unemployment is a push factor for self-employment. The other variable explaining the change in self-employment, the labor income share, has the expected effect: the estimate of b_3 is negative. The effect is insignificant, though. This means that we fail to find evidence for our variable of business profitability to act as a pull factor for business ownership. The remaining variable in the business ownership equation, the "Italy-dummy", shows a significant positive coefficient. The rate of business ownership in Italy rises faster *ceteris paribus* than in other countries.

Another important characteristic of the estimation results is the deviation of the actual number of business owners from the equilibrium rate having a negative impact on economic growth: the estimate of c_1 is significantly negative.[24] This implies that economies with a business ownership rate below the equilibrium may benefit from stimulating new start-ups. In case this rate exceeds the equilibrium, it suggests that there are important impediments to growth for small and medium-sized enterprises. In the growth equation, the per capita income parameter c_2 is estimated to be negative. This might reflect the convergence of countries hypothesis. However, it may also be a within (regression-to-the-mean) effect: a higher value of GDP per capita in a certain year leads to a smaller economic growth in the subsequent period. Finally, the constant term c_0 is positive.

A comparison of the third and sixth column of Table I shows that in 1988 most countries had too few self-employed relative to the equilibrium value. An obvious exception is Italy. It indicates that the high level of self-employment in Italy is not efficient: it has a relatively large negative impact on economic growth.[25] Another exception is Australia. But as opposed to Italy, Australia moved in the direction of equilibrium between 1988 and 1996, as can be seen from the fourth column of Table I. Countries which experienced very low business ownership rates compared to the equilibrium include the Scandinavian countries. These economies are chacterized by a large public sector, relatively low entry and exit rates and high taxes. Eliasson (1995) and Braunerhjelm and Carlsson (1999) blame part of Sweden's relatively bad economic performance in the 1980s on limited private initiative and a lack of structural adjustment. Another country with a relatively low business ownership rate is Germany. In Figure 1 it is shown that, at least until recently, Germany has failed to restructure where for example the United Kingdom has. Klodt (1990) blames (West) German industrial policy for repressing structural change in supporting large-scale industries with subsidies. An important reason for the lack of a vibrant sector of new firms and industries in Germany up till the mid 1990s has been the high barriers to innovative activity (Audretsch, 2000). An example of important economic reforms transforming an economy from a regulated one to a market-orientated one with increasing business ownership rates is New Zealand (see e.g. Evans et al., 1996). Carlsson (1996) shows the strong increase in the number of firms as a result of the reforms, certainly when compared to countries like Sweden. After a painful transition period the New Zealand's reforms appear to ultimately have generated economic growth (McMillan, 1998; and Silverstone et al., 1996). The data in Table I suggest that, indeed, business ownership rates were below equilibrium values for New Zealand before the start of the reforms in 1984. The increase in business ownership rates has been fierce in the period thereafter and may be "over-

shooting", making some "shake-out" of newly entered entrepreneurs likely.

6. Discussion

Business ownership has received considerable attention from policy makers in European countries. The high unemployment rate coupled with limited economic growth in Europe has triggered a plea by policy makers for rethinking the policy approach that fostered prosperity during the postwar era. In two ways globalization has reduced the ability of the European countries to generate economic growth and create jobs. On the one hand the advent of new competition from low-cost countries in Asia and Central and Eastern Europe has flooded the EU markets. On the other hand, the telecommunications and computer revolutions have drastically reduced the cost of shifting capital and information out of the high-cost locations of Europe and into lower-cost locations around the globe (Audretsch and Thurik, 2000).

It is deeply embedded in the current European policy approach that the creativity and independence of the self-employed contribute to higher levels of economic activity. In modern economies a great variety of organizations is involved in making innovative products. This is the case particularly in niche markets like in the ICT sector. The more organizations are active in such markets, the greater the chance that an innovation takes place. Variety and selection play a dominant role in this mechanism. Therefore, major funds of governmental institutions and independent donor organizations are being channeled towards young and small firms. The present paper aims at achieving some first insights into whether such policies are justified in different phases of economic development.

We seek to explain the interrelationship between economic progress and the size class structure of firms. The present paper zooms in on one specific linkage: that between the number of business owners and economic development. Three aspects of this linkage are investigated. First, we investigate whether there is a long-term equilibrium relation between the number of business owners and the stage of economic development. This conjecture arises from analysing empirical and theoretical work in this area. The relation is hypothesized to initially be a decreasing function of economic development in that the self-employment rate is high in low-developed economies whereas more highly developed countries where mass production and scale economies thrive have lower self-employment rates. A large literature points at a still later phase of economic development where the business ownership rate is increasing again. This phase is characterized by "the reversal of the trend" towards increasing economies of scale and scope. Therefore we formulate the equilibrium business ownership to have a U-shaped relation with respect to economic development. Second, we investigate whether there is a correction mechanism when the rate of business ownership is out of equilibrium and compute the speed of convergence. Deviations from equilibrium can occur due to exogenous shocks and institutional divergences, for instance, because "government regulation of market activity is likely to obstruct and frustrate the spontaneous, corrective forces of entrepreneurial adjustments" (Kirzner, 1997, p. 81). Third, we investigate whether deviating from the equilibrium rate of business ownership leads to lower economic growth. The three aspects are tested using a two-equation model. The first equation explains the growth of the number of business owners using the deviation between the actual and the equilibrium rate of business ownership, unemployment as a push factor and the labor income share as a measure of business profitability. The second equation explains economic growth using the deviation between the actual and the equilibrium rate of business ownership, and the per capita income level. The model is tested using a data panel of 23 OECD countries.

We find evidence for a long-term equilibrium relation between economic development and business ownership. However, U-shaped equilibrium functions cannot be distinguished from L-shaped functions in a statistical sense. In fact, the large majority of countries has levels of economic development smaller than that at which the U-curve reaches its "minimum", making the "equilibrium function" largely L-shaped.

We find evidence for an error correction mechanism between the actual rate of business ownership and the equilibrium rate. Lagged unemployment appears to be a significant push

factor of business ownership. Italy plays an exceptional role in our sample of 23 OECD countries in that there appears to be an additional autonomous increase of the rate of self-employment which may have frustrated economic growth.

The rate of business ownership is found to influence economic growth through deviations from the equilibrium rate. This result supports the view that size distribution differences across countries matter when explaining economic performance (Davis and Henrekson, 1999). As a consequence, economies can have both too few or too many business owners and both situations can lead to a growth penalty. By and large, a five percent point deviation implies a growth loss of three percent over a period of four years.

An important policy implication of our exercises is not only that "To induce dynamic entrepreneurial competition we require the fulfillment of only one condition: guaranteeing free entrepreneurial entry into any market where profit opportunities may be perceived to exist" (Kirzner, 1997, p. 74), but also that exit free of stigma and financial burdens has to be safeguarded. See also Acs et al. (1999). Low barriers to entry and exit of business owners are a necessary condition for the equilibrium seeking mechanisms which are vital in our model of the relation between business ownership and economic development.

The results presented in this study should be interpreted with caution. The very concept of the economy-wide rate of business ownership entails several difficulties of interpretation. For example, it is impossible to make the rates perfectly statistically comparable across countries. In addition, the composition of the rates are unclear: high-tech start-ups are indistinguishable from old mom-and-pop businesses in the retail sector (with the same number of employees). Nevertheless, we argue that this paper may provide a good starting point for a promising line of research. As an important issue we mention that while the present research is based upon country-wide composites, sectoral diversity between countries probably plays a role when explaining differences in equilibrium situation and differences in the equilibrium restoring mechanism.

Acknowledgements

The authors are grateful to an anonymous referee for helpful comments on an earlier draft. Martin Carree is grateful to the Royal Netherlands Academy of Arts and Sciences (KNAW) for financial support. Earlier versions of this paper have been read at the EARIE conference (Turin, 1999), the AEA meetings (Boston, 2000), the Jönköping international workshop (Jönköping, 2000), the Tinbergen Institute (Rotterdam, 2000) and at the Young Economists' Conference (Oxford, 2000).

Appendix: Weighted regressions

Estimation results are obtained by weighting the observations with the number of inhabitants. In this appendix we provide the rationale. For simplicity we consider the case of cross sectional data (i.e. no time dimension).

Suppose that there are N regions in L countries with $L \ll N$. In our case, L would be 23 because we have 23 countries in our data set. We assume that these N regions are all of the same size. Thus, for example, the U.S. would have many regions the size of Luxembourg. If we would dispose of data per region, we would propose the following model for a linear relationship between two variables x and y:

$$y_{R,i} = \beta x_{R,i} + \varepsilon_{R,i}, \quad i = 1, \ldots, N \text{ (regions)}. \quad \text{(a)}$$

The subscript R is used to denote that the data are assumed to be available at the regional level. The OLS-estimator of β in (a) is then

$$b_{OLS}(a) = \frac{\sum_{i=1}^{N} x_{R,i} y_{R,i}}{\sum_{i=1}^{N} x_{R,i} x_{R,i}}.$$

However, we have data at the aggregated level of countries and not at the level of regions. Given our assumption that the regions are equally large, we write the model with the variables x and y at the country level (subscript C) as

$$y_{C,j} = \beta x_{C,j} + \varepsilon_{C,j}, \quad j = 1, \ldots, L \text{ (countries), with} \quad \text{(b)}$$

$$y_{C,j} = \frac{\sum_{D_{i,j}=1} y_{R,i}}{N_j} \quad \text{and} \quad x_{C,j} = \frac{\sum_{D_{i,j}=1} x_{R,i}}{N_j}.$$

The variable $D_{i,j}$ is defined as follows: $D_{i,j} = 1$ if region i lies in country j and 0 otherwise. Furthermore, N_j denotes the number of regions in country j ($\sum_{j=1}^{L} N_j = N$). Hence, we assume that the variables x and y at the country-level can be written as the averages of the variables over the regions of the country. When we translate these country-level variables $y_{C,j}$ and $x_{C,j}$ in (b) back to the regional level variables $y_{R,i}$ and $x_{R,i}$ in (a), we obtain the following observations for our original model (a) at the regional level:

Observations for which:

$$D_{i,1} = 1: \quad y_{R,i}^* = y_{C,1} \quad x_{R,i}^* = x_{C,1} \quad (N_1 \text{ observations})$$

$$\cdot$$

$$D_{i,L} = 1: \quad y_{R,i}^* = y_{C,L} \quad x_{R,i}^* = x_{C,L} \quad (N_L \text{ observations})$$

Writing the data at the regional level in this manner, it is implicitly assumed that *within* countries, the various regions are identical. With these observations, the OLS-estimator can be written as:

$$b_{OLS}^*(a) = \frac{\sum_{i=1}^{N} x_{R,i}^* y_{R,i}^*}{\sum_{i=1}^{N} x_{R,i}^* x_{R,i}^*} = \frac{\sum_{j=1}^{L} N_j x_{C,j} y_{C,j}}{\sum_{j=1}^{L} N_j x_{C,j} x_{C,j}}.$$

Thus, here it is assumed that there are N observations where for every observation (region) within a country, the variables have identical values. However, we have only L observations and then the OLS-estimator of β from (b) reads as

$$b_{OLS}(b) = \frac{\sum_{j=1}^{L} x_{C,j} y_{C,j}}{\sum_{j=1}^{L} x_{C,j} x_{C,j}}.$$

We see that this estimator is different from $b_{OLS}^*(a)$, which we would like to have. The estimator $b_{OLS}(b)$ does not take into account that different countries have different numbers of regions, or stated differently, that the various countries are not equally large. Therefore, we weight the observations by pre-multiplying the variables x_C and y_C from (b) with the square root of the number of regions. The (weighted) least squares estimator $b_{WLS}(b)$ reads as

$$b_{WLS}(b) = \frac{\sum_{j=1}^{L} \sqrt{N_j} x_{C,j} \sqrt{N_j} y_{C,j}}{\sum_{j=1}^{L} \sqrt{N_j} x_{C,j} \sqrt{N_j} x_{C,j}}.$$

We see that the WLS-estimator of (b) is exactly the same as the OLS-estimator of (a), $b_{OLS}^*(a)$. Clearly, we do not know the number of regions per country. We use the population size as a proxy.

Notes

[1] There is considerable controversy about the number of U.S. self-employed. Publications which deal with various issues on estimating the actual number of business owners in the U.S. include Fain (1980), Bregger (1996), Dennis (1997) and Chapter 3 of *The State of Small Business; a Report of the President 1996*, Washington: U.S. Government Printing Office. Most controversy is about measuring the number of incorporated self-employed. In the present paper we basically follow the approach taken by USSBA (2000), p. 5, in which the number of incorporated self-employed is estimated by the number of *employer firms*.

[2] Audretsch and Thurik (2001) characterize this period as one where stability, continuity and homogeneity were the cornerstones and label it the managed economy.

[3] See also the various editions of *The European Observatory for SMEs* that provide an account of the state of small business in Europe, for instance EIM/ENSR (1997).

[4] Brock and Evans (1986) were the first to provide an elaborate overview.

[5] Entrepreneurial energy as such may not suffice for economic progress. Baumol (1990) stressed the importance of entrepreneurship being led into productive channels.

[6] Small deviations are unlikely to have much impact. See e.g. Simon (1991, pp. 41–42): "organization size and degree of integration, and the boundaries between organizations and markets, are determined by rather subtle forces. The wide range of organizational arrangements observable in the world suggests that the equilibrium between these two alternatives may often be almost neutral, with the level highly contingent on a system's history".

[7] Schultz (1990) reports having found statistical evidence for a quadratic relationship between the share of wage earners and the stage of economic development.

[8] In case the "minimum" is reached at a level of per capita income exceeding those attained in the data set, the relation can be better described as L-shaped.

[9] Alba-Ramirez (1994) shows that for both Spain and the U.S. the duration of unemployment increases the probability of becoming self-employed. His analysis suggests that the effect of unemployment duration on the probability of becoming self-employed is not very different for the two countries, albeit stronger for the U.S. The results are interesting especially since the Spanish economy has a higher degree of unemployment and self-employment when compared to the American economy. The results suggest that the influence of unemployment on business ownership is a common feature across economies. Alba-Ramirez also notes that legislation aimed to help the jobless starting up their own businesses has been implemented across developed countries and provides the example of the Spanish 1985 law giving lump-sum unemployment insurance to workers becoming self-employed.

[10] Acs et al. (1999) point at differences in competition and entrepreneurship when comparing the more successful U.S. economy to that of Europe and Japan.

[11] The excess growth of small firms in that study is defined as the percentage change in the value-of-shipments accounted for by small firms minus that accounted for by large firms.

[12] A subset of small firms which are assumed to improve economic performance are the so-called New Technology-Based Firms (NTBFs). Many of the businesses can be found on Science Parks of which the number in many countries has increased strongly during the 1980s and 1990s. Storey and Tether (1998) show that most of the NTBFs are, in fact, small firms. They report the average number of employees to be around 20 both in France and the U.K. The two countries were the first in Europe (in 1969) to establish science parks (Cambridge Science Park in the U.K. and Sophia Antipolis in France). They claim that Italy serves as an example of lagging behind in the establishment of "advanced" science parks and relate this to the relatively low proportion of university research that is financed by the Italian private sector.

[13] See for example Russia's Shatalin Plan, which "is built on the assumption that society needs small enterprises to orient production to the needs of every person, to fight the dictatorship of monopolies in consumer and production markets, and to create a favourable environment for quick introduction of new scientific and technological ideas" (Nolan, 1995, p. 82).

[14] In Carree et al. (2000) we compare four different specifications of the relationship between the equilibrium business ownership rate and GDP per capita, based upon an earlier version of our business ownership dataset (COMPENDIA 1999; in the present paper we use COMPENDIA 2000.1, see Section 4). The log-quadratic specification adopted in the present paper was found to outperform the other specifications in terms of goodness of fit, although not by much. The estimates of the error-correction parameter b_1 and the growth penalty parameter c_1 did not differ much between the four specifications.

[15] Audretsch and Thurik (1998), in an earlier empirical investigation for 23 OECD countries find a positive effect of the (lagged) change of unemployment on the change of the self-employment rate.

[16] In Carree et al. (2000) we consider an alternative penalty function based on the squared instead of the absolute deviation. For each of the shapes of the equilibrium function the absolute deviation penalty structure outperformed the squared deviation case.

[17] For the unemployment rate and the labor income share we also use data of 1974.

[18] This topic is dealt with in Chapter 5 of *OECD Employment Outlook June 2000*.

[19] For the United States, sources include The State of Small Business; a Report of the President 1996.

[20] Contact André van Stel for further information about these business ownership data (ast@eim.nl). The data set is referred to as COMPENDIA 2000.1.

[21] Separate data for Northern and Southern Italy are obtained from *Eurostat Regions Statistical Yearbook*.

[22] The size of newly established firms in Italy is very small in comparison with the size of incumbent firms (see Santarelli and Sterlacchini, 1994).

[23] We have also run a regression of equation (4) with dummy-variables included for *all* countries in the sample. We found the error-correction effect to increase to 0.20 and the growth penalty to become insignificant (*t*-value below unity). Because one possible interpretation of such a regression is that every country has its own unique equilibrium level, these results are not surprising. However, this type of country-specific equilibrium levels is not the focus of this study, since we are investigating a "universal" equilibrium function which should be valid for all countries. Indeed, as we described earlier, we do not even interpret the "Italy-dummy" as reflecting a country-specific equilibrium. Instead, we interpret it as an autonomous additional rise in the number of business owners, not necessarily favouring economic growth.

[24] We do not include country-specific dummies in Eq. (2). However, when including such dummies the coefficient of c_1 remains negative and the value of the estimate barely changes, both in the "Two yearly" case and the "Four yearly" case. This is also found for both cases when the "Italy-dummy" in the first equation is excluded (as in Table II). Likelihood ratio test statistics testing whether or not to include country-specific dummies in equation (2) have values between 34.0 and 46.5

for the four cases of Table II and III. These values are close to the critical values at 5% (33.9) and 1% (40.3).

[25] In Italy, research and development expenditures are by far the lowest among the largest OECD countries as a percentage of gross national product. This is in line with the idea that when there are too many business owners, the scale advantages in research and development are not utilized. See Cohen and Klepper (1996).

References

Acs, Z. J., 1996, 'Small Firms and Economic Growth', in P. H. Admiraal (ed.), *Small Business in the Modern Economy, De Vries Lectures in Economics*, Oxford, U.K.: Blackwell Publishers.

Acs, Z. J. and D. B. Audretsch, 1987, 'Innovation, Market Structure, and Firm Size', *Review of Economics and Statistics* 69, 567–574.

Acs, Z. J. and D. B. Audretsch, 1993, 'Conclusion', in Z. J. Acs and D. B. Audretsch (eds.), *Small Firms and Entrepreneurship; an East-West Perspective*, Cambridge, U.K.: Cambridge University Press.

Acs, Z. J., D. B. Audretsch and D. S. Evans, 1994, *The Determinants of Variation in the Self-employment Rates across Countries and over Time*, mimeo (fourth draft).

Acs, Z. J., B. Carlsson and Ch. Karlsson, 1999, 'The Linkages among Entrepreneurship, SMEs and the Macroeconomy', in Z. J. Acs, B. Carlsson and Ch. Karlsson (eds.), *Entrepreneurship, Small and Medium-Sized Enterprises and the Macroeconomy*, Cambridge, U.K.: Cambridge University Press.

Aiginger, K. and G. Tichy, 1991, 'Small Firms and the Merger Mania', *Small Business Economics* 3, 83–101.

Alba-Ramirez, A., 1994, 'Self-Employment in the Midst of Unemployment: The Case of Spain and the United States', *Applied Economics* 26, 189–204.

Amit, R., L. Glosten and E. Muller, 1993, 'Challenges to Theory Development in Entrepreneurship Research', *Journal of Management Studies* 30, 815–834.

Audretsch, D., 2000, 'Entrepreneurship in Germany', in D. L. Sexton and H. Landström (eds.), *The Blackwell Handbook of Entrepreneurship*, Oxford: Blackwell Publishers.

Audretsch, D. B. and A. R. Thurik, 1998, *The Knowledge Society, Entrepreneurship and Unemployment*, Research Report 9801/E, Zoetermeer, NL: EIM.

Audretsch, D. B. and A. R. Thurik, 2000, 'Capitalism and Democracy in the 21st Century: from the Managed to the Entrepreneurial Economy', *Journal of Evolutionary Economics* 10(1), 17–34.

Audretsch, D. B. and A. R. Thurik, 2001, 'What is New about the New Economy: Sources of Growth in the Managed and Entrepreneurial Economies', *Industrial and Corporate Change* 10(1), 267–315.

Baumol, W. J., 1990, 'Entrepreneurship: Productive, Unproductive and Destructive', *Journal of Political Economy* 98, 893–921.

Blau, D., 1987, 'A Time Series Analysis of Self-Employment', *Journal of Political Economy* 95, 445–467.

Braunerhjelm, P. and B. Carlsson, 1999, 'Industry Structure, Entrepreneurship and the Macroeconomy: A Comparison of Ohio and Sweden, 1975–1995', in Z. J. Acs, B. Carlsson and C. Karlsson (eds.), *Entrepreneurship, Small & Medium-Sized Enterprises and the Macroeconomy*, Cambridge: Cambridge University Press.

Bregger, J. E., 1996, 'Measuring Self-Employment in the United States', *Monthly Labor Review* 119(1), 3–9.

Brock, W. A. and D. S. Evans, 1986, *The Economics of Small Businesses: Their Role and Regulation in the U.S. Economy*, New York: Holmes and Meier.

Calvo, G. A. and S. Wellisz, 1980, 'Technology, Entrepreneurs, and Firm Size', *Quarterly Journal of Economics* 95, 663–677.

Carree, M. A. and A. R. Thurik, 1998, 'Small Firms and Economic Growth in Europe', *Atlantic Economic Journal* 26(2), 137–146.

Carree, M. A. and A. R. Thurik, 1999, 'Industrial Structure and Economic Growth', in D. B. Audretsch and A. R. Thurik (eds.), *Innovation, Industry Evolution and Employment*, Cambridge; Cambridge University Press, pp. 86–110.

Carree, M. A, A. J. van Stel, A. R. Thurik and A. R. M. Wennekers, 2000, *Business Ownership and Economic Growth in 23 OECD Countries*, Tinbergen Institute Discussion Paper TI 2000-01/3, Tinbergen Institute Rotterdam, NL.

Carlsson, B., 1989, 'The Evolution of Manufacturing Technology and Its Impact on Industrial Structure: An International Study', *Small Business Economics* 1, 21–37.

Carlsson, B., 1996, 'Differing Patterns of Industrial Dynamics: New Zealand, Ohio and Sweden, 1978–1994', *Small Business Economics* 8, 219–234.

Chandler, A. D. Jr., 1990, *Scale and Scope: The Dynamics of Industrial Capitalism*, Cambrdge: Harvard University.

Cohen, W. M. and S. Klepper, 1996, 'A Reprise of Size and R&D', *Economic Journal* 106, 925–951.

Davis, S. J. and M. Henrekson, 1999, 'Explaining National Differences in the Size and Industry Structure of Employment', *Small Business Economics* 12, 59–83.

Dennis, W. J. Jr., 1997, 'More than you think: an Inclusive Estimate of Business Entries', *Journal of Business Venturing* 12(3), 175–196.

EIM/ENSR, 1994, *The European Observatory for SMEs: Second Annual Report*, Zoetermeer, The Netherlands: EIM.

EIM/ENSR, 1996, *The European Observatory for SMEs: Fourth Annual Report*, Zoetermeer, The Netherlands: EIM.

EIM/ENSR, 1997, *The European Observatory for SMEs: Fifth Annual Report*, Zoetermeer, The Netherlands: EIM.

Eliasson, G. E., 1995, *Economic Growth through Competitive Selection*, paper presented at 22nd Annual E.A.R.I.E. Conference 3–6 September 1995.

Evans, D. S. and L. S. Leighton, 1989, 'Some Empirical Aspects of Entrepreneurship', *American Economic Review* 79, 519–535.

Evans, L., A. Grimes, B. Wilkinson and D. Teece, 1996, 'Economic Reform in New Zealand 1984–95: The Pursuit of Efficiency', *Journal of Economic Literature* 34, 1856–1902.

Fain, T. S., 1980, 'Self-employed Americans: Their Number has Increased', *Monthly Labor Review* 103(11), 3–8.

Freeman, C. and C. Perez, 1988, 'Structural Crises of Adjustment: Business Cycles and Investment Behavior', in G. Dosi et al. (eds.), *Technical Change and Economic Theory*, London: Pinter Publishers.

Fiegenbaum, A. and A. Karnani, 1991, 'Output Flexibility – A Competitive Advantage for Small Firms', *Strategic Management Journal* **12**, 101–114.

Holmes, T. J. and J. A. Schmitz Jr., 1990, 'A Theory of Entrepreneurship and its Application to the Study of Business Transfers', *Journal of Political Economy* **98**, 265–294.

Henrekson, M. and D. Johansson, 1999, 'Institutional Effects on the Evolution of the Size Distribution of Firms', *Small Business Economics* **12**, 11–23.

Inman, R. P. (ed.), 1985, *Managing the Service Economy*, Cambridge: Cambridge University Press.

Iyigun, M. F. and A. L. Owen, 1998, 'Risk, Entrepreneurship, and Human Capital Accumulation', *American Economic Review, Papers and Proceedings* **88**, 454–457.

Jackson, L. F., 1984, 'Hierarchic Demand and the Engle Curve for Variety', *Review of Economics and Statistics* **66**, 8–15.

Jensen, M. C., 1993, 'The Modern Industrial Revolution, Exit, and the Failure of Internal Control Systems', *Journal of Finance* **68**, 831–880.

Jovanovic, B., 1993, 'The Diversification of Production', *Brookings Papers: Microeconomics* (1993), 197–235.

Kihlstrom, R. E. and J. J. Laffont, 1979, 'A General Equilibrium Entrepreneurial Theory of Firm Formation Based on Risk Aversion', *Journal of Political Economy* **87**, 719–748.

Kirchhoff, B. A., 1996, 'Self-Employment and Dynamic Capitalism', *Journal of Labor Research* **17**, 627–643.

Kirzner, I. M., 1997, 'Entrepreneurial Discovery and the Competitive Market Process: An Austrian Approach', *Journal of Economic Literature* **35**, 60–85.

Klodt, H., 1990, 'Industrial Policy and Repressed Structural Change in West Germany', *Jahrbücher für National-ökonomie und Statistik* **207**, 25–35.

Klomp, L. and J. J. M. Pronk, 1998, *Kennis en Economie 1998*, Voorburg/Heerlen: Statistics Netherlands.

KPMG/ENSR, 2000, *The European Observatory for SMEs: Sixth Report*, Zoetermeer, NL: EIM.

Kuznets, S., 1971, *Economic Growth of Nations, Total Output and Production Structure*, Cambridge, MA: Harvard University Press/Belknapp Press.

Lever, M. H. C. and H. R. Nieuwenhuijsen, 1999, 'The Impact of Competition on Productivity in Dutch Manufacturing', in D. B. Audretsch and A. R. Thurik (eds.), *Innovation, Industry Evolution and Employment*, Cambridge: Cambridge University Press, pp. 111–128.

Lloyd-Ellis, H. and D. Bernhardt, 2000, 'Enterprise, Inequality and Economic Development', *Review of Economic Studies* **67**, 147–168.

Loveman, G. and W. Sengenberger, 1991, 'The Re-emergence of Small-Scale Production; an International Comparison', *Small Business Economics* **3**, 1–37.

Lucas, R. E., 1978, 'On the Size Distribution of Firms', *BELL Journal of Economics* **9**, 508–523.

Maslow, A. H., 1970, *Motivation and Personality*, New York: Harper and Row.

McMillan, J., 1998, 'Managing Economic Change: Lessons from New Zealand', *World Economy* **21**, 827–843.

Meredith, J., 1987, 'The Strategic Advantages of New Manufacturing Technologies for Small Firms', *Strategic Management Journal* **8**, 249–258.

Nickell, S. J., 1996, 'Competition and Corporate Performance', *Journal of Political Economy* **104**, 724–746.

Nickell, S., P. Nicolitsas and N. Dryden, 1997, 'What Makes Firms Perform Well?', *European Economic Review* **41**, 783–796.

Nolan, P., 1995, *China's Rise, Russia's Fall: Politics, Economics and Planning in the Transition from Stalinism*, New York: St Martin's Press.

Nooteboom, B, 1994, 'Innovation and Diffusion in Small Firms', *Small Business Economics* **6**, 327–347.

OECD, 1995, *Competition Policy in OECD Countries 1992–1993*, Paris.

OECD, 1998, *Fostering Entrepreneurship*, Paris.

Oughton, C. and G. Whittam, 1997, 'Competition and Cooperation in the Small Firm Sector', *Scottish Journal of Political Economy* **44**, 1–30.

Peretto, P. F., 1999, 'Industrial Development, Technological Change and Long-Run Growth', *Journal of Development Economics* **59**, 389–417.

Phillips, B. D., 1985, 'The Effect of Industry Deregulation on the Small Business Sector', *Business Economics* **20**, 28–37.

Piore, M. J. and C. F. Sabel, 1984, *The Second Industrial Divide Possibilities for Prosperity*, New York: Basic Books.

Prusa, T. J. and J. A. Schmitz Jr., 1991, 'Are New Firms an Important Source of Innovation? Evidence from the Software Industry', *Economics Letters* **35**, 339–342.

Rothwell, R., 1983, 'Innovation and Firm Size: A Case for Dynamic Complementarity; Or, Is Small Really So Beautiful?', *Journal of General Management* **8**, 5–25.

Rothwell, R., 1984, 'The Role of Small Firms in the Emergence of New Technologies', *OMEGA* **12**, 19–29.

Santarelli, E. and A. Sterlacchini, 1994, 'New Firm Formation in Italian Industry: 1985–89', *Small Business Economics* **6**, 95–106.

Schaffner, J. A., 1993, 'Rising Incomes and the Shift from Self-Employment to Firm-Based Production', *Economics Letters* **41**, 435–440.

Schiller, B. R. and P. E. Crewson, 1997, 'Entrepreneurial Origins: A Longitudinal Inquiry', *Economic Inquiry* **35**, 523–531.

Schmitz, J. A. Jr., 1989, 'Imitation, Entrepreneurship, and Long-Run Growth', *Journal of Political Economy* **97**, 721–739.

Schultz, T. P., 1990, 'Women's Changing Participation in the Labor Force: A World Perspective', *Economic Development and Cultural Change* **38**, 457–488.

Schumpeter, J. A., 1934, *The Theory of Economic Development*, Cambridge, MA: Harvard University Press.

Schumpeter, J. A., 1950, *Capitalism, Socialism and Democracy*, New York: Harper and Row.

Shepherd, W. G., 1982, 'Causes of Increased Competition in the U.S. Economy, 1939–1980', *Review of Economics and Statistics* **64**, 613–626.

Silverstone, B., A. Bollard and R. Lattimore (eds.), 1996, *A Study of Economic Reform: The Case of New Zealand, Contributions to Economic Analysis*, vol. 236, Amsterdam: Elsevier North-Holland.

Simon, H. A., 1991, 'Organizations and Markets', *Journal of Economic Perspectives* 5(2), 25–44.

Stopford, J. M. and C. W. F. Baden-Fuller, 1994, 'Creating Corporate Entrepreneurship', *Strategic Management Journal* 15, 521–536.

Storey, D. J., 1991, 'The Birth of New Enterprises – Does Unemployment Matter? A Review of the Evidence', *Small Business Economics* 3, 167–178.

Storey, D. J. and B. S. Tether, 1998, 'Public Policy Measures to Support New Technology-based Firms in the European Union', *Research Policy* 26, 1037–1057.

Thurik, A. R., 1996, 'Small Firms, Entrepreneurship and Economic Growth', in P. H. Admiraal (ed.), *Small Business in the Modern Economy, De Vries Lectures in Economics*, Oxford: Blackwell Publishers.

Thurik, A. R., 1999, 'Entrepreneurship, Industrial Transformation and Growth', in G. D. Libecap (ed.), *The Sources of Entrepreneurial Activity: Vol. 11, Advances in the Study of Entrepreneurship, Innovation, and Economic Growth*, JAI Press, pp. 29–65.

United States Small Business Administration, Office of Advocacy (USSBA), 2000, *Small Business Economic Indicators 1998*, Washington: SBA.

Wennekers, A. R. M. and A. R. Thurik, 1999, 'Linking Entrepreneurship and Economic Growth', *Small Business Economics* 13, 27–55.

Yamada, G., 1996, 'Urban Informal Employment and Self-Employment in Developing Countries: Theory and Evidence', *Economic Development and Cultural Change* 44, 289–314.

[20]

Regional Studies, Vol. 38.8, pp. 911–927, November 2004

Carfax Publishing
Taylor & Francis Group

Employment Growth and Entrepreneurial Activity in Cities

ZOLTAN J. ACS*†‡ and CATHERINE ARMINGTON‡

*Merrick School of Business, University of Baltimore, 1420 North Charles Street, BC 491, Baltimore, MD 21201, USA.
Email: zacs@ubalt.edu

†Max Planck Institute for Research into Economic Systems, Jena D-07745, Germany

‡US Bureau of the Census, Washington, DC, USA

(Received September 2003: in revised form March 2004)

Acs Z. J. and Armington C. (2004) Employment growth and entrepreneurial activity in cities, *Regional Studies* **38**, 911–927. Recent theories of economic growth have stressed the role of externalities in generating growth. Using data from the Census Bureau that tracks all employers in the whole US private-sector economy, the impact of these externalities, as measured by entrepreneurial activity, on employment growth in Local Market Areas are examined. Differences in levels of entrepreneurial activity, diversity among geographically proximate industries and the extent of human capital are positively associated with variation in growth rates, but the manufacturing sector appears to be an exception.

Economic growth   Knowledge spillovers   Entrepreneurship   Industry diversity

Acs Z. J. et Armington C. (2004) La croissance de l'emploi et l'esprit d'entreprise dans les grandes villes, *Regional Studies* **38**, 911–927. Des théories récentes de la croissance économique ont souligné l'importance des effets externes. A partir des données provenant du Census Bureau, institut national de la statistique qui fait le suivi de tous les employeurs dans toute l'économie privée aux Etats-Unis, cet article cherche à examiner les retombées de ces effets externes-là, mesurés en termes de l'esprit d'entreprise, sur la croissance de l'emploi dans les bassins d'emplois locaux. Il s'avère que les écarts des les niveaux de l'esprit d'entreprise, la diversité des industries à proximité, et l'importance du capital humain sont en corrélation étroite avec la variation des taux de croissance, à une exception près, le secteur industriel.

Croissance économique   Retombées de connaisance   Esprit d'entreprise   Diversité industrielle

Acs Z. J. und Armington C. (2004) Zunahme der Arbeitsstellen und Unternehmertätigkeit in Städten, *Regional Studies* **38**, 911–927. Kürzlich aufgekommene Theorien wirtschaftlichen Wachstums haben die Rolle externer Effekte bei der Wachstumsentwicklung betont. Mit Hilfe von Daten des Census Bureau, das sämtliche Arbeitgeber des Privatsektors der Wirtschaft der USA erfaßt, wird die Auswirkung dieser externen Effekte auf die Zunahme von Erwerbsstellen in 'Local Market Areas' durch Messung an Hand unternehmerischer Aktivität untersucht. Es wird festgestellt, daß Unterschiede der Stufen unternehmerischer Aktivität, Vielfalt in geographisch benachbarten Industrien und der Umfang des Menschenkapitals in positiver Verbindung mit Abweichungen bei Zuwachsraten auftreten, obschon der herstellende Sektor hierbei eine Ausnahme darstellt.

Wirtschaftswachstum   Verbreitung von Fachkenntnissen   Unternehmerschaft   industrielle Vielfalt

Acs Z. J. y Armington C. (2004) Crecimiento en el empleo y actividad emprendedora en las ciudades, *Regional Studies* **38**, 911–927. Las teorías recientes sobre el crecimiento económico han enfatizado el rol de las externalidades en la generación de crecimiento. Utilizando datos de la Oficina del Censo que siguen la trayectoria de todos los empresarios en la totalidad de la economía del sector privado en los Estados Unidos, examinamos el impacto de estas externalidades, medido por medio del grado de actividad emprendedora, en el crecimiento del empleo en Áreas de Mercado Local. Encontramos que las diferencias en los niveles de actividad empresarial, la diversidad entre industrias que están geográficamente próximas, y el grado de capital humano están positivamente asociados a una variación en los índices de crecimiento, pero el sector manufacturero parece presentar una excepción.

Crecimiento económico   Desbordamientos de conocimiento   Actividad emprendedora   Diversidad industrial

JEL classifications: C8, M13, O40, R11

0034-3404 print/1360-0591 online/04/080911-17 ©2004 Regional Studies Association
http://www.regional-studies-assoc.ac.uk

DOI: 10.1080/0034340042000280938

INTRODUCTION

What is the relationship between economic growth and entrepreneurial activity – the process of creating a new business (REYNOLDS *et al.*, 2002)? Neoclassical growth theory had no mechanism to explain the relationship between entrepreneurial activity and economic growth (SOLOW, 1956). Because scale economies operate at the establishment level, in the traditional Solow model, economic growth relied on physical capital investment in larger establishments. However, capital accumulation can explain only a small amount of the variation in economic growth across regions (CICCONE and HALL, 1996).

Recent theories of economic growth focus on the importance of knowledge and view knowledge externalities, as opposed to scale economies, as the primary engine of economic growth (ROMER, 1986). This suggests that if the domestic economy is endogenously growing, and if one believes in competitive markets, then it almost follows that knowledge spillovers feature in the economic landscape. This concept of spillovers solves the technical problem in economic theory of reconciling increasing returns (which are generally needed to generate endogenous growth) with competitive markets.

The concept of knowledge spillovers leads to several theoretical issues. First, for analysis of endogenous growth, cities and their broader integrated economic areas provide much more suitable units than states or nations (LUCAS, 1988). The local economic areas centred on primary cities tend to function as open economies, with a tremendous internal mobility of capital, labour and ideas. These city-based economic areas are much more homogeneous units than those defined by the political boundaries of states, and they frequently cross-state boundaries. National boundaries that bar factor mobility and national policies that encourage industrial diversification reduce the gains from factor mobility. These forces complicate analysis with cross-national samples. Cities allow us to look at units of economic growth without these concerns (GLAESER *et al.*, 1995).

Second, not all type of industrial structure can promote knowledge spillovers equally. GLAESER *et al.* (1992), FELDMAN and AUDRETSCH (1999) and ACS *et al.* (2002) examined the role of externalities associated with knowledge spillovers as an engine of regional economic growth. They found that local competition and industrial variety, rather than regional specialization and monopoly, encouraged employment growth. Their evidence suggested that knowledge spillovers might occur predominately between, rather than within, industries, consistent with the theories of JACOBS (1969).

Third, knowledge spillovers do not appear to be constant over time, and affect mature and young industries differently. The empirical and theoretical literature suggests that knowledge spillovers are more important in the early stages of the industry life cycle, when young firms flourish (UTTERBACK, 1994). If knowledge spillovers are more important in the early stages of the industry life cycle, the mechanics by which local spillovers are achieved should receive more attention. One potential interpretation is that cities that are endogenously growing may have higher levels of entrepreneurial activity. Organization ecology supports the latter, suggesting that typically entrepreneurs enter the local economy through a new organization that involves some degree of local knowledge spillovers and benefits from local network externalities (HANNAN and FREEMAN, 1989).[1]

The purpose of the present paper is to examine variations in regional employment growth rates in the context of an endogenous growth model with a particular emphasis on knowledge spillovers. The paper focuses on the early stage of the product life cycle, when competition is fiercer and technology is more fluid (JOVANOVIC, 2001).[2] The 1990s was a period when several industries were in the early stage of the industry life cycle, e.g. semiconductors, computers and communications equipment and software – the Information Age (JORGENSON, 2001) – and these resulted in substantial product and process changes in many other sectors of the economy (BRESNAHAN *et al.*, 2001).

The present paper tests the hypothesis that increased entrepreneurial activity in the early stages of the industry life cycle leads to higher growth rates of regional economies. The next section further examines some of the theories explaining variation in growth rates across local economies. The third section discusses the data for Labor Market Areas (LMAs) and measurement of the employment growth rate. The fourth section examines the aggregate data showing the contribution of new firms to economic growth. The fifth section presents the regression model and empirical results are given in the sixth section. Conclusions are made in the final section. Higher levels of employment growth rates are found to be strongly and positively associated with entrepreneurial activity and human capital and negatively associated with agglomeration effects (specialization and density) in all sectors of the economy except manufacturing.

WHY DO LOCAL EMPLOYMENT GROWTH RATES VARY?

The growth of cities and regions has many facets, and this paper focuses on continuing the search for an understanding of why some areas persistently show much higher growth than others. Three theories in the literature that have an important impact on variation in regional growth will be built upon. First, several papers in the last decade have confirmed the connection between the initial level of human capital in an area and the more rapid employment growth of that area (RAUCH, 1993; GLAESER *et al.*, 1995), demonstrating the link between human capital (knowledge) and employment growth. Second, knowledge spillovers can occur between firms in the same or different industries, fuelling the debate on the contributions to growth of specialization versus diversity (ROMER, 1990). Finally, no matter how richly endowed is an economic environment with intellectual, social, human and financial resources, someone has to organize these resources to pursue market opportunities (BAUMOL, 1993).

Where do market opportunities come from? They come from the information and knowledge that accumulates in every local economy. In the endogenous growth model at the micro level, knowledge – just like any other good – is produced by profit-maximizing firms, i.e. knowledge production is endogenized. At the macro level, the production of knowledge carries obvious implications for growth. It is channelled into growth through two main mechanisms. First, firms run their firms more efficiently; second, knowledge spills over across firms acting as a shift factor in their production functions. Both levels tend to increase firm-level productivity. However, in the endogenous growth models, the opportunity to exploit knowledge spillovers accruing from aggregate knowledge investment is not adequately explained. In essence, these models assume that knowledge – defined as codified and tacit research and development automatically transforms into commercial activity. However, the imposition of this assumption lacks intuitive as well as empirical backing. ACS and VARGA (2002, 2004) and ACS *et al.* (2003) argue that it is one thing for technological opportunities to exist, but an entirely different matter for them to be discovered, exploited and commercialized.

One of the key features of an urban economy is the partitioning of knowledge among individuals. Even if the total stock of knowledge was freely available, spatially and temporally unbounded, knowledge about the existence of any particular information would still be limited (HAYEK, 1945). Because of asymmetric information, knowledge is not uniformly at everyone's disposal, and no two individuals share the identical scope of knowledge or information about the economy. Thus, only a few people might know about a new invention, a particular scarcity or resources lying fallow. Such knowledge is typically idiosyncratic because it is acquired through each individual's own channels, including jobs, social relationships and daily life. It is this specific knowledge, frequently obtained through knowledge spillovers, that can lead to a profit-making opportunity.

However, many more opportunities are recognized than are actively pursued. Bringing new products and services into existence usually involves considerable risk. By definition, entrepreneurship requires making investments today without assurance of what the returns

will be tomorrow. Despite the absence of current markets for future goods and services, and in spite of the moral hazard when dealing with investors, suppliers and customer markets for future goods and services, many individuals succeed in creating new businesses. The ability to overcome these barriers to entrepreneurship varies among individuals, and such skill is not evenly distributed across economic areas. The market dynamics associated with entrepreneurship are not, it appears, so much those associated with changes in the size of the population of firms or products in the market as they are those associated with changes in the population characteristics of firms or products. At least in some, if not most, cases, entrepreneurs represent *agents of change* in the market (GEROSKI, 1995, p. 431).

Thus, a model is proposed where local employment growth is dependent on the various information externalities present in the regional knowledge base – the set of technical and non-technical information inputs, knowledge and capabilities about new technologies and processes. A model is estimated that explains differences in regional employment growth rates as a function of the regional levels of entrepreneurial activity, agglomeration effects and human capital:

$$\text{Employment growth}_{srt+1} = f(\text{entrepreneurial activity}_{srt},$$

$$\text{agglomeration effects}_{srt}, \text{ human capital}_{rt}) \quad (1)$$

where s is the industrial sector, r is for regions and t is for time.

While the present model suggests that causation runs from entrepreneurial activity to economic growth, several authors have suggested that it might run the other way with economic growth causing new firm formation. However, in neither the SOLOW (1956) nor the ROMER (1990) models is new firm formation the outcome of economic growth. In fact, in the Solow models, it can be argued that existing firms through the expansion of new establishments will accommodate all new growth with no need for new firms. In the Romer model, although the number of firms, entry rates and the scale of operation cannot be determined in the model – the number of firms is given (i.e. it is equal to the number of individuals) – no entry occurs (labour being constant) and all firms operate at the same level. In principle, these models typically assume what amounts to a 'representative firm', which is supposed to capture microeconomic behaviour.

Strictly speaking, the concept of entrepreneurship operates at the individual level. While requiring skills and other resources, essentially entrepreneurship has to do with people's behaviour. Entrepreneurial action, or the pursuit of opportunity, takes us from the individual to the firm level. A new business in which the entrepreneur has a controlling interest and strictly protected property rights provides a vehicle transforming personal skills and ambitions into actions. Underlying the start-up of each new organization is an entrepreneur who acquired the knowledge to recognize and pursue a good business opportunity (LAZEAR, 2002). Firms create output (and jobs as a by-product), and entrepreneurs create firms. Framing the challenge this way sheds light on new firm birth and the entrepreneurs that start them, providing a new focus for addressing an old question: where does growth come from in local economies (HART, 2003)?

MEASUREMENT OF EMPLOYMENT GROWTH RATE IN REGIONS

Data and measurement units

The present study uses a fairly new database that the Bureau of the Census, Washington, DC, has constructed for study of birth, survival and growth in different types of establishments. The Longitudinal Establishment and Enterprise Microdata (LEEM) has multiple years of annual data for every US private-sector (non-farm) business with employees. This analysis is based on a LEEM file that tracked employment, payroll, and firm affiliation and (employment) size for the more than 11 million establishments that had employees at some time during 1989–99.

This LEEM file was constructed by the Bureau of the Census from its Statistics of US Business (SUSB) files,[3] which were developed from the annual files of microdata underlying the aggregate data in the Census's County Business Patterns. These annual data were linked using the Longitudinal Pointer File associated with the SUSB, which facilitates tracking establishments over time, even when they change ownership and identification numbers.

The basic unit of the LEEM data is a business establishment (location or plant). An establishment is a single physical location where business is conducted or where services or industrial operations are performed. The microdata include the year each establishment first had payroll expenses and describe each establishment for each year of its existence in terms of its March employment, annual payroll, location (state, county and metropolitan area) and primary industry. Additional data for each establishment and year identify the firm to which the establishment belongs and the total employment of that firm.

A firm (or enterprise or company) is the largest aggregation (across all industries) of business legal entities under common ownership or control. Establishments are owned by legal entities, which are typically corporations, partnerships or sole proprietorships. Most firms are composed of only a single legal entity that operates a single establishment – their establishment data and firm data are identical, and they are referred to as 'single-unit' establishments or firms. Only 4% of firms have more than one establishment, and they and their establishments are both described as multi-location or multi-unit.

The LEEM data cover all US private-sector businesses with employees, with the exception of those in agricultural production, railroads and private households. This is the same universe covered in the Census's annual County Business Patterns publications, but for this project, the establishments with positive payroll during a year and no employment in March of that year are not counted as active.[4]

The geographic unit of analysis used for this study is Labor Market Areas (LMAs). These are aggregations of all the 3141 counties[5] in the USA into 394 geographical regions, each containing a high proportion of the locale's residential–work commutes, as defined for 1990 by TOLBERT and SIZER (1996) for the Department of Agriculture. Many of the 394 LMAs cut across state boundaries to represent better the functioning of local economic areas. (States themselves are too broad to function as integrated economic areas, and their borders frequently cut through highly integrated areas.) Some relatively isolated smaller Commuting Zones have been grouped with adjacent areas so that all LMAs had a minimum population of 100 000 people. Despite considerable differences across LMAs in terms of area, population density and total population, most are quite similar in their economic structures. Their percentage of workers in different economic sectors shows little variation for transportation, communications, wholesale and retail trade, consumer services, health, education, social services, and government employees, which together account for 56–60% of all workers in each LMA (REYNOLDS, 1999). For a discussion of alternative units of observation, see GLAESER (2000).[6]

The present paper distinguishes six broad industry sectors to facilitate analysis of different industries' sensitivities to factors affecting their growth, and to control better for aggregation effects in regions with different shares of weak industries: manufacturing, agriculture and mining sectors. It expands both the scope and the industrial detail beyond that of previous studies, most of which were limited to manufacturing. Industry codes are based on the most recently reported four-digit Standard Industrial Classifications (SIC) code for each establishment, except for new multi-unit firms the SIC of their primary location is used. Most new firms are single location firms. There are very few new multi-unit firms, and for most of them, the industry classification of their primary location is the same as that of their secondary locations. The most recently reported SIC code is used rather than the first reported SIC, because the precision and accuracy of the codes tend to increase over time (Table 1).[7]

These six broad sectors distinguish industries that might differ in their sensitivity to local market conditions. For instance, local consumer services and construction are more dependent on local regional demand than are manufacturing and distributive services, while manufacturing and distributive services may have greater

Table 1.   Industry classification

Sector	Standard Industrial Classifications
Distributive	4000–5199 (transportation, communication, public utilities and wholesale trade)
Manufacturing	2000–3999
Business services	7300–7399 and 8700–8799 (including engineering, accounting, research and management services)
Extractive	0700–1499 (agricultural, services and mining)
Retail trade	5200–5999
Local market	1500–1799 and 6000–8999 excluding business services (construction, consumer and financial services)

dependence on the supply of semi- and unskilled labour. Growth in extractive industries is limited by the local supply of natural resources and arable land.

Variation in growth of local economic areas

Employment in an area tends to keep pace with the growth of population in that area, *ceteris parebus*, so it is useful to examine both the rate of increase in employment and how it differs from the rate of increase in population. It is not clear whether the growing economy is attracting the increasing population, or if the growing population is simply causing the economy to expand to keep up with local demand and supply. Table 2 focuses on the LMAs whose employment growth rates from 1991 to 1996 were among the highest or lowest in the country. Further, the last column shows the extent to which each area's employment growth exceeded its population growth rate. For the LMA growth rate comparisons in Tables 2 and 3, rates of change of both employment and population are expressed as the 5-year change divided by the 1991 level.

There is considerable variation in regional growth rates during this period. Employment change ranged from a low of −5.9% for the LMA containing Hilo, HI (i.e. Hawaii), to a high of 47.1% for St George, UT (Utah). The highest excess of employment growth over population growth was the 35.2% in Kankakee, IL (Illinois), followed by Laurel, MS (Mississippi), with 30.9%. There were also many cases where employment change did not appear to be closely related to population change. About 50 LMAs had lower growth in employment than in population in the first half of the 1990s. The poor employment growth of the Hilo LMA cited above was accompanied by a population growth of 9.7%, so that its relative employment growth was −15.7% over the 5 years. Note that two of the 10 LMAs with the highest employment growth had relatively low population growth, while only three of the 10 LMAs with the highest rates of employment loss also had population losses.

Table 3 shows the 5-year growth rates for the ten largest and smallest LMAs, based on their total employment in 1991. Employment growth rates appear to be substantially higher in the smallest LMAs, averaging 19.6% compared with the 3.9% average of the largest LMAs. In the largest LMAs, employment growth just barely kept up with population growth, so their 5-year relative employment growth was a mere 0.6%. The population growth rates of the largest and smallest LMAs were quite similar, so even after controlling for population growth, the smallest LMAs had significantly higher relative employment growth.

CONTRIBUTION OF ENTREPRENEURSHIP TO ECONOMIC GROWTH

It is important to clarify our definition of the entrepreneurial firm. A cursory review of entrepreneurial studies illustrates the multiple ways in which researchers have conceptualized the entrepreneurial firm (DAILY *et al.*, 2002). These range from a high-growth firm to an owner-managed firm to a founder-run business. Inconsistency in the treatment of what constitutes an entrepreneurial firm may cloud empirical and theoretical advances in the field, as it is difficult to synthesize across studies where there is little commonality in firms defining characteristics. The definition of the entrepreneurial firm on which this study is based is consistent with the concept of independent entrepreneurship (SHARMA and CHRISMAN, 1999), defined as the process whereby an individual or group of individuals acting independently of any association with an existing organization, create a new organization. Thus, the definition operates outside the context of a previously established organization.

What is the relative contribution of entrepreneurial firms to economic growth?[8] It is evident from Table 4 that new firm start-ups play a far more important role in the economy than has previously been recognized. For the economy as a whole, over the 5 years of the early 1990s, employment in 1996 of establishments that started up after 1991 accounted for 26.3% of the mean employment over that period. The growth from expanding establishments that existed in 1991 was only 17.7% (including high and low growth), and this increase was offset by the loss of 13.5% of their employment from shrinking establishments, and another 20.5% loss from the deaths of some of those 1991 establishments.

In the traditional Solow model, the entry of new large plants played a predominant role, while in the Romer model, the focus has shifted from scale economies to externalities. Support for this is found when growth is distinguished by the type of business – organized in single- versus multi-unit firms. The employment growth rate from new single-unit firms/ establishments is much greater than that from new

Entrepreneurship and Economic Growth

916 *Zoltan J. Acs and Catherine Armington*

Table 2. Five-year growth rates for 1991–96 by Labor Market Area (LMA) for LMAs with the highest and lowest employment growth rates

LMA		State	1991 Employment	Employment growth (A) (%)	Population growth (B) (%)	(A)−(B)ᵃ (%)
Highest employment growth						
359	St George	UT	34 400	47.1	24.0	23.0
298	Monett	MO	27 362	39.9	18.6	21.4
312	Austin	TX	321 222	38.8	18.5	20.3
242	Kankakee	IL	41 609	38.8	3.6	35.2
360	Provo	UT	87 500	37.2	18.1	19.1
379	Las Vegas	NV	391 494	35.9	28.1	7.8
284	Colorado Springs	CO	138 892	35.8	18.9	16.9
352	Grand Junction	CO	45 682	34.5	15.0	19.5
354	Flagstaff	AZ	60 529	34.4	18.5	15.9
28	Laurel	MS	24 645	32.9	2.0	30.9
Lowest employment growth						
177	Syracuse	NY	401 336	−1.5	−2.0	0.5
383	Los Angeles	CA	5 639 265	−1.6	3.9	−5.5
208	Springfield	MA	241 400	−2.0	−1.4	−0.6
187	Sunbury	PA	60 697	−2.5	3.0	−5.6
371	Bakersfield	CA	138 692	−3.1	8.5	−11.6
183	Watertown	NY	60 656	−3.5	1.3	−4.8
179	Binghamton	NY	103 907	−3.6	−3.4	−0.1
347	Honolulu	HI	400 509	−3.8	4.3	−8.1
193	Poughkeepsie	NY	238 525	−5.8	1.6	−7.4
356	Hilo	HI	41 089	−5.9	9.7	−15.7

Notes: ᵃRate at which employment increased in excess of the overall growth rate of the population.
   Growth is measured as a 5-year change divided by the 1991 level.
Source: 1989–96 LEEM File, US Bureau of the Census.

Table 3. Five-year growth rates for 1991–96 by Labor Market Area (LMA) for the largest and the smallest LMAs

LMA		State	1991 Empoyment	Employment growth (A) (%)	Population growth (B) (%)	(A)−(B) (%)
Largest LMAs						
383	Los Angeles	CA	5 639 265	−1.6	3.9	−5.5
194	New York	NY	4 290 264	0.6	1.1	−0.5
243	Chicago	IL	3 302 354	7.0	4.5	2.5
113	ArlntonWashBalt	VA	2 639 292	7.4	3.8	3.6
196	Newark	NJ	2 359 911	3.1	2.4	0.7
197	Philadelphia	PA	2 154 296	2.5	0.4	2.0
205	Boston	MA	2 143 471	7.1	1.9	5.1
116	Detroit	MI	1 921 754	13.0	3.6	9.4
378	San Francisco	CA	1 772 575	3.1	3.6	−0.5
320	Houston	TX	1 567 212	8.2	9.8	−0.5
Average of 10 largest				3.9	3.3	0.6
Smallest LMAs						
77	Lake City	FL	27 522	15.1	11.7	3.4
298	Monett	MO	27 362	39.9	18.6	21.4
158	Athens	OH	26 508	10.7	3.2	7.6
337	Ardmore	OL	26 068	16.4	3.5	12.9
258	Blytheville	AR	25 229	19.9	−5.8	25.7
283	North Platte	NE	24 722	15.9	1.5	14.4
28	Laurel	MS	24 645	32.9	2.0	30.9
327	Brownwood	TX	23 711	19.6	5.4	14.2
324	Big Spring	TX	21 698	10.7	1.9	8.8
245	FortLeonardWood	MO	19 895	11.9	−1.0	12.9
Average of 10 smallest				19.6	4.4	15.2

Notes: ᵃRate at which employment increased in excess of the overall growth rate of the population.
   Growth is measured as a 5-year change divided by the 1991 level.
Source: 1989–96 LEEM File, US Bureau of the Census.

Employment Growth and Entrepreneurial Activity in Cities 917

Table 4. *Establishment employment and 1991–96 net and gross job flows, by firm type and by industry sector*

| | Employment | | 1991—96 employment change as a percentage of mean employment | | | | | | |
| | | | | | Expansion | | | |
Establishment class	1991	1996	Net (%)	Birth (%)	High (%)	Low (%)	Shrink (%)	Death (%)
All	92 265 576	102 149 281	10.2	26.3	8.9	8.8	−13.5	−20.5
Firm type								
Single unit	38 532 294	44 811 609	15.1	31.3	9.8	10.3	−11.1	−25.3
Multi-unit	53 731 429	57 324 994	6.5	22.6	8.3	7.7	−15.3	−16.9
Industry sector								
Business services	7 780 445	10 385 762	28.7	43.6	7.4	17.8	−14.6	−25.5
Distributon	11 887 375	12 719 155	6.8	23.4	9.4	10.5	−14.8	−21.7
Extractive	1 269 551	1 237 600	−2.5	24.5	8.6	10.7	−18.5	−27.9
Local market	33 434 183	37 773 144	12.2	25.8	9.4	8.5	−12.8	−18.7
Manufactures	18 450 502	18 556 546	0.6	13.3	9.4	7.6	−14.2	−15.5
Retail trade	19 443 520	21 477 074	9.9	33.3	8.0	5.4	−12.3	−24.4

Notes: All growth rates are based on the mean of 1991 and 1996 employment for the class of establishments.
Size classified in 1991, except new establishements classified in 1996; type = multi if multi-unit in either year.
¹High-growth establishments expanded by an average of at least 15% per year (adding at least five employees).
Source: 1989–96 LEEM file, US Bureau of the Census.

branch plants/locations, 31.3 versus 22.6%. This same 9% difference is maintained between the net employment growth rates for single-unit firms versus establishments in multi-location firms, 15.1 versus 6.5%. These differences strongly suggest that the role of externalities leading to new firms and plants is greater than that of scale economies as a driving factor behind growth.

Each of the six sectors had similar patterns of gross employment change rates, with the notable exception of the very high rates of increase in business services employment from both births (43.6%) and expansions (25.2%, including both high and low expansion rates). The exceptionally low rate of increase from births in manufacturing (13.3%) supports GEROSKI's (1995) analysis that new firm births do not appear to play an important role in manufacturing.

These data also allow us to evaluate the frequent claim that the majority of new jobs are created by a relatively small number of rapidly growing establishments (BHIDE, 2000). If this assessment was limited to gross job growth from the expansion of existing establishments, then it is true that a small number of high-growth establishments created more jobs than the much larger number of low-growth establishments – increases of 8.9% from high- versus 8.8% from low-growth establishments. Only about 4% of establishments had high average growth rates (at least 15% per year for 5 years). However, the total employment growth from the expansion of existing establishments was much less than that from the birth of new establishments, except for the manufacturing sector. And the rates of job loss from the population of existing establishments greatly exceeded their gains from expansions. These patterns are also consistent across sectors and firm types.

To gain further insight into the contribution of new organizations to economic growth, the employment and growth of all establishments that are single-unit firms have been distinguished from those owned by multi-unit firms (whose secondary establishments are commonly called plants or branches), and then these are separated into age groups according to the age of each establishment. Fig. 1 shows the distribution of total US private non-farm employment in 1995 by the age of establishments for those in both single- and multi-unit firms. It also shows a number of interesting characteristics of US businesses. First, new establishments less than 2 years old account for only 3% of total employment; those that are new firms (single-unit establishments) account for just 1% of employment, or one-third of the total. However, in the subsequent 2 years, the balance between new firms and new multi-unit locations changes, so that establishments under 4 years old of each type account for 7% of total employment. Obviously, both *de novo* firms and new secondary-location establishments contribute new employment opportunities.[9]

At the other extreme, note that establishments at least 10 years old account for 60% of total employment – most people are employed in older establishments. Contrary to a popular image of insecure jobs in obsolete production facilities, the typical older establishment offers jobs with good prospects for continued employment. Note also that the majority (36 versus 24%) of employment in these older establishments is in those belonging to multi-unit firms. Because many successful single-unit firms expand by starting up secondary locations, this dominance by multi-unit firms is to be expected for older businesses.

Fig. 2 shows net job growth for 1995–96 distributed

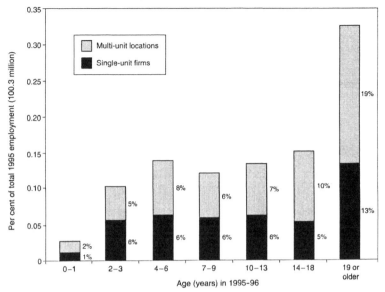

Fig. 1. *Distributions of employment in 1995 by age and type of establishment*

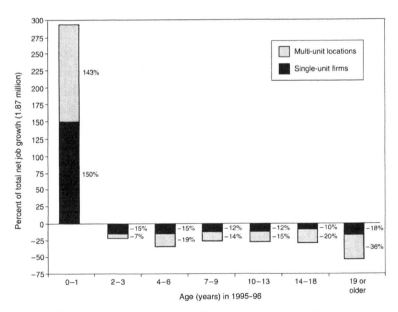

Fig. 2. *Net job growth distribution in 1995–96 by age and type of establishment*

by the age and type of establishments. The class of establishments less than 2 years old accounts for all net job growth. Establishments in all other age classes lost employment on average, whether they were single-unit firms or multi-unit locations. Among the older age classes, the share of losses by firm type was roughly proportional to their share of employment, with the exception of the oldest group. Establishments incurred a disproportionately large share of losses over 18 years old that belong to multi-unit firms. This is consistent with the trend of the 1980 s and 1990s that saw a shift towards both smaller plants and less large firms.

According to HALTIWANGER and KRIZAN (1999, p. 94),

> for employment growth, it looks as if the more important factor is age and not size. Put differently, most small establishments are new. Thus, the role of small business in job creation may simply reflect the role of births and in turn young establishments. ... One clear pattern that emerges is that net job creation rates decline with plant age.[10]

It is clear from Figs 1 and 2 that new firms play an important role in employment growth.

EMPIRICAL MODEL

From the above discussion, it should be clear that the major hypotheses concerning the regional variation in growth rates are related to dynamic externalities, and one way to capture the extent of these spillovers is to examine how the growth rates vary across regions. The literature suggests that higher employment growth rates should be associated with increased entrepreneurial activity, increased industry diversity and higher levels of human capital. Detailed definitions of these explanatory (independent or exogenous) variables are given below.

The flow of entrepreneurial activity is measured as the new firm birth rate, including both new single-unit firms (establishments or locations) with less than 500 employees, and the primary locations of new multi-unit firms with less than 500 employees firm-wide (ARMINGTON and ACS, 2002).[11] Firm birth rates are calculated for each of the 394 LMAs, for each industry sector and for the total private sector (all industry). The number of new firms in each LMA would tend to be proportional to the size of the LMA, so these numbers are standardized by dividing by the size of the local labour force (in thousands) in the central year. Labour force is preferred to population or employment as a size indicator, because it is a better measure of the number of potential entrepreneurs. Thus, birth rates represent the number of new firms per 1000 of labour force in each LMA. This labour market approach has a particular appeal in that it is based on the theory of entrepreneurial choice. That is, someone starts each new business in the local economy

that has chosen entrepreneurship over employment in an existing firm. The entrepreneur starting a new business is assumed to live in the same LMA as the new firm and to have benefited from spillovers within that region. Higher rates of entrepreneurial activity are expected to be associated with higher employment growth in the same region. This approach has the added property that there is a clear lower bound of 0.00 (for no new businesses) and a theoretical upper bound of 1.00, which would represent the extreme case where every worker within a region started a new business during a year.

There are two important qualifications to be noted concerning firm birth rate. The first has to do with the timing of the recognition of the new firm. While firms enter the regional economy continuously, the LEEM file annually reports only the first quarter employment of each establishment and firm, representing their employees during their 15 March pay-period each year. If an establishment hires its first employee after March, the new firm is not counted as active until the following year. Therefore, the new firms being counted have had employees for an average of 6 months by the time the LEEM file records their 'first' employment (ACS and ARMINGTON, 1998). Second, the average time between an entrepreneur's decision to create a new organization and the initial operation of the business is about 2 years (REYNOLDS *et al.*, 2002). Therefore, much of the entrepreneurial activity has taken place 2–3 years earlier than the first appearance of the firm's employment in the LEEM file.

The second measure of entrepreneurial activity measures the share of business owners in the area. This measure has been used in several European studies (e.g. WENNEKERS and THURIK, 1999). It is less of a measure of entrepreneurship and more a measure of the local dominance of business ownership. Proprietors are members of the labour force who are also business owners. In addition to those who own firms with employees, this measure includes the self-employed with no employees. The share of proprietors is defined for each LMA as the number of proprietors in 1991 divided by the labour force in 1991. This share averaged 20.5% nationally and varied from a low of 9.9% to a high of 44.8% across LMAs.

Two measures of agglomeration effects that characterized local economies are included. Many studies have attempted to measure industry specialization within an economic area with a simple measure of establishment density per square mile of the area, but this may be more indicative of the extent of physical crowding of businesses, which is related to the probable relative costs of doing business there. Therefore, specialization is measured' as the relative intensity of the sectors establishments, defined as the number of establishments in the sector in a region divided by the region's population. After standardizing by the national average, this measure is identical to the specialization measure used by GLAESER *et al.* (1992). Industry intensity should be positively related to employment growth if specialization is important for regional growth. A negative relationship would suggest that the competitive effects of specialization are stronger than its contribution to knowledge spillovers.

To control for the vast differences in the physical density of economic activity, establishment density, defined as the number of establishments per square mile in that industry in 1991, was used. If firms in cities or other areas with high concentrations of businesses benefit from the closeness of other businesses in the same sector, then higher establishment densities should be positively related to employment growth. Since the regression analysis uses each area's relative levels of establishment density in each industry rather than absolute levels, there is no need to correct for differences in national industry presence or demand. Establishment density should be positively related to local growth rates if agglomerations drive demand or increase network externalities (CICCONE and HALL, 1996).

Two measures of human capital were included that have been found to have a positive impact on regional growth in previous studies (SIMON and NARDINELLI, 2002). The first is the share of adults with at least a high-school degree, with adults defined as those 25 years or older. Those adults without high-school degrees are the principal supply of unskilled and semiskilled labour for work in manufacturing branch plants and retail or unskilled service establishments. Higher shares of high-school graduates indicate a generally higher level of human capital in the area. In 1990, 73.0% of adults nationally had at least a high-school degree.

The second measure of educational attainment is the share of college graduates, defined as the number of adults with college degrees in 1990 divided by the total number of adults. This is a proxy measure of both the technical skills needed in the economy, and the skills needed to start and build a business. In 1990, an average of 15.9% of the adult population had a college degree. Naturally, the number of college degree holders is included in the number of high-school degree holders, so these two measures will suffer from collinearity, and they will be tested separately. It is expected that employment growth will be positively related to higher average levels of education at both the high-school and the college levels (GLAESER *et al.*, 1995).

To control for differences in the size distribution of businesses in each industry and region, average local establishment size, measured for each industry sector and economic area by dividing the number of local employees in 1991 by the number of local establishments in 1991 in each sector, is included. Mean establishment sizes vary nationally from 11 employees for the local market sector to 55 for manufacturing. Regions dominated by large branch plants or firms are likely to be less competitive than those with many smaller

establishments. The spatial division of labour within multi-site enterprises has resulted in some areas being dominated by externally owned branch plants performing routine assembly and production services or by large-scale retail outlets.

All variables are used in the regressions in their standardized form, so that the national mean is subtracted from each variable and the resulting relative rate is divided by its standard deviation across all LMAs. Thus, each standardized variable measures how the area differs from the national average in terms of the standard deviation of that variable. Standardizing their distribution over LMAs so that each has a mean of zero and a standard deviation of 1 allows us to make direct comparisons of the estimated standardized β-coefficients for different industry sectors in Tables 6–9. Each coefficient can then be interpreted as the share of the independent variable's standard deviation that is reflected in the local deviation of the employment change rate from average rates.

Of course, some variables might be endogenous or correlated with other variables. The share of the regional population with high-school degrees is highly correlated with the share holding college degrees. Certainly, the average size of establishments is smaller when the share of proprietors is higher, as confirmed by their simple correlation of -0.63. Both industry intensity and establishment density are partially the effect of firm start-ups in the past, as well as contributing factors during the period under study. Some of these econometrically will be controlled by separately estimating a birth equation and then including the predicted value of births in the employment growth equation. For others, alternative models with subsets of these variables are estimated.

The counts of firm births and numbers of establishments and employees were tabulated by LMA, industry sector and year from the LEEM file at the Center for Economic Studies, US Bureau of the Census. All other variables were tabulated from county-level data collected (often from other agencies) on a CD-ROM entitled 'USA Counties 1998' by the US Census Bureau. Table 5 presents summary statistics for all variables. Correlation coefficients reveal three important findings. First, firm formation rates are highly correlated, e.g. the correlation between 1990–93 and 1993–96 is 0.96 and between 1993–96 and 1996–99 it is 0.96. Second, the correlation of employment growth rates over the same period is 0.40, 0.31 and 0.18, respectively. In fact, from year to year, there is no correlation between employment growth rates. Third, the correlation between human capital and employment growth increased over the decade for both college and high-school graduation rates suggesting that the source of employment growth has been shifting to more knowledge-based activities. A data appendix with additional detail is available from the authors.

Table 5. *Summary statistics for Labour Market Area (LMA) level regional variables*

	Mean	Standard deviation	Minimum	Maximum
Three-year average employment growth rate: $e(t+3)/e(t)^{\star 1/3}-1$				
1990	0.0188	0.0196	−0.0278	0.1390
1993	0.0273	0.0149	−0.0243	0.0902
1996	0.0214	0.0150	−0.0207	0.0989
Entrepreneurial activity: average firm formations/LF$(t)\star 1000$				
1990	3.605	0.872	2.192	9.239
1993	3.710	0.932	2.060	9.870
1996	3.477	0.876	1.984	9.876
Business specialization: establishments(t)/population$(t)\star 1000$				
1990	2.146	0.332	1.151	4.123
1993	2.176	0.347	1.155	4.464
1996	2.214	0.364	1.131	4.728
Business density: ln(establishments(t)/square miles)				
1990	0.352	1.168	−3.82	4.80
1993	0.397	1.159	−3.73	4.78
1996	0.441	1.157	−3.67	4.82
Establishment size: employment(t)/establishments(t)				
1990	14.93	2.97	8.14	21.51
1993	15.05	2.87	8.19	21.03
1996	15.58	2.90	8.25	22.67
Share of proprietors: proprietors(t)/labour force(t)				
1990	0.205	0.058	0.106	0.390
1993	0.203	0.055	0.099	0.389
1996	0.212	0.057	0.106	0.404
1990 Human capital (share of adults 25 years and over)				
Basic (high school degrees)	0.721	0.080	0.459	0.883
Higher (college degress)	0.159	0.050	0.069	0.320

Sources: 1989–99 LEEM file, US Bureau of the Census, US Bureau of Labor Statistics.

EMPIRICAL RESULTS

A regression model is estimated where the dependent variable is (compounded) average annual employment growth rates over three 3-year periods of the 1990s. This is measured as the third root of the ratio of 1993 employment to 1990 employment minus one in each LMA and sector, repeated for three 3-year periods. The annual average growth rate of each local economic area is defined as:

$$\text{Average annual employment growth rate}_{srt+1}$$
$$= (empl_{srt+1}/empl_{srt})^{\star 1/3}-1 \qquad (2)$$

For all industries together, the local growth rates varied from −1.2% annual average to 8.0%. The equations are estimated for 394 LMAs for all industries together for three different periods, for lagged employment

growth as well as for each of the six industry sectors separately.

Table 6 presents three important results in the estimated model of local growth differences. First, the coefficient on the firm birth rate is positive, large and statistically significant, as hypothesized for all three periods. Note that the standard deviation of the employment growth rate is about 0.015 and that of firm formation rates is about 0.9. Therefore, the estimated standardized coefficient of entrepreneurial activity of about 0.55 indicates that a difference of one firm formation per 1000 labour force in a region's average is associated with a difference of about three-quarters of a point in the region's growth rate. The findings of positive relationships between firm birth and local economic growth rate differences are inconsistent with FRITSCH (1997), who found no relationship between firm birth and employment growth in Germany, but they are consistent with REYNOLDS (1999), who found a similar relationship.

The coefficient on the share of proprietors is positive and statistically significant for 1990. However, it is insignificant for the later two periods, suggesting that the greater the share of proprietors in a region, the higher the growth rate only in recession years. The coefficient for the share of proprietors is much smaller than that for entrepreneurial activity, suggesting that it is not so much the accumulated stock of entrepreneurial activity but the flow that is important for economic growth. This result suggests that it is younger firms (age and not smaller size per se) that are more important for promoting growth and productivity. These results are inconsistent with CARREE et al. (2002).

Second, the negative and statistically significant coefficient on industry specialization suggests that greater geographic specialization (or less industrial diversity) leads to less growth rather than to greater growth. These results are consistent for the whole decade. This suggests that specialization does not generally lead to higher levels of technological externalities or other knowledge spillovers that promote growth in the same industry sector. This is consistent with the findings of GLAESER et al. (1992), FELDMAN and AUDRETSCH (1999) and ACS et al. (2002).

The negative and statistically significant coefficients on establishment density suggest that when other factors are the same, employment growth will be greater in regions with less physical crowding in their industry. Thus, when measured by the number of establishments per square mile, the agglomeration effect on growth seems negative for LMAs. This is in contrast with the findings of GLAESER et al. (1992) and CICCONE and HALL (1996), who used growth in other industries in each area as an indication of the size of the agglomeration effect and found a positive relationship with growth. Indeed, it contrasts with much of the theoretical literature on agglomerations

Table 6. Analysis of factors associated with differences in employment growth rates in Labor Market Areas (LMAs) by 3 year period

Three-year employment change rate (t to $t+3$)	1990	1993	1996
Adjusted R^2	0.397	0.298	0.319
Observations	394	394	394
Entrepreneurial activity: average annual $t+1$ to $t+3$ formation rate	**0.498** 9.47	**0.639** 11.38	**0.555** 10.15
Share of proprietors: proprietors(t)/labour force(t)	**0.273** 4.44	0.082 1.26	0.124 1.84
Business specialization: establishment(t)/population(t)	**−0.382** −6.17	**−0.201** −3.00	**−0.392** −6.14
Business density: ln(establishment(t)/square miles)	**−0.411** −6.76	**−0.243** 3.79	0.094 1.50
Basic human capital 1990: high-school degree/adults (25 years and older)	**0.144** 2.32	**0.205** 3.03	**0.293** 4.32
Higher human capital 1990: college degree/adults (25 years and older)	−0.056 −0.88	−0.119 −1.60	0.097 1.41
Establishment size: employment(t)/establishments(t)	**0.255** 4.00	**0.427** 6.59	**0.143** 2.25

Notes: Employment was derived from the Census's Country Business Patterns.
Data are estimated standardized β-coefficients with t-ratios below, **bold** if significant at $p=0.05$.

(KRUGMAN, 1991). Perhaps these older studies' inability to measure adequately the impact of differences in the level of competition resulted in the agglomeration variables serving instead as proxies for competition.

Third, human capital appears important for employment growth. The greater the proportion of the area's adults with a high-school degree, the higher the employment growth rates. During the early 1990s, the additional impact of higher proportions of college graduates was negative but insignificant. However, by the latter part of the decade, the coefficient on college degree was positive and significant. These results are consistent with GLAESER et al. (1995) and SIMON and NARDINELLI (2002). The importance of regional differences in the share of proprietors, and the importance of business density, appears to be falling during the 1990s, while the importance of human capital is increasing.

To address the endogeneity issue, the model has been re-estimated with 3- and 6-year lags using employment growth for two subsequent periods. It has also averaged growth rates over 3 years to control for the business cycle effects (i.e. positive intertemporal correlation between regional growth rates that often exists) that might be erroneously captured by the firm entry rate resulting from positive correlation between growth and subsequent firm entry rates. The results from Table 6 for 1990–93 are repeated in Table 7 for reasons of comparison. The adjusted R^2 drops off as expected as one moves away from the start-up year. Most of the other variables become weaker compared with Table 6. The results are consistent with the simple correlation results of the start-up rate being invariant over time across regions.

Table 8 presents results for six industry sectors.[12] The coefficient on entrepreneurial activity is positive and statistically significant for five of the six industry sectors, with the exception of manufacturing, where it was insignificant. This exception explains the prior findings of industrial organization economists that new firm start-ups are not important for employment growth in manufacturing (e.g. GEROSKI, 1995). This also does not support some of the research on clusters. Much of the research in industrial organization, labour economics and regional science has been limited to analysis of data from the manufacturing sector, and these results have been frequently generalized to the whole economy. It appears that those generalizations from the behaviour of manufacturing firms are not always valid, but may be valid for other industries dominated by large plants. Certain aspects of the results are consistent with both AUDRETSCH and FRITSCH (2002) and GLAESER et al. (1992), who found the impact of competition on growth stronger outside of manufacturing than in manufacturing.[13] The coefficient on the share of the proprietor is small, inconsistent and mostly insignificant, suggesting the presence of business owners does not lead to employment growth.

The negative and statistically significant coefficient on industry specialization suggests that greater geographic specialization lead to less rather than to greater growth. These results are again robust for all industry sectors with the exception of manufacturing, where the coefficient is positive but not significant. This suggests that specialization does not generally lead to higher levels of technological externalities or other knowledge spillovers that promote growth in the same industry sector. This is consistent with the findings of

Table 7. Analysis of local factors associated with differences in lagged employment growth rates in Labor Market Areas

Three-year employment change rate	1990–93	1993–96	1996–99
Adjusted R^2	0.397	0.215	0.282
Observations	394	394	394
Entrepreneurial activity: average annual formation rate 1991–93	**0.498**	**0.535**	**0.516**
	9.47	8.92	9.00
Share of proprietors 1990: proprietors/labour force	**0.273**	0.081	0.080
	4.44	1.15	1.19
Business specialization 1990: establishments/population	**−0.382**	**−0.217**	**−0.347**
	−6.17	−3.07	−5.13
Business density 1990: ln(establishments/square miles)	**−0.411**	**−0.244**	0.076
	−6.76	3.51	1.15
Basic human capital 1990: high-school degree/adults (25 years or older)	**0.144**	**0.170**	**0.235**
	2.32	2.39	3.46
Human human capital 1990: college degree/adults (25 years or older)	−0.056	−0.023	**0.176**
	−0.88	−0.32	2.53
Establishment size 1990: employment/establishments	**0.255**	**0.347**	**0.146**
	4.00	4.77	2.10

Notes: Employment was derived from the Census's Country Business Patterns.
Data are estimated standardized β-coefficients with t-ratios below, **bold** if significant at $p = 0.05$.

Table 8. Analysis of factors associated with differences in employment growth rates in Labor Market Areas by industry sectors

1991–96 Employment change rate	All industries	Business services	Distributive	Extractive	Local market	Manufac-turing	Retail
R^2	0.33	0.10	0.13	0.31	0.44	0.14	0.25
Observations	394	394	394	394	394	394	394
Entrepreneurial activity: average annual 1991–96 births/1993 labour force	**0.62**	**0.57**	**0.41**	**0.42**	**0.54**	−0.04	**0.54**
	11.3	4.96	6.86	5.19	11.3	−0.59	8.98
Share of proprietors: 1991 proprietors/labour force	**0.16**	**−0.14**	0.01	0.01	0.03	**0.21**	0.02
	2.81	−2.54	0.10	0.09	0.61	3.79	0.34
Business specialization: 1991 industry establishment/population	**−0.30**	**−0.57**	**−0.28**	**−0.53**	**−0.50**	0.14	**−0.34**
	−4.78	−3.97	−4.10	−6.30	−8.40	1.92	−5.19
Density: 1991 industry establishment/square mile	**−0.22**	−0.05	**−0.11**	**−0.14**	**−0.13**	**−0.15**	**−0.23**
	−4.61	−0.91	−1.97	−2.84	−2.91	−2.75	−4.78
Basic human capital: 1990 high-school degree/ adults (25 years and over)	**0.14**	0.12	**0.16**	0.03	−0.08	0.06	−0.04
	2.02	1.61	2.06	0.40	−1.23	0.87	−0.56
Higher human capital: 1990 college degree/adults	−0.11	−0.03	0.06	0.13	0.10	**−0.15**	0.02
	−1.66	−0.34	0.73	1.87	1.51	−2.02	0.22
Establishment size: 1991 industry employment/ industry establishment	**0.20**	**−0.17**	−0.07	**−0.41**	**−0.25**	−0.09	0.07
	3.26	−3.02	−1.03	−9.30	−4.55	−1.61	0.96

Note: Data are estimated standardized β-coefficients with t-ratios below, **bold** if significant at $p = 0.05$.

GLAESER *et al.* (1992), FELDMAN and AUDRETSCH (1999) and ACS *et al.* (2002).

The alternative model formulations shown in Table 9 allow closer examination of the association between entrepreneurship and employment growth. When the all-industry regression was run without the college graduate measure, the results were virtually unchanged. Both these human capital variables were dropped and this act also had no substantial impact on the estimated parameters for the remaining variables. Therefore, the results are robust with respect to the inclusion or exclusion of the human capital variables.[14]

While birth seems the best available measure of the relative levels of competition (low barriers to entry) within industries and areas, it also involves some new employment in the new firms, adding directly to the growth of the region. Earlier work found that local rates of new firm birth were strongly related to many of these same characteristics of local economic areas (ARMINGTON and ACS, 2002). The local firm birth rate could be substantially predicted as a function of local industry intensity and establishment density, average establishment size, share of proprietors, local income and population growth, unemployment rate,

Table 9. *Alternative models of Labor Market Area (LMA) employment growth rates*

1991–96 Employment change rate	A	B	C	D	E	F
R^2	0.33	0.31	0.30	0.35	0.29	0.08
Observations	394	394	394	394	394	394
Entrepreneurial activity: average annual 1991–96 births/1993 labour force	**0.62**	**0.59**	**0.59**		**0.56**	
	11.3	11.40	11.3		10.7	
Share of proprietors: 1991 proprietors/labour force	**0.16**	**0.18**	**0.18**		0.07	**0.16**
	2.81	3.04	3.14		1.45	2.31
Business specialization: 1991 establishment/population	**−0.30**	**−0.30**	**−0.26**	**−0.35**	**−0.31**	−0.05
	−4.78	−4.82	−4.87	−6.43	−5.01	−0.71
Density: 1991 establishment/square mile	**−0.22**	**−0.24**	**−0.23**	**−0.23**	**−0.20**	**−0.22**
	−4.61	−5.13	−5.10	−5.16	−4.25	−4.16
Basic human capital: 1990 high-school degree/adults (25 years and older)	**0.14**	0.07			**0.14**	−0.05
	2.02	1.25			2.11	−0.65
Higher human capital: 1990 college degree/adults	−0.11				−0.06	0.14
	−1.66				−0.91	1.87
Establishment size: 1991 employment/established	**0.20**	**0.17**	**0.19**	**0.15**		−0.04
	3.26	2.95	3.35	3.11		−0.56
Predicted firm birth rate[a]: 1995–96 average annual births/labour force				**0.72**		
				12.5		
Unexplained birth rate[a]: actual–predicted 1995–96 birth				**0.12**		
				2.91		

Notes: [a]Based on an estimate of the average of 1995 and 1996 firm births per 1000 local labour force as a function of establishment size, industry intensity, growth in personal income and in population, share of proprietors, unemployment rate, share of adults with high-school degrees, and college degrees. The unexplained variation is primarily associated with less easily quantified economic, social and geographic factors not correlated with these other factors.
Data are estimated standardized β-coefficients with t-ratios below, **bold** if significant at $p = 0.05$.

and both high-school and college educational attainment shares. By substituting into equation (D) both the predicted firm birth rates and the unexplained (or residual) component of the actual firm birth rates in place of the actual firm birth rates, the explanatory power of the regression increases while the qualitative results are unchanged.

The coefficient on the predicted firm birth rate is very similar to that on the actual firm birth rate. It can be seen that even the unexplained portion of the firm birth[15] has a significant positive relationship to local area growth rate variation, indicating that other local characteristics (missing variables in the birth rate model) that lead to higher firm birth rates also lead to higher growth rates, although the coefficient on this is small.

Because establishment size and the share of proprietors are negatively correlated, equation (E) was also estimated without the establishment size variable. The results are again robust with respect to this specification of the model. Finally, equation (F) estimates equation (A) without the firm birth rate. The results are unequivocal: without the new firm birth rate, the equation loses most of its explanatory power and most of the other coefficients become insignificant. Regional growth rate variation is closely associated with the regional variation in new firm start-up rates.

CONCLUSIONS

Recent theories of economic growth view local externalities, as opposed to scale economies, as the primary engine in generating growth in cities and their closely integrated surrounding counties (LMAs). While scale economies operate at the plant level, externalities operate at the firm level, primarily through entrepreneurial activity. The impact of these externalities on regional employment growth was examined from an entrepreneurial perspective by examining the relationship of local economic growth to local entrepreneurial activity. Using data on 394 local economic areas and six industrial sectors, covering the entire (non-farm) private-sector economy of the USA, it was found that higher rates of entrepreneurial activity were strongly associated with faster growth of local economies.

Analysis suggests that new organizations play an important role in taking advantage of knowledge externalities within a region, and that entrepreneurship may be the vehicle by which these spillovers contribute to economic growth. Specifically, it is found that new firms are more important than the stock of small firms in a region, but the manufacturing sector appears to be an exception. These results, while preliminary, suggest that theories of growth should study entrepreneurship to understand better how knowledge spillovers operate.

Several qualifiers are in order. Perhaps most importantly, employment growth is not the same as economic growth. Therefore, the issue of productivity growth is still unanswered. While the direct aggregate impact of new firms may be small, nevertheless the survivors play an important role in employment creation.

Acknowledgements – Research was initiated and supported by the Kauffman Center for Entrepreneurial Leadership, Ewing Marion Kauffman Foundation, as the first step of a larger project to analyse the causes of regional differences in new firm formation rates in the USA. Research was carried out at the Center for Economic Studies (CES), US Bureau of the Census, Washington, DC, under the title 'U.S. Geographical Diversity in Business Entry Rates'. The results and conclusions are those of the authors and do not necessarily indicate concurrence with the Bureau of the Census or the Center for Economic Studies. The authors thank Andre van Stel, Philip Cooke, David Storey, David B. Audretsch, Attila Varga, Paul Reynolds, Olav Sorenson and seminar participants at the University of Maryland at College Park, the University of Pécs, Ohio State University, the School of Advanced Studies, Pisa, Italy, The 2002 Babson Entrepreneurship Research Conference and the 2003 American Economic Association Meetings for valuable comments. The paper was the winner of the 2002 Babson Kauffman Entrepreneurship Research Conference's National Federation of Independent Business Award for Excellence in Research.

NOTES

1. Broad local differences in entrepreneurial activity have historically contributed to variation in regional growth rates. For example, between 1960 and 1983, the number of corporations and partnerships in the USA more than doubled (from 2.0 million to 4.5 million), but this growth was not evenly distributed geographically. The regional differences in business formation rates, in turn, reflect regional differences in a number of other local economic factors, such as rates of return on investment, productivity, unit labour costs and levels of competition (ACS, 2002).

2. According to Jovanovic, we are entering the era of the young firm. The average age of all companies in the stock market is shrinking. The younger firm will thus resume a role that, in its importance, is greater than it has been at any time in the last 70 years or so.

3. The SUSB data and their Longitudinal Pointer File were constructed by the Census under contract to the Office of Advocacy of the US Small Business Administration. For documentation of the SUSB files, see ACS and ARMINGTON (1998).

4. The LEEM data do not include new firm start-ups without employees (i.e. the self-employed). The self-employed should be included as new firm start-ups, but the data do not allow for this.

5. Businesses that report operating statewide (county = 999) have been placed into the largest LMA in each state.

6. LMAs divide the entire USA into areas within which labour is very mobile, so that LMA functionally is an integrated region for both supply and demand. While

in many cases LMAs are similar to Metropolitan Statistical Areas (PMSA, CMSA), they include the hinterlands of each metropolitan area, and also distinguish economic areas within the non-metropolitan parts of the country. Counties or census tracts are frequently very interdependent with adjacent units that are parts of the same economic region. LMAs cover the whole country and do not focus solely on cities.

7. There is a small number (10 000–16 000) of new firms each year for which no industry code is available. Most firms are small and short lived. These have been added to the local market category, which is, by far, the largest of our sectors.

8. While the primary contributions of new firms are probably in the area of facilitating innovation and increasing productivity (see SCHUMPETER's, 1942, discussions on 'creative destruction'), the present study is limited to analysing their impact on local employment as a proxy for local growth.

9. A long tradition of studies of the determinants of new plant entry (secondary location) has focused on tax rates, transportation costs and scale economies at the plant level (BARTIK, 1989). The present study will not examine the impact of multi-unit establishments, since it focuses on the entrepreneurial behaviour of individuals who create new firms with employees.

10. During the past 25 years, there has been a significant research agendum examining the relationship between on-job creation and firm size. This literature suggests that size is an important variable and that there is an inverse relationship between firm size and job creation (KIRCHHOFF and GREEN, 1998). However, several studies have concluded that the earlier claims of job creation by small firms was overstated and that there was in fact no relationship between job creation and firm size, after controlling for age (DAVIS et al., 1996). While these findings are not without their critics (CARREE and KLOMP, 1996, among others), firms of all size do appear to create jobs.

11. When the new primary location of a multi-unit firm has less than one-third of the total employment of the firm, it is not counted as a birth. Such relatively small new headquarters establishments are usually created to manage a new firm created as the result of a merger or joint venture, involving the restructuring of older firms.

12. The average birth rates for 1991–96 were calculated from the average of the number of births in 1992, 1993, 1995 and 1996 divided by the labour force in 1993, in thousands. The number of firm births by LMA and sector in 1994 was not easily available, but it has been shown to be consistent with the previous and subsequent years for more aggregated annual birth data.

13. Note that by using start-up rates, one measures a different kind of competition than that by GLAESER et al. (1992). That is, one mainly measures competition between and/ or induced by new firm start-ups, and by doing so, one does not take account of the theoretical possibility of strong competition between incumbent firms without regard to start-ups.

14. ARMINGTON and ACS (2002) regressed agglomeration effects on the firm birth rate. The results were positive, suggesting that greater density leads to more new firm formation. This suggests that higher density leads to

greater creativity and spillovers (LUCAS, 1988). However, it appears that growth is promoted by lower density.

15. The unexplained portion represents the impact of a
variety of less easily quantified economic and social
factors that were omitted from the prediction model,
plus stochastic variation. Thus, the unexplained portion
is strictly orthogonal to all of the other exogenous
variables in the growth model.

REFERENCES

ACS Z. J. (2002) *Innovation and the Growth of Cities*. Edward Elgar, Cheltenham.

ACS Z. J. and ARMINGTON C. (1998) *Longitudinal Establishment and Enterprise Microdata (LEEM) Documentation*. CES 98-9. Center for Economic Studies, US Bureau of the Census, Washington, DC.

ACS Z. J., AUDRETSCH D. B., BRAUNERHJELM P. and CARLSSON B. (2003) *The Missing Link: The Knowledge Filter and Entrepreneurship in Endogenous Growth*. Center for Business and Policy Studies, Stockholm.

ACS Z. J., FITZROY F. and SMITH I. (2002) High technology employment, and R&D in cities: heterogeneity vs. specialization, *Annals of Regional Science* **36**, 269–371.

ACS Z. J. and VARGA A. (2002) Geography, endogenous growth and innovation, *International Regional Science Review* **25**, 132–148.

ACS Z. J. and VARGA A. (2004) Entrepreneurship, agglomeration and technological change. Paper presented at the GEMs Research Conference, Berlin, Germany.

ARMINGTON C. and ACS Z. J. (2002) The determinants of regional variation in new firm formation, *Regional Studies* **36**, 33–45.

AUDRETSCH D. and FRITSCH M. (2002) Growth regimes over time and space, *Regional Studies* **36**, 113–124.

BARTIK T. J. (1989) Small business start-ups in the U.S.: estimates of the effects of characteristics of states, *Southern Economic Journal* **55**, 1004–1018.

BAUMOL W. J. (1993) *Entrepreneurship, Management, and the Structure of Payoffs*. MIT Press, Cambridge, MA.

BHIDE A. (2000) *The Origin and Evolution of New Businesses*. Oxford University Press, New York.

BRESNAHAN T., GAMBARDELLA A. and SAXENIAN A. (2001) 'Old Economy' inputs for 'New Economy' outcomes: cluster formation in the New Silicon Valleys, *Industrial and Corporate Change* **10**, 835–860.

CARREE M. and KLOMP L. (1996) Small business and job creation: a comment, *Small Business Economics* **8**, 317–322.

CARREE M., VAN STEL A., THURIK R. and WENNEKERS S. (2002) Economic development and business ownership: an analysis using data of 23 OECD countries in the period 1976–1996, *Small Business Economics* **19**, 271–290.

CICCONE C. and HALL R. E. (1996) Productivity and the density of economic activity, *American Economic Review* **86**, 54–70.

DAILY C. M., MCDOUGALL P. P., COVIN J. G. and DALTON D. R. (2002) Governance and strategic leadership in entrepreneurial firms, *Journal of Management* **28**, 387–412.

DAVIS S., HALTIWANGER J. and SCHUH S. (1996) *Job Creation and Job Destruction*. MIT Press, Cambridge, MA.

FELDMAN M. P. and AUDRETSCH D. B. (1999) Innovation in cities: science-based diversity, specialization and localized competition, *European Economic Review* **43**, 409–429.

FRITSCH M. (1997) New firms and regional employment change, *Small Business Economics* **9**, 437–447.

GEROSKI P. (1995) What do we know about entry?, *International Journal of Industrial Organization* **13**, 421–441.

GLAESER E. L. (2000) The new economics of urban and regional growth, in CLARK G. L., FELDMAN M. P. and GERTLER M. S. (Eds) *The Oxford Handbook of Economic Geography*, pp. 83–98. Oxford University Press, New York.

GLAESER E. L., KALLAL H. D., SCHEINKMAN J. A. and SHLEIFER A. (1992) Growth in cities, *Journal of Political Economy* **100**, 1126–1152.

GLAESER E. L., SCHEINKMAN J. A. and SHLEIFER A. (1995) Economic growth in a cross-section of cities, *Journal of Monetary Economics* **36**, 117–143.

HALTIWANGER J. and KRIZAN C. J. (1999) Small business and job creation in the United States: the role of new and young business, in ACS Z. J. (Ed.) *Are Small Firms Important?*, pp. 52–79. Kluwer, Boston.

HANNAN M. T. and FREEMAN J. (1989) *Organizational Ecology*. Harvard University Press, Cambridge, MA.

HART D. (2002) *The Emergence of Entrepreneurship Policy: Governance, Start-ups, and Growth in the Knowledge Economy*. Cambridge University Press, New York (in press).

HAYEK F. (1945) The use of knowledge in society, *American Economic Review* **35**, 519–530.

JACOBS J. (1969) *The Economy of Cities*. Vintage, New York.

JORGENSON D. W. (2001) Information technology and the U.S. economy, *American Economic Review* **91**, 1–32.

JOVANOVIC B. (2001) New technology and the small firm, *Small Business Economics* **16**, 53–55.

KIRCHHOFF B. and GREENE P. G. (1998) Understanding the theoretical and empirical content of critiques of U.S. job creation research, *Small Business Economics* **10**, 153–159.

KRUGMAN P. (1991) Increasing returns and economic geography, *Journal of Political Economy* **99**, 483–499.

LAZEAR E. P. (2002) *Entrepreneurship*. Working Paper 9106. National Bureau of Economic Research, Cambridge, MA.

LUCAS JR R. E. (1988) On the mechanisms of economic development, *Journal of Monetary Economics* **22**, 3–39.

RAUCH J. E. (1993) Productivity gains from geographic concentration of human capital: evidence form the cities, *Journal of Urban Economics* **34**, 380–400.

REYNOLDS P. D. (1999) Creative destruction, in ACS Z. J., CARLSSON B. and KARLSSON C. (Eds) *Entrepreneurship, Small & Medium-sized Enterprises and the Macroeconomy*, pp. 97–136. Cambridge University Press, Cambridge.

REYNOLDS P. D., BYGRAVE W. D., AUTIO E. and HAY M. (2002) *Global Entrepreneurship Monitor*. London Business School, London.

ROMER P. (1986) Increasing returns and long run growth, *Journal of Political Economy* **94**, 1002–1037.

ROMER P. (1990) Endogenous technological change, *Journal of Political Economy* **98**, S71–S102.

SCHUMPETER J. A. (1942) *Capitalism, Socialism and Democracy.* Harper & Row, New York.

SHARMA P. and CHRISMAN J. J. (1999) Towards a reconciliation of the definitional issues in the field of corporate entrepreneurship, *Entrepreneurship Theory and Practice* **23**, 11–27.

SIMON C. J. and NARDINELLI C. (2002) Human capital and the rise of American cities, 1900–1990, *Regional Science and Urban Economics* **32**, 59–96.

SOLOW R. M. (1956) A contribution to the theory of economic growth, *Quarterly Journal of Economics* **94**, 614–623.

TOLBERT C. M. and SIZER M. (1996) *U.S. Commuting Zones and Labor Market Areas: A 1990 Update.* Rural Economy Division, Economic Research Service, US Department of Agriculture, Washington, DC.

UTTERBACK J. M. (1994) *Mastering the Dynamics of Innovation.* Harvard Business School Press, Cambridge, MA.

WENNEKERS S. and THURIK R. (1999) Linking entrepreneurship and economic growth, *Small Business Economics* **13**, 27–55.

[21]

Do Entrepreneurs Create Jobs?

Stefan Fölster

ABSTRACT. Many countries support the creation of new firms. Such policy is based on the presumption that the total number of jobs increases when a person moves from unemployment or regular employment to self-employment. In this paper the link between self-employment and overall employment is analyzed. The empirical analysis, based on panel data of Swedish counties from 1976–1995, pays particular attention to simultaneity issues. The results suggest that self-employment may have a significant positive effect on overall employment.

1. Introduction

Does total employment increase when more people decide to become entrepreneurs and be their own employers? Or does this merely replace existing jobs with self-employment? These are important policy questions since many countries attempt to promote self-employment as a way of combatting unemployment. Many countries have introduced subsidies and loans to newly started firms. Many countries also allow unemployed people to receive unemployment insurance compensation during the initial phase of a business start-up. Further there are moves to lighten regulation and reduce taxes for self-employed.

In spite of this policy interest the question has received relatively little attention in economic research. Much of the literature on entrepreneurship has concerned effects on technological innovation and productivity growth, e.g. Schumpeter (1911) or Baumol (1990, 1993). In general equilibrium models, however, it remains ambiguous whether technological innovation and productivity growth increases or decreases employment.

Final version accepted on December 1, 1999

The Swedish Research Institute of Trade
103 29 Stockholm
Sweden
E-mail: stefan.folster@hui.se

One strand of literature has debated the extent of job creation in small firms (summarized e.g. in Storey, 1994).[1] Typically this literature has analyzed to what extent new jobs are created in small or large firms. But new jobs in small firms may merely substitute jobs in larger firms. In that sense this literature has not directly adressed the question whether restructuring from large to small firms increases or decreases total employment.[2]

There is also a sizable empirical literature on the determinants of self-employment (e.g. Blau, 1987; Rees and Shah, 1986; Blanchflower and Meyer, 1994). These studies usually formulate models that draw on Knight's (1921) notion that the individual responds to the risk-adjusted relative earnings opportunities associated with employment and self-employment.[3] These models are then tested using aggregate time series data on the frequency of self-employment in different branches or data from household surveys.

Some papers in this literature also indirectly estimate a relationship between self-employment and employment. For example, Parker (1996) finds a positive relation between unemployment and self-employment using cointegration techniques on aggregate U.K. time series.[4] This approach has been criticized by Meager (1994) who argues that these studies are biased by business cycle effects. In a slump some self-employed will go out of business, while unemployment grows simultaneously.

This critique raises two issues. One is that there may be correlations of unemployment and self-employment over the business cycle. The other issue is that there may be a simultaneous relation between self-employment and employment. On the one hand low employment may induce people who have a hard time finding work to become self-employed. On the other hand, increased self-employment may affect employment. The point of this paper is to disentangle these simultaneous relationships and to identify the long-run structural effect that self-employment may have on employment.

To this end we explore two simultaneous structural equations that link self-employment with the overall employment rate. The first captures individuals' choice of self-employment. This may be affected by the fact that a fall in employment makes self-employment relatively more attractive or provides an alternative to those unable to secure a job, thus increasing the rate of self-employment.[5] This is sometimes called the "push effect". In addition self-employment may vary due to demand fluctuations over the business cycle or structural shifts in business conditions. This is sometimes called the "pull effect" into self-employment.

The second structural equation models the demand for labor as a function of the wage rate, business conditions, but also the share of self-employed. A number of possible mechanisms have been mentioned in the literature. For example, a number of models link entrepreneurship to productivity growth.[6] If the self-employed create productive firms some of which in turn hire additional workers, then the aggregate marginal product of labor may increase for a given total employment. At the current wage rate the demand for labor will then increase. While a higher demand for labor will also drive wages this may be moderated by the fact that higher wages can attract more people into the labor force.[7]

In addition there are a variety of microeconomic and political mechanisms through which self-employment may affect overall employment. For example, there is no principal-agent problem between the firm owner and the employee for the self-employed. This means that there is no need for an efficiency wage and the equilibrium unemployment that is normally associated with efficiency wages. Further, there are no employment protection laws for self-employed. This means that firms may be more prone to engage people if there is a good supply of self-employed that can be contracted, instead of having to employ people who then may be costly to lay off. An additional indirect mechanism could be that a greater share of self-employed exerts a political influence which makes policy more favourable to business in general.[8]

In appendix I it is shown how these two structural equations can be derived from microfoundations, starting with a labor market modelled in the tradition of Layard-Nickell-Jackman (1991), and extended by allowing employees to become self-employed. The main aim of the paper, however, is to empirically disentangle the simultaneous nature of the equations linking self-employment and employment.

One could try to analyze our model using country data for e.g. OECD countries. Unfortunately, there are considerable problems in comparing self-employment data between countries. The definitions of self-employment and employment vary considerably between countries. The same is true for the various variables that one might use as instruments and controls.

Instead, the model is applied to Swedish panel data of regional employment and self-employment. Using this data base it is possible to estimate cross-section, time-series regressions without encountering the considerable variation in the definition of the self-employed that plague cross-country comparisons. Also there is a fair supply of variables in this data base that can be used as instruments to disentangle the simultaneous relationships.

The analysis indicates that self-employment may indeed have a significant positive impact on overall employment. Section 2 presents empirical approach, Section 3 describes how the simultaneity problem is adressed, and Section 4 presents the results.

2. The empirical approach

The starting point is a modified version of the Layard-Nickell-Jackman (1991) model of a labour-market distinguishing between a wage-setting and a labour-demand relationship.[9] In Appendix I we show in greater detail how the macroeconomic expressions could be derived from a microeconomic model.

In the Layard-Nickel-Jackman model wages for employees (w) are thought of as being derived either from a bargaining (monopoly-union) model or from an efficiency-wage framework. The (real) wage is a positive function (1) of employment, n, and other variables. Employment is defined as the share of the labor force that is either in regular employment or is self-employed.

$$w_{i,t} = \omega_i + \omega_t + \omega n_{i,t} + u_{i,t} \qquad (1)$$

We express these relationships directly in the linear form that we assume in empirical estimation. We do not use the logarithmic form since the main variables $n_{i,t}$ and $s_{i,t}$ are already ratios of the labour force. Thus the coefficients (ω, λ) are easily interpreted as the effects of changes in employment and self-employment in terms of percent of the labour force rather than percent changes of absolute levels of these variables. Since we use panel data there is an observation for each region i and each time period t. It is natural to assume that there is a fixed component for each region, denoted by ω_i, a fixed component for each time period, denoted by ω_t, and stochastic and a normally distributed error $u_{i,t}$. The regional and period dummies go some way to correcting for differences in the business structure and economy-wide business cycles.[10]

The main modification in our model is that we assume that employment consists of regular employment and self-employment. We do not make any particular assumptions about the characteristics of firms operated by self-employed. They may be one-man operations, or they may in turn hire regular employees. The self-employed may work in the same branches as regular employees, or they may be concentrated in particular branches.

It is assumed, however, that entrepreneurial competence, and access to promising business ideas, varies among people. Suppose people can be ranked by their competence and the quality of their business idea in terms of the profit they earn if they become self-employed. Then the profit of the marginal self-employed, π', is a (decreasing) function of the share of self-employed of the labour force, s.[11] Here $v_{i,t}$ is a normally distributed stochastic error.

$$\pi'_{i,t} = p_i + p_t + p s_{i,t} + v_{i,t} \qquad (2)$$

The share of self-employed, s, is determined by a relation between w and π'. The exact equilibrium relationship will depend on what the likelihood is that unemployed have business opportunities and how high unemployment benefits are in relation to wages. We assume simply that $\pi'_{i,t} = a w_{i,t}$. This

allows combining and substituting (1) and (2) into equation (3), giving s as a negative function of n. Equation 3 expresses that a decrease in n lowers wages w (and income to unemployed) and thus makes it relatively more profitable to become self-employed. Equation (3) incorporates both the push effect – which makes self-employment more attractive when employment falls, and the pull effect captured by level shifts which may make self-employment (and sometimes employment) more attractive as business policy becomes more favorable or business conditions change. These shifts are captured by the region and period dummies ω_i and ω_t as well as the error term. Here the error term $\mu_{i,t}$ is a function of $u_{i,t}$ and $v_{i,t}$.

$$s_{i,t} = \frac{a(\omega_i + \omega_t)}{p} - \frac{p_i + p_t}{p} + \frac{\omega a}{p n_{i,t}} + \mu_{i,t} \qquad (3)$$

Finally, the labor demand relationship is assumed to follow from profit-maximizing behaviour of firms. The share of employment as a proportion of the labor force, $n_{i,t}$, is a decreasing function of the wage level and a vector of other variables.[12] In addition employment may be a function of the share of self-employment. Most directly the self-employed add to employment themselves, but some of them also employ others. To some extent this may replace employment in other firms. But at least in a Keynesian setting s also influences n directly to the extent that those that become self-employed do not crowd out other employed or self-employed persons. In addition self-employed may behave differently from regular employees in ways that affect employment, for example by not demanding negotiated wages and employment protection, or by having greater incentives to improve productivity.

Equation (4) shows the empirical implementation of this relationship between overall employment and self-employment. Here we also introduce lagged employment as a variable in order to capture lingering effects of self-employment that arises when start-ups grow and hire labour.

$$n_{i,t} = \eta_i + \eta_t + \mu_{t-1} \eta_{i,t-1} + \eta w_{i,t}$$
$$+ \lambda s_{i,t} + z_{i,t} \qquad (4)$$

Figure 1 illustrates the model. The downward sloping line captures the determination of self-employment in equation (3) which increases the number of self-employed as employment and

140   *Stefan Fölster*

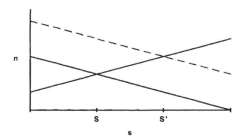

Figure 1. The relationship between self-employment *s* and employment *n*.

wages fall. The upward sloping line captures the employment function expressed in equation (4).

If policy is made more conducive to self-employment for other reasons then π' will rise for a given *s*. This would shift the downward-sloping line outward to the dotted line in Figure 1. The number of self-employed then increases from *S* to *S'* and employment increases also.

In this paper we do not analyze what causes different regions to end up in different employment/self-employment locations. Rather, we estimate the relationship given by equation (4), trying to isolate this from the simultaneous relationship given by (3) and business cycle and other effects that might affect the error terms in (3) and (4) simultaneously. Thus we seek an answer to the following question: What is the overall employment effect of a policy change, or of improved entrepreneurial opportunities, that increase self-employment by a certain amount?

3. The simultaneity issue and other econometric problems

We exploit a pooled time-series cross-section data set containing information on the 24 Swedish counties (län) in order to study the covariation between employment and self-employment. The estimates concern the period 1976 to 1995 for which data are available. The self-employment data exclude agriculture. The data are described in more detail in Appendix II.

Clearly, estimation of the system described by equations (3) and (4) as it is does not allow identification of the coefficients. Since we use county data the bias need not be all that large. The wage

may be determined more by the national wage rate, and thus not be influenced very much by fluctuations in local employment. Further, for the decision to become self-employed the comparison with the national wage may be more important than with the county wage. If $w_{i,t}$ were exogenous rather than being endogenous then the system would be recursive, and (4) could be estimated as it is. However, that would still leave a risk of business cycle and other effects that could simultaneously vary the error term in both equations.

If there is a simultaneity bias in estimating equation (4) we do know something about the direction of the bias. The coefficients ω in equation (1) and *p* in equation (2) are negative by assumption. We can rewrite (3) and (4) as

$$n_{i,t} = -\frac{\omega_i + \omega_t}{\omega} + \frac{1}{\omega w_{i,t}} + u_{i,t} \qquad (5)$$

$$n_{i,t} = -\frac{\omega_i + \omega_t}{\omega} + \frac{p_i + p_t}{\omega a} + \frac{p}{\omega} a s_{i,t} + u_{i,t} \qquad (6)$$

Here we know that the coefficient $1/\omega$ on $w_{i,t}$ will be negative and $p/\omega a$ on $s_{i,t}$ is positive. Following the discussion in e.g. Maddala (1977, p. 242) this implies that the bias in estimating η leads to overestimation, while for λ in (4) the bias leads to underestimation. This means that the true coefficient λ is as least as large as the estimated ones.[13] This will be interesting if we find a rather large positive estimate for λ.

Of course the picture is complicated if there are other biases as well. For example, if county employment rates are measured with an error these may be correlated with errors in the measure of self-employment since both are employment and self-employment are measured in the same survey. But these surveys are quite extensive and not likely to contain significant errors. In any case such a measurement error would also lead to underestimation of λ.

More worrisome is our specification of the lag structure as a Koyck lingering effects model. It is well known that the lingering effects specification may give plausible, but misleading, coefficient estimates if the true lag structure is a current effect model with an autoregressive error scheme. This possibility, however, we test for and reject the current effect model. A remaining problem, however, is that the error term in the lingering effect model is a moving average process and is therefore correlated with the lagged value of the dependent variable, $n_{i, t-1}$. Estimation by OLS leads to biased estimates.[14]

We adress the biases that may arise due to including the lagged dependent variable and simultaneity by using three types of instrument variable estimation methods, that are applied both to levels and first differences.

First, we use a 2SLS estimation, replacing the lagged dependent variable $n_{i, t-1}$ by its estimated value, using the second lag of employment as an instrument. This mainly adresses the issue of biased estimates due to the Koyck lingering effects specification.

Our second approach adresses both the lingering effects specification and the simultaneity problem. η and λ in equation (12) can be identified if instruments can be found that are exogenous determinants of $w_{i, t}$ and $s_{i, t}$. Therefore we use a 2SLS procedure using instruments for all three independent variables in (12). For $w_{i, t}$ we use regional dummies, the national wage rate and the ratio between county unemployment and non-employment as a share of the population age 16–64. Unemployment is a measure of how many people without employment are immediately available in the labour market. Non-employment includes people in labour market programmes and people in early retirement (often due to previous unemployment). The ratio of unemployment to non-employment is thus a measure of the labour market policy stance, which we take as exogenously given.[15]

As instruments for $s_{i, t}$ we use regional dummies, the second lag of $s_{i, t}$, and the share of public work that is contracted out, and a dummy for the introduction of a subsidy to unemployed for firm start-ups. Different counties have pursued quite different policies in terms of allowing entrepreneurs to compete for contracts. In some counties most work is done by public employees, while in other counties a sizable share is contracted out. Contracting out generally increases the number of self-employed. We take the choice of contracting out to be an exogenous policy variable.

Third, the availability of instruments allows us to use GMM as an estimation method. Apart from adressing the presence of the lagged dependent variable and the simultaneity problem, this pro-

cedure is also considered to be robust against autocorrelation and heteroscedasticity. GMM exploits the idea that the disturbances in the equations are uncorrelated with the instruments. The GMM estimator is the one that sets the calculated correlations of the instruments and disturbances as close to zero as possible, according to a criterion provided by a heteroscedasticity and autocorrelation corrected weighting matrix.

Two other econometric concerns should be discussed before we report results. First, one could argue that a number of regional variables that ought to be important are omitted from our regressions. These include population density, government production subsidies, public sector employment, labour market programmes, tax rates, and other factors. Many such differences between regions are, however, captured by our dummy variables. Also, this argument carries less weight the longer the periods of observation. The reason is that the actual rate of unemployment is then likely to be closer to the equilibrium rate, the main determinants of which are usually taken to be only a number of structural labour-market parameters.[16] For this reason we perform som regressions on averages over several years instead of on yearly observations. Also, to be on the safe side a number of potential explanatory variables, such as population density, are tested.

Second, a concern one might have is that regions with much self-employment increase their employment share merely by acting as a magnet for attractive employees. This possibility should be borne in mind when interpreting our results. Essentially the question is whether there is a supply restriction at the national level for certain types of labor, which is not binding at the regional level. One could argue, however, that if all regions increased self-employment and become "magnets" for attractive labor then it would become more profitable for the individual and for the nation to invest in the scarce human capital, so that supply would also increase. One should also note that the problem would be bigger if the regions we use as units of observations were smaller. The regions we use as units of observations are generally too large for employment figures to be affected merely by commuters.

142   *Stefan Fölster*

4. Results

The first column in Table I shows OLS estimates of equation (4). The coefficient for self-employment is significant at the one percent level. The coefficient estimate for self-employment implies a short-run effect of around 0.5. This means that when self-employment increases by an additional one percent of the work force, then total employment increases by one half percent of the workforce. The long-run effect is calculated by taking into account the dynamics that arise because an increase in total employment also affects next year's total employment and so forth. The long run effect based on a self-employment coefficient of 0.5 would be 1.3. This would mean that when self-employment increases by one percent more of the work force, then total employment eventually increases by 1.3 percent of the workforce. A typical region with high self-employment, say 10 percent of the labor force, would then have total employment of 6.5 percentage points higher than a typical region with low self-employment with

say, 5 percent of the labor force in self-employment.

As noted above this estimate is probably biased, but the presumption is that the bias is downward, and that the effect of self-employment may be underestimated.

In column (2) the second lag of employment is used as an instrument for lagged employment. In columns (3) to (5) all the instruments discussed above are used for the three explanatory variables. Column (5) uses the GMM estimation procedure.[17] As it turns out the coefficient estimates are not that different. The estimates for the self-employment coefficient are slightly higher when self-employment is instrumented. This is what one might expect, given that the simultaneity problem implies that OLS underestimates the coefficient. The difference, however, is quite small. A Hausman specification test, for example, does not detect any significant correlation between the explanatory variables and the error term.[18] This is again not a great surprise in light of the arguments given above, implying that the simultaneity bias

TABLE I
Estimated equation for the regional employment rate, 1976–1995, levels

Independent variables	OLS (1)	2SLS (2)	2SLS (3)	2SLS (4)	GMM (5)
Regional Employment rate, lagged	0.62*	0.60*	0.69*	0.63*	0.67*
	(17.91)	(17.94)	(29.81)	(20.76)	(16.14)
Self-employment	0.50*	0.50*	0.53*	0.54*	0.57*
	(8.09)	(8.03)	(7.21)	(7.42)	(6.89)
Relative wages	0.019	0.014	−0.035	−0.038	−0.041
	(0.36)	(0.37)	(−1.31)	(−1.34)	(−1.01)
Regional dummies	Yes	Yes	Yes	Random	Yes
Time dummies	Yes	Yes	Yes	Yes	Yes
R^2-adj	0.98	0.98	0.98	0.98	0.98
Ljung-box Q-stat	1.99	2.16	1.67	1.22	0.16

Notes:
(i)   *, indicates significance at the 1%-level.
(ii) *T*-ratios within parentheses.
(iii) The regressions have 480 observations.
(iv) Equations (1) and (2) are estimated with fixed, regional, effects.
(v)   Equation (4) is estimated with "random effects" for each region.
(vi) Relative wages is the ratio between regional to national wages.
(vii) In column (2) the second lag of employment is used as an instrument for lagged employment.
(viii) In column (3), (4) and (5) instruments are the second lags of employment, self-employment and wage, regional dummies, the national wage rate and the ratio between county unemployment and non-employment as a share of the population age 16–64, the share of public work that is contracted out, and a dummy for the introduction of a subsidy to unemployed for firm start-ups.

may not be all that great. The instrumental variable technique also corrects for simultaneous variation in the error term, due to business cycles or other effects.

We also test whether the lingering effects model is correct by running the regression including lagged self-employment as an explanatory variable. The estimated coefficient for lagged self-employment is, however, never significantly different from zero. This supports the use of the lingering effects specification.

Population density has also been tried as a separate explanatory variable, but the estimated coefficient is always near zero and insignificant and is therefore not shown. This is what should be expected given that fixed effects are controlled for and population density is quite stable.

Since a Durbin-Watson test statistic is biased in regressions with lagged dependent variables, we use a Ljung-Box Q statistic to test for autocorrelation, with 3 lags. The Q-statistic is distributed as a Chi-square with three degrees of freedom. The statistic does not indicate presence of serial correlation in any specification.

To throw some light on the robustness of the

estimates above, Table II shows the same regressions in first differences. First differences is the most radical way of eliminating fixed effects between regions. The first-difference form, using the second-lag of the dependent variable as an instrument for the lagged dependent variable is also suggested by Anderson and Hsiao (1981) as a solution to the bias in estimating regressions with lagged dependent variables and fixed effects.

Table III displays the estimates using non-overlapping four year periods as the unit of observation. In these regressions the coefficient on self-employment becomes much larger, since the lagged effects are included. On the other hand the coefficient on the lagged regional employment variable becomes much smaller. If one calculates the long run effect of self-employment on total employment based on Table III, the effect is on the same order of magnitude as the calculation based on Table I; that is, an increased share of self-employment by one percent of the population increases total employment by about 1.3 percent of the population.

There is a remaining concern that the estimates may be an artifact of business cycle swings or of

TABLE II
Estimated equation for the regional employment rate, 1976–1995, first differences

Independent variables	OLS (1)	2SLS (2)	2SLS (3)	2SLS (4)	GMM (5)
Regional Employment rate, lagged	−0.025	−0.025	−0.011	−0.0009	−0.0009
	(−0.511)	(−0.515)	(−0.228)	(−0.019)	(−0.019)
Self-employment	0.49*	0.49*	0.51*	0.51*	0.53*
	(6.19)	(6.16)	(5.44)	(5.33)	(5.11)
Relative wages	−0.01	−0.04	−0.05	−0.044	−0.044
	(−0.67)	(−0.50)	(−0.61)	(−0.547)	(−0.47)
Regional dummies	Yes	Yes	Yes	Random	Yes
Time dummies	Yes	Yes	Yes	Yes	Yes
R2-adj	0.93	0.93	0.93	0.93	0.93
Ljung-Box Q stat.	0.99	0.84	0.69	1.44	1.31

Notes:
(i)   *, indicates significance at the 1%-level.
(ii)   *T*-ratios within parentheses.
(iii) The regressions have 457 observations.
(iv)   Equation (4) is estimated with random, regional, effects.
(v)   Relative wages is the ratio between regional to national wages.
(vii) In column (2) the second lag of employment is used as an instrument for lagged employment.
(viii) In column (3), (4) and (5) instruments are the second lags of employment, self-employment and wage, regional dummies, the national wage rate and the ratio between county unemployment and non-employment as a share of the population age 16–64, the share of public work that is contracted out, and a dummy for the introduction of a subsidy to unemployed for firm start-ups.

TABLE III

Estimated equation for the regional employment rate, 1976–1995 (4-year intervals), levels

Independent variables	OLS (1)	2SLS (2)	2SLS (3)	2SLS (4)	GMM (5)
Regional Employment rate, lagged	0.20**	0.21**	0.20**	0.20**	0.21**
	(2.98)	(2.09)	(2.15)	(2.12)	(2.99)
Self-employment	1.14*	1.16*	1.19*	1.17*	1.21*
	(5.85)	(5.87)	(5.00)	(5.13)	(5.22)
Relative wages	−0.07	−0.11	−0.17	−0.93	−0.13
	(−1.41)	(−1.35)	(−1.09)	(−1.05)	(−0.86)
Regional dummies	Yes	Yes	Yes	Random	Yes
Time dummies	Yes	Yes	Yes	Yes	Yes
R2-adj	0.95	0.95	0.97	0.97	0.95
Ljung-Box Q stat.	2.41	1.89	1.49	1.77	1.89

Notes:

(i)   * and **, indicates significance at the 1% and 5%-level respectively.

(ii) T-ratios within parentheses.

(iii)   The regressions have 120 observations.

(iv)   Equations (3) and (4) are estimated with fixed, regional, effects.

(v)   Equation (5) is estimated with "random effects" for each region.

(vi)   Relative wages is the ratio between regional to national wages.

(vii)   In column (2) the second lag of employment is used as an instrument for lagged employment.

(viii)   In column (3), (4) and (5) instruments are the second lags of employment, self-employment and wage, regional dummies, the national wage rate and the ratio between county unemployment and non-employment as a share of the population age 16-64, the share of public work that is contracted out, and a dummy for the introduction of a subsidy to unemployed for firm start-ups.

reverse causality rather than long-term effects. One way of looking at this issue more closely is to perform a Granger causality test. While this is not a foolproof method, a negative result would significantly weaken our case. This is shown in Table IV. This test indicates that self-employment Granger-causes employment, but employment does not Granger-cause self-employment. We have also used a Box-Jenkins pre-whitening procedure to calculate Granger-causality. This led to quite similar conclusions, and is therefore not reported.

Table IV supports the notion that self-employment Granger-causes employment, and this effect is more significant with a few years lag. This is precisely what one would expect. Some self-employed begin to employ with a lag. A few of the self-employed even employ many other after some time. The hypothesis that self-employment does not Granger-cause employment is significantly rejected. On the other hand the test provides no indication that employment Granger-causes self-employment.

TABLE IV

Granger causality tests for the relation between self-employment and employment for different lags of self-employment, F-statistic

Null hypothesis	1 lag	2 lags	3 lags	4 lags	5 lags
1. Self-employment does not Granger-cause employment	2.96	6.89	9.33	10.41	11.13
	(0.08)	(0.04)	(0.02)	(0.006)	(0.003)
2. Employment does not Granger-cause self-employment	1.77	1.09	0.97	0.94	1.01
	(0.29)	(0.33)	(0.37)	(0.39)	(0.37)

Comment: Probabilities in parentheses.

5. Conclusion

There are a number of mechanisms that link self-employment to total employment. We have attempted to capture these in a simple framework in the Layard-Nickell tradition. Some micro-foundations for the link between self-employment and employment are provided in Appendix II. But clearly more theoretical development of the mechanisms involved would be desirable.

As an empirical matter, however, we find significant support for the notion that increased self-employment has a positive effect on employment. A key issue in this empirical study is to identify parameters in the presence of simultaneity. We adress this problem with the use of instruments. As a word of caution, the choice of instruments may be important.

Another cautionary note concerns the characteristics of self-employment. Our results concern the effects of the pattern of self-employment that actually occurred. If one implemented public programs to increase self-employment it is not at all certain that this artificially created self-employment has the same characteristics, and the same employment effects, as we find here.

This raises a wider issue, namely which types of self-employment are most entrepreneurial and how business conditions for those could be improved. That may be an avenue for future research.

Appendix I: Some microfoundations.

The starting point is a modified version of the Layard-Nickell-Jackman (1991) model of a labour-market, distinguishing between a wage-setting and a labour-demand relationship.[19] In this type of model wages for employees (w) are thought of as being derived either from a bargaining (monopoly-union) model or from an efficiency-wage framework. The (real) wage is a positive function of employment, n^d, and a negative function of labour supply n^s. In the following equations we ignore other structural and business cycle variables. Employment, n^d, is defined as the share of the labor force that is either in regular employment or is self-employed. The difference between n^d and n^s constitutes unemployment.

$$w = f(n^d, n^s) \quad \frac{\partial f}{\partial n^d} > 0, \quad \frac{\partial f}{\partial n^s} < 0, \quad (A1)$$

Individuals choose whether to enter the labor force, and they choose whether to seek employment or to become self-employed. It is assumed, however, that entrepreneurial competence, and access to promising business ideas, varies among people. Suppose people can be ranked by their competence and the quality of their business idea in terms of the profit they earn if they become self-employed. Then the profit of the marginal self-employed , π', is a (decreasing) function of the share of self-employed, s.

$$\pi' = h(s) \quad \frac{\partial h}{\partial s} < 0, \quad (A2)$$

Each individual maximizes utility in choosing between employment and self-employment. In equilibrium the number of self-employed is then determined by a market clearing condition $\pi' = k(w)$. If the individual is risk averse the expected profit for the marginal self-employed will be higher than the wage. But this could be reversed if self-employment is thought to be attractive in other ways. Individuals for whom $\pi' \geq k(w)$ are assumed to always be in the labor force and self-employed.[20] Other individuals merely choose whether to be in the labour force or not. For these utility maximization implies that more enter the labor force when the wage increases, $n^s = q(w)$.

Combining equations (A1) and (A2) and the equilibrium conditions yields equation (A3) which expresses that a decrease in n^d lowers wages w (and income to unemployed) and thus makes it relatively more profitable to become self-employed.

$$s = g(n^d, n^s) \quad \frac{\partial g}{\partial n^d} < 0, \quad (A3)$$

Finally, the labour demand relationship is assumed to follow from profit-maximizing behaviour of firms.

In order to model the demand for labor, assume that there is a size distribution of firms which is determined by economies of scale in the firm, or by the scarce supply of managerial talent as modelled in Lucas (1978). It is assumed that firms merge if they can better exploit economies of scale. Thus the size distribution of firms at any point in time is optimal. Each firm i, however, operates in the range of diminishing marginal returns, and employs up to the point where the marginal product of labour equals the market wage, $m_i' = w$. For simplicity assume that each firm is operated by a self-employed person.

If an employee starts a new firm and becomes self-employed one of two things can happen. Either the new size distribution of firms may not be optimal, which implies that there will be a merger and the number of self-employed will remain unchanged. Or the new size distribution is optimal. This means that the marginal product of labor increases which increases the demand for labour. This labor demand function is expressed in (A4).

$$n^d = y(w, s). \tag{A4}$$

It is now obvious that an increase in the number of self-employed leads to a higher marginal product of labor for a given wage rate, and thus increases labour demand n^d. The increase in the wage rate is, however, moderated by the fact that more people enter the labour force, according to $n^s = q(w)$.

Equations (A3) and (A4) correspond to the empirical equations (1) and (2) in the main text. There, however, n^d and s are expressed as a share of the labor force n^s, which therefore does not enter the equations explicitly. In the empirical work unobservable structural and business cycle variables that also determine $g(\ )$ and $y(\ )$ are captured by region and period dummies.

Appendix II: Data description

We have taken data for the number of self-employed, total employment, and people employed in agriculture in different counties from the labor force survey (AKU). The share of self-employment is calculated by dividing the number of self-employed minus self-employment in agriculture by the labor force. County variables are obtained from the Statistical Central Bureau Yearbook.

Relative wages are calculated as, regional wages for ISIC (SNI) 2 and 3, divided by national wages for ISIC (SNI) 2 and 3.

All observations are yearly from 1976–95.

Notes

[1] Birch (1979) first found that small and newly founded firms create most jobs. The results by Birch and others were criticized by Davis, Haltiwanger and Schuh (1996a, 1996b). But their criticism is partly refuted by Davidsson, Lindmark and Olofsson (1998). This issue is also surveyed e.g. in Acs (1996) and Acs, Carlsson and Karlson (1998).

[2] An exception is a paper by Thurik (1999) who studies the timing of changes in the share of entrepreneurs and unemployment in 23 OECD countries. He finds that a change in the number of entrepreneurs Granger causes a change in the rate of unemployment.

[3] More recent theoretical models in this tradition consider explicitly how stochastic shocks in demand or cost functions affect the decision to become self-employed (Appelbaum and Katz, 1986; Kihlstrom and Laffont, 1979).

[4] See also Crouchley et al., 1994.

[5] This mechanism is common in models of the choice of self-employment versus regular employment, e.g. Blau (1987). A number of authors describe this effect in terms of self-employment as a safety valve for unemployed people or people that are discriminated in the labour market, e.g. Moore (1983).

[6] E.g. Baumol, 1993.

7 An additional mechanism is that if unemployment is caused by rigid wages, it may be important that the self-employed generally have flexible incomes, e.g. they do not have a negotiated wage. This means that they will meet temporary slumps with reduced income rather than unemployment.

[8] Such political equilibria have been analyzed in Fölster and Trofimov, 1997.

[9] The model has been modified in other ways, e.g. to include participation in labour market programs by Calmfors (1994) and Calmfors and Skedinger (1995).

[10] Other variables that play a role are unemployment compensation, total factor productivity, the capital stock, and taxes, the quality of business opportunities, taxes, employment regulation and other policies that affect business. These are not explicitly included because many may be endogenous functions of self-employment. Instead an instrumental variables technique is used to isolate the exogenous effect of self-employment on total employment.

[11] B includes the quality of business opportunities, taxes, employment regulation and other policies that affect business.

[12] Such other variables might include productivity and the capital stock.

[13] This reasoning assumes that the covariances between the error terms u, v, and z are zero.

[14] Nickell (1981) also shows more generally that dynamic models with fixed effects yield biased estimates of order $1/T$.

[15] Calmfors and Skedinger (1995) provide a closer analysis of the link between labour market policy and the jobless rate.

[16] It is argued that since there seem to be no secular trends in unemployment, changes in the variables discussed must in equilibrium be fully shifted on to the real consumption wage (e.g. Layard et al., 1991; Bean, 1994; Calmfors and Skedinger, 1995).

[17] The GMM module in E-views was used. For the estimations reported here the Bartlett kernel was chosen in

combination with Andrew's automatic bandwidth procedure. We have also run GMM on a pre-whitened residual. This hardly affected the results.

[18] The Hausman specification test implies that a reduced form equation is estimated by OLS with self-employment as dependent variable and the instruments used in columns (3) to (5) of Table I as explanatory variables. The fitted values from this regression are then included in the employment equation (column 1). The Hausman test then consists of testing whether the coefficient on the fitted value is significantly different from one.

[19] The model has been modified in other ways, e.g. to include participation in labour market programs by Calmfors (1994) and Calmfors and Skedinger (1995). Labour supply is often assumed constant in these models. Here we let labour supply vary.

[20] In a more sofisticated model one might take into account that some unemployed individuals may choose self-employment even if $\pi' < k(w)$. This is the so-called "push-effect".

References

Acs, Z. J. (ed.), 1996, *Small Firms and Economic Growth*, Cheltenham: Edward Elgar.

Acs, Z. J., B. Carlsson and C. Karlsson (eds.), 1998, *Entrepreneurship, Small and Medium-Sized Enterprises and the Macro Economy*, Cambridge University Press.

Anderson, T. W. and C. Hsiao, 1981, 'Estimation of Dynamic Models with Error Components', *Journal of American Statistical Association* **76**.

Baumol, W. J., 1990, 'Entrepreneurship: Productive, Unproductive, and Destructive', *Journal of Political Economy* **98**(5).

Baumol, W. J., 1993, *Entrepreneurship, Management, and the Structure of Payoffs*, Cambridge, MA: MIT Press.

Birch, D., 1979, *The Job Generation Process. Final Report to Economic Development Administration*, Cambridge, MA: MIT Program on Neighborhood and Regional Change.

Blanchflower, D. G. and B. D. Meyer, 1994, 'A Longitudinal Analysis of the Young Self-employed in Australia and the United States', *Small Business Economics* **6**(1), 1–19.

Blanchflower, D. G. and A. J. Oswald, *Does Access to Capital Help Make an Entrepreneur?*, NBER Working Paper, No. 3252, 1991.

Blau, D. M., 1989, 'A Time-series Analysis of Self-employment in the United States', *Journal of Political Economy* **95**(3), 445–467.

Calmfors, L., 1994, *Active Labour Market Policy and Unemployment – A Framework for the Analysis of Cirucial Design Features*. OECD Economic Studies, No. 22, 1994.

Calmfors, L. and P. Skedinger, 1995, 'Does Active Labour-market Policy Increase Employment?', *Oxford Review of Economic Policy* **11**, 91–109.

Crouchley, R., P. Abell, and D. Smeaton, 1994, *An Aggregate Time Series Analysis of Non-agricultural Self-employment in the U.K.*, Discussion Paper No. 209, Centre for Economic Performance, London School of Economics, London.

Davidsson, P., L. Lindmark and C. Olofsson, 1998, 'The Extent of Overestimation of Small Firm Job Creation – An Empirical Examination of the Regression Bias', *Small Business Economics* **11**, 87–100.

Davis, S. J., J. Haltiwanger and S. Schuh, 1996a, 'Small Business and Job Creation: Dissecting the Myth and Reassessing the Facts', *Small Business Economics* **8**(4), 297–315.

Davis, S. J., J. Haltiwanger and S. Schuh, 1996b, *Job Creation and Destruction*, Boston, MA: The MIT Press.

Evans, D. S. and B, Jovanovic, 1989, 'An Estimated Model of Entrepreneurial Choice under Liquidity Constraints', *Journal of Political Economy* **97**(4).

Fölster, S. and G. Trofimov, G., 1997, *Does the Welfare State Discourage Entrepreneurs?*, IUI Working Paper.

Grubb D. and Wells, W., Employment regulation and patterns of work in EC countries. OECD Economic Studies, no. 21, 1993.

Holtz-Eakin, D., D. S. Joulfaian and H. S. Rosen, 1994a, 'Sticking It Out: Entrepreneurial Survival and Liquidity Constraints', *Journal of Political Economy* **102**(1), 53–75.

Holtz-Eakin, D., D. Joulfaian and H. S. Rosen, 1994b, 'Entrepreneurial Decisions and Liquidity Constraints', *Rand Journal of Economics* **25**(2), 334–347.

Kihlstrom, R. E. and J. J. Laffont, 1979, *A General Equilibrium Entrepreneurial Theory of Firm Foundation Based on Risk Aversion*, vol. 87, 719–748.

Knight, F. H., 1921, Risk, *Uncertainty and Profit*, New York: Houghton Mifflin.

Koskela, E. and M. Virén, 1994, 'Taxation and Household Saving in Open Economies – Evidence from the Nordic Countries', *Scandinavian Journal of Economics* **96**(3), 425–441.

Kotlikoff, L. J., 1995, *Privatization of Social Security: How It Works and Why It Matters*, NBER Working Paper No. 5330.

Laussel, D. and M. Le Breton, 1995, 'A General Equilibrium Theory of Firm Formation Based on Individual Unobservable Skills', *European Economic Review* **39**, 1303–1319.

Layard, R., R. Jackman and S. Nickell, 1991, *Unemployment*, Oxford: Oxford University Press.

Lindh, T. and H. Ohlsson, 1995, 'Self-employment and Self-financing', *Economic Journal*.

Lindh, T. and H. Ohlsson, 1996, *Self-employment and Self-financing*, Department of Economics, Uppsala University, Working Paper.

Lucas, R. Jr., 1978, 'On the Size Distribution of Business Firms', *Bell Journal of Economics* **9**, 508–523.

Maddala, G. S., 1977, *Econometrics*, McGraw Hill International.

Meager, N., 1994, *Self-employment Schemes for the Unemployed in the European Community: The Emergence of a New Institution and Its Evaluation*, I Schmid, G., red., Labor Market Institutions in Europe – a Socioeconomic evaluation of performance, M.E. Sharpe, New York.

Moore, R. L., 1983, 'Employer Discrimination: Evidence from Self-employed Workers', *Review of Economics and Statistics* **65**, 496–501.

Murphy, K. M., A. Schleifer and R. W. Vishny, 1991, 'The Allocation of Talent: Implications for Growth', *Quarterly Journal of Economics*, 503–530.

Nickell, S., 1981, 'Biases in Dynamic Models with Fixed Effects', *Econometrica* **49**.

OECD Employment Outlook, July 1992, p. 158.

Parker, S. C., 1996, 'A Time Series Model of Self-employment under Uncertainty', *Economica* **63**(251), 459–475.

Quadrini, V., *Entrepreneurship, Saving and Social Mobility*, Mimeo, Department of Economics, University of Pennsylvania.

Rees, H. and A. Shah, 1986, 'An Empirical Analysis of Self-employment in the U.K.', *Journal of Applied Econometrics* 1, 95–108.

Schumpeter, J. A., 1911, *The Theory of Economic Development*. Cambridge, MA: Harvard University Press, English translation, 1936.

Storey, D. J., 1994, *Understanding the Small Business Sector*, New York: Routledge.

Thurik, R., 1999, *The Dutch Polder Model: Shifting from the Managed Economy to the Entrepreneurial Economy*, Paper presented at AEA meeting in New York, January.

Regional Studies, Vol. 38.8, pp. 949–959, November 2004

Entrepreneurship Capital and Economic Performance

DAVID B. AUDRETSCH* and MAX KEILBACH†

*Max-Planck Institut zur Erforschung von Wirtschaftssystemen, Kahlaische Str. 10, D-07745 Jena, Germany.
Email: audretsch@mpiew-jena.mpg.de

†Max-Planck Institut zur Erforschung von Wirtschaftssystemen, Kahlaische Str. 10, Research Group on Entrepreneurship, Growth and Public Policy, D-07745 Jena, Germany.
Email: keilbach@mpiew-jena.mpg.de

(Received September 2003: in revised form June 2004)

AUDRETSCH D. B. and KEILBACH M. (2004) Entrepreneurship capital and economic performance, *Regional Studies* **38**, 949–959. The neoclassical model of the production function, as applied by Solow when building the neoclassical model of growth, linked labour and capital to output. More recently, Romer and others have expanded the model to include measures of knowledge capital. This paper introduces a new factor, entrepreneurship capital, and links it to output in the context of a production function model. It explains what is meant by entrepreneurship capital and why it should influence economic output. A production function model including several different measures of entrepreneurship capital is then estimated for German regions. The results indicate that entrepreneurship capital is a significant and important factor shaping output and productivity. The results suggest a new direction for policy that focuses on instruments to enhance entrepreneurship capital.

Production function   Entrepreneurship capital   Regional economic performance

AUDRETSCH D. B. et KEILBACH M. (2004) Le capital entrepreneurial et la performance économique, *Regional Studies* **38**, 949–959. Le modèle néo-classique de la fonction de production selon Solow, qui l'a employé dans le but de construire le modèle néo-classique de croissance, relie le travail et le capital au rendement. Plus récemment, Romer, parmi d'autres, a développé le modèle afin de comporter des mesures du capital de connaissance. Cet article cherche à présenter un noveau facteur, le capital entrepreneurial, et à le relier au rendement économique sur la base d'un modèle de fonction de production. D'abord, cet article cherche à expliquer la notion du capital entrepreneurial et les raisons pour lesquelles il pourrait influencer le rendement économqiue. Il s'ensuit une estimation d'un modèle de fonction de production qui se rapporte aux régions allemandes et qui utlise differents mesures du capital entrepreneurial. Les résultats montrent que le capital entrepreneurial excerce un effet positif et signifiant sur le rendement économique des regions. Ces résultats laissent supposer une nouvelle orientation pour la politique qui porte sur des outils destinés à augmenter le capital entrepreneurial.

Fonction de production   Capital entrepreneurial   Performance économique régionale

AUDRETSCH D. B. und KEILBACH M. (2004) Entrepreneurship Kapital und wirtschaftliche Leistungsfähigkeit, *Regional Studies* **38**, 949–959. Das neoklassische Modell der Produktionsfunktion, wie es von Solow zur Konstruktion des neoklassischen Wachstumsmodell benutzt wurde, verband Arbeit und Kapital mit wirtschaftlichem Output. In jüngster Zeit haben Romer und andere das Modell dahingehend erweitert, dass Wissenskapital einbezogen wird. In diesem Aufsatz wird ein weiterer Faktor eingeführt, der des Entrepreneurship Kapitals und die Produktionsfunktion mit diesem Faktor erweitert. Der Aufsatz erklärt zunächst, was mit Entrepreneurship Kapital gemeint ist, und inwiefern es den wirtschaftlichen Output einer Region beeinflussen kann. Es wird sodann ein Produktionsfunktionsmodell einschließlich mehrerer verschiedener Maße für Entrepreneurship Kapital für deutsche Regionen geschätzt. Die Ergebnisse weisen darauf hin, dass Entrepreneurship Kapital einen signifikanten und wichtigen Beitrag zur Beeinflussung des wirtschaftlichen Outputs der Regionen darstellt. Die Ergebnisse legen nahe, neue Wege der Wirtschaftspolitik zu beschreiten, die sich auf Instrumente zur Erhöhung des Entrepreneurship Kapitals konzentrieren.

Produktionsfunktion   Entrepreneurship Kapital   Regionalwirtschaftliche Leistungsfähigkeit

AUDRETSCH D. B. y KEILBACH M. (2004) Capital entrepreneurial y comportamiento económico, *Regional Studies* **38**, 949–959. El modelo neoclásico de la función de producción, tal como ha sido aplicado por Solow para desarrollar el modelo neoclásico de crecimiento, vinculó trabajo y capital a producción. Más recientemente, Romer y otros han expandido el modelo para incluir medidas de capital intelectual. En este artículo nosotros introducimos un nuevo factor, el capital empresarial, y lo vinculamos a la producción en el contexto de un modelo de función de producción. Este artículo explica qué es a lo que nosotros nos referimos cuando hablamos de capital empresarial y por qué debería influir en la producción económica. A

0034-3404 print/1360-0591 online/04/080949-11 ©2004 Regional Studies Association
http://www.regional-studies-assoc.ac.uk

DOI: 10.1080/0034340042000280956

950   *David B. Audretsch and Max Keilbach*

continuación se estima un modelo de función de producción que incluye varias medidas diferentes de capital empresarial para las regiones alemanas. Los resultados indican que el capital empresarial es un factor importante y significativo a la hora de determinar producción y productividad. Estos resultados sugieren una nueva dirección para las políticas que se centran en instrumentos dirigidos a aumentar el capital empresarial.

Función de producción   Capital empresarial   Comportamiento económico regional

JEL classifications: M13, O32, O47

The Entrepreneur is the single most important player in a modern economy.

(LAZEAR, 2002, p. 1)

INTRODUCTION

Ever since SOLOW (1956) based his model of economic growth on the neoclassical production function with its key factors of production, capital and labour, economists have relied upon the model of the production function as a basis for explaining the determinants of economic growth. ROMER's (1986) critique of the Solow approach was not with the basic model of the neoclassical production function, but rather with what Romer perceived to be omitted from that model – knowledge. Not only did Romer along with LUCAS (1988) and others argue that knowledge was an important factor of production, along with the traditional factors of labour and capital, but because it was endogenously determined as a result of externalities and spillovers, it was particularly important.

The purpose of the paper is to suggest that another key factor has been omitted from the neoclassical production function: entrepreneurship capital. Entrepreneurship has typically been referred to as an action, process or activity. It is proposed that it can also be considered to constitute a stock of capital, since it reflects a number of different factors and forces, legal, institutional and social, which create a capacity for this activity (HOFSTEDE et al., 2002). ACS and AUDRETSCH (2003) suggest that entrepreneurship capital might be something of a missing link in explaining variations in economic performance. However, while a rich literature has emerged identifying the determinants of entrepreneurship, led by the pioneering study of EVANS and LEIGHTON (1989), the link between entrepreneurship capital and performance remains largely anecdotal or based on case studies. For example, SAXENIAN (1994) provides compelling case study evidence attributing the superior performance of Silicon Valley, CA, USA, to a high capacity for promoting entrepreneurship, which could be viewed as a rich endowment of entrepreneurship capital.

BAUMOL (2002, pp. 58–59) has argued that entrepreneurial activity might account for a significant amount of the growth left unexplained in traditional production function models. While the traditional factors of labour and capital, and even the addition of knowledge capital, are important in shaping output, the capacity to harness new ideas by creating new enterprises is also essential to economic output. A counter-example is instructive. In the former Soviet Union, while the exact measures of the stocks of capital and labour, and even knowledge, were questionable, their existence was not. By contrast, entrepreneurship capital, at least as it could be legally applied, was minimal.

The paper is organized as follows. The second section is devoted to defining entrepreneurship capital and to explaining why is should be linked to output in the context of a production function model. The third section specifies the production function to be estimated and it exposes the data. A production function model is estimated for German regions in the fourth section. The final section provides a summary and conclusion. In particular, the evidence suggests that various measures of entrepreneurship capital in fact contribute to output. Those regions with a higher level of entrepreneurship capital exhibit higher levels of output and productivity, while those with a paucity of entrepreneurship capital tend to generate lower levels of output and productivity.

ENTREPRENEURSHIP CAPITAL

What is entrepreneurship capital?

While it has become widely acknowledged that entrepreneurship is a vital force in the economies of developed countries, there is little consensus about what actually constitutes entrepreneurial activity. Scholars have proposed a broad array of definitions, which when operationalized have generated a number of different measures (HEBERT and LINK, 1989). Similarly, there is no generally accepted definition of entrepreneurship for the developed countries of the Organisation for Economic Co-operation and Development (OECD, 1998). The failure of a single definition of entrepreneurship to emerge undoubtedly reflects the fact that it is a multidimensional concept. The actual definition used to study or classify entrepreneurial activities reflects a particular perspective or emphasis. For example, definitions of entrepreneurship typically vary between the economic and management perspectives. From the economic perspective, Hebert and Link distinguish between the supply of financial capital, innovation, allocation of resources among alternative uses and decision-making. Thus, an entrepreneur is someone encompassing the entire spectrum of these functions: 'The entrepreneur is someone who specializes in taking responsibility for and making judgmental decisions that affect the location, form, and the use of goods, resources or institutions' (HEBERT and LINK, 1989, p. 213).

The most prevalent and compelling views of entrepreneurship focus on the perception of new economic opportunities and the subsequent introduction of new ideas in the market. Just as entrepreneurs are agents of change, entrepreneurship is thus about the process of change. This corresponds to the definition of entrepreneurship proposed by the OECD (1998, p. 11):

> Entrepreneurs are agents of change and growth in a market economy and they can act to accelerate the generation, dissemination and application of innovative ideas. ... Entrepreneurs not only seek out and identify potentially profitable economic opportunities but are also willing to take risks to see if their hunches are right.

Or as GARTNER and CARTER (2003) state:

> Entrepreneurial behavior involves the activities of individuals who are associated with creating new organizations rather than the activities of individuals who are involved with maintaining or changing the operations of on-going established organizations.

While the entrepreneur undertakes a definitive action, starting a new business, his/her action cannot be viewed in a vacuum devoid of context. Rather, as AUDRETSCH *et al.* (2002) show, the determinants of entrepreneurship are shaped by a number of forces and factors, including legal and institutional and also social factors. The study of social capital and its impact on economic decision-making and actions stems from classic literatures in economics and sociology in which social and relational structure influence market processes (GRANOVETTER, 1983). SAXENIAN (1994) and THORTON and FLYNNE (2003) attribute the high economic performance of Silicon Valley not only to single individuals, but also to their interaction within formalized networks (e.g. firms) and unformalized ones:

> It is not simply the concentration of skilled labour, suppliers and information that distinguish the region. A variety of regional institutions – including Stanford University, several trade associations and local business organizations, and a myriad of specialized consulting, market research, public relations and venture capital firms – provide technical, financial, and networking services which the region's enterprises often cannot afford individually. These networks defy sectoral barriers: individuals move easily from semiconductor to disk drive firms or from computer to network makers. They move from established firms to start-ups (or vice versa) and even to market research or consulting firms, and from consulting firms back into start-ups. And they continue

to meet at trade shows, industry conferences, and the scores of seminars, talks, and social activities organized by local business organizations and trade associations. In these forums, relationships are easily formed and maintained, technical and market information is exchanged, business contacts are established, and new enterprises are conceived. ... This decentralized and fluid environment also promotes the diffusion of intangible technological capabilities and understandings.

(SAXENIAN, 1990, pp. 96–97)[1]

The present paper defines entrepreneurship capital as a region's endowment with factors conducive to the creation of new businesses. This involves aspects such as a high endowment with individuals willing to take the risk of starting up a new business. It also implies the existence of a regional milieu that encourages start-up activities such as an innovative milieu, the existence of formal and informal networks, but also a general social acceptance of entrepreneurial activity and the activity of bankers and venture capital agents willing to share risks and benefits involved. Such contexts generating a high propensity for economic agents to start new firms can be characterized as being rich in entrepreneurship capital. Other contexts, where the start-up of new firms is inhibited, can be characterized as being weak in entrepreneurship capital.

Impacts of entrepreneurship capital

Entrepreneurship capital can be expected to exert a positive impact on economic output for a number of reasons. The first is that it is a mechanism for knowledge spillovers. ROMER (1986), LUCAS (1988, 1993) and GROSSMAN and HELPMAN (1991) establish that knowledge spillovers are an important mechanism underlying endogenous growth. However, they shed little light on the actual mechanisms by which knowledge is transmitted across firms and individuals. The answer to this question is important, because a policy implication commonly drawn from the new economic growth theory is that as a result of convexities in knowledge and the resultant increasing returns, knowledge factors, such as research and development (R&D), should be publicly supported. While this may be valid, it is also important to recognize that the mechanisms for spillover transmission may also play a key role and might also serve as a focus for public policy enhancing economic growth and development.

The literature identifying mechanisms actually transmitting knowledge spillovers is sparse and remains underdeveloped. However, one important area where such transmission mechanisms have been identified involves entrepreneurship. Entrepreneurship involves the start-up and growth of new enterprises.

Why should entrepreneurship serve as a mechanism for the spill over of knowledge from the source of origin? At least two major channels or mechanisms for knowledge spillovers have been identified in the literature. Both spillover mechanisms revolve around the issue of appropriability of new knowledge. COHEN and LEVINTHAL (1989) suggest that firms develop the capacity to adapt new technology and ideas developed in other firms and, therefore, can appropriate some of the returns accruing to investments in new knowledge made externally. This view of spillovers is consistent with the traditional model of the knowledge production function, where the firm exists exogenously and then undertakes (knowledge) investments to generate innovative output.

By contrast, AUDRETSCH (1995) proposes shifting the unit of observation away from exogenously assumed firms to individuals, such as scientists, engineers or other knowledge workers, i.e. agents with endowments of new economic knowledge. When the lens is shifted away from the firm to the individual as the relevant unit of observation, the appropriability issue remains, but the question changes: How can economic agents with a given endowment of new knowledge best appropriate the returns from that knowledge? If the scientist or engineer can pursue the new idea within the organizational structure of the firm developing the knowledge and appropriate roughly the expected value of that knowledge, he/she has no reason to leave the firm. On the other hand, if he/she places a greater value on his/her ideas than does the decision-making bureaucracy of the incumbent firm, he/she might choose to start a new firm to appropriate the value of his/her knowledge. Small enterprises can compensate for their lack of R&D through spillovers and spinoffs. Typically, an employee from an established large corporation, often a scientist or engineer working in a research laboratory, will have an idea for an invention and ultimately for an innovation. Accompanying this potential innovation is an expected net return from the new product. The inventor would expect to be compensated for his/her potential innovation accordingly. If the company has a different, presumably lower, valuation of the potential innovation, it might decide either not to pursue its development, or that it merits a lower level of compensation than that expected by the employee.

In either case, the employee will weigh the alternative of starting his/her own firm. If the gap in the expected return accruing from the potential innovation between the inventor and the corporate decision-maker is sufficiently large, and if the cost of starting a new firm is sufficiently low, the employee might decide to leave the large corporation and establish a new enterprise. Since the knowledge was generated in the established corporation, the new start-up is considered to be a spin-off from the existing firm. Such start-ups typically do not have direct access to a large R&D laboratory. Rather, these small firms succeed in exploiting the knowledge and experience accrued from the R&D laboratories with their previous employers.

The research laboratories of universities provide a source of innovation-generating knowledge that is available to private enterprises for commercial exploitation. JAFFE (1989) and AUDRETSCH and FELDMAN (1996) find that the knowledge created in university laboratories 'spills over' to contribute to the generation of commercial innovations by private enterprises. ACS *et al.* (1994) find persuasive evidence that spillovers from university research contribute more to the innovative activity of small firms than to the innovative activity of large corporations.

In the metaphor provided by HIRSCHMAN (1970), if a voice proves ineffective within incumbent organizations and loyalty is sufficiently weak, a knowledge worker might resort to exit the firm or university where the knowledge was created to form a new company. In this spillover channel, the knowledge production function is actually reversed. The knowledge is exogenous and embodied in a worker. The firm is created endogenously in the worker's effort to appropriate the value of his/her knowledge through innovative activity. Thus, entrepreneurship serves as the mechanism by which knowledge spills over from the source by the creation of a new firm where it is commercialized.

A second way that entrepreneurship capital exerts a positive influence on economic output is through increased competition by an increased number of enterprises. JACOBS (1969) and PORTER (1990) argue that competition is more conducive to knowledge externalities than is local monopoly. It should be emphasized that by local competition, Jacobs does not mean competition within product markets as has traditionally been envisioned within the industrial organization literature. Rather, Jacobs is referring to the competition for the new ideas embodied in economic agents. Not only does an increased number of firms provide greater competition for new ideas, but also greater competition across firms facilitates the entry of a new firm specializing in some particular new product niche. This is because the necessary complementary inputs and services are likely to be available from small specialist niche firms, but not necessarily from large, vertically integrated producers.

Both FELDMAN and AUDRETSCH (1999) and GLAESER *et al.* (1992) find empirical evidence supporting the hypothesis that an increase in competition, as measured by the number of enterprises, in a city increases the growth performance of that city.

A third way that entrepreneurship capital generates economic output is by providing diversity among the firms. Not only does entrepreneurship capital generate a greater number of enterprises, but also it increases the variety of enterprises in the location. A key assumption made by HANNAN and FREEMAN (1989) in the population ecology literature is that each new organization represents a unique approach. A series of theoretical arguments suggests that the degree of diversity, as opposed to homogeneity, in a location will influence the growth potential.

The theoretical basis linking diversity to economic performance is provided by JACOBS (1969), who argues that the most important source of knowledge spillovers is external to the industry in which the firm operates and that cities are the source of considerable innovation because the diversity of these knowledge sources is greatest in cities. According to Jacobs, it is the exchange of complementary knowledge across diverse firms and economic agents that yields a greater return on new economic knowledge. Jacobs develops a theory that emphasizes that the variety of industries within a geographic region promotes knowledge externalities and ultimately innovative activity and economic growth.

The first important test linking diversity to economic performance, measured in terms of employment growth, was by GLAESER *et al.* (1992), who used a data set on the growth of large industries in 170 cities between 1956 and 1987 to identify the relative importance of the degree of regional specialization, diversity and local competition play in influencing industry growth rates. They find evidence that diversity promotes growth in cities. FELDMAN and AUDRETSCH (1999) identify the extent to which the extent of diversity influences innovative output. They link the innovative output of product categories within a specific city to the extent to which the economic activity of that city is concentrated in that industry or, conversely, diversified in terms of complementary industries sharing a common science base.

Entrepreneurship capital therefore can contribute to output and growth by serving as a conduit for knowledge spillovers, increasing competition and by injecting diversity. Inclusion of measures of entrepreneurship capital would be expected to be positively related to output.

PRODUCTION FUNCTION MODEL AND MEASUREMENT ISSUES

The goal of the paper is to state that a region's endowment with entrepreneurship capital exerts a positive impact on the region's economic output. It bases a test of this hypothesis on an often tested approach, i.e. it augments a production function with entrepreneurship capital. Using a specification of the Cobb–Douglas type, one obtains:

$$Y_i = \alpha K_i^{\beta_1} L_i^{\beta_2} R_i^{\beta_3} E_i^{\beta_4} e^{\varepsilon_i} \qquad (1)$$

where K is the factor of physical capital, L is labour, R is knowledge capital, E is entrepreneurship capital and i refers to German regions. Data derive from a cross-section of 327 West German *Kreise* (regions) for 1992, if not indicated otherwise. Table 1 has some summary statistics for these variables. The sources and construction of the data are as follows (for further details, see KEILBACH, 2000):

- Output: measured as gross value added corrected for purchases of goods and services, Value Added Tax (VAT) and shipping costs. Statistics are published every 2 years for *Kreise* by the Working Group of the Statistical Offices of the German *Länder* (Federal States) under 'Volkswirtschaftliche Gesamtrechnungen der Länder'.
- Physical capital: stock of capital used in the manufacturing sector of the *Kreise* has been estimated using a perpetual inventory method, which computes the stock of capital as a weighted sum of past investments. In the estimates, a β-distribution was used with $p = 9$ and a mean age of $q = 14$. The type of survival function as well as these parameters was provided by the German Federal Statistical Office, Wiesbaden. This way, we attempted to obtain maximum coherence with the estimates of the capital stock of the German producing sector as a whole as published by the Federal Statistical Office. Data on investment at the level of *Kreise* are published annually by the Federal Statistical Office in the 'E I 6' series. These figures, however, are limited to firms of the producing sector, excluding the mining industry, with more than 20 employees. The vector of the producing sector as a whole was estimated by multiplying these values such that the capital stock of Western Germany – as published by STATISTISCHES BUNDESAMT (1993) – was attained. Note that this procedure implies that estimates for *Kreise* with a high proportion of mining might be biased. Note also that for protection purposes, some *Kreise* did not publish data on investment (like, for example, the city of Wolfsburg, whose producing sector is dominated by the car-maker Volkswagen). Therefore, five *Kreise* are treated as missing.
- Labour: data are published by the Federal Labor Office, Nuremberg, which reports number of employees liable to social insurance by *Kreise*.
- Knowledge capital: expressed as number of employees engaged in R&D in the public (1992) and the private (1991) sectors. With this approach, the examples of GRILICHES (1979), JAFFE (1989) and AUDRETSCH and FELDMAN (1996) are followed. Data have been communicated by the Stifterverband für die Wissenschaft, Essen, under obligation of data protection. With these data, it was impossible to make a distinction between research and development employees in both the producing and nonproducing sectors. Regression results, therefore, will implicitly include spillovers from R&D of the nonproducing sector to the producing sectors. It is presumed, however, that this effect is rather low.
- Entrepreneurship capital: measurement of entrepreneurship capital is no less complicated than is measuring the traditional factors of production. Just as measuring capital, labour and knowledge invokes numerous assumptions and simplifications, creating a metric for entrepreneurship capital presents a

954   *David B. Audretsch and Max Keilbach*

Table 1. *Summary statistics of variables used in regression*

	Mean	Standard deviation	Minimum	Maximum
Gross Domestic Product (Y) (DM millions)	2351.89	2621.77	95.00	22 258.00
Capital (K) (DM millions)	4248.25	5038.72	211.20	37 295.64
Number of employees (L)	27 022.48	24 080.32	2562	171 938
Number of R&D employees (R)	840.76	2223.75	0	29 863
Entrepreneurship capital (E)^a	9.406	2.805	4.793	24.635
High-technology (HT) E^a	0.755	0.398	0.011	6.004
Information and Communication Technology (ICT) E^a	0.565	0.310	0.157	2.520

Note: ^{a}Entrepreneurship capital is measured as the sum of the number of start-ups in the respective industry in 1989–92 divided by 1000 of the population. Hence, on average, there were 9.4 start-ups per 1000 population in all industries in these years.

challenge. Many of the elements that determine entrepreneurship capital in the present definition defy quantification. In any case, entrepreneurship capital, like all the other types of capital, is multifaceted and heterogeneous. However, it manifests itself singularly: the start-up of new enterprises. Thus, using new-firm start-up rates as an indicator of entrepreneurship capital, the latter being an unobservable (i.e. latent) variable, is proposed. *Ceteris paribus*, higher start-up rates reflect higher levels of entrepreneurship capital. Entrepreneurship capital is computed as the number of start-ups in the respective region relative to its population, which reflects the propensity of inhabitants of a region to start a new firm. From the background of the present definition of entrepreneurship capital, alternative measures would be possible. A number of aspects of this definition being difficult to quantify, a natural candidate would be a region's stock of young firms. However, this measure would implicitly reflect exit and shakeout dynamics. Hence, a measure along these lines would inevitably be influenced by factors external to entrepreneurship capital such as the quality of management or business ideas and, thus, be biased. The number of start-ups is therefore considered as being the most appropriate measure of entrepreneurship capital.

The data on start-ups are taken from the start-up panel that is developed by the Centre for European Economic Research (ZEW), Mannheim, Germany on the basis of data provided biannually from the largest German credit-rating agency, Creditreform (Neuss, Germany). These data contain virtually all entries – hence start-ups – in the German Trade Register, especially for firms with large credit requirements as, for example, high-technology firms.[2] By now, there are 1.6 million entries for Western Germany. Since the number of start-ups is subject to a greater level of stochastic disturbance over short periods, it is prudent to compute the measure of entrepreneurship capital based on start-up rates over a longer period. The number of start-ups between 1989 and 1992 is therefore used.

One might argue that in the set-up of equation (1),

the use of entrepreneurship capital invokes a simultaneity problem in the sense that it is not only entrepreneurship capital that drives output, but also high output drives start-ups. The argument would imply that entrepreneurs move to locations where economic performance is high. However, a similar argumentation would hold for all variables used in this approach. If this effect holds for entrepreneurs, it will certainly also apply to labour, but probably even more to capital, which is a sum of past monetary investments and money migrating more easily across borders, hence moving more quickly to productive regions. Thus, the present measure of entrepreneurship capital fits well with the tradition of production function regressions. The use of lagged start-up rates avoids some of the degree of simultaneity between output and entrepreneurship.

While the present paper argues that entrepreneurship capital should include start-up activity in any industry, some scholars have suggested that it should only apply to start-ups involving innovative activity. Therefore, two modified measures of entrepreneurship are computed. The first restricts entrepreneurship capital to include only start-up activity in high-technology manufacturing industries (whose research and development intensity is above 2.5%). The second restricts entrepreneurship capital to include only start-up activity in the information and communication industries, i.e. firms in the hard- and software business. Some of these industries are also classified under high-technology manufacturing. Hence, there exists an intersection between the two measures. The measures will place more emphasis on the aspect of risk involved in the present definition of entrepreneurship capital since R&D-intensive activities are more uncertain in outcome and a larger financial commitment is also necessary to engage in R&D-intensive industries. Therefore, the expected monetary loss is larger.

The spatial distribution of the measure of entrepreneurship capital based on all industries is shown in Fig. 1. It makes evident that entrepreneurship capital is a phenomenon of agglomerated regions, Frankfurt, Munich, Hamburg and Düsseldorf, with their surrounding regions showing the highest start-up intensity. This is reflected in the correlation matrix shown in

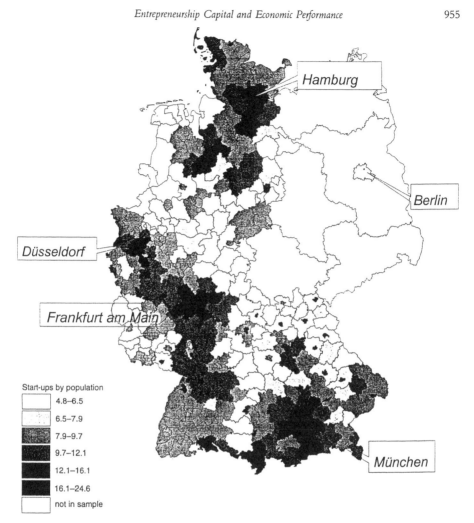

Fig. 1. *Spatial distribution of entrepreneurship capital measured as the number of start-ups in all industries in 1989–92 per 1000 population*

Table 2 where entrepreneurship capital shows a positive and significant correlation with population density, measured as inhabitants per square kilometre.

Table 3 ranks the regions according to their endowment with entrepreneurship capital. This makes again evident that Frankfurt, Munich, Hamburg and Düsseldorf, together with their surrounding regions, are those with the strongest endowment. This ranking will differ slightly, though not fundamentally if start-ups in high-technology manufacturing industries or in ICT industries are used instead of start-ups in all industries.

This is indicated by the positive and significant correlations between all three measures of entrepreneurship shown in Table 2. Tables A1 and A2 (in the Appendix) show the ranking of regions (showing again the 20 strongest and 20 weakest regions) when using the two alternative measures of entrepreneurship capital.

EMPIRICAL RESULTS

Estimation of the production function model of equation (1) produced the results shown in Table 4. The

Table 2. *Correlation between variables used in regression and between these variables and population density for 327 German Kreise*

	Population density	Y	K	L	R	E	High-technology E
Y	0.5539 (0.000)						
K	0.5978 (0.000)	0.9172 (0.000)					
L	0.5252 (0.000)	0.9437 (0.000)	0.9244 (0.000)				
R	0.5068 (0.000)	0.7838 (0.000)	0.7250 (0.000)	0.6922 (0.000)			
E	0.3376 (0.000)	0.2671 (0.000)	0.2133 (0.000)	0.2203 (0.000)	0.3036 (0.000)		
HT E	0.2668 (0.000)	0.3179 (0.000)	0.2292 (0.000)	0.2756 (0.000)	0.3404 (0.000)	0.8153 (0.000)	
ICT E	0.2870 (0.000)	0.3167 (0.000)	0.2224 (0.000)	0.2579 (0.000)	0.3396 (0.000)	0.8164 (0.000)	0.9138 (0.000)

Notes: For abbreviations, see Table 1.
Numbers in parentheses are probabilities (*p*) of correlations not differing significantly from zero.

Table 3. *Regions ranked by start-up intensity (start-ups in 1989–92 per 1000 population) for all industries*

Rank	Region	Start-up intensity
1	Munich, surrounding area	24.634 561
2	Düsseldorf, city	20.241 409
3	Hamburg, city	19.669 706
4	Offenbach, surrounding area	18.606 913
5	Wiesbaden, city	17.671 311
6	Starnberg	17.101 142
7	Munich, city	16.081 293
8	Frankfurt am Main, city	15.956 175
9	Hochtaunuskreis	15.866 653
10	Speyer, city	15.395 183
11	Passau, city	15.254 072
12	Freising	14.850 592
13	Memmingen, city	14.805 079
14	Landsberg a. Lech	14.792 960
15	Offenbach am Main, city	14.620 285
16	Segeberg	14.572 237
17	Diepholz	14.435 722
18	Main-Taunus-Kreis	14.232 831
19	Ebersberg	13.811 470
20	Dachau	13.779 904
...		
308	Wesermarsch	6.006 103
309	Wolfsburg, city	6.001 654
310	Cham	5.991 514
311	Sankt Wendel	5.919 445
312	Neckar-Odenwald-Kreis	5.912 736
313	Donnersbergkreis	5.896 884
314	Schweinfurt	5.896 509
315	Emsland	5.774 027
316	Uelzen	5.758 620
317	Salzgitter, city	5.668 607
318	Lichtenfels	5.551 670
319	Trier-Saarburg	5.541 770
320	Herne, city	5.526 887
321	Grafschaft Bentheim	5.428 270
322	Höxter	5.287 556
323	Bremerhaven, city	5.258 049
324	Tirschenreuth	5.198 918
325	Coburg	5.193 940
326	Cuxhaven	5.168 823
327	Kusel	4.793 161

equation estimates the traditional Solow model of the production function. As the positive and statistically significant coefficients suggest, both physical capital and labour are important factors of production in determining output in German regions. In the second column of Table 4, the factor of knowledge capital is added. The positive and statistically significant coefficients of all three variables lend support to the Romer view that knowledge-intensive inputs matter as a factor of production.

The third column of Table 4 shows the results when entrepreneurship capital is included in the production function model (1). The positive and statistically significant coefficient indicates that entrepreneurship is a key factor in explaining variations in output across German regions. Equation (1) specifies the impact of production factors on output in terms of production elasticities, i.e. an increase of a factor j by 1% implies an increase of output by β_j%. Thus, it can be deduced from the estimates that an increase of a region's entrepreneurship capital by 1% increases output, *ceteris paribus*, by 0.12%. On the basis of the present definition, which involves a number of aspects, it is not yet possible to state what should actually be increased to increase a region's entrepreneurship capital; this is left for further research. However, the estimates evidence that the impact of entrepreneurship capital is stronger than that of knowledge capital, the production elasticity of entrepreneurship capital being roughly five times larger than that of knowledge capital. This would imply that investments in entrepreneurship capital are more productive compared with investments in knowledge capital, which in turn would suggest a shift in public policy to increasing entrepreneurship capital. Of course, this first evidence should be interpreted carefully. In addition, estimates do not allow the derivation of specific policy measures; however, they give important directions for further research.

Table 4, columns (4) and (5), shows the results for equation (1) if start-up rates in high-technology manufacturing or in ICT industries are used instead of the start-up rates of all industries. The results indicate

Table 4. Results of the estimation of the production function model (1) for German counties: the dependent variable is Gross Domestic Product (Y)

	(1)	(2)	(3)	(4)	(5)
Y	−2.755*** (0.000)	−2.380*** (0.000)	−1.863*** (0.000)	−1.620*** (0.000)	−1.549*** (0.000)
K	0.270*** (0.000)	0.261*** (0.000)	0.258*** (0.000)	0.265*** (0.000)	0.267*** (0.000)
L	0.805*** (0.000)	0.755*** (0.000)	0.767*** (0.000)	0.753*** (0.000)	0.756*** (0.000)
R		0.034** (0.011)	0.026* (0.063)	0.021 (0.133)	0.019 (0.179)
E			0.120** (0.026)		
HT E				0.043*** (0.003)	
ICT E					0.105*** (0.001)
Adjusted R^2	0.9108	0.9124	0.9134	0.9156	0.9150

Notes: For abbreviations, see Table 1.

Numbers in parentheses denote the probability (p) of estimates being stochastically equal to zero. Hence, statistically significant for the two-tailed test: *90%, **95% and ***99% levels of confidence

that using these two alternative measures of entrepreneurship capital still generates a positive and statistically significant coefficient, suggesting that entrepreneurship capital is an important addition to the model of the production function.

SUMMARY AND CONCLUSION

Subsequent to publication of SOLOW's (1956) seminal paper depicting the neoclassical model of the production function as a basis for analysing economic growth, a series of new policy directions were developed to enhance the two traditional factors of production, physical capital and labour. Similarly, endogenous growth theory has triggered a new policy direction focusing on enhancing knowledge capital through investments in R&D, education and human capital. The present paper suggests that these approaches neglect an important factor that also shapes the economic performance of a region: the entrepreneurship capital of that region. It gives a definition of entrepreneurship capital and measures the regions' endowment with this factor by the regions' start-ups of new businesses in different industries, taking this as an indicator of the underlying latent variable. Based on a Cobb–Douglas production function, empirical evidence is found that entrepreneurship capital indeed exerts a positive impact on regions' output as measured in terms of Gross Domestic Product. This finding holds for different measures of entrepreneurship capital, be they general or more risk oriented. Indeed, a larger production elasticity is measured for entrepreneurship capital than for the present measure of knowledge capital, suggesting that the impact of a 1% increase in entrepreneurship capital on Gross Domestic Product is larger than the increase of knowledge capital by the same amount.

The results suggest, at least in the case of Germany, a different and new policy direction: the enhancement of entrepreneurship capital. While these findings certainly do not contradict the conclusions of earlier studies linking growth to factors such as labour, capital and knowledge, the present evidence points to an additional factor, entrepreneurship capital, that also plays an important role in the model of the production function. Although on the basis of analysis the present authors cannot yet provide detailed policy recommendations such as, for example, what specific measures should be taken and what aspect of entrepreneurship capital they should address, it can be stated that under certain conditions, policies focusing on enhancing entrepreneurship capital can prove to be more effective than those targeting more traditional factors. A detailed analysis of the components of entrepreneurship capital and how public policy can address them will be dealt with in further research. This research needs to map out more precisely the exact links and channels that policy can influence and augment entrepreneurship in such a way as to raise productivity and growth, as suggested by the results of the present paper.

Acknowledgements – The paper was written during a research stay at the Centre for European Economic Research (ZEW) in Mannheim, Germany. The authors gratefully acknowledge the support from the ZEW and financial support of the Deutsche Forschungsgemeinschaft (DFG) within the research focus Interdisziplinäre Gründungsforschung under Contract Number STA 169/10-1.

NOTES

1. SAXENIAN (1990, pp. 97–98) claims that even the language and vocabulary used by technical specialists can be specific to a region: 'a distinct language has evolved in the region and certain technical terms used by semiconductor production engineers in Silicon Valley would not even be understood by their counterparts in Boston's Route 128'.
2. Firms with low credit requirements, with a low number of employees or with unlimited liability legal forms are registered only with a time lag. These are typically retail stores or catering firms. For more detail on the ZEW foundation panels, see HARHOFF and STEIL (1997).

APPENDIX

Table A1. Regions ranked by start-up intensity (start-ups in 1989–92 per 1000 population) of high-technology manufacturing industries

Rank	Region	High-technology manufacturing start-up intensity
1	Tuttlingen	6.00 451
2	Munich	5.82 258
3	Aachen, krfr. St.	5.17 982
4	Ravensburg	4.42 391
5	Landsberg a. Lech	4.38 991
6	Starnberg	4.04 163
7	Enzkreis	3.77 389
8	Miesbach	3.61 141
9	Ebersberg	3.58 143
10	Solingen, krfr. St.	3.55 480
11	Bad Tölz-Wolfratshausen	3.54 417
12	Offenbach	3.51 651
13	Darmstadt, krfr. St.	3.45 167
14	Bodenseekreis	3.44 225
15	Speyer, krfr. Stadt	3.43 462
16	Fürstenfeldbruck	3.39 916
17	Aachen	3.38 475
18	Herford	3.38 254
19	Segeberg	3.37 696
20	Rottweil	3.33 336
...	...	
308	Salzgitter, krfr. Stadt	0.50 916
309	Werra-Meissner-Kreis	0.50 894
310	Gifhorn	0.50 387
311	Neuburg-Schrobenhausen	0.47 102
312	Haßberge	0.46 271
313	Cochem-Zell	0.46 240
314	Trier-Saarburg	0.45 116
315	Hersfeld-Rotenburg	0.45 077
316	Schwalm-Eder-Kreis	0.41 891
317	Uelzen	0.41 881
318	Donnersbergkreis	0.39 844
319	Wittmund	0.36 625
320	Wolfsburg, krfr. Stadt	0.31 505
321	Aschaffenburg, krfr. St.	0.30 290
322	Kusel	0.25 294
323	Regen	0.24 462
324	Lüchow-Dannenberg	0.19 536
325	Emden, krfr. St.	0.19 303
326	Freyung-Grafenau	0.12 302
327	Kitzingen	0.11 511

Table A2. Regions ranked by start-up intensity (start-ups in 1989–92 per 1000 population) of ICT industries (hardware, software, consulting, database services)

Rank	Region	ICT industry start-up intensity
1	Munich	2.519 525
2	Offenbach	2.030 401
3	Starnberg	1.835 573
4	Ebersberg	1.561 137
5	Karlsruhe, krfr. St.	1.483 696
6	Freising	1.472 786
7	Darmstadt, krfr. St.	1.423 815
8	Hamburg	1.383 457
9	Hochtaunuskreis	1.366 637
10	Fürstenfeldbruck	1.332 686
11	Wiesbaden, krfr. St.	1.319 147
12	Munich, krfr. St.	1.309 578
13	Aachen, krfr. St.	1.218 066
14	Landsberg a. Lech	1.214 881
15	Darmstadt-Dieburg	1.160 630
16	Main-Taunus-Kreis	1.139 757
17	Frankfurt am Main, krfr. St.	1.105 130
18	Koblenz, krfr. Stadt	1.095 390
19	Rheingau-Taunus-Kreis	1.091 414
20	Offenbach am Main, krfr. St.	1.081 712
...	...	
308	Cloppenburg	0.241 666
309	Wilhelmshaven, krfr. St.	0.241 149
310	Emsland	0.234 035
311	Lichtenfels	0.228 346
312	Wesermarsch	0.225 632
313	Trier-Saarburg	0.225 581
314	Kelheim	0.224 252
315	Bremerhaven, krfr. St.	0.221 633
316	Salzgitter, krfr. Stadt	0.212 148
317	Südwestpfalz	0.209 798
318	Freyung-Grafenau	0.209 128
319	Helmstedt	0.206 010
320	Neustadt a.d. Waldnaab	0.202 612
321	Kusel	0.202 350
322	Wittmund	0.201 439
323	Regen	0.195 700
324	Cham	0.178 735
325	Coburg	0.177 571
326	Donnersbergkreis	0.159 375
327	Cuxhaven	0.157 092

REFERENCES

ACS Z. J. and AUDRETSCH D. B. (2003) The International Handbook of Entrepreneurship. Kluwer, Dordrecht.
ACS Z. J., AUDRETSCH D. B. and FELDMAN M. P. (1994) R&D spillovers and recipient firm size, Review of Economic and Statistics 76, 336–340.
AUDRETSCH, D. B. (1995) Innovation and Industry Evolution. MIT Press, Cambridge, MA.
AUDRETSCH D. B. and FELDMAN M. P. (1996) R&D spillovers and the geography of innovation and production, American Economic Review 86, 630–640.
AUDRETSCH D. B., THURIK R., VERHEUL I. and WENNEKERS S. (2002) Entrepreneurship: Determinants and Policy in a European–U.S. Comparison. Kluwer, Boston.
BAUMOL W. J. (2002) Free Market Innovation Machine: Analysing the Growth Miracle of Capitalism. Princeton University Press, Princeton.
COHEN W. and LEVINTHAL D. (1989) Innovation and learning: the two faces of R&D, Economic Journal 99, 569–596.
EVANS, D. S. and LEIGHTON, L. S. (1989) Some empirical aspects of entrepreneurship, American Economic Review 79, 519–535.

FEDERAL STATISTICAL OFFICE (annually) E I 6 series.

FELDMAN M. P. and AUDRETSCH D. B. (1999) Innovation in cities: science based diversity, specialization and localized competition, *European Economic Review* **43**, 409–429.

GARTNER W. B. and CARTER N. M. (2003) Entrepreneurship behavior: firm organizing processes, in ACS Z. J. and AUDRETSCH D. B. (Eds) *The International Handbook of Entrepreneurship*, pp. 195–221. Kluwer, Dordrecht.

GLAESER E., KALLAL H., SCHEINKMAN J. and SHLEIFER A. (1992) Growth of cities, *Journal of Political Economy* **100**, 1126–1152.

GRANOVETTER M. S. (1983) The strength of weak ties: a network theory revisited, in COLLINS R. (Ed.) *Sociological Theory,* pp. 201–233. Jossey-Bass, San Francisco.

GRILICHES Z. (1979) Issues in assessing the contribution of R&D to productivity growth, *Bell Journal of Economics* **10**, 92–116.

GROSSMAN G. M. and HELPMAN E. (1991) *Innovation and Growth in the Global Economy,* MIT Press, Cambridge MA.

HANNAN M. T. and FREEMAN J. (1989) *Organizational Ecology*. Harvard University Press, Cambridge, MA.

HARHOFF D. and STEIL F. (1997) Die ZEW-Gruendungspanels: Konzeptionelle Ueberlegungen und Analysepotential, in HARHOFF D. (Ed.) *Unternehmensgruendungen – Empirische Analysen fuer die alten und neuen Bundeslaender,* 7. Nomos, Baden-Baden.

HEBERT R. F. and LINK A. N. (1989) In search of the meaning of entrepreneurship, *Small Business Economics* **1**, 39–49.

HIRSCHMAN A. O. (1970) *Exit, Voice, and Loyalty*. Harvard University Press, Cambridge, MA.

HOFSTEDE G., NOORDERHAVEN N. G., THURIK A. R., WENNEKERS A. R. M., UHLANER L. and WILDEMAN R. E. (2004) Culture's role in entrepreneurship, in ULIJN J. and BROWN T. (Eds) *Innovation, Entrepreneurship and Culture: The Interaction between Technology, Progress and Economic Growth*, pp. 162–203. Edward Elgar, Brookfield.

JACOBS, J.(1969) *The Economy of Cities*. Vintage, New York.

JAFFE A. B. (1989) Real effects of academic research, *American Economic Review* **79**, 957–970.

KEILBACH M. (2000) *Spatial Knowledge Spillovers and the Dynamics of Agglomeration and Regional Growth*. Physica, Heidelberg.

LAZEAR E. (2002) *Entrepreneurship*. Working Paper No. 9109. National Bureau of Economic Research, Cambridge, MA.

LUCAS Jr R. E. (1993) Making a miracle, *Econometrica* **61**, 251–272.

LUCAS R. E. (1988) On the mechanics of economic development, *Journal of Monetary Economics* **22**, 3–39.

ORGANISATION FOR ECONOMIC CO-OPERATION AND DEVELOPMENT (1998) *Fostering Entrepreneurship*. OECD, Paris.

PORTER M. (1990) *The Comparative Advantage of Nations*. Free Press, New York.

ROMER P. M. (1986) Increasing returns and long-run growth, *Journal of Political Economy* **94**, 1002–1037.

SAXENIAN A. (1990) Regional networks and the resurgence of Silicon Valley, *California Management Review* **33**, 89–111.

SAXENIAN A. (1994) *Regional Advantage*. Harvard University Press, Cambridge, MA.

SOLOW R. (1956) A contribution to the theory of economic growth, *Quarterly Journal of Economics* **70**, 65–94.

STATISTISCHES BUNDESAMT (1993) *Statistisches Jahrbuch 1993*. Metzler-Poeschel, Stuttgart.

THORTON P. H. and FLYNN K. H. (2003) Entrepreneurship, networks and geographies, in ACS Z. J. and AUDRETSCH D. B. (Eds) *The International Handbook of Entrepreneurship*, pp. 401–433. Kluwer, Dordrecht.

Name Index